CBSE
CHAPTERWISE QUESTION BANK
2024-2010

Biology

Class 12

Authors
Juhi Bhatia • Md. Shadab

arihant
SUCCESS AND NOTHING LESS

arihant
SUCCESS AND NOTHING LESS

ARIHANT PRAKASHAN
(School Division Series)

ADMINISTRATIVE & PRODUCTION OFFICES

Regd. Office
'Ramchhaya' 4577/15, Agarwal Road, Darya Ganj, New Delhi -110002
Tele: 011- 47630600, 43518550

Head Office
Kalindi, TP Nagar, Meerut (UP) - 250002, Tel: 0121-7156203, 7156204

SALES & SUPPORT OFFICES

Agra, Ahmedabad, Bengaluru, Bareilly, Chennai, Delhi, Guwahati, Hyderabad, Jaipur, Jhansi, Kolkata, Lucknow, Nagpur & Pune.

PO No : TXT-XX-XXXXXXX-X-XX

Published By Arihant Publications (India) Ltd.

For further information about the books published by Arihant, log on to www.arihantbooks.com or e-mail at info@arihantbooks.com

PRICE

Follow us on

Achieving 99+ Marks in Board Exams

Achieving 99+ marks in board exams is definitely an ambitious goal, but with the right approach and these 7 tips from toppers, you can definitely increase your chances of success!

Here are the 7 Topper Tips to ace your board exams:

1. Master the art of consistency

Consistency builds understanding and confidence, both crucial for excelling in exams.

2. Build a winning study strategy

Create a personalised timetable that prioritises subjects based on your strengths and weaknesses.

3. Befriend the syllabus

Focus on high-weightage topics and prioritise mastering core concepts before moving on to advanced ones.

4. Embrace active learning

Explain concepts to yourself or in study groups to solidify understanding.

5. Conquer the past

Solve Past years' papers and Sample Papers under timed conditions to practice time management and understand paper pattern.

6. Seek help, when needed!

Don't hesitate to clarify doubts with teachers, tutors, or study groups. Asking questions strengthens your understanding and prevents confusion.

7. Prioritise well-being

Eat nutritious meals, get enough sleep, have regular exercise practice stress management techniques like meditation to stay calm and focused during exams.

These tips are just a starting point, and you can personalise them to fit your learning style and preferences.

Description of

Newly Added Features

01

Sexual Reproduction in Flowering Plants

TREND ANALYSIS 3 YEARS

TOPIC 01 Flower and its Parts

Average No. of Questions Across all Sets

Types of Questions	2024	2023	2020
1 Mark	0	0	1
2 Marks	0	0	0
3 Marks	0	0	0
4 Marks (Case Based)	0	0	0
5 Marks	1	1	0

Trend Analysis

At the start of each chapter, Trend Analysis is given to indicate the types of Questions asked from different topics of the chapter. This feature helps students to know the importance of different topics of the given chapter from exam point of view and helps them to prepare accordingly.

47. Angiospermic flowers may be monoecious, cleistogamous or show self-incompatibility. Describe the characteristic features of each one of them and state which one of these flowers promotes inbreeding and outbreeding, respectively. **All India 2014C**

> **KEY idea**
>
> Monoecious plants have both male and female flowers in some plants.
> Cleistogamous flowers are closed flowers. Self incompatibility promotes out-crossing.

Ans. The characteristic features of angiospermic flowers

(i) **Monoecious flowers** are unisexual, i.e. they have either the male reproductive or female reproductive part in separate flowers, both produced on same plant. The flowers (male and female) are separate. It prevents self- pollination and promotes cross-pollination.

Key Idea

'Key idea is given with selected questions with the purpose to help students to get the approach 'to answer the question'. This feature help students to develop the systematic approach to answer difficult/ complex questions.

107. (i) List three different allelic forms of gene 'I' in human. Explain the different phenotypic expressions, controlled by these three forms.

(ii) A woman with blood group A marries a man with blood group O. Discuss the possibilities of the inheritance of the blood group in the following starting with 'yes' or 'no' for each.

> **Common Mistakes** Students usually get confused between alleles and genes, but genes are segments of DNA which control specific trait in organisms.

Common Mistakes

It focuses on some of the general but critical mistakes that students commit while answering the questions. This feature helps students to develop the habit of avoiding mistakes while answering questions

7. Assertion Apomictic embryos are genetically identical to the parent plant.

Reason Apomixis is the production of seeds without fertilisation. **CBSE SQP 2023**

Ans. (a) Both Assertion and Reason are true and Reason is the correct explanation of Assertion

Very Short Answer Type Questions

8. Why does endosperm development precede embryo development? **CBSE SQP 2021-22**

Ans. Endosperm develops before the embryo development because it provides nutrition to the developing embryo.

9. How many meiotic divisions are required to produce 76 seeds in a guava fruit? **CBSE SQP 2021-22**

Ans. 95 meiotic divisions are required to produce 76 seeds in a guava fruit.

> **Concept Enhancer** In females, 76 meiotic divisions will produce 76 haploid cells.
> In males, 1 meiotic division will produce 4 haploid cells, i.e. 19 meiotic divisions will produce 76 haploid cells. Therefore 76 + 19 meiotic divisions are required to produce 76 seeds in a guava fruits.

Concept Enhancer

Concept Enhancer gives the brief description of the concept, which has been used to answer the question. This feature provides revision of important concept along with practice of question solving.

Mastering

CBSE Board Exams

Tips and Strategies From Top Scorers!

Raksha Gopal
Class 12 Topper

Hansika Shukla
Class 12 Topper

Karishma Arora
Class 12 Topper

Students put their heart, soul, and sweat into their board exam preparation. In a bid to score the best they can, aspirants often look to previous toppers to draw inspiration from them.

Here we have covered some tips & strategies shared by few former toppers - Raksha Gopal, Hansika Shukla, and Karishma Arora. So, what makes them special? Did they study for 24 hours a day? Did they burn the midnight oil days before the exam? Or even lock themselves up inside a room to avoid distractions? No, they did none of these things.

How to handle the exam pressure?

Raksha: The best way to handle pressure is to not overthink. Treat the board exams as a stepping stone in your life and do not let them define your entire life. It is helpful to keep a calm mind and if you can meditate for some time, nothing like it.

Hansika: One should have a healthy conversation with parents in this situation and reach out for help. Studying excessively won't help and it will blur your mind.

Karishma: It is important to keep aside some time for relaxation. Pursuing your hobby even while preparing for the exams act as a stress reliever.

Top time management skills while writing the exams

Raksha: Try to answer the questions according to the marks allocated to them. Do not spend too much time on one question neglecting other questions. And always keep some buffer time to review your answers.

Hansika: Time management is important, especially for language papers, as one cannot predict how long a paper will be. For instance, students can always divide the papers into different sections such as section A, section B, and so on. They must aim to finish a section within a certain time limit

Karishma: While writing the exam, keep in mind that the length of your answers should be according to the weightage of marks allotted for it.

How to approach the exams - attempt the easy and known answers first and then try to solve the difficult ones or take on each question chronologically?

Raksha: Try to attempt the questions chronologically as it is easier for the examiner to check.

Hansika: It depends on the student. Solving the questions chronologically may help. However, a preferred method would be tackling the easy answers first before moving to the difficult ones.

Karishma: Usually, I try to answer the questions in chronological order.

Is it true 'Neat and clean answer sheets have more chances of getting good marks than untidy ones'.

Raksha: Yes, of course! An examiner should be able to read your answers easily. Good handwriting or not, you should present your answers in a neat manner.

Hansika: Whether neat and clean papers would get more marks depends on the examiner. In most cases, having neat and clear handwriting does help.

Karishma: When the examiner checks an answer sheet and it has good handwriting and neat and clean work, he or she will assume that the student is well-prepared. Often there is a chance that the examiner might even miss your careless mistakes.

Should student should review the paper again after completing it, to check if any mistakes have been committed

Raksha: You should keep the last 5-10 minutes to review your answers again and check for any mistakes. But once you are out of the exam hall, no point going through the paper again to check for mistakes.

Hansika: I firmly believe that one should review the paper thoroughly after the exam. This way, any errors committed during the exam can be rectified.

Karishma: Revising the answers before submitting your sheet is important to check for any last-minute mistakes.

Some miscellaneous exam writing tips for Students.

Raksha: Always underline the important points of your answer. It helps in scoring. And try to mark your answers neatly.

Hansika: Students should remain calm and tackle one question at a time. In case they come across a question which they find difficult, they should try to write what would be the most relevant and appropriate answer.

Karishma: Make sure that you know the distribution of marks for all the topics in that subject. This way you can plan the length of your answers accordingly.

Please Note that all the information is collected from different websites.

Most Important Topics

from each Chapter

On the basis of analysis of last 4 Years' Board Examination Papers, we have identified Important Topics from each chapter.

Chapter Name	Important Topics	Weightage in Last 4 Years' Boards			
		2024	2023	2020	2019
Sexual Reproduction in Flowering Plants	Flower and its Parts	5M	5M	1M	2M, 3M, 5M (2Q)
	Pollination	1M	1M, 3M	2M(2Q), 3M	2M(3Q), 3M(4Q)
	Post-fertilisation: Structures and Events	2M		2M(2Q), 5M	2M, 3M, 5M
Human Reproduction	Reproductive System		1M		3M
	Gametogenesis	1M, 4M, 5M	2M, 3M	3M(2Q)	2M, 3M
	Fertilisation, Pregnancy and Embryonic Development		5M	3M,5M	1M,3M, 5M
Reproductive Health	Reproductive Health : Problems and Strategies	1M, 3M	1M(2Q), 3M, 5M	3M	
	Sexually Transmitted Diseases (STDs) and Infertility	1M, 2M	1M	5M	5M
Principles of Inheritance & Variation	Mendel's Laws of Inheritance	1M, 5M	2M, 5M(3Q)	2M, 3M(2Q), 5M(4Q)	1M(2Q), 2M, 3M(3Q), 5M(2Q)
	Sex-determination and Genetic Disorders	1M	1M, 4M	1M,2M,5M	2M(2Q)
Molecular Basis of Inheritance	The DNA and RNA World	1M, 5M		1M,3M (2Q), 5M	2M, 3M(3Q)
	Genetic Code, Human Genome Project and DNA Fingerprinting	1M, 3M	1M,3M, 5M(3Q)	2M,3M,5M	3M(2Q), 5M(2Q)
Evolution	The Origin of Life and Evidences of Evolution	3M	3M(2Q)	3M	1M
	Theories of Evolution and Biological Evolution	2M	1M, 3M	3M	1M(2Q), 2M, 3M(2Q), 5M
Human Health & Diseases	Health, Common Diseases in Humans and Immunity	1M, 2M 3M, 5M	1M(4Q), 2M(3Q), 3M(2Q), 4M	2M(2Q), 3M(4Q), 5M	1M(2Q), 2M(2Q)
	Adolescence and Drug/ Alcohol Abuse			2M, 3M	
Microbes in Human Welfare	Microbes in Household Products, Industrial Products and in Sewage Treatment	1M, 5M	1M	1M	1M, 3M
	Microbes in Production of Biogas, as Biocontrol Agents and Biofertilisers	2M	2M(2Q)	1M,3M	1M, 3M(2Q)
Biotechnology: Principles and Processes	Principles of Biotechnology and Tools of Recombinant DNA Technology	3M	1M, 2M, 5M	2M(2Q), 3M (2Q)	1M(2Q), 2M, 3M(6Q)
	Processes of Recombinant DNA Technology	1M, 4M	1M,2M, 5M	2M	2M, 3M(2Q)

Biotechnology and Its Applications	Biotechnological Applications in Agriculture and Medicine	1M(3Q)	2M, 3M(3Q)	3M(2Q), 5M	1M, 2M, 3M(2Q)
	Transgenic Animals and Ethical Issues	1M, 3M		2M(2Q)	
Organisms and Populations	Population		1M	3M	3M, 5M(2Q)
	Population Interactions	1M	1M(3Q), 2M(2Q)	2M, 3M	2M, 3M
Ecosystem	Ecosystem: Structure and Function, Productivity and Decomposition	3M	1M(2Q)	2M(2Q),3M	2M
	Energy Flow in Ecosystem			2M	5M
Biodiversity & Its Conservation	Biodiversity	2M	1M(3Q)		2M(2Q)
	Conservation of Biodiversity	4M	3M	3M(2Q)	3M

Contents

CBSE Chapterwise Question Bank 2024-2010

1. Sexual Reproduction in Flowering Plants 1-38

Flower and Its Parts
Pollination
Post-Fertilisation : Structures and Events
Chapter Test

2. Human Reproduction 39-70

Reproductive System
Gametogenesis
Fertilisation, Pregnancy and Embryonic Development
Chapter Test

3. Reproductive Health 71-88

Reproductive Health : Problems and Strategies
Sexually Transmitted Diseases (STDs) and Infertility
Chapter Test

4. Principles of Inheritance and Variation 89-132

Mendel's Laws of Inheritance
Sex Determination and Genetic Disorders
Chapter Test

5. Molecular Basis of Inheritance 133-182

The DNA and RNA World
Genetic Code, Human Genome Project and DNA Fingerprinting
Chapter Test

6. Evolution 183-206

The Origin of Life and Evidences of Evolution
Theories of Evolution and Biological Evolution
Chapter Test

7. Human Health and Diseases 207-243
Health, Common Diseases in Human and Immunity
Adolescence and Drug/Alcohol Abuse
Chapter Test

8. Microbes in Human Welfare 244-263
Microbes in Household Products, Industrial Products and in Sewage Treatment
Microbes in Production of Biogas, as Biocontrol Agents and Biofertilisers
Chapter Test

9. Biotechnology : Principles and Processes 264-295
Principles of Biotechnology and Tools of Recombinant DNA Technology
Processes of Recombinant DNA Technology
Chapter Test

10. Biotechnology and Its Applications 296-317
Biotechnological Applications in Agriculture and Medicine
Transgenic Animals and Ethical Issues
Chapter Test

11. Organisms and Populations 318-340
Population
Population Interactions
Chapter Test

12. Ecosystem 341-356
Ecosystem : Structure and Function, Productivity and Decomposition
Energy Flow in Ecosystem
Chapter Test

13. Biodiversity and Its Conservation 357-375
Biodiversity
Conservation of Biodiversity
Chapter Test

- 3 Sample Papers 376-390

Latest Syllabus

Class 12 (2024-25)

Paper: One **Time: 3 Hrs** **Max. Marks : 70**

Units		Marks
I	Reproduction	16
II	Genetics and Evolution	20
III	Biology and Human Welfare	12
IV	Biotechnology and its Applications	12
V	Ecology and Environment	10
	TOTAL	70

UNIT I Reproduction

Chapter 2 : Sexual Reproduction in Flowering Plants

Flower structure; development of male and female gametophytes; pollination - types, agencies and examples; out breeding devices; pollen-pistil interaction; double fertilisation; post- fertilisation events - development of endosperm and embryo, development of seed and formation of fruit; special modes- apomixis, parthenocarpy, polyembryony; Significance of seed dispersal and fruit formation.

Chapter 3 : Human Reproduction

Male and female reproductive systems; microscopic anatomy of testis and ovary; gametogenesis - spermatogenesis and oogenesis; menstrual cycle; fertilisation, embryo development upto blastocyst formation, implantation; pregnancy and placenta formation (elementary idea); parturition (elementary idea); lactation (elementary idea).

Chapter 4 : Reproductive Health

Need for reproductive health and prevention of Sexually Transmitted Diseases (STDs); birth control - need and methods, contraception and Medical Termination of Pregnancy (MTP); amniocentesis; infertility and assisted reproductive technologies - IVF, ZIFT, GIFT (elementary idea for general awareness).

UNIT II Genetics and Evolution

Chapter 5 : Principles of Inheritance and Variation

Heredity and variation: Mendelian inheritance; deviations from Mendelism – incomplete dominance, co-dominance, multiple alleles and inheritance of blood groups, pleiotropy; elementary idea of polygenic inheritance; chromosome theory of inheritance; chromosomes and genes; Sex determination - in humans, birds and honeybee; linkage and crossing over; sex linked inheritance - haemophilia, colour blindness; Mendelian disorders in humans - thalassemia; chromosomal disorders in humans; Down's syndrome, Turner's and Klinefelter's syndromes.

Chapter 6 : Molecular Basis of Inheritance
Search for genetic material and DNA as genetic material; Structure of DNA and RNA; DNA packaging; DNA replication; Central Dogma; transcription, genetic code, translation; gene expression and regulation - *lac* operon; Genome, Human and rice genome projects; DNA fingerprinting.

Chapter 7 : Evolution
Origin of life; biological evolution and evidences for biological evolution (paleontology, comparative anatomy, embryology and molecular evidences); Darwin's contribution, modern synthetic theory of evolution; mechanism of evolution - variation (mutation and recombination) and natural selection with examples, types of natural selection; Gene flow and genetic drift; Hardy - Weinberg's principle; adaptive radiation; human evolution.

UNIT III Biology and Human Welfare

Chapter 8 : Human Health and Diseases
Pathogens; parasites causing human diseases (malaria, dengue, chikungunya, filariasis, ascariasis, typhoid, pneumonia, common cold, amoebiasis, ring worm) and their control; Basic concepts of immunology - vaccines; cancer, HIV and AIDS; Adolescence - drug and alcohol abuse.

Chapter 10 : Microbes in Human Welfare
Microbes in food processing, industrial production, sewage treatment, energy generation and microbes as bio-control agents and bio-fertilisers. Antibiotics; production and judicious use.

UNIT IV Biotechnology and Its Applications

Chapter 11 : Biotechnology - Principles and Processes
Genetic Engineering (Recombinant DNA Technology).

Chapter 12 : Biotechnology and its Application
Application of biotechnology in health and agriculture: Human insulin and vaccine production, stem cell technology, gene therapy; genetically modified organisms - *Bt* crops; transgenic animals; biosafety issues, biopiracy and patents.

UNIT V Ecology and Environment

Chapter 13 : Organisms and Populations
Population interactions - mutualism, competition, predation, parasitism; population attributes - growth, birth rate and death rate, age distribution. (Topics excluded: Organism and its Environment, Major Aboitic Factors, Responses to Abioitic Factors, Adaptations)

Chapter 14 : Ecosystem
Ecosystems: Patterns, components; productivity and decomposition; energy flow; pyramids of number, biomass, energy (Topics excluded: Ecological Succession and Nutrient Cycles)

Chapter 15 : Biodiversity and its Conservation
Biodiversity-Concept, patterns, importance; loss of biodiversity; biodiversity conservation; hotspots, endangered organisms, extinction, Red Data Book, Sacred groves, biosphere reserves, national parks, wildlife sanctuaries and Ramsar sites.

01

Sexual Reproduction in Flowering Plants

TREND ANALYSIS 3 YEARS

Average No. of Questions Across all Sets

Topic	Types of Questions	2024	2023	2020
TOPIC 01 Flower and its Parts	1 Mark	0	0	1
	2 Marks	0	0	0
	3 Marks	0	0	0
	4 Marks (Case Based)	0	0	0
	5 Marks	1	1	0
TOPIC 02 Pollination	1 Mark	1	1	0
	2 Marks	0	0	2
	3 Marks	0	1	1
	4 Marks (Case Based)	0	0	0
	5 Marks	0	0	0
TOPIC 03 Post-Fertilisation : Structures and Events	1 Mark	0	0	0
	2 Marks	1	0	2
	3 Marks	0	0	0
	4 Marks (Case Based)	0	0	0
	5 Marks	0	0	1

Sexual reproduction is the process of fusion of haploid gametes, resulting in the production of a diploid zygote, which ultimately develops into a new organism. All flowering plants show sexual reproduction.

TOPIC 1

Flower and its Parts

Flowers

- These are the site of sexual reproduction in flowering plants.
- A flower has parts namely; sepals, petals, stamens and pistils arranged in four whorls, i.e. calyx (sepals), corolla (petals), androecium (stamens) and gynoecium (pistils). These whorls are attached on central axis called **thalamus.**
- Flowers may contain both male (stamens) and female (carpels or pistils) reproductive parts or organs in it and such flowers are called **bisexual.**

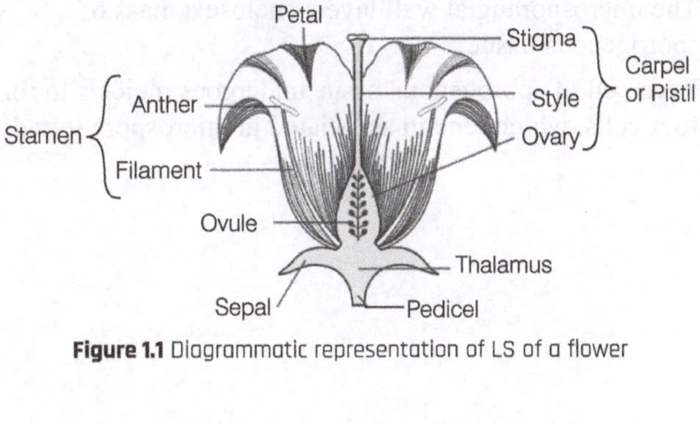

Figure 1.1 Diagrammatic representation of LS of a flower

- In **unisexual flowers**, only either of the reproductive parts is present, e.g. in corn, the tassels represent the male flowers (stamens) and the ears or silk represent the female flower (styles and stigma).

Development of Male Gametophyte

Development of male gametophyte involves the study of following

Stamen

It is the male reproductive unit of angiosperm. It consists of following two parts

- The long and slender stalk called the **filament.**
- The terminal generally bilobed structure called the **anther**.

Structure of Anther

It is a bilobed structure with each lobe having two **theca**, therefore it is called **dithecous**. In a cross-section, it appears four sided, i.e. tetragonal.

It consists of four microsporangia, located at four corners (two in each lobe). **Microsporangia** after development become pollen sacs by producing pollen grains.

Microsporangium

Structure of microsporangium contains following features in a transverse section

- It appears nearly circular in outline.
- It is surrounded by four wall layers.
  The outer three layers are **epidermis**, **endothecium** and **middle layers**. These three wall layers are protective in function and they also help in dehiscence of anther to release the pollen. The fourth and innermost layer called the **tapetum**, which nourishes developing pollen grains. It contains cells with dense cytoplasm and more than one nuclei.
- The microsporangial wall layers enclose a mass of sporogenous tissue.
- Each cell of sporogenous tissue undergoes meiosis to form four cells, which remain associated in microspore tetrad.

Each cell of this tetrad after separation develops into pollen grains that represent male gametophyte.

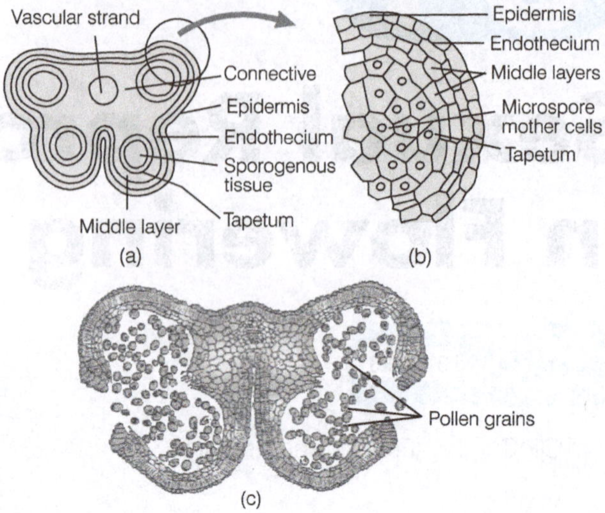

Figure 1.2 (a) TS of a young anther, (b) Enlarged view of one microsporangium, (c) TS of mature dehised anther

Microsporogenesis

The process of the formation of microspores from a **Pollen Mother Cell** (PMC) through meiosis is called microsporogenesis.

Microspores are arranged as tetrad. As the anthers mature and dehydrate, they dissociate from each other and develop into pollen grains. Pollen grains or the male gametophytes are later released during dehiscence of anther.

Male Gametophyte (Pollen Grain)

- Pollen grains have the following characteristic features
  - Generally **spherical**, about 25-50 micrometres in diameter.
  - Mature pollen grain consists of an outer covering called **sporoderm**.
- It is differentiated into two layers
  (i) Outer hard layer, i.e. **exine** is made up of one of the most resistant organic material **sporopollenin,** that enables them to resist high temperatures and action of strong acids and alkalis.

Further no enzyme is yet known to degrade sporopollenin, because of which pollen grains are well-preserved as fossils.

The regions on exine, where sporopollenin is absent are called **germ pores**. These help in the formation of pollen tube, while the pollen grain germinates on stigma.

(ii) Inner thin, continuous layer, i.e. **intine** is made up of cellulose and pectin.

- A mature pollen grain contains two cells, that are formed *via* mitosis. These are

(i) **Vegetative cell or Tube cell** It is larger as compared to other cells and possesses vacuolated cytoplasm, which is rich in reserve food, i.e. starch, protein, fat and cell organelles. The nucleus is large and irregular.

(ii) **Generative cell** It is smaller cell usually spindle-shaped or spherical with thin dense cytoplasm and prominent nuclei.

It divides mitotically to form two non-motile male gametes, prior to release of pollen grain. The process of the formation of male gametes from generative cell is called **microgametogenesis**.

- In about 60% of angiosperms, pollen grains shed at 2-celled stage (1 vegetative cell +1 generative cell).
- In about 40% flowering plants, the generative cell divides mitotically to give rise to the two male gametes before pollen grains are shed at 3-celled stage (1 vegetative cell +2 male gametes).

Some Important Aspects of Pollen Grain

- Pollen grains of many species (e.g. *Parthenium* or carrot grass) cause severe allergy and chronic respiratory disorders like asthma, bronchitis, etc.
- **Viability of pollen grains** depends on temperature and humidity. In cereals such as rice and wheat, viability is for 30 minutes whereas in members of Rosaceae, Leguminosae and Solanaceae, pollen grains maintain viability for months.
- Pollen grains are rich in nutrients and are used as food supplements in the form of pollen tablets and syrups. Consumption of pollens has been claimed to increase the performance of athletes and race horses.
- Pollen grains of many species are stored for years in liquid nitrogen (–196°C), in order to use them in crop breeding programmes. Such pollens are stored in pollen banks.

Development of Female Gametophyte

It involves the study of the following

Pistil/Gynoecium

It is the female unit of flower. A flower may be **monocarpellary** (having one pistil) or **multicarpellary** (having more than one pistil). Pistils may be **syncarpous** (fused together) or **apocarpous** (free).

The main parts of pistil are

- **Stigma** is the topmost receptive part that receives pollen grains.
- **Style** is the elongated slender part beneath the stigma.
- **Ovary** is the bulged part at the base of style that contains ovules or megasporangia. Ovules are connected to ovary by means of placenta, which is located inside the **ovarian cavity** or **locule**.

Megasporangium (Ovule)

It arises from the placenta. Ovule is attached to the placenta by a stalk called **funicle**. The number of ovules in an ovary may be one (wheat, paddy and mango) to many (papaya, watermelon and orchids).

The main parts of megasporangium (ovule) are

- **Hilum** is a junction between ovule and funicle.
- Each ovule has one or two protective envelopes called **integuments**.
- **Micropyle** is an opening present at the tip where integument is absent.
- **Chalaza** is opposite to the micropylar end representing the basal part of the ovule.

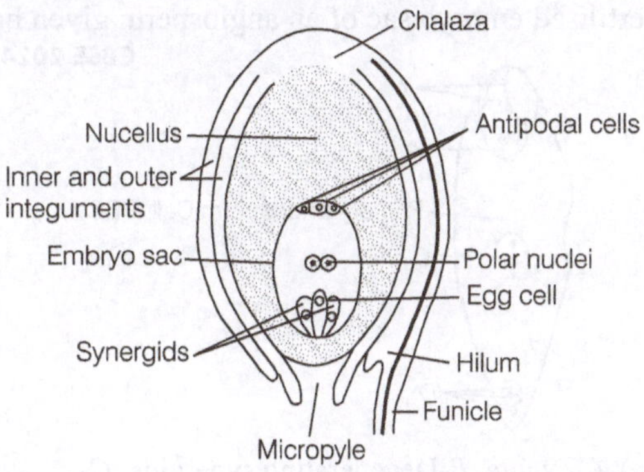

Figure 1.3 Diagrammatic view of a typical anatropous ovule

- The integument encloses a mass of cells called the **nucellus,** which have food reserves.
- **Embryo sac** or **Female gametophyte** is located in the nucellus (generally one formed from a megaspore through reductional division).

Megasporogenesis

It is the process of formation of **megaspores** from the **Megaspore Mother Cell** (MMC). The MMC is a large cell with dense cytoplasm and prominent nucleus. It undergoes meiosis resulting in the production of four megaspores.

Female Gametophyte (Embryo Sac)

- Out of the four magaspores, only one is functional, while the other three degenerate in majority of angiosperms.
- Only the functional megaspore develops into the **female gametophyte** or **embryo sac**. This is called **monosporic development.**
- Nucleus of the functional megaspore divides mitotically to form two nuclei, which move to the opposite poles forming the **2-nucleate** embryo sac.
- Nuclear divisions result into the formation of first **4-nucleate** and later **8-nucleate** stages of the embryo sac.
- Six of the eight nuclei are surrounded by cell walls and organised into cells. The remaining two nuclei called **polar nuclei**, are situated below the egg apparatus in the large **central cell**.
- Three cells group together at the micropylar end and constitute the **egg apparatus**.
- The egg apparatus consists of two **synergids** and one **egg cell.**
- A **filiform apparatus** made of cellular thickenings of synergids at the micropylar end, plays an important role in guiding the pollen tubes into the **synergid.**
- At the chalazal end, three cells are present called **antipodals.**
- Thus, a typical angiosperm embryo sac at maturity is **8-nucleate** and **7-celled.**

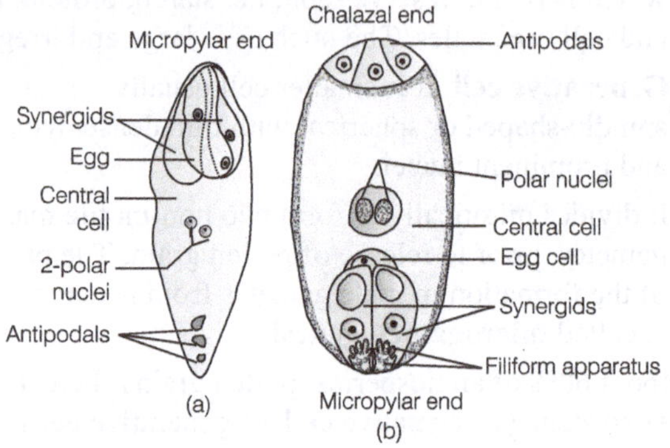

Figure 1.4 (a) 8-nucleate stage of embryo sac, (b) Diagrammatic representation of the mature embryo sac

PYQs Previous Years' Questions

1 Mark Questions

Multiple Choice Questions

1. Identify the correct labellings in the figure of a fertilised embryo sac of an angiosperm given below. **CBSE 2024 (Set-II)**

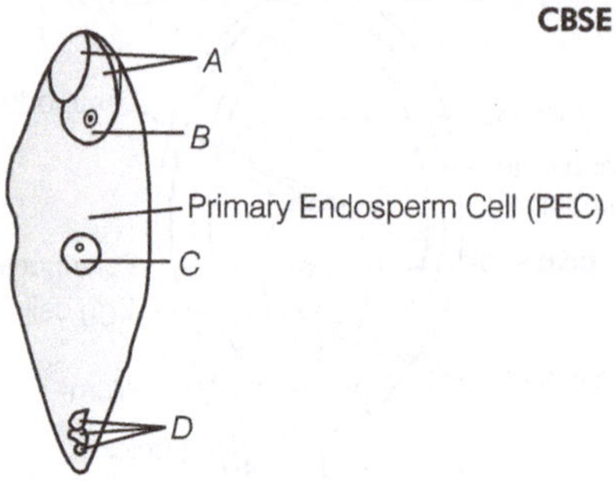

(a) *A*-Zygote, *B*-Degenerating synergids, *C*-Degenerating antipodals, *D*-PEN

(b) *A*- Degenerating synergids, *B*- Zygote, *C*-PEN, *D*-Degenerating antipodals

(c) *A*-Degenerating antipodals, *B*-PEN, *C*-Degenerating synergids, *D*-Zygote

(d) *A*-Degenerating synergids, *B*-Zygote, *C*-Degenerating antipodals, *D*-PEN

Ans. (b) The correct labelling for the given figure showing post-fertilisation events is as follows
A-Degenerating synergids, *B*-Zygote *C*-PEN, *D*-Degenerating antipodals.

2. The wall layer of microsporangium which nourishes the pollen grain is **CBSE SQP 2023**

(a) epidermis (b) endothecium
(c) middle layers (d) tapetum

Ans. (d) tapetum

3. The structure of bilobed anther consists of **CBSE SQP 2021-22 Term-I**

(a) 2 thecae, 2 sporangia (b) 4 thecae, 4 sporangia
(c) 4 thecae, 2 sporangia (d) 2 thecae, 4 sporangia

Ans. (d) 2 thecae, 4 sporangia

4. In the figure of anatropous ovule given below, choose the correct option for the characteristic distribution of cells within the typical embryo sac. **CBSE SQP 2021-22 Term-I**

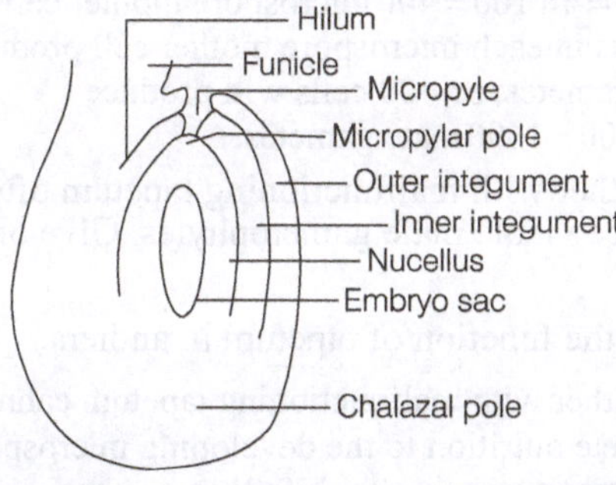

	Number of cells at chalazal end	Number of cells at micropylar end	Number of nuclei left in central cell
(a)	3	2	3
(b)	3	3	2
(c)	2	3	3
(d)	2	2	4

Ans. (b) 3, 3, 2

5. Pollen grains are well preserved as fossils because of presence of **CBSE SQP 2021-22 Term-I**
(a) sporopollenin (b) cellulose
(c) lignocellulose (d) pectocellulose

Ans. (a) sporopollenin

6. During megasporogenesis, potential megaspore mother cell undergoes following cell divisions to form gametophyte female **CBSE SQP 2021-22 Term-I**
(a) two meiotic divisions and three mitotic divisions
(b) one meiotic and one mitotic divisions
(c) one meiotic and three mitotic divisions
(d) one meiotic and two mitotic divisions

Ans. (c) one meiotic and three mitotic divisions

7. In the transverse section of a young anther shown below, identify the correct sequence of wall layers from outside to inside. **CBSE 2021-22 Term-I**

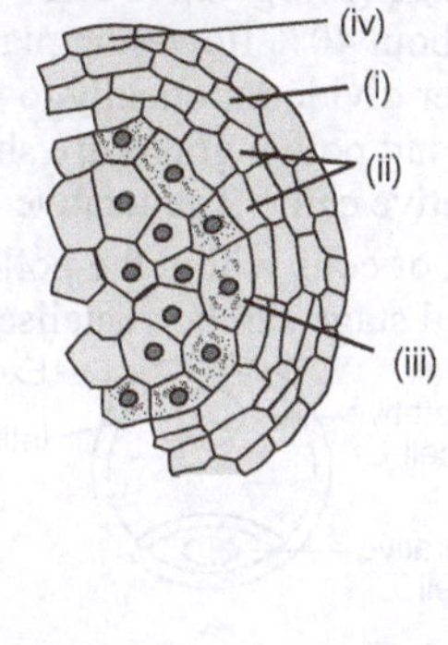

	(i)	(ii)	(iii)	(iv)
(a)	Middle layers	Endothecium	Epidermis	Tapetum
(b)	Tapetum	Middle layers	Endothecium	Epidermis
(c)	Epidermis	Endothecium	Middle layers	Tapetum
(d)	Endothecium	Middle layers	Tapetum	Epidermis

Ans. (d)

8. Pollen grains retain viability for months in plants belonging to different families given below.
(i) Solanaceae (ii) Leguminosae
(iii) Gramineae (iv) Rosaceae
(v) Liliaceae
The correct option is **CBSE 2021-22 Term-I**
(a) (i), (ii) and (v) (b) (i), (ii) and (iv)
(c) (ii), (iv) and (v) (d) (i), (iii) and (v)

Ans. (b) (i), (ii) and (iv)

9. Enclosed within the integuments of a typical anatropous ovule is a diploid mass of cellular tissue known as **CBSE 2021-22 Term-I**
(a) megaspore mother cell (b) nucellus
(c) synergids (d) embryo sac

Ans. (b) nucellus

10. Which one of the following is not found in a female gametophyte of an angiosperm? **Delhi 2020**
(a) Germ pore (b) Synergids
(c) Filiform apparatus (d) Central cell

Ans. (a) Germ pore

Very Short Answer Type Questions

11. How many pollen grains and ovules are likely to be formed in the anther and the ovary of an angiosperm bearing 25 microspore mother cells and 25 megaspore mother cells, respectively? **CBSE SQP 2019**

Ans. 100 pollen grains and 25 ovules are likely to be formed in the anther and the ovary of an angiosperm bearing 25 microspore mother cells and 25 megaspore mother cells, respectively. (½ + ½)

12. Angiosperms bearing unisexual flowers are said to be either monoecious or dioecious. Explain with the help of one example each. **All India 2016**

Ans. Plant bearing flowers of both sexes, i.e. staminate and pistillate flowers are called monoecious, e.g. *Zea mays* (maize).

When both sexes, i.e. staminate and pistillate flowers, are present on different plants; these plants are called dioecious, e.g. *Carica papaya* (papaya). (½ + ½)

13. These pictures show the gynoecium of *Papaver* (*A*) and *Michelia* (*B*) flowers. Write the difference in the structure of their ovaries. **Delhi 2015C**

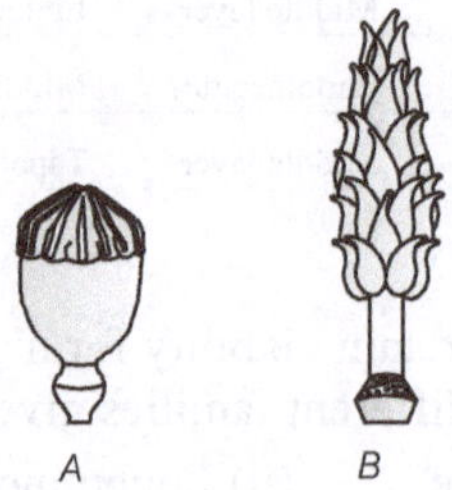

Ans. The gynoecium of *Papaver* is multicarpellary and syncarpous (pistils are fused together), the ovary can be unilocular to multilocular. The gynoecium of *Michelia* is multicarpellary and apocarpus (pistils are free) and the ovary is always unilocular. (½ + ½)

14. Name the parts of the flower which the tassels of corn cob represent. **All India 2014**

Ans. The parts of the flower that represent the tassels of corn cob are stigma and style which wave in the wind to trap pollen grains flowing with the wind.

15. Draw a diagram of a mature microspore of an angiosperm. Label its cellular components only. **Foreign 2014**

Or Draw a labelled diagram of a mature pollen grain. **Delhi 2013C**

Ans. The labelled diagram of a mature microspore of an angiosperm with its cellular components is given below

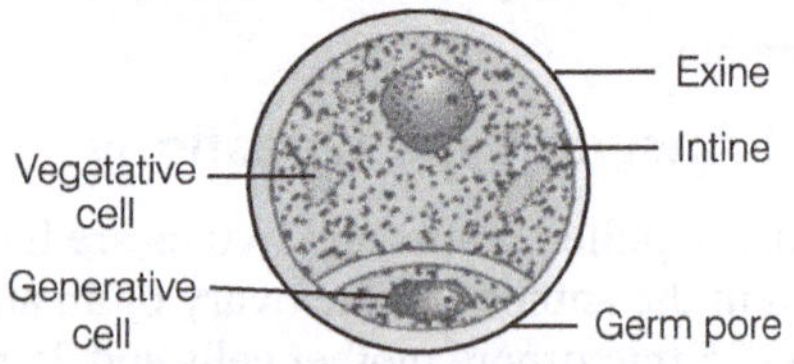

16. State the function of filiform apparatus found in mature embryo sac of an angiosperm. **Foreign 2014**

Ans. The special cellular thickenings present in synergids at the micropylar tip are called filiform apparatus. They are found in mature embryo sac of an angiosperm and help in guiding the entry of pollen tubes upto the synergids.

17. Give an example of a plant which came into India as a contaminant and is a cause of pollen allergy. **All India 2014**

Ans. *Parthenium* or Carrot grass is a major contaminant which came to India and caused pollen allergy.

18. A bilobed, dithecous anther has 100 microspore mother cells per microsporangium. How many male gametophytes this anther can produce? **Delhi 2010**

Ans. An anther is a four-sided (tetragonal) structure consisting of four microsporangia.
Each microsporangium has 100 microspore mother cells, so total number of microspore mother cells in anther $= 4 \times 100 = 400$ microspore mother cells.
Meiosis in each microspore mother cell produces 4 male gametes, so 400 cells will produce $= 4 \times 400 = 1600$ male gametes.

19. An anther with malfunctioning tapetum often fails to produce viable male gametophytes. Give one reason. **Delhi 2010**

Or Write the function of tapetum in anthers. **Delhi 2012**

Ans. The anther with malfunctioning tapetum cannot provide complete nutrition to the developing microspores or male gametophytes. So, it fails to produce viable male gametophyte.

2 Marks Questions

20. In the TS of a mature anther given below, identify '*a*' and '*b*' and mention their functions. **All India 2019**

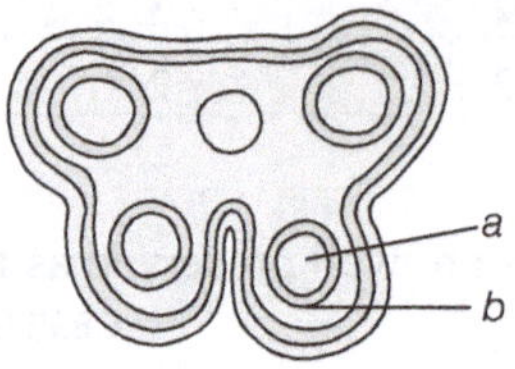

Ans. In the given figure, *a* is sporogenous tissue and *b* is tapetum.

(i) **Sporogenous tissue** has cells which are potential Pollen Mother Cells (PMC) or microspore mother cells and give rise to microspore tetrad after meiotic cell division. (1)

(ii) **Tapetum** nourishes the developing microspores or pollen grains. (1)

21. A pollen grain in angiosperm at the time of dehiscence from an anther could be 2-celled or 3-celled. Explain, how are the cells placed within the pollen grain when shed at a 2-celled stage? **All India 2017**

Ans. In about 60% of angiosperms, pollen grains are shed at the 2-celled stage (1 vegetative cell + 1 generative cell). However, in about 40% flowering plants, the generative cell may further divide mitotically to give rise to two male gametes and pollen grains are shed at this 3-celled stage (1 vegetative cell + 2 generative cells).
The placement of cells within the pollen grain when shed at 2-celled stage can be visualised as shown below

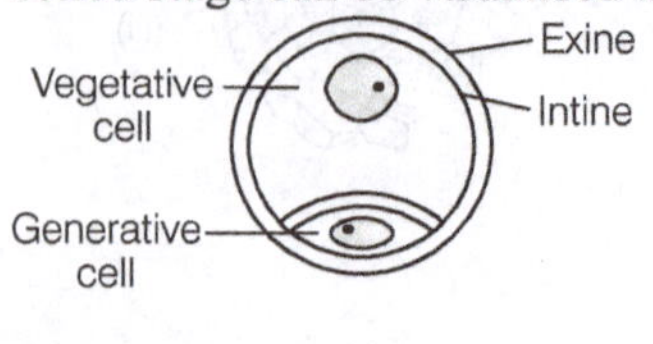

22. A mature embryo sac in a flowering plant may possess 7-cells, but 8-nuclei. Explain with the help of a diagram only. **Delhi 2017**

Ans. A typical angiospermic embryo sac is 8-nucleated and 7-celled shown below.

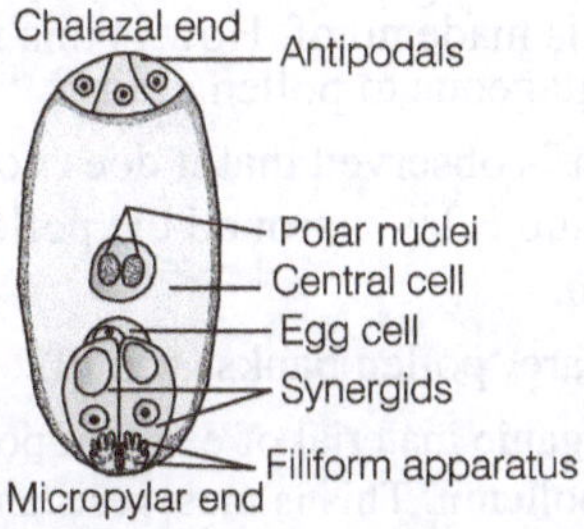

23. In a flowering plant, a microspore mother cell produces four male gametophytes while a megaspore mother cell forms only one female gametophyte. Explain. **Delhi 2017**

Ans. In flowering plants, microspore mother cells undergo meiosis and give rise to four microspores that remain together in a microspore tetrad.

After attaining maturity, these microspores separate from each other and each microspore develops into a male gametophyte or pollen grain.

On the other hand, megaspore mother cell divides by meiotic division to produce four megaspores. From these, three degenerate while, one undergoes further development to produce female gametophyte.

Thus, in a flowering plant, a microspore mother cell produces four male gametophytes while, megaspore mother cell produces one female gametophyte.

24. Gynoecium of a flower may be apocarpous or syncarpous. Explain with the help of an example each. **Delhi 2016**

Ans. Gynoecium of a flower is called as apocarpous when the carpels are free, e.g. apocarpus in *Ranunculus.* On the other hand, it is called syncarpous when the carpels are fused, e.g. syncarpous in *Petunia*.

25. Draw a diagram of a section of a megasporangium of an angiosperm and label funiculus, micropyle, embryo sac and nucellus. **All India 2016**

Ans. Diagrammatic view of a megasporangium (anatropous ovule)

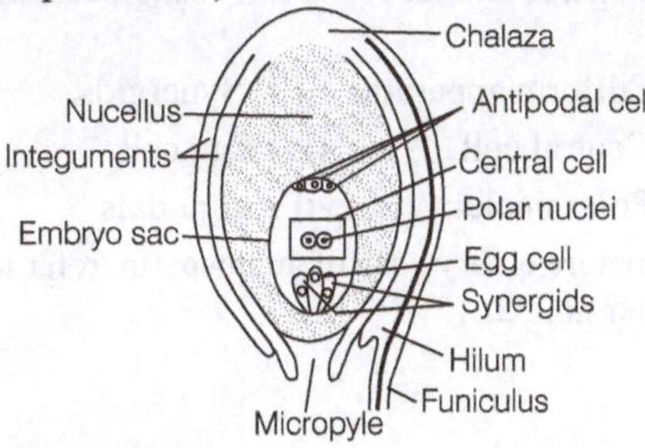

26. Differentiate between the two cells enclosed in a mature male gametophyte of an angiosperm. **All India 2013**

Ans. Haploid pollen grains represent the male gametophyte. It contains two cells, i.e. vegetative cell and generative cell.

The vegetative or tube cell is larger in size as compared to generative cell and have a vacuolated cytoplasm. The generative cell on the other hand has thin dense cytoplasm with prominent nuclei that gives rise to two male gametes, while vegetative cell does not.

27. Name all the haploid cells present in an unfertilised mature embryo sac of a flowering plant. Write the total number of cells in it. **All India 2013**

Or How many haploid cells are present in mature female gametophyte of a flowering plant? Name them. **Delhi 2013C**

Ans. An unfertilised embryo sac of angiosperm is composed of 7 cells, i.e. 7-celled and 8-nucleated. Among 8-nuclei, 6 are enclosed by cell walls and organised into cells, which are haploid in number (3 antipodals, 2 synergids and 1 egg cell) and a large central cell with 2 polar nuclei.

28. Draw a labelled schematic diagram of the transverse section of a mature anther of an angiosperm plant. **Delhi 2013**

Ans. TS of mature dehised anther shown below

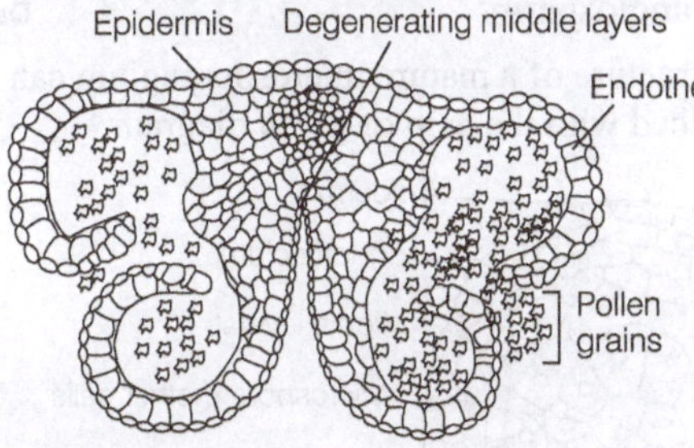

29. Explain the function of germ pores. **All India 2012**

Ans. Germ pores are prominent apertures of pollen grain exine where sporopollenin is absent. These are the regions where intine comes out forming a pollen tube to release male gametes in the embryo sac.

3 Marks Questions

30. Pollen banks are playing a very important role in promoting plant breeding programme the world over. How are pollens preserved in the pollen banks? Explain. How are such banks benefitting our farmers? Write any two ways. **Delhi 2019**

Ans. Pollen grains are stored for years in liquid nitrogen (–196°C) in pollen banks for later use in plant breeding programmes. Plant breeding is a technique of manipulation of plant species in order to create desired plant types that are better suited for cultivation, give better yield and are disease resistant. **(1)**

The objectives of such pollen banks include incorporation of certain traits or characters into crop plants in order to enhance the food production such as

(i) Increased tolerance to environmental stresses such as salinity, extreme temperature, drought, etc.

(ii) Resistance to pathogens like viruses, fungi and bacteria. **(2)**

31. The embryo sac in female gametophyte is seven celled and eight nucleated structure. Justify the statement with the help of a labelled diagram. **CBSE SQP 2019**

Ans. Refer to text on page no. 4.

32. Draw the diagram of microsporangium of an angiosperm and label any four parts. State the function of its innermost wall layer. **CBSE SQP 2018**

Or Draw a labelled diagram of a section of an enlarged view of microsporangium of an angiosperm. **All India 2016 C**

Or Why are angiosperm anthers called dithecous? Describe the structure of its microsporangium. **Delhi 2014**

Or Describe the structure of a mature microsporangium of an angiosperm. **Delhi 2014**

Ans. The structure of a mature microsporangium can be described with the help of given diagram

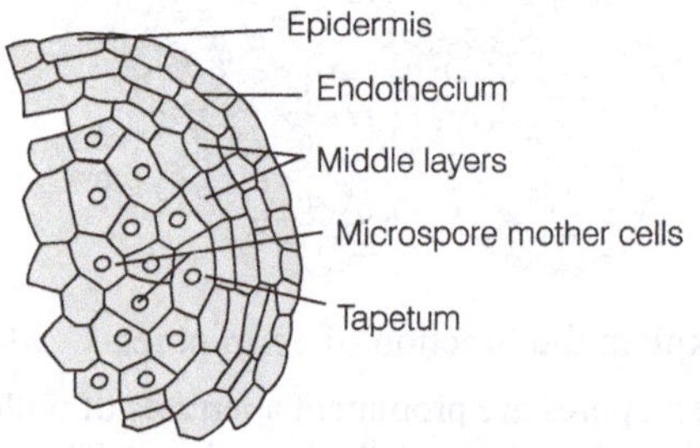

The angiosperm's anthers are bilobed, each lobe bearing two thecae. Thus, they are referred to as dithecous. Microsporangium appears circular in outline and is usually surrounded by four wall layers. The outer three layers epidermis, endothecium and middle layers are protective in function. They also help in dispersal of pollens by dehiscing themselves. While, the innermost layer tapetum is nutritive in function and nourishes the developing pollen grains. The centre of the microsporangium comprises of compact sporogenous tissue. The cells of this sporogenous tissue undergo meiotic divisions to form microspore tetrads, that further develop to form pollen grains.

33. (i) Name the organic material exine of the pollen grain is made up of. How is this material advantageous to pollen grain?

(ii) Still it is observed that it does not form a continuous layer around the pollen grain. Give reason.

(iii) How are 'pollen banks' useful? **All India 2016C**

Ans. (i) The organic material of exine of pollen grain is sporopollenin. This is most resistant biological material known so far. It protects pollen grains from damages. **(1)**

(ii) Exine of pollen grain is not a continuous layer. It is thin at places and pollen tube germinates by growth of intine through these thin parts of exine called germ pores. **(1)**

(iii) Pollen banks are used to store pollen grains for short as well as long period of time in viable conditions. **(1)**

34. Draw a labelled diagram of a typical anatropous ovule. **Delhi 2014**

Ans. For structure or labelled diagram of anatropous ovule, refer to answer no. 25.

35. Explain the process of microsporogenesis in angiosperms. **Delhi 2013C**

Ans. The formation of microspores from a pollen mother cell through meiosis is called microsporogenesis. **(1)**

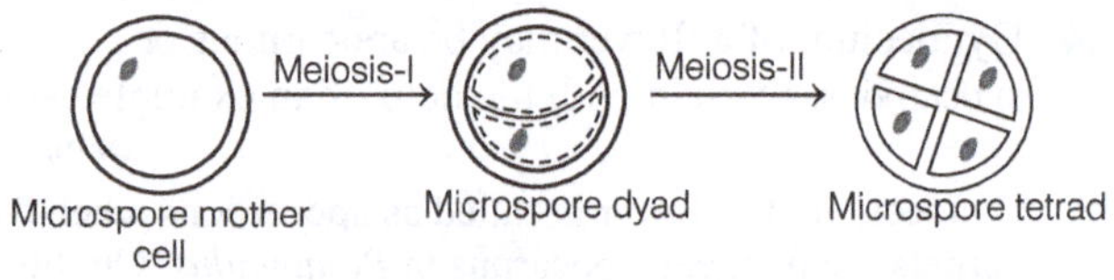

Microspores are arranged as tetrad. As the anthers mature and dehydrate, they dissociate from each other and develop into mature pollen grains. Pollen grains or the male gametophytes are released by dehiscence of anther. **(2)**

36. Draw a diagram of a mature embryo sac of an angiosperm and label the following parts in it. **Delhi 2013**

(i) Filiform apparatus (ii) Synergids
(iii) Central cell (iv) Egg cell
(v) Polar nuclei (vi) Antipodals

Ans. For mature embryo sac of angiosperm, refer to figure in answer no. 22.

5 Marks Questions

37. (i) Explain the development of male gametophyte in an angiosperm.

(ii) Draw a labelled diagram of a three-celled male gametophyte. **CBSE 2024 (Set-I)**

Ans. (i) Refer to text on page no. 2 and 3. **(2½)**

(ii)

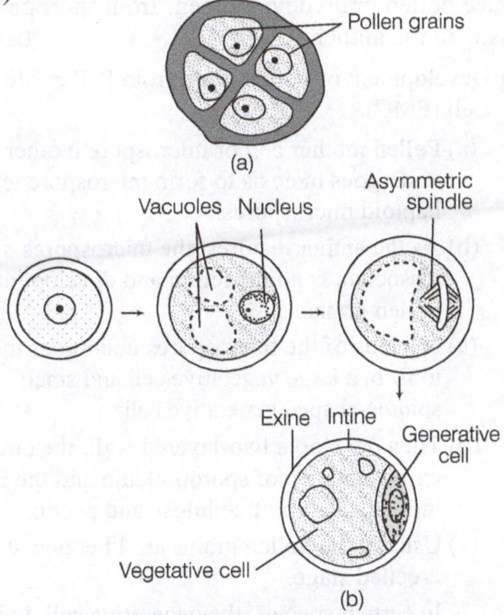

(a) Enlarged view of a pollen grain tetrad
(b) Stages of a microspore maturing into a pollen **(2½)**

38. (i) Show the development of megaspore mother cell upto the formation of mature embryo sac in flowering plants with the help of labelled diagrams only.

(ii) How does geitonogamy differ from xenogamy?

(iii) Name the type of flowers that are invariably autogamous. **CBSE 2024 (Set-II)**

Ans. (i) Refer to text on page no. 4.

(ii) Differences between geitonogamy and xenongamy are

Geitonogamy	Xenogamy
It is the pollination between flowers on same plant.	It is the pollination between flowers on different plants.
The flowers are genetically similar.	The genetic makeup of flower is different.
It is a type of self-pollination.	It is a cross-pllination.

(2)

(iii) Cleistogamous flowers are invariably autogamous as there is no chance of cross-pollen landing on the stigma. These flowers do not open at all and produce assured seed set even in the absence of pollinators. **(2)**

39. (i) Explain the monosporic development of embryo sac in the ovule of an angiosperm.

(ii) Draw a diagram of the mature embryo sac of an angiospermic ovule and label any four parts in it. **CBSE 2023**

Or (i) Describe the process of megasporogenesis, in an angiosperm.

(ii) Draw a diagram of a mature embryo sac of angiosperm, label its any six parts. **All India 2020**

Ans. (i) Refer to text on page no. 4.

(ii) Refer to figure 1.4 on page no. 4.

40. Trace the development of a 2-celled pollen grain of an angiosperm within an anther. Draw a labelled diagram to substantiate your answer. **Delhi 2020**

Ans. Refer to answer no. 43.

41. Describe the process of megasporogenesis upto fully developed embryo sac formation in an angiosperm. **All India 2019**

Or Where does the process of megasporogenesis start in an angiosperm? Describe the process upto the formation of embryo sac. **Delhi 2019**

Ans. In angiosperms, the process of megasporogenesis starts inside the nucellus of the ovule. During megasporogenesis, the Megaspore Mother Cell (MMC) undergoes meiosis resulting in the production of four megaspores. Out of the four megaspores, only one is functional while the other three degenerate.

The functional megaspore undergoes mitosis to form two nuclei, which migrate to opposite poles, forming a 2-nucleate embryo sac.

Further, mitotic divisions lead to the formation of 4-nucleate and 8-nucleate stages of the embryo sac. In these mitotic divisions, nuclear division is not followed by cell division.

After the 8-nucleate stage, cell walls are laid down and a typical female gametophyte or embryo sac is formed. Among the 8 nuclei, 6 are enclosed by cell walls and organised into cells, while the remaining 2 nuclei (polar nuclei) are situated above the egg apparatus in a large central cell.

Out of the six cells, three are grouped at the micropylar end and constitute the egg apparatus. It is made up of two synergids and one egg cell. The other three cells are located at the chalazal end and are called antipodals.

Thus, a typical angiosperm embryo sac after maturity is 8-nucleate and 7-celled.

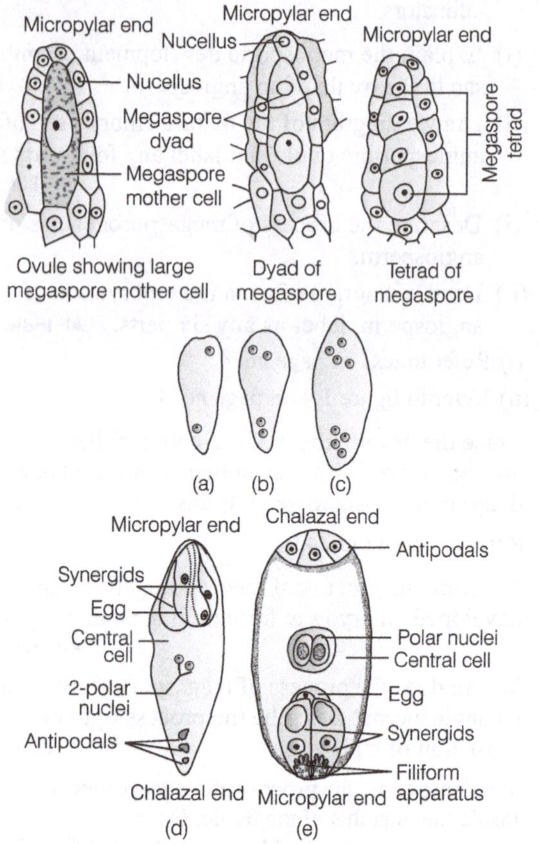

Stages of development of embryo sac (a to e)

42. (i) Draw a diagrammatic sketch of a transverse section of an anther of an angiosperm. Label its different walls and the tissue forming microspore mother cells.

(ii) Describe the process of microsporogenesis upto the formation of a microspore.

(iii) Write the function of 'germ pore' in a pollen grain of an angiosperm. **2018C**

Ans. (i)

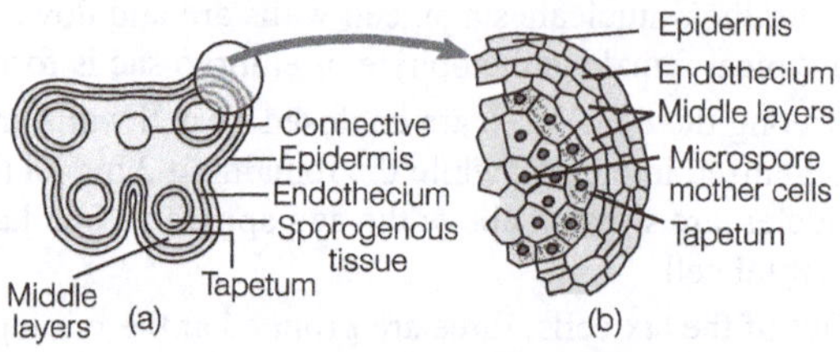

(a) TS of an anther, (b) Enlarged view of a microsporangium showing four wall layers

(2)

(ii) Refer to answer no. 35. **(2)**

(iii) Refer to answer no. 29. **(1)**

43. (i) Describe the sequence of the process of microsporogenesis in angiosperms.

(ii) Draw a labelled diagram of a 2-celled final structure formed. **Delhi 2015C**

Or

Trace pollen grain development from sporogenous tissue in the anther. **Delhi 2012**

Ans. (i) Development of pollen grain from Pollen Mother Cell (PMC).

(a) Pollen mother cell or microspore mother cell undergoes meiosis to form microspore tetrad or haploid microspores.

(b) As the anther matures, the microspores dissociate from the tetrad and develop into pollen grains.

(c) Nucleus of the microspores undergoes mitosis to form a large vegetative cell and small spindle-shaped generative cell.

(d) They develop a two-layered wall, the outer exine made up of sporopollenin and the inner intine made up of cellulose and pectin.

(e) Usually the pollen grains are liberated at this 2-celled stage.

In certain species, the generative cell divides mitotically to form two male gametes and the pollen grains are 3-celled during liberation. **(3)**

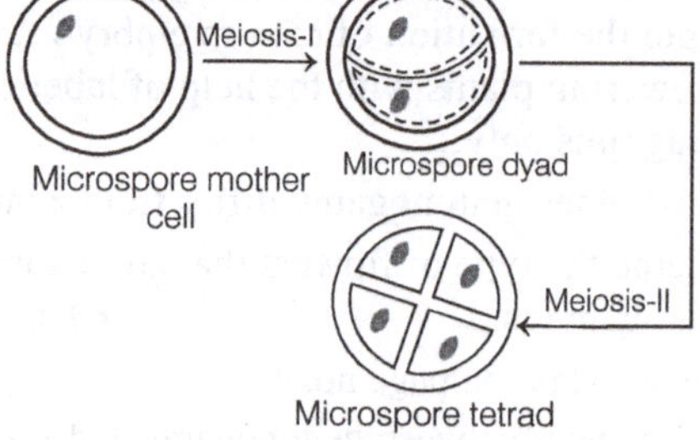

Microsporogenesis

(ii)

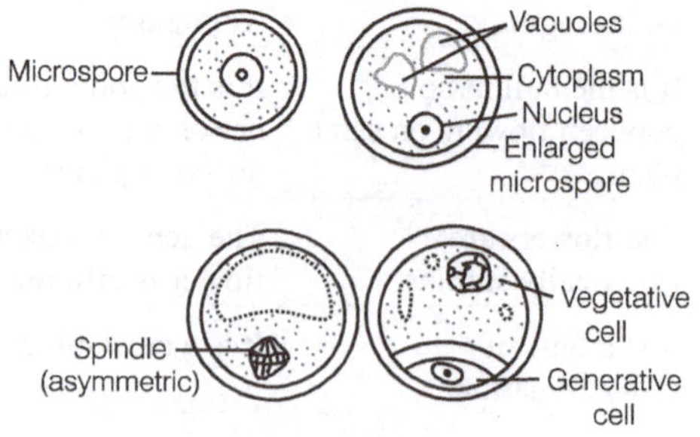

(2)

44. (i) Describe the formation of mature female gametophyte within an ovule in angiosperms.
(ii) Describe the structure of cell that guides the pollen tube to enter the embryo sac. **All India 2014**

Ans. (i) The functional megaspore undergoes mitosis to form 2 nuclei, which migrate to opposite poles, forming a 2-nucleate embryo sac. Further, mitotic divisions lead to the formation of 4-nucleate and 8-nucleate stages of the embryo sac. In these mitotic divisions, nuclear division is not followed by cell wall formation. After the 8-nucleate stage, cell walls are laid down and a typical female gametophyte or embryo sac is formed. Among the eight nuclei, six are enclosed by cell wall and organised into cells, while the remaining two nuclei (polar nuclei) are situated above the egg apparatus in a large central cell.

Out of the six cells, three are grouped at the micropylar end and constitute the egg apparatus made up of two synergids and one egg cell. The other three cells are located at the chalazal end and are called antipodals. Thus, a typical angiosperm embryo sac after maturity is 8-nucleate and 7-celled. **(3)**

(ii) The egg apparatus present towards the micropylar end, comprises of two synergids and an egg cell. These synergids possess special cellular thickenings at their micropylar tip and called filiform apparatus. This filiform apparatus guides the pollen tube to enter into embryo sac.
For figure, refer to answer no. 41 fig (e). **(2)**

Common Mistakes Generally students get confused that female gametophyte and female gamete are same, but female gametophyte is the embryo sac in the ovule and is 7-celled and 8-nucleated structure.
7-celled = 3 antipodals + 2 synergids + 1 egg cell + 1 central cell.
The egg cell is the female gamete.

45. Draw a labelled diagram of sectional view of a mature embryo sac of an angiosperm. **Delhi 2014**

Ans. Refer to figure in answer no. 22.

46. How does the megaspore mother cell develop into 7-celled and 8-nucleate embryo sac in an angiosperm? Draw a labelled diagram of a mature embryo sac. **Delhi 2012**

Or Explain with the help of diagram the development of mature embryo sac from a megaspore mother cell in angiosperm. **Foreign 2012; All India 2010C**

Or Describe the process of megasporogenesis in angiosperm until 8-nucleate stage. **All India 2013C**

Ans. For development of megaspore mother cell, refer to answer no. 41.

47. (i) Draw a diagram of an enlarged view of TS of one microsporangium of an angiosperm and label the following parts
(a) Tapetum
(b) Middle layers
(c) Endothecium
(d) Microspore mother cell
(ii) Mention the characteristic features and function of tapetum.
(iii) Explain the following giving reasons
(a) Pollen grains are well-preserved as fossils.
(b) Pollen tablets are in use of people these days. **Foreign 2011**

Ans. (i) For diagram, refer to answer no. 32. **(2)**
(ii) Tapetum is the inner most nourishing layer of microsporangial wall. The cells of tapetum have dense cytoplasm and more than one nucleus. These cells nourish the developing pollen grains. **(1)**
(iii) (a) The outer exine layer of pollen grain is highly resistant because of sporopollenin. It is an organic material which can withstand harsh conditions, action of alkalis and acids. No enzyme can degrade sporopollenin. Thus, pollen grains are well-preserved as fossils.
(b) Pollen grains are rich in nutrients. So, they are used by people as health tablets or food supplements. **(2)**

Concept Enhancer Pollen is recognised as an excellent dietary supplement for human nutrition. Thus, it is found in various forms like capsule, tablets, powders, etc. The high content of carbohydrates, lipids etc., makes pollen an ideal natural supplement that not only provides energy, but also has a good nutritional value.

TOPIC 2

Pollination

It is the transfer of pollen grains from anther to the stigma of a pistil.

Types of Pollination

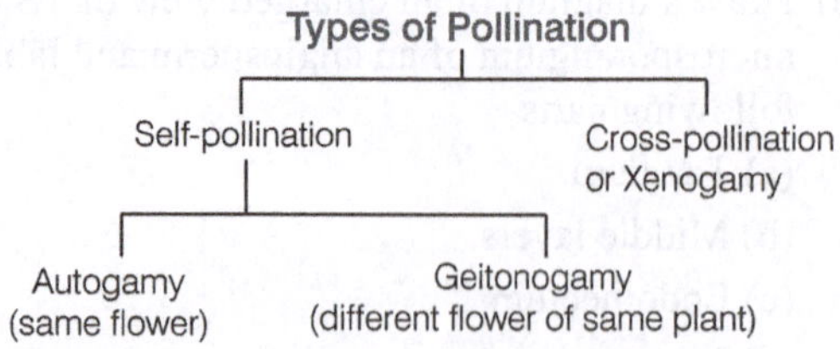

Depending upon the source of pollen grains, pollination is of following types

(i) **Autogamy** is the transfer of pollen grains from anther to the stigma of the same flower. In these flowers the anthers and the stigma lie close to each other in a way that self-pollination occurs, i.e. cleistogamous flowers and assure seed-set even in the absence of pollinators.

(ii) **Geitonogamy** is the transfer of pollen grains from anther to the stigma of another flower of same plant. Continuous geitonogamy leads to inbreeding depression. It is genetically similar to autogamy, but functionally related to cross-pollination.

(iii) **Xenogamy** is the transfer of pollen grains from anther of one plant to the stigma of another plant.

Agents of Pollination

There are following two agents which are responsible for pollination

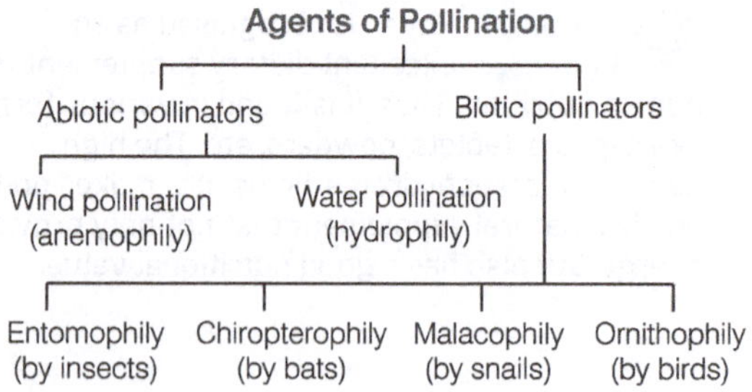

Abiotic Agents of Pollination

Non-living or abiotic agents of pollination include water and wind. Flower to get pollinated by abiotic factors have special adaptations as given below

1. **Wind pollinated** flowers have
   - Light and non-sticky pollen grains.
   - Generally a single ovule in each ovary and numerous flowers are packed into an inflorescence, e.g. corn cob.
   - Well-exposed stamens and large feathery stigma to trap air-borne pollen grains.
   - Common in grass, maize, date palm, etc.
2. **Water pollination** occurs in mostly monocotyledons (in about 30 genera). Some examples of water pollinated plants are *Hydrilla*, *Vallisneria* and *Zostera*.
   - In majority of aquatic plants, the flowers emerge above the level of water and are pollinated by insects or wind, e.g. water hyacinth and water lily.
   - The female flower reaches the surface of water by the long stalk and pollen grains are released onto the surface of water, e.g. *Vallisneria*.
   - In most of the water pollinated species, pollen grains are protected from wetting by mucilaginous covering.

Biotic Agents of Pollination

These (insects, animals, etc), adaptations for pollination include.

- Insect pollinated flowers are generally large, colourful, fragrant and rich in nectar.
- The pollen grains and stigmatic surface are sticky.
- The animal pollinated flowers offer certain rewards to the pollinators.
- Some of these rewards include
  - nectar and (edible) pollen grains.
  - safe place for laying eggs, e.g. *Amorphophallus* and *Yucca*.

A relationship exists between a species of moth and the plant *Yucca,* where both species–moth and the plant cannot complete their life cycles without each other.
The moth deposits its eggs in the locule of the ovary and the flower, in turn, gets pollinated by the moth. The larvae of the moth come out of the eggs as the seeds start developing.

- Many insects may consume pollen or the nectar without bringing about pollination. Such floral visitors are referred to as **pollen/nectar robbers**.

> Plants like *Viola, Oxalis* and *Commelina* produce two types of flowers
> (i) **Chasmogamous** Similar to flowers of other species with exposed anther and stigma.
> (ii) **Cleistogamous** Flowers do not open at all. Anthers and stigma lie close to each other to affect self-pollination. There is no chance of cross-pollination.

Outbreeding Devices

These are developed by the bisexual flowers to avoid self-pollination and promote cross-pollination because continuous self-pollination results in poor yield and poor quality of seeds or **inbreeding depression.**

These devices are

- Dichogamy (Production of male and female reproductive parts at diffferent times)
- Self-sterility
- Unisexuality
- Chasmogamous flowers
- Protandry (Maturation of male parts prior to female parts)
- Protogyny (Maturation of female parts before male parts)

NOTE In castor and maize, unisexuality prevents autogamy. In papaya, it prevents both autogamy and geitonogamy.

Pollen-Pistil Interaction

It is mediated by chemical components of the pollen interacting with those of pistil.

It involves events mentioned below

- Following compatible pollination, pollen grain germinates on the stigma to produce a pollen tube through a germ pore.
- The pollen tube grows and reaches the ovary, enters the ovule through micropyle and then enters one of the synergids.

Artificial Hybridisation

In this desired pollen grains are used for pollination and the stigma is protected from contamination (from unwanted pollen). This is done by emasculation and bagging.
Artificial hybridisation creates new genetic recombination with better qualities.

- In **emasculation**, anthers are removed from the flower bud with the help of a pair of forceps before they dehisce.
- Emasculated flowers are covered by a bag to prevent contamination of the stigma by unwanted pollens. This process is called **bagging**.

Double Fertilisation

It occurs after the pollen tube reaches the ovary. It is the characteristic of angiosperms.

- The pollen tube releases two male gametes into the cytoplasm of a synergid.
- One of the male gamete fuses with egg cell (syngamy) which results in the formation of zygote.
- The second male gamete fuses with the two polar nuclei to form a triploid **Primary Endosperm Nucleus** (PEN). This is called **triple fusion**.
- Since, two fusions, i.e. syngamy and triple fusion occur in an embryo sac, this is called **double fertilisation.**
- Central cell and primary endosperm nucleus called as Primary Endosperm Cell (PEC) develops into the **endosperm** and zygote develops into an **embryo**.

PYQs Previous Years' Questions

1 Mark Questions

Multiple Choice Questions

1. In which of the following plants are both male and female flowers born on the same plant and the mode of pollination can be geitonogamy or xenogamy? **CBSE 2024 (Set-I)**

(a) Papaya (b) Date palm
(c) Maize (d) Spinach

Ans. (c) In maize plant, both male and female flowers are born on the same plant and the mode of pollination can be geitonogamy (pollination on same plant, different flowers) or xenogamy (pollination in different flower on different plant). Other plants mentioned in the options are all dioecious (bisexual) where no geitonogamy is possible.

2. Select the option that shows the correctly identified *U*, *X*, *Y* and *Z* in a developing dicot embryo. **CBSE 2023**

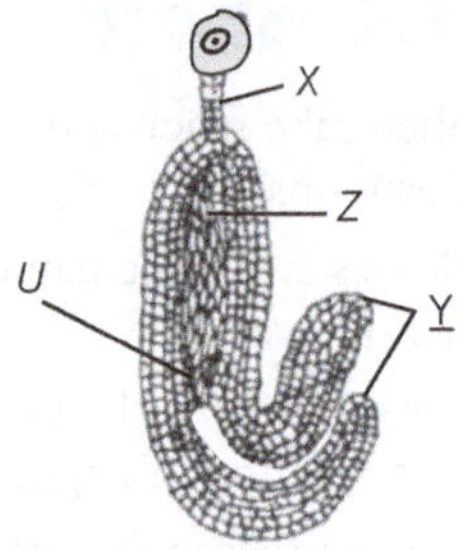

(a) *X*–Plumule (2*n*), *Y*–Suspensor (*n*), *Z*–Cotyledon (2*n*), *U*–Radicle (2*n*)
(b) *X*–Plumule (2*n*), *Y*–Suspensor (2*n*), *Z*–Radicle (2*n*), *U*–Cotyledon (2*n*)
(c) *X*–Suspensor (2*n*), *Y*–Cotyledon (2*n*), *Z*–Radicle (2*n*), *U*–Plumule (2*n*)
(d) *X*–Cotyledon (2*n*), *Y*–Radicle (*n*), *Z*–Plumule (*n*), *U*–Suspensor (*n*)

Ans. (c) X–Suspensor (2*n*), *Y*–Cotyledon (2*n*), *Z*–Radicle (2*n*), *U*–Plumule (2*n*)

3. Remnants of nucellus are persistent during seed development in **CBSE SQP 2023**

(a) pea (b) groundnut
(c) wheat (d) black pepper

Ans. (d) black pepper

4. A botanist studying *Viola* (common pansy) noticed that one of the two flower types withered and developed no further due to some unfavourable condition, but the other flower type on the same plant survived and it resulted in an assured seed set. Which of the following will be correct? **CBSE SQP 2021-22 Term-I**

(a) The flower type which survived is cleistogamous and it always exhibits autogamy
(b) The flower type which survived is chasmogamous and it always exhibits geitonogamy
(c) The flower type which survived is cleistogamous and it exhibits both autogamy and geitonogamy
(d) The flower type which survived is chasmogamous and it never exhibits autogamy

Ans. (a) The flower type which survived is cleistogamous and it always exhibits autogamy

5. On observing the pollen grain under the microscope, it was found to be long and ribbon-shaped. The flower bearing these pollen grain will be pollinated by **CBSE SQP 2021-22 Term-I**

(a) insects (b) water
(c) air (d) birds

Ans. (b) The flower bearing long and ribbon-shaped pollen grain will be pollinated by water.

6. In the dioecious aquatic plant shown, identify the characteristics of the male flowers that reach the female flowers for pollination. **CBSE SQP 2021-22 Term-I**

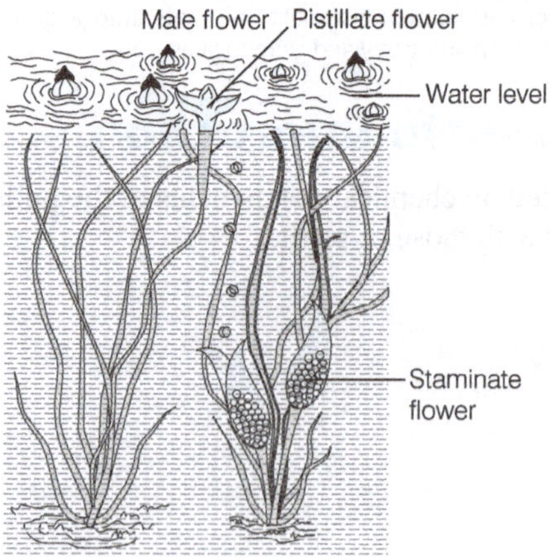

	Sizes of the flower	Colours of the flower	Characteristic features of pollen grain
(a)	Small	Brightly coloured	Light weight and non-sticky
(b)	Large	Colourless	Large and sticky
(c)	Small	White	Small, covered with mucilage
(d)	Large	Colourless	Non-sticky

Ans. (c) Small and white flower, Small pollen covered with mucilage

7. In a fertilised ovule, n, $2n$ and $3n$ conditions occur respectively in **CBSE SQP 2021-22 Term-I**
(a) antipodal, zygote and endosperm
(b) zygote, nucellus and endosperm
(c) endosperm, nucellus and zygote
(d) antipodals, synergids and integuments

Ans. (a) antipodal, zygote and endosperm

8. Floral reward(s) provided by insect pollinated flowers to sustain animal visit is/are **CBSE 2021-22 Term-I**
(a) nectar and fragrance
(b) nectar and pollen grains
(c) pollen grains and fragrance
(d) fragrance and bright colour

Ans. (b) nectar and pollen grains

9. The aquatic plant having long and ribbon like pollen grains is **CBSE 2021-22 Term-I**
(a) *Vallisneria* (b) *Hydrilla*
(c) *Eichhornia* (d) *Zostera*

Ans. (d) *Zostera*

10. Which of the following outbreeding devices are used by majority of flowering plants to prevent inbreeding depression? **CBSE 2021-22 Term-I**
(i) Pollen release and stigma receptivity are not synchronised.
(ii) Different positions of anther and stigma.
(iii) Production of different types of pollen grains.
(iv) Formation of unisexual flowers along with bisexual flowers.
(v) Preventing self-pollen from fertilising the ovules by inhibiting pollen germination.
(a) (i), (ii) and (v) (b) (ii), (iii) and (v)
(c) (i), (iii) and (v) (d) (iii), (iv) and (v)

Ans. (a) (i), (ii) and (v)

11. To overcome incompatible pollinations so as to get desired hybrids, a plant breeder must have the knowledge of .... **CBSE 2021-22 Term-I**
(a) pollen-nucellar interaction
(b) pollen-egg cell interaction
(c) pollen-pistil interaction
(d) pollen-embryo sac interaction

Ans. (c) pollen-pistil interaction

12. Choose the correct labellings for the parts X, Y and Z in the given figure of the stages in embryo development in a dicot. **CBSE 2021-22 Term-I**

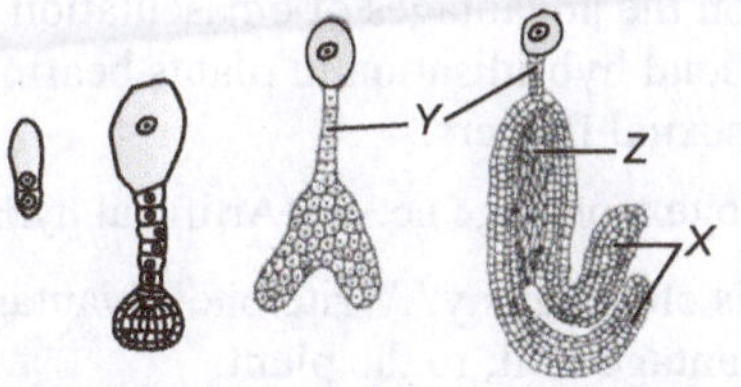

(a) X is suspensor, Y is radicle and Z is cotyledon
(b) X is radicle, Y is cotyledon and Z is suspensor
(c) X is cotyledon, Y is suspensor and Z is radicle
(d) X is zygote, Y is radicle and Z is cotyledon

Ans. (c) X is cotyledon, Y is suspensor and Z is radicle

Very Short Answer Type Questions

13. How does pollination take place in water hyacinth and water lily? **CBSE SQP 2021-22**

Ans. In water hyacinth and water lily, pollination takes place by insects or wind.

14. Write one advantage and one disadvantage of cleistogamy to flowering plants. **CBSE 2018C**

Ans. The advantage of cleistogamy is that it ensures pollination even in the absence of pollinators. Disadvantage of cleistogamy is that there is no chance of variation to occur. (½ + ½)

15. What is pollen-pistil interaction and how is it mediated? **Foreign 2014**

Ans. Pollen-pistil interaction is a chain or group of events that takes place from the falling of pollen over the stigma to the formation of pollen tube and its entry into the ovule. It is mediated by chemical components of pollen grain, interacting with that of pistil. (½ + ½)

16. Differentiate between xenogamy and geitonogamy. **Delhi 2014C**

Ans. **Xenogamy** is the transfer of pollen grains from anther of one flower to the stigma of another flower of a different plant, while **geitonogamy** is the transfer of pollen grains from anther of one flower to the stigma of another flower on the same plant.

2 Marks Questions

17. Describe the process of pollination in *Vallisneria*. **Delhi 2020, 2019, 2016 C**

Ans. **Process of pollination in *Vallisneria*** It is a water pollinated plant. In *Vallisneria spiralis*, flowers are borne under water. The male flower gets detached from the parent plant after maturation. Female flowers at the time of pollination, are brought to the surface by their long stalks. As they arrive on the surface, they form a cup-like depression to gap male flowers and complete the pollination.

18. Mention the advantages of emasculation and bagging in artificial hybridisation in plants bearing unisexual and bisexual flowers. **Delhi 2020**

Ans. Refer to text on page no. 13 (Artificial hybridisation).

19. What is cleistogamy? Write one advantage and one disadvantage of it, to the plant. **All India 2019**

Or State one advantage and one disadvantage of cleistogamy. **All India 2012**

Ans. Cleistogamy is a type of self-pollination that occurs in a permanently closed flower. (1)

Advantage and disadvantage of cleistogamy are as follows

(i) **Advantage** Cleistogamous flowers produce assured seed-set even in the absence of pollinators.

(ii) **Disadvantage** Cleistogamous flowers are invariably autogamous.

So, there is no chance of cross-pollination. Hence, less variations are generated in the progeny. (½+½)

20. You are conducting artificial hybridisation on papaya and potato. Which one of them would require the step of emasculation and why ? However for both you will use the process of bagging. Justify giving one reason. **Delhi 2019**

Ans. Papaya produces unisexual flowers and potato produces bisexual flowers. Therefore, the step of emasculation will be done on potato because emasculation is done on bisexual flower to avoid self-pollination. But, bagging is done on unisexual flowers, so as to dust suitable pollen grains on the stigma when the stigma turns receptive and the flowers are rebagged. (1+1)

21. Comment upon the mode of pollination in *Vallisneria* and *Eichhornia* which have emergent flowers. **CBSE SQP 2019**

Ans. In *Vallisneria*, long stalk and pollen grains are released onto the surface of water and pollination takes place by water. Whereas in *Eichhornia*, the flowers emerge above the level of water and are pollinated by insects or wind. (1+1)

22. A farmer maintained bee hives in his *Brassica* field during its flowering season. How will be he benefitted? **CBSE SQP 2019**

Ans. Bee hives are kept in a crop field during flowering period to enhance the pollination of the crop. Farmer will be benefitted from both increased crop yield and honey production.

23. A single pea plant in your kitchen garden produces pods with viable seeds, but the individual papaya plant does not. Explain. **All India 2016**

Or Out of many papaya plants growing in your garden, only a few bear fruits. Give reason.

Ans. A single pea plant produces pods with viable seeds because the pea plant is autogamous, i.e. they have the ability of self-pollination.

Whereas the individual papaya plant is prevented from both autogamy and geitonogamy. In this plant, male and female flowers are present on different plants, i.e. each plant is either male or female.

24. List the different types of pollination depending upon the source of pollen grain. **Delhi 2016**

Or Differentiate between autogamy, geitonogamy and xenogamy. **All India 2012C**

Ans. Depending on the source of pollen grain, pollination can be classified into

(i) **Autogamy** It is the transfer of pollen grain from anther to the stigma of the same flower.

(ii) **Geitonogamy** It is the transfer of pollen grains from anther of one flower to the stigma of another flower on the same plant.

Geitonogamy is functionally cross-pollination involving pollinating agent, but genetically it is equivalent to autogamy since the pollen grains come from the same plant.

(iii) **Xenogamy** It is the transfer of pollen grains from anther to the stigma of different plants of same species. It brings genetically different types of pollen grains to the stigma.

25. In angiosperms, zygote is diploid, while primary endosperm cell is triploid. Explain. **All India 2013**

Or Mention the reasons for difference in ploidy of zygote and primary endosperm nucleus in an angiosperm. **Delhi 2010**

Ans. In angiosperms or flowering plants, zygote is diploid and primary endosperm nucleus is triploid. It is because in these plants, one of the male gametes fuses with egg cell, which results in the formation of zygote.

So, zygote is diploid, while primary endosperm cell is triploid because the nucleus of the second male gamete

(n) fuses with the two haploid polar nuclei or diploid secondary nucleus ($2n$) of the central cell to form a triploid primary endosperm nucleus ($3n$). This process is referred to as triple fusion. The central cell is now called primary endosperm cell.

26. Explain triple fusion in angiosperm. **Delhi 2013C**

Ans. Refer to answer no. 25.

27. Why should a bisexual flower be emasculated and bagged prior to artificial pollination? **Foreign 2010**

Or Why does a breeder need to emasculate a bisexual flower? Mention a condition in a flower where emasculation is not necessary. **Delhi 2011C**

Ans. **Emasculation** in a bisexual flower is required to prevent contamination of the stigma with self-pollen grains.

Bagging is done to prevent contamination of the stigma of the emasculated flower with any other unwanted pollen grains. That is why a bisexual flower should be emasculated and bagged prior to artificial pollination.

Emasculation is not required in unisexual flowers.

3 Marks Questions

28. One of the major approaches of crop improvement programme is artificial hybridisation. Explain the steps involved in making sure that only the desired pollen grain pollinate the stigma of a bisexual flower by a plant breeder. **CBSE 2023**

Ans. The steps involved in making sure that only the desired pollen grain pollinate the stigma of a bisexual flower by a plant breeder are as follows

(i) **Isolation** The first step is to isolate the bisexual flower to be pollinated from other flowers to prevent cross-pollination.

(ii) **Emasculation** In the next step, breeder removes the anthers from the flower bud before they dehisce. This is done to prevent the self-pollination and to ensure that the desired pollen grains pollinate the flower.

(iii) **Pollination** The desired pollen grain is then collected from the male flower and dusted on to the stigma of the emasculated bisexual flower.

(iv) **Bagging** After pollination emasculated flowers are covered by a bag to prevent the contamination of the stigma by unwanted pollens.

(v) **Monitoring** Development of flowers is monitored and observations are recorded.

(vi) **Harvesting** After the maturation of seeds, they are harvested from the plant and stored for further use in the crop improvement programme.

29. State the agent(s) which helps in pollinating in the following plants. Explain the adaptations in these plants to ensure pollination. **CBSE SQP 2023**

(i) Corn

(ii) Water hyacinth

(iii) *Vallisneria*

Ans. (i) **Corn** Pollinating agent is wind. Numerous flowers are packed into inflorescence with well exposed stamens and large feathery stigma to trap air born pollen grains.

(ii) **Water hyacinth** In this plant, the flowers emerge above the level of water and are pollinated by insects or wind.

(iii) ***Vallisneria*** In this plant, pollinating agent is water. The female flower reaches the surface of water by long stalk and pollen grains are released onto the surface of water. (1 × 3)

30. Explain three different modes of pollination that can occur in a chasmogamous flower. **All India 2020**

KEY idea

Chasmogamous flowers have exposed anther and stigma.

Ans. In chasmogamous flower, three different modes of pollination that can occur are

(i) **Anemophily** It is the pollination that takes place by wind, e.g. *Zea mays* (maize). In such plants, the flowers are small, colourless, inconspicuous and nectarless. The anthers are well-exposed to facilitate easy dispersal of pollens by wind. Pollen grains are small, light, dry and even sometimes winged.

(ii) **Hydrophily** It is the pollination that takes place by water, e.g. *Vallisneria*. Flowers are small, incospicuous and nectarless, stigmas are long and sticky pollen grains are covered by a mucilaginous covering.

(iii) **Entomophily** It is the pollination that takes place through insects, e.g. *Salvia*. In such plants, flowers are large, colourful, fragrant and nectar-rich, pollen grains are sticky and get attached to insect's body and are transferred from one plant to another. (1 × 3)

31. Draw a well labelled diagram of LS of a pistil showing the passage of growing of pollen tube upto its destination. **CBSE SQP 2020**

Or (i) Draw a LS of pistil showing pollen tube entering into the embryo sac. Label the following

(a) Nucellus (b) Antipodals

(c) Synergids (d) Micropyle

(ii) Write the functions of the following

(a) Synergids (b) Micropyle **All India 2019**

Ans. (i) For pollen-pistil diagram, refer to answer no. 35 (ii).

(ii) (a) **Synergids** These possess special cellular thickenings at their micropylar tip called filiform apparatus. This filiform apparatus guides the pollen tube to enter embryo sac.

(b) **Micropyle** It facilitates the entry of pollen tube and thus fertilisation.

32. Emasculation and bagging are the two important steps carried during artificial hybridisation to obtain superior varieties of desired plants. Explain giving reasons, in which types of flowers and at what stages are the two processes carried out? **All India 2019**

Ans. For emasculation and bagging, refer to answer no. 27. If the plant bears bisexual flowers, emasculation and bagging are carried out before the anther dehisces.

If the plant bears unisexual flowers, emasculation is not required. The female flower buds are bagged before the opening of flowers.

33. (i) Differentiate between geitonogamy and xenogamy.

(ii) Write the difference in the characteristics of the progeny produced as a result of the two processes. **Delhi 2019**

Ans. (i) Differences between geitonogamy and xenogamy are

Geitonogamy	Xenogamy
It is the transfer of pollen grains from the anther to the stigma of another flower of same plant.	It is the transfer of pollen grains from the anther to the stigma of different plants.
The pollen grains are genetically similar to the plant.	The pollen grains are genetically different from the plant.

(1½)

(ii) **Geitonogamy** results in progenies which are purelines, e.g. homozygous. They are genetically similar. **Xenogamy** results in hybrids, e.g. heterozygous. They show variations in characters. (1½)

34. How does a bisexual flowering plant ensure cross-pollination? Explain. **Delhi 2019**

Ans. Refer to answer no. 38.

35. (i) Can a plant flowering in Mumbai be pollinated by pollen grains of the same species growing in New Delhi? Provide explanation to your answer.

(ii) Draw the diagram of a pistil where pollination has successfully occurred. Label the parts involved in reaching the male gametes to its desired destination. **All India 2017**

Ans. (i) Yes, a plant flowering in Mumbai can be pollinated by pollen grains of the same species growing in New Delhi. It is mainly because there are certain agents of pollination that can carry pollen grains to long distance.

Plants can use either abiotic or biotic agents for pollination. Abiotic pollinators include wind and water, while biotic pollinators are insects, birds, animals and even humans. It is believed that pollination by wind (anemophily) is more common because transport by wind-current can take pollens to distant places.

(ii) The parts involved in transferring the male gametes to their desired destination are stigma, style, micropyle, filiform apparatus and synergids.

Longitudinal Section (LS) of a post-pollinated pistil is given below

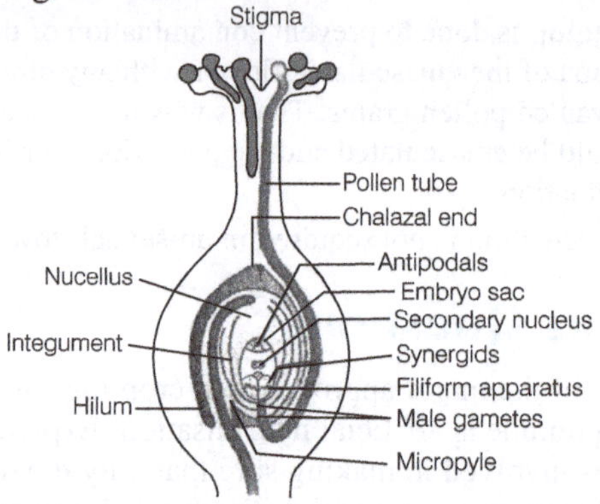

(1½ × 2)

36. What does an interaction between pollen grains and its compatible stigma result in after pollination? List two steps in sequence that follow after the process. **Delhi 2016C**

Ans. When the pollen grains fall on the stigma, the pollen tube enters one of the synergids and releases two male gametes.

(i) One of the male gametes moves towards the egg cell and fuses with it to complete syngamy to form the zygote.

(ii) The other male gamete fuses with the two polar nuclei and forms triploid Primary Endosperm Nucleus (PEN). This is termed as triple fusion.

(iii) Since, two kinds of fusion–syngamy and triple fusion takes place, the process is known as double fertilisation and is a characteristic of flowering plants. (1 × 3)

37. As a senior biology student you have been asked to demonstrate to the students of secondary level in your school, the procedure(s) that shall ensure cross-pollination in a hermaphrodite flower. List the different steps that you would suggest and provide reasons for each one of them. **All India 2016**

Ans. Cross-pollination is done to mix two desired characters of two different species of a plant. For example, purple and white flowers of a pea plant.

(i) Select two pea plants one with white and other with purple flower.

(ii) Label them as male (white flowered) and female (purple flowered) plant.

(iii) Cut anthers from purple flower with the help of scissors before their dehiscence to avoid self-pollination and cover the flower with white paper bag.

(iv) Now collect pollens from the white flower (male plant) with the help of brush.

(v) Dust the pollens on the stigma of female (purple) flower.

(vi) Cover it again with paper bag till seed formation.

38. Flowering plants have developed many devices to discourage self-pollination and to encourage cross-pollination. Explain three such devices. **Delhi 2016C**

Or Why do hermaphrodite angiosperms develop outbreeding devices? Explain any two such devices with the help of examples. **All India 2015C**

Or Make a list of any three outbreeding devices that flowering plants have developed and explain how they help to encourage cross-pollination. **All India 2014**

Ans. Hermaphrodites or Bisexual flowers develop outbreeding devices to ensure cross-pollination and avoid self-pollination.

The three outbreeding devices that flowering plants have developed to discourage self-pollination are

(i) **Unisexuality** (Dicliny) Flowers are unisexual, so that self-pollination is not possible.

The plants may be monoecious (bearing both male and female flowers, e.g. maize) or dioecious (bearing male and female flowers on different plants, e.g. mulberry, papaya).

(ii) **Dichogamy** Anthers and stigmas mature at different times in a bisexual flower for preventing self-pollination.

(a) **Protandry** Anthers mature earlier than stigma of the same flower. The pollens thus become available to stigmas of the older flowers, e.g. sunflower, *Salvia*.

(b) **Protogyny** Stigma becomes receptive earlier, so that it gets pollinated before the anthers of the same flower develop pollen grains, e.g. *Mirabilis jalapa, Gloriosa, Plantago*.

(iii) The third device to prevent self-pollination is **self-incompatibility**. It is a genetic mechanism that prevents self-pollen from fertilising the ovules by preventing pollen germination or pollen tube growth in the pistil.

All these methods encourage cross-pollination. Thus, causing genetic variations among them. (1 × 3)

39. Explain the phenomenon of double fertilisation. **Delhi 2014**

Ans. The phenomenon of double fertilisation occurs in following steps

(i) In an angiospermic plant, two male gametes are discharged by a pollen tube into the cytoplasm of a synergid of the embryo sac.

(ii) One of the male gametes fuses with the egg to form a zygote. This process is called syngamy.

(iii) Other male gamete fuses with the secondary nucleus to form the primary endosperm nucleus, this process is called triple fusion.

(iv) Since, there are two fusions (syngamy and triple fusion) inside an ovule during fertilisation, it is known as double fertilisation.

40. Write the differences between wind pollinated and insect pollinated flowers. Give an example of each type. **Foreign 2014**

Ans. The differences between wind pollinated and insect pollinated flowers are

Wind pollinated flowers	Insect pollinated flowers
These are small and sometimes grow in groups called inflorescence.	These are large and mostly grow individually.
Usually inconspicuous due to dull colours.	The corolla, calyx or bracts are brightly coloured to attract insects.
They are odourless and devoid of nectar.	Strongly odoured and usually possess nectar or edible pollen.
Pollens are produced in large numbers.	Fewer pollen grains are produced.
e.g. *Urtica*, maize, *Parthenium*.	e.g. rose, snapdragon, *Calotropis*.

41. Differentiate between geitonogamy and xenogamy in plants. Which one between the two will lead to inbreeding depression and why? **Delhi 2011**

Ans. For difference, refer to answer no. 33 (i).

Geitonogamy will lead to inbreeding depression because the pollen grains are genetically similar resulting into inbreeding. Continuous inbreeding reduces fertility.

Concept Enhancer Inbreeding depression refers to the decrease or loss in the fitness of an individual caused when mating occurs between the relatives in a small population. It is a very common phenomenon seen both in plant and animal species. Inbreeding results in a reduction in fertility and therefore productivity of an individual.

42. (i) Write the characteristic features of anther, pollen and stigma of wind pollinated flowers.

(ii) How do flowers reward their insect pollinators? Explain. **All India 2010**

Ans. (i) In wind pollinated flowers,

(a) Anthers are well-exposed for easy dispersal of pollen grains.

(b) Pollen grains are light and non-sticky, so that they can be transported by wind currents.

(c) Stigma is large and feathery to trap pollens. **(2)**

(ii) Flower rewards their insect pollinators easily by offering

(a) nectar and edible pollen grains.

(b) safe place for insects to lay eggs, e.g. *Amorphophallus* and *Yucca*. **(1)**

5 Marks Questions

43. (i) Describe any two devices in a flowering plant which prevent both autogamy and geitonogamy.

(ii) Explain the events upto double fertilisation after the pollen tube enters one of the synergids in an ovule of an angiosperm. **CBSE 2018**

Ans. (i) The two devices that prevent both autogamy and geitonogamy in flowering plants are as follows

(a) **Self-incompatibility** In some plants when pollen from same flower or other flowers of the same plant comes on the stigma, it is incapable of bringing about fertilisation.
It is due to the presence of similar self-sterile gene, e.g. tobacco, potato, etc. It prevents autogamy and geitonogamy.

(b) **Dioecy** In several species such as papaya, male and female flowers are present on different plants. Thus, each plant is either male or female. This condition also prevents both autogamy and geitonogamy. **(2)**

(ii) In the ovule, the pollen tube is attracted by secretions of synergids. Usually the pollen tube enters the embryo sac by passing into one of the two synergids which starts degenerating. The pollen tube bursts up by absorbing hydrolytic substances secreted by degenerating synergids. It is followed by double fertilisation in flowering plants.

Double fertilisation It is the fusion of two male gametes to two different cells of the same female gametophyte in order to produce two different structures.

Nawaschin (1898) was the first to show that both the male gametes are involved in fertilisation in *Fritillaria* and *Lilium*. Double fertilisation consists of two events that are as follows

(a) **Syngamy or Amphimixis** Fusion of the egg nucleus with one male gamete is called syngamy. This fusion results in the formation of diploid cell, the zygote.

(b) **Triple fusion** Along with syngamy, the other male gamete moves towards the two polar nuclei located in the central cell and fuses with them to produce a triploid Primary Endosperm Nucleus (PEN). In this way, fertilisation occurs in flowering plants. **(3)**

44. Draw the longitudinal section of a flower showing growth of pollen tube upto the embryo sac. Label the following parts

(i) Stigma
(ii) Pollen tube
(iii) Integument
(iv) Chalazal end
(v) Nucellus
(vi) Synergids **Delhi 2015**

Ans. For LS of flower, refer to answer no. 35 (ii).

45. (i) Plan an experiment and prepare a flowchart of the steps that you would follow to ensure that the seeds are formed only from the desired sets of pollen grains. Name the type of experiment that you carried out.

(ii) Write the importance of such experiments. **All India 2015**

Ans. (i) **Artificial hybridisation** is carried out to ensure that seeds are formed from the desired set of pollen grains. This is done by **emasculation** and **bagging**. The flowchart below shows the steps to be followed

Emasculation–stamens are removed in bud condition from a bisexual flower.

↓

Female flower is obtained.

↓

Emasculated flower is enclosed in a bag made up of butter paper or plastic (Bagging).

↓

Mature and viable pollen grains are collected from male plant.

↓

Bag is opened, pollen grains are dusted on the stigma.

↓

Bag replaced immediately.

↓

Artificial pollination takes place. **(3)**

(ii) Importance of such experiments are

(a) Creation of new genetic recombination with better quality.

(b) Incorporation of a large number of desirable characters into a single variety. **(2)**

46. Draw a diagram of a fertilised embryo sac of a dicot flower. Label all its cellular components. **Delhi 2015C**

Or (i) Why is the process of fertilisation in angiosperms termed as double fertilisation? Explain.

(ii) Draw a diagram of an angiospermic embryo sac, where fertilisation is just completed.

Label the following parts

(a) Micropylar end of embryo sac

(b) The part that develops into an embryo

(c) The part that develops into an endosperm

(d) The degenerating cells at the chalazal end

(iii) Draw a labelled diagram of globular embryonic stage of an angiosperm. **Foreign 2011**

Ans. (i) Refer to answer no. 49. **(2)**

(ii) Fertilised angiospermic embryo sac with its cellular component is given below

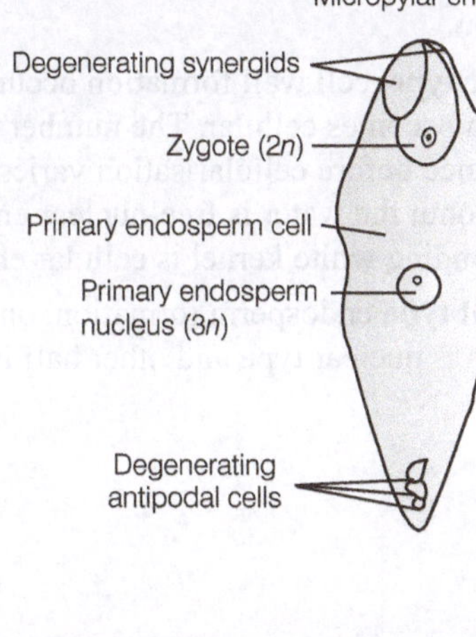

(1½)

(iii)

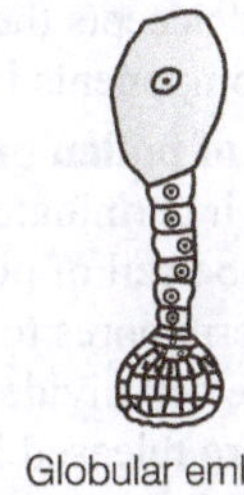

Globular embryo **(1½)**

47. Angiospermic flowers may be monoecious, cleistogamous or show self-incompatibility. Describe the characteristic features of each one of them and state which one of these flowers promotes inbreeding and outbreeding, respectively. **All India 2014C**

KEY idea

Monoecious plants have both male and female flowers in some plants.
Cleistogamous flowers are closed flowers. Self incompatibility promotes out-crossing.

Ans. The characteristic features of angiospermic flowers

(i) **Monoecious flowers** are unisexual, i.e. they have either the male reproductive or female reproductive part in separate flowers, both produced on same plant. The flowers (male and female) are separate. It prevents self- pollination and promotes cross-pollination. **(2)**

(ii) **Cleistogamous flowers** are those flowers which do not open at all, even at maturity. These flowers are invariably autogamous as the anther and stigma lie closely to each other. Such flowers promote inbreeding depression as there is no chance for cross-pollination at all. **(2)**

(iii) **Self-incompatible** In angiospermic flowers, there is a genetic mechanism, wherein the flowers prevent the self-pollens from fertilising the ovules or inhibit their germination on stigma. This device or mechanism promotes outbreeding. **(1)**

48. (i) Draw a longitudinal section of a pistil of an angiosperm showing the growth of pollen tube upto the micropyle of ovule. Label (a) stigma, (b) embryo sac (c) pollen tube (d) micropyle.

(ii) Explain the events that occur, upto fertilisation, when the compatible pollen grain lands on the stigma. **Delhi 2014C**

Ans. (i) For LS of flower, refer to answer no. 35 (ii). **(2)**

(ii) The events that occur when compatible pollen grains fall on stigma in the sequence are as follows

(a) **Pollen-pistil interaction** Once the compatible pollen grain falls on receptive stigma, the latter recognises and accepts the pollen with the aid of chemical components interacting with pollen.

(b) **Germination of pollen grain** Once the pollen is recognised, it germinates on the stigma of flower. The tube cell of pollen grain protrudes out through germ pores to form a pollen tube. The generative cell divides to form two male gametes that are released into the tube.

(c) **Growth of pollen tube** The pollen tube grows down through the tissues of stigma and style and enters ovule, usually through micropyle. Inside ovule, the filiform apparatus guides the pollen tube, carrying gametes to the egg cell.

(d) **Double fertilisation** After releasing the two male gametes into the synergids, one of them fuses with egg to form a diploid zygote (syngamy) and other male gamete fuses with two polar nuclei to form triploid primary endosperm cell (triple fusion). Because of the occurrence of these two types of fusions, it is called double fertilisation. **(3)**

49. Why is fertilisation in an angiosperm referred to as double fertilisation? Mention the ploidy of the cells involved. **All India 2012**

Ans. In fertilisation (in angiosperm), two types of fusion occur, i.e. syngamy and triple fusion, in the embryo sac. That is why it is called double fertilisation

Ploidy of cells involved in double fertilisation.

Zygote is formed as a result of syngamy, i.e. fusion of two haploid gametes (male gamete + egg). Thus, it is diploid ($2n$).

Primary endosperm nucleus ($3n$) is formed as a result of triple fusion, i.e. fusion of two haploid polar nucleus with male gamete.

50. (i) Geitonogamy is functionally a cross-pollination, but genetically similar to autogamy. Explain.

(ii) Why do flowering plants need to develop outbreeding devices? Explain any three such devices developed by flowering plants. **All India 2010C**

Ans. (i) Transfer of pollen grains from the anther to stigma of another flower of the same plant is called geitonogamy. It is functionally cross-pollination as it involves a pollinating agent, but genetically similar to autogamy since, the pollen grains come from the same plant (genetically same parent). **(2)**

(ii) Continued self-pollination results in inbreeding depression because majority of flowering plants produce hermaphrodite flowers and pollen grains generally come in contact with the stigma of same flower. **(1½)**

To discourage this, flowering plants developed many devices. For some of these devices, refer to answer no. 38. **(1½)**

TOPIC 3

Post-Fertilisation: Structures and Events

After double fertilisation, the following changes occur

- Endosperm and embryo development.
- Maturation of ovule(s) into seed(s).
- Maturation of ovary into fruit.

These events are collectively termed as **post-fertilisation events**.

Post-fertilisation changes in floral parts

- Sepals fall down or persist in few.
- Petals, stamen, stigma and style fall down.
- Ovary changes into fruit.
- Ovules become seeds.
- Synergids and antipodal cells degenerate.
- Central cell becomes endosperm. It may persist or get consumed.

Development of Endosperm

It takes place by three methods

(i) **In nuclear type**, which is a common method, the **Primary Endosperm Nucleus** (PEN) undergoes repeated mitotic division without cytokinesis. At this stage, the endosperm is called **free-nuclear endosperm.**

(ii) **In cellular type**, cell wall formation occurs and the endosperm becomes cellular. The number of free nuclei formed before cellularisation varies greatly, e.g. in coconut the water is free-nuclear endosperm and surrounding white kernel is cellular endosperm.

(iii) **In helobial type** endosperm formation, one half of endosperm is nuclear type and other half is cellular type.

Development of Embryo

(i) **Formation of embryo** occurs when certain amount of endosperm is formed, because endosperm provides nutrition for embryo development.
- Zygote divides by mitosis and forms **proembryo**.
- This results in the formation of globular and heart-shaped embryo that finally becomes horse shoe-shaped (mature embryo) having cotyledon.

(ii) Dicot embryo consists of two cotyledons and an embryonal axis between them
- The part of embryonal axis above the level of cotyledons is the **epicotyl** which becomes **plumule** (shoot).
- The part of embryonal axis below the level of cotyledons is the **hypocotyl** which becomes **radicle** (root tip).

(iii) Monocot embryo consists of only one cotyledon (called **scutellum** in grass family), e.g. rice, maize plants, etc.
- Embryonal axis has the radicle on its lower end (hypocotyl), the radicle is covered by an undifferentiated sheath called **coleorhiza**.
- At the upper end (epicotyl), the embryonal axis has plumule. It is covered by a hollow foliar sheath called **coleoptile**.

Maturation of Ovule into Seed

A seed is also referred to as fertilised ovule as it is the final product of sexual reproduction. Following features are possessed by a seed.

- It consists of seed coat, cotyledons and an embryo axis.
- **Non-albuminous seeds** have no residual endosperm as it is completely consumed in embryo development, e.g. pea, groundnut.
- **Albuminous seeds** retain a part of endosperm as it is not completely used up during embryo development, e.g. wheat, maize, castor, sunflower, etc.
- In some seeds such as black pepper and beet, remnants of nucellus are also persistent which is called **perisperm**. Integuments of ovules harden as tough protective seed coat.
- Micropyle remains as a small pore in the seed coat to allow the entry of oxygen and water.
- During seed maturation, its water content is reduced and seeds become relatively dry (10-15% moisture by mass). The general metabolic activity of the embryo slows down. The embryo may enter a state of inactivity called **dormancy**.
- On the availability of favourable conditions, seeds germinate and are later dispersed by abiotic and biotic agents.

Seeds have following advantages

- Seeds help the species to spread in other areas by dispersal.
- They generate new combinations leading to variations.
- Seeds are stored and used as food throughout the year.
- They can be used in favourable seasons depending on their viability.

Formation of Fruits

Ovary develops into a fruit. The wall of the ovary develops into the fruit's wall called **pericarp**.

Types of Fruits

(i) **True fruits** These fruits develop only from ovary, e.g. grapes, cucumber, etc.

(ii) **False fruits** In such fruits, thalamus also contributes in fruit formation, e.g. apple, strawberry, cashewnuts, etc.

(iii) **Parthenocarpic fruits** These fruits develop without fertilisation, e.g. banana.

Parthenocarpy can be induced through growth hormones and such fruits are seedless.

Special Mechanisms of Reproduction

(i) **Apomixis** is a form of asexual reproduction that mimics sexual reproduction. It is useful for the hybrid industry, e.g. grass.

The modes by which apomictic seeds can be produced are agamospermy, adventive embryony, etc.

(ii) **Polyembryony** is the presence of more than one embryo in a seed. In many *Citrus* and mango varieties, some of the nucellar cells surrounding the embryo sac start dividing, protrude into the embryo sac and develop into embryos.

PYQs Previous Years' Questions

1 Mark Questions

Multiple Choice Questions

1. Which of the following statements are true related to seeds *X* and *Y*? **CBSE SQP 2021-22 Term-I**

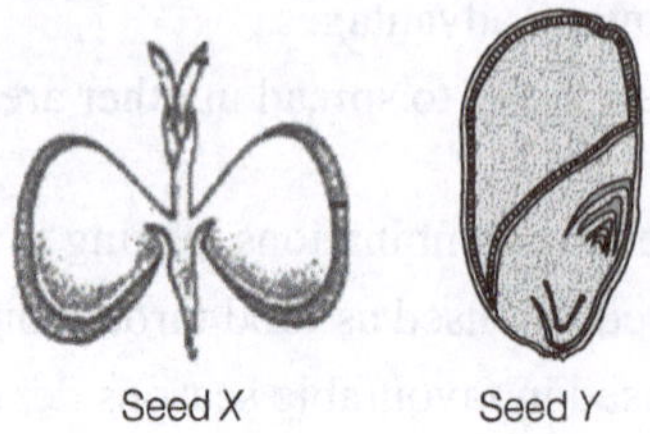

(i) Seed *X* is dicot and endospermic or albuminous.
(ii) Seed *X* is dicot and non-endospermic or non-albuminous.
(iii) Seed *Y* is monocot and endospermic or albuminous.
(iv) Seed *Y* is monocot and non-endospermic or non-albuminous.

Choose the correct option with respect to the nature of the seed.

(a) (i) and (iii) (b) (ii) and (iii)
(c) (i) and (iv) (d) (ii) and (iv)

Ans. (b) (ii) and (iii)

2. The thalamus contributes to the fruit formation in **CBSE SQP 2021-22 Term-I**

(a) banana (b) orange
(c) strawberry (d) guava

Ans. (c) strawberry

3. To produce 400 seeds, the number of meiotic divisions required will be **CBSE SQP 2021-22 Term-I**

(a) 400 (b) 200
(c) 500 (d) 800

Ans. (c) 500

4. In a typical dicotyledonous embryo, the portion of embryonal axis above the level of cotyledons is **CBSE 2021-22 Term-I**

(a) plumule (b) coleoptile
(c) epicotyle (d) hypocotyle

Ans. (c) epicotyle

5. Researchers the world over are trying to transfer apomictic genes to hybrid varieties as hybrid characters in the progeny **CBSE 2021-22 Term-I**

(a) do not segregate
(b) segregate
(c) develop genetic variations
(d) will remain unexpressed

Ans. (c) develop genetic variations

Assertion-Reason Type Questions

Direction (Q. Nos. 6-7) *consist of two statements Assertion (A) and Reason (R). Answer these questions selecting the appropriate option given below.*

(a) Both Assertion and Reason are true and Reason is the correct explanation of Assertion
(b) Both Assertion and Reason are true, but Reason is not the correct explanation of Assertion
(c) Assertion is true, but Reason is false
(d) Assertion is false, but Reason is true

6. **Assertion** Primary endosperm nucleus is diploid.

Reason It is the product of double fertilisation. **CBSE SQP 2023**

Ans. (d) Assertion is flase, but Reason is true. Assertion can be corrected as

Primary endosperm nucleus is formed by the fusion of two polar nuclei ($2n$) and one male nucleus (n). Thus, it is triploid ($3n$).

7. **Assertion** Apomictic embryos are genetically identical to the parent plant.

Reason Apomixis is the production of seeds without fertilisation. **CBSE SQP 2023**

Ans. (a) Both Assertion and Reason are true and Reason is the correct explanation of Assertion

Very Short Answer Type Questions

8. Why does endosperm development precede embryo development? **CBSE SQP 2021-22**

Ans. Endosperm develops before the embryo development because it provides nutrition to the developing embryo.

9. How many meiotic divisions are required to produce 76 seeds in a guava fruit? **CBSE SQP 2021-22**

Ans. 95 meiotic divisions are required to produce 76 seeds in a guava fruit.

Concept Enhancer In females, 76 meiotic divisions will produce 76 haploid cells. In males, 1 meiotic division will produce 4 haploid cells, i.e. 19 meiotic divisions will produce 76 haploid cells. Therefore 76 + 19 meiotic divisions are required to produce 76 seeds in a guava fruits.

10. Given below is a section of maize grain. Identify *A* and state its function. **All India 2016C**

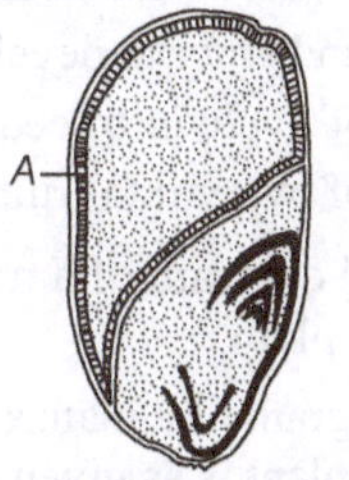

Ans. *A* is endosperm. It provides nutrition to the developing embryo.

11. Identify *A* in the figure showing a stage of embryo development in a dicot plant and mention its function. **All India 2016**

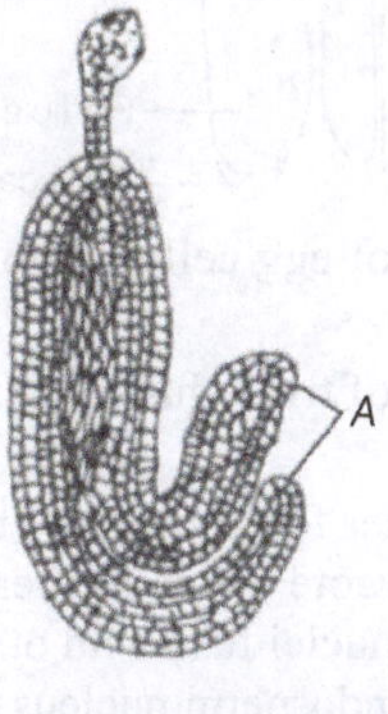

Ans. *A* is cotyledon. It is the storehouse of food.

12. Mention the function of coleorhiza. **Delhi 2015C; All India 2012**

Ans. Coleorhiza is a protective sheath covering the young root of the embryo in plants of the grass family.

13. The meiocyte of rice has 24 chromosomes. Write the number of chromosomes in its endosperm. **All India 2013C**

Ans. The meiocyte is a diploid cell and has 24 chromosomes. Thus, its haploid chromosome number is 12.

Number of chromosomes in endosperm ($3n$) is

$12 \times 3 = 36$

14. Write the function of coleoptile. **CBSE 2012**

Ans. Coleoptile is a conical sheath present in the monocot seeds. Its function is to protect the developing ovule.

15. Give reason for the following

Some organisms like honeybees are called parthenogenetic animals. **CBSE 2012**

Ans. In honeybees, the drone bees are developed parthenogenetically from an unfertilised egg. Since, they develop from unfertilised diploid eggs (and do not undergo fertilisation), they are called parthenogenetic animals.

16. Why is banana considered a good example of parthenocarpy? **All India 2012**

Or

Banana is a true fruit, but is also a parthenocarpic fruit. Give reason. **Foreign 2010**

Ans. The fruit of banana is formed from the ovary, so it is a true fruit. It is a parthenocarpic fruit because the ovary develops into fruit without fertilisation and banana is thus seedless.

17. Write the function of scutellum. **Delhi 2012**

Ans. The cotyledon of embryo of grass family is called scutellum. It is an embryonic leaf.

18. Why is apple referred to as a false fruit? **All India 2010C**

Ans. In apple, the thalamus also contributes to fruit formation. So, apples are called false fruits.

19. Name the mechanism responsible for the formation of seed without fertilisation in angiosperms. Give an example of a species of flowering plants with such seed formation. **Delhi 2010**

Ans. Apomixis is the mechanism responsible for the formation of seeds without fertilisation in angiosperms, e.g. grasses.

2 Marks Questions

20. Do you think apomixis can be compared to asexual reproduction ? Justify your answer. State the benefits of apomixis to the farmers. **CBSE 2024 (Set-I)**

Ans. Yes, apomixis can be compared to asexual reproduction. It is a form of asexual reproduction that mimics sexual reproduction as it involves seed formation, but do not involve fusion of gametes, e.g. grasses and Asteraceae. **(1)**

Apomixis is beneficial to the farmers as

(i) It is genetically similar to the parents producing them. Thus, useful traits can be maintained over generations.

(ii) It is a cost-effective method for producing seeds.

(iii) Apomictic seeds can be used years after year to raise new crops. **(1)**

21. "Farmers prefer apomictic seeds to hybrid seeds". Justify giving two reasons. **CBSE 2024 (Set-II)**

Ans. Farmer prefer apomictic seeds to hybrid seeds because of the following advantages of apomictic seeds

(i) It reduces the cost of input in farming as farmers can retain and replant seeds from their apomictic crops. Unlike hybrid seeds which needs to be bought every years. **(1)**

(ii) Maintenance of superior characters in the crops can be done easily as apomictic seeds are produced asexually and plant produced are genetically identical to the parent plant, unlike hybrid plants which are result of cross-pollination and contain genetic variability in their offsprings. **(1)**

22. (i) Name the structure seen on the surface of black pepper and beet roots, not seen on a bean seed. Mention the part of the ovule it is a remnant of.

(ii) Name the outer layer of a maize grain and state where generally does this layer get developed in a flowering plant. **Delhi 2020**

Ans. (i) The structure seen on the surface of black pepper and beet root, but not seen in bean seed is remnant of nucellus. This is also called perisperm or residual nucellus. **(1)**

(ii) The name of outer layer of maize grain is pericarp. It develops from the ovary wall. **(1)**

23. State two advantages of apomictic seed to a farmer. **All India 2020**

Or Suggest two advantages to a farmer using apomictic seeds of hybrid varieties. **Foreign 2015**

Ans. Advantages of an apomictic seed to a farmer are

(i) These seeds drastically reduce the cost of hybrid production. **(1)**

(ii) Apomictic seeds help to maintain hybrid characters. **(1)**

24. It is said apomixis is a type of asexual reproduction. Justify. **Delhi 2019**

Ans. Through apomixis, viable seeds can be produced without fertilisation and zygote formation through gametic fusion. This is not the case during sexual reproduction. In sexual reproduction, seeds are produced through gametic fusion following fertilisation. So, apomixis is called a type of asexual reproduction.

25. Name the type of fruit apple is categorised under and why? Mention two other examples which belong to the same category as apple. **Delhi 2015C**

Ans. Apple is categorised as false fruit because it does not develop from the ovary, but thalamus. Cashew and strawberry belong to the same category as apple.

26. Write the difference between the tender coconut water and the thick, white kernel of a mature coconut and their ploidy. **Delhi 2015C**

Ans. The tender coconut water represents the free nuclear endosperm while, the white kernel is the cellular endosperm. The water and kernel of the endosperm are both triploid.

27. List the post-fertilisation events in angiosperms. **Delhi 2014**

Ans. The post-fertilisation events in angiosperms include

(i) Endosperm and embryo development.

(ii) Maturation of ovule into seed.

(iii) Maturation of ovary into fruit.

28. Draw a labelled diagram of a matured embryo of a dicotyledonous plant. **All India 2014C**

Ans. The labelled diagram of a mature embryo of a dicotyledonous plant is as given below

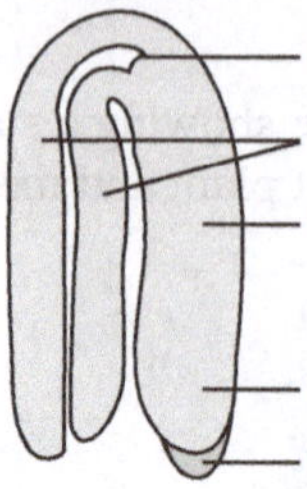

29. Write the fate of egg cell and polar nuclei after fertilisation. **Delhi 2013**

Or Write the fate of triple fusion in mature fruit of coconut. **Delhi 2012**

Ans. The egg cell after fertilisation with one of the two male nuclei forms zygote which further develops into an embryo. Polar nuclei fuse with other male nuclei to form primary endosperm nucleus which further develops into endosperm. In case of coconut, the endosperm is watery.

30. Some angiospermic seeds are said to be 'albuminous', whereas few others are said to have a perisperm. Explain each with the help of an example. **Foreign 2012**

Ans. Some angiospermic seeds are albuminous as they retain endosperm even after embryo development, i.e. endosperm is not completely consumed by embryo, e.g. wheat, maize, castor.

While in some angiospermic seeds, remnants of nucellus are persistent which is referred to as perisperm, e.g. black pepper and beet.

31. Differentiate between albuminous and non-albuminous seeds, giving one example of each. **Delhi 2011**

Ans. Difference between albuminous and non-albuminous seeds is

Albuminous seed	Non-albuminous seed
Endosperm is not completely consumed by the developing embryo, so a portion of it remains in the seed, e.g. coconut, castor and maize.	Endosperm is completely consumed by the developing embryo before the maturation of seed, so there is no endosperm left in the seed, e.g. pea, bean and mustard.

3 Marks Questions

32. If the cells in the leaves of a maize plant contain 10 chromosomes each, write the number of chromosomes in its endosperm and zygote. Name and explain the process by which an endosperm and a zygote are formed in maize. **CBSE 2024 (Set-II)**

Ans. Leaves of a maize plant contains 10 chromosomes each, so

$2n = 10$ (as leaf is diploid in nature)

Haploid no. $n = 5$

Gametes will be $\rightarrow n = 5$, each

Chromosome no. in endosperm $(3n) = 3 \times 5 = 15$ chromosomes

Chromosome no. in zygote $(2n) = 2 \times 5 = 10$ chromosomes

Maize is an angiosperm and exhibit double fertilisation as its characteristic feature in which two processes called syngamy and triple fusion occurs to form zygote and endosperm, respectively.

One male gametes + Egg cell ↓ Syngamy → Zygote $(2n)$

One male gamete + Central polar nuclei ↓ Triple fusion → Endosperm/PEN/PEC $(3n)$

Zygote $(2n)$ and Endosperm/PEN/PEC $(3n)$ ↓ Double fertilisation

The pollen tube releases two male gametes into the synergids in which one male gamete moves towards egg cell and fuses to form a diploid zygote. The other male gametes move towards the central nuclei and fuses with them to form a triploid Primary Endosperm Nucleus (PEN). (3)

33. Apomixis is a form of asexual reproduction that mimics sexual reproduction in plants. Explain with the help of a suitable example. **CBSE SQP 2020**

Ans. Refer to answer no. 38 (Apomictic seeds).

34. State what is apomixis. Write its significance. How can it be commercially used? **All India 2019**

Or State what is apomixis. Comment on its significance. How can it be commercially used? **All India 2015**

Ans. **Apomixis** is a special mechanism to produce seeds without fertilisation. It is a form of asexual reproduction that mimics sexual reproduction. (1)

Significance

(i) It helps in fixing heterosis or hybrid vigour in plants permanently.

(ii) Rapid multiplication of genetically uniform individuals can be achieved without risk of segregation. (1)

Commercial use Apomixis is used in plant breeding. It increases the chance of developing superior gene combinations and facilitates the rapid incorporation of desirable traits. (1)

35. Differentiate between parthenocarpy and parthenogenesis. Give one example of each. **CBSE 2018**

Or

Differentiate between parthenogenesis and parthenocarpy. **All India 2014C**

Ans. The differences between parthenocarpy and parthenogenesis are

Parthenocarpy	Parthenogenesis
It is the phenomenon of formation of fruits, without fertilisation.	It is the phenomenon in which the unfertilised female gamete (ovum) develops into an adult.
It occurs in plants only.	It occurs in both plants and animals.
Fruits produced by this procedure are of normal type, e.g. pineapple fruits.	Individuals produced by parthenocarpy are usually weak or non-viable, e.g. Plants–*Datura*, Animals–drones (honeybee).

36. If the meiocyte of a maize plant contains 20 chromosomes. Write the number of chromosomes in the endosperm and embyro of the maize grain and give reasons in support of your answer. **2018 C**

> **KEY idea**
> Embryo $= 2n$, Endosperm $= 3n$

Ans. If the meiocyte of a maize plant contains 20 chromosomes, then the number of chromosomes in the endosperm and the embryo of maize grain will be 30 and 20, respectively.

The meiocyte is a diploid cell and have 20 chromosomes. Thus, its haploid chromosome is 10.

Number of chromosome in endosperm is $3n$, $10 \times 3 = 30$.

Number of chromosomes in embryo is $2n$, $2 \times 10 = 20$.

37. Do you think apomixis can be compared with asexual reproduction? Support your answer, giving one reason. How is apomixis beneficial to farmers? Explain. **2018C**

Ans. Yes, apomixis can be compared with asexual reproduction. It is also called a form of asexual reproduction that mimics sexual reproduction.

In apomixis, seeds are produced without fertilisation and zygote formation occurs through gametic fusion. So, it can be called as a form of asexual reproduction.

Two advantages of apomictic seeds (apomixis) to farmers are

(i) It lowers the cost of production.

(ii) Apomictic seeds do not have to be produced every year.

38. How are parthenocarpic fruits produced by some plants and apomictic seeds by some other? Explain. **Delhi 2016**

Ans. **Parthenocarpic Fruits**

Some fruits that develop without undergoing fertilisation, are called parthenocarpic fruits, e.g. banana. The process of formation of fruit without fertilisation is called parthenocarpy. It can be induced through the application of growth hormones and such fruits are seedless. **(1½)**

Apomictic Seeds

These are formed by apomixis. It is a form of asexual reproduction that mimics sexual reproduction, but produces viable seeds without fertilisation. It does not involve formation of zygote through the gametic fusion. It occurs in some species of Asteraceae and grasses.

These are produced from segments of fruit (mango stem), male gametic content of pollen (*Cyperus*) and other vegetative parts. In some species, the diploid egg cell is formed without reduction division and develops into embryo without fertilisation. In some species like *Citrus,* some of the nucellar cells surrounding the embryo sac start dividing and develop into embryos. **(1½)**

39. Double fertilisation is reported in plants of both, castor and groundnut. However, the mature seeds of groundnut are non-albuminous and castor are albuminous. Explain the post-fertilisation events that are responsible for it. **Delhi 2015**

Ans. Double fertilisation is reported in both castor and groundnut, but their mature seeds are different in terms of endosperm. The primary endosperm nucleus formed after fertilisation divides mitotically without cytokinesis to initiate the formation of endosperm. At this stage, the endosperm is called **free-nuclear endosperm**.

Then, cell wall formation occurs and the endosperm becomes **cellular type**. The number of free nuclei formed before cellularisation varies greatly. Endosperm may be completely utilised by the developing embryo before the maturation of seeds as in groundnut. Such seeds are called **non-albuminous** or **non-endospermic seeds**, e.g. bean. When a portion of endosperm remains in seeds and is used up during seed germination, such seeds are called **albuminous** or **endospermic seeds,** e.g. castor.

40. Describe endosperm development in angiosperm. **Foreign 2014**

Ans. Endosperm development takes place by three methods

(i) **In nuclear type**, which is a common method, the Primary Endosperm Nucleus (PEN) undergoes repeated mitotic division without cytokinesis. At this stage, the endosperm is called **free-nuclear endosperm.**

(ii) **In cellular type**, cell wall formation occurs and the endosperm becomes cellular.

The number of free nuclei formed before cellularisation varies greatly, e.g. in coconut, the water is free nuclear endosperm and surrounding white kernel is cellular endosperm.

(iii) **In helobial type** endosperm formation, one half of endosperm is nuclear type and other half is cellular type. **(1 × 3)**

41. (i) How is apomixis different from parthenocarpy?

(ii) Describe any two modes by which apomictic seeds can be produced. **Delhi 2014C**

Ans. (i) Parthenocarpy is the development and production of seedless fruits in the absence of fertilisation, whereas apomixis refers to development of seeds and fruits, without fertilisation. So, the main difference between apomixis and parthenocarpy is that seeds are formed in former, while absent in latter. **(1)**

(ii) The two modes by which apomictic seeds can be produced are

(a) **Agamospermy** It is the process in which the seed or embryo derived from diploid egg cell, is formed without meiosis and syngamy. This diploid egg cell develops into embryo without undergoing fertilisation, e.g. apple, *Rubus*.

(b) **Adventive embryony** The method in which diploid cells surrounding the embryo sac, e.g nucellus and integument protrude into the sac and develop into embryo. This may also lead to the formation of more than one embryos in an embryo sac or ovule, leading to a condition called polyembryony, e.g. *Citrus, Opuntia*. **(2)**

42. (i) Describe the endosperm development in coconut.

(ii) Why is tender coconut considered as healthy source of nutrition?

(iii) How are pea seeds different from castor seeds with respect to endosperm? **All India 2013**

Ans. (i) Coconut endosperm formation is nuclear type. The primary endosperm nucleus undergoes free nuclear division without cell wall formation.

(ii) Soft coconut is an endosperm. It is rich in nutrients like fats, proteins, carbohydrates, minerals, vitamins, etc. Hence, it is considered as a healthy source of nutrition.

(iii) The seeds of pea are non-endospermic, while castor seeds are endospermic. The endosperm in pea seeds is consumed completely during embryo development, but endosperm is not utilised in castor seeds. (1 × 3)

43. Differentiate between perisperm and endosperm giving one example of each. **All India 2012**

Ans. Differences between perisperm and endosperm are

Perisperm	Endosperm
It represents persistent remains of nucellus (of ovule) in the seed.	It develops from Primary Endosperm Nucleus (PEN).
It is a part that belongs to seed.	It contains reserve food materials for developing seed.
It is usually dry.	It is usually in fluid form or soft.
e.g. black pepper.	e.g. water of coconut.

5 Marks Questions

44. (i) Describe the process of double fertilisation in angiosperms.

(ii) Trace the development of polyploidal cell that is formed after double fertilisation in a non-albuminous seed and albuminous seed. **All India 2020**

Ans. (i) Refer to text on page no. 13.

(ii) Refer to answer no. 39.

Common Mistakes Usually students get confused that double fertilisation results in the formation of two zygotes but in double fertilisation, one male gamete fused with egg cell forms **zygote**. Second male gamete fused with two polar nuclei forms PEN.

45. (i) Explain any two ways by which apomictic seed can develop.

(ii) List one advantage and one disadvantage of an apomictic crop.

(iii) Why do farmers find production of hybrid seeds costly? **Delhi 2019**

Ans. (i) Apomictic seed can develop in two ways as follows

(a) These are produced from segments of fruit (mango stem), male gametic content of pollen (*Cyperus*) and other vegetative parts.

(b) In some species, the diploid egg cell is formed without reduction division and develops into embryo without fertilisation. (2)

(ii) **Advantage of apomictic seed** These are the products of asexual reproduction in the absence of pollinators and takes place in extreme environment.
Disadvantage of apomictic seed During the production of apomictic crop, there is no segregation of characters in the hybrid progeny. (2)

(iii) Apomixis produces hybrid seeds and it is a costly process. Since, hybrid seeds do not maintain hybrid characters, the apomictic seeds are to be produced year after year. This is the reason why farmers find production of hybrid seeds costly. (1)

46. (i) When a seed of an orange is squeezed, many embryos, instead of one are observed. Explain, how it is possible.

(ii) Are these embryos genetically similar or different? Comment. **All India 2017**

Ans. (i) It is true that when we squeeze a seed of an orange, many embryos, instead of one are observed. It occurs mainly due to a process named **polyembryony**.

It is a phenomenon of occurrence of more than one embryo in a seed. It was first described by Antony van Leeuwenhoek (1719) in *Citrus*.

Polyembryony can be spontaneous or induced experimentally. The polyembryony may arise by the following reasons

- Formation of additional embryos from synergids or from antipodals and polar nuclei (very rare).
- Some embryos can also be derived by the activation of some sporophytic cells of ovule such as nucellus or integument.
- Embryos can also be developed from an additional embryo sac in the same ovule. (2½)

(ii) The embryos formed as a result of polyembryony are genetically similar to one another. However, the embryos arising from gametophytic tissues are similar to each other, but not to their parents. The embryos that are derived from sporophytic tissues are usually similar to each other as well as their parents. (2½)

47. (i) Explain the different ways apomictic seeds can develop. Give an example of each.

(ii) Mention one advantage of apomictic seeds to farmers.

(iii) Draw a labelled mature stage of a dicotyledonous embryo. **All India 2014**

Ans. (i) For apomictic seeds, refer to answer no. 41 (ii).

(ii) For advantage of apomictic seeds, refer to answer no. 23.

(iii) For diagram, refer to answer no. 28.

48. (i) Why does endosperm development precede embryo development in angiosperm seeds? State the role of endosperm in mature albuminous seeds.

(ii) Describe with the help of three labelled diagrams the different embryonic stages that include mature embryo of dicot plants. **Delhi 2014**

Ans. (i) The embryo development starts only after a certain amount of endosperm is formed. It is an adaptation for assured nutrition of the developing embryo therefore, endosperm development precedes embryo development. The role of endosperm in mature albuminous seeds is storage of reserve food for growing embryo. **(2)**

(ii) The embryonic stages during the development of mature embryo sac.

For figure, refer to answer no. 4 (ii) in Miscellaneous section. **(3)**

49. (i) Mature seeds of legumes are non-albuminous. Then, can it be assumed that double fertilisation does not occur in legumes? Explain your answer.

(ii) List the differences between the embryos of dicot (pea) and monocot (grass) families. **Delhi 2014C**

Ans. (i) Seeds of legumes are non-albuminous that implies that endosperm in such seeds is completely used up in providing nutrition to developing embryo. The endosperm is formed as a result of triple fusion, i.e. between a male gamete and two polar nuclei. This makes it obvious that it cannot be formed in the absence of double fertilisation.

Therefore, though the seeds of legumes are non-albuminous, it clearly states the occurrence of double fertilisation in them. **(2)**

(ii) The differences between the embryos of pea and grass can be summarised as follows

Dicot embryo (Pea)	**Monocot embryo** (Grass)
The basal cell forms a 6-10 celled suspension.	Basal cell produces a single-celled suspension.
Terminal cell produces embryo, except the radicle.	Forms the whole of embryo.
First division of terminal cell is longitudinal.	First division is transverse.
It possesses two cotyledons.	It possesses one cotyledon.
Plumule is terminal and is present between the elongated cotyledons.	Plumule is laterally present to excessive growth of single cotyledon.

(3)

50. (i) Why are seeds of some grasses called apomictic? Explain.

(ii) State two reasons to convince a farmer to use an apomictic crop. **Delhi 2014C**

Ans. (i) The seeds of some grasses develop without fertilisation. It may be because a diploid egg cell develops into an embryo directly (without undergoing meiosis and syngamy) or some diploid cells of nucellus or integument surrounding the embryo sac, protrude inside and develop into embryos. This phenomenon of developing embryo and seeds without fertilisation is called apomixis and such seeds produced are referred to as apomictic. **(3)**

(ii) For advantage of apomictic seeds, refer to answer no. 23. **(2)**

51. Give reasons why

(i) Most zygotes in angiosperms divide only after certain amount of endosperm is formed.

(ii) Groundnut seeds are exalbuminous and castor seeds are albuminous.

(iii) Micropyle remains as a small pore in the seed coat of a seed.

(iv) Integuments of an ovule harden and the water content is highly reduced as the seed matures.

(v) Apple and cashewnuts are not called true fruits. **All India 2011**

Ans. (i) Zygotes in angiosperms mostly divide only after a certain amount of endosperm is formed as an adaptation strategy to assure nutrition for the developing embryo.

(ii) Groundnut seeds are exalbuminous because the developing embryo utilises the endosperm completely. So, there is no endosperm left in the seed.

Castor seeds are albuminous because endosperm is not completely used up by the developing embryo. There is some amount of endosperm left in the seeds always.

(iii) Micropyle remains as a small pore in the seed coat to allow the entry of water and oxygen during seed germination.

(iv) During unfavourable conditions, seeds become dormant. The loss of water reduces the metabolic activity of seeds and hardens the integuments.

(v) In fruit-like cashewnuts and apple, thalamus contributes in fruit formation. So, they are not called true fruits. **(1 × 5)**

52. (i) Draw a labelled longitudinal view of an albuminous seed.

(ii) How are seeds advantageous to flowering plants? **All India 2010**

Ans. (i) LS of an albuminous seed (castor) is

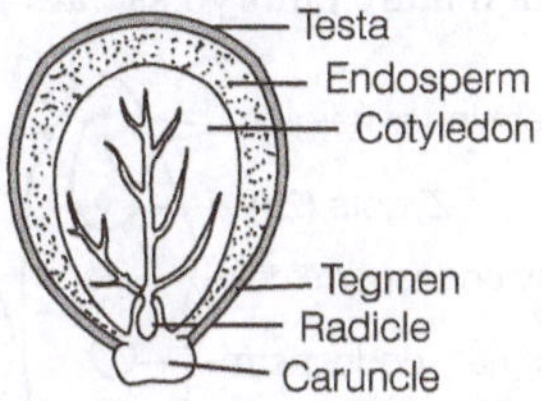

(2)

(ii) Advantages of seeds to flowering plants are

(a) Provide protection to embryo in most delicate stage.

(b) Help in dispersal and spread in new habitats.

(c) Contain sufficient food reserves.

(d) Produce genetic variations.

(e) Seeds are related to pollination and fertilisation. **(3)**

53. Explain the development of the zygote into an embryo and of the primary endospermic nucleus into an endosperm in a fertilised embryo sac of a dicot plant. **All India 2010C**

Ans. Development of endosperm refer to answer no. 40.

Embryo Development in Dicot Seed

(i) Embryo formation starts after a certain amount of endosperm is formed.

(ii) Zygote divides by mitosis to form a proembryo.

(iii) Formation of globular and heart-shaped embryo occurs, which finally becomes horseshoe-shaped mature embryo.

(iv) In dicot plants, embryo consists of two cotyledons and an embryonal axis between them.

(v) The portion of embryonal axis above the level of attachment of cotyledons is epicotyl and terminates in the plumule.

(vi) The portion of embryonal axis below the level of attachment of cotyledon is the hypocotyl, it becomes radicle (root tip).

Miscellaneous Questions

3 Marks Question

1. Name two end products of double fertilisation in angiosperms. How are they formed? Write their fate during the development of seed. **Delhi 2014C**

Ans. The two end products of double fertilisation in angiosperms are diploid zygote and a triploid Primary Endosperm Nucleus (PEN). **(1)**

Diploid zygote is formed by the fusion of haploid gametes, i.e. male gamete and egg, while another male gamete and two polar nuclei of central cell fuse to form triploid primary endosperm nucleus. **(1)**

During the development of seed, the zygote undergoes mitotic divisions to form a mature embryo while, the primary endosperm cell gives rise to nutritive tissue called endosperm, which provides nourishment to growing embryo. **(1)**

5 Marks Questions

2. (i) Explain the process of double fertilisation in angiosperms.

(ii) Why does the development of endosperm precedes that of embryo?

(iii) List the parts of a typical dicot embryo.

Ans. (i) **Double fertilisation** After the release of the two male gametes into the synergids from a pollen tube, one of them fuses with egg to form a diploid zygote (syngamy) and other male gamete fuses with 2 polar nuclei to form triploid primary endosperm cell (triple fusion). Because of the occurrence of these two types of fusions this process is called double fertilisation.

Refer to figure in answer no. 35 (ii) in Topic 2. **(1½)**

(ii) The embryo development starts only after a certain amount of endosperm is formed. It is an adaptation to assure availability of nutrition for the developing embryo. Therefore, endosperm development precedes embryo development.

The role of endosperm in mature albuminous seeds is storage of reserve food for growing embryo. **(1½)**

(iii) Parts of a typical dicot embryo are

(a) Plumule (b) Radicle

(c) Cotyledons (d) Hypocotyl **(2)**

3. Read the following statement and answer the questions that follows.

'A guava fruit has 200 viable seeds'.

(i) What are viable seeds?

(ii) Write the total number of

(a) Pollen grains

(b) Gametes are producing 200 viable guava seeds.

(iii) Prepare a flowchart to depict the post-pollination events leading to viable seed production in a flowering plant. **Delhi 2017**

Ans. (i) Viable seeds are seeds having the ability to germinate when favourable conditions are present. **(1)**

(ii) (a) Number of pollen grains = 200

(b) Gametes are producing 200 viable guava seeds = 400 **(1)**

(iii) Post-pollination events include

(a) Double fertilisation

(b) Formation of embryo

(c) Formation of endosperm **(1)**

Flowchart depicting post-pollination events is as follows

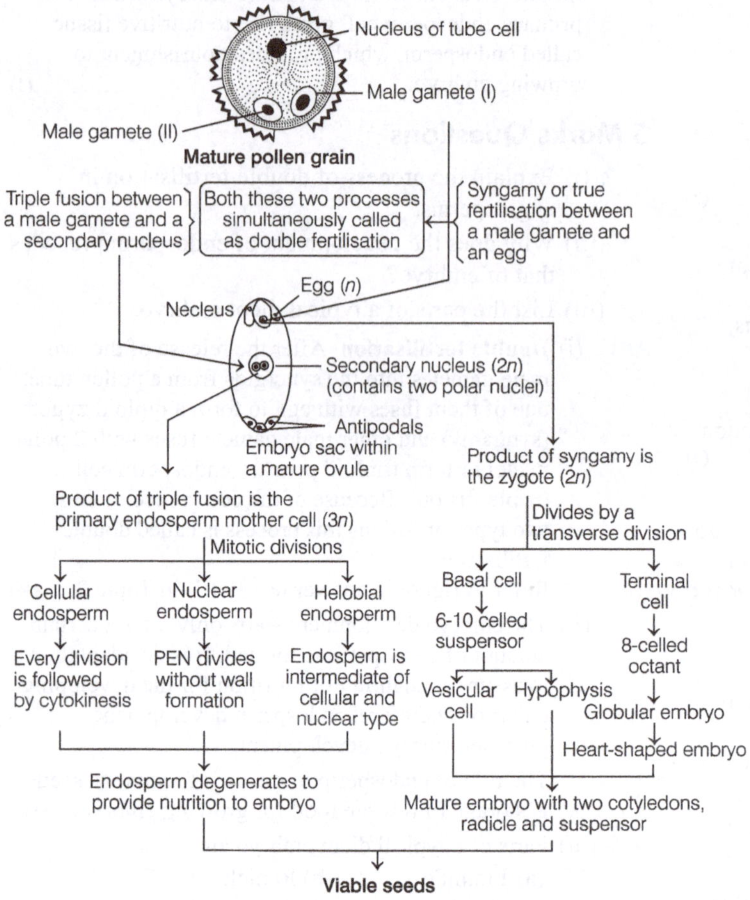

(2)

4. Read the statement and answer the questions that follows

A flower of brinjal has 520 ovules in its ovary. However, it produces a fruit with only 480 viable seeds.

(i) What could have prevented the rest of the 40 ovules from maturing into viable seeds? Explain giving a reason.

(ii) Describe the development of a dicot embryo in a viable seed.

(iii) Why certain angiospermic seeds are albuminous, while others are exalbuminous? Explain. **Delhi 2017**

Ans. (i) Ovules can develop into viable seeds having the ability to germinate under suitable environmental conditions, however often ovules do not develop into viable seeds because of the following reasons

(a) Excessive dry weather or high temperature.

(b) Damage to embryo.

(c) Starvation due to exhaustion of food in ovule. **(1½)**

(ii) For development of a dicot embryo, refer to answer no. 53 in Topic 3.

The embryonic stages during the development of a mature embryo sac are

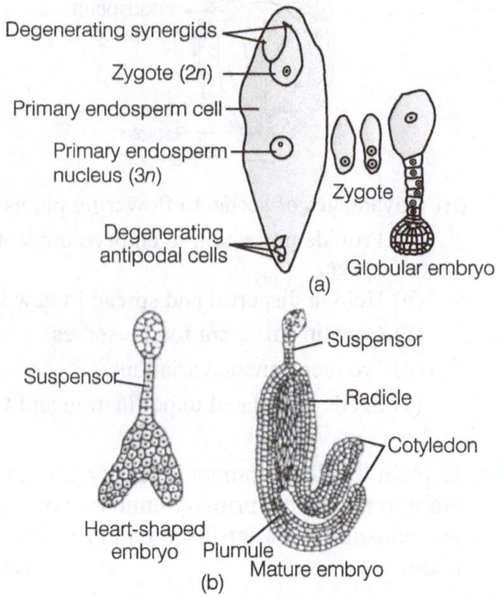

(a) Fertilised embryo sac showing zygote and Primary Endosperm Nucleus (PEN). (b) Stages in embryo development in a dicot.

(2)

(iii) In flowering plants, during the development of seeds, along with embryo, a nutritive tissue called endosperm is also formed. During embryo development, endosperm degenerates to release its content that helps in the growth of embryo. In some plants, the endosperm is completely used up in embryo development.

In such seed, endosperm is absent, e.g. pea, gram, beans, etc. These seeds are called exalbuminous seeds. On the other hand, in some plants, the endosperm tissue persists in the viable seeds. These are called as albuminous seeds, e.g. castor. **(1½)**

5. (i) Explain the post-pollination events leading to seed production in angiosperms.

(ii) List the different types of pollination depending upon the source of pollen grain. **Delhi 2016**

Ans. (i) Post-pollination events include pollen-pistil interaction, double fertilisation, formation of endosperm, development of embryo, seed and fruit.

For pollen-pistil interaction, refer to answer no. 15 of Topic 2.

For double fertilisation, refer to answer no. 39 of Topic 2.

Development of an endosperm The development of endosperm precedes embryo development. The primary endosperm cell divides repeatedly to form a **triploid endosperm tissue.**

Development of an embryo The embryo develops at the micropylar end of the embryo sac where the zygote is situated. Most zygotes divide only after certain amount of endosperm is formed. It is an adaptation to assure availability of nutrition for the developing embryo.

Development of a seed Double fertilisation in angiosperms triggers the transformation of ovule into a seed. These seeds are formed inside the fruits.

Formation of a fruit A fruit is formed as a result of cell division and differentiation in the ovary, which is transformed into fruit. **(2)**

(ii) Depending upon the source of pollen grains, pollination is of following three types

(a) **Autogamy** (Self-pollination) It is the kind of pollination achieved within the same flower. The pollen from the anthers of a flower is transferred to the stigma of the same flower, e.g. wheat, rice, pea, etc. Autogamy is further classified as

Cleistogamy In some plants, flowers never open up and the anthers dehisce inside the closed flowers to ensure pollination. Thus, cleistogamous flowers are invariably autogamous as there is no chance of cross-pollination. These flowers produce assured seed sets even in the absence of pollinators, e.g. *Oxalis*, *Viola*, etc.

Homogamy In this method, both the anthers and the stigma of bisexual flowers mature at the same time, e.g. *Mirabilis*.

(b) **Geitonogamy** The pollination where the pollen grains from the anther of a flower are transferred to the stigma of another flower borne on the same plant, but at different branches. It usually occurs in plants, which show monoecious condition, e.g. *Cucurbita*. It is functionally cross-pollination (involves a pollinating agent), but genetically it is similar to autogamy (since pollen grains come from same plant).

(c) **Xenogamy** (Cross-pollination) It involves the transfer of pollen grains from the anther of one plant to the stigma of another plant. This is the only type of pollination, which brings genetically different types of pollen grains to the stigma during pollination, e.g. papaya, maize, etc. **(3)**

6. (i) Explain the events after pollination leading to the formation of a seed in angiosperms.

(ii) Mention the ploidy levels of the cells of different parts of an albuminous seed. **Foreign 2015**

Ans. (i) The following events take place between pollination and formation of a seed in angiosperms

(a) **Double fertilisation**
refer to answer no. 39 of Topic 2.

(b) **Endosperm formation**
refer to answer no. 5 (i) of this section only.

(c) **Embryo development**
refer to answer no. 5 (i) of this section only.

(d) **Seed formation** Seeds are fertilised ovules that are developed inside a fruit. Each seed consists of a seed coat, an embryonal axis and cotyledon. **(1 × 4)**

(ii) The ploidy of the endosperm of an albuminous seed is $3n$ and ploidy of the embryo is $2n$. **(1)**

7. A flower of tomato plant following the process of sexual reproduction produces 240 viable seeds.

Answer the following questions giving reasons

(i) What would have been the minimum number of ovules present in per pollinated pistil?

(ii) How many microspore mother cells would minimally be required to produce requisite number of pollen grains?

(iii) How many pollen grains must have minimally pollinated the carpel?

(iv) How many male gametes would have used to produce these 200 viable seeds?

(v) How many megaspore mother cells were required in this process? **Delhi 2015**

Ans. (i) The minimum number of ovules would also have been 240, as 240 viable seeds are formed. After fertilisation, the ovule turns into seeds.

(ii) The minimum number of microspore mother cells in the above case would be 60. This is because each microspore mother cell gives rise to 4 microspores.
Thus, to obtain 240 microspores, 60 cells are required.

(iii) The minimum number of pollen grains that must have been involved are 240, as 240 viable seeds are formed. This is because each pollen grain contains 2 male gametes, out of which one fuses with the egg forming zygote that gives rise to seeds.

(iv) The number of male gametes involved would be 240. Each male gamete fuses with one egg nuclei to form zygote that gives rise to seed.

(v) 240 megaspore mother cells were involved. They undergo meiotic division to form 4 haploid megaspores. Out of them, only 1 becomes functional megaspore, rest 3 degenerate. (1 × 5)

8. A flower of brinjal plant following the process of sexual reproduction produces 300 viable seeds. Answer the following questions giving reasons

(i) How many ovules are minimally involved?

(ii) How many megaspore mother cells are involved?

(iii) What is the minimum number of pollen grains that must land on stigma for pollination?

(iv) How many male gametes are involved in the above case?

(v) How many microspore mother cells must have undergone reduction division prior to dehiscence of anther in the above case? **Delhi 2015**

Ans. (i) The minimum number of ovules would be 300 as 300 viable seeds are formed.

(ii) 300 megaspore mother cells were involved.

(iii) The minimum number of pollen grains that must have been involved are 300.

(iv) The number of male gametes involved in seed formation are 300.

(v) Minimum 75 microspore mother cells must have been involved to form 300 pollen grains. (1 × 5)

9. (i) Draw a LS of a pistil showing pollen tube entering the embryo sac in an angiosperm and label the six parts other than stigma, style and ovary.

(ii) Write the changes a fertilised ovule undergoes within the ovary in an angiosperm plant.

All India 2013

Ans. (i) **Diagram** refer to answer no. 35 (ii) of Topic 2. (2)

(ii) Changes taking place in a fertilised ovule within the ovary in an angiospermic plant are

Fertilised ovule	—	Seed
Funiculus	—	Stalk of ovule
Integument	—	Seed coat
(a) outer	—	Testa
(b) inner	—	Tegmen
Polar nuclei	—	Endosperm
Nucellus	—	Utilised or remaining perisperm
Antipodal	—	Degenerate
Synergid	—	Degenerate
Egg	—	Embryo

(3)

10. (i) Name the structures which the parts *A* and *B* shown in the diagram given below, respectively develop into.

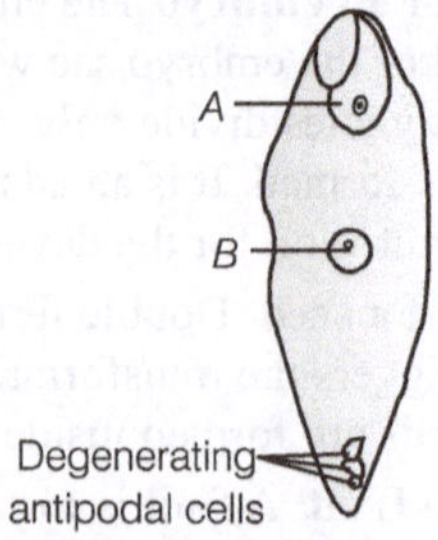

(ii) Explain the process of development which *B* undergoes in albuminous and exalbuminous seeds. Give one example of each of these seeds.

Foreign 2011

Ans. (i) The part *A* is zygote which develops into the embryo. The part *B* is primary endosperm nucleus which develops into the endosperm. (1)

(ii) **Endosperm Formation**

(a) Primary endosperm cell divides repeatedly and forms triploid primary endosperm nucleus. (½)

(b) Primary endosperm nucleus undergoes successive free nuclear divisions to give rise to a number of free nuclei. At this stage, it is called free nuclear endosperm. (1)

(c) Wall formation takes place from the periphery and proceeds towards the centre and the endosperm becomes cellular. (½)

(d) In albuminous seeds, some amount of endosperm persists in the mature seed as the developing embryo does not consume it completely, e.g. wheat, maize. (1)

(e) In exalbuminous seeds, the endosperm is completely consumed by the developing embryo before seed maturation, e.g. in pea/groundnut. (1)

11. (i) Draw a labelled diagram of LS of an embryo of grass (any six labels).

(ii) Give reason for each of the following

(a) Anthers of angiosperm flowers are described as dithecous.

(b) Hybrid seeds have to be produced year after year. **All India 2011**

Ans. (i) LS of grass embryo is given below

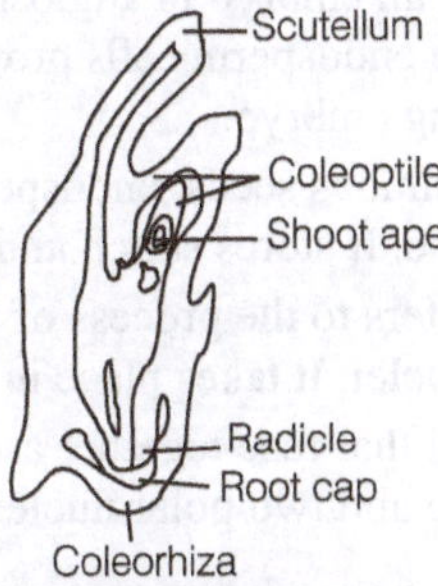

(2)

(ii) (a) A typical angiosperm anther is bilobed with each lobe having two thecae. So, anther is called dithecous. (1)

(b) Hybrid seeds show segregation of traits and do not maintain the hybrid character in plants. So, they need to be produced every year and cannot be stored. (2)

12. Explain double fertilisation and trace the post-fertilisation events in sequential order leading to seed formation in a typical dicotyledonous plant. **Foreign 2010**

Ans. For double fertilisation, refer to answer no. 39 of Topic 2.

Post-fertilisation events can be traced as

- Development of endosperm, enlargement of seeds and fruit formation.
- Zygote develops into an embryo.
- Central cell becomes primary endosperm cell and the primary endosperm nucleus develops into the endosperm.
  - Antipodals and synergids degenerate.
  - Integuments develop into seed coat.
  - Ovules ripen into seeds.
  - Ovary ripens to form the fruit.

For development of embryo, refer to answer no. 5 (i) of this section only.

Case Based/Source Based/Passage Based Questions (Based on Complete Chapter)

1. Read the following and answer the questions given below

Continued self-pollination may lead to the chance of inbreeding depression. Hence, flowering plants have developed many devices to discourage self-pollination and to encourage cross-pollination. This may either include the non-synchronisation of pollen release or stigma receptivity or prevention of pollens from fertilising the ovule or anything else.

(i) Which outbreeding device out of these is mainly seen in orchids where the sex organs themselves prove to be a barrier to prevent self-pollination?

(a) Dioecy (b) Herkogamy
(c) Dicliny (d) Both (a) and (b)

(ii) In heterostyly

(a) pollens are prevented to fertilise ovules
(b) anther becomes receptive earlier
(c) pollens are released earlier
(d) anther and stigma are placed at different locations

(iii) The condition where pollen is released first is called

(a) protandry (b) protogyny
(c) heterostyly (d) dicliny

(iv) Dicliny effectively prevents

(a) cross pollination
(b) self-pollination
(c) inbreeding depression
(d) Both (a) and (c)

(v) In dioecy each plant is

(a) Male (b) Female
(c) Either male or female (d) Both male and female

Ans. (i)-(c), (ii)-(d), (iii)-(a), (iv)-(b), (v)-(c)

2. Read the following and answer the questions given below

The ovule is an integumented megasporangium that undergoes meiotic division to form megaspore. It is found attached to the placenta with the help of a stalk like structure called funicle. The junction between an ovule and funicle is called hilum that later becomes a scar on the seed when it develops after fertilisation.

(i) The ovule of an angiosperm is technically

(a) megasporophyll (b) MMC
(c) megasporangium (d) megaspore

(ii) Consider the diagram of embryo sac below.

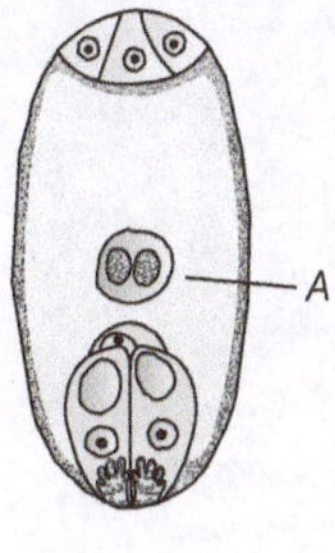

The part labelled as *A* in the ovule is

(a) synergids
(b) egg cells
(c) antipodal
(d) central cell

(iii) The ovule generally has
(a) single embryo sac (b) three embryo sac
(c) two embryo sac (d) four embryo sac

(iv) The megaspore mother cell is
(a) haploid (b) diploid
(c) haplo-diploid (d) triploid

(v) The integuments encircle the complete ovule excepting
(a) antipodal (b) chalazal end
(c) micropyle (d) Both (b) and (c)

Ans. (i)-(c), (ii)-(d), (iii)-(a), (iv)-(b), (v)-(c)

3. Study the diagram given below and answer the questions that follows.

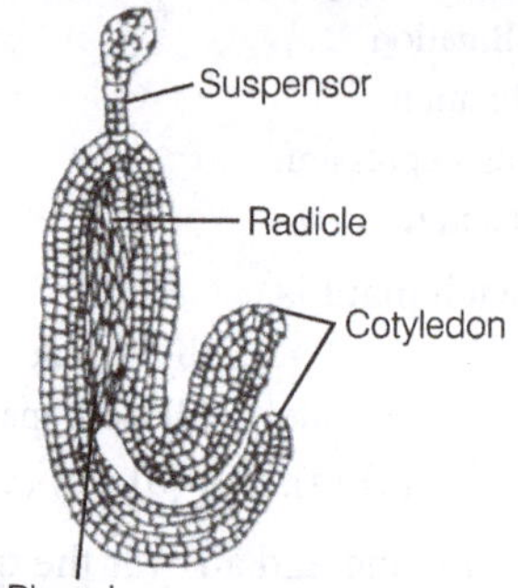

(i) Which of the following, an endosperm or an embryo, develops first in an angiospermic seed? Give reason for the precedence.

(ii) State the role of endosperm in mature albuminous seed.

(iii) What is triple fusion? Where and how does it take place?

(iv) Give the name of nuclei involved in triple fusion.

Ans. (i) The development of endosperm is followed by the development of an embryo in angiospermic seeds. It is because the endosperm cells provide nutrition to the developing embryo.

(ii) In mature albuminous seeds, endosperm exists as the storage tissue. It stores starch and fat.

(iii) Triple fusion refers to the process of fusion of three haploid nuclei. It takes place in embryo sac.

(iv) The three nuclei that fuse together are nucleus of the male gamete and two polar nuclei of the central cell.

4. During botany lecture, teacher told students that an embryo sac contains 8 nucleus, but it is 7-celled structure. Teacher further told about antipodals, synergids and polar nuclei so as to clear the confusion of students.

(i) What is the alternative term used for embryo sac?

(ii) Name the structure in which embryo sac is found and the cell, which upon division form embryo sac.

(iii) Name the structures found at the micropylar and chalazal ends of embryo sac.

(iv) Mention the function of filiform apparatus in embryo sac.

Ans. (i) Female gametophyte.

(ii) Embryo sac is present in the ovule of flowering plants. It is formed when haploid megaspore nucleus divide.

(iii) At micropylar end, egg apparatus is found. It consists of two synergids and one egg cell. At chalazal end, three antipodals are present.

(iv) Filiform apparatus helps to guide the pollen tubes into the synergids during fertilisation process.

(1 × 4)

CHAPTER TEST

01 Mark Questions

Multiple Choice Questions

1 There are 10 flowers in one individual plant of *Crotalaria*. In each microsporangium of every stamen of all the flowers, there are 30 micropsore mother cells. How many pollen grains are formed from that plant?

(a) 4000 (b) 10,000
(c) 24,000 (d) 48,000

2 Which of the following statements is not true about pollen grains?

(a) They form well preserved fossil due to the presence of sporopollenin
(b) They can be cryopreserved at –196°C in liquid nitrogen
(c) Their allergy causes pneumonia
(d) They can be shed in two or three-celled stages

3 Which of the following pairs is not correctly matched?

(a) Anemophily – Grasses, maize
(b) Hydrophily – *Vallisneria, Hydrilla*
(c) Malacophily – Rose, poppy
(d) Ornithophily – *Erythrina, Marcgravia*

4 What is *A, B* and *C* in the given figure of an embryo sac?

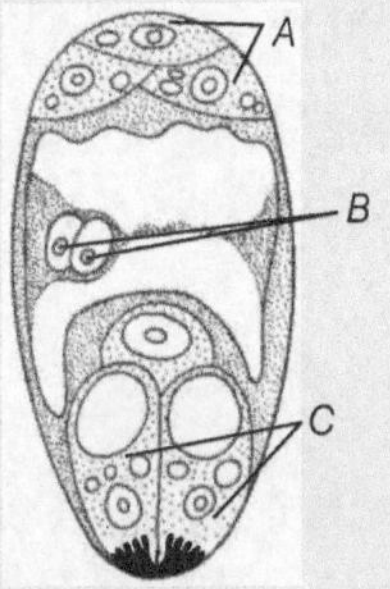

(a) *A*–Antipodals, *B*–Polar nuclei, *C*–Synergids
(b) *A*–Antipodals, *B*–Central cells, *C*–Egg cells
(c) *A*–Synergids, *B*–Polar nuclei, *C*–Egg cells
(d) *A*–Synergids, *B*–Egg cells, *C*–Filiform apparatus

5 One advantage of cleistogamy is that

(a) it leads to gene flow as pollination results in transfer of hundreds of greater genetic diversity
(b) seed dispersal is more efficient and widespread
(c) seed set is not dependent on pollinators
(d) it is used to obtain variabilities in traits

Assertion-Reason Type Questions

Direction (Q. Nos. 6-9) *In the questions given below two statements an* ***Assertion*** (A) *and a* ***Reason (R)*** *are given. Give the appropriate response as*

(a) If both A and R are true and R is the correct explanation of A
(b) If both A and R are true, but R is not the correct explanation of A
(c) If A is true, but R is false
(d) If A is false, but R is true

6 **Assertion** (A) In hemianatropous type of ovule, the funicle lies parallel to the body of ovule.

Reason (R) The body of ovule has rotated through 90° angle.

7 **Assertion** (A) Synergids of embryo sac help in fertilisation in angiosperms.

Reason (R) Filiform apparatus of synergids secrete certain chemotropically active substances due to which pollen tube grows towards the embryo sac.

8 **Assertion** (A) Nocturnal flowers are pollinated by moth.

Reason (R) Nocturnal flowers are highly fragrant and dull in colour.

9 **Assertion** (A) Endosperm is formed by the fusion of one male gamete and two polar nucleus.

Reason (R) In pea, the seed retains a part of endosperm as it is not completely used up during embryo development.

2/3 Marks Questions

10 Name the component cells of the egg apparatus in an embryo sac.

11 Which parts of pistil form fruits and seeds?

12 What do you mean by self-incompatiblity?

13 Define the term polyembryony.

14 How many meiotic divisions are required to produce 400 seeds in a fruit?

15 Identify the diagram given below. Label the parts *P* and *Q* correctly and state the function of *Q*.

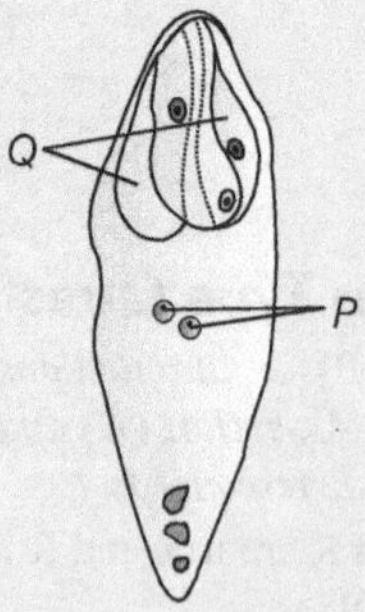

16 Briefly describe the male gametophyte and give any one difference between vegetative cell and generative cell.

17 Describe any three biotic agents of pollination.

18 How does a chasmogamous bisexual flower prevent self pollination?

19 State the function of Primary Endosperm Nucleus (PEN) found in fertilised embryo sac of an angiosperm.

05 Marks Questions

20 Draw a well-labelled diagram of longitudinal section of a flower and write the functions of any three parts of it.

21 Describe the structure of microsporangium. How many meiotic divisions are required to produce 80 seeds in a guava fruits?

22 What do you mean by self-pollination and cross pollination? Write the any three differences between water pollinated and insects pollinated flowers.

23 Can a fruit produce without fertilisation? Explain in your words.

Answers

1. (d)	**2.** (c)	**3.** (c)	**4.** (a)	**5.** (c)
6. (d)	**7.** (a)	**8.** (a)	**9.** (c)	

02 Human Reproduction

TREND ANALYSIS 3 YEARS

Topic	Types of Questions	2024	2023	2020
TOPIC 01 Reproductive System	1 Mark	0	1	0
	2 Marks	0	0	0
	3 Marks	0	0	0
	4 Marks (Case Based)	1	0	0
	5 Marks	0	0	0
TOPIC 02 Gametogenesis	1 Mark	1	0	0
	2 Marks	0	1	0
	3 Marks	0	1	2
	4 Marks (Case Based)	0	0	0
	5 Marks	1	0	0
TOPIC 03 Fertilisation, Pregnancy and Embryonic Development	1 Mark	0	0	0
	2 Marks	0	0	0
	3 Marks	0	0	1
	4 Marks (Case Based)	0	0	0
	5 Marks	0	1	1

Average No. of Questions Across all Sets

TOPIC 1

Reproductive System

Male Reproductive System

It includes a pair of testes, accessory ducts, glands and the external genitalia.

1. Testes

These are located outside the abdominal cavity within a pouch called **scrotum**. This maintains the low temperature of the testes (2-2.5°C lower than the normal body temperature) required for spermatogenesis.

- Each testis is an oval-shaped structure having a length of 4-5 cm and width of 2-3 cm. These are covered by a dense covering called **tunica albuginea**.
- Internally, testis are divided into about 250 compartments known as **testicular lobules**.
- Each lobule contains 1-3 highly coiled structural and functional units of testis called **seminiferous tubules**. In these tubules sperms are produced.
- Seminiferous tubule is lined on its inside by two types of cells called **male germ cells** or spermatogonia and **Sertoli cells**.
- Male germ cells undergo meiotic divisions leading to the formation of spermatozoa.
- Sertoli cells provide nutrition to the germ cells and hence, called **nurse cells**.

- Interstitial spaces are present in between the seminiferous tubules. These spaces contain small blood vessels and **interstitial cells** or **Leydig cells**.
- Leydig cells synthesise and secrete the testicular hormones called **androgens**.

2. Male Accessory Ducts

These include rete testis, vasa efferentia, epididymis and vas deferens.

- The intratesticular duct system starts with segments recti, which are short, straight end segments of the seminiferous tubules. These segments connect the seminiferous tubules to the highly anastomosing, cuboidal epithelium-lined channels called **rete testis**.
- From rete testis, 10-25 fine tubules called **vasa efferentia** arise. These leave the testis and open into the epididymis.

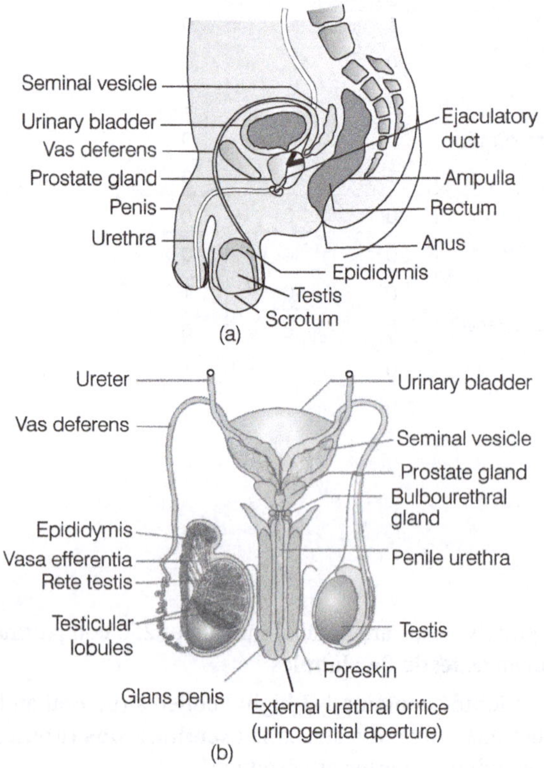

Figure 2.1 (a) Diagrammatic sectional view of male pelvis showing reproductive system, (b) Diagrammatic view of male reproductive system (part of testis is open to show inner details)

- The epididymis leads to vas deferens that ascends to the abdomen and loops over the urinary bladder. It receives a duct from the seminal vesicle to form **ejaculatory duct** that runs through the prostate gland and opens into urethra.
- **Urethra** receives the ducts of prostate gland and the bulbourethral gland (Cowper's glands). It runs through the penis to its external opening called **urethral meatus**.

3. The Accessory Glands

Male reproductive system include a pair of seminal vesicle, a prostate gland and a pair of bulbourethral gland (Cowper's glands).

- The secretions of all these glands constitute **seminal plasma**.
- **Seminal vesicles** secrete alkaline seminal fluid that contains fructose, citrate, prostaglandins, etc.
- **Prostate gland** secretes slightly acidic (pH-6.5), milky fluid containing calcium, proteolytic enzymes, etc. This fluid nourishes and activates spermatozoa to swim in female reproductive tract, providing sperm motility.
- Secretion of **bulbourethral glands** is alkaline. It helps in the lubrication of the urogenital tract. It also neutralises any acid of urine present in urethra.
- Seminal plasma along with sperms is called **semen**.

4. External Genitalia

It is the penis. It is made up of special erectile tissues that help in the erection of penis. The enlarged tip of the penis is called **glans penis**. It is covered by a loose fold of skin called **foreskin** or **prepuce**.

Female Reproductive System

It consists of a pair of ovaries, secondary sex organs, external genitalia and mammary glands.

1. Ovaries

These are primary female sex organs. They produce female gametes called ova and secrete the female sex hormones.

- These are located one on each side of the lower abdomen.
- These are almond-shaped, 2-4 cm in length and 1.5 cm in width.
- Each ovary is connected to the pelvic wall and uterus by ligaments.
- Each ovary is covered by a thin epithelium which encloses the **ovarian stroma**.
- Ovarian stroma is divided into two regions, i.e. **peripheral cortex** and **inner medulla**.

2. Accessory Ducts

The following parts constitute the accessory ducts in females

(i) **Fallopian tube** or **Oviducts** is about 10-12 cm long and extends from the periphery of each ovary to the uterus.

- The part of oviduct closer to the ovary is funnel-shaped structure known as **infundibulum**.
- The edges of infundibulum possess finger-like projections called **fimbriae**. These projections help in the collection of ovum after ovulation.
- Infundibulum leads to a wider part of the oviduct called **ampulla**.
- **Isthmus** is the last part of the oviduct. It has a narrow lumen which joins the uterus.

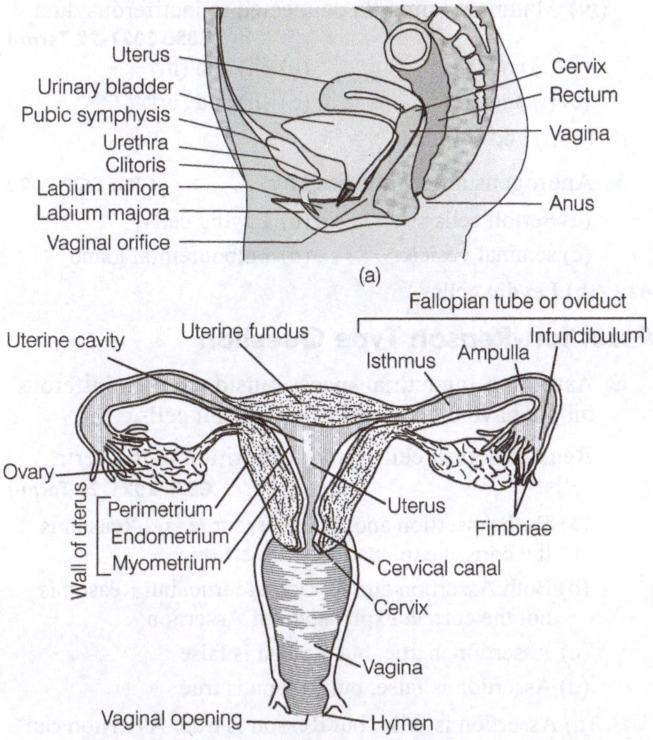

Figure 2.2 Female reproductive system (a) Lateral view (b) Sectional view

(ii) **Uterus** or womb is a pear-shaped muscular organ. It is about 7.5 cm long and 5 cm wide. It is attached to the pelvic wall and supported by ligaments.

- Wall of the uterus has three layers, i.e. **Perimetrium** the outermost thin membranous layer, **myometrium** the middle thick layer of smooth muscles and **endometrium** the innermost glandular layer which lines the uterine cavity.
- Uterus opens into the **vagina** through a narrow **cervix**. Its cavity is called **cervical canal**, which along with vagina forms **birth canal**.
- Endometrium layer undergoes cyclic changes during menstrual cycle.
- Smooth muscles in myometrium contract during parturition to deliver the baby.

(iii) **Vagina** is a muscular tube-like structure that opens to the outside. It receives spermatozoa during insemination and also serves as birth canal.

3. Female External Genitalia

It include mons pubis, labia majora, labia minora, clitoris and hymen.

(i) **Mons pubis** is a cushion of fatty tissues covered by skin and pubic hair.

(ii) **Labia majora** are fleshy folds of tissues. It extends down from the mons pubis and surround the vaginal opening.

(iii) **Labia minora** are paired folds of tissue under the labia majora.

(iv) **Hymen** is a membrane that covers the opening of vagina partially. It gets ruptured during vigorous physical activities or during the first coitus.

(v) **Clitoris** is a tiny finger-like structure. It lies at the upper junction of the two labia minora above the urethral opening. It is homologous to male penis.

4. Mammary Glands (Breasts)

- These are paired structures that contain glandular tissue and variable amount of fat.
- Glandular tissue of each mammary gland is divided into 15-20 mammary lobes containing the cluster of cells called **alveoli**.
- The cells of alveoli secrete milk, which is stored in the cavities (lumen) of alveoli.
- The alveoli open into **mammary tubules**. The each lobe of the tubule join to form a **mammary duct**.
- Several mammary ducts join to form a wider **mammary ampulla**. The ampulla is connected to the lactiferous duct through which milk is sucked out.

PYQs Previous Years' Questions

1 Mark Questions

Multiple Choice Questions

1. Given below are the structural details of a human mammary gland. **CBSE 2023**

   (i) The glandular tissue in the breast has 15-20 clusters of cells called alveoli.

   (ii) The milk is stored in the lumen of alveoli.

   (iii) The alveoli join to form the mammary ducts.

   (iv) Mammary ampulla is connected to lactiferous ducts.

   Choose the option that gives the correct detail of human mammary gland.

   (a) (i) and (ii) (b) (ii) and (iii)
   (c) (ii) and (iv) (d) (i) and (iii)

Ans. (c) (ii) and (iv)

2. Given below is a diagrammatic view of the human male reproductive system.

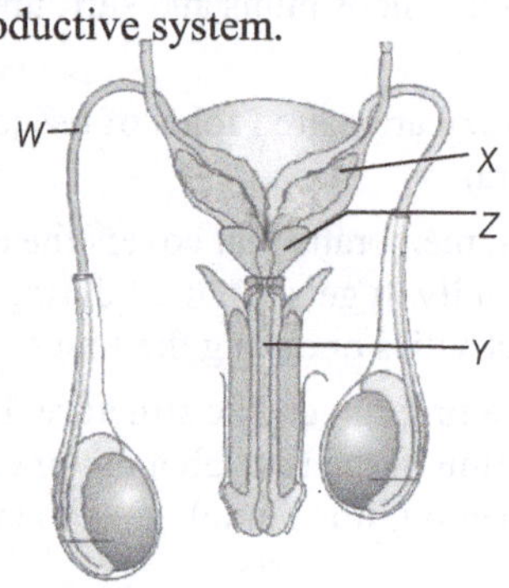

Identify the correct labelling for W, X, Y and Z and choose the correct option from the table below. **CBSE 2021-22 Term-I**

	W	*X*	*Y*	*Z*
(a)	Epididymis	Prostate gland	Glans penis	Bulbourethral gland
(b)	Bulbourethral gland	Glans penis	Prostate gland	Epididymis
(c)	Vas deferens	Seminal vesicle	Urethra	Prostate gland
(d)	Rete testis	Bulbourethral gland	Epididymis	Glans penis

Ans. (c)

3. The uterus opens into the vagina through a narrow **CBSE 2021-22 Term-I**

   (a) ampulla (b) isthmus
   (c) cervix (d) infundibulum

Ans. (c) cervix

4. Choose the correct option for the features of functional mammary gland of all female mammals from the statements below.

   (i) Glandular tissue with variable amount of fat.

   (ii) Mammary lobes, 30-40 in number called alveoli.

   (iii) Mammary ducts joining to form mammary tubules.

   (iv) Mammary ampulla connected to lactiferous duct. **CBSE 2021-22 Term-I**

   (a) (i) and (iii) (b) (ii) and (iii)
   (c) (i) and (iv) (d) (ii) and (iv)

Ans. (c) (i) and (iv)

5. Androgens are synthesised by **CBSE SQP 2020**

   (a) Sertoli cells (b) Leydig cells
   (c) seminal vesicles (d) bulbourethral gland

Ans. (b) Leydig cells

Assertion-Reason Type Question

6. **Assertion** Interstitial spaces outside the seminiferous tubule have blood vessels and sertoli cells.

   Reason Sertoli cells provide nutrition to the germ cells. **CBSE 2021-22 Term-I**

   (a) Both Assertion and Reason are true and Reason is the correct explanationof Assertion

   (b) Both Assertion and Reason are true, but Reason is not the correct explanation of Assertion

   (c) Assertion is true, but Reason is false

   (d) Assertion is false, but Reason is true

Ans. (d) Assertion is false, but Reason is true. Assertion can be corrected as

The region outside the seminiferous tubules called interstitial spaces which contains small blood vessels and masses of cells called Leydig cells or interstitial cells.

Sertoli cells are tall, pyramidal cells which provide nutrition to the developing germ cells.

Very Short Answer Type Questions

7. Name the glands that contribute to human seminal plasma. **CBSE SQP 2021**

Ans. Seminal vesicles, prostate gland and bulbourethral glands all contribute to human seminal plasma.

8. Why are human testes located outside the abdominal cavity? Name the pouch in which they are present. **All India 2014**

Ans. Human testes are located outside the abdominal cavity as it helps in maintaining the low temperature of the testes (2-2.5°C lower than body temperature) required for spermatogenesis.

Testes are enclosed in a pouch called scrotum.

9. Write the location and functions of the following in human testes **All India 2014**

(i) Sertoli cells
(ii) Leydig cells

Ans. (i) **Location of Sertoli cells** Within the lining of seminiferous tubule of testis.

Function of Sertoli cells They provide nutrition to the developing sperms or germ cells.

(ii) **Location of Leydig cells** In the interstitial spaces between the seminiferous tubules.

Function of Leydig cells They synthesise and secrete male hormones, i.e. androgens, testosterone.

10. Name the cells that nourish the germ cells in the testes. Where are these cells located in the testes? **All India 2013C**

Ans. Cells which nourish the germ cells in the testes are sertoli cells. Refer to answer no. 9(i).

11. Write the function of the seminal vesicle. **Delhi 2012**

Ans. Seminal vesicle produces an alkaline secretion containing prostaglandins, proteins and fructose. The high fructose content provides energy to the spermatozoa.

12. Give reasons for the following.

The human testes are located outside the abdominal cavity.

Ans. Testes are located outside the abdominal cavity within a pouch called scrotum. It maintains low temperature of the testes (2-2.5°C lower than normal body temperature) required for spermatogenesis.

2 Marks Questions

13. List the different parts of human oviduct through which the ovum travels till it meets the sperm for fertilisation. **Delhi 2014C**

Ans. The different parts of human oviduct through which the ovum travels, till it gets fertilised are given below in the sequence

(i) **Fimbriae**, finger-like projections which collects the ovum from the ovary after ovulation.

(ii) **Infundibulum** Ovum from fimbriae is guided into funnel-shaped infundibulum, part of Fallopian tube.

(iii) **Ampulla** A wider part of oviduct that leads ovum into isthmus.

(iv) **Isthmus** It has a narrow lumen which opens into uterus. In the junction of **ampulla- isthmus** where the ovum gets fertilised.

14. Write the function of each one of the following.
(i) Fimbriae (oviducal) (ii) Oxytocin **Delhi 2012**

Ans. (i) **Fimbriae** are the feathery finger-like projections present at the end of Fallopian tubes. They help to collect the ovum after its release from the ovary during ovulation.

(ii) **Oxytocin** is a hormone secreted by the posterior pituitary that stimulates the contraction of uterine muscles during child birth (parturition).

3 Marks Questions

15. Explain the functions of the following structures in the human male reproductive system. **CBSE SQP 2023**

(i) Scrotum (ii) Leydig cells
(iii) Male accessory glands

Ans. (i) **Scrotum** Testes are located outside the abdominal cavity within a pouch called scrotum. This maintains the low temperature of testes (2-2.5° C lower than the normal body temperature) required for spermatogenesis.

(ii) **Leydig cells** The interstitial spaces are present in between the seminiferous tubules. They contain small blood vessels and interstitial cells or Leydig cells. These cells synthesise and secretes the testicular hormones called androgens.

(iii) **Male accessory glands** The male accessory glands includes paired seminal vessicles, a prostate and paired bulbourethral glands. Secretions of these glands consistute the human seminal plasma responsible for the mobility of sperms. **(1+1+1)**

16. Draw a labelled diagram to show interrelationship of four accessory ducts in a human male reproductive system.

Ans. Refer to figure 2.1 (b) on page no. 40. **Delhi 2019**

17. The below diagram shows human male reproductive system (one side only).

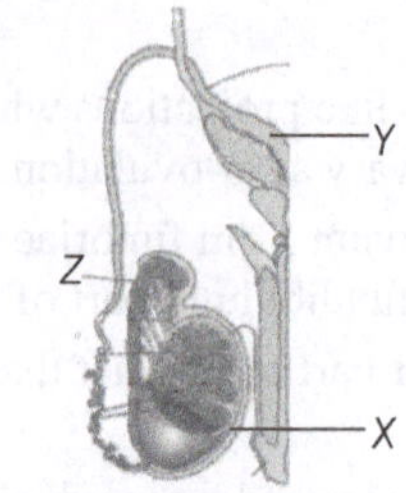

(i) Identify *'X'* and write its location in the body.

(ii) Name the accessory gland *'Y'* and its secretion.

(iii) Name and state the function of *'Z'*. **Delhi 2015C**

Ans. (i) ***X*–Testis** It is located outside the abdominal cavity within a pouch called scortum. **(1)**

(ii) ***Y*–Seminal vesicle** It produces an alkaline secretion rich in fructose and constitutes 60% of the volume of the semen. **(1)**

(iii) ***Z*–Epididymis** It stores the sperms and secretes a fluid which helps in the maturation of sperms. **(1)**

18. (i) Draw a labelled diagrammatic view of human male reproductive system.

(ii) Differentiate between vas deferens and vasa efferentia. **Delhi 2014**

Ans. (i) Refer to figure 2.1 on page no. 40. **(2)**

(ii) Differentiate between vas deferens and vasa efferentia

Vas deferens	Vasa efferentia
It is a tube-like structure which conducts the spermatozoa from the epididymis to the penis.	It connects the rete testis to the epididymis.
They arise from the rete testis.	They arise from the cauda epididymis.
They are only 2 in number.	They vary from 15-20 in number.

(1)

19. Name and explain the role of inner and middle walls of human uterus. **Delhi 2014**

Ans. The innermost wall of uterus is called endometrium.

Role of Endometrium

(i) It lines the uterine cavity and is glandular in nature.

(ii) It undergoes cyclic changes during menstrual cycle. **(1½)**

The middle wall or layer of uterus is called myometrium.

Role of Myometrium

(i) It is made up of thick layer of smooth muscles.

(ii) It shows strong contractions during the delivery of baby. **(1½)**

20. Draw a labelled diagram of reproductive system in a human female. **All India 2011**

Ans. Refer to figure 2.2 on page no. 41.

TOPIC 2

Gametogenesis

It is the process of formation of haploid gametes from diploid germ cells in the gonads, i.e. sperms and ova. These are produced in the testis and ovary, respectively.

It is of following two types

(i) Spermatogenesis (ii) Oogenesis

Spermatogenesis

It is the production of sperms in male gonads.

- In testes, the immature male germ cells (spermatogonia) produce sperms by **spermatogenesis** at puberty.
- Spermatogonia (sing. spermatogonium) present on the inside wall of seminiferous tubules multiply by mitotic division and increase in number.

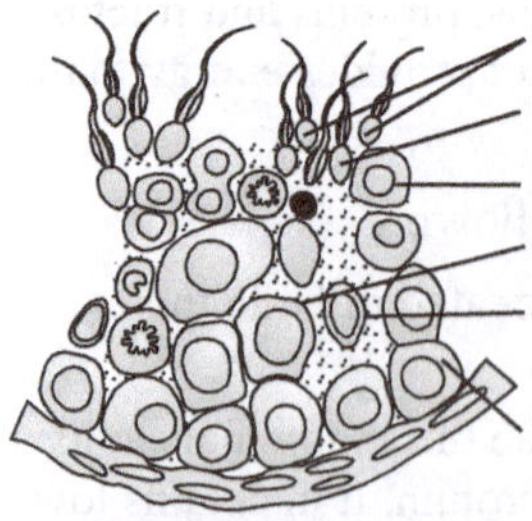

Figure 2.3 Diagrammatic sectional view of a seminiferous tubule (enlarged)

- Each spermatogonium is diploid and contains 46 chromosomes. Some of the spermatogonia called **primary spermatocytes**, undergo first meiotic division leading to two equal haploid cells called **secondary spermatocytes.**

- The secondary spermatocytes (23 chromosomes) undergo the second meiotic division to produce four equal, haploid **spermatids** containing 23 chromosomes each.
- The spermatids are transformed into spermatozoa (sperms) by the process called **spermiogenesis**. Thus, each sperm too contains only 23 chromosomes.
  A schematic representation of spermatogenesis is given below

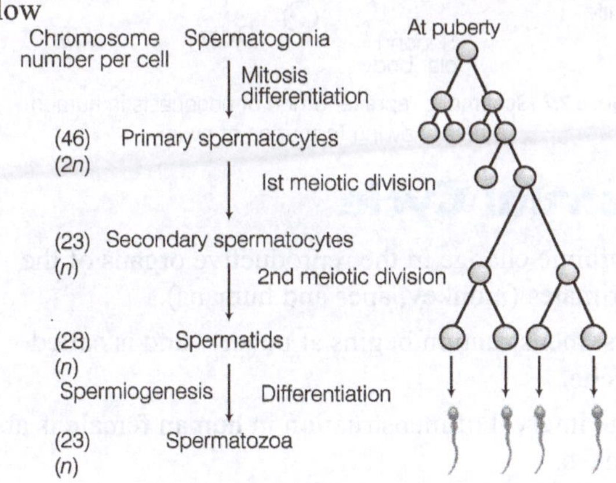

Figure 2.4 Schematic representation of spermatogenesis in human male

- After spermiogenesis, sperm heads are embedded in the Sertoli cells and are finally released from the seminiferous tubules by the process called **spermiation.**

Role of Hormones in Spermatogenesis

The following hormones play an essential role in spermatogenesis

- Spermatogenesis starts with the significant increase in hypothalamic hormone called **Gonadotropin Releasing Hormone** (GnRH).
- The increased level of GnRH acts on the anterior pituitary gland and stimulates the secretion of two gonadotropins, i.e. **LH** (Luteinizing Hormone) and **FSH** (Follicle Stimulating Hormone).
- LH acts on the Leydig cells and stimulates the synthesis and secretion of androgens. It stimulate the process of spermatogenesis.
- FSH acts on Sertoli cells and stimulates them to secrete Androgen Binding Protein (ABP) which help in the process of spermiogenesis.

Structure of a Sperm

- A plasma membrane encloses the whole body of sperm.
- A sperm is composed of a **head, neck,** a **middle piece** and a **tail**.
- Sperm head contains an elongated haploid nucleus. Its anterior portion is covered by a cap-like structure called **acrosome.**
- The acrosome is filled with enzymes that helps in the fertilisation of ovum.

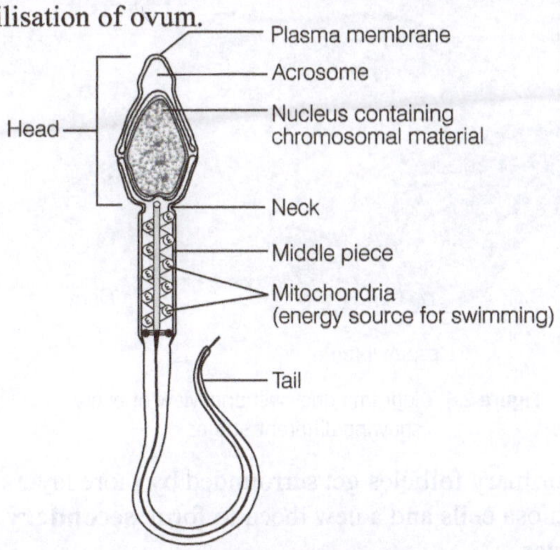

Figure 2.5 Structure of a sperm

- Neck contains two centrioles, i.e. a proximal one which is necessary for first cleavage division of zygote and a distal one, which gives rise to axial filament of the tail.
- Middle piece possesses many mitochondria to produce energy for the sperm motility.
- Tail of the sperm consists of an axial filament. It helps in the movement of sperm.

Oogenesis

It is the process of formation of a female gamete or ova in the ovary.

- It starts during the embryonic stage, but get completed only after fertilisation.
- About a million **oogonia** are formed in the ovary of the female foetus which is 25 weeks old. No new oogonia are formed after birth.
- The oogonial cells start meiotic division. They enter into prophase-I, get temporarily arrested at that stage and are called as **primary oocytes.**

- Each primary oocyte then gets surrounded by a layer of granulosa cells and hence, called as **primary follicle**.
- A large number of primary follicles degenerate during the period from birth to puberty. As a result, about 60,000-80,000 primary follicles are left in each ovary at puberty.

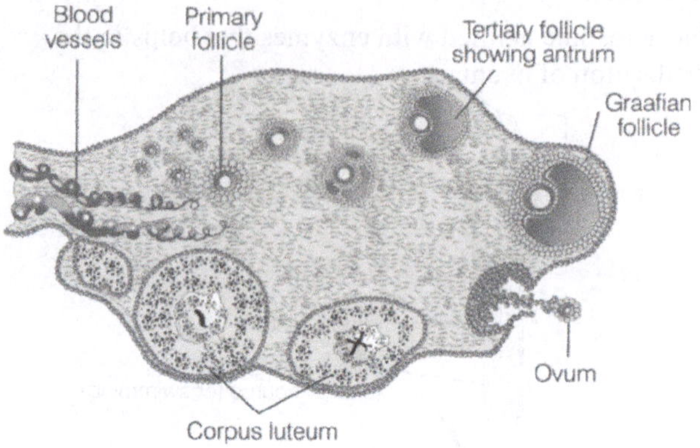

Figure 2.6 Diagrammatic sectional view of ovary showing different stages

- The primary follicles get surrounded by more layers of granulosa cells and a new theca to form **secondary follicles**.
- The theca layer in secondary follicles becomes organised into an outer **theca externa** and an inner **theca interna**. At this stage follicle is called **tertiary follicle**.
- Tertiary follicle is characterised by a fluid-filled cavity called **antrum**.
- At this stage, the primary oocyte within the tertiary follicle grows in size and completes its first meiotic division.
- The first meiotic division is an unequal division. It results in the formation of haploid **secondary oocyte** and a tiny first polar body.
- Secondary oocyte retains bulk of the nutrient rich cytoplasm of the primary oocyte.
- The tertiary follicle develops into a mature follicle or **Graafian follicle.**
- The secondary oocyte forms a new membrane called **zona pellucida** surrounding it.
- The Graafian follicle ruptures to release the secondary oocyte (ovum) from the ovary by the process called **ovulation**.

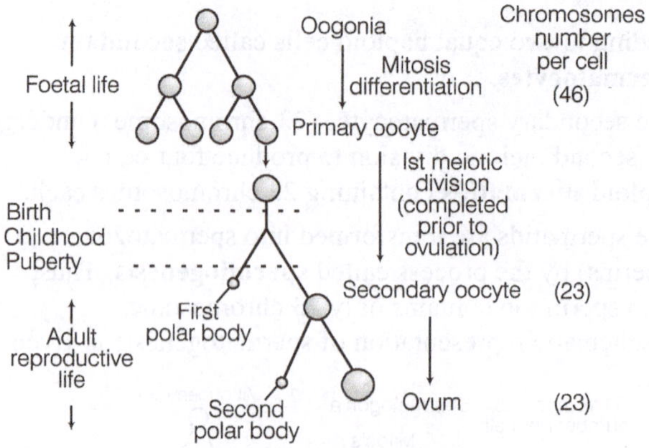

Figure 2.7 Schematic representation of oogenesis in human female showing formation of ovum

Menstrual Cycle

It is a rhythmic change in the reproductive organs of the female primates (monkey, apes and humans).

- The first menstruation begins at puberty and is called **menarche.**
- Average interval of menstruation in human female is about 28-29 days.
- The cyclic events starting from one menstruation till the next one constitute one menstrual cycle.

The four phases of menstrual cycle are as follows

1. Menstrual Phase

- Cycle starts with this phase and the menstrual flow occurs for 3-5 days.
- It occurs due to the breakdown of endometrial lining of the uterus and blood vessels which along with unfertilised ovum comes out through the vagina.
- Menstruation occurs only if fertilisation does not take place.
- Lack of menstruation generally indicates pregnancy. It may also be due to stress, poor health, diseases, etc.

2. Follicular or Proliferative Phase

- Menstrual phase is followed by the follicular phase.
- The primary follicle in the ovary grows to become a fully mature Graafian follicle and simultaneously the endometrium of uterus regenerates through proliferation.
- Pituitary and ovarian hormones induce the changes in ovary and uterus.
- LH and FSH levels increase gradually during this phase and stimulate follicular development.
- The growing follicles secrete oestrogens.

- Both LH and FSH attain highest level during mid-cycle (about 14th day).

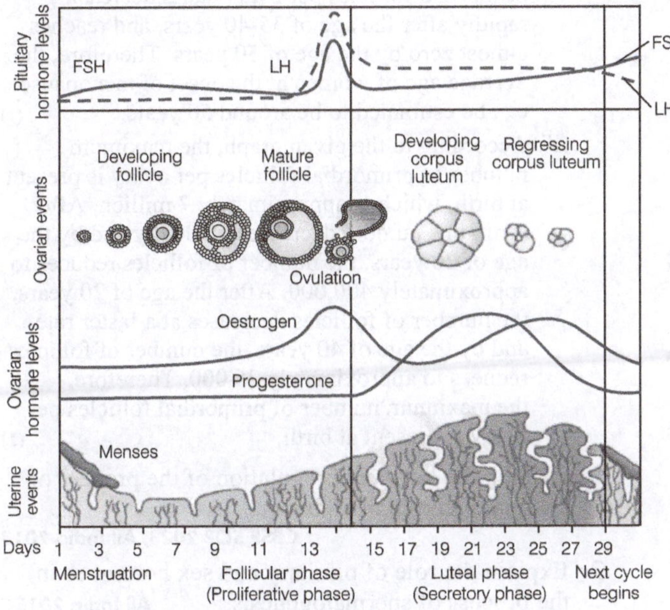

Figure 2.8 Diagrammatic representation of various events during a menstrual cycle

3. Ovulatory Phase

- Rapid secretion of LH leading to its maximum level during the mid-cycle is called **LH surge**.
- The LH surge induces rupture of Graafian follicle, releasing the ovum. This process is known as **ovulation**.

4. Luteal Phase/Secretory Phase

- Ovulatory phase is followed by the luteal phase.
- The remaining parts of the ruptured Graafian follicle change into **corpus luteum**.
- Corpus luteum secretes large amount of progesterone, which is required for the maintenance of endometrium.
- The thickened endometrium is necessary for the implantation of fertilised ovum and maintenance of pregnancy.
- During pregnancy, all the events of menstrual cycle stop and menstruation does not occur.
- If fertilisation does not occur, the corpus luteum degenerates to form **corpus albicans**, which does not secrete progesterone. This causes rupture of endometrium leading to menstruation, i.e. initiation of a new cycle.

> - In human females, menstrual cycle stops around the age of 50 years and this phase is called as **menopause**.
> - Menstrual cycle is absent temporarily during pregnancy and lactation periods and permanently after menopause.
> - Menstruation is also called '**Weeping of uterus for the lost ovum**' or '**Funeral of unfertilised eggs**'.

PYQs Previous Years' Questions

1 Mark Questions

Multiple Choice Questions

1. Select the option that has the correct sequence of events of human female reproductive cycle. **CBSE 2024 (Set-I)**
   (i) Secretion of FSH
   (ii) Ovulation
   (iii) Growth of corpus luteum
   (iv) Growth of follicle and oogenesis
   (v) Sudden increase in LH
   Options
   (a) i-iii-v-iv-ii (b) i-iv-v-ii-iii
   (c) iv-i-v-iii-ii (d) v-ii-iii-iv-i

Ans. (b) The correct order of events of human female reproductive cycle is -
(i) Secretion of FSH → (iv) Growth of follicle and oogenesis → (v) Sudden increase in LH → (ii) Ovulation → (iii) Growth of corpus luteum.

2. Penetration of the sperm in the ovum is followed by **CBSE SQP 2021-22 Term-I**
   (a) formation of first polar body
   (b) completion of meiosis-II
   (c) first meiosis
   (d) dissolution of zona pellucida

Ans. (b) Completion of meiosis-II.

3. The correct sequence of hormone secretion from beginning of menstruation is **CBSE SQP 2021-22 Term-I**
   (a) FSH, progesterone, oestrogen
   (b) oestrogen, FSH, progesterone
   (c) FSH, oestrogen, progesterone
   (d) oestrogen, progesterone, FSH

Ans. (c) FSH, oestrogen, progesterone

4. The nature of meiotic division during oogenesis in a human female is **CBSE SQP 2021-22 Term-I**

(a) equal cell division (b) suspended cell division
(c) continuous cell division (d) rapid cell division

Ans. (b) suspended cell division

Very Short Answer Type Questions

5. When do the oogenesis and the spermatogenesis initiate in human females and males, respectively? **Delhi 2012**

Ans. **Oogenesis** initiates during foetal or embryonic stage in females, whereas **spermatogenesis** in males starts at puberty. (½ + ½)

6. Mention the differences between spermiogenesis and spermiation. **Delhi 2012**

Ans. Difference between spermiogenesis and spermiation is

Spermiogenesis	Spermiation
It is the process of transforming spermatids into mature spermatozoa or sperms through differentiation.	Sperm heads are embedded in Sertoli cells to obtain nourishment and finally released from seminiferous tubules by the process called spermiation.

7. List the changes of the primary oocyte undergoes in the tertiary follicular stage in human embryo. **Foreign 2011**

Ans. The primary oocyte within the tertiary follicle grows in size and completes its first meiotic division to produce two daughter nuclei in which larger haploid cell is called secondary oocyte and the tiny one is called first polar body.

2 Marks Questions

8. The graph given below shows the number of primordial follicles per ovary in women at different ages. Study the graph and answer the questions that follow. **CBSE 2023**

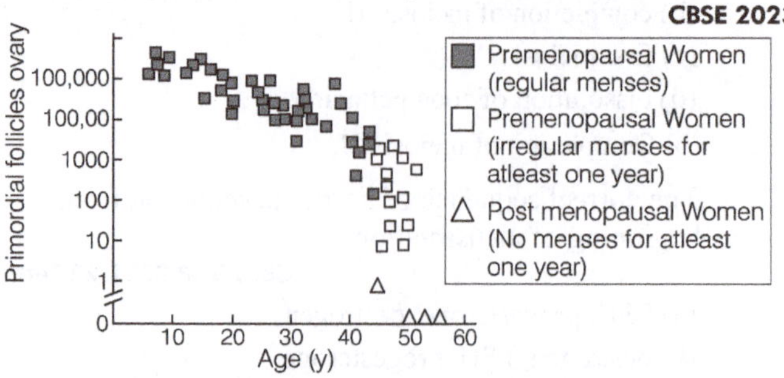

(i) What is the average age of the women at the onset of menopause?

(ii) At what age are maximum primordial follicles present in the ovary, according to the given graph?

Ans. (i) It is clear from the graph that the primordial follicles per ovary starts decreasing rapidly after the age of 35-40 years, and reaches almost zero by the age of 50 years. Therefore, the average age of women at the onset of menopause can be estimated to be around 50 years. **(1)**

(ii) According to the given graph, the maximum number of primordial follicles per ovary is present at birth, which is approximately 7 million. After birth, this number decreases gradually and by the age of 20 years, the number of follicles reduces to approximately 400,000. After the age of 20 years, the number of follicles decreases at a faster rate and by the age of 40 years, the number of follicles reduces to approximately 25,000. Therefore, the maximum number of primordial follicles per ovary is present at birth. **(1)**

9. Explain the hormonal regulation of the process of spermatogenesis in humans. **CBSE SQP 2023, All India 2013**

Or Explain the role of pituitary and sex hormones in the process of spermatogenesis. **All India 2015C**

Or Spermatogenesis in human males is a hormone regulated process. Justify. **Delhi 2014**

Ans. Hormonal control of spermatogenesis in human males is as follows

(i) Gonadotropin Releasing Hormone (GnRH) is released significantly from the hypothalamus during puberty.

(ii) GnRH stimulates anterior pituitary to secrete gonadotropins, i.e. LH and FSH or Interstitial Cell Stimulating Hormone (ICSH).

(iii) Luteinizing Hormone (LH) acts on Leydig cells to stimulate the synthesis and secretion of androgens which then stimulate the process of spermatogenesis.

(iv) Follicle Stimulating Hormone (FSH) acts on Sertoli cells and stimulates them to secrete inhibin which then stimulates the process of spermiogenesis.

10. In the figure given below, parts *A* and *B* show the level of hormones which influence the menstrual cycle. Study the figure and answer the questions that follow. **CBSE SQP 2021-22 Term-I**

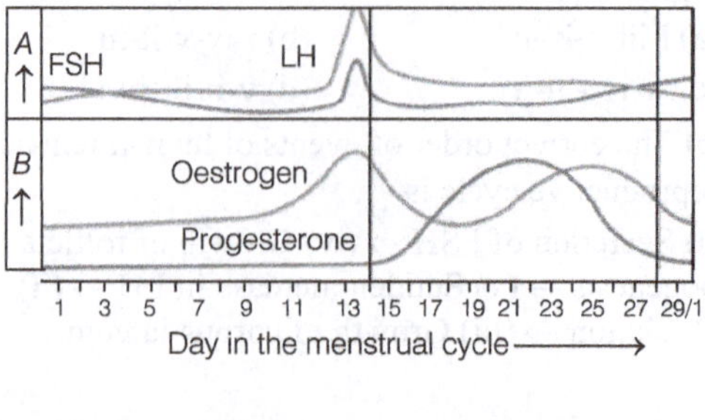

(i) Name the organs which secrete the hormones represented in parts *A* and *B*.

(ii) State the impact of the hormones in part *B* on the uterus of the human female during 6 to 15 days of menstrual cycle?

Ans. (i) Hormones represented in part *A* is secreted by pituitary gland and in part *B* is secreted by ovary. **(1)**

(ii) Endometrium of the uterus regenerates through proliferation. **(1)**

11. Draw a sectional view of human ovary showing the different stages of developing follicles, corpus luteum and ovulation. **Delhi 2019**

Or

(i) Draw a sectional view of human ovary and label the following parts.

(a) Primary follicle (b) Secondary oocyte
(c) Graafian follicle (d) Corpus luteum

(ii) Name the hormones influencing follicular development of corpus luteum. **All India 2019**

Ans. (i) Refer to figure 2.6 on page no. 46.

(ii) The hormones influencing follicular development of corpus luteum are FSH, oestrogen and progesterone.

12. What happens to corpus luteum in human female if the ovum is (i) fertilised, (ii) not fertilised? **Delhi 2015**

Or

Mention the fate of corpus luteum and its effect on the uterus in the absence of fertilisation of the ovum in human female. **Foreign 2010**

Ans. (i) In case of fertilisation, the corpus luteum continues secreting progesterone which is required for the maintenance of endometrium during pregnancy. **(1)**

(ii) In the absence of fertilisation, the corpus luteum degenerates and gets converted into corpus albicans this does not secrete progesterone. Lack of progesterone causes disintegration of the endometrium leading to menstruation and thus, a new cycle starts. **(1)**

13. Draw a diagram of a mature human sperm. Label any three parts and write their functions.

Or Draw a labelled diagram of a human sperm. **Foreign 2015, 2011**

Or Draw a diagram of human sperm. Label only those parts along with their functions that assist the sperm to reach and gain entry into the female gamete. **Foreign 2014**

Ans. For structure of a human sperm refer to figure 2.5 on page no. 45.

The parts of sperm are as follows

(i) **Tail** Its wiggling movement helps the sperm to swim in female reproductive tract.

(ii) **Middle piece** It contains mitochondria that provide energy for sperm movement.

(iii) **Head** It contains acrosome loaded with sperm lysins. These help to dissolve the layers of female gamete or egg.

Concept Enhancer The production of the spermatozoa takes place in about 64 days. The sperm can live upto 5 days in female reproductive system.

14. Write the effect of high concentration of LH on a mature Graafian follicle. **All India 2014**

Ans. The high concentration of LH (also known as LH surge) induces the rupture of Graafian follicle, which results in the release of secondary oocyte hence, causing **ovulation** in females.

15. Differentiate between spermatogenesis and spermiogenesis. **Delhi 2014**

Ans. Differences between spermatogenesis and spermiogenesis are

Spermatogenesis	Spermiogenesis
It is a process of formation of sperms from immature germ cells.	It is a process of transformation of a circular spermatid to a motile spermatozoa.
Number of cells increases as each spermatogonium produces four spermatids.	No change in number of cells as only one spermatid develops into a spermatozoa.

16. Draw and label the parts of the head region only of a human sperm. **Delhi 2014C**

Ans. Diagram showing head of human sperm is given below

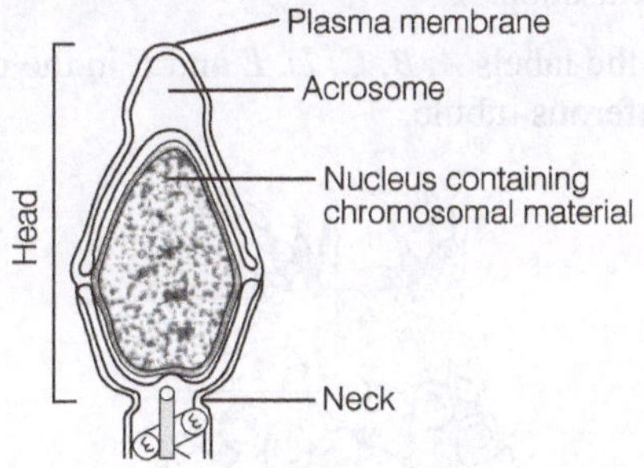

17. Identify *A*, *B*, *C* and *D* with reference to gametogenesis in humans, in the flowchart given below. **All India 2012C**

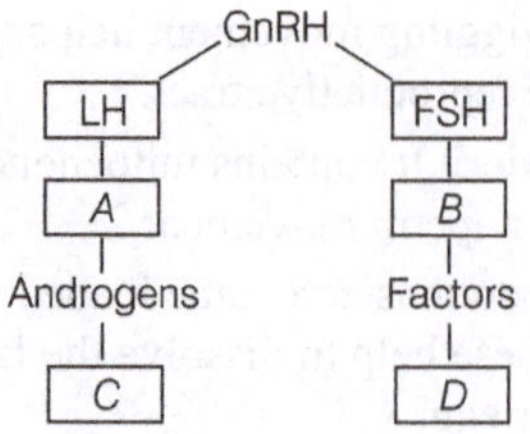

Ans. *A* – Leydig's cell
B – Sertoli cell
C – Spermatogenesis
D – Spermiogenesis

18. Write the function of each of the following.
(i) Middle piece in human sperm.
(ii) Luteinizing hormone in human males. **Delhi 2012**

Ans. (i) **Middle piece** in human sperm contains several mitochondria which produce energy for the motility of the sperm. **(1)**
(iii) **Luteinizing hormone in human males** stimulates the Leydig cells to produce testosterone which is necessary to complete the process of spermatogenesis. **(1)**

19. Write the function of each of the following.
(i) Seminal vesicle.
(ii) Acrosome of human sperm. **Delhi 2012**

Ans. (i) **Seminal vesicle** During spermatogenesis, it secretes an alkaline fluid rich in fructose and prostaglandins. High level of fructose provides energy to sperms. **(1)**
(ii) **Acrosome of human sperm** It is the cap-like structure that is present at the tip of the sperm (male gamete) in head region. The acrosome contains hydrolytic enzyme, which helps the sperm to enter into the cytoplasm of the ovum and thus, helps in fertilisation. **(1)**

20. Name the labels *A*, *B*, *C*, *D*, *E* and *F* in the diagram of seminiferous tubule. **Delhi 2011**

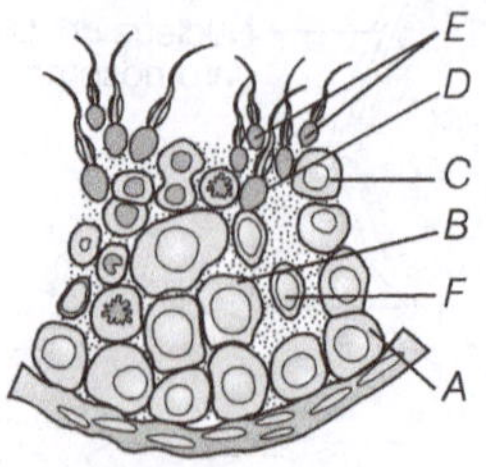

Ans. In the given diagram of seminiferous tubule the name of labels parts are as follows
A – Spermatogonium
B – Primary spermatocyte
C – Secondary spermatocyte
D – Spermatid
E – Spermatozoa
F – Sertoli cell

21. Differentiate between menarche and menopause. **All India 2010**

Ans. Differences between menarche and menopause are

Menarche	Menopause
It refers to the beginning of menstrual cycle in human female at puberty.	It refers to the stoppage of menstrual cycle at the age of about 45-50 in human female.
It indicates the start of reproductive phase.	It indicates the end of reproductive phase.

22. Study the sectional view of human testis showing seminiferous tubules given below.

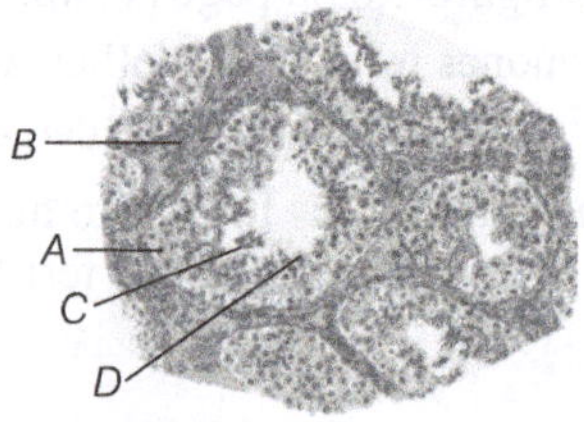

(i) Identify *A*, *B* and *C*.
(ii) Write the function of *A* and *D*. **Foreign 2010**

Ans. (i) *A*–Spermatogonia,
B–Interstitial cells
C–Spermatozoa. **(1)**
(ii) *A*–Spermatogonia undergo meiosis to produce spermatozoa (sperms).
D–Sertoli cells provide nutrition to the germ cells. **(1)**

23. How and at what stage of menstrual cycle is corpus luteum formed in human females? When does it regress? **Delhi 2010C**

Ans. After ovulatory phase (ovulation), the luteal phase starts. The remaining parts of ruptured Graafian follicle transform into corpus luteum in this phase. The corpus luteum secretes large amount of progesterone which is essential for the maintenance of endometrium. **(1½)**
In the absence of fertilisation, the corpus luteum degenerates in the ovary and gets converted into corpus albicans. **(½)**

3 Marks Questions

24. Explain the role of pituitary and ovarian hormones in the menstrual cycle of human females. **Delhi 2020**

Ans. The cycle of events starting from one menstruation till next in female primates like humans is called menstrual cycle. It comprises of following four phases which are regulated by both pituitary (LH and FSH) and ovarian hormones (oestrogen and progesterone).

With the start of menstrual cycle the pituitary produces FSH hormone that stimulates the ovaries to start the formation and maturation of eggs. With the maturation of these follicles oestrogen levels rises in the body indicating the formation of the mature egg. This leads to the completion of follicular phase.

The pituitary gland now produces LH hormone which causes the release of an egg from ovary by the process of ovulation. After ovulation luteal phase begins during which the level of progesterone in the body start increasing. The progesterone hormone, thus maintains the lining of the wall of the uterus for pregnancy. If pregnancy does not take place then progesterone level falls and menstrual flow begins.

25. Draw a labelled diagrammatic sectional view of a human seminiferous tubule. **Delhi 2017**

Ans. Refer to figure 2.3 on page no. 44.

26. (i) How many primary follicles are left in each ovary in a human female at puberty?

(ii) Draw a sectional view of the ovary showing the different follicular stages of a human female in her preovulatory phase of menstrual cycle. **Outside Delhi 2016C**

Ans. (i) A large number of primary follicles degenerate in females during the period from birth to puberty. As a result, about 60000-80000 primary follicles are left in each ovary at puberty. (1½)

(ii) Refer to figure 2.6 on page no. 46. (1½)

27. Explain the events in a normal woman during her menstrual cycle on the following days **Delhi 2015C**

(i) Ovarian event from 13-15 days.

(ii) Ovarian hormones level from 16-23 days.

(iii) Uterine events from 24-29 days.

Ans. (i) In the ovarian event from 13-15 days, an immature ovum (egg cell) is released from the Graafian follicle. Both LH and FSH attain maximum peak. FSH helps Graafian follicle to attain maturity and LH helps in its rupture. Ovum covered by a number of layer and a yellow fat layer forms corpus luteum. It releases (secretes) progesterone. (1)

(ii) During menstrual cycle, the period from 16-23 days is called luteal phase (secretory phase). In which the corpus luteum secretes large amount of progesterone, essential for the maintenance of endometrium. (1)

(iii) Uterine events from 24-29 days are under the influence of progesterone hormone. It influences the maintenance of the endometrium for any pregnancy to occur. In the absence of pregnancy, the corpus luteum degenerates and endometrium sheds off. It causes the menstrual flow or bleeding. (1)

28. Explain the events in a normal woman during her menstrual cycle on the following days **All India 2015C, Outside Delhi 2015C**

(i) Pituitary hormone levels from 8-12 days.

(ii) Uterine events from 13-15 days.

(iii) Ovarian events from 16-23 days.

Ans. (i) The period of 8-12 days after the onset of menstruation is the follicular phase. During this phase, GnRH from hypothalamus stimulates anterior pituitary to release FSH and LH. FSH stimulates the ovarian follicles to secrete oestrogen, which in turn stimulates the proliferation of the endometrium of the uterine wall. This causes the endometrial lining to thicken. (1)

(ii) The uterine events between day 13 and 15 are governed by the high LH and FSH levels. The endometrium is intact due to the effect of these gonadotropin hormones and also prepares itself for pregnancy, if fertilisation occurs. (1)

(iii) During 16-23 days, ruptured Graafian follicle gets converted into corpus luteum in the ovary. It starts secreting progesterone which maintains the endometrium, necessary for the implantation of fertilised ovum followed by other events of pregnancy. (1)

29. Explain the hormonal control of spermatogenesis in humans. **Foreign 2014**

Ans. Refer to answer no. 9.

30. Explain the steps in the formation of an ovum from oogonium in humans. **All India 2013**

Ans. In human females, primary oocytes are formed from the oogonia during the embryonic developmental stages in the foetal ovaries.

(i) Oogonial cells start dividing and enter prophase-I of meiosis. They remain suspended at this stage as primary oocytes.

(ii) Each primary oocyte is surrounded by a layer of granulosa cells and becomes the primary follicle.

(iii) The primary follicle when surrounded by more layers of granulosa cells, is called a secondary follicle which transforms into a tertiary follicle.

(iv) Granulosa cells become organised into an outer theca externa and an inner theca interna.

(v) Now, primary oocyte completes meiosis-I and forms a larger haploid secondary oocyte and a tiny first polar body.

(vi) Tertiary follicle grows and becomes a mature follicle called Graafian follicle.

(vii) Secondary oocyte secretes a new membrane called zona pellucida around it.

(viii) At this stage, follicle ruptures to release the secondary oocyte, which moves into the cytoplasm.

(ix) Secondary oocyte completes meiosis-II only when a sperm enters its cytoplasm and forms the ootid and the second polar body. This event occurs in the ampulla of Fallopian tube.

5 Marks Questions

31. (i) Draw a diagrammatic sectional view of ovary of human female and label the following

(1) Blood vessels (2) Primary follicle

(3) Tertiary follicle (4) Ovum

(ii) At which state of life are primary follicles formed in a human female?

(iii) Explain the events (both hormonal and structural) that occur at the time of ovulation till the onset of the next menstrual cycle. **CBSE 2024 (Set-I)**

Ans. (i) Refer to fig 2.6 on page no. 46. **(2)**

(ii) Primary follicles are formed in a human female at the foetal stage only. **(½)**

(iii) Refer to text on page no. 46 and 47. **(2½)**

32. (i) Describe the events of spermatogenesis with the help of a schematic diagram.

(ii) Explain the role of hormone in spermatogenesis. **CBSE 2024 (Set-II)**

Ans. (i) Refer to text on page no. 44 and 45.

(ii) Refer to text on page no. 45.

33. Study the graph given below related with menstrual cycle in females

(i) Identify ovarian hormones *X* and *Y* mentioned in the graph and specify their source.

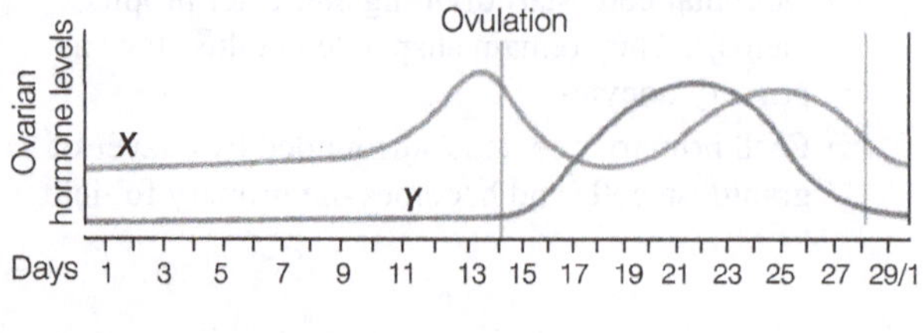

(ii) Correlate and describe the uterine events that take place according to the ovarian hormone levels *X* and *Y* mentioned in the graph on

(a) 6–15 days

(b) 16–25 days

(c) 26–28 days (when ovum is not fertilised) **CBSE SQP 2021-22**

Ans. (i) Hormones '*X*' in the graph identify as, *X* is oestrogen secreted by growing follicles, and *Y* is progesterone secreted by corpus luteum. **(2)**

(ii) Uterine events that take place according to the ovarian hormone levels *X* and *Y* on.

(a) **6-15 days** endometrium of the uterus regenerates by proliferation under the influence of oestrogen.

(b) **16-25 days** under the influence of progesterone the endometrium of the uterus is maintained for implantation of fertilised ovum and other events of pregnancy.

(c) **26-28 days** (when ovum is not fertilised). In the absence of fertilisation, corpus luteum degenerates which causes disintegration of endometrium leading to menstruation, marking a new cycle. **(3)**

34. (i) Where and how in the testes the process of spermatogenesis occur in humans?

(ii) Draw diagram of human sperm and label the four parts. **All India 2020**

Ans. (i) Refer to text on page no. 44 and 45.

(ii) Refer to figure on 2.5 on page no. 45.

Common Mistakes Students commonly got confused that spermatogenesis and spermiogenesis are same. But, spermiogenesis is the final stage of spermatogenesis which sees the maturation of spermatids into mature, motile spermatozoa.

35. Differentiate between spermatogenesis and oogenesis. **CBSE SQP 2019**

Ans. Differentiate between spermatogenesis and oogenesis are as follows

Spermatogenesis	Oogenesis
It produces male gametes (sperm).	It produces female gametes (oocyte).
It occurs in the seminiferous tubules (in testes).	It occurs in the ovaries.
Meiosis occurs throughout the life after puberty.	Meiosis occurs after puberty until menopause.
It may produce 1,00,00,000 sperms per day.	Human females normally produce one oocyte during each ovarian cycle.

Spermatogenesis	Oogenesis
Primary spermatocyte divides equally to form two similar secondary spermatocytes.	Primary oocyte divides unequally to form one large secondary oocyte and a small polar body.
One spermatogonium produces four functional spermatozoa.	An oogonium produces one functional ovum and two non-functional polar bodies.

36. The graph given below shows the variations in the levels of ovarian hormones during various phases of menstrual cycle.

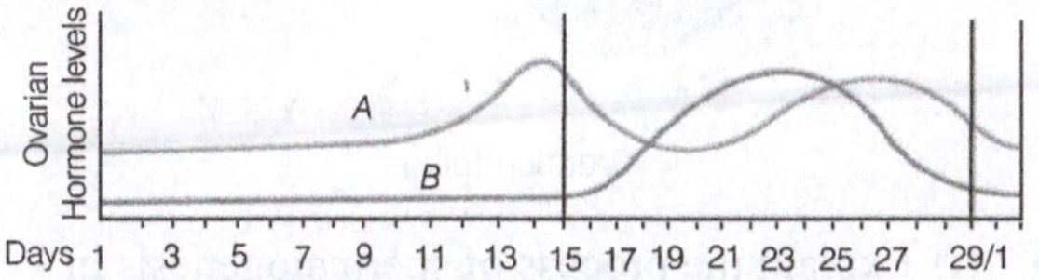

(i) Identify '*A*' and '*B*'.

(ii) Specify the source of the hormones marked in the diagram.

(iii) Reason out why *A* peaks before *B*.

(iv) Compare the roles of *A* and *B*.

(v) Under which condition will level of *B* be continue to remain high on the 28th day? **CBSE SQP 2018**

Ans. (i) *A* is hormone oestrogen.
B is hormone progesterone.

(ii) Oestrogen is secreted by the granulosa cells of maturing Graafian follicles. Progesterone is secreted by corpus luteum.

(iii) The release of oestrogen hormone is followed by the formation and release of progesterone hormone.

(iv) **Oestrogen** hormone brings about changes in the lining of endometrium through its proliferation.
Progesterone hormone maintains endometrium for implantation of the fertilised ovum.

(v) The level of progesterone remains high during fertilisation has occurred which leads to pregnancy. This is because, it is produced by the placenta to maintain the development of foetus. **(1 × 5)**

37. (i) Explain menstrual cycle in human females.

(ii) How can the scientific understanding of the menstrual cycle of human females help as a contraceptive measure? **CBSE 2018**

Ans. (i) **Menstrual Cycle** The cycle of events starting from one menstruation till next is called menstrual cycle. A typical menstrual cycle completes in an average of about 28 days. It starts at the age of 13 or 15 and continues till about 50 years of age. Menstrual cycle occurs in three major phases namely menstrual phase, follicular phase and secretory phase.

(a) **Menstrual phase** (from 3rd-5th day in a 28 day cycle) Initiated by reduced secretion of LH, progesterone and oestrogen. The endometrium breaks down and blood along with unfertilised ovum constitutes menstrual flow.

(b) **Follicular phase** (from 6th-13th day in a 28 day cycle) The FSH (Follicle Stimulating Hormone) secreted by anterior pituitary stimulates ovarian follicle to secrete oestrogens.
These oestrogens stimulate proliferation of uterine walls as a result of which endometrium gets thickened (due to rapid cell division and increase in uterine glands and blood vessels).

(c) **Ovulatory phase** (14th day in 28 day cycle) Pituitary hormones, i.e. LH and FSH reach the highest level in middle of the cycle. Rapid secretion of LH causes ovulation thus, inducing the rupture of Graafian follicle to release secondary oocyte and a polar body.

(d) **Luteal or secretory phase** (from 15th-28th day in a 28 day cycle) The pituitary hormone LH stimulates the remaining cells of ovarian follicles to develop into corpus luteum. This corpus luteum secretes large amount of progesterone and maintains endometrium thickening for the implantation of fertilised ovum during pregnancy. In the absence of fertilisation, the hormone levels are reduced (LH and progesterone) and endometrium disintegrates leading to onset of another menstrual cycle. **(3)**

(ii) The scientific understanding of the menstrual cycle of human females helps as a contraceptive method by the process known as periodic abstinence. In this method, the couples avoid or abstain the coitus from day 10 to 17 of the menstrual cycle when ovulation could be expected. The chances of fertilisation are very high during this period. **(2)**

38. (i) Arrange the following hormones in the sequence of their secretion in a pregnant woman.
hCG, LH, FSH, Relaxin

(ii) Mention their source and the function they perform. **Delhi 2017**

Ans. (i) The sequence of secretion of the given hormones in a pregnant woman is
FSH → LH → hCG → Relaxin **(1)**

(ii)

Hormone	Source	Function
FSH	Anterior pituitary lobe	Stimulates the growth of ovarian follicles in ovary.
LH	Anterior pituitary lobe	It triggers ovulation.
hCG	Placenta	It stimulates the corpus luteum to secrete progesterone.
Relaxin	Placenta	It facilitates parturition by softening the connective tissue of symphysis pubic.

(4)

39. (i) Explain the menstrual phase in a human female. State the level of ovarian and pituitary hormones during this phase.

(ii) Why is follicular phase in the menstrual cycle also referred as proliferative phase? Explain.

(iii) Explain the events that occur in a Graafian follicle at the time of ovulation and thereafter.

(iv) Draw a Graafian follicle and label antrum and secondary oocyte. **Delhi 2016**

Ans. (i) The reproductive cycle in female primates, e.g. monkeys, apes and human beings is called **menstrual cycle.**

Menstrual phase starts from 3rd day and ends on 5th day of the menstrual cycle. It is initiated due to the reduced secretion of progesterone and oestrogen from the regressing corpus luteum in the ovary. The endometrium breaks down and blood along with degenerated ovum constitutes the menstrual flow.

The secretion of pituitary hormones, i.e. FSH and LH is also reduced during this phase. **(2)**

(ii) In follicular phase, primary follicles in the ovary grow under the influence of Follicle Stimulating Hormone (FSH). It starts from 6th day and ends on 13th or 14th day of 28 day cycle. FSH also stimulates the ovarian follicles to secrete oestrogen which in turn stimulates endometrium to proliferate, so that it becomes thicker and highly vascularised. Thus, it is also called **proliferative stage** of menstrual cycle. **(1)**

(iii) **Graafian Follicle at Ovulation** At the time of ovulation, following events occur

(a) LH and FSH reach at their peak levels (about 14th-16th day of cycle).

(b) High level of LH induces Graafian follicle to rupture and the release of secondary oocyte from it.

(c) **After ovulation** The remaining cells of Graafian follicle are stimulated by LH to develop corpus luteum (an endocrine gland which secrete progesterone hormone). **(1)**

(iv) **Diagrammatic sectional view of Graafian follicle**

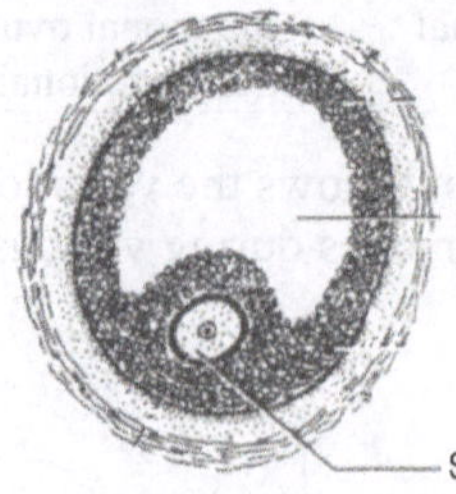

Graafian follicle **(1)**

40. (i) Explain the process of spermatogenesis in humans.

(ii) Draw a human sperm and label acrosome and middle piece. Mention their functions.

Outside Delhi 2016C

Ans. (i) **Spermatogenesis** is the production of sperms in males.

(a) In testis, the immature male germ cells (spermatogonia) produce sperms by **spermatogenesis.** It begins at puberty due to significant increase in the secretion of gonadotropins, i.e. Luteinizing hormone and follicle stimulating hormone under the influence of Gonadotropin Releasing Hormone (GnRH) released from hypothalamus.

(b) Spermatogonia (sing. spermatogonium) present on the inside wall of seminiferous tubules multiply by mitotic division and increases in numbers.

(c) Each spermatogonium is diploid and contains 46 chromosomes. Some of the spermatogonia transform to primary spermatocytes.

(d) The primary spermatocyte undergoes meiosis-I and forms two haploid secondary spermatocytes containing 23 chromosomes each.

(e) The secondary spermatocytes undergo meiosis-II and form four equal sized haploid spermatids.

(f) Spermatids transform into the spermatozoa by spermiogenesis.

(g) After spermiogenesis, the sperm heads get embedded in the Sertoli cells and released from the seminiferous tubules *via* spermiation process. **(3)**

(ii)

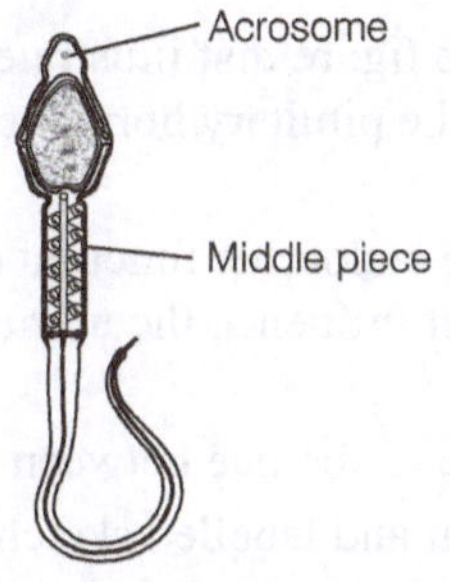

(a) The acrosome is filled with hydrolytic enzymes that help the sperm to penetrate the ovum.

(b) Middle piece possesses many mitochondria to produce energy for the movement of tail to facilitate sperm motility. (2)

41. Describe the roles of pituitary and ovarian hormones during the menstrual cycle in a human female. **Delhi 2015**

Or Explain the ovarian and uterine events that occur during a menstrual cycle in a human female under the influence of pituitary and ovarian hormones, respectively. **Delhi 2014**

Or Explain the different phases of menstrual cycle and correlate the phases with the different levels of pituitary hormones in a human female. **Delhi 2014C**

Or With the help of graphical illustration only, show the changes in the levels of the pituitary hormone during menstrual cycle in humans. **Delhi 2011C**

Ans. The cycle of events starting from one menstruation till next in female primates is called menstrual cycle. It comprises of four phases which are regulated by both pituitary (LH and FSH) and ovarian (oestrogen and progesterone) hormones that affect ovaries and uterus, respectively. The events occurring in a menstrual cycle refer to answer no. 37.

For graphical illustration of menstrual cycle; refer to figure 2.8 on page no. 47.

42. Explain the development of a secondary oocyte (ovum) in a human female from the embryonic stage up to its ovulation. Name the hormones involved in this process. **Delhi 2015**

Or When and where are primary oocytes formed in a human female? Trace the development of these oocytes till ovulation (in menstrual cycle). How do gonadotropins influence this developmental process? **Delhi 2010**

Ans. Refer to text on page no. 45 and 46.

Influence of Gonadotropins on Oogenesis

(i) Gonadotropins, i.e. LH and FSH stimulate follicular development and secretion of oestrogen by the growing follicles.

(ii) Both LH and FSH attain a peak level in the middle of the cycle (14th day).

(iii) Rapid release of LH during mid-cycle causes ovulation.

(iv) LH also stimulates the formation of corpus luteum from the ruptured follicle and secretion of progesterone from corpus luteum. (2)

43. (i) How is 'oogenesis' markedly different from 'spermatogenesis' with respect to the growth till puberty in the humans?

(ii) Draw a sectional view of human ovary and label the different follicular stages, ovum and corpus luteum. **Delhi 2014**

Ans. (i) Oogenesis is markedly different from spermatogenesis in the following aspects

Spermatogenesis	Oogenesis
It occurs in males, starting from puberty till the complete life cycle.	It starts before birth during embryonic development and occurs till menopause.
A single spermatogonium after second meiotic division forms four haploid spermatids that mature to form four spermatozoa.	A single oogonium, after second meiotic division, produces one ovum and two non-functional polar bodies.
The process of spermatogenesis, i.e. second meiotic division completes in testes and releases mature sperms.	The second meiotic division of oogenesis completes in Fallopian tube when sperm enters the secondary oocyte.

(3)

(ii) Refer to figure 2.6 on page no. 46. (2)

44. The following is the illustration of the sequence of ovarian events (*A-I*) in a human female.

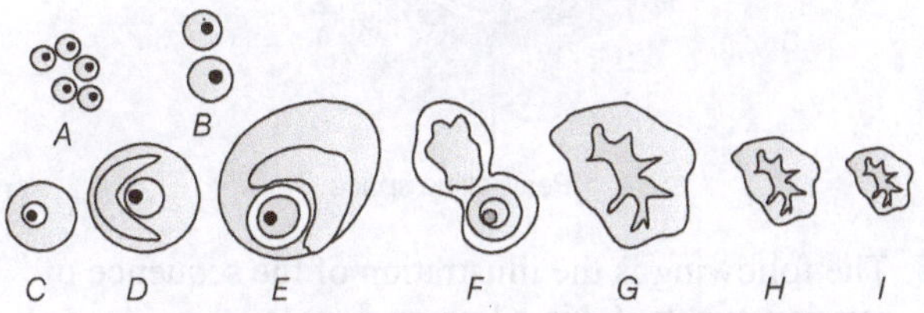

(i) Identify the figure that illustrates ovulation and mention the stage of oogenesis it represents.

(ii) Name the ovarian hormone and the pituitary hormone that have caused the above mentioned event.

(iii) Explain the changes that occur in the uterus simultaneously in anticipation.

(iv) Write the differences between *C* and *H*.

(v) Draw a labelled sketch of the structure of a human ovum prior to fertilisation. **Delhi 2012**

Ans. (i) Figure *F* illustrates ovulation. It represents the ovulatory stage of oogenesis. **(½)**

(ii) Ovarian and pituitary hormones involved in causing ovulation are

Ovarian hormone Oestrogen.

Pituitary hormone LH and FSH. **(½)**

(iii) In anticipation of receiving the fertilised egg, the endometrium of the uterus gets thickened and also the blood supply to the endometrium increases. **(1)**

(iv) In the figure, *C* stage represents the secondary follicle and the *H* stage represents the degenerating corpus luteum.

Secondary follicle	Corpus luteum
It is surrounded by the layers of granulosa cells and theca layer.	Layers of granulosa cells and theca cells are absent.
It contains an oocyte in developing stage.	It does not contain oocyte as it is formed after the release of secondary oocyte.
It does not secrete progesterone.	It secretes progesterone.

(1½)

(v) Structure of a human ovum surround by few sperms

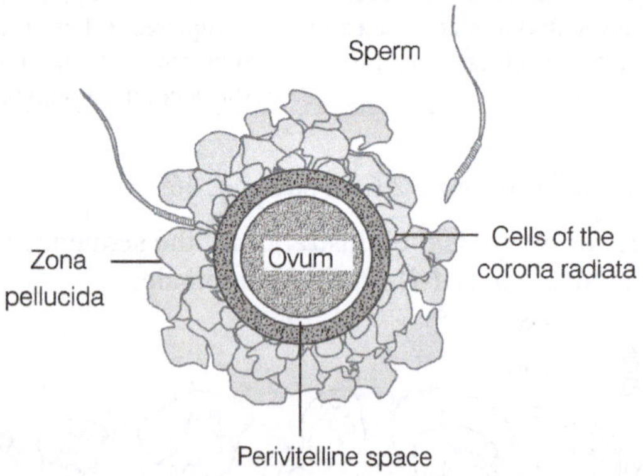

(1½)

45. The following is the illustration of the sequence of ovarian events *A-I* in a human female.

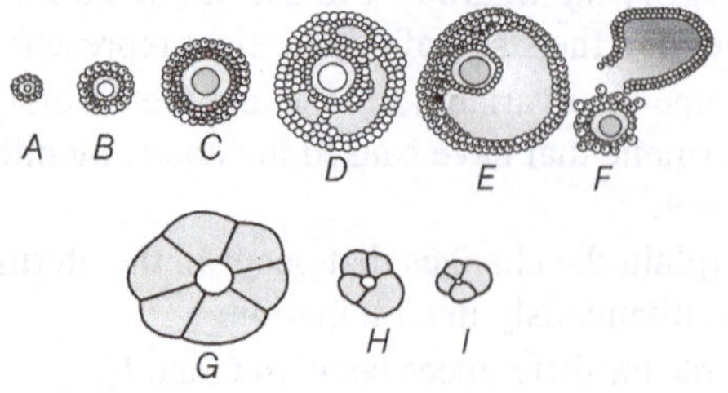

(i) Identify the figure that illustrates corpus luteum and name the pituitary hormone that influences its formation.

(ii) Specify the endocrine function of corpus luteum. How does it influence the uterus? Why is it essential?

(iii) What is the difference between *D* and *E*?

(iv) Draw a neat and labelled sketch of Graafian follicle. **Delhi 2012**

Ans. (i) *G* represents corpus luteum. LH secreted by anterior pituitary influences its formation. **(1/2 + 1/2)**

(ii) The endocrine function of corpus luteum is to secrete progesterone which is essential for the maintenance of endometrium layer of uterus. Thickened endometrium is necessary for the implantation of fertilised ovum and other events of pregnancy. **(2)**

(iii) *D* is a developing secondary follicle containing primary oocyte and undifferentiated thecal cells. *E* is a mature tertiary follicle that contains a secondary oocyte and differentiated theca cells. **(1)**

(iv) Structure of a Graafian follicle

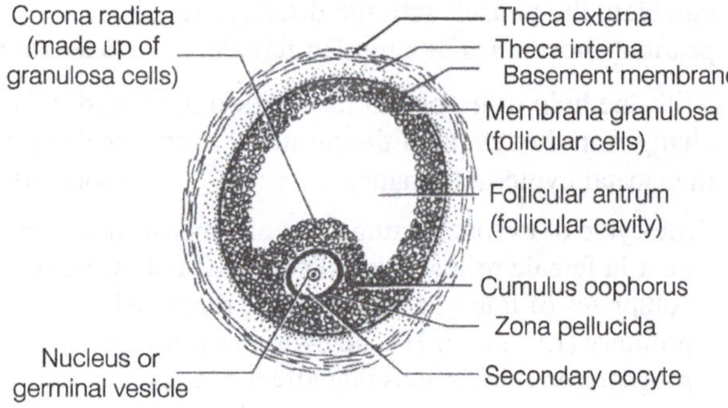

(1)

46. (i) Describe the stages of oogenesis in human females.

(ii) Draw a labelled diagram of a human ovum released after ovulation. **Delhi 2012**

Ans. (i) **For oogenesis,** Refer to answer no. 30.

(ii) **Human ovum** Refer to answer no. 44 (v).

47. (i) Draw a diagrammatic labelled sectional view of a seminiferous tubule of a human.

(ii) Describe in sequence the process of spermatogenesis in humans. **All India 2010**

Ans. (i) **Sectional view of a seminiferous tubule** Refer to figure 2.3 on page no. 44.

(ii) Refer to answer no. 40 (i).

TOPIC 3

Fertilisation, Pregnancy and Embryonic Development

Fertilisation

The process of fusion of a sperm with an ovum is called **fertilisation**. The semen of a male is transferred by the penis to the vagina of female during copulation (coitus). This process is called **insemination.**

The events leading to fertilisation are as follows

- During fertilisation, a sperm comes in contact with the **zona pellucida** layer of the ovum. It induces changes in the membrane that blocks the entry of other sperms. It ensures that only one sperm fertilises an ovum.
- The secretions of the acrosome help the sperm to enter into the cytoplasm of the ovum as it digests the zona pellucida and the plasma membrane.
- This induces the completion of the meiotic division of the secondary oocyte. This results in the formation of a haploid ovum (ootid) and a small **second polar body**.
- The haploid nucleus of the sperms and that of ovum fuse together to form a **diploid zygote**.

Sex Determination

After the fusion of male and female gametes, the zygote would carry either XX or XY chromosomes, depending on whether the sperm carrying X or Y chromosome fertilised the ovum. The zygote carrying XX would develop into a female baby and that carrying XY would form a male baby.

Hence, the sex of the baby is determined by the father and not by the mother.

Implantation

The implantation of zygote in uterus occurs in the following steps

- The mitotic division within the zygote is termed as **cleavage**. It starts as the zygote moves towards the uterus through the isthmus of the oviduct.
- It forms 2, 4, 8 and 16 daughter cells called **blastomeres**.
- The embryo with 8-16 blastomeres is called a **morula**.
- Morula continues to divide and transforms into **blastocyst** as it moves further into the uterus.
- Blastomeres in the blastocyst are arranged into an outer layer called **trophoblast**.
- The inner group of cells attached to trophoblast constitute the **inner cell mass.**

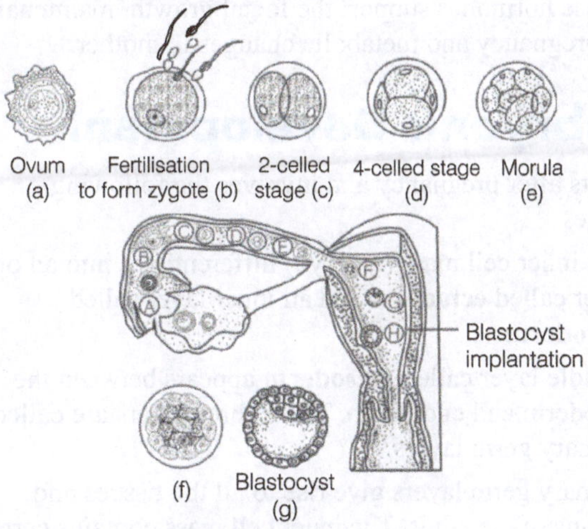

Figure 2.9 Implantation

- Trophoblast layer then gets attached to the endometrium and the inner cell mass gets differentiated as the embryo.
- After attachment, the uterine cells divide rapidly and cover the blastocyst. This leads to embedding of blastocyst in the endometrium of the uterus. This is called **implantation.**

Changes During Pregnancy

After implantation, following changes occur in uterus and embryo during pregnancy

- The finger-like projections appear on the trophoblast called **chorionic villi.** These are surrounded by the uterine tissue and maternal blood.
- Both the uterine tissue and chorionic villi become interdigitated with each other. They jointly form a structural and functional unit between developing embryo and maternal body called **placenta.**
- Placenta transports oxygen and nutrients to the foetus and removes carbon dioxide and excretory waste materials produced by it.
- Placenta also acts as an endocrine tissue. It secretes hormones like human Chorionic Gonadotropin (hCG), human Placental Lactogen (hPL), oestrogen, progesterone, etc.

- A hormone called **relaxin** is secreted by the ovary, in the later phase of pregnancy.
- Umbilical cord connects the placenta with foetus and helps in the transpont of substances to form embryo.
- During pregnancy, the levels of other hormones like oestrogen, progesterone, cortisol, prolactin, thyroxine, etc. are increased many times in the maternal blood. These hormones support the foetal growth, maintenance of pregnancy and metabolic changes in mother.

Embryonic Development

It starts after pregnancy and involves the following changes

- The inner cell mass (embryo) differentiates into an outer layer called **ectoderm** and an inner layer called **endoderm**.
- Middle layer called **mesoderm** appears between the ectoderm and endoderm. These three layers are called primary germ layers.
- Primary germ layers give rise to all the tissues and organs of the adult. The inner cell mass contains certain cells called **stem cells**. These cells have the potency to give rise to all the tissues and organs.
- In humans, after one month of pregnancy, the embryo's heart is formed. The sign of growing foetus can be ensured by listening to the heartbeat after 5-7 week of pregnancy.
- By the end of second month, limbs and digits develop.
- By the end of third month (first trimester), most of the major organ systems are formed.
- During the fifth month, the first movement of foetus and appearance of hair on the head are observed.

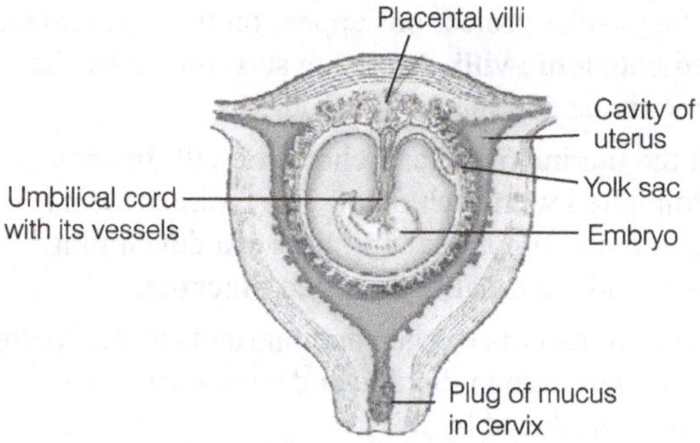

Figure 2.10 Human foetus within the uterus

- By the end of sixth month (second trimester), the body gets covered with fine hair, eyelids separate and eyelashes are formed.
- By the end of eight months, the testes in male foetus descend into the scrotum.
- By the end of nine months, the foetus is fully developed and ready for the birth.

Parturition

The process of delivery of foetus (childbirth) is called **parturition.**

- The average duration of human pregnancy is about 9 months, which is called **gestation** period.
- Vigorous contraction of the uterus at the end of pregnancy causes expulsion/delivery of the foetus.
- Parturition is induced by complex neuroendocrine mechanism.
- Relaxin hormone is secreted by the ovary and placenta to facilitate parturition by softening the connective tissue of symphysis pubica.
- Foetus and the placenta induce mild uterine contractions called **foetal-ejection reflex**. This initiates the release of oxytocin hormone from the posterior pituitary.
- Oxytocin acts on uterine muscles to cause stronger contractions, which in turn stimulate further secretion of oxytocin. This causes more stronger contractions leading to the expulsion of the baby out of the uterus through the birth canal.
- After the baby is delivered, the placenta is also expelled out of the uterus.

Lactation

Parturition is followed by the lactation which requires certain changes in the mother's body.

- Mammary glands of the female undergo differentiation during pregnancy.
- By the end of pregnancy, these glands start producing milk by the process called lactation.
- During the initial few days of lactation, the yellow coloured milk is produced and is called **colostrum.**
  It contains several antibodies (IgA) and nutrients essential to develop resistance in the newborn baby.

PYQs Previous Years' Questions

1 Mark Questions

Multiple Choice Questions

1. Figure *A* shows the front view of the human female reproductive system and figure *B* shows the development of a fertilised human egg cell.

Figure A

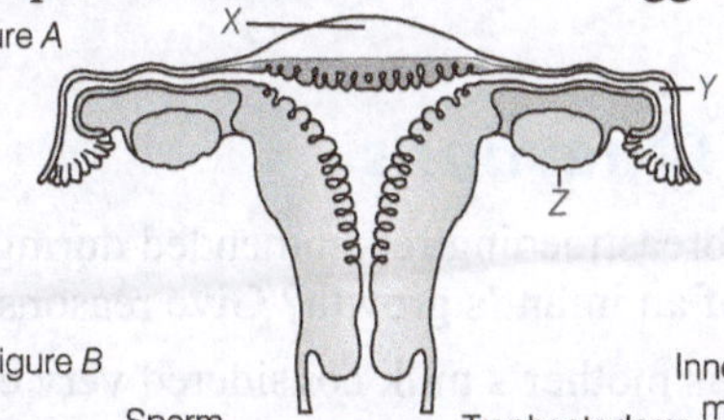

Figure B

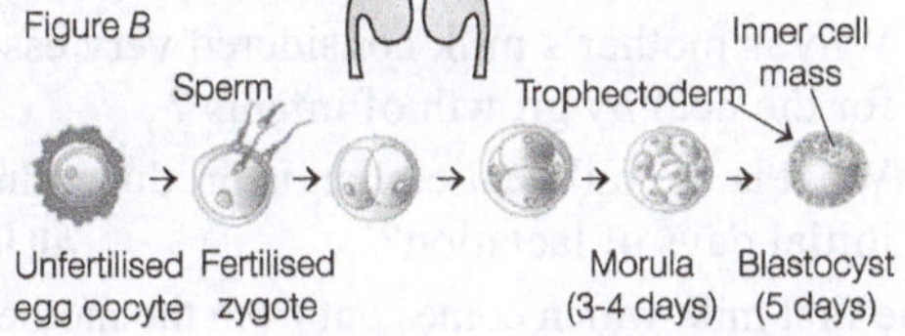

Identify the correct stage of development of human embryo (Figure B) that takes place at the site *X*, *Y* and *Z*, respectively in the human female reproductive system (Figure *A*).

Choose the correct option from the table below.

	X	*Y*	*Z*
(a)	Morula	Fertilised egg	Blastocyst
(b)	Unfertilised egg	Fertilised egg	Morula
(c)	Blastocyst	Fertilised egg	Unfertilised egg
(d)	Fertilised egg	Morula	Blastocyst

CBSE SQP 2021-22 Term-I

Ans. (c) Blastocyst, fertilised egg, unfertilised egg.

2. Which of the following statements are correct with respect to hormones secreted by placenta?

(i) Placenta secretes relaxin during later stage of pregnancy.

(ii) Placenta secretes high amount of FSH during pregnancy.

(iii) Placenta secretes relaxin during initial stage of pregnancy.

(iv) Placenta secretes hCG and hPL during pregnancy.

CBSE SQP 2021-22 Term-I

(a) (i) and (iv) (b) (i), (ii) and (iv)

(c) (iii) and (iv) (d) (ii), (iii) and (iv)

Ans. (a) (i) and (iv)

3. Concentration of which of the following substances will decrease in the maternal blood as it flows from embryo to placenta through the umbilical cord?

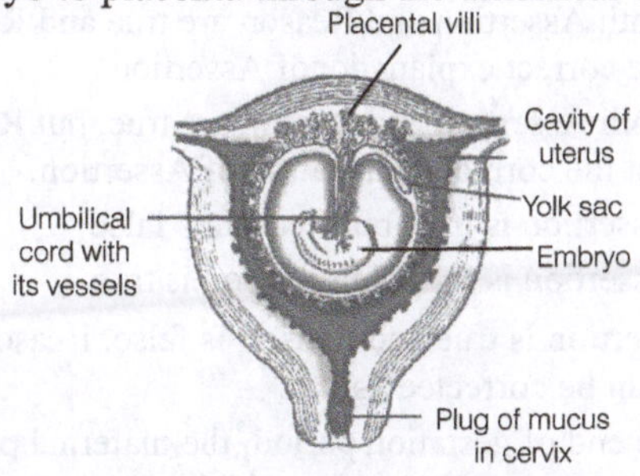

(i) Oxygen (ii) Amino acids

(iii) Carbon dioxide (iv) Urea

CBSE SQP 2021-22 Term-I

(a) (i) and (ii) (b) (ii) and (iv)

(c) (iii) and (iv) (d) (i) and (iv)

Ans. (a) (i) and (ii)

4. Choose the correct option wherein, the correct stages of the development of human embryo takes place.

	Ovary	Fallopian tube	Uterus
(a)	Morula	Fertilised egg	Blastocyst
(b)	Unfertilised egg	Fertilised egg	Morula
(c)	Unfertilised egg	Fertilised egg	Blastocyst
(d)	Fertilised egg	Morula	Blastocyst

CBSE SQP 2021-22 Term-I

Ans. (c) Unfertilised, fertilised egg, blastocyst.

5. During human embryonic development the heart in the embryo is formed after **CBSE SQP 2021-22 Term-I**

(a) 15 days of pregnancy (b) 30 days of pregnancy

(c) 45 days of pregnancy (d) 60 days of pregnancy

Ans. (b) 30 days of pregnancy.

6. During parturition, a pregnant woman is having prolonged labour pains and child birth has to be fastened. It is advisable to administer a hormone that can **CBSE SQP 2021-22 Term-I**

(a) increase the metabolic rate

(b) release glucose in the blood

(c) stimulate the ovary

(d) activate smooth muscles

Ans. (d) activate smooth muscles

Assertion-Reason Type Question

7. **Assertion** Parturition is induced by a complex neuroendocrine mechanism.

Reason At the end of gestation period, the maternal pituitary releases prolactin which causes uterine contractions. **CBSE SQP 2021-22 Term-I**

(a) Both Assertion and Reason are true and Reason is the correct explanationof Assertion.

(b) Both Assertion and Reason are true, but Reason is not the correct explanation of Assertion.

(c) Assertion is true, but Reason is false

(d) Assertion is false, but Reason is true

Ans. (c) Assertion is true and Reason is false. Reason is false and can be corrected as

At the end of gestation period, the maternal pituitary releases oxytocin hormone which causes uterine contractions.

Very Short Answer Type Questions

8. State from where do the signals for parturition originate in human females. **All India 2019**

Ans. Foetal-ejection reflex generated by fully developed foetus and placenta stimulates pituitary to release the hormone oxytocin responsible for parturition.

9. Mention the function of zona pellucida. **Delhi 2015, 2013**

Ans. During fertilisation, zone pellucida allows the entry of one sperm into the cytoplasm of the ovum and induces change to prevent entry of additional sperms.

10. How does the sperm penetrate through the zona pellucida in human ovum? **Delhi 2013C**

Ans. The sperm penetrates through the zona pellucida by releasing sperm lysins (hyaluronidase and protease) present in the acrosome.

11. How is the entry of only one sperm ensured into an ovum during fertilisation in humans? **All India 2012**

Ans. Presence of zona pellucida layer ensures that only one sperm can fertilise an ovum.

12. Write the function of oxytocin. **Delhi 2012**

Ans. Oxytocin secreted by posterior pituitary helps in parturition by inducing and enhancing uterine muscle contractions.

13. Mention the function of trophoblast in human embryo. **Delhi 2011**

Ans. Trophoblast is the outer layer of blastocyst which helps in the attachment of blastocyst to the endometrium of the uterus.

14. Name the embryonic stage that gets implanted in the uterine wall of a human female. **All India 2011**

Ans. Blastocyst gets implanted in the uterine wall of human female.

15. What stimulates pituitary to release the hormone responsible for parturition? Name the hormone. **All India 2011**

Ans. Foetal-ejection reflex stimulates pituitary to release the hormone responsible for parturition. This hormone is oxytocin.

2 Marks Questions

16. Why is breastfeeding recommended during the initial period of an infant's growth? Give reasons. **Delhi 2016**

Or (i) Why is mother's milk considered very essential for the healthy growth of infants ?

(ii) What is the milk called that is produced in the initial days of lactation? **All India 2016**

Ans. The first milk which comes out from the mother's mammary glands just after childbirth is called **colostrum.** This is a thin, yellowish, opalescent fluid. It is rich in proteins and energy along with several antibodies (IgA) that provide passive immunity to the newborn.

Hence, breastfeeding during the initial period of infant growth is highly recommended by the doctors for bringing up a disease-free, healthy baby.

17. Where does fertilisation occur in humans? Explain the events that occur during this process. **All India 2014**

Or Explain the events that occur during fertilisation of an ovum in humans. How is it that only one sperm enters the ovum? **All India 2014C**

Ans. In humans, the fertilisation of ovum takes place in ampullary-isthmic junction of the Fallopian tube. (½)

The events that occur during the process of fertilisation are

(i) The sperm reaches the junction of ampulla and isthmus and comes in contact with zona pellucida layer of ovum.

(ii) Acrosome of sperm head releases sperm lysin enzyme that dissolves corona radiata and digests zona pellucida layer to enter the cytoplasm of ovum.

(iii) After the entry of sperm into the ovum, zona pellucida induces changes in membrane and blocks the entry of additional sperms.

(iv) Entry of sperm stimulates the secondary oocyte to complete its suspended second meiotic division thus, producing haploid egg or ovum and second polar body.

(v) Nucleus of sperm and of ovum fuse to form a diploid zygote. **(1½)**

18. When and where do chorionic villi appear in humans? State their function. **Delhi 2013**

Ans. After implantation in the uterus, finger-like projections called chorionic villi appear on the trophoblast of blastocyst. It interdigitates with uterine tissue to form placenta that transports oxygen and nutrients to foetus and remove waste products and carbon dioxide produced by the foetus.

19. (i) Where do the signals for parturition originate in humans?

(ii) Why is it important to feed the newborn babies on colostrum? **All India 2012**

Ans. (i) The signals for parturition originate from the fully developed foetus and the placenta, which induces mild uterine contraction called foetal-ejection reflex. **(1)**

(ii) Colostrum contains necessary antibodies (IgA) that provide protection against disease to infants. **(1)**

20. Explain the function of umbilical cord. **All India 2012**

Ans. The placenta is connected to developing embryo through an umbilical cord, which helps in the transport of substances like oxygen, nutrients, etc. to and from the developing embryo. Blood in umbilical cord can be collected during delivery and stored to treat various diseases in future because it is rich in stem cells.

21. Mention the number of cells in the following stages.

Embryonic stage	Number of cells
Zygote	(i)
Morula	(ii)
Blastocyst	(iii)

Delhi 2011

Ans. (i) 1 (ii) 16 (iii) 64

22. Name the hormones produced only during pregnancy in human female. Mention their source organs. **Foreign 2011**

Ans. The hormones produced only during pregnancy in human female are human Chorionic and placenta Gonadotropin (hCG), human Placental Lactogen (hPL) and relaxin. **(1)**

The source of hCG and hPL is placenta and that of relaxin is ovary and placenta.

23. Why is parturition called a neuroendocrine mechanism? **All India 2011C**

Ans. Process of parturition is induced by both neural system and endocrine system therefore, it is called a neuroendocrine mechanism.

Foetus and placenta induce mild uterine contractions called foetal-ejection reflex. This initiates the release of oxytocin hormone which acts on unterine muscles to cause stronger contractions.

Vigorous contraction of the uterus at the end of pregnancy causes expulsion/delivery of the foetus. The process of delivery of foetus (childbirth) is called parturition.

3 Marks Questions

24. The figure given below shows 3 sperms *A*, *B* and *C*.

(i) Which one of the three sperms will gain entry into the ovum?

(ii) Describe the associated changes induced by it on *P* and *Q*. **CBSE SQP 2024**

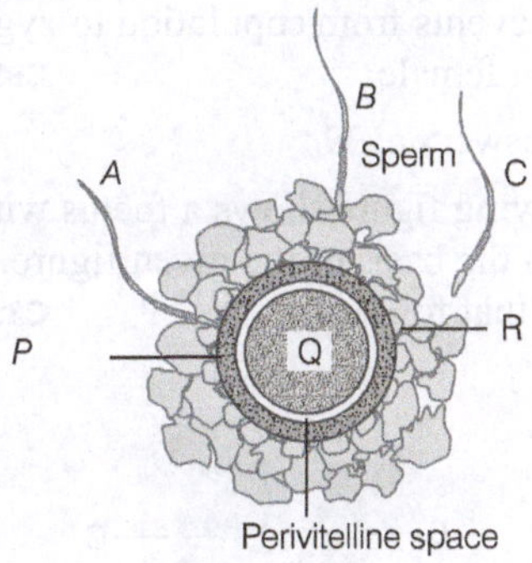

Ans. (i) Sperm *A* **(1)**

(ii) In the figure given, Sperm *A* has come in contact with the zona pellucida layer (*P*) of the ovum (*Q*). It will induce changes in the membrane that will block the entry of additional sperms (*B* and *C*). Thus, it ensures that only one sperm can fertilise the ovum.

The secretions of the acrosome of sperm *A* will help it to enter into the cytoplasm of the ovum (*Q*) through the zona pellucida (*P*) and the plasma membrane, this will induce the completion of the meiotic division of the secondary oocyte (*Q*).

The second meiotic division in *Q* being unequal will result in the formation of a second polar body and a haploid ovum. Then, the haploid nucleus of the sperm *A* and that of the ovum (Q) will fuse together to form a diploid zygote. **(2)**

25. Explain the phases of the embryonic development from morula stage till the establishment of pregnancy in human female. **CBSE SQP 2024**

Ans. Refer to text on page no. 57 and 58.

26. A fully developed foetus initiates its delivery from the mother's womb'. Justify the statement. **CBSE SQP 2021-22**

Ans. During the end days of gestation period, signals of parturition are initiated by fully developed foetus and vigorous contractions of uterus by the hormones released by placenta. It is known as foetal-ejection reflex. Firstly, the uterine contractions causes the release of oxytocin from the maternal posterior pituitary gland. Oxytocin causes stronger uterine contractions. The foetal pituitary gland also secretes increasing amount of oxytocin and its adrenal gland secretes cortisol. These hormones act as uterine stimulant. Beside these, oestrogen to progesterone ratio also increase sufficiently. All these hormonal changes initiate the delivery of fully developed foetus from the mother's womb.

27. Trace the events from copulation to zygote formation in a human female. **CBSE SQP 2021-22**

Ans. Refer to answer no. 39.

28. The following figure shows a foetus within the uterus. On the basis of the given figure, answer the questions that follows. **CBSE SQP 2021-22**

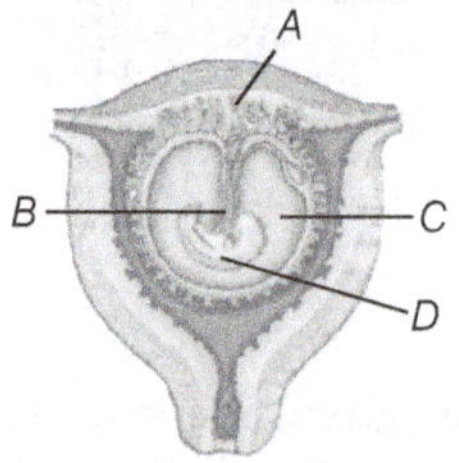

(i) In the above figure, choose and name the correct part (*A*, *B*, *C* or *D*) that acts as a temporary endocrine gland and substantiate your answer. Why is it also called the functional junction?

(ii) Mention the role of *B* in the development of the embryo.

(iii) Name the fluid surrounding the developing embryo. How is it misused for sex-determination?

Ans. (i) In the given figure, *A* represents placenta that acts as a temporary endocrine gland. It forms intimate connection between maternal blood and foetus and also produces several hormones like human Chorionic Gonadotropin (hCG), human Placental Lactogen (hPL), oestrogen and progesterone. Placenta is also called the functional junction because it supplies the nutrients and oxygen from maternal blood to the embryo. It also removes CO_2 and other excretory products produced by the embryo. **(1)**

(ii) The structure *B* represents umbilical cord. It connects the placenta to the embryo and helps in the transportation of various substances to and from the embryo. **(1)**

(iii) The fluid surrounding the developing embryo is called amniotic fluid. This fluid contains the cells of foetus which are used to study the chromosome pattern of developing foetus. It is often misused to determine the sex of the foetus and facilitates the sin of female foeticide. **(1)**

29. Explain the formation of placenta after implantation in a human female. **All India 2020**

Ans. Refer to text on page no. 57 and 58 (Changes during pregnancy).

> **Concept Enhancer** The human placenta is also known as chorionic placenta as chorion is involved in its formation.

30. (i) Explain the process of fertilisation in human.

(ii) Name the embryonic stage that gets implanted in human females. Explain the process of implantation. **Delhi 2019**

Ans. (i) Refer to answer no. 39 (i).

(ii) Blastocyst gets implanted in the uterine wall. **(1)**

Process of implantation, refer to answer no. 39 (i). **(2)**

31. The given diagram shows a part of the human female reproductive system.

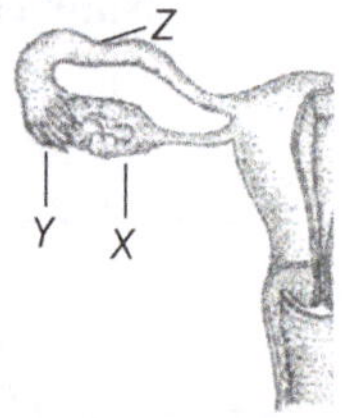

(i) Name the gamete cells that would be present in '*X*' if taken from a newborn baby.

(ii) Name '*Y*' and write its function.

(iii) Name '*Z*' and write the events that take place here. **All India 2015C**

Ans. (i) Primary oocytes are present in *X*, i.e. ovary of a newborn baby. **(1)**

(ii) *Y* is fimbriae. It helps in the collection of ovum from ovary after ovulation. **(1)**

(iii) *Z* is the ampullary–isthmic junction. It is the site of fertilisation in humans. **(1)**

32. Describe the process of parturition in human. **Delhi 2015**

Ans. Refer to answer no. 23.

33. (i) How is placenta formed in human female?

(ii) Name any two hormones which are secreted by it and are also present in a non-pregnant woman. **Foreign 2014**

Ans. (i) After implantation of blastocyst, the finger-like projections called chorionic villi, appear on the trophoblast. They get surrounded by uterine tissue and maternal blood which become interdigitated with each other to form placenta. **(1)**

(ii) The two hormones secreted by placenta that are also present in a non-pregnant woman are oestrogen and progesterone. **(2)**

5 Marks Questions

34. (i) Explain the formation of placenta after the implantation in a human female.

(ii) Draw a diagram showing human foetus within the uterus and label any four parts in it. **CBSE 2023**

Ans. (i) The development of the placenta is called placentation. In humans, placental formation starts in the third week of pregnancy. At the stage of the blastocyst, the embryo has two different cell types trophoblast cells and inner cell mass. The inner cell mass forms the foetus and the trophoblast forms the placenta. From trophoblast, some processes develop that connect with the uterine wall. From the placenta, the umbilical cord is developed that is also connected to the foetus. **(3)**

(ii) Refer to figure no 2.10 on page no. 58. **(2)**

35. Where does fertilisation occur in the oviduct of a human female? Explain the embryonic development from fertilised ovum up to its implantation. **Delhi 2020**

Ans. Refer to text on page no. 57-58.

36. Given below is the diagram of a human ovum surrounded by a few sperms. Study the diagram and answer the following questions.

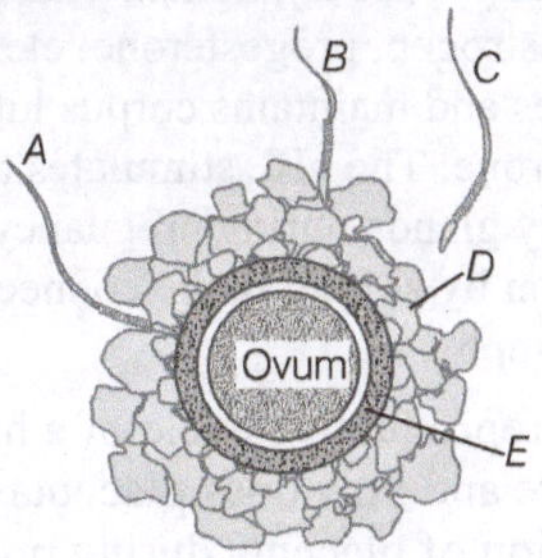

(i) Which one of the sperms would reach the ovum earlier?

(ii) Identify '*D*' and '*E*'. Mention the role of '*E*'.

(iii) Mention what helps the entry of sperm into the ovum and write the changes occurring in the ovum during the process.

(iv) Name the specific region in the female reproductive system where the event represented in the diagram takes place. **All India 2019**

Ans. (i) The sperm '*A*' would reach the ovum earlier. **(1)**

(ii) *D*–Corona radiata, *E*–Zona pellucida-During fertilisation, a sperm comes in contact with zona pellucida layer of the ovum and induces changes in the membrane that block the entry of additional sperms. Hence, *E* helps to prevent polyspermy. **(1)**

(iii) The hydrolytic secretions of the acrosome help the sperm to enter into the cytoplasm of the ovum through the zona pellucida and the plasma membrane. This induces the completion of the meiotic division of the secondary oocyte. **(2)**

(iv) These events take place in the ampullary-isthmic junction of the Fallopian tube of uterus. **(1)**

37. Given below is the diagram of a human ovum surrounded by a few sperms. Observe the diagram and answer the following questions.

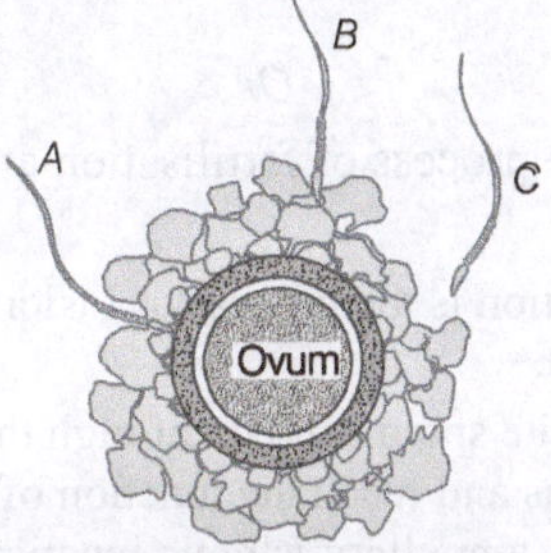

(i) Compare the fate of sperms shown in the diagram.

(ii) What is the role of zona pellucida in this process?

(iii) Analyse the changes occurring in the ovum during this process.

(iv) How is the entry of sperm into the ovum facilitated?

(v) Specify the region of female reproductive system where the event represented in the diagram takes corone place. **CBSE SQP 2018**

Ans. (i) The sperm *A* has already penetrated the cells of corona radiata present around the ovum and about to reach layer zona pellucida. It will succeed to fertilise the egg. Sperm *B* and *C* are unable to penetrate the layers around the egg cell and will get degenerated.

(ii) Zona pellucida prevents polyspermy thus, allowing only one sperm to enter the ovum and fertilise the egg.

(iii) After the entry of the sperm into the ovum, the anaphase-II of meiosis of oocytes comes to end and meiotic division gets completed.

(iv) The acrosome of sperm releases an enzyme, hyaluronidase, which digests the cells of corona radiata and makes path for sperm entry in the ovum to complete fertilisation.

(v) The event of fertilisation takes place in the ampullary– isthmic junction of the Fallopian tube. **(1 × 5)**

38. (i) Draw a diagram of the adult human female reproductive system and label the different
(a) parts of Fallopian tube
(b) layers of uterus wall

(ii) Explain the events during fertilisation of an ovum in humans. **CBSE 2018C**

Ans. (i) Refer to figure 2.2 on page no. 41.
(ii) Refer to answer no. 39 (i).

39. (i) Briefly explain the events of fertilisation and implantation in an adult human female.

(ii) Comment on the role of placenta as an endocrine gland. **Delhi 2016**

Or

Explain the process of fertilisation and implantation in human. **Foreign 2015**

Ans. (i) Fertilisation is the process of fusion of a sperm with an ovum.

(a) The motile sperms move through the cervix, enter the uterus and reach the junction of the isthmus and ampulla (ampullary-isthmic junction) of the Fallopian tube.

(b) The ovum released from the ovary also reaches the ampullary-isthmic junction where fertilisation takes place.

(c) Fertilisation can only occur if the ovum and sperms are transported simultaneously to this junction. This explains why all copulations do not lead to fertilisation and pregnancy.

(d) The sperm comes in contact with the **zona pellucida** of the ovum and releases sperm lysins which induces changes in the egg membrane and blocks the entry of the other sperms.

(e) The secretions of the acrosome help the sperm to enter into the cytoplasm of the ovum.

(f) This induces the completion of meiotic division of the secondary oocyte.
The secondary meiotic division results in the formation of a **secondary polar body** and a haploid ovum (**ootid**).

(g) The haploid nucleus of the sperm and that of ovum fuse together to form a diploid **zygote**.

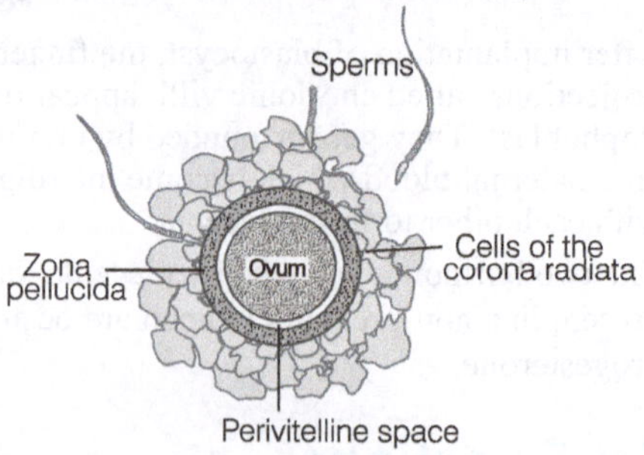

Implantation The mitotic division starts as the zygote moves through the isthmus of the oviduct towards the uterus. This is called **cleavage** thus, forming 2, 4, 8, 16 daughter cells called **blastomeres**.

(a) The embryo with 8-16 blastomeres is called **morula**. But, it is not larger than a zygote.

(b) The morula continues to divide and transforms into **blastocyst** as it moves further into the uterus.

(c) The blastomeres in the blastocyst gets arranged into an outer layer called **trophoblast** and the inner group of cells attached to trophoblast called the **inner cell mass**.

(d) The trophoblast layer then gets attached to the endometrium and the inner cell mass differentiates into the **embryo**. After attachment, the uterine cells divide rapidly and cover the blastocyst.
As a result, the blastocyst becomes embedded in the endometrium of the uterus. This is called **implantation** and it leads to pregnancy. **(4)**

(ii) Placenta also acts as an **endocrine tissue** and produces several hormones like human Chorionic Gonadotropin (hCG), human Placental Lactogen (hPL) oestrogen, progesterone, etc. The hCG stimulates and maintains corpus luteum to secrete progesterone. The hPL stimulates the growth of mammary glands during pregnancy. Relaxin helps in parturition by softening the connective tissue of pubic symphysis. **(1)**

40. During the reproductive cycle of a human female when, where and how does placenta develop? What is the function of placenta during pregnancy and embryo development? **Delhi 2015**

Ans. Placenta is an organ that connects the developing foetus to the uterine wall of mother for supporting pregnancy.

After implantation, finger-like projections appear on the trophoblast called chorionic villi, which are surrounded by the uterine tissue and maternal blood. The chorionic villi and the uterine tissue become interdigitated with each other and jointly form a structural and functional unit between foetus and maternal body, i.e. placenta. (1)

Functions of Placenta

(i) It facilitates the supply of oxygen and nutrients to the developing embryo.

(ii) It also facilitates the removal of carbon dioxide and waste materials produced by the foetus.

(iii) The placenta is connected to the developing embryo through the **umbilical cord**, which helps in the transport of substances to and from the developing embryo.

(iv) Placenta also acts as an **endocrine tissue** and produces several hormones like human Chorionic Gonadotropin (hCG), human Placental Lactogen (hPL), oestrogen, progesterone, etc.

The production of these hormones is necessary to support foetal growth, metabolic changes in the mother and maintenance of pregnancy (4)

41. (i) Explain the events taking place at the time of fertilisation of an ovum in a human female.

(ii) Trace the development of the zygote up to its implantation in the uterus.

(iii) Name and draw a labelled sectional view of the embryonic stage that gets implanted. **Delhi 2010**

Ans. (i) Refer to answer no. 39 (i).

(ii) Refer to answer no. 39 (i).

(iii) Blastocyst is the stage that implanted in the uterus.

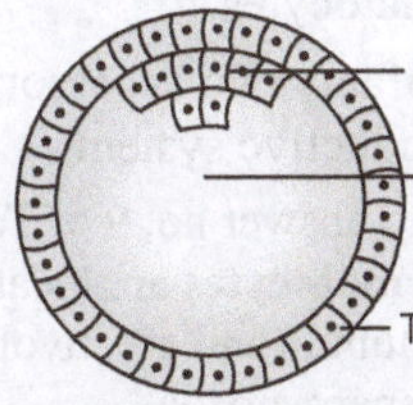

42. Describe the post-zygotic events leading to implantation and placenta formation in humans. Mention any two functions of placenta. **All India 2010**

Or Explain the process of fertilisation in human female and trace the post-fertilisation events in a sequential order up to implantation of the embryo.

Ans. Post-zygotic events leading to implantation and placenta formation.

Refer to answer no. 39 (i).

Events leading to formation of placenta and functions of placenta, refer to answer no. 29 and 40.

43. (i) Mention the event that induces the completion of the meiotic division of the secondary oocyte.

(ii) Trace the journey of the ovum from the ovary, its fertilisation and further development until the implantation of the embryo. **All India 2010C**

Ans. (i) Secondary oocyte completes meiosis-II only when a sperm enters into its cytoplasm. It forms a larger cell, the ootid and a small cell, the second polar body. (1)

(ii) (a) The secondary oocyte is released by the rupture of the Graafian follicle in the process called ovulation. (½)

(b) It is moved into the Fallopian tube with the help of fimbriae. (½)

(c) It reaches the ampullary-isthmic junction of the Fallopian tube where fertilisation takes place. (½)

(d) After fertilisation, cleavage starts in the zygote. (½)

(e) Cleavage results in the formation of 2, 4, 8 and 16 daughter cells called blastomeres. The embryo with 8-16 blastomeres is a solid spherical structure called **morula**. (½)

(f) Morula continues to divide and blastomeres rearrange themselves as it moves further into the uterus. (½)

(g) As a result, **blastocyst** is formed, which contains trophoblast (outer layer) and inner cell mass. (½)

(h) The trophoblast attaches to endometrium and blastocyst gets embedded in it (implantation) (½)

Miscellaneous Questions

3 Marks Question

1. Draw a diagrammatic sectional view of the female reproductive system of human and label the parts.

(i) Where does the secondary oocyte develop?

(ii) Which help in the collection of ovum after ovulation?

(iii) Where does fertilisation occur?

(iv) Where does implantation of embryo occur? **Delhi 2013**

Ans. For diagram, refer to the figure 2.2 on page no. 41.

(i) The secondary oocyte develops in **ovary**.

(ii) **Fimbriae** help in the collection of ovum after ovulation.

(iii) In the junction of **ampulla-isthmus**, the ovum gets fertilised.

(iv) Implantation of embryo occurs in the cavity of **uterus**.

5 Marks Questions

2. (i) Explain the following phases in the menstrual cycle of a human female.
   (a) Menstrual phase (b) Follicular phase
   (c) Luteal phase

   (ii) A proper understanding of menstrual cycle can help immensely in family planning. Do you agree with the statement? Provide reasons for your answer. **All India 2017**

Ans. (i) (a) **Menstrual phase** The menstrual cycle starts with menstrual phase. It lasts for about 3-5 days. The menstrual flow results due to the breakdown of endometrial lining of the uterus and its blood vessels that come out through vagina. **(1)**

(b) **Follicular phase** It lasts till about 13th day of menstrual cycle. In this phase, the primary follicles in the ovary grow to become a fully mature **Graafian follicle**.

The secretion of gonadotropins (LH and FSH) from anterior pituitary increases gradually during the follicular phase. They stimulate follicular development as well as secretion of oestrogen by the growing follicles. **(1)**

(c) **Luteal phase** This phase lasts for about 10-14 days. In this phase, the ruptured Graafian follicle transforms into **corpus luteum**. It secretes large amount of progesterone which is essential to maintain endometrium. **(1)**

(ii) Yes, a proper understanding of menstrual cycle can help in family planning as this knowledge can be used to avoid the meeting of sperms and ovum. This is known as periodic abstinence or rhythm method of birth control, i.e. temporary avoidance of sex.

In this method, a couple can avoid or abstain the coitus from day 10 to 17 of the menstrual cycle because ovulation occurs during this period. The chances of fertilisation are very high during this period **(2)**

3.

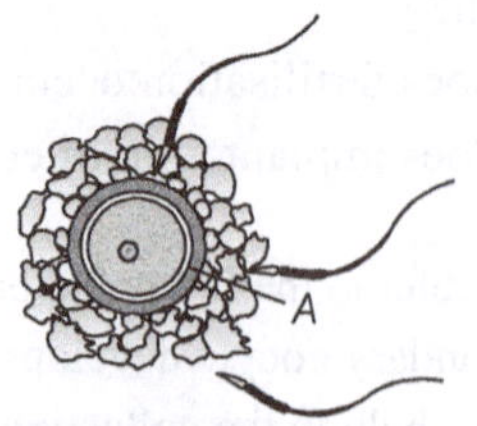

(i) One of the sperms is observed to penetrate '*A*' of the ovum, as shown in the above diagram. Name '*A*'.

(ii) How is the sperm able to do so?

(iii) Where exactly in the Fallopian tube does this occur?

(iv) Explain the events thereafter up to morula stage. **All India 2013C**

Ans. (i) *A* is zona pellucida. **(1)**

(ii) Sperm is able to penetrate the egg with the help of sperm lysins contained in acrosome. **(1)**

(iii) Ampullary-isthmic junction. **(1)**

(iv) As soon as the sperm enters the egg, meiotic division of secondary oocyte gets completed. As a result a second polar body and a haploid ovum are formed. Then, haploid sperm and ovum fuse together to form a diploid zygote which undergoes cleavage *via* mitotic division. At 8-16 cell stage, the embryo is called morula. **(2)**

4. (i) Draw a labelled diagram of the human female reproductive system.

   (ii) Enumerate the events in the ovary of a human female during **Delhi 2012**
   (a) follicular phase
   (b) luteal phase of menstrual cycle

Ans. (i) Refer to figure 2.2 on page no. 41. **(3)**

(ii) (a) **Follicular phase** The primary follicle in the ovary grows to become fully mature Graafian follicle. Endometrium gets thickened and the follicular cells secrete oestrogen. **(1)**

(b) **Luteal phase** The remaining part of ruptured Graafian follicle transforms into corpus luteum that secretes progesterone. **(1)**

5. (i) Write the specific location and the functions of the following cells in human males **Delhi 2011**
   (a) Leydig cells (b) Sertoli cells
   (c) Primary spermatocytes

   (ii) Explain the role of any two accessory glands in human male reproductive system

Ans. (i) (a) and (b) Refer to answer no. 9 of Topic 1.

(c) **Primary spermatocytes** are located inside the seminiferous tubule and are involved in the formation of spermatozoa. **(3)**

(ii) Accessory glands of human male reproductive system are

(a) **Prostate and seminal vesicles** Their secretions provide a fluid medium for the sperms to swim towards the ovum. They provide nutrition to sperms.

(b) **Bulbourethral glands** Their secretion helps in the lubrication and neutralising the acidity of urogenital tract. **(2)**

6. (i) When does oogenesis begin?
(ii) Differentiate between the location and function of the Sertoli cells and Leydig cells. **All India 2012**

Ans. (i) Oogenesis begins during the embryonic development stage when a million gamete mother cells (oogonia) are formed within each foetal ovary. **(2)**

(ii) (a) Sertoli cells are located on the inside lining of seminiferous tubule. These cells provide nutrition to the germ cells.
(b) Leydig cells or interstitial cells are located in the regions outside the seminiferous tubule called interstitial spaces. These cells synthesise and secrete testicular hormone called androgens. **(3)**

Case Based/Source Based/Passage Based Questions (Based on Complete Chapter)

1. In a human female, the reproductive phase starts on the onset of puberty and ceases around middle age of the female. Study the graph given below regarding menstrual cycle and answer the questions that follow **CBSE 2024 (Set-II)**

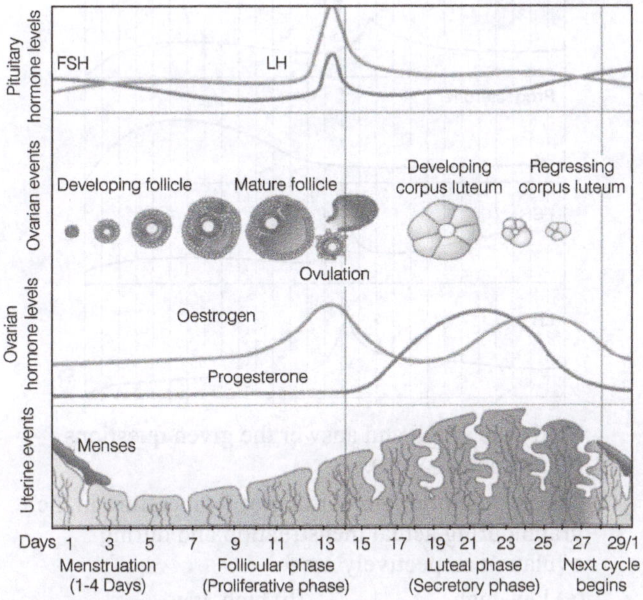

(i) Name the hormones and their source organ, which are responsible for menstrual cycle at puberty.
(ii) For successful pregnancy, at what phase of the menstrual cycle an early embryo (upto 3 blastomeres) should be implanted in the uterus (IUT) of a human female who has opted for Assisted Reproductive Technology (ART)? Support your answer with a reason.
(iii) Name the hormone and its source organ responsible for the events occurring during proliferative phase of menstrual cycle. Explain the event.

Or (iii) In a normal human female, why does menstruation only occurs if the released ovum is not fertilised? Explain.

Ans. (i) At puberty, the menstrual cycle is regulated by hormones produced by various organs
(a) Follicle-Stimulating Hormone (FSH)-produced by anterior pituitary.
(b) Luteinizing Hormone (LH)-produced by anterior pituitary.
(c) Oestrogen-produced by ovaries (developing follicles)
(d) Progesterone-produced by ovaries (corpus luteum) **(1)**

(ii) For successful pregnancy through Assisted Reproductive Technology (ART), the early embryo (upto 3 blastomeres) should be implanted in the uterus (IUT) of a human female in the luteal phase of the menstrual cycle, mostly around 6-8 days after ovulation. This is due to
(a) Elevated levels of progesterone during luteal phase is preparing the endometrium for embryo implantation.
(b) Endometrium becomes receptive to blastocyst implantation and remains receptive during this phase.
This increases the chances of embryo implantation and pregnancy. **(1)**

(iii) The main hormone during follicular (proliferative) phase is oestrogen whose source organ is developing ovarian follicle. Oestrogen stimulates the proliferation of the endometrium (inner lining of uterus) and uterus starts preparation for another pregnancy. **(2)**

Or

(iii) In a normal human female, menstruation occurs when the released ovum is not fertilised. In absence of fertilisation, corpus luteum that is formed from the ruptured follicle after ovulation degenerates. Regression or degeneration of the corpus luteum leads to a decrease in progesterone and oestrogen level. The decrease in hormone level causes disintegration of the endometrium leading to menstruation, marking a new cycle. So, menstruation occurs due to withdrawal of hormonal support and subsequent shedding of the uterine lining when the released ovum is not fertilised. **(2)**

2. To answer the questions, study the graphs below for Subject 1 and 2 showing different levels of certain hormones.

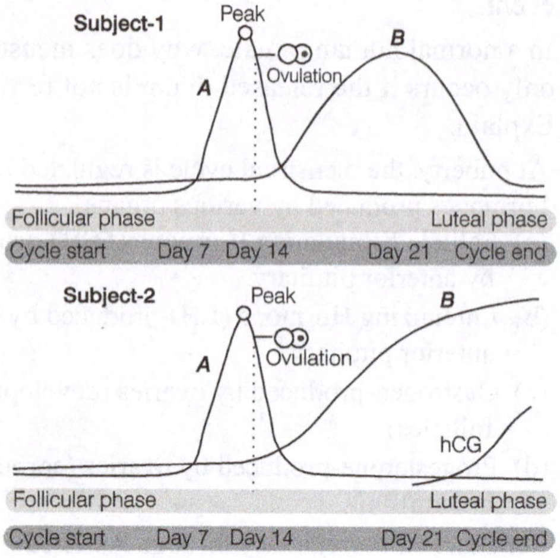

(i) The peak observed in subjects 1 and 2 is due to **CBSE SQP 2021-22 Term-I**
   (a) oestrogen
   (b) progesterone
   (c) Luteinizing hormone
   (d) follicle stimulating hormone

(ii) Subject 2 has higher level of hormone *B*, which is
   (a) oestrogen
   (b) progesterone
   (c) Luteinizing hormone
   (d) follicle stimulating hormone

(iii) If the peak of hormone *A* does not appear in the study for subject 1, which of the following statement is true?
   (a) Peak of hormone *B* will be observed at a higher point in the graph
   (b) Peak of hormone *B* will be observed at a point lower than what is given in the graph
   (c) There will be no observed data for hormone *B*
   (d) The graph for hormone *B* will be a sharp rise followed by a plateau

(iv) Which structure in the ovary will remain functional in subject 2?
   (a) Corpus luteum
   (b) Tertiary follicle
   (c) Graafian follicle
   (d) Primary follicle

(v) For subject 2, it is observed that the peak for hormone *B* has reached the plateau stage. After approximately, how much time will be the curve for hormone *B* descend?
   (a) 28 days (b) 42 days
   (c) 180 days (d) 280 days

(vi) Which of the following statements is true about the subjects?
   (a) Subject 1 is pregnant
   (b) Subject 2 is pregnant
   (c) Both subjects 1 and 2 are pregnant
   (d) Both subjects 1 and 2 are not pregnant

Ans. (i)-(c), (ii)-(b), (iii)-(c), (iv)-(a), (v)-(d), (vi)-(b)

3. A group of medical students carried out a detailed study on the impact of various factors on the different hormones during the menstrual cycle in a human female. They collected the data with different factors. Given below is the graph plotted from the data collected showing the morning temperature and concentration of hormones FSH, LH, oestrogen and progesterone during normal menstrual cycle in a woman. **CBSE 2021-22 Term-I**

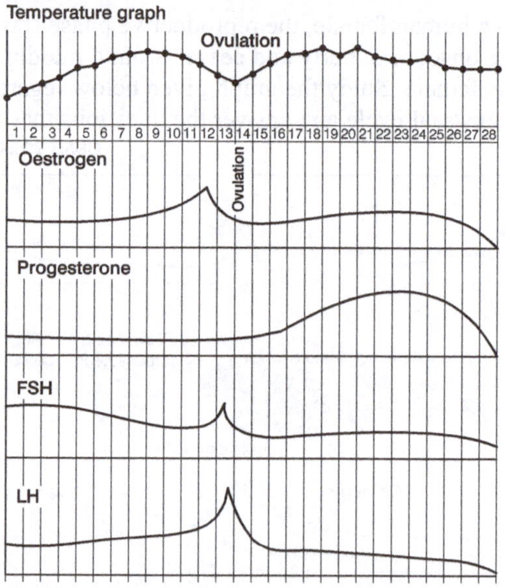

Study the graph and answer the given questions (Question nos. i-vi).

(i) The early morning recording of temperature in the graph during actual menstruation and during ovulation respectively are
   (a) low, high (b) high, low
   (c) low, low (d) high, high

(ii) The time of ovulation is of importance in cases of
   I. couples having difficulty in conception.
   II. to know the safe period for prevention of pregnancy.
   III. to inhibit the process of ovulation.
   IV. to stimulate ovarian follicular development.
   (a) I and IV (b) II and IV
   (c) I and II (d) III and IV

(iii) The increase in the level of progesterone is maximum under the influence of LH during
(a) secretory phase (b) follicular phase
(c) menstruation (d) proliferation phase

(iv) Which of the following hormone/hormones is/are showing rapid surge leading to changes in Graafian follicle just before ovulation?
(a) LH (b) FSH
(c) FSH and oestrogen (d) FSH and LH

(v) The human corpus luteum starts regressing .... days after ovulation (Identify the correct choice for the blank).
(a) 10–11 (b) 14–15
(c) 16–17 (d) 18–20

(vi) As per the data plotted in the graph, in which period of the menstrual cycle is the chance of fertilisation very high in human female?
(a) 3rd – 9th days (b) 10th – 17th days
(c) 18th – 23rd days (d) 23rd – 28th days

Ans. (i)-(a), (ii)-(c), (iii)-(a), (iv)-(d), (v)-(a), (vi)-(b)

4. Read the following and answer the questions given below

A mature spermatozoa or sperm cell is a microscopic tadpole shaped structure about 2-5 µm in diameter and 60 µm long. A plasma membrane encloses the entire sperm. It consist of four different parts, i.e. head, neck middle piece and a tail.

(i) The small cap-like structure called acrosome contains
(a) glucose
(b) fructose
(c) hydrolytic enzymes
(d) semen

(ii) According to estimate, for normal fertility about 60% of them must have normal .... and size and 40% of them must show ....
(a) shape, fertility (b) structure, vigorus motility
(c) shape, vigorus fertility (d) shape, vigorus motility

(iii)

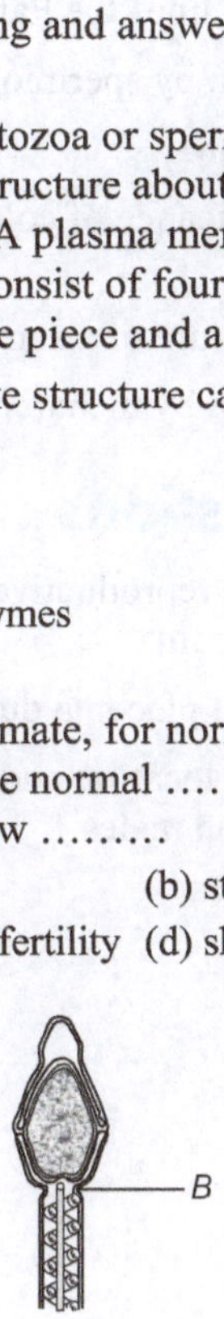

What does part *B* contains?
(a) Acrosome (b) Mitochondria
(c) Two centrioles (d) Ribosomes

(iv) From where does the axial filament found on the tail of the sperm arises?
(a) Anterior centriole (b) Posterior centriole
(c) Neck (d) Head

(v) The acrosome is formed of which component?
(a) Mitochondria (b) Golgi complex and ribosome
(c) Golgi complex (d) Both (a) and (c)

Ans. (i)-(c), (ii)-(d), (iii)-(c), (iv)-(b), (v)-(c)

5. Read the following and answer the questions given below

The development of an embryo from the fertilised ovum involves various different events. The fertilised ovum first undergoes mitotic division starting as the zygote moves through the isthmus of the oviduct towards the uterus forming 2,4,8,16 daughter cells called blastomeres.

This process is called cleavage on the above situation. Study the figure given below and answer the questions that follows.

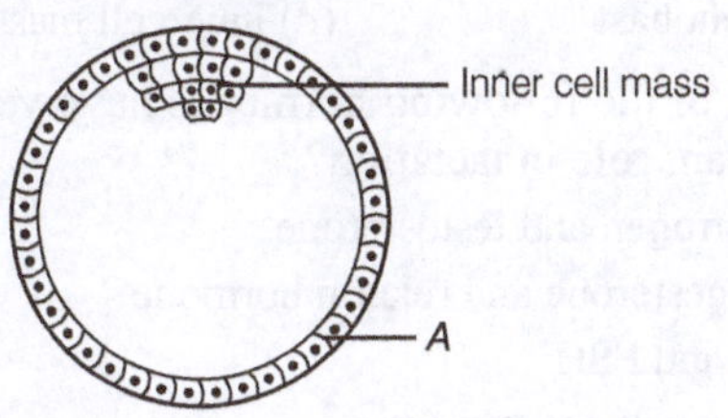

(i) Name the stage of human embryo the figure represents.
(ii) Identify '*A*' in the figure.
(iii) Mention the function of part *A*.
(iv) Mention the fate of the inner cell mass after implantation in the uterus.
(v) Where are the stem cells located in this embryo?

Ans. (i) Blastocyst. (½)
(ii) '*A*' is trophoblast. (½)
(iii) The trophoblast layer gets attached to endometrium and later forms chorionic villi. (1)
(iv) The inner cell mass gets differentiated into an embryo. (1)
(v) Inner cell mass. (1)

CHAPTER TEST

01 Mark Questions

Multiple Choice Questions

1 In humans, at the end of the first meiotic division, the male germ cells differentiate into the
(a) primary spermatocytes
(b) secondary spermatocytes
(c) spermatids
(d) spermatogonia

2 Which of the following cells present in the mammalian testes forms the sperms?
(a) Leydig cells (b) Spermatogonia
(c) Interstitial space (d) Sertoli cells

3 Nebenkern is part of
(a) foetus (b) ovum
(c) sperm (d) Graafian follicle

4 Embryo at 16-32 cell stage is called
(a) blastula (b) morula
(c) trophobast (d) innercell mass

5 Which of the following hormones have very important role in lactation?
(a) Oestrogen and testosterone
(b) Progesterone and relaxin hormone
(c) LH and FSH
(d) Oxytocin and prolactin

Assertion-Reason Type Questions

Directions (Q. Nos. 6-9) *In the questions given below two statements an **Assertion** and a **Reason** are given. Give the appropriate response as*

(a) If both Assertion and Reason are true and Reason is the correct explanation of Assertion
(b) If both Assertion and Reason are true, but Reason is not the correct explanation of Assertion
(c) If Assertion is true, but Reason is false
(d) If both Assertion and Reason are false

6 **Assertion** Interstitial spaces outside the seminiferous tubule have blood vessels and Sertoli cells.

Reason Sertoli cells provide nutrition to the germ cells. **CBSE 2021-22 Term-I**

7 **Assertion** Generally, a woman does not conceive during lactation period.

Reason The hormone prolactin initiates and maintains lactation in a woman.

8 **Assertion** Before fusion, spermatozoa has to penetrate egg membrane.

Reason The activated spermatozoa undergo acrosomal reactions and release sperm lysin.

9 **Assertion** During fertilisation, only head of spermatozoa enters the egg.

Reason If several spermatozoa hit the egg at same time, all can enter.

2/3 Marks Questions

10 Mention the function of Sertoli cells.

11 Which epithelium lines the Fallopian tube?

12 What do you mean by spermiogenesis?

13 Define capacitation.

14 What is the significance of colostrum in new born baby?

15 Describe the structure of a seminiferous tubule.

16 What do you mean by menarche?

05 Marks Questions

17 Describe the male reproductive system with well-labelled diagram.

18 Explain the role of placenta during the pregnancy.

19 Write the specific location and the functions of the following in human males.
(a) Tunica albuginea
(b) Leydig cells
(c) Epididymis

Answers

1.	(b)	2.	(b)	3.	(c)	4.	(b)	5.	(d)
6.	(b)	7.	(b)	8.	(a)	9.	(c)		

03

Reproductive Health

TREND ANALYSIS 3 YEARS

Average No. of Questions Across all Sets

Topic	Types of Questions	2024	2023	2020
TOPIC 01 Reproductive Health: Problems and Strategies	1 Mark	1	2	0
	2 Marks	0	0	0
	3 Marks	1	1	1
	4 Marks (Case Based)	0	0	0
	5 Marks	0	1	0
TOPIC 02 Sexually Transmitted Diseases (STDs) and Infertility	1 Mark	1	1	0
	2 Marks	1	0	0
	3 Marks	0	0	0
	4 Marks (Case Based)	0	0	0
	5 Marks	0	0	1

TOPIC 1

Reproductive Health: Problems and Strategies

The word 'Reproductive health' simply refers to healthy reproductive organs with normal functioning. According to the **World Health Organisation** (WHO), reproductive health means a total well-being in all aspects of reproduction, i.e. physical, emotional, behavioural and social.

The improved reproductive health of society requires following factors

- better awareness about sex related matters.
- increased number of medically assisted deliveries and better postnatal care.
- increased number of couples with small families.
- better detection and cure of STDs (Sexually Transmitted Diseases).

Awareness of Reproductive Health

Some of the measures taken for the awareness of reproductive health are as follows

- The family planning programmes were initiated in India in 1951 and were periodically assessed over the past decades. These programmes were improved and later included reproduction related areas under the popular name **Reproductive and Child Healthcare** (RCH) programmes. It was launched in 1997. Major tasks of RCH programme are
  - creating awareness among people about reproduction related aspects.
  - providing facilities and support for building up a reproductively healthy society.

- In schools, introducing sex education is a good step to provide right information to adolescents and to discourage them from believing in myths and misconceptions about sex related issues.
- Married couple or those in marriageable age group should be educated about available birth control options, care of pregnant mothers, postnatal care of the mother and child, importance of breast feeding, equal opportunities for the male and female child, etc.
- Successful implementation of action plans like providing medical assistance and care to reproduction related problems, pregnancy, delivery, STDs, abortions, contraception, menstrual problems, infertility, etc. need strong support and infrastructural facilities.

Amniocentesis

- It is a prenatal diagnostic technique based on chromosomal pattern.
- In this technique, a sample of amniotic fluid is taken from the uterus of a pregnant woman to detect the early development of foetus.
- The benefits of amniocentesis include the diagnosis of chromosomal abnormalities and developmental disorders of foetus. However, it is being misused for the sex- determination of foetus, as it leads to female foeticides.
- Therefore, statutory ban on amniocentesis for sex-determination keeps check on female foeticides.

Population Explosion

The tremendous increase in the size and growth rate of population is called population explosion. It occurs due to increased health facilities and better living conditions of population.

- Other reasons for population explosion include
  - Decreased death rate.
  - Declined **Maternal Mortality Rate** (MMR).
  - Decreased **Infant Mortality Rate** (IMR).
  - Increase in the number of people in reproductive age.
- According to the 2001 census report, the population growth rate was around 1.7%, i.e. 17/1000/year. By this rate, our population could double in 33 years. The 15th census of India was conducted in 2011 which showed decadal growth of 17.70%.

Methods to prevent population explosion include

- Raising the marriageable age, i.e. **18** years for females and **21** years for males.
- Couples with small families should be given some incentives.
- Birth control is an important step to control the population growth by motivating smaller families to use contraceptive methods.

Birth Control (Contraception) Methods

Contraceptive methods are ideal if they are user friendly, easily available, effective, reversible with no side effects and non-interfering with the sexual drive, desire and the sexual act. There are several methods of birth control that can be categorised as follows

1. Natural Methods

The natural methods of birth control involve the prevention of sperm and ovum meeting during coitus or reproductive phase.

(i) **Periodic abstinence** or **rhythm method** In this method, couples avoid coitus from day 10-17 (fertile period) of the menstrual cycle.

(ii) **Coitus interruptus** or 'rejected sexual intercourse' or 'pull-out'/withdrawl method. In this method, the penis is withdrawn just before ejaculation, to avoid insemination.

(iii) **Lactational amenorrhea** It is the absence of menstruation during the period of intense lactation following parturition.

2. Barrier Methods

These methods are based on the prevention of ovum and sperm from physically meeting with the help of barriers. The barriers may be mechanical or chemical and can be used by both males and females.

Mechanical Barriers

(i) **Condoms** They are made of thin rubber or latex sheath to cover the penis in male or vagina and cervix in females (femidom). They prevent meeting of sperm and ova. Condoms provide protection from sexually transmitted diseases.

(ii) **Diaphragms, cervical caps and vaults** They are made up of rubber and are inserted into the female reproductive tract to cover the cervix during coitus. They are reusable.

Chemical Barriers

They include spermicidal creams, jellies and foams. They are usually used along with the barriers to increase their contraceptive efficiency.

3. Intra Uterine Devices (IUDs)

These devices are placed in the uterus through vagina by doctors or expert nurses. IUDs are ideal contraceptives for females who want to delay pregnancy.

These are one of the most widely accepted contraception methods in India. These are of following types

- Non-medicated IUDs, e.g. lippes loop.
- Copper-releasing IUDs, e.g. Cu-T, Cu-7 and multiload 375.
- Hormone-releasing IUDs, e.g. progestasert, LNG-20.

IUDs prevent contraception in the following ways

- Increase phagocytosis of sperms within the uterus.
- Copper-releasing IUDs suppress sperm motility and fertilising ability of sperm by releasing copper ions.
- The hormone releasing IUDs make uterus unsuitable for implantation and make the cervix hostile for sperms.

4. Oral Contraceptives

These are hormonal preparations in the form of pills. Their major features include

- Pills are of two types-combined pills and mini pills. **Combined pills** (Mala-D and Mala-N) contain synthetic progesterone and oestrogen whereas **mini pills** contain progestin (progesterone like synthetic hormone) only.
- Oral pills inhibit ovulation and modify the quality of cervical mucus to prevent/retard the motility of sperms. They also modify uterine endometrium by making it unsuitable for implantation.
- Oral pills have to be taken daily for a period of 21 days starting within the first five days of menstrual cycle.
- **Saheli**, an oral contraceptive pill developed by scientists at **Central Drug Research Institute** (CDRI), Lucknow, contains a non-steroid called **centchroman**. It is once-a-week pill, with very few side effects and high contraceptive value.

5. Implants or Injections

These are effective for longer period and their mode of action is similar to that of oral contraceptives. Progesterone alone or in combination with oestrogen is used by females as injections (Depo Provera) or implants under the skin.

6. Emergency Contraceptives

These include administration of high dose of progesterone or progestogen-oestrogen combinations within 72 hours of coitus. These have been found to be very effective in preventing possible pregnancy due to unprotected intercourse.

7. Sterilisation or Surgical Methods

Sterilisation methods are used by male or female partner as a terminal, permanent and stable method to prevent pregnancies. These methods block the transport of gametes and prevent conception. These are of following two types

(i) **Vasectomy** is applied in case of males. In this method, a small portion of vas deferens is removed or cut and tied up through an incision on the scrotum to prevent the passage of sperms from the testes to copulatory organ, i.e penis.

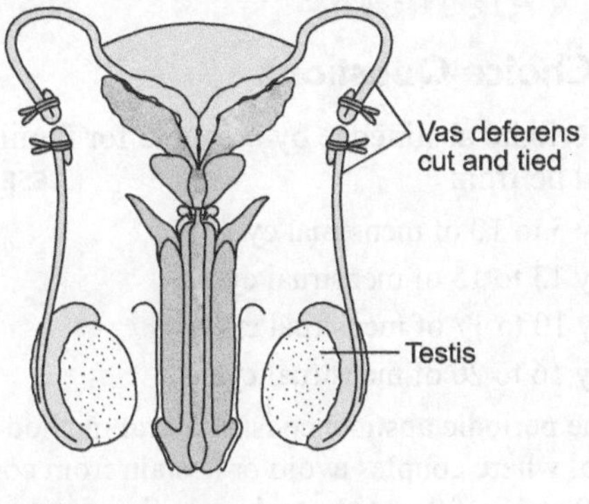

Figure 3.1 Vasectomy in male

(ii) **Tubectomy** is applied in case of females, where a small part of Fallopian tube is removed or cut and tied up through a small incision in the abdomen or through vagina to prevent the passage of ova from ovary to Fallopian tube.

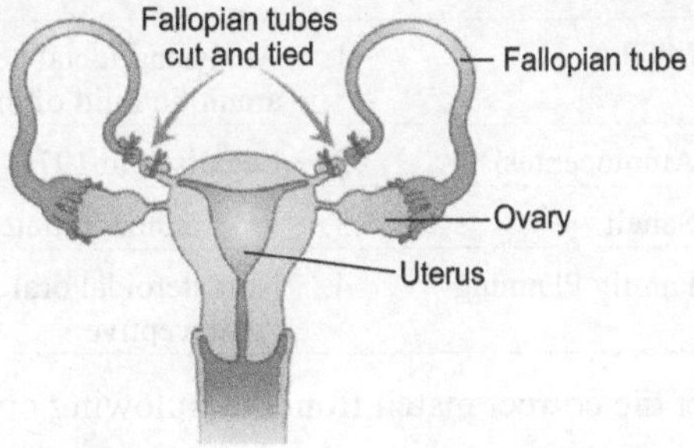

Figure 3.2 Tubectomy in female

Both of these methods are highly effective, but poorly reversible.

Medical Termination of Pregnancy (MTP)

It is the intentional or voluntary termination of pregnancy (induced abortion) before the full term. MTP has following characteristics

- The Government of India had legalised MTP in **1971** with some strict conditions to avoid its misuse. These are important to check indiscriminate and illegal female foeticides, which are reported to be high in India.
- MTP is done in certain cases where pregnancy can be harmful and even fatal either to the mother or to the foetus or both or due to the failure of contraceptive used during coitus.
- MTPs are considered relatively safe during the first trimester (upto 12 weeks) of pregnancy.
- During second trimester, MTPs are unsafe and could be fatal too.
- About 45-50 million MTPs are carried out in a year all over the world. These have a significant role in decreasing population though they are not meant for that purpose.
- Drawback of MTP is that it is being misused to abort the normal female foetus. It has also raised many emotional, ethical and social issues too.

PYQs Previous Years' Questions

1 Mark Questions

Multiple Choice Questions

1. The periodic abstinence by a couple for family planning should be from **CBSE 2024 (Set-I)**
   (a) day 5 to 10 of menstrual cycle
   (b) day 13 to 15 of menstrual cycle
   (c) day 10 to 17 of menstrual cycle
   (d) day 16 to 20 of menstrual cycle

Ans. (c) The periodic abstinence is a natural method of birth control where couples avoid or abstain from coitus from day 10 to 17 of the menstrual cycle (i.e. fertile period) when ovulation could be expected.

2. Given below are four aspects of Reproductive Health in Column A and their related information in Column B.

	Column A (Terms used in reproductive health)		Column B (Significant information)
A.	MTP	1.	Analysing foetal cells from amniotic fluid of the foetus
B.	Amniocentesis	2.	Legalised in 1971
C.	Saheli	3.	Programme initiated in 1951
D.	Family Planning	4.	Non-steroidal oral contraceptive

Select the correct match from the following options.

Codes **CBSE 2023**

	A	B	C	D
(a)	4	2	3	1
(b)	2	1	4	3
(c)	1	3	2	4
(d)	2	1	3	4

Ans. (b) A–2, B–1, C–4, D–3

3. Given below are four contraceptive methods and their modes of action. Select the correct match.

	Methods		Mode of action
A.	Condom	1.	Ovum not able to reach Fallopian tube
B.	Vasectomy	2.	Prevents ovulation
C.	Pill	3.	Prevents sperm reaching the cervix
D.	Tubectomy	4.	Semen contains no sperms

CBSE SQP 2023

	A	B	C	D
(a)	1	2	3	4
(b)	2	3	4	1
(c)	3	4	2	1
(d)	4	1	3	2

Ans. (c) A–3, B–4, C–2, D–1

4. The mode of action of the copper ions in an IUD is to **CBSE SQP 2021-22 Term-I**
   (a) increase the movement of sperms
   (b) decrease the movement of the sperms
   (c) make the uterus unsuitable for implantation
   (d) make the cervix hostile to the sperms

Ans. (b) decrease the movement of the sperms

5. An IUD recommended to promote the cervix hostility to the sperms is **CBSE 2021-22 Term-I**
   (a) Cu-T
   (b) Multiload-375
   (c) LNG-20
   (d) Cu7

Ans. (d) Cu7

Assertion-Reason Type Questions

Direction (Q. Nos. 6-9) consist of two statements Assertion and Reason. Answer these questions selecting the appropriate option given below

(a) Both Assertion and Reason are true and Reason is the correct explanation of Assertion

(b) Both Assertion and Reason are true and Reason is not the correct explanation of Assertion

(c) Assertion is true, but Reason is false

(d) Assertion is false, but Reason is true

6. **Assertion** Determining the sex of an unborn child followed by MTP is an illegal practice.

Reason Amniocentesis is a practice to test the presence of genetic disorders also. **CBSE 2023**

Ans. (b) Both Assertion and Reason are true, but Reason is not correct explanation of Assertion.

7. **Assertion** Lactational amenorrhea is the natural method of contraception.

Reason It increases the phagocytosis of sperm. **CBSE SQP 2021-22**

Ans. (c) Assertion is true, but Reason is false.

Lactational amenorrhea is the natural method of contraception, as ovulation does not occur in this period and the chances of contraception are nil. This method is reliable for a maximum period of 6 months after delivery.

8. **Assertion** Vasectomy is a sterilisation procedure advised for females as a terminal method.

Reason In vasectomy, a small part of the vas deferens is removed or tied by blocking gamete transport therefore preventing conception. **CBSE 2021-22 Term-I**

Ans. (d) Assertion is false, but Reason is true.

9. **Assertion** Saheli, an oral contraceptive for females, contains a steroidal preparation.

Reason It is 'once a week' pill with very few side effects. **CBSE SQP 2021-22**

Ans. (d) Assertion is false, but Reason is true.

Saheli is a non-steroidal oral contraceptive pill for females, developed by scientists at CDRI, Lucknow.

Very Short Answer Type Questions

10. Our government has intentionally imposed strict conditions for MTP in our country. Justify giving a reason. **Delhi 2017**

Ans. MTP or induced abortion is the termination of pregnancy due to certain medical reasons. Government of India legalised MTP in 1971 with strict conditions to avoid its misuse, i.e. to check indiscriminate and illegal female foeticides.

11. Name an IUD that you would recommend to promote the cervix hostility to sperms. **Delhi 2014C**

Ans. The hormone releasing IUDs, e.g. progestasert and LNG-20 are recommended to promote the cervix hostility to sperms.

12. State one reason, why breastfeeding the baby acts as a natural contraceptive for the mother. **Delhi 2014C**

Ans. **Lactation** or **Breastfeeding** the baby delays the onset or return of menstruation and ovulation cycle due to interference of hormone prolactin. Therefore, the chances of conception are nil during this period, i.e. up to six months. Hence, breastfeeding the baby (lactational amenorrhea) may act as a natural contraceptive for mother.

13. Mention one positive and one negative application of amniocentesis. **Delhi 2010**

Ans. Applications of amniocentesis are

(i) **Positive application** It can be used to diagnose any chromosomal abnormality or genetic disorder in foetus. (½)

(ii) **Negative application** It can be used to determine the sex of foetus and lead to female foeticide. (½)

2 Marks Questions

14. Mention one advantage and one disadvantage of amniocentesis. **CBSE 2024 (Set-II)**

Ans. Amniocentesis is a pre-natal medical procedure where amniotic fluid is used as a sample to diagnose chromosomal abnormalities, foetal infections and sex determination.

Advantages of Amniocentesis It helps in finding out genetic disorders such as Down's syndrome, sickle-cell anaemia, etc. in the baby. (1)

Disadvantages of Amniocentesis It may be used to determine the sex of the unborn child and be misused to selectively abort female foetus. (1)

15. State the composition and principle of oral pills as a contraceptive measure taking the example of Saheli. **CBSE SQP 2021-22**

Or Name an oral pill used as a contraceptive by human females. Explain, how does it prevent pregnancy? **Delhi 2011**

Or Why is Saheli a well-accepted contraceptive pill? **Foreign 2010**

Ans. Saheli is a non-steroidal preparation that contains centchroman to carryout effective contraceptive functions. Other contraceptive oral pills like mala-D contains either progestogens or the combination of progestogen and oestrogen. These pills inhibit ovulation and implantation and alter the quality of cervical mucus to prevent or retard the entry of sperm.

16. Name any two copper related IUDs. Explain how it acts as a contraceptive? **CBSE SQP 2020**

Or Why is Cu-T considered a good contraceptive device to space children? **Delhi 2011**

Ans. Copper-T (Cu-T) and multiload 375 are copper releasing Intra Uterine Devices (IUD) that are inserted by experts and serve as an effective contraceptive in the following ways

(i) Increase phagocytosis of sperms within the uterus.

(ii) Copper ions released by Cu-T suppress the motility of sperms and their fertilising ability. **(1+1)**

17. The alarming population growth is leading to scarcity of basic requirements. Suggest with reason, any two population control measures other than contraception to address the situation. **CBSE SQP 2018**

Ans. The population control methods other than contraceptives are

(i) Statutory raising of marriageable age to 21 years for males and 18 years for females. This will delay new births.

(ii) Government should provide some incentives to the couples having small families.

18. Mention the problems that are taken care by Reproduction and Child Healthcare Programme. **All India 2016**

Ans. Reproduction and Child Healthcare (RCH) programmes cover wide range of reproduction related areas. They include

(i) creating awareness among people about various reproduction related aspects.

(ii) support for building up a reproductively healthy society by providing increased medical facilities, better postnatal care, better detection and cure of diseases like STDs, etc.

19. What do oral pills contain and how do they act as effective contraceptives? **Delhi 2014C**

Ans. Oral contraceptives or pills contain either progestogens or progesterone-oestrogen combinations. **(1)**

They function as contraceptives by

(i) inhibiting ovulation.

(ii) inhibiting implantation.

(iii) altering the quality of cervical mucus to prevent the motility of sperms in female reproductive tract. **(1)**

Concept Enhancer Oral contraceptives do not prove to be a good form of birth control when doses are missed frequently. Side effects of these contraceptives vary depending on the pills hormone levels and types.

20. Describe the lactational amenorrhea method of birth control. **All India 2011**

Ans. Lactation amenorrhea refers to the absence of menstruation during the period of intense lactation following parturition. It is a birth control method because

(i) ovulation and other events of menstrual cycle are stopped at this time.

(ii) As long as the mother breastfeeds her child, chances of conception are nil because of the suppressed gonadotropin activity.

However, this method is generally reliable up to only six months after delivery.

21. At the time of Independence, the population of India was 350 million, which exploded to over 1 billion by May 2000.

List any two reasons for this rise in population and any two steps taken by the government to check this population explosion. **Foreign 2011**

Ans. Reasons for rise in population include

(i) All-round development in various fields and increased health facilities along with better living conditions.

(ii) Reduced maternal and infant mortality rate.

Two major steps taken by the government to check this population growth are

(a) People are educated and support the idea of small family by using various contraceptive methods.

(b) There is statutory raising of marriageable age of females to 18 years and of males to 21 years.

22. How do copper and hormone releasing IUDs act as contraceptives? Explain. **All India 2010**

Ans. Copper and hormone releasing IUDs act as contraceptives because

(i) Copper IUDs (Cu-T, Cu-7) release Cu ions, which suppress sperm motility and the fertilising capacity of sperms.

(ii) Hormone releasing IUDs (progestasert, LNG-20)

(a) inhibit ovulation.

(b) make the cervix unreceptive to sperms.

(iii) They both increase the phagocytosis of sperms within the uterus.

3 Marks Questions

23. Explain the mode of action of contraceptive pills taken by human females. Mention the schedule to be followed for effective outcome. **CBSE 2024 (Set-I)**

Ans. Contraceptive pills contain small dosage of either progestogens or progestogen - oestrogen combinations. These pills inhibit ovulation and implantation as well as alter the quality of cervical mucus to prevent/retard entry of sperms.

These pills have to be taken daily for a period of 21 days starting preferably within the first five days of menstrual cycle. After a gap of 7 days (during which menstruation occurs) it has to be repeated in the same pattern till the female desires to prevent conception. Saheli, a new oral contraceptive pill is 'once a week pill'. (3)

24. Name and explain a surgical contraceptive method that can be adopted by the male partner of a couple. **CBSE 2023**

Ans. Vasectomy is a surgical contraceptive method that can be adopted by the male partner of a couple. It is a sterilisation method in which a small portion of vas deferens is removed or tied up through a cut or incision on scrotum, thus blocking the transport of sperms from the testes to the copulatory organ.

This method is highly effective as it blocks the transport of gametes. The main disadvantage of this method is that this surgical procedure cannot be reversed.

25. (i) Explain the mode of action of Cu^{++} releasing IUDs as a good contraceptive. How is hormone releasing IUD different from it ?

(ii) Why is 'Saheli' a preferred contraceptive by women (any two reasons)? **All India 2020**

Ans. (i) Cu^{++} ions-releasing IUDs are more efficient methods of contraception because

(a) Cu^{++} ions suppress sperm motility and fertilising capacity of sperms.

(b) Cu-releasing IUDs increase phagocytosis of sperms within the uterus.

(c) It is one of the safest, longterm, most effective, convenient and least expensive reversible contraceptives available.

(d) It has no systemic effects and can be safely used by breastfeeding women.

The hormone releasing IUDs on the other hand make the uterus unsuitable for implantation and the cervix hostile to sperms. (2)

(ii) Saheli is a preferred contraceptive method by women because

(a) it is taken once in a week. (½)

(b) it has very few side effects and high contraceptive value. (½)

26. (i) List any four characteristics of an ideal contraceptive.

(ii) Name two intrauterine contraceptive devices that affect the motility of sperms. **All India 2016**

> **KEY idea**
> Intra Uterine Devices (IUDs) are the ideal contraceptive.

Ans. (i) An ideal contraceptive must have the following four characteristics.

(a) It must be safe and user friendly.

(b) It must be easily available.

(c) It must be reversible with little or no side effects.

(d) It must not interfere with the sexual drive, desire or sexual act of the user. (2)

(ii) Cu-T and Cu-7 are the two examples of IUDs that affect the motility of sperms. (½ + ½)

27. Name two hormones that are constituents of contraceptive pills. Why do they have high and effective contraceptive value? Name a commonly prescribed non-steroidal oral pill. **All India 2014**

Ans. The two hormones that are the constituents of oral pills are

(i) progesterone (ii) oestrogen (1)

They inhibit ovulation and fertilisation and also modify the quality of cervical mucus to prevent or retard the entry of sperms. Hence, they have high and effective contraceptive value.

Saheli is the most commonly prescribed new oral contraceptive pill for females. It contains a non-steroidal preparation called **centchroman**. It is once a week pill with few side effects and high contraceptive value. It was developed by CDRI (Central Drug Research Institute), Lucknow. (2)

28. If implementation of better techniques and new strategies are required to provide more efficient care and assistance to people, then why is there a statutory ban on amniocentesis? Write the use of this technique and give reason to justify the ban. **All India 2014**

Ans. Though implementation of better techniques and new strategies is required to provide more efficient care and assistance to people still, there is a statutory ban on amniocentesis. The test helps to determine any chromosomal abnormalities or genetic disorders, sex of foetus and foetal infections, etc. by using minute amount of amniotic fluid surrounding the foetus.

This prenatal diagnostic test is particularly useful for those women who are at increased risk or have high chances of giving rise to child with genetic disorders or chromosomal problems.

However, this is also misused to determine the sex of foetus which had ultimately lead to increased female foeticides. Therefore, government has imposed a statutory ban to prevent its further misuse and to balance the unequal sex-ratio prevailing in human population.

29. A woman has certain queries as listed below, before starting with contraceptive pills. Answer them.

(i) What do contraceptive pills contain and how do they act as contraceptives?

(ii) What schedule should be followed for taking these pills? **Delhi 2014**

Ans. (i) Refer to answer no. 19. (1)

(ii) The oral contraceptive pills are to be taken daily for 21 days, preferably within the first five days of menstrual cycle. After the onset of menstruation cycle, i.e. 5-7 days, the process is to be repeated in the same pattern (again for 21 days). This schedule is to be followed till the woman wants to avoid conception. (2)

30. (i) Name any two copper releasing IUDs.

(ii) Explain, how do they act as effective contraceptives in human females? **All India 2014**

Ans. (i) The copper releasing IUDs are Cu-T, Cu-7 and multiload-375. (1)

(ii) Refer to answer no. 16. (2)

31. Name and explain the surgical method advised to human males and females as a means of birth control. Mention its one advantage and one disadvantage. **Foreign 2014**

Ans. The surgical or sterilisation methods advised to human males and females as effective means of birth control are

(i) **Vasectomy** (in males) A sterilisation method in which a small portion of vas deferens is removed or cut and tied up through a cut or incision on scrotum. Thus, blocking the transport of sperms from the testes to the copulatory organ. (1)

(ii) **Tubectomy** (in females)- A sterilisation method in which small part of Fallopian tube is removed or cut and tied up through incision in abdomen or through vagina. It blocks the passage of ova from ovary to the site of fertilisation. (1)

The **advantage** of these two methods is that both methods prevent conception as they block the transport of gametes.

The **disadvantage** of this method is that this surgical procedure cannot be reversed, so it is helpful for only those who already have children and do not want to extend their family further. (1)

32. How do 'implants' act as an effective method of contraception in human females? Mention its one advantage over contraceptive pills. **Delhi 2012C**

Ans. Subcutaneous 'implants' contain synthetic progesterone and are placed under the skin. They are an effective contraceptive method as they check ovulation and thicken cervical mucus to prevent sperm transport.

'Subcutaneous implants' are more advantageous than contraceptive pills as they are long lasting and once implanted, they are effective for upto 5 years.

5 Marks Questions

33. Given below are certain situations. Analyse the situation and suggest the name of suitable contraceptive device along with mode of action. **CBSE SQP 2024**

Situation	Requirement of contraceptive for	Name of contraceptive device	Mode of action
1	Blocking the entry of sperms through cervix		
2	Spacing between children		
3	Effective emergency contraceptive		
4	Terminal method to prevent any more pregnancy in female		
5	Sterilization in male		

Ans.

S No.	Requirement of contraceptive for	Name of contraceptive device	Mode of action
1	Blocking the entry of sperms through cervix	Diaphragms/ cervical caps/ vaults	Cover the cervix during coitus
2	Spacing between children	Cu or hormone releasing IUDs such as Cu T/Cu7/ Multiload 375/ Progestasert/L NG 20	Cu ions from Cu containing IUDs increase phagocytosis of sperms within uterus, suppress sperm motility and fertilising capacity/ hormone releasing IUDs make uterus unsuitable for implantation
3	Effective emergency contraceptive	Pills containing Progestogens or progestogen-oestrogen combination or IUDs within 72 hours of coitus	Pills inhibit ovulation and implantation as well as alter the quality of cervical mucus to prevent the entry of sperms/IUDs - Cu ions increase phagocytosis of sperms within uterus, suppress sperm motility and fertilising capacity/ hormone releasing IUDs make uterus unsuitable for implantation.
4	Terminal method to prevent any more pregnancy in female	Tubectomy	Block gamete transport and prevent conception.
5	Sterilisation in male	Vasectomy	Blocks sperm transport.

34. Your school has been selected by the Department of Education to organise and host an interschool seminar on 'Reproductive Health Problems and Practices'. However, many parents are reluctant to permit their wards to attend it. Their argument is that the topic is 'too embarrassing'.

Put forth four arguments with apporpriate reasons and explanation to justify the topic to be very essential and timely. **All India 2015**

Ans. Parents should encourage their children to attend such seminar as they will get right information regarding myths and misconceptions about sex related aspects. Following are the four points to justify this topic to be essential

(i) Awareness of problems due to uncontrolled population growth, social evils like sex abuse and sex related crimes, etc. need to be created so that children should think and take up necessary steps to prevent them and thereby build up a reproductively healthy society.

(ii) Large group of school students comprises of adolescents who have attained puberty. Therefore, these seminars are necessary to provide medical help and care for reproduction related problems like menstrual problems, infertility, pregnancy, delivery, contraception, abortions, etc.

(iii) Knowledge about Sexually Transmitted Diseases (STDs) is essential as children should be aware that unprotected sex with multiple partners results in the transmission of sex related problems.

(iv) Increasing population is a major problem of India which is directly related with reproductive health. Children should be aware of family planning programmes such as Reproductive and Child Healthcare (RCH) programmes.

TOPIC 2

Sexually Transmitted Diseases (STDs) and Infertility

STDs are those diseases or infections, which are transmitted through sexual intercourse. These are also called as **Venereal Diseases** (VDs) or **Reproductive Tract Infections** (RTIs). Some common STDs are gonorrhoea, syphilis, genital herpes, trichomoniasis, hepatitis-B, AIDS, etc.

Among the above mentioned STDs, three viral infections, i.e. AIDS, genital herpes and hepatitis-B are not curable, while others are curable.

The early general symptoms of STDs are

- itching in genital area.
- fluid discharge.
- slight pain in genital areas.
- swellings in the genital region.

The patients with STDs remain undetected and untreated due to

- the absence or less significant symptoms in the early stages of infection.
- social stigma attached to the STDs.

The late detection leads to the complications like Pelvic Inflammatory Diseases (PIDs), abortions, still births, ectopic pregnancies, infertility and the cancer of the reproductive tract.

The incidence of these diseases is high in the persons of age group 15-24 years. These infections can be avoided or prevented by the following ways

- Avoid sexual practices with unknown partners or multiple partners.
- Use of condoms during coitus.
- In case of any doubt, visit a doctor immediately for the detection and treatment.

Infertility

The inability to produce children inspite of unprotected sexual practices is called infertility. It is one of the major aspects of reproductive health.

The reasons of infertility can be physical, congenital diseases, drugs, immunological or even psychological.

Common causes of infertility in males include oligospermia (low sperm count), azoospermia, cryptorchidism (failure of testes to descend into the scrotum), etc.

Assisted Reproductive Technologies (ARTs)

Sometimes corrective treatments do not lead to the treatment of infertility. In such cases, ARTs are used. Some of the ARTs are

IVF (*In Vitro* Fertilisation) or Test-Tube Baby Programme

(i) Ova from wife/donor female and sperms from the husband/donor male are made to fertilised to form zygote in the laboratory under same conditions as in the body (*in vivo*). This is called *in vitro* fertilisation (fertilisation outside the body).

(ii) Zygote or early embryo is transferred into Fallopian tube or uterus for further development. This is called **Embryo Transfer** (ET). It can be of following two types, namely

(a) **ZIFT** (Zygote Intra Fallopian Transfer) in which embryos up to 8 blastomeres are transferred into the Fallopian tubes.

(b) **IUT** (Intra Uterine Transfer) in which embryos of more than 8 blastomeres are transferred into the uterus.

ICSI (Intra Cytoplasmic Sperm Injection)

It is carried out by directly injecting the sperm into the ovum to form an embryo in the laboratory. Embryo transfer is done later on by IUT technique in woman.

In Vivo Fertilisation

It is performed by the fusion of gametes within the female and then this zygote can be used for ZIFT or IUT.

GIFT (Gamete Intra Fallopian Transfer)

It is done by the transfer of an ovum collected from a donor female into the Fallopian tube of another female, who is unable to produce ova, but can provide suitable conditions for fertilisation and further development of the foetus.

PYQs Previous Years' Questions

1 Mark Questions

Multiple Choice Questions

1. Observe the schematic representation of assisted reproductive technology given below

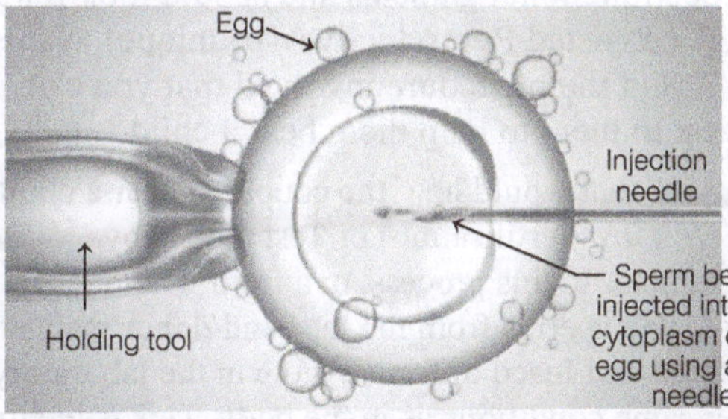

Identify the most appropriate technique depicted in the above diagram. **CBSE 2024 (Set-II)**

(a) IUT (b) IUI
(c) ICSI (d) ZIFT

Ans. (c) The given schematic representation of assisted reproductive technology belongs to ICSI, i.e. Intra Cytoplasmic Sperm Injection. In ICSI, sperm is directly injected into the ovum to form an embryo in the laboratory followed by embryo transfer.

2. Given below are Column A with a list of certain Assisted Reproductive Technologies (ART) and in Column B the procedures followed during ART.

	Column A (Names of ART)		Column B (Procedures)
A.	GIFT	1.	Transfer of ovum from a donor into the Fallopian tube of another female.
B.	ICSI	2.	Transfer of semen from the donor into the vagina of the female.
C.	ZIFT	3.	Injecting sperms directly into the ovum.
D.	IUI	4.	Transfer of early embryos into the Fallopian tube.

Choose the option where ART correctly matches with the procedure. **CBSE 2023**

	A	B	C	D
(a)	1	2	3	4
(b)	4	1	2	3
(c)	4	3	1	2
(d)	1	3	4	2

Ans. (d) A–1, B–3, C–4, D–2.

3. An infertile couple was advised to undergo *in vitro* Fertilisation by the doctor. Out of the options given below, select the correct stage for transfer to the Fallopian tube for successful results. **CBSE SQP 2023**

(a) Zygote only
(b) Zygote or early embryo upto 8 blastomeres
(c) Embryos with more than 8 blastomeres
(d) Blastocyst stage

Ans. (b) Zygote or early embryo upto 8 blastomeres.

4. A female undergoing IVF treatment has blocked Fallopian tubes. The technique by which the embryo with more than 8 blastomeres will be transferred into the female for further development is **CBSE SQP 2021-22 Term-I**

(a) ZIFT (b) GIFT (c) IUT (d) AI

Ans. (c) IUT

5. Identify the disease which is not a sexually transmitted disease. **CBSE 2021-22 Term-I**

(a) Gonorrhea (b) Syphilis
(c) Amoebiasis (d) Chlamydiasis

Ans. (c) Amoebiasis

6. A procedure that finds use in testing for genetic disorders, but is also miused for foeticide is **CBSE SQP 2020**

(a) lactational amenorrhea (b) amniocentesis
(c) artificial insemination (d) parturition

Ans. (b) amniocentesis

Assertion-Reason Type Questions

Direction (Q. Nos. 7-8) *consist of two statements, Assertion (A) and Reason (R). Answer these questions selecting the appropriate option given below.*

(a) Both Assertion and Reason are true and Reason is the correct explanation of Assertion
(b) Both Assertion and Reason are true, but Reason is not the correct explanation of Assertion
(c) Assertion is true, but Reason is false
(d) Assertion is false, but Reason is true

7. **Assertion** The laws of our country permit legal adoption and it is as yet, one of the best methods for childless couples looking for parenthood.

Reason Emotional, religious and social factors are no deterrents to the legal adoption of orphaned and destitute children in India. **CBSE 2024 (Set-I)**

Ans. (a) Both A and R are true and R is the correct explanation of A.

Our laws permit legal adoption and it is as yet, one of the best methods for couples looking for parenthood. Emotional, religious and social factors are no deterrents to the legal adoption of orphaned and destitute children in India unlike the Assisted Reproductive Technologies (ARTs) that face emotional, religious and social issues.

8. **Assertion** Very often persons suffering from Sexually Transmitted Diseases (STD) do not go for timely detection and proper treatment.

Reason Absence or less significant symptoms in the early stages of STDs and the social stigma attached to the disease. **CBSE 2021-22 Term-I**

Ans. (a) Both Assertion and Reason are true and Reason is the correct explanation of Assertion

Very Short Answer Type Question

9. In case of an infertile couple, the male partner can inseminate normally, but the mobility of sperms is below 40 per cent. Judge, which kind of ART is suitable in this situation to form an embryo in the laboratory, without involving a donor. **CBSE SQP 2018**

Ans. In case of male infertility, which occurs due to low motility of sperm, the effective ART used is Intra Cytoplasmic Sperm Injection (ICSI).

2 Marks Questions

10. Write the basic steps followed in the Assisted Reproductive Technologies (ART) programme to help childless couples. Why is it also known as test-tube baby programme? **CBSE 2024 (Set-I)**

Ans. Assisted Reproductive Technologies (ARTs) programmes or *In Vitro* Fertilisation (IVF) is very helpful to such couples who cannot have a baby by natural means.

The steps of ART are as follows

(i) The sperm from male donor and ova from female donor is collected.

(ii) They are fertilised outside the body in similar condition as that of the body.

(iii) Embryo transfer takes place.
The early embryo sac upto 8 blastomeres is transferred into the Fallopian tube and more than 8 blastomeres embryos are transferred into uterus.

(iv) Further development of embryo takes place inside the womb of mother in usual manner.
The baby formed by ARTs is called test tube baby because embryo is formed in the lab in a test tube, instead of the woman's Fallopian tube. The programme is thus called test tube baby programme.

11. After a brief medical examination a healthy couple came to know that both of them are unable to produce functional gametes and should look for an 'ART' (Assisted Reproductive Technique). Name the 'ART' and the procedure involved that you can suggest to them to help them bear a child. **Delhi 2015**

Ans. The ART that would help the couple to bear a child is IVF (*In Vitro* Fertilisation) or Test tube baby programme. In this process, ova from wife/donor female and sperms from the husband/donor male are collected and fused to form zygote in the laboratory under same conditions as in the body. This is *in vitro* fertilisation (fertilisation outside the body).

Zygote or early embryo is transferred into Fallopian tube or uterus for further development. This is called **Embryo Transfer** (ET). It can be Zygote Intra Fallopian Transfer (ZIFT) or Intra Uterine Transfer (IUT).

12. An infertile couple is advised to adopt test tube baby programme. Describe two principal procedures adopted for such technologies. **Delhi 2015**

Ans. Refer to text on page no. 80. (Assisted reproductive technologies).

13. A childless couple has agreed for a test tube baby programme. List only the basic steps the procedure would involve to conceive the baby. **Delhi 2015C**

Or (i) Give any two reasons for infertility among young couple.

(ii) Test tube baby programme is a boon to such couples. Explain the steps followed in the procedure. **All India 2010C**

Ans. (i) The reasons of infertility in young people can be physical, congenital diseases, use of drugs, immunological or even psychological factors.

(ii) In test tube programme,

(a) Ova from the wife or a donor female and the sperms from the husband or a donor male are allowed to fuse under simulated conditions in the laboratory. It is called *in vitro* fertilisation.

(b) Embryo is then transferred into the uterus or Fallopian tube for further development.

The process of embryo transfer is done in following ways

Zygote or embryo up to 8 blastomeres is transferred into Fallopian tube (ZIFT).

Embryo with more than 8 blastomeres is transferred into uterus (IUT).

14. 'Intra Cytoplasmic Sperm Injection (ICSI)' and 'Gamete Intra Fallopian Transfer (GIFT)' are two assisted reproductive technologies. How is one different from the other? **All India 2014C**

Ans. In Gamete Intra Fallopian Transfer (GIFT), the ovum from a healthy donor female is transferred to a female, who cannot produce ova. However, she can provide suitable environment for fertilisation and embryo development (*in vivo* fertilisation).

In Intra Cytoplasmic Sperm Injection (ICSI), the fertilisation is done *in vitro* by injecting sperms directly into the ovum from a donor female, under simulated conditions. The embryo is thus, formed in laboratory and which is later transferred to the uterus or Fallopian tube for further development.

15. Why is ZIFT a boon to childless couples? Explain the procedure. **Delhi 2013C**

Ans. ZIFT (Zygote Intra Fallopian Transfer) is a boon to childless couples as it helps them to become parents. In this technique, ova from wife/donor female and sperms from husband/donor male are fused to form zygote in laboratory. Zygote is allowed to divide up to 8 blastomeres stage and it is at this stage, that the zygote or early embryo is transferred into the Fallopian tube. Implantation takes place in the uterus where further development takes place.

16. State any four methods to overcome infertility in human couples. **Delhi 2011C**

Ans. Following are the four methods to overcome infertility problems in human couples

(i) **Test tube baby programme** In this method, the fusion of ovum and sperm is done outside the body of a woman (*in vitro* fertilisation) to form zygote. This zygote further divides to form embryo. The embryo is then implanted in the uterus where it develops into a foetus and then into the child.

(ii) **Intra Cytoplasmic Sperm Injection** (ICSI) In this technique, embryo is formed in the laboratory by directly injecting the sperm into the ovum followed by embryo transfer.

(iii) **Artificial Insemination Technique** (AIT) In this technique, semen (containing sperms) from husband or donor is artificially introduced into the vagina or uterus (IUI).

(iv) **Gamete Intra Fallopian Transfer** (GIFT) In this, sperm and the unfertilised ova are transferred into the Fallopian tube of the female and they are allowed to fuse naturally.

Concept Enhancer Infertility is very common and can affect people of all sexes and ages. A lot of possible causes of infertility include

- Chemotherapy
- Excessive drug/alcohol use
- Smoking cigarette
- Improper diet

3 Marks Questions

17. Suggest and explain the assisted reproductive techniques which will help a couple to have children, where the female had a blockage in the Fallopian tube and the male partner had a low sperm count. **CBSE SQP 2019**

Ans. ART stands for the Assisted Reproductive Techniques used for the treatment of infertility. These include GIFT, ZIFT, IVF and ICSI, etc.

As the female partner is having blockage in the Fallopian tube, *in vitro* fertilisation technique will help her conceive. In this method, ova from female partner and sperms from male partner are made to fertilise in the laboratory under same conditions as in human body.

As the male partner is suffering from low sperm count, Intra cytoplasmic sperm injection (ICSI) technique should be used to directly inject sperm into the ovum.

18. A couple where both husband and wife are producing functional gametes, but the wife is still unable to conceive, is seeking medical aid. Describe any one method that you can suggest to this couple to become happy parents. **All India 2014**

Ans. In case, if both husband and wife are producing functional gametes, but wife is not able to conceive, the IVF technique can be employed to bless them with child.

Method of *in vitro* fertilisation is given below

(i) Gametes from both husband and wife, i.e. sperm and ova are collected, i.e. these are fused to form zygote under laboratory conditions. As the fertilisation takes place outside the female body, it is referred to as *in vitro* fertilisation.

(ii) The zygote or embryo is then either transferred to Fallopian tubes (if up to 8 blastomeres), i.e. ZIFT or to the uterus (more than 8 blastomeres), i.e. IUT.

Concept Enhancer IUT and IVF embryo transfer are the most popular techniques for treating male factor infertility.

19. Suggest and explain any three Assisted Reproductive Technologies (ART) to an infertile couple. **All India 2013**

Ans. Refer to text on page no. 80.

5 Marks Questions

20. Placed below are case studies of some couples who were not able to have kids. These couples are not ready for adoption or taking gametes from donors. After thoroughly examining the cases, which Assisted Reproductive Technology will you suggest to these couples as a medical expert? Explain briefly with justification of each case. **CBSE SQP 2024**

Couple	Test reports of female partner	Test reports of male partner
Couple 1	Normal reports	Normal sperms in testes, Missing connection in epididymis and Vas deferens
Couple 2	Blockage in the Fallopian tube	Normal reports
Couple 3	Normal reports	Poor semen parameters in terms of count, motility and morphology
Couple 4	low ovarian reserve	Normal reports
Couple 5	Sterilisation in male	Morphologically abnormal sperms

Ans. **Couple 1** Normal reports of female, Normal sperms in testes, Missing connection in epididymis and Vas deferens in male.

Assisted Reproductive Technology

Semen will be devoid of sperms in this case. So, *In Vitro* Fertilisation (IVF) by collecting the sperms from epididymis, followed by ZIFT or IUT (Test Tube Baby) is suggested. ZIFT is the transfer of zygote or early embryo up to 8 blastomeres in Fallopian tube and IUT refers to transfer of embryos with more than 8 blastomeres in uterus.

Couple 2 Blockage in the Fallopian tube in the female, Normal reports of male.

Assisted Reproductive Technology

Blockage of Fallopian tube will not allow the transfer of sperms to the site of fertilisation. *In Vitro* Fertilisation (IVF) followed by IUT (Test Tube Baby) is suggested. It would involve transfer of embryo with more than 8 blastomeres in uterus.

Couple 3 Normal reports of female, Poor semen parameters in terms of count, motility and morphology in male partner.

Assisted Reproductive Technology

Intracytoplasmic sperm injection (ICSI) in which sperm is directly injected into the ovum. Artificial insemination procedure is used mainly when sperms have poor characteristic or low sperm count.

Couple 4 Low ovarian reserve in female, Normal reports in male

Assisted Reproductive Technology

In Vitro Fertilisation (IVF) by selection of normal blastocysts from ovary followed by Zygote intra-fallopian transfer involving transfer of zygote or early embryos up to 8 blastomeres (ZIFT) or transfer of embryo with more than 8 blastomeres in the uterus (IUT) is suggested.

Couple 5 Poor ovarian reserve in female, morphologically abnormal sperms in male partner.

Assisted Reproductive Technology

ICSI intracytoplasmic sperm injection in which selected normal sperms will be injected into the selected blastocyst. Intracytoplasmic sperm injection (ICSI) procedure is used mainly when sperms have poor characteristic or low sperm count.

21. (i) List any two reasons other than physical and congenital disorders for causing infertility in couples.

(ii) Explain how IVF as a technique helped childless couples in having children?

(iii) Compare GIFT with ICSI. **All India 2020**

Ans. (i) Reasons of infertility in couples (other than physical and congenital) are

(a) Drugs, alcoholism suppress gametogenesis.

(b) Immunological. **(1)**

(ii) *In vitro* fertilisation refers to reproductive procedure that is performed outside the organism's body. In this technique, egg cells are fertilised by sperms outside the woman's womb in a test tube.

It is a major treatment for infertility in couples especially when other methods of achieving conception have failed. The process involves removal of ova (eggs) from the woman's ovaries and their fusion with the sperms in a fluid medium.

Once fertilisation has occurred, the embryo is allowed to develop for 3-5 days. It is then transferred to the patient's uterus. **(2)**

(iii) Comparison between GIFT and ICSI are

GIFT	ICSI
It is Gamete Intra Fallopian Transfer.	It is Intra Cytoplasmic Sperm Injection.
The technique is suitable for couples where woman is unable to produce egg, but can provide suitable conditions for fertilisation and further foetal development.	This technique is used to assist fertilisation of an egg.
Ovum is collected from donor and transferred to Fallopian tube of recipient female.	Sperm is injected into the cytoplasm of an egg with a microscopic needle to allow fertilisation after which the embryo is placed in uterus of female.

(2)

22. (i) Explain one application of each one of the following. **Delhi 2019**

(a) Amniocentesis (b) Lactational amenorrhea
(c) ZIFT

(ii) Prepare a poster for the school programme depicting the objectives of 'Reproductive and Child Healthcare Programme'.

Ans. (i) (a) Amniocentesis is often performed to diagnose chromosomal abnormalities and developmental disorders of foetus.

(b) Lactational amenorrhea is the absence of menstruation during the period of intense lactation following parturition. Since ovulation does not occur in this period, the chances of conception are nil. It is a natural method to avoid unwanted pregnancy.

(c) **ZIFT** (Zygote Intra Fallopian Transfer) is related to embryo transfer in the test tube programme. In this technique, the zygote or embryo up to 8 blastomeres is transferred into the Fallopian tube. (3)

(ii)

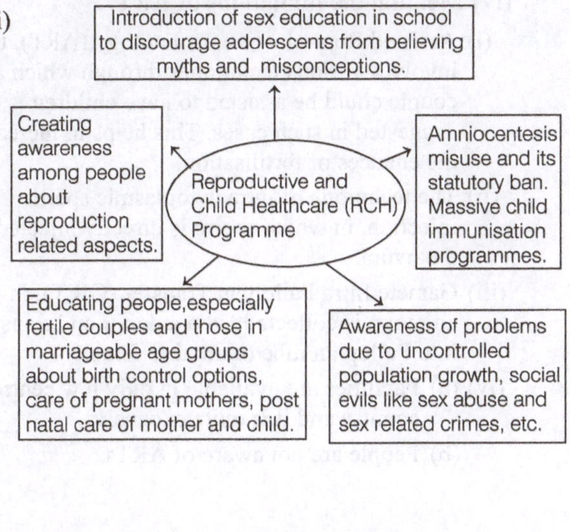

(2)

Case Based/Source Based/Passage Based Questions

(Based on Complete Chapter)

1. Read the following and answer the questions given below

India was amongst the first few countries to initiate action plans and programmes at the national level to attain total reproductive health as a social goal. These programmes are called family planning programmes.

(i) The programmes of family planning were initiate in the year
(a) 1941
(b) 1951
(c) 1952
(d) 1956

(ii) Identify the incorrect statement out of the following.
(a) The major task of RCH programme was to create awareness among people about various aspects of reproduction
(b) The government and non- government agencies use A-V and print media for creating awarenes among people
(c) Introducing sex education in schools
(d) Not imposing ban on amniocentesis

(iii) The population size increases due to
(a) immigration
(b) natality
(c) emigration
(d) Both (a) and (b)

(iv) Mortality is also called
(a) birth rate
(b) population/ area
(c) death rate
(d) movement of people into area

(v) The reason behind population explosion can be
(a) rapid increase in death rate
(b) increase in number of people of reproducible age
(c) rapid decline in death rate
(d) Both (b) and (c)

Ans. (i) (b) 1951
(ii) (d) Not imposing ban on amniocentesis
(iii) (d) Both (a) and (b)
(iv) (c) death rate
(v) (d) Both (b) and (c)

2. Consider the following graph showing the trend of sexually transmitted diseases in a country '*X*' in both males and females.

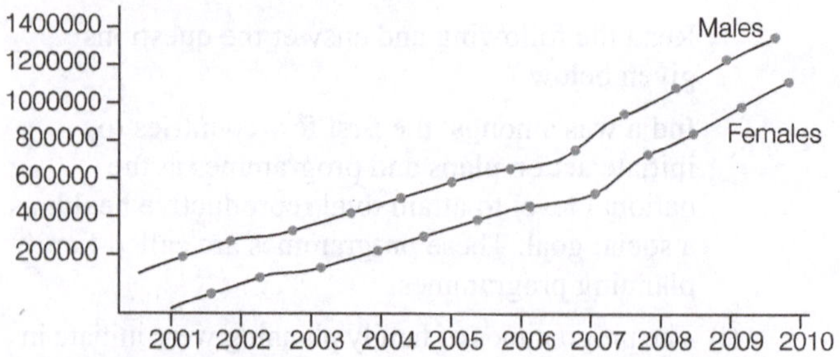

(i) Which of the following is not a cause of rising case of STDs in men?
(a) Unprotected sexual intercouses
(b) Not using femidoms
(c) Intercouses with multiple partners
(d) Use of condoms

(ii) The sexually transmitted infection that can affect both the male and female genital and may damage the eyes of new born babies born of infected mothers is
(a) AIDS (b) syphilis
(c) gonorrhoea (d) hepatitis

(iii) Hepatitis B is transmitted through
(a) blood transfusion (b) intimate physical contact
(c) sexual contact (d) All of these

(iv) Which of the following should not be avoided to prevent contracting STIs?
(a) Using condoms during intercourse
(b) Sex with unknown partners
(c) Sex with multiple partners
(d) Sharing needles during blood transfusion

Ans. (i) (b) (ii) (c)
(iii) (d) (iv) (a)

3. With reference to the diagram of (a) tubectomy and (b) vasectomy, answer the following questions.

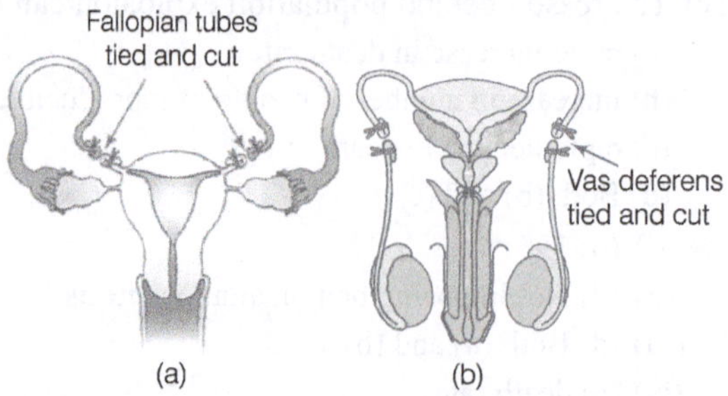

(i) Define sterilisation or surgical method of contraception.

(ii) Describe the process of tubectomy and vasectomy.

(iii) Why these methods are generally not recommended to couples?

Ans. (i) Sterilisation involves the terminal and permanent modification of reproductive ducts, e.g. tubectomy in women and vasectomy in men. **(1)**

(ii) Tubectomy is a sterilisation procedure in females, where a small part of the Fallopian tube is removed or cut and tied up through a small incision in the abdomen/vagina. Thus, preventing the ovulated egg to enter Fallopian tube.

Vasectomy is sterilisation procedure in males, where a small part of the vas deferens is removed or cut and tied up through a small incision on the scrotum, thereby preventing sperms to reach urethra. **(2)**

(iii) Though the above described methods are highly effective as they block transport and fusion of gametes, but are irreversible. Thus, they are not advised to couples. **(1)**

4. Read the following and answer the questions given below

During a temple visit, Neha came across her old friend. She learnt that her friend had been visiting different temples and praying to get a child. Neha was astonished and told her friend about the various techniques that assist the childless couples to conceive.

(i) What is ART?

(ii) How is ART helpful, if the male partner has low sperm count in ejaculate?

(iii) Which ART is prescribed to woman who cannot produce ovum but can provide suitable environment for fertilisation?

(iv) Mention the limitations of ART.

Ans. (i) Assisted Reproductive Technology (ART), that involves various techniques through which a couple could be assisted to have children is usually suggested in such cases. This helps in increasing the chances of fertilisation.

(ii) The technique of intra cytoplasmic sperm injection, in which sperm is directly injected into the ovum.

(iii) Gamete Intra Fallopian Transfer (GIFT), in which an ovum is collected from a donor and transferred into Fallopian tube of another female.

(iv) (a) Facilities are available in only few centres in country and it is quite expensive.
(b) People are not aware of ARTs. **(1 × 4)**

CHAPTER TEST

01 Mark Questions

Multiple Choice Questions

1 Intensely lactating mothers do not generally conceive due to the
(a) suppression of gonadotropins
(b) hypersecretion of gonadotropins
(c) suppression of gametic transport
(d) suppression of fertilisation

2 Which of the following is included under barrier methods of birth control?
(a) Vaginal pouch (b) Diaphragm
(c) Cervical cap (d) All of these

3 Which of the following hormones is/are maintained at high level during hormonal method of birth control?
(a) FSH (b) LH
(c) Progesterone (d) Both (a) and (b)

4 LNG-20 is
(a) IUDs with progesterone
(b) IUDs with Cu
(c) IUDs with Cu and progesterone
(d) IUD with prolactin

5 The test-tube baby programme employs which one of the following techniques?
(a) Intra Uterine Insemination (IUI)
(b) Gamete Intra Fallopian Transfer (GIFT)
(c) Zygote Intra Fallopian Transfer (ZIFT)
(d) Intra Cytoplasmic Sperm Injection (ICSI)

Assertion-Reason Type Questions

Direction (Q. Nos. 6-9) *In the questions given below two statements an **Assertion** and a **Reason** are given. Give the appropriate response as*

(a) If both Assertion and Reason are true and Reason is the correct explanation of Assertion
(b) If both Assertion and Reason are true, but Reason is not the correct explanation of Assertion
(c) If Assertion is true, but Reason is false
(d) If Assertion is false, but Reason is true

6 **Assertion** One in every six persons in the world is an Indian.

Reason A rapid decline in MMR and IMR are probable reasons for it.

7 **Assertion** IUDs need to be replaced more frequently.

Reason Using IUDs for long have chances of perforation, infection and expulsion.

8 **Assertion** IUDs are very effective contraceptive method.

Reason These do not allow sperm to enter uterus.

9 **Assertion** Inability to produce children inspite of unprotected sexual practices is called infertility.

Reason The reasons for this could be physical, congenital disease, drugs, etc.

2/3 Marks Questions

10 Why were family planning programmes initiated in India?

11 How do Cu-T, multiload 375 and LNG-20 differ in contraceptive action?

12 Why is tubectomy considered a contraceptive method?

13 Give some reasons for infertility among young couples.

14 Expand the following
(i) IVF
(ii) STDs
(iii) ZIFT
(iv) GIFT

15 Mention any two events that are inhibited by the intake of oral contraceptive pills to prevent pregnancy in humans.

16 Mention two significant differences between tubectomy and vasectomy.

17 Explain how IVF is useful in case of an infertile women?

18 Observe the relation between first two words given below and give suitable word for blank.

(i) Male : Vasectomy : : Female : ....

(ii) Condom : Nirodh : : Oral pill : ....

19 State true/false with explanation.

(i) Abortions could happen spontaneously too.

(ii) Complete lactation could help as a natural method of contraception.

(iii) Creating awareness about sex-related aspects is an effective method to improve reproductive health of the people.

20 Read the following statements carefully and give an appropriate term for each of the following.

(i) Low sperm count in males.

(ii) Introduction of artificially collected semen into the vagina.

(iii) Reusable rubber sheath that covers the cervix during intercourse.

(iv) The absence of sperms in males.

21 What is amniocentesis? How was being misused in earlier times? What is the initiative of the government regarding this test?

22 What do you mean by infertility? Give two reasons for infertility in male and females.

05 Marks Questions

23 What are STDs? Describe any two.

24 How are the assisted reproductive techniques practised to help infertile couples? Describe any three techniques.

25 Answer the following questions on Medical Termination of Pregnancy (MTP).

(i) Though MTP can check population growth, it is not meant for this purpose. Give reason.

(ii) Why MTP is not legalised in many countries of the world?

(iii) Why MTP is legalised in India?

(iv) Is MTP considered safe at all stages of pregnancy? Comment.

26 Write the notes on any two of the following

(i) Barrier Methods

(ii) Intra Uterine Devices

(iii) Oral Contraceptives

27 Describe the sterilisation methods in both male and female with the help of diagrams.

Answers

1. (a)	**2.** (d)	**3.** (c)	**4.** (a)	**5.** (c)
6. (a)	**7.** (a)	**8.** (c)	**9.** (b)	

04

Principles of Inheritance and Variation

TREND ANALYSIS 3 YEARS

Average No. of Questions Across all Sets

Topic	Types of Questions	2024	2023	2020
TOPIC 01 Mendel's Laws of Inheritance	1 Marks	1	0	0
	2 Marks	0	1	1
	3 Marks	0	0	2
	4 Marks (Case Based)	0	0	0
	5 Marks	1	3	4
TOPIC 02 Sex-Determination and Genetic Disorders	1 Marks	1	1	1
	2 Marks	0	0	1
	3 Marks	1	0	0
	4 Marks (Case Based)	0	1	0
	5 Marks	0	0	1

TOPIC 1

Mendel's Laws of Inheritance

- **Genetics** is the branch of biology which deals with the study of pattern of inheritance as well as variation of characters from parents to offsprings.
- **Inheritance** is the process by which characters or traits are transferred from one generation to the next.
- **Variation** is the degree by which progenies differ from each other and from their parents. Humans knew from as early as 8000-1000 BC, that one of the causes of variation was hidden in sexual reproduction.
- **Gregor Johann Mendel** for the first time conducted experiments to understand the pattern of inheritance of variation in living beings.

Mendel's Experiment

Experimental Material

(i) He conducted experiments on garden pea plant (*Pisum sativum*) for seven years, i.e. from 1856-1863. Based on this, he proposed the laws of inheritance in living organisms.

(ii) He selected garden pea plant as experimental material because

- It is easily available on a large scale.
- Many varieties are available with distinct characteristics.
- They are self-pollinated and can be cross-pollinated easily.

- Pea plant has a shorter life cycle. This enables the geneticists to study many generations of the pea plant in a short time period.

(iii) Mendel selected **14 true-breeding** pea plant varieties, as pairs. These pairs which were similar except for one character with contrasting traits.

Seven contrasting characters and their traits as taken by Mendel are listed in the table given below

Contrasting Characters Studied by Mendel in Pea

Character	Contrasting character (Dominant/Recessive)
Stem height	Tall/Dwarf
Flower colour	Violet/White
Flower position	Axial/Terminal
Pod shape	Inflated/Constricted
Pod colour	Green/Yellow
Seed shape	Round/Wrinkled
Seed colour	Yellow/Green

Procedure

- He studied one trait or character at a time.
- Mendel hybridised plants with alternate forms of a single trait (monohybrid cross). The seeds produced by these crosses were grown to develop into plants of **Filial$_1$** progeny or F_1-generation.
- He then self-pollinated the tall F_1 plants to produce plants of **Filial$_2$** progeny or F_2-generation.
- Mendel also self-pollinated the F_2 plants.
- Mendel used procedures like emasculation and bagging to avoid unwanted pollination in his experiments.
- In later experiments, Mendel crossed pea plants with two contrasting characters, such a cross is known as **dihybrid cross**.

Observations

- In F_1-generation, Mendel found that all pea plants were tall and none were dwarf.
- He found that F_1 always resembled one of its parents.
- In F_2-generation, he found that some of the offsprings were dwarf. This means that the characters which were not seen in F_1-generation were now expressed in F_2-generation.
- These contrasting traits (tall/dwarf) did not show any mixing either in F_1 or in F_2-generation.
- Similar results were obtained with the other traits that he studied. Only one of the parental traits was expressed in F_1-generation, while in F_2-generation, both the traits were expressed in the ratio of 3 : 1.
- Mendel also found identical results in dihybrid cross as in monohybrid cross.
- On self-pollinating F_2 plants, he found that dwarf F_2 plants continued to generate dwarf plants in F_3 and F_4-generations.

Inferences

- Mendel observed that something was being passed down unchanged from parents to offsprings through the gametes over successive generations. He called these as 'factors'. The Mendelian 'factors' are now known as **genes** (units of inheritance).
- Genes which code for a pair of contrasting traits are called **alleles** or **allelomorphs**. The alleles are the alternative forms of the same gene.
- TT and tt represent **genotype** of a trait.
- The observable external features, e.g. tall and dwarf represent the **phenotype**.
- When the tall (TT) and dwarf (tt) pea plants produce gametes, the alleles of the parental pair **segregate** from each other and only one allele is transmitted to a gamete.
- The gametes of the tall (TT) plants have the allele T and that of dwarf (tt) plants have the allele t.
- This segregation of alleles is a random process. There is 50% chance of a gamete containing either allele, as verified by the results of crossing. After fertilisation of plant with TT and tt traits, hybrids are formed that contain Tt. The cross between TT and tt is a monohybrid cross.
- Mendel found the phenotype of Tt to be similar as TT parent in appearance. He proposed that in a pair of dissimilar factors, one factor is able to express itself and is known as **dominant**, while another factor is unable to express itself and is known as **recessive**.

- Alleles can be similar in case of **homozygous** condition like TT or tt and dissimilar in case of **heterozygous** condition like Tt.
- Dominant character is expressed in homozygous as well as in heterozygous condition, while recessive character is expressed only in its homozygous condition.

Test Cross

It is a method devised by Mendel to determine the genotype of an organism. It is performed to know whether an organism is homozygous dominant (TT) or heterozygous dominant (Tt).

A test cross is conducted between unknown dominant genotype and the recessive parent. It is a type of **backcross** where F_1-progeny is crossed to one of its parent.

(i) For example, F_1 hybrid (Tt- heterozygous of a pure tall plant, i.e. TT and a pure dwarf plant, i.e. tt) is crossed with a pure dwarf parent plant.

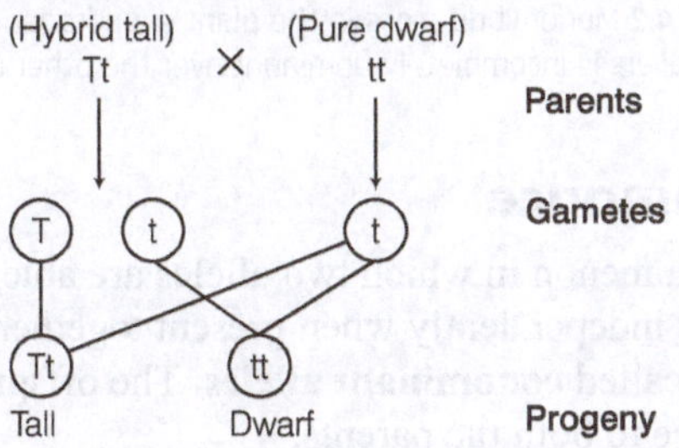

In this example, the progeny consists of tall and dwarf plants in the ratio of 1:1. Thus, monohybrid test cross ratio is 1:1.

(ii) In case of both homozygous parents, i.e. TT and tt, the progeny obtained will have all tall plants.

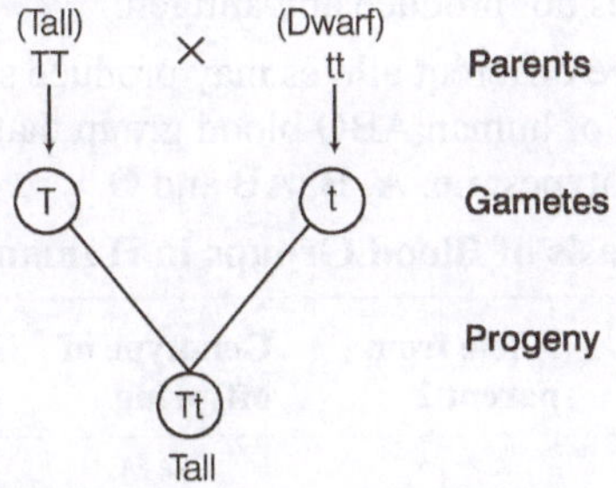

(iii) In case of dihybrid test cross, a heterozygous individual is crossed with a homozygous recessive parent, the dihybrid test cross ratio comes as 1:1:1:1.

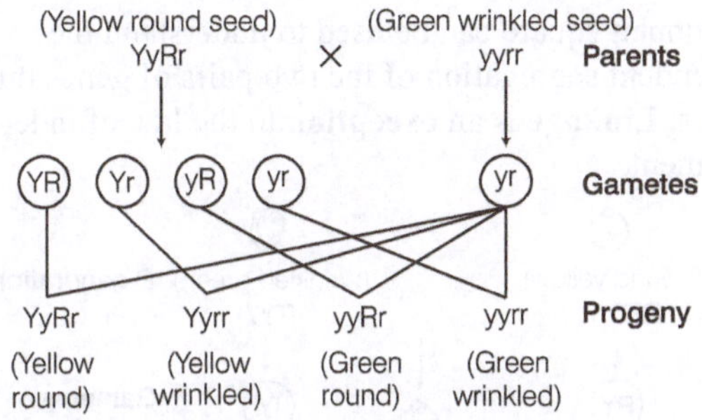

Mendel's Laws of Inheritance

Based on the observations of monohybrid (first and second law) and dihybrid crosses (third law). Mendel proposed following three laws

Law of Dominance (First Law)

It explains expression of genes in a monohybrid cross. When two genes or alleles are present in an organism, only one factor (dominant) expresses itself in F_1-generation, while the other factor (recessive) remains hidden. This is known as law of dominance. In such a cross, in the F_2-generation, phenotypic ratio is 3 : 1, while genotypic ratio is 1 : 2 : 1. There are two **exceptions** to law of dominance. These include **incomplete dominance** and **codominance.**

Law of Segregation (Second Law)

It states that the factors or alleles of a pair segregate from each other during gamete formation. They segregate in such a way that a gamete receives only one of the two factors. They do not show any blending or mixing. It is also known as law of purity of gametes. There is no exception to law of segregation.

Law of Independent Assortment (Third Law)

It is based on the inheritance of two genes, i.e. **dihybrid cross.** It states that when two pairs of contrasting traits are combined in a hybrid, segregation of one pair of characters is independent of the other pair of characters and both the characters assort independently. Thus, the genes get randomly rearranged in the offsprings, producing both parental and new combinations of characters.

The Punnett square can be used to understand the independent segregation of the two pairs of genes during meiosis. **Linkage** is an **exception** to the law of independent assortment.

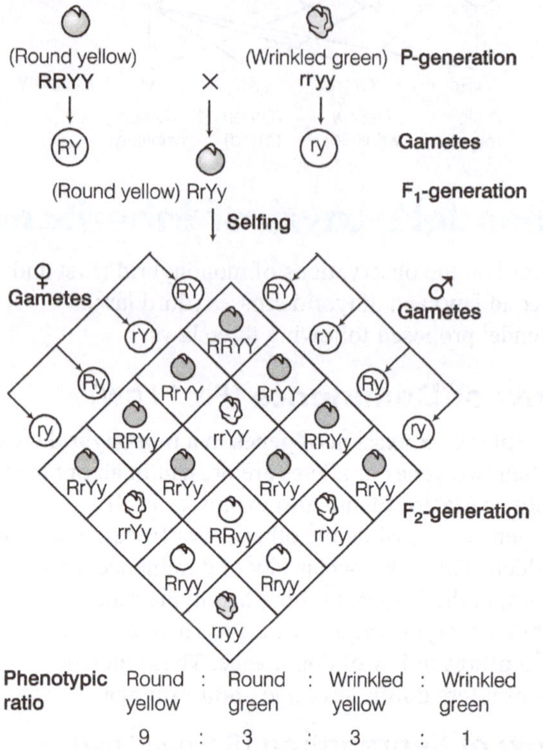

Figure 4.1 A Punnett square (graphical representation used to calculate the probability of all possible genotypes of offspring) used to understand Mendel's law of Independent assortment

Deviation from Mendelism

The inheritance patterns that show deviation from Mendelism are discussed below

Incomplete Dominance

- It is a phenomenon in which the dominant allele is not able to mask the characters of recessive allele completely. This F_1- hybrid shows characters intermediate to the parental type. In this process, the phenotypic ratio of F_2-generation deviates from the Mendel's monohybrid ratio.
- For example, inheritance of flower colour in the dog flower (snapdragon or *Antirrhinum* sp.) and four O' clock plant (*Mirabilis jalapa*).
  - In snapdragon, cross between red flower (RR) and white flower (rr) plant, produces the F_1-generation containing pink (Rr) flower. When F_1 plants are self-pollinated, the F_2-generation containing red, pink and white flowers in the ratio of 1 : 2 : 1 obtained.
- In incomplete dominance, genotypic ratio of F_2 remains same as Mendel's monohybrid cross, i.e. 1 : 2 : 1, but phenotypic ratio changes from 3 : 1 to 1 : 2 : 1. Hence, in this case, both phenotypic and genotypic ratios are similar.

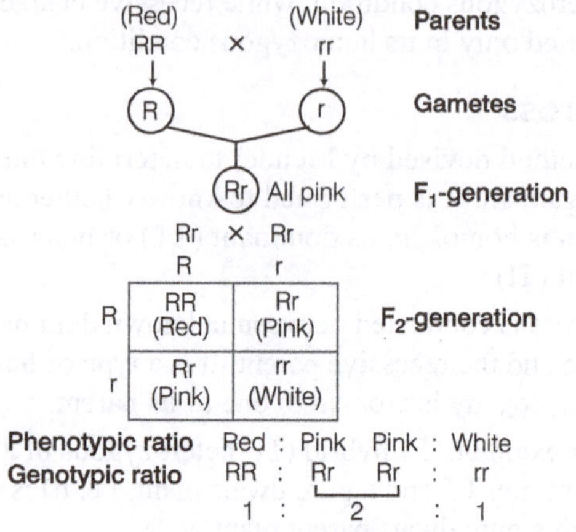

Figure 4.2 Monohybrid cross in the plant snapdragon where one allele is incompletely dominant over the other allele

Codominance

It is a phenomenon in which two alleles are able to express themselves independently when present together. These alleles are called **codominant alleles**. The offsprings show resemblance to both the parents.

- A common example of codominance is ABO blood grouping in humans, which is controlled by the gene I (I^A, I^B and i).
- I^A and I^B (dominant alleles) produce RBC surface antigens A and B, respectively, whereas 'i' (recessive allele) does not produce any antigen.
- These three different alleles may produce six different genotypes of human ABO blood group that may show four phenotypes, i.e. A, B, AB and O.

Genetic Basis of Blood Groups in Human Population

Allele from parent 1	Allele from parent 2	Genotype of offspring	Blood types of offspring
I^A	I^A	I^AI^A	A
I^A	I^B	I^AI^B	AB
I^A	i	I^A i	A
I^B	I^A	I^AI^B	AB
I^B	I^B	I^BI^B	B
I^B	i	I^B i	B
i	i	ii	O

Multiple Allelism

When more than two alleles are present for a character then, the condition is known as multiple allelism. It can be explained by ABO blood grouping. In this case, more than two, i.e. three alleles are governing the same character.

Pleiotropy

It is the phenomenon in which a single gene exhibits multiple phenotypic expressions. It means that a single pleiotropic gene may produce more than one effect.

For example, Phenylketonuria, which is a disorder caused by the mutation in the gene encoding for enzyme phenylalanine hydroxylase. In the absence of this enzyme, phenylalanine is not converted into tyrosine and accumulation of phenylalanine takes place.

The affected individuals show hair reduction and skin pigmentation and mental retardation.

Polygenic Inheritance

- The concept of polygenic inheritance was given by **Galton** in 1833. In this, traits are controlled by three or more genes (multiple genes). Such traits are called **polygenic traits**.
- The phenotype is produced as a result of participation of several genes and is also influenced by the environment. It is also called **quantitative inheritance** as the character or phenotype can be quantified. For example, human skin colour is produced by a pigment melanin.
- The quantity of melanin is due to three pairs of polygenes (A, B and C). If a black or very dark (AA BB CC) and white or very light (aa bb cc) individuals marry each other, the offspring shows intermediate colour who are often called **mulatto** (Aa Bb Cc). A total of eight allele combinations are possible in the gametes forming 27 distinct genotypes.

Complementary Genes

These genes complement the effect of each other to produce a phenotype. For example, in case of sweet pea (*Lathyrus*), the flower colour is due to complementary genes. Here, one gene complements the expression of another gene, but neither of them produces the trait in the absence of other. Phenotypic ratio obtained in this case is 9 : 7.

Rediscovery of Mendel's Laws

(i) Though, Mendel published his work on inheritance of characters in 1865, it remained unrecognised for several reasons till 1900. Some of these reasons are as follows

- Communication was difficult, so his work could not be widely publicised.
- His concept of genes as stable units that control the expression of traits and that, of the pair of alleles that did not blend was not accepted due to continuous variations seen in nature.
- His idea of using mathematics to explain biological phenomenon was new and unacceptable.
- He could not provide any physical proof for the existence of factors, i.e. where these factors are located in the cell.

(ii) In 1900, **Hugo de Vries, Correns** and **Erich von Tschermak** rediscovered Mendel's results independently. Due to advanced microscopy, they carefully observed cell division.

(iii) This led to discovery of **chromosomes** (structure in the nucleus that gets double and divides just before each cell division).

Chromosomal Theory of Inheritance

This theory was proposed independently by **Walter Sutton** and **Theodore Boveri** in 1902. They united the knowledge of chromosomal segregation with Mendelian principles and called it **chromosomal theory of inheritance**.

The main points of this theory are as follows

- Gametes (sperm and egg) carry and transmit hereditary characters from one generation to another.
- Nucleus is the site where hereditary factors are present.
- Chromosomes as well as genes occur in pairs.

- The two alleles of a gene pair are located on homologous sites on the homologous chromosomes. During meiotic anaphase-I, separation of homologous chromosomes takes place.

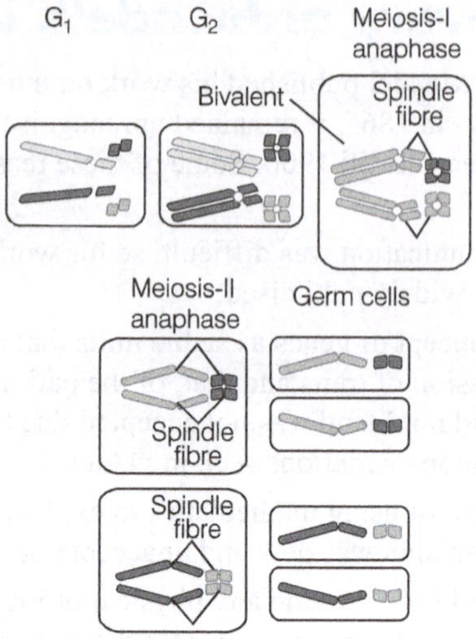

Figure 4.3 Meiosis and germ cell formation in a cell with four chromosomes

- Homologous chromosomes synapse during meiosis and get separated to pass into different cells. It is the basis of segregation and independent assortment during meiosis.

Sutton and **Boveri** said that the pairing and separation of a pair of chromosomes would lead to the segregation of a pair of factor they carry.

Experimental Verification of the Chromosomal Theory of Inheritance

This was done by Thomas Hunt Morgan and his colleagues. Morgan selected fruitfly, *Drosophila melanogaster* for his experiments because of the following reasons

- They could be grown on simple artificial medium in the laboratory.
- Their life cycle is only about two weeks.
- A single mating could produce a large number of flies.
- There was a clear differentiation of the sexes, i.e. male (smaller) and female (bigger).
- It has many types of hereditary variations that can be easily seen through low power microscopes.

Linkage and Recombination

The diagram given below represents the linkage result of the experiments conducted by Morgan.

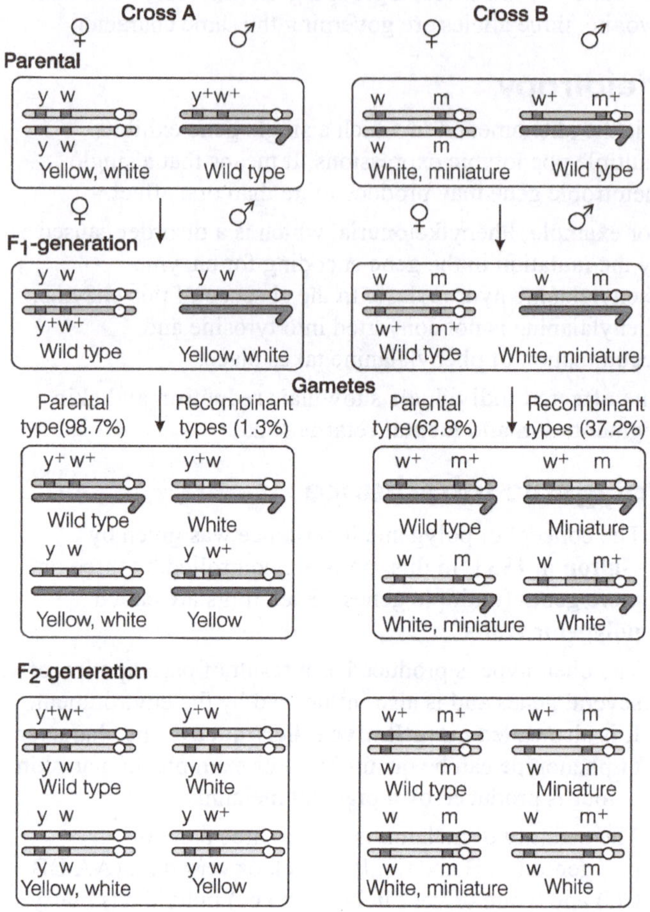

Figure 4.4 Linkage result of two dihybrid crosses conducted by Morgan, Cross 'A' shows crossing between genes y and w ; Cross 'B' shows crossing between genes w and m. Here, dominant wild type alleles are represented with (+) sign in superscript. The strength of linkage between y and w is higher than w and m.

- The physical association of two or more genes on a chromosome is called **linkage**. In other words, when two or more genes are closely located on a chromosome, then both the genes are passed on together in the next generation.
This type of inheritance of genes is known as linkage. It is an exception of Mendel's law of independent assortment.
- **Recombination** involves the generation of non-parental gene combinations.

- To explain the phenomena of linkage and recombination, Morgan carried out several dihybrid crosses in *Drosophila* to study genes that were sex-linked. He mainly studied the genes that are located on X-chromosome.
- He observed that
  - two closely located genes did not segregate independently of each other.
  - When two genes in a dihybrid cross were situated on the same chromosome the proportion of parental gene combinations were much higher than the non-parental types. Morgan concluded this as a physical association or linkage.
- Linkage $\propto \dfrac{1}{\text{Distance between two genes}}$

  If two genes are very close to each other, then they are tightly linked and there are very less chances of recombination and vice versa.
- Morgan and his group also found that even when genes were grouped on the same chromosome, some genes were very tightly linked (very low recombination), while others were loosely linked (high recombination).
- Recombination of linked genes occurs by crossing over, i.e. exchange of corresponding parts between the chromatids of homologous chromosomes.
- **Alfred Sturtevant** (Morgan's student) used the frequency of recombination between gene pairs on the same chromosome as a measure of the distance between genes and 'mapped' their position on the chromosome.

Genetic maps are now used as a starting point in the sequencing of whole genomes. The same were used in case of **Human Genome Sequencing Project**.

PYQs Previous Years' Questions

1 Mark Questions

Multiple Choice Questions

1. In human beings, where genotype AABBCC represents dark skin colour, aabbcc represents light skin colour and AaBbCc represents intermediate skin colour; the pattern of genetic inheritance can be termed as **CBSE SQP 2021-22 Term-I**

   (a) pleiotropy and codominance
   (b) pleiotropy and incomplete dominance
   (c) polygenic and qualitative inheritance
   (d) polygenic and quantitative inheritance

Ans. (d) polygenic and quantitative inheritance.

2. How many types of gametes would be produced if the genotype of a parent is AaBB? **CBSE SQP 2021-22 Term-I**

   (a) 1 (b) 2 (c) 3 (d) 4

Ans. (b) 2 types of gametes would be produced

3. Which of the following statements indicates parallelism in genes and chromosomes? **CBSE SQP 2021-22 Term-I**

   (i) They occur in pairs
   (ii) They segregate during gamete formation
   (iii) They show linkage
   (iv) Independent pairs segregate independently

   (a) (i) and (iii) (b) (ii) and (iii)
   (c) (i), (ii) and (iii) (d) (i), (ii) and (iv)

Ans. (d) Statements i, ii and iv indicates parallelism in genes and chromosomes.

4. A cross is made between tall pea plants having green pods and dwarf pea plants having yellow pods. In the F_2-generation, out of 80 plants, how many are likely to be tall plants? **CBSE SQP 2021-22 Term-I**

   (a) 15 (b) 20 (c) 45 (d) 60

Ans. (d) 60

5. In *Antirrhinum,* RR is phenotypically red flowers, rr is white and Rr is pink. Select the correct phenotypic ratio in F_1-generation, when a cross is performed between RR × Rr. **CBSE SQP 2021-22 Term-I**

   (a) 1 red : 1 pink : 1 white (b) 2 pink : 1 white
   (c) 2 red : 2 pink (d) All pink

Ans. (c) 2 Red : 2 Pink

6. What would be the genotype of the parents if the offspring have the phenotypes in 1:1 proportion? **CBSE SQP 2021-22 Term-I**

   (a) Aa × Aa (b) AA × AA
   (c) Aa × AA (d) Aa × aa

Ans. (d) Aa ×aa

7. Genotypic ratio of 1:2:1 is obtained in a cross between **CBSE SQP 2021-22 Term-I**

(a) AB × AB (b) Ab × Ab
(c) Ab × ab (d) ab × ab

Ans. (b) Ab × Ab

8. The following are results of crossing a females fly (AaBb) with a male fly (aabb). **CBSE SQP 2021-22 Term-I**

AaBb 1005 aabb 1000
Aabb 200 aaBb 210

Which two genotypes are the recombinant offsprings?

(a) AaBb and Aabb (b) AaBb and aaBb
(c) Aabb and aaBb (d) AaBb and aabb

Ans. (c) Aabb and aaBb are the recombinant offspring.

9. The gene that controls the ABO blood group system in human beings has three alleles, I^A, I^B and i. A child has blood group O. His father has blood group A and mother has blood group B. Genotypes of other offsprings can be **CBSE SQP 2021-22 Term-I**

(i) I^BI^B (ii) I^Ai
(iii) I^Bi (iv) I^AI^B
(v) ii

(a) i, ii, iii and V (b) ii, iii, iv and v
(c) iii, iv and v (d) i, iii and iv

Ans. (b) Genotypes of other offspring can be I^Ai, I^Bi, I^AI^B, ii

10. Given below is a dihybrid cross performed on *Drosophila*. **CBSE SQP 2021-22 Term-I**

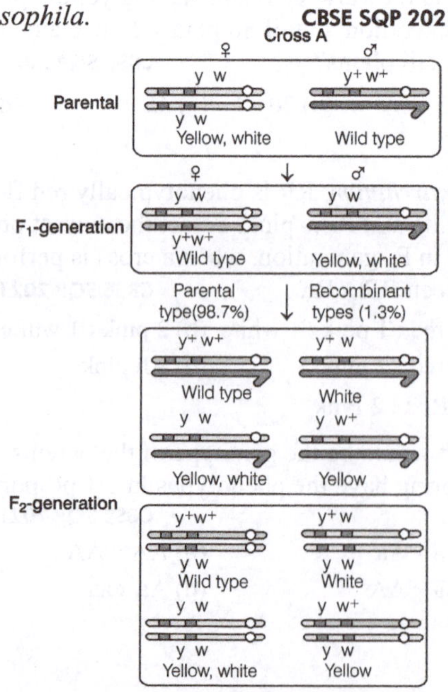

Which of the following conclusions can be drawn on the basis of this cross? When yellow bodied (y), white eyed (w) *Drosophila* females were hybridised with brown bodied (y^+), red eyed males (w^+) and F_1 progenies were intercrossed, F_2-generation would have shown the following ratio.

(a) 1 : 2 : 1 because of linkage of genes
(b) 9 : 3 : 3 : 1 because of recombination of genes
(c) Deviation from 9 : 3 : 3 : 1 ratio because of segregation of genes
(d) Deviation from 9 : 3 : 3 : 1 ratio because of linkage of genes

Ans. (d) Deviation from 9 : 3 : 3 : 1 ratio because of linkage of genes.

11. Given below are the pairs of contrasting traits in *Pisum sativum* as studied by Mendel. Identify the incorrect pair of traits. **CBSE 2021-22 Term-I**

Characters	Dominant	Recessive
(a) Stem height	Tall	Dwarf
(b) Seed shape	Round	Wrinkled
(c) Pod colour	Yellow	Green
(d) Flower position	Axial	Terminal

Ans. (c)

12. According to Mendel, the nature of the unit factors that control the expression of traits were **CBSE 2021-22 Term-I**

(a) stable
(b) blending
(c) stable and discrete
(d) discrete

Ans. (c) Stable and discrete

13. In *Pisum sativum*, the flower position may be axial (allele A) or terminal (allele a). What would be the percentage of the offspring with respect to axial flower position, if a cross is made between parents Aa × aa? **CBSE 2021-22 Term-I**

(a) 25% (b) 50%
(c) 75% (d) 100%

Ans. (b) 50%

14. The probability of all possible genotypes of offsprings in a genetic cross can be obtained with the help of **CBSE 2021-22 Term-I**

(a) test cross (b) back cross
(c) Punnett square (d) linkage cross

Ans. (c) Punnett square

15. Possibility of the blood groups of the children in a family where the father is heterozygous for blood group 'A' and the mother is heterozygous for blood group 'B' would be **CBSE 2021-22 Term-I**

(a) blood groups A, B (b) blood groups A, B, O
(c) blood group AB, O (d) blood groups A, B, AB, O

Ans. (d) Blood Groups A, B, AB, O

16. The number of different type of gametes that would be produced from a parent with genotype AABBCc is **CBSE 2021-22 Term-I**

(a) 1 (b) 2 (c) 3 (d) 4

Ans. (b) 2

Assertion-Reason Type Questions

Direction (Q. Nos. *17-19) consist of two statements, Assertion (A) and Reason (R). Answer these questions selecting the appropriate option given below.*

(a) Both Assertion and Reason are true and Reason is the correct explanation of Assertion
(b) Both Assertion and Reason are true, but Reason is not the correct explanation of Assertion
(c) Assertion is true, but Reason is false
(d) Assertion is false, but Reason is true

17. **Assertion** Linked genes do not show dihybrid F_2 ratio 9 : 3 : 3 : 1.

Reason Linked genes do not undergo independent assortment. **CBSE 2024 (Set-I)**

Ans. (d) Assertion is false, but Reason is true. A can be corrected as

Linked genes do not show dihybrid F_2 ratio 9 : 3 : 3 : 1 as they do not follow independent assortment. Linked genes act and move as a unit rather than independently.

18. **Assertion** When white eyed, yellow bodied *Drosophila* females were hybridised with red eyed, brown-bodied males; and F_1-progeny was intercrossed, F_2 ratio deviated from 9 : 3 : 3 : 1.

Reason When two genes in a dihybrid are on the same chromosome, the proportion of parental gene combinations is much higher than the non-parental type. **CBSE SQP 2023**

Ans. (a) Both Assertion and Reason are true and Reason is the correct explanation of Assertion.

19. **Assertion** When the two genes in a dihybrid cross are situated on the same chromosome, the proportion of parental gene combinations is much higher than non-parental type.

Reason Higher parental gene combinations can be attributed to crossing over between two genes. **CBSE SQP 2021-22 Term-I**

Ans. (c) Assertion is true, but Reason is false.

When two genes in a dihybrid cross were situated on the same chromosome, the proportion of parental gene combination were much higher than the non-parental type. This is due to the physical association or linkage of the two genes.

Very Short Answer Type Questions

20. A snapdragon plant with violet flowers was crossed with another such plant with white flowers. The F_1-progeny obtained had pink flowers. Explain in brief, the inheritance pattern seen in offspring of F_1-generation. **CBSE SQP 2020**

Ans. The inheritance pattern seen in offspring of F_1-generation in the question is incomplete inheritance. In such inheritance pattern, new intermediate phenotype between two parental phenotypes is obtained because one allele for a specific trait do not express completely over the other allele.

21. Name the pattern of inheritance where F_1-phenotype

(i) resembles only one of the two parents.
(ii) does not resemble either of the two parents and is in between the two. **All India 2019**

Or Name the respective pattern of inheritance, where F_1 phenotype

(i) does not resemble either of the two parents and is in between the two.
(ii) resembles only one of the two parents. **All India 2012**

Ans. (i) Dominance (ii) Incomplete dominance
Or (i) Incomplete dominance (ii) Dominance (½ + ½)

22. British geneticist RC Punnett developed a graphical representation of a genetic cross called 'Punnett Square'. Mention the possible result this representation predicts of the genetic cross carried. **Delhi 2019**

Ans. Punnett square helps to predict the probability of all the possible genotypes of the offspring in a genetic cross.

23. A cross was carried out between two pea plants showing the contrasting traits of height of the plant. The result of the cross showed 50% of parental characters. Name the type of cross. **CBSE SQP 2018**

Ans. In a cross of two pea plants showing contrasting traits of height, i.e. cross between tall pea plant (Tt) and dwarf pea plant (tt), 50% progenies are of parental characters (Tall). This is only possible in case of test cross (a cross is made of unknown dominant genotype with recessive parent).

24. Name the type of cross that would help to find the genotype of a pea plant bearing violet flowers. **All India 2017**

Ans. To find the genotype of a pea plant bearing violet flowers, test cross would be carried out in which the plant with dominant trait, i.e. violet flowers, will be crossed with its recessive parent.

25. State a difference between a gene and an allele. **All India 2016**

Ans. A unit of inheritance which is passed down from parent to offspring through the gametes over successive generations is known as **gene**. (½)

Genes consist of a pair of contrasting forms for a character that are known as **alleles**. (½)

26. Give an example of polygenic trait in humans. **Delhi 2016C**

Ans. An example of a polygenic trait in humans is skin colour.

27. On what basis is the skin colour in humans considered polygenic? **Delhi 2016**

Ans. Skin colour is considered to be a polygenic trait because it is under the control of many genes.

28. A geneticist interested in studying variations and patterns of inheritance in living beings prefers to choose organisms for experiments with shorter life cycle. Provide a reason. **Delhi 2015**

Ans. A geneticist interested in studying variations and patterns of inheritance in living beings prefers to choose organisms with shorter life cycle, because it enables the geneticist to study many generations of the organism in a short time period.

29. Mention any two contrasting traits with respect to seeds in pea plant that were studied by Mendel. **All India 2014**

Ans. Two contrasting seed traits studied by Mendel are

(i) **Seed shape** Round and wrinkled. (½)

(ii) **Seed colour** Yellow and green. (½)

30. What are 'true-breeding lines' that are used to study inheritance pattern of traits in plants. **Delhi 2014**

Ans. True-breeding lines are those plants, which have undergone continuous self-pollination and show stable trait inheritance and expression for several generations.

31. How many kinds of phenotype would you expect in F_2-generation in a monohybrid cross exhibiting codominance? **All India 2014**

Ans. In codominance, alleles are able to express themselves independently when present together. Thus, in a monohybrid cross there would be three kinds of phenotype in the F_2-generation showing codominance.

32. Name the stage of cell division where segregation of an independent pair of chromosomes occurs. **All India 2014**

Ans. During meiotic anaphase-I of cell division, the separation of independent pair of chromosomes occurs.

33. Name the event during cell division cycle that results in the gain and loss of chromosomes. **Delhi 2011**

Ans. Non-disjunction of chromosomes during anaphase-I of meiosis results in the gain or loss of chromosomes.

34. A garden pea plant produced axial white flowers another of the same species produced terminal violet flowers. Identify the dominant traits. **All India 2012**

Ans. The dominant trait in the pea plant is axial violet flowers, while the recessive trait is terminal white flowers.

35. In a dihybrid cross, when would the proportion of parental gene combinations be much higher than non-parental types, as experimentally shown by Morgan and his group? **All India 2012**

Ans. The proportion of parental gene combination is much higher than non-parental types, when the two genes show linkage and are inherited together.

36. Write possible genotypes Mendel got when he crossed
F_1 tall plant with a dwarf pea plant. **Foreign 2012**

Ans. The cross is a test cross. Here Tt and tt (in ratio of 1:1) genotypes were obtained on crossing F_1 tall plant with a dwarf parent plant.

37. Garden pea plant produced round, green seed. Another of same species produced wrinkled yellow seeds. Identify dominant traits. **Foreign 2012**

Ans. The dominant trait in pea plant is round and green seeds, while the recessive trait is wrinkled and yellow seeds.(1)

38. Mention two contrasting flower related traits studied by Mendel in his pea plant experiments. **All India 2011C**

Ans. The two contrasting flower traits in pea plant are

(i) Violet flowers and white flowers. (½)

(ii) Axial flowers and terminal flowers. (½)

39. Name the contrasting pod related traits studied by Mendel in his pea plant experiment. **All India 2011C**

Ans. The two contrasting pod related traits in pea plant are

(i) Inflated/Constricted shape. (½)

(ii) Green/Yellow colour. (½)

40. Mention the type of allele that expresses itself only in homozygous state in an organism. **Foreign 2011**

Ans. Recessive allele expresses itself only in homozygous condition because in the presence of a dominant allele its effect is masked.

41. Pea flowers produce assured seed sets. Give a reason. **All India 2010**

Ans. Pea flowers produce assured seed sets because they have cleistogamous flowers, which undergo natural self-pollination.

2 Marks Questions

42. By using Punnett square depict the genotypes and phenotypes of the test crosses [when green pod colour (G) is dominant over yellow pod colour (g)] in garden pea with unknown genotype. **CBSE 2023**

Ans. A test cross is conducted between unknown dominant genotype and the recessive parent.

When unknown genotype is crossed with a homozygous recessive (gg) individual.

	g	g
G	Gg	Gg
g	gg	gg

The possible genotypes of the offspring are Gg and gg. Gg individual will have green pods colour while the gg individual will have yellow pods. The phenotype ratio of the offspring is 1 : 1 , i.e. half of the offspring have green pods and half have yellow pods.

43. A true-breeding pea plant, homozygous dominant for inflated green pods is crossed with another pea plant with constricted yellow pods (ffgg). With the help of Punnett square show the above cross and mention the results obtained phenotypically and genotypically in F_1 - generation. **CBSE SQP 2023**

Ans. As per the question, genotype of the P_1 (Parent) generation would be

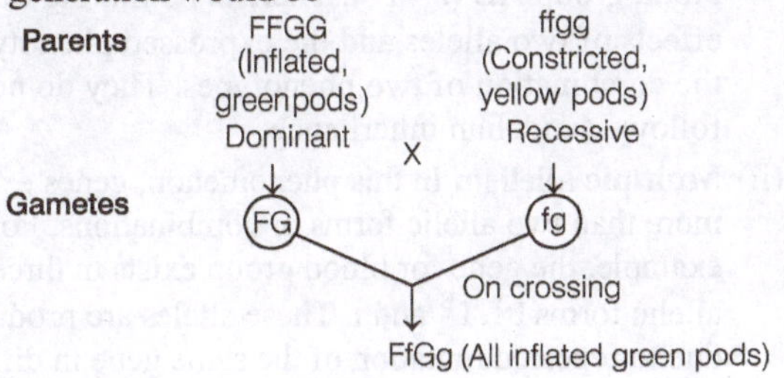

	FG	FG
fg	FfGg	FfGg
fg	FfGg	FfGg

Phenotype – All inflated green pods

Genotype – FfGg

44. Two children one with blood group 'AB' and other with blood group 'O' are born to parents, where the father has blood group 'A' and the mother has blood group 'B'. Work out a cross to show how is it possible? **Delhi 2020**

Ans. Parents must be heterozygous, since blood group 'O' appears in progeny as two children have blood group 'AB' and 'O'.

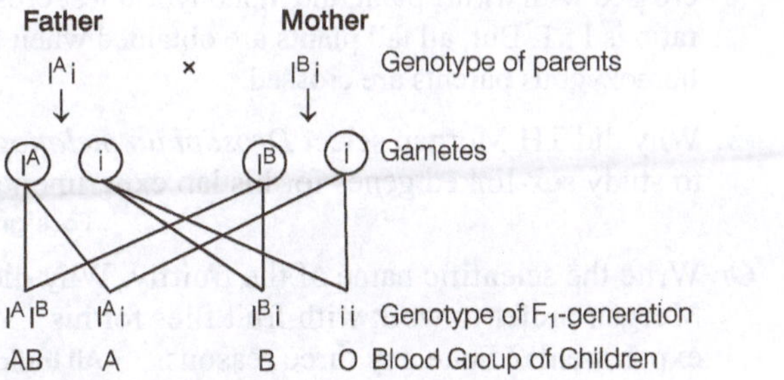

There are three alleles of the gene controlling blood group character, i.e. I^A , I^B and i. Where, I^A and I^B are dominant over i and together they are codominant to each other.

45. Why is it not possible to study the inheritance pattern of traits in human beings, the same way as it is done in pea plant? Name the alternate method employed for such an analysis of human traits. **CBSE SQP 2020**

Ans. In humans, it is not possible to study the pattern of inheritance in the same way as it is done in pea plants as

(i) The progeny produced is very small.

(ii) Controlled crosses cannot be performed. (1½)

An alternate method for analysis of human traits is pedigree analysis. (½)

46. Explain polygenic inheritance with the help of an example. **All India 2019**

Ans. Refer to text 'Polygenic Inheritance, on page no. 93.

47. State the Mendelian principle which can be derived from a dihybrid cross and not from monohybrid cross. **CBSE SQP 2019**

Ans. Law of independent assortment is based on the inheritance of two genes, i.e. dihybrid cross.

It states that when two pairs of contrasting traits are combined in a hybrid, segregation of one pair of characters is independent of the other pair of characters.

48. When does a geneticist need to carry a test cross? **Foreign 2015**

Or How would you find the genotype of an organism exhibiting a dominant phenotype? **Delhi 2012C**

Ans. A geneticist needs to carry a test cross when he/she wants to determine the genotype of an organism, with a dominant phenotype trait, whether it is homozygous or heterozygous.

Or Genotype of the dominant phenotype is determined by a test cross. In it, the F_1 progeny is crossed to its recessive parent. When F_1 progeny (heterozygous) crossed with dwarf plant, the monohybrid test cross ratio is 1 : 1. But, all tall plants are obtained when both homozygous parents are crossed.

49. Why did TH Morgan select *Drosophila melanogaster* to study sex-linked genes for his lab experiments. **Foreign 2015**

Or Write the scientific name of the fruitfly. Why did Morgan prefer to work with fruit flies for his experiments? State any three reasons. **All India 2014**

Ans. The scientific name of fruitfly is *Drosophila melanogaster.* **(½)**

TH Morgan preferred this organism for his study because of the following reasons

(i) It has fast and short life cycle.

(ii) It has only four pairs of chromosomes.

(iii) It reproduces quickly. **(1½)**

50. Give an example of a gene responsible for multiple phenotypic expressions. What are such genes called? State the cause that is responsible for such an effect. **Foreign 2015**

Or Explain pleiotropy with the help of an example. **Foreign 2014**

Ans. Pleiotropy is the phenomenon in which a single gene exhibits multiple phenotypic expressions.

The genes exhibiting pleiotropy are called pleiotropic genes. Pleiotropism occurs mainly because of mutation in a particular gene, e.g. phenylketonuria which is a disorder caused by mutation in the gene coding for the enzyme phenylalanine hydroxylase. In the absence of this enzyme, phenylalanine is not converted into tyrosine and accumulation of phenylalanine takes place. The affected individual shows hair reduction and skin pigmentation and mental problems.

51. The F_2 progeny of a monohybrid cross showed phenotypic and genotypic ratio as 1 : 2 : 1, unlike that of Mendel's monohybrid F_2 ratio. With the help of a suitable example, work out a cross and explain how it is possible. **All India 2015**

Or Why are F_2 phenotypic and genotypic ratios are same in a cross between red flowered snapdragon and white flowered snapdragon plants? Explain with the help of cross. **Delhi 2010**

Ans. The given condition represents the case of incomplete dominance. In snapdragon, the inheritance of flower colour shows incomplete dominance.

Neither of the alleles of gene for flower colour is completely dominant over the other and hybrid shows an intermediate phenotype. Therefore, F_2 phenotypic and genotypic ratios are same in a cross between red flowered snapdragon and white flowered snapdragon plants. **(1)**

It can be explained with the help of a cross given below

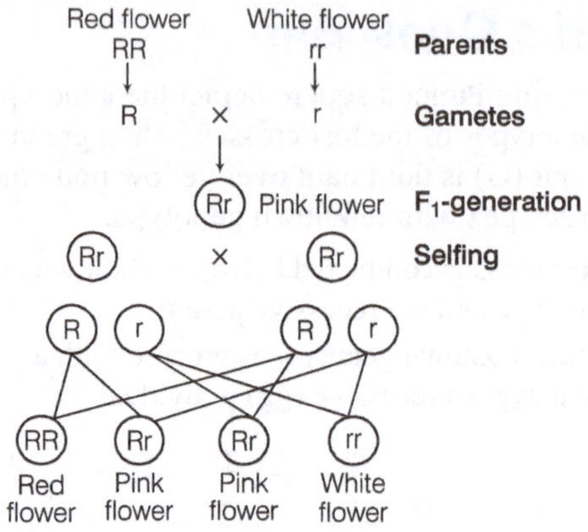

Phenotypic ratio	Red flower	:	Pink flowers	:	White flower
Genotypic ratio	RR 1	: :	Rr 2	: :	rr 1

(1)

52. With the help of one example, explain the phenomena of codominance and multiple allelism in human population. **All India 2014**

Ans. In human population, the phenomena of codominance and multiple allelism can be explained by the inheritance pattern of ABO blood groups which are controlled by three alleles, i.e. I^A, I^B and i.

(i) **Codominance** I^A and I^B both are codominant as both of them express themselves independently in blood group AB (I^A I^B). There is no mixing of the effects of two alleles and the expressed phenotype is the combination of two phenotypes. They do not follow Mendelian inheritance. **(1)**

(ii) **Multiple allelism** In this phenomenon, genes exist in more than two allelic forms or combinations, For example, the gene for blood group exists in three allelic forms I^A, I^B and i. These alleles are produced due to repeated mutation of the same gene in different direction. They do not follow Mendelian pattern of inheritance. **(1)**

53. Linkage and crossing over of genes are alternatives of each other. Justify with the help of an example. **All India 2014**

Ans. Linkage is the tendency of certain loci or alleles (genes) to be inherited together. While crossing over is the segregation of genes. The former helps to preserve parental characters in offsprings whearas the latter produces new combination of characters.

The genes on a chromosome either follow linkage path or crossing over to form the gametes during gametogenesis in human. Therefore, linkage and crossing over of genes are alternatives of each other.

54. In snapdragon, a cross between true-breeding red flowered (RR) plants and true-breeding white flowered (rr) plants showed a progeny of plants with all pink flowers.

(i) The appearance of pink flowers is not known as blending. Why?

(ii) What is this phenomenon known as? **All India 2014**

Ans. (i) Blending is the mixing of two colours, but in this example red and white colours appear independently at cellular level. Thus, no blending occurs. The red and white colours reappear in F_2-generation. **(1)**

(ii) This phenomenon is known as incomplete dominance. **(1)**

55. A cross was carried out between two pea plants showing the contrasting traits of height of the plants. The results of the cross showed 50% parental characters.

(i) Work out the cross with the help of a Punnett square.

(ii) Name the type of the cross carried out. **Delhi 2014**

Ans. (i) A Punnett square representing the cross given in the question is as follows

(Tall) Tt × (Dwarf) tt

Gametes: T t   t t

♀ \ ♂	t	t
T	Tt (Tall)	Tt (Tall)
t	tt (Dwarf)	tt (Dwarf)

(1)

(ii) The type of cross carried out here is a test cross, in which an individual with an unknown dominant phenotype is crossed with a homozygous recessive for that trait. **(1)**

56. How does the gene 'I' control ABO blood group in humans? Write the effect the gene has on the structure of red blood cells. **Delhi 2014**

Ans. In humans, the ABO blood groups are controlled by a gene called gene 'I'. It has three alleles, i.e. I^A, I^B and i. A person possesses any two of the three alleles. I^A and I^B are codominant and they both are dominant over i. These alleles help to determine the blood group of a person. The plasma membrane of red blood cells has sugar polymers that protrude out from its surface and the kind of sugar is regulated by the gene 'I' of ABO blood group. The alleles I^A and I^B produce enzymes that produce A and B types of sugar respectively on the surface of red blood cells, while allele i does not produce any sugar.

57. Study the figures given below and answer the question.

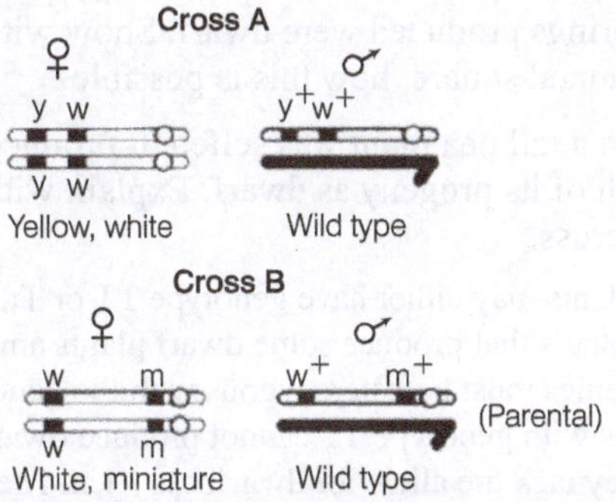

Identify in which of the crosses, the strength of linkage between the genes is higher. Give reasons in support of your answer. **Foreign 2014**

Ans. The strength of linkage is higher in the cross A than in cross B because linkage is higher when two genes are present closely on the same chromosome than those genes which are far apart. In cross B, the chances of crossing over or recombination are higher because the genes are loosely linked. **(1+1)**

58. A cross between a red flower bearing plant and a white flower bearing plant of *Antirrhinum* produced all plants having pink flowers. Work out a cross to explain how this is possible. **All India 2013**

Or Explain the mechanism of inheritance of the progeny produced when two *Antirrhinum* pink flowers were crossed. **All India 2012**

Ans. Cross of red flowered *Antirrhinum* with white flowered plant produces pink flowered plants. This shows incomplete dominance. **(1)**

For cross, refer to answer no. 51. **(1)**

59. Work out a cross to find the genotype of a tall pea plant. Name the type of cross. **All India 2013**

Ans. To know the genotype of tall pea plant, test cross is to be performed. It is the cross between F_1-hybrid and its recessive parent.

For cross, refer to answer no. 55 (i).

60. Differentiate between multiple allelism and pleiotropy with the help of an example of each. **Delhi 2013C**

Ans. Differences between multiple allelism and pleiotropy are

Multiple allelism	Pleiotropy
This occurs when one trait is controlled by more than two alleles.	This occurs when one gene controls many traits.
e.g. ABO blood grouping.	e.g. Phenylketonuria (PKU).

61. In a cross between two tall pea plants, some of the offsprings produced were dwarf. Show with the help of Punnett square, how this is possible. **Delhi 2013**

Or When a tall pea plant was selfed, it produced one fourth of its progeny as dwarf. Explain with the help of a cross. **Delhi 2010**

Ans. Tall plants may either have genotype TT or Tt. Two tall pea plants that produce some dwarf plants among their progenies must be heterozygous with the genotype Tt. Plants with genotype TT cannot produce dwarf offspring as they lack the allele for dwarfness (t) and hence, cannot transfer it to the progeny. But, if both the parents are heterozygous tall (Tt), 25% of F_1 progeny would contain 't' allele in homozygous (tt) condition. It can be represented using Punnett square as follows

Tt × Tt
↓

♂ / ♀	T	t
T	TT Tall	Tt Tall
t	Tt Tall	tt Dwarf

62. In a typical monohybrid cross, the F_2 population ratio is written as 3 : 1 for phenotype, but expressed as 1 : 2 : 1 for genotype. Explain with the help of an example. **All India 2013**

Or Tallness of pea plant is dominant trait, while dwarfness is the alternate recessive trait. When a pureline tall is crossed with a pureline dwarf, what fraction of tall plants in F_2-generation shall be heterozygous? Give reasons. **Delhi 2011C**

Ans. In a monohybrid cross, when a pureline tall plant is crossed with a pureline dwarf plant, following ratios are produced

The phenotypic ratio 3 : 1 represents that 3/4th of F_2 plants are tall, whereas 1/4th plants are dwarf.

The genotypic ratio 1 : 2 : 1 represents 1 true-breeding dominant, 2 heterozygous dominant and 1 true-breeding recessive progeny.

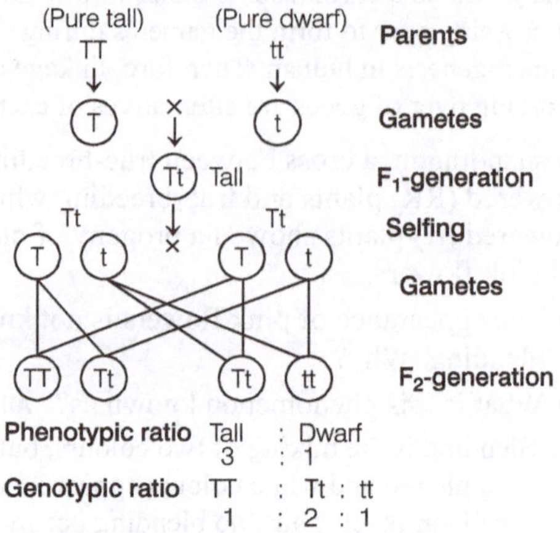

Two-third of tall progenies are heterozygous because gene for tallness (T) is dominant and also expresses itself in heterozygous condition. It is due to this reason that a difference is observed in F_2 phenotypic and genotypic ratio.

63. How is the phenotypic ratio of F_2-generation in a dihybrid cross is different from monohybrid cross? **All India 2012**

Ans. In a monohybrid cross, the phenotypic ratio of F_2-generation is 3 : 1, whereas in dihybrid cross, the pheonotypic ratio of F_2-generation is 9 : 3 : 3 : 1. **(1+1)**

64. In a dihybrid cross, white-eyed, yellow-bodied female *Drosophila* crossed with red-eyed, brown-bodied male *Drosophila* produced in F_2-generation 1.3% recombinants and 98.7% progeny with parental type combinations. This observation of Morgan deviated from Mendelian F_2-phenotypic dihybrid ratio. Explain, giving reasons Morgan's observation. **Foreign 2011**

Ans. The results obtained were due to the linkage. It is the phenomenon in which two or more linked genes are inherited together and their frequency of recombination in a test cross progeny is less than the expected 50%. In Morgan's experiment on *Drosophila*, the genes for eye colour and body colour show linkage and do not allow crossing over during gamete formation. Hence, parental type progeny is in greater ratio than that of recombinants.

3 Marks Questions

65. Expression of different genes for different traits may show dominance, incomplete dominance or co-dominance. Write about expression of such genes with the help of one example each. **CBSE 2024 (Set-II)**

Ans. Expression of different genes for different traits may show dominance, incomplete dominance or co-dominance based on expression of genes.

(i) **Dominance** In this, one allele of a gene dominates (dominant) the other (recessive) and is able to express itself in the heterozygous condition also. e.g. a pea plant with two alleles of stem height- T (tall; dominant) and t (short; recessive).

For cross see page no. 91.

(ii) **Incomplete dominance** Refer to text on page no. 92.

(iii) **Co-dominance** Refer to text on page no. 92. **(3)**

66. How would you find out the genotype of a pea plant with violet flowers? Explain with the help of Punnett square showing crosses. **CBSE SQP 2021**

Ans. The genotype of an individual is determined by the test cross. In such cross, the individual whose genotype is to be determined is crossed with the homozygous recessive parent. To find out the genotype of a pea plant with violet flowers, it is crossed with the homozygous recessive parent. The possible genotype of violet flower plant would be Ww or WW.

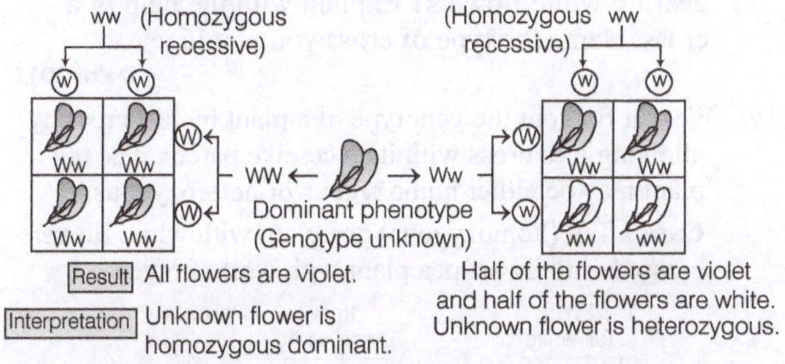

Diagrammatic representation of a test cross

67. State Mendel's law of dominance. How did he deduce the law? Explain with the help of a suitable example. **All India 2020**

Ans. Mendel's law of dominance states that when two individuals of a species, differing in a pair of contrasting forms of a trait are crossed, the form of the trait that appears in the F_1-hybrid is dominant and the other form that remains hidden is called as recessive trait. Mendel deduced this law through a monohybrid cross in a pea plant. He observed that only dominant trait for tallness expresses itself whether present in homozygous (TT) or heterozygous (Tt) state, while recessive trait, i.e. dwarfness expresses itself only in homozygous (tt) state. **(1)**

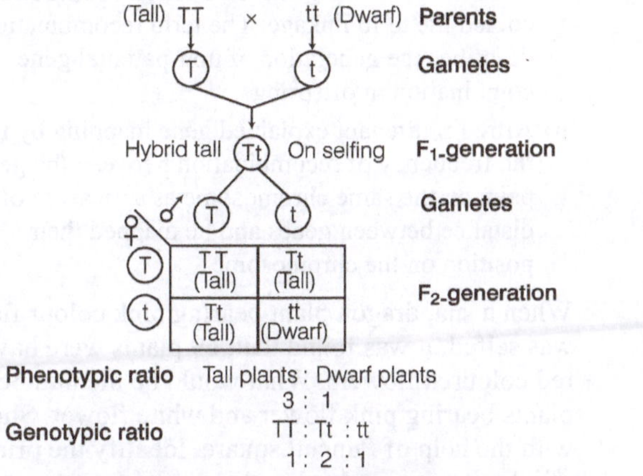

A monohybrid cross of true-breeding pea plant **(2)**

68. Explain Mendel's law of segregation in a typical monohybrid cross with the help of a suitable example. **All India 2020**

Ans. Refer to answer no. 99 (i).

69. Explain the phenomena of dominance, multiple allelism and codominance taking human ABO blood group as an example. **All India 2019**

Ans. Refer to text on page no. 91-93.

70. Compare in any three ways the chromosomal theory of inheritance as proposed by Sutton and Bovery with that of experimental results on pea plant presented by Mendel. **Delhi 2019**

Ans. Through any of the given ways chromosomal theory of inheritance and experimental results presented by Mendel can be compared

(i) In a diploid organism, the factors (genes) and chromosomes occur in pairs.

(ii) Both chromosomes as well as genes segregate at the time of gamete formation such that only one of each pair is transmitted to a gamete.

(iii) The paired condition of both chromosomes as well as Mendelian factors is restored during fertilisation. **(1 × 3)**

71. (i) Explain the linkage and recombination as put forth by TH Morgan based on his observations with *Drosophila melanogaster* crossing experiment.

(ii) Write the basis on which Alfred Sturtevant explained gene mapping. **Delhi 2019**

Ans. (i) TH Morgan studied X-linked gene in *Drosophila* and saw that when the two genes in a dihybrid cross were situated on the same chromosome, the proportion of parental gene combinations were much higher than the non-parental type.

He attributed this due to the physical association or linkage of the two genes on a chromosome and coined the term linkage. The term recombination describes the generation of non-parental gene combination in offsprings. **(1½)**

(ii) Alfred Sturtevant explained gene mapping by using the frequency of recombination between the gene pairs on the same chromosome as a measure of the distance between genes and he mapped their position on the chromosome. **(1½)**

72. When a snapdragon plant bearing pink colour flower was selfed, it was found that, 69 plants were having red coloured flowers. What would be the number of plants bearing pink flower and white flower. Show with the help of Punnett square. Identify the principle of inheritance involved in this experiment. **CBSE SQP 2018**

Ans. In a self-cross of snapdragon plant bearing pink flower, 69 plants were having red coloured flowers, 69 plants were having white coloured flowers and 138 plants were having pink coloured flowers. This can be shown as

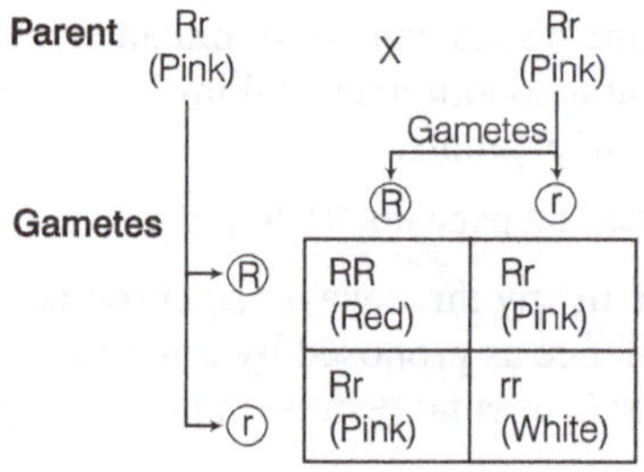

Genotypic ratio — 1 : 2 : 1
(RR : Rr : rr)

Phenotypic ratio — 1 : 2 : 1 **(1)**
(Red : Pink : White)

If, plants having red coloured flower are 69 then plants having pink coloured flower

$= 2 \times 69$
$= 138$

Plants having white coloured flower = 69 **(1)**

The principle of inheritance involved in this cross is **incomplete dominance.** **(1)**

73. What is a test cross? How can it decipher the heterozygosity of a plant? **All India 2016**

Ans. Test cross is a method devised by Mendel to determine the genotype of an organism. In this cross, the organism with an unknown dominant genotype is crossed with the recessive parent, instead of self-crossing.

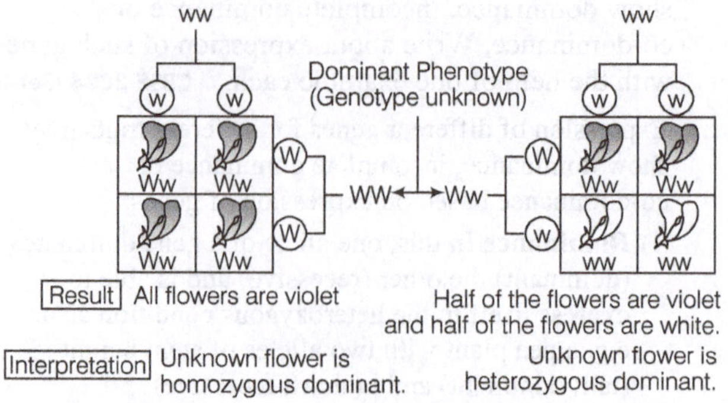

For example, in a monohybrid cross, between violet colour flower (W) and white colour flower (w), the F_1-hybrid was a violet colour flower.

If all the F_1-progenies are of violet colour, then the dominant flower is homozygous and if the progenies are in 1 : 1 ratio, then it is deciphered that dominant flower is heterozygous.

Common Mistakes Students usually get confused between a test cross and a back cross.

Back Cross: F_1 generation × parents (dominant or recessive) while, **test cross :** F_1-generation × recessive parents.

74. How would you find genotype of a tall pea plant bearing white flowers? Explain with the help of a cross. Name the type of cross you would use. **Delhi 2016**

Ans. We can find out the genotype of a plant by test cross by allowing it to cross with its recessive parent. The tall plant may be either homozygous or hetorozygous.

Case I Tall (homozygous) pea plant with white flowers crossed with dwarf pea plant with white flowers.

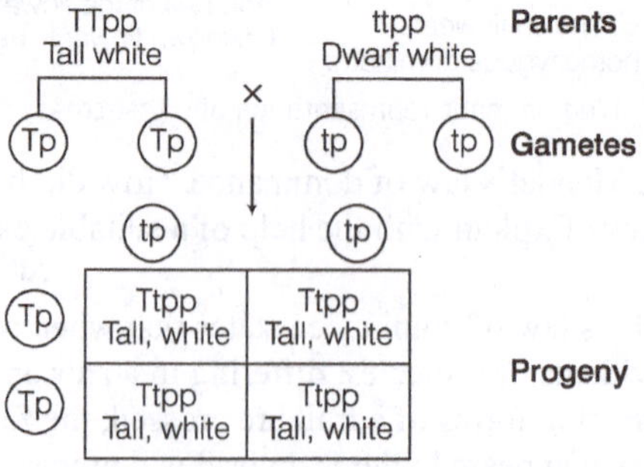

If plant produces all tall plants with white flowers as offspring, then genotype of plant is TTpp, i.e. homozygous tall plant with white flowers.

Case II Tall (heterozygous) pea plant with white flowers is crossed with dwarf pea plant with white flowers. If plant produces both tall plant with white flowers and dwarf plant with white flowers, then genotype of plant is Ttpp, i.e. heterozygous tall pea plant with white flowers.

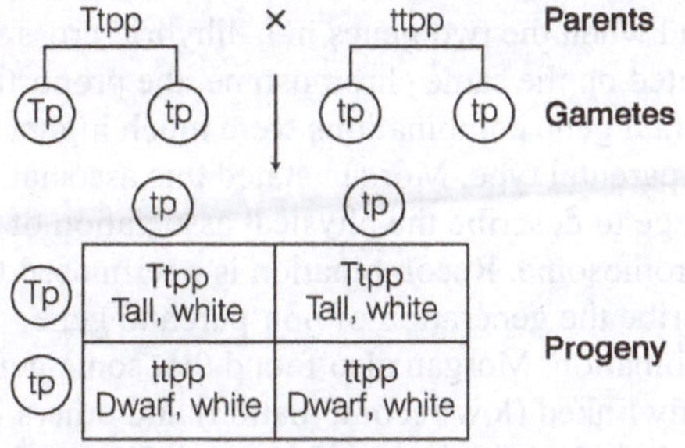

75. Although Mendel published his work on inheritance of characters in 1865 but for several reasons, it remained unrecognised till 1900. Explain giving three reasons, why did it take so long. **Delhi 2016C**

Or Mendel published his work on inheritance of characters in 1865, but it remained unrecognised till 1900. Give three reasons for the delay in accepting his work. **Delhi 2014**

Ans. The following are the three reasons that led to delay in accepting Mendel's work.

(i) Lack of communication and less published work. **(1)**

(ii) His concept of factors (genes) as discrete units that did not blend with each other was not accepted in the light of variations occurring continuously in nature. **(1)**

(iii) Mendel's approach to explain biological phenomenon with the help of mathematics was also not accepted. **(1)**

76. Explain the laws that Mendel derived from his monohybrid crosses. **Delhi 2016C**

Ans. From monohybrid crosses, Mendel derived law of dominance and law of segregation.

Refer to text on page no. 91 for detailed description of these laws.

77. A teacher wants his/her students to find the genotype of pea plants bearing purple coloured flowers in their school garden. Name and explain the cross that will make it possible. **Delhi 2015**

Ans. Test cross is a method devised by Mendel to determine the genotype of a plant with dominant phenotype (purple flower in this case). In a test cross, the unknown dominant genotype is crossed with recessive parent (white, ww in the given case). **(1)**

(i) If the progeny consists of purple and white flowers in ratio of 1:1, the purple flower is a hybrid with Ww genotype. It can be seen from the given cross.

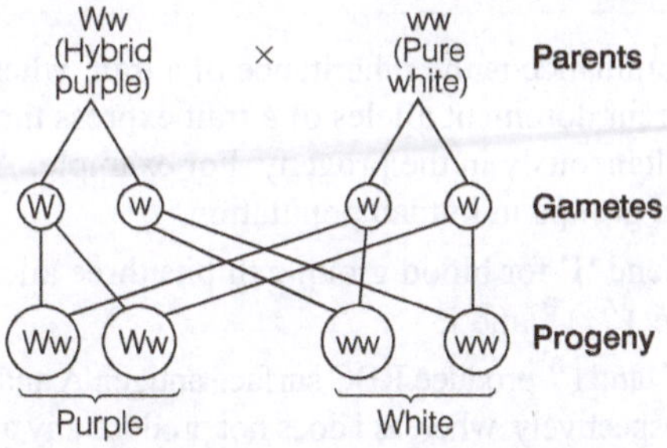

(1)

(ii) If the progeny obtained have all purple flowers, both parents are homozygous, i.e. genotype of purple flower is WW.

It can be seen from the cross that follows

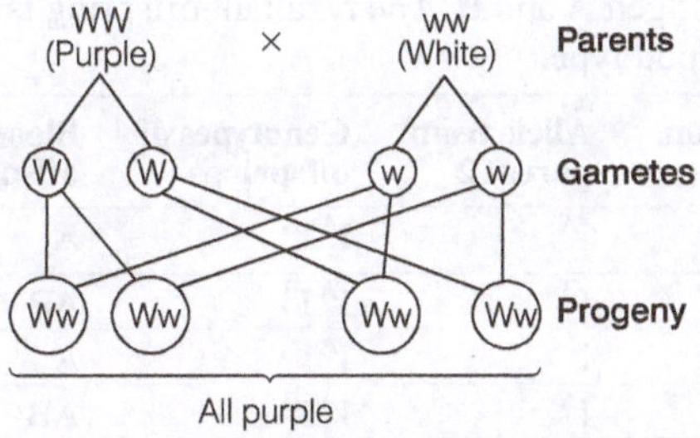

(1)

78. During a monohybrid cross involving a tall pea plant with a dwarf pea plant, the offspring populations were tall and dwarf in equal ratio. Work out a cross to show how it is possible? **All India 2015**

Ans. In a monohybrid test cross, involving a heterozygous tall plant (Tt) and a pure dwarf plant (tt), the progeny consists of tall and dwarf plants in the ratio of 1 : 1. This can be shown as follows **(1)**

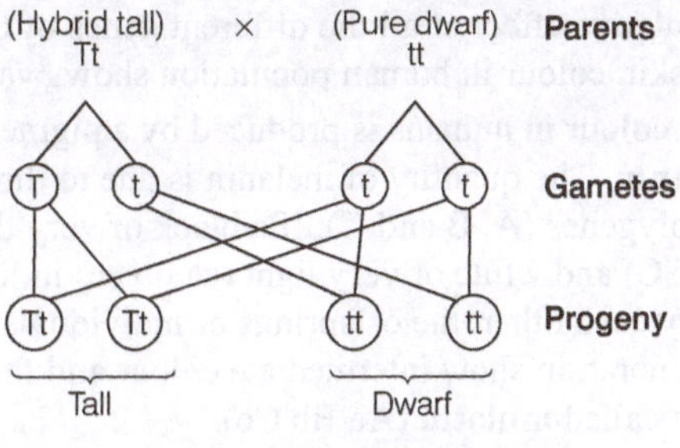

(2)

79. Explain with the help of a suitable example, the inheritance of a trait where two different dominant alleles of a trait express themselves simultaneously in the progeny. Name this kind of inheritance pattern.
All India 2014C

> **KEY idea**
> Incomplete dominance and codominance show the deviation from Mendelian principles.

Ans. Codominance is the inheritance of a trait where two different dominant alleles of a trait express themselves simultaneously in the progeny. For example, ABO blood groups in human population.

(i) Gene 'I' for blood group exhibits three allelic forms, i.e. I^A, I^B and i.

(ii) I^A and I^B produce RBC surface antigen A and B respectively, whereas i does not produce any antigen.

(iii) I^A and I^B are codominant alleles, and they both are dominant over 'i' which is a recessive allele.

(iv) In case I^A and I^B are present together, both express themselves equally and produce both surface antigen A and B. The resultant offspring is of 'AB' blood type.

Allele from parent 1	Allele from parent 2	Genotypes of offsprings	Blood types of offsprings
I^A	I^A	I^AI^A	A
I^A	I^B	I^AI^B	AB
I^A	i	I^Ai	A
I^B	I^A	I^AI^B	AB
I^B	I^B	I^BI^B	B
I^B	i	I^Bi	B
i	i	ii	O

80. Explain polygenic inheritance with the help of a suitable example. **All India 2014**

Ans. Polygenic inheritance is an inheritance pattern controlled by three or more genes (multiple genes) and the graded phenotypes are due to the additive or cumulative effect of all the different genes of the trait, e.g. skin colour in human population shows variation.

Skin colour in humans is produced by a pigment called **melanin**. The quantity of melanin is due to three pairs of polygenes (A, B and C). If a black or very dark (AA BB CC) and white or very light (aa bb cc) individuals marry each other, the offsprings or individuals of F_1-generation show intermediate colour and they are often called **mulatto** (Aa Bb Cc).

A total of eight allele combinations are possible in the gametes forming 27 distinct genotypes distributed into 7 phenotypes, i.e. 1 very dark, 6 dark, 15 fairly dark, 20 intermediate, 15 fairly light, 6 light and 1 very light.

81. Morgan carried out several dihybrid crosses in *Drosophila* and found F_2 ratios deviated very significantly from the expected Mendelian ratio. Explain his finding with the help of an example.
All India 2014C; Delhi 2010

Ans. Morgan's studies on *Drosophila* were based on the genes that were located on the X-chromosome. He found when the two genes in a dihybrid cross were situated on the same chromosome, the proportion of parental gene combinations were much higher than the non-parental type. Morgan stated this association as linkage to describe the physical association of genes on a chromosome. Recombination is a term used to describe the generation of non-parental gene combination. Morgan also found that some genes were tightly linked (low recombination) and others were loosely linked (high recombination). He concluded that in case of inheritance of linked genes, the phenotypic ratio deviates from expected 9 : 3 : 3 : 1 ratio of Mendel's dihybrid cross.

To prove his findings, Morgan hybridised yellow-bodied and white-eyed females with brown-bodied and red-eyed males (wild type) and intercrossed their F_1-progeny (cross A). It was observed that the two genes did not segregate independently from each other and the F_2-ratio deviated significantly from 9 : 3 : 3 : 1 ratio.

In F_2-generation, parental combinations were 98.7% and the recombinants were 1.3%. In another cross (cross B), between white-bodied female fly with miniature wing and a male fly with yellow body and normal wing, parental combinations were 62.8% and recombinants were 37.2% in F_2-generation. Thus, it was proved from the crosses that the linkage between genes for yellow body and white eyes was stronger than the linkage between the white, 6 light body and miniature wing.

> **Common Mistakes** Students usually get confused between linkage and recombination, in **Linkage**, two or more linked genes are always inherited together in the same combination for more than two generation.
>
> In **Recombination** process, pieces of DNA are broken and recombined to produce new combinations of alleles.

82. (i) Write the conclusion Mendel arrived at on dominance of traits on the basis of monohybrid crosses that he carried out in pea plants.

(ii) Explain why a recessive allele is unable to express itself in a heterozygous state. **Foreign 2014**

Ans. (i) In a monohybrid cross in pea plant, Mendel found that only dominant trait expresses itself in offspring no matter whether it is present in homozygous state (TT) or in heterozygous state (Tt). Dominant trait does not require another similar allele to produce its effect on the phenotype, in fact it has the ability to mask the effect of recessive allele.

Based on this observation, Mendel proposed the law of dominance. **(1½)**

(ii) Since, the characters are controlled by genes which occur in pair, when two alternate forms of a trait or character (genes or alleles) are present in an organism, only one factor expresses itself in F_1-generation. This factor is dominant, while the other factor that remains masked by the dominant factor is called as recessive.

The recessive allele is unable to express itself in a heterozygous state because it forms an incomplete or defective polypeptide or enzyme, so its expression does not contain any effect. In contrast, dominant allele can form complete polypeptide or enzyme to express its effect. **(1½)**

83. In pea plants, the colour of the flower is either violet or white, whereas human skin colour shows many gradation. Explain giving reasons how it is possible. **Delhi 2013C**

Ans. In pea plants, the colour of the flower is either violet or white because the colour is purely dependent on two alleles and the crossing between them, i.e. violet and white in the parents generation, which results in F_1-generation. Thus, the resultant offsprings are either violet or white coloured. Hence, the inheritance pattern of flower colour in pea plant follows the law of dominance. **(1)**

But in case of humans, skin colour is produced by polygenes. Such inheritance is controlled by one or more genes in which dominant alleles have cumulative effect with each dominant allele expressing a part of the trait. The full trait is shown only when all the dominant alleles are present together. **(1)**

The quantity of human skin pigment melanin determines the human skin colour (i.e. very dark, dark, fairly dark, intermediate, fairly light, light and very light). Refer to answer no. 80. **(1)**

84. A pea plant with purple flowers was crossed with white flowers producing all plants with only purple flowers. On selfing, these plants produced 482 plants with purple flowers and 162 with white flowers. What genetic mechanism accounts for these results? Explain. **Delhi 2011**

Ans.

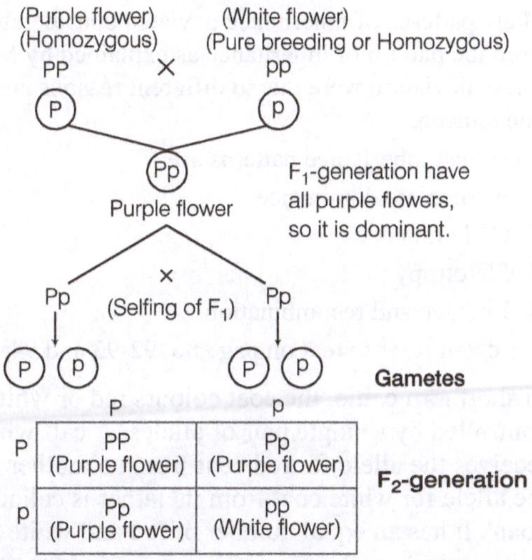

Purple flowered plants : White flowered plants are in the ratio of 482 : 162 which is approximately equal to 3 : 1. **(2)**

The genetic mechanism for these results is explained below

(i) Factors segregate from each other during gamete formation that remain together in a parent.

(ii) A homozygous parent produces all gametes that are similar, while heterozyogous parent produces two kinds of gametes in equal ratio. **(1)**

85. Work out a cross between true-breeding red and white flowered dog flower plants (snapdragon) upto F_2 progeny. Explain the results of F_1 and F_2-generations. **Foreign 2010**

Ans. For cross, refer to answer no. 51. **(1)**

In F_1-generation Pink flowered plants are obtained. It is due to incomplete dominance. **(1)**

In F_2-generation Alleles of the hybrid (F_1) segregate during gamete formation and the parental characters reappear. So, the phenotypic and genotypic ratios in F_2-generation are same.

RR	:	Rr	:	rr
1	:	2	:	1

(1)

5 Marks Questions

86. Many patterns of inheritance deviate considerably from the pattern of inheritance as explained by Mendel. List any four such inheritance patterns and explain any three with the help of an example each. **CBSE 2024 (Set-I)**

Ans. Many patterns of inheritance deviated considerably from the pattern of inheritance as explained by Mendel. These deviation were due to different reasons and phenomena. **(2)**

Four such inheritance patterns are

1. Incomplete dominance
2. Codominance
3. Pleiotropy
4. Linkage and recombination **(3)**

For detail refer to text on page no. 92-93 and 94.

87. In shorthorn cattle, the coat colours red or white are controlled by a single pair of alleles. A calf which receives the allele for red coat from its mother and the allele for white coat from its father is called a 'roan'. It has an equal number of red and white hairs in its coat. **CBSE SQP 2023**

(i) Is this an example of codominance or of incomplete dominance?

(ii) Give a reason for your answer.

(iii) With the help of genetic cross explain what will be the consequent phenotype of the calf when

(a) red is dominant over white

(b) red is incompletely dominant.

Ans. (i) Codominance. **(½)**

(ii) Codominance is a condition in which two different alleles for a genetic trait are expressed. Individuals receive one version of a gene, called an allele, from each parent. **(½)**

(iii) (a) If pure breeding red coated cattles are represented as 'RR' and pure breeding white coated as 'rr'. If red is dominant over white. A cross between 'RR' and 'rr' would produce red coated cattles (Rr) in F_1-generation. Red and white coated cattle in the ratio of 3 : 1 in F_2-generation.

Parents RR (Red) × rr (White)
Gametes R r
F_1-generation Rr
Gametes R r
Selfing

	R	r
R	RR Red coat	Rr Red coat
r	Rr Red coat	rr White coat

F_2-generation 3 : 1 **(2)**

(b) If the red and white coated cattles produce pink colour on a cross then, they exhibit incomplete dominance in the inheritance of coat colour due to which they produce pink coloured coat upon hybridisation.

If pure breeding red coated cattles are represented as 'RR' and pure breeding white coated as 'rr', then the pink coated cattles are 'Rr'.

A cross between 'RR' and 'rr' would produce red coated catties (RR), pink coated cattles (Rr) and white coated cattle (rr) in the ratio of 1 :2: 1

Parents RR (Red) × rr (White)
Gametes R r
F_1-generation Rr
Gametes R r
Selfing

	R	r
R	RR Red coat	Rr Pink coat
r	Rr Pink coat	rr White coat

F_2-generation 1 : 2 : 1 **(2)**

88. Describe the dihybrid cross upto F_2-generation as conducted by Gregor Mendel using pure lines of garden pea for characters seed shape and seed colour. **CBSE 2023**

Or State and explain the 'law of independent assortment' in a typical Mendelian dihybrid cross. **Delhi 2017**

Or Using Punnett square show the F_2 result of a dihybrid cross where the pure breed parents have contrasting traits with reference to seed shape and seed colour in *Pisum sativum*. Give the phenotypic ratio. **Delhi 2013C**

Or Workout a typical Mendelian dihybrid cross and state the law that he derived from it. **All India 2014**

Ans. **Law of Independent Assortment** (Third law) is based on the inheritance of two genes, i.e. dihybrid cross which states that when two pairs of contrasting traits are combined in a hybrid, segregation of one pair of characters is independent of the other pair of characters. **(2)**

These factors randomly rearrange in the offspring producing both parental and new combination of characters. It means inheritance of one character does not affect the inheritance of another character and both characters assort independently during gamete formation. The Punnett square can be used to understand the independent segregation of the two pairs of genes during meiosis.

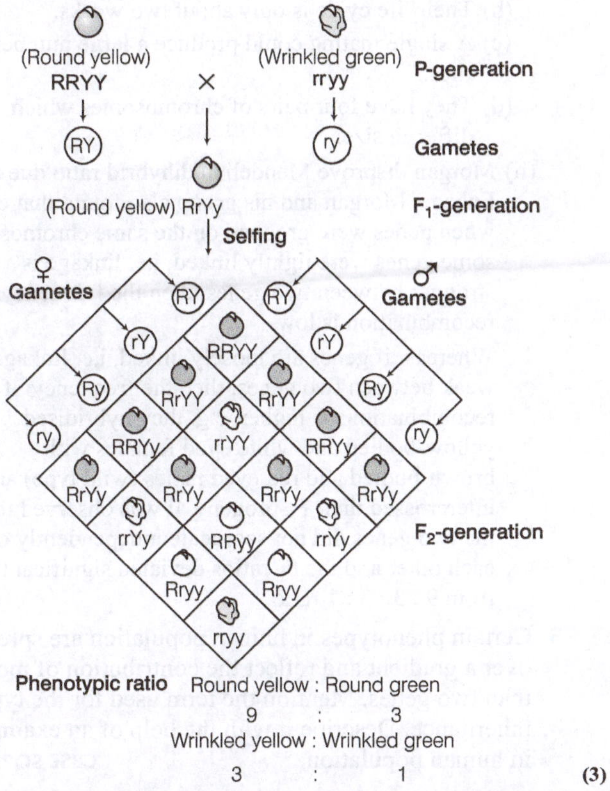

(3)

89. It is sometimes observed that the F_1 - progeny has a phenotype that does not resemble either of the two parents and has intermediate phenotype. Explain by taking a suitable example and working out the cross upto F_2 - progeny. **CBSE 2023**

Ans. The phenomenon described in the question is called incomplete dominance or partial dominance. It is a phenomenon, in which dominant alleles is not able to mask the characters of recessive allele completely, hence an intermediate phenotype is obtained. It is an exception to Mendel's law of dominance. (2)

For example, inheritance of flower colour in the dog flower (snapdragon or *Antirrhinum* sp.) and four O clock plant (*Mirabilis jalapa*).

In snapdragon, cross between red flower (RR) and white flower (rr) plant, produces the F_1 - generation containing pink (Rr) flower. When F_1 plants are self-pollinated, the F_2 - generation containing red, pink and white flowers in the ratio of 1 : 2 : 1 is formed. In incomplete dominance, genotypic ratio of F_2 remains same as mendel's monohybrid cross, i.e. 1 : 2 : 1, but phenotypic ratio changes from 3 : 1 to 1 : 2 : 1. hence, in this case, both phenotypic and genotypic ratios are similar.

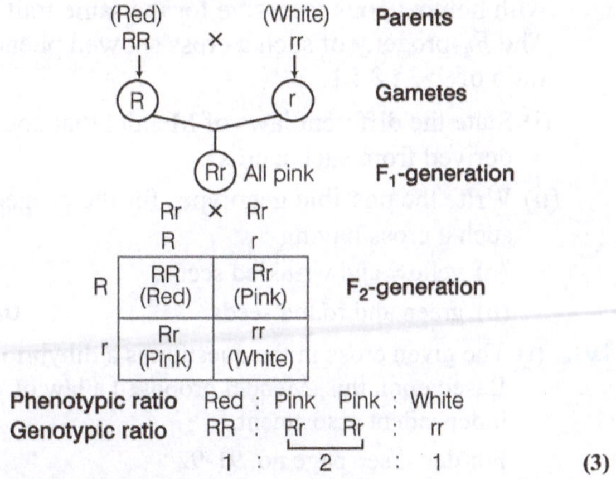

(3)

90. "It is sometimes observed that the F_1 - progeny shows a phenotype that resembles both the parents." Explain this type of inheritance using the example of A, B, O blood groups in human **CBSE 2023**

Ans. Codominance is the inheritance of a trait where F_1 -progeny shows a phenotype that resembles both the parents. In this type of inheritance two different alleles of a trait express themselves simultaneously in the progeny. For example, ABO blood groups in human population.

(i) Gene I for blood group exhibits three allelic forms, i.e. I^A, I^B and i.

(ii) I^A and I^B produce RBC surface antigen A and B respectively, whereas i does not produce any antigen.

(iii) I^A and I^B are codomiant alleles, and they both are dominant over i which is a recessive allele.

(iv) In case I^A and I^B are present together, both express themselves equally and produce both surface antigen A and B. The resultant offspring is of AB blood type. (2)

Allele from parent 1	Allele from parent 2	Genotype of offspring	Blood types of offspring
I^A	I^A	I^AI^A	A
I^A	I^B	I^AI^B	AB
I^A	i	I^A i	A
I^B	I^A	I^AI^B	AB
I^B	I^B	I^BI^B	B
I^B	i	I^B i	B
i	i	ii	O

(3)

91. A cross was carried out between two pea plants homozygous dominant for yellow and round seeds with homozygous recessive for the same trait. The F_2-progeny of such a cross showed phenotypic ratio of 9: 3 : 3 : 1.

(i) State the different laws of Mendel that could be derived from such a cross.

(ii) Write the possible genotypes for the progeny for such a cross having

(a) yellow and wrinkled seeds.

(b) green and round seeds. **Delhi 2020**

Ans. (i) The given cross in the question is a dihybrid cross. Based upon this, Mendel proposed a law of independent assortment.

For detail see page no. 91-92. **(2)**

(ii) The possible genotype of the progeny in the above given dihybrid cross for different phenotypes are as follow

(a) Yellow and wrinkled seeds – YYrr, Yyrr.

(b) Green and round seed – yyRR, yyRr. **(3)**

92. A group of F_1 pea plants produce round and yellow seeds. However, when selfed their offspring provided a 9 : 3 : 3 : 1 phenotypic ratio for seed shape and colour, with some seeds being wrinkled and green and others wrinkled and yellow.

(i) Explain with the help of a Punnett square their phenotypes, genotypes and respective given phenotypic ratios of F_2-population.

(ii) State Mendel's law that can be deduced only from such a cross. **Delhi 2020**

Ans. Refer to text on page no. 91-92 and figure 4.1.

93. How do certain phenotypes appear in F_2 populations when none of the parents originally exhibited them in a dihybrid cross conducted by G Mendel in pea plants? Explain.

Prepare Punnett square to substantiate your answer. **Delhi 2020**

Ans. Certain phenotypes appear in F_2 populations when none of the parents originally exhibited them in a dihybrid cross conducted by G Mendel in pea plants due to law of independent assortment (third law).

For this refer to text on page no. 91-92.

94. (i) Why did TH Morgan select *Drosophila melanogaster* for his experiments ?

(ii) How did he disprove Mendelian dihybrid F_2 phenotypic ratio of 9 : 3 : 3 : 1 ? Explain giving reasons. **All India 2020**

Ans. (i) TH Morgan selected fruitfly (*Drosophila melanogaster*) for his experiments because

(a) They could be grown on simple artificial medium in the laboratory.

(b) Their life cycle is only about two weeks.

(c) A single mating could produce a large number of flies.

(d) They have four pairs of chromosomes which differ in size. **(2)**

(ii) Morgan disprove Mendelian dihybrid ratio due to linkage. Morgan and his group also found that even when genes were grouped on the same chromosome, some genes were tightly linked, i.e. linkage is stronger between two genes, then the frequency of recombination is low.

Whereas, if genes are loosely linked, i.e. linkage is weak between two genes, then the frequency of recombinations is higher, e.g. they hybridised yellow-bodied and white eyed females with brown-bodied and red eyed males (wild type) and intercrossed their F_1-progeny. It was observed that the two genes did not segregate independently of each other and the F_2 ratios deviated significantly from 9 : 3 : 3 : 1 ratio. **(3)**

95. Certain phenotypes in human population are spread over a gradient and reflect the contribution of more than two genes. Mention the term used for the type of inheritance. Describe it with the help of an example in human population. **CBSE SQP 2020**

Or (i) What is polygenic inheritance? Explain with the help of a suitable example.

(ii) How are pleiotropy and Mendelian pattern of inheritance different from polygenic pattern of inheritance?

Ans. (i) **Polygenic Inheritance** It was proposed by **Galton** in 1833 and he suggested that many instances of continuous variations are heritable. In this case, a trait is controlled by three or more genes and the graded phenotypes develop due to the additive or cumulative effect of all the different genes of the trait, e.g. human skin colour, height, intelligence, etc.

Polygene is a gene where one dominant allele controls only a unit or partial quantitative expression of a trait.

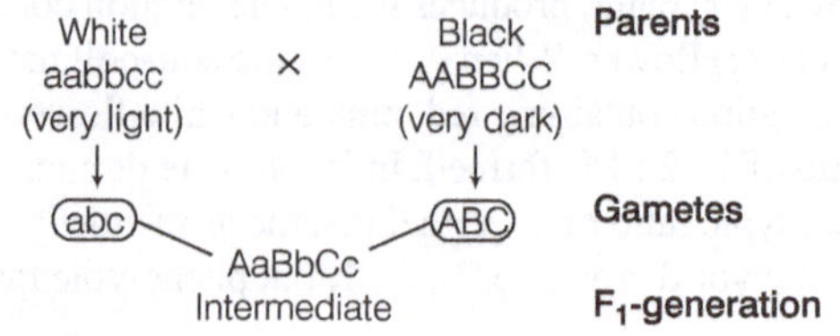

It also takes into account the influence of environment and is also called as **quantitative inheritance**, as the character or phenotype can be quantified, like the amount of pigment, intelligence in human beings and milk yield in animals. These characters have been found to be determined by many genes and their effects have been cumulative. These traits are called **polygenic traits**, e.g. human skin colour explains the phenomenon of polygenic inheritance.

Skin colour in human is produced by a pigment called **melanin**. The quantity of melanin is due to three pairs of polygenes (A, B and C). If black or very dark (AABBCC) and white or very light (aabbcc) individuals marry each other, the offsprings or individuals of F_1-generation show intermediate colour which are often called **mulatto** (AaBbCc). A total of eight allele combinations are possible in the gametes forming 27 distinct genotypes distributed into 7 phenotypes, i.e. 1 very dark, 6 dark, 15 fairly dark, 20 intermediate, 15 fairly light, 6 light and 1 very light. **(3)**

(ii) In pleiotropy, a single gene product may produce multiple or more than one phenotypic effect whereas in polygenic inheritance a single phenotypic trait (human skin colour) is controlled by 3 pairs of genes (A, B and C). In Mendelian inheritance, one gene controls one phenotypic character (flower colour red or white). However, in polygenic inheritnace one phenotype is controlled by more than one gene. **(2)**

96. (i) Work out the crosses so as to obtain the phenotypic ratios given below :

(a) 1 : 2 : 1 (in F_2-generation)

(b) 3 : 1 (in F_2-generation)

(c) 1 : 1 (in F_1-generation)

(ii) Differentiate between pleiotropy and polygenic inheritance patterns. **All India 2019**

Ans. (i) (a) 1 : 2 : 1 (in F_2-generation) is the phenotypic ratio of incomplete dominance.

Refer to figure 4.2 on page no. 92.

(b) 3 : 1 (in F_2-generation) is the phenotypic ratio of monohybrid cross.

Refer to answer no 62.

(c) 1 : 1 (in F_1-generation) is the phenotypic ratio of test cross.

Refer to text and figure of 'Test cross' on page no. 91. **(2½)**

(ii) Differences between pleiotropy and polygenic inheritance are

Pleiotropy	Polygenic inheritance
Single gene product confers many physiological effects.	Single phenotypic effect is under the control of many genes.
The genes involved are called pleiotropic genes.	The genes involved are called polygenes.
e.g. phenylketonuria.	e.g. human skin colour.

(2½)

97. Differentiate between incomplete dominance and codominance. Substantiate your answer with one example of each. **Delhi 2019**

Ans. Differences between codominance and incomplete dominance are

Codominance	Incomplete dominance
It is the appearance of both parental phenotypes together in the offspring when a cross is done between individuals with two different phenotypes.	It is the appearance of an intermediate phenotype, which is a combination of both parental alleles when a cross is done between individuals with two different phenotypes.
Both parental alleles produce their effect independently.	Effect of the two parental alleles is intermediate on the offspring.
Both parental alleles can be observed in the offspring.	None of parental alleles can be observed in the offspring.
Examples include ABO blood group, etc. Six different genotypes of human ABO blood group show four phenotypes–A, B, AB and O.	Examples include inheritance of flower colour in the dogflower, etc. Here, the genotypic ratio of F_2 remains same as Mendel's monohybrid cross, i.e. 1: 2 : 1, but phenotypic ratio changes from 3:1 to 1 : 2 : 1.

98. (i) Write the scientific name of the organism Thomas Hunt Morgan and his colleagues worked with for their experiments.

Explain the correlation between linkage and recombination with respect to genes as studied by them.

(ii) How did Sturtevant explain gene mapping while working with Morgan? **CBSE 2018**

Ans. (i) **Thomas Hunt Morgan** and his colleagues worked on *Drosophila melanogaster.*

Relation between Linkage and Recombination

Morgan carried out dihybrid crosses in *Drosophila* to study sex-linked genes. Morgan hybridised yellow-bodied, white-eyed females to brown-bodied, red-eyed males. He intercrossed their F_1- progeny. It was observed that the two genes did not segregate independently of each other. The F_2 ratio deviated from the ratio of 9 : 3 : 3 : 1.

It was known to Morgan and his colleagues that genes were located on X-chromosomes. They noticed that when the two genes in a dihybrid cross were situated on the same **chromosome**, the proportion of parental combination was very high in comparison to non-parental type. He attributed this due to the physical association or linkage of the two genes. To describe this physical association of gene, he coined the term **linkage**. Recombination term was used to describe the generation of non-parental gene combinations. In his experiments, he observed that even when genes were grouped on the same chromosome, some genes were very tightly linked and showed very low recombination. On the other hand, loosely linked genes showed higher recombination. **(3)**

(ii) **Sturtevant**, a student of Morgan, used the frequency of recombination between the gene pairs on the same chromosomes as a measure of the distance between genes. He mapped the position of genes on the chromosome by using this information. **(2)**

99. (i) A couple with blood group A and B, respectively have a child with blood group O. Work out a cross to show how it is possible and the probable blood groups that can be expected in their other offspring?

(ii) Explain the genetic basis of blood groups in human population. **All India 2015C, Delhi 2015**

Ans. (i) Parents must be heterozygous since blood group 'O' appears in progeny. The progeny can have all the four blood groups, A, B, AB and O. There are three alleles of the gene controlling blood group character, i.e. I^A, I^B and i. I^A and I^B are dominant over i and together they are codominant to each other.

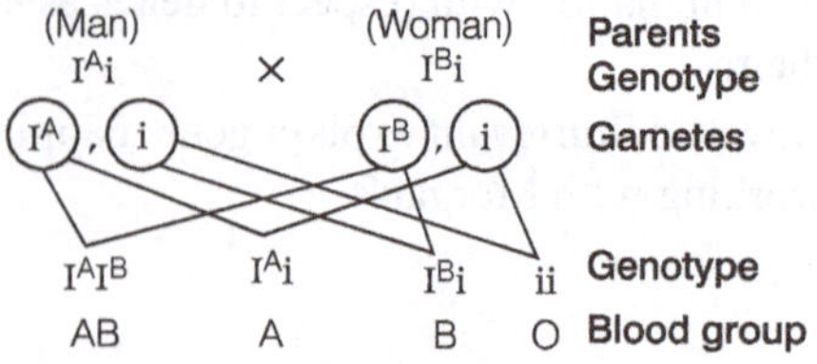

(3)

(ii) ABO blood grouping in humans shows the phenomenon of codominance. Refer to answer no. 78. **(2)**

Concept Enhancer A non-Mendelian trait does not pass on to successive generations. This is because, some genes may disobey Mendelian laws of inheritance and not seggregate in accordance to Mendel's laws, e.g. blood types, hair colour, height, etc.

100. (i) State and explain the law of segregation as proposed by Mendel in a monohybrid cross.

(ii) Write the Mendelian F_2 phenotypic ratio in a dihybrid cross. State the law that he proposed on the basis of this ratio. How is this law different from the law of segregation? **Foreign 2015**

Ans. (i) Law of segregation states that the factors or alleles of a pair segregate from each other during gamete formation in a way that a gamete receives only one of the two factors. They do not show any blending.

The pattern of inheritance can be understood by crossing F_1-hybrid (Tt heterozygous) of a tall plant with a dwarf plant.

Here, hybrid tall makes two types of gametes (T) and (t), while pure dwarf makes only one type of gamete, i.e. (t). It is because only one allele can enter in a gamete for a character. **(2)**

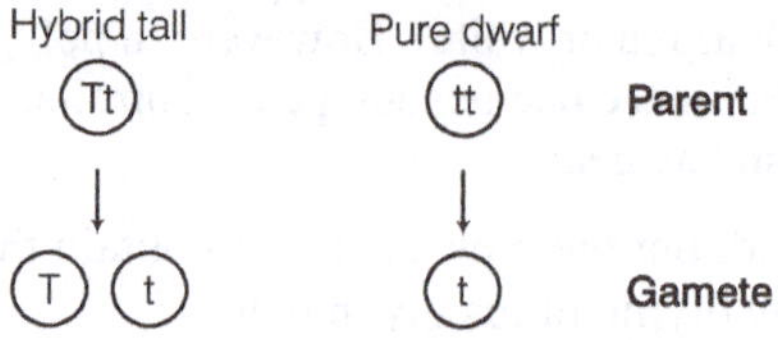

(ii) (a) Mendelian F_2 phenotypic ratio in a dihybrid cross is 9 : 3 : 3 : 1. **(1)**

(b) Law of independent assortment was proposed on the basis of dihybrid cross. It states that when two pairs of contrasting traits are combined in a hybrid, segregation of one pair of characters is independent of the other pair of characters. **(1)**

Differences between law of segregation and law of independent assortment are

Law of segregation	Law of independent assortment
It is based on the monohybrid cross.	It is based on the dihybrid cross.
It explains non-mixing of two alleles of a gene at the time of gamete formation.	It explains non-mixing of characters during their inheritance to the next generation.

(1)

101. Give a genetic explanation for the following cross. When a tall pea plant with round seeds was crossed with a dwarf pea plant with wrinkled seeds then all the individuals of F_1-population were tall with round seeds. However, selfing among F_1-population led to a 9 : 3 : 3 : 1 phenotypic ratio. **All India 2015**

Ans. The cross given in the question is a dihybrid cross, which explains the third law of Mendel, i.e. law of independent assortment. In a **dihybrid cross** inheritance pattern of two traits are considered simultaneously. This law states that when two pairs of traits are combined in a hybrid, segregation of one pair of character is independent of the other pair of characters at the time of gamete formation. The alleles controlling these characters also get randomly rearranged in the offspring producing both parental and new combinations of characters. (2)

Parents: Tall plant Round seeds (TTRR) × Dwarf plant Wrinkled seeds (ttrr)

Gametes: TR, tr

F_1-progeny: TtRr

Selfing: TtRr × TtRr

F_2-generation

♀ \ ♂	TR	Tr	tR	tr
TR	TTRR	TTRr	TtRR	TtRr
Tr	TTRr	TTrr	TtRr	Ttrr
tR	TtRR	TtRr	ttRR	ttRr
tr	TtRr	Ttrr	ttRr	ttrr

Phenotypic ratio 9 : 3 : 3 : 1

The ratio 9 : 3 : 3 : 1 was obtained because the factors of height of plant and those for shape of seeds have segregated independently and each gamete has one factor for each of these two traits. (3)

102. A cross was carried out between a pea plant heterozygous for round and yellow seeds with a pea plant having wrinkled and green seeds.

(i) Show the cross in a Punnett square.

(ii) Write the phenotype of the progeny of this cross.

(iii) What is this cross known as? State the purpose of conducting such a cross.

All India 2014C; Foreign 2014

Ans. (i) RrYy (Heterozygous round and yellow) × rryy (Wrinkled and green seeds)

♀ \ ♂	RY	Ry	rY	ry
ry	RrYy	Rryy	rrYy	rryy

Phenotypic ratio 1 : 1 : 1 : 1

Genotypic ratio 1 : 1 : 1 : 1 (2)

(ii) **Phenotypic ratio** Round yellow : Round green : Wrinkled yellow : Wrinkled green = 1 : 1 : 1 : 1

Genotypic ratio 1 : 1 : 1 : 1 (1)

(iii) This cross is known as dihybrid test cross. The purpose of this cross is to determine the relationship between different allelic pairs. (2)

103. Work out a monohybrid cross up to F_2-generation between two pea plants and two *Antirrhinum* plants both having contrasting traits with respect to colour of flower.

Comment on the pattern of inheritance in the crosses carried above. **All India 2014C**

Ans. Refer to answer no. 84 for cross showing inheritance pattern of flower colour in garden pea plant.

Phenotypic ratio Purple : White
3 : 1

Genotypic ratio PP : Pp : pp
1 : 2 : 1

Inheritance of flower colour in garden pea shows true dominance. In F_1-generation, dominant colour purple is expressed and in F_2-generation, both dominant (purple) and recessive (white) colours are expressed in the ratio of 3 : 1. (2½)

Inheritance pattern of flower colour in *Antirrhium* (snapdragon), refer to answer no. 88.

Inheritance in snapdragon flower colour shows incomplete dominance. In this phenomenon, neither of the two alleles is completely dominant over the other and the hybrid is intermediate between the two. Hence, red is homozygous dominant, white is homozygous recessive, while hybrid is intermediate, i.e. pink. (2½)

104. (i) Differentiate between dominance and codominance.

(ii) Explain codominance taking an example of human blood groups in the population. **All India 2013**

Ans. (i) Difference between dominance and codominance is

Dominance	Codominance
Out of the two contrasting alleles of a gene, only one can produce effect in heterozygous condition, e.g. trait of tallness in pea plants.	Both the alternative forms of a gene can produce effect in heterozygous condition, e.g. ABO blood grouping in humans.

(2)

(ii) Refer to answer no. 79. (3)

105. (i) Explain Mendel's law of independent assortment by taking a suitable example.

(ii) How did Morgan show the deviation in inheritance pattern in *Drosophila* with respect to this law? **All India 2013**

Ans. (i) Refer to answer no. 88. **(3)**

(ii) Morgan found that linkage is an exception to the law of independent assortment.

Conclusion of Morgan's studies, refer to answer no. 80. **(2)**

> **Concept Enhancer** The recombination frequency and linkage between gene is inversely proportional. That is, if any two genes are completely linked, their recombination frequency is almost 0%.

106. What is the inheritance pattern observed in the size of starch grains and seed shape of *Pisum sativum*. Work out the monohybrid cross showing the above traits. How does this pattern of inheritance deviate from that of Mendelian law of dominance? **Delhi 2013**

Or Pea seeds with BB alleles have round seeds and large starch grains, while seeds with bb alleles have wrinkled seeds with small starch grains.

Work out the cross between these two parents. Explain the phenotypic ratio of the progeny with respect to seed shape and the starch grain size of the progeny produced. **All India 2012C**

Ans. The starch synthesis in pea plants is controlled by a single gene. It has two alleles B and b.

BB homozygotes produce large starch grains as compared to that produced by bb homozygotes.

After maturation, it was observed that BB seeds were round and bb were wrinkled. When they were crossed, the resultant progeny have intermediate sized (Bb) seeds. **(2)**

The cross involved is

BB × bb — P-generation

↓

Bb — F_1-generation

↓ Selfing

F_2-generation:

	B	b
B	BB	Bb
b	Bb	bb

Phenotypic ratio is

1 : 2 : 1

Large : Inter mediate : Wrinkled **(2)**

Deviation from Mendel's law of dominance If starch grain size is considered as the phenotype, then the alleles show incomplete dominance.

Thus, dominance is not an autonomous feature of a gene, it depends on gene product and production of particular phenotype from this product. **(1)**

107. Differentiate between the following.

(i) Polygenic inheritance and pleiotropy.

(ii) Dominance, codominance and incomplete dominance. **All India 2013C; Delhi 2011**

Ans. (i) Differences between polygenic inheritance and pleiotropy are

Polygenic inheritance	Pleiotropy
Single phenotypic effect is under the control of many genes.	Single gene product confers many phenotypic effects.
The genes involved are called polygenes, e.g. human skin colour.	The genes involved are called pleiotropic genes, e.g. phenylketonuria.

(2)

(ii) Differences between dominance, codominance and incomplete dominance are

Dominance	Codominance	Incomplete dominance
It is a relationship between alleles of a single gene, in which one allele masks the phenotypic expression of another allele at the same gene locus, e.g. tallness in pea plant.	It is the phenomenon of expression of both the alleles in heterozygous condition. In this, alleles do not show dominant-recessive relationship and are able to express themselves independently, e.g. ABO blood group in humans.	It is also known as partial or mosaic dominance where none of the two contrasting alleles or factors is dominant, e.g. incomplete dominance in 4 'O' clock plant.

(3)

108. (i) List three different allelic forms of gene 'I' in human. Explain the different phenotypic expressions, controlled by these three forms.

(ii) A woman with blood group A marries a man with blood group O. Discuss the possibilities of the inheritance of the blood group in the following starting with 'yes' or 'no' for each.

(a) They produce children with blood group A only.

(b) They produce children, some with O blood group and some with A blood group. **Delhi 2012**

Ans. (i) In humans, the ABO blood groups are controlled by a gene called 'I'. It has three alleles. These are I^A, I^B and i. **(1)**

Table showing the genetic basic of blood groups in human population Refer to answer no. 79. **(2)**

(ii) (a) No, its not necessary as mother could have a genotype I^AI^A or I^Ai. If the genotype is $I^A I^A$, all the offsprings would have A blood group, but in the second case, offsprings can have either 'A' or 'O' blood group as their father has 'O' blood group. **(1)**

(b) Yes, if the mother is of genotype I^Ai and father is 'O' (genotype ii), blood group of some children can be 'O' and some can be 'A'. **(1)**

Common Mistakes Students usually get confused between alleles and genes, but genes are segments of DNA which control specific trait in organisms.

While alleles are particular variant or alternative of the gene.

It can be explained as the hair colour is a trait which is expressed by a gene while different hair colours are possible because of different alleles of the gene for hair colour.

109. (i) Explain monohybrid cross taking seed coat colour as a trait in *Pisum sativum*. Work out the cross up to F_2-generation.

(ii) State the law of inheritance that can be derived from such a cross.

(iii) How is the phenotypic ratio of F_2-generation different in a dihybrid cross?

All India 2012

Ans. (i) In a monohybrid cross, when homozygous dominant and homozygous recessive parents are crossed, F_1-hybrid would be heterozygous for the trait and would express the dominant allele.

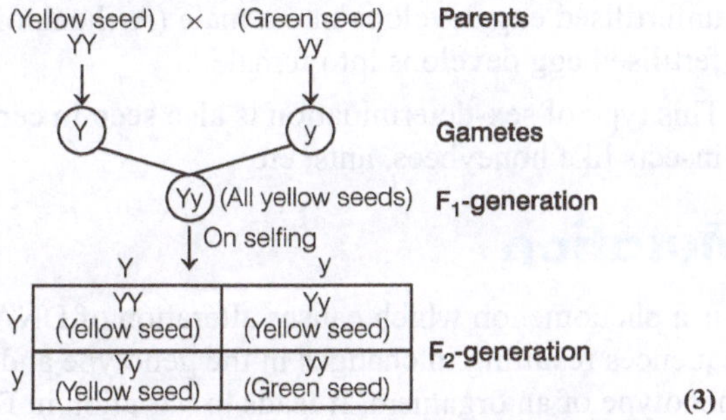

(3)

(ii) The laws of inheritance that can be derived from such a cross are

(a) Law of dominance

(b) Law of segregation (1)

(iii) Phenotypic ratio in F_2-generation.

In monohybrid cross — 3 : 1

In dihybrid cross — 9 : 3 : 3 : 1 (1)

110. When a garden pea plant with violet flowers was crossed with another plant with white flowers, 50% of the progeny bear violet flowers.

(i) Work out the cross.

(ii) Name the type of cross and mention its significance.

(iii) How does the inheritance pattern of flower colour in snapdragon differ from the above? **Delhi 2010C**

Ans. (i) The test cross ratio is 1 : 1.

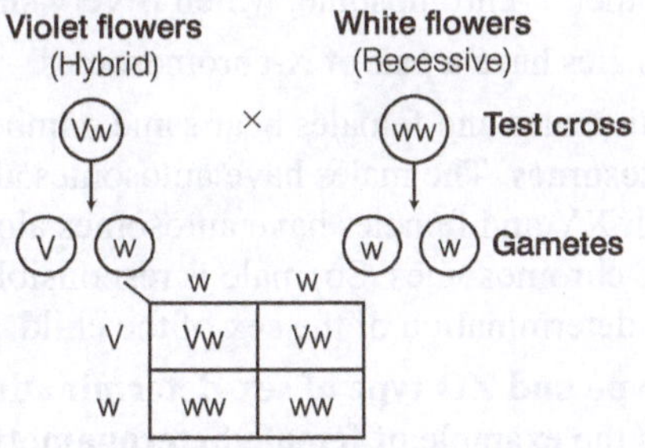

50% flowers are violet. The dominant plant is heterozygous, i.e. Vw. On crossing with white flower, 50% dominant violet colour is expressed. (2)

(ii) Type of cross-Test cross.

Significance The cross is used to determine the genotype of the unknown dominant parent. (1)

(iii) In this test cross, violet and pure white flower when crossed produce violet and white flowers. Whereas in snapdragon, the F_1-generation hybrid was pink coloured. F_2-generation consists of red, pink and white flowers in the ratio of 1 red : 2 pink : 1 white. This is due to incomplete dominance. Similar type of cross can be made for plants with green and yellow pods. (2)

TOPIC 2

Sex-Determination and Genetic Disorders

Sex-Determination

The establishment of sex through differential development in an individual at the time of zygote formation is called **sex-determination.**

Henking (1891) traced a specific nuclear structure all through spermatogenesis in few insects.

- He observed that 50% of sperms received this specific structure after spermatogenesis, whereas the other 50% sperms did not receive it.
- He named this structure as X-body. Scientists further explained this X-body as **X-chromosome**.
- There are different types of sex-determination mechanisms observed in various organisms. These mechanisms are mainly dependent on whether the parents are **homogametic**, i.e. with similar gametes or **heterogametic**, i.e. with different type of gametes. Some of the sex-determination mechanisms are as follows

(i) **XY type of sex-determination** shows the example of **male heterogamety**. This means that in both cases, males produce two different types of gametes
- Some gametes with X-chromosome and some with Y-chromosome.
- This type sex-determination is found in many insects like *Drosophila melanogaster* and in mammals including man. This type of sex-determination includes homogametic females and heterogametic males.
- In males, an X-chromosome is present along with another Y-chromosome, which is very small.
- Females have a pair of X-chromosomes.
- Both males and females bear same number of **autosomes**. The males have autosomes along with XY and females have autosomes along with XX-chromosomes. So, male is responsible for the determination of the sex of the child.

(ii) **ZW type and ZO type of sex-determination** shows the example of **female heterogamety**.
- **ZW type of sex-determination** is found in certain birds, fowls and fishes.
- Females have Z and W-chromosomes along with autosomes and the males have a pair of Z-chromosomes.
- In this type, sex is determined by the type of ovum that is fertilised to produce offspring.
- **ZO type of sex-determination** is seen in butterflies and moths. In this type, the female have only one Z-chromosome, while the male have a pair of Z-chromosomes.

Sex-Determination in Humans

- In humans, 23 pairs of chromosomes are present, out of which 22 pairs are exactly same in both males and females. These are known as **autosomes**.
- A pair of X-chromosome (XX) is present in females, whereas one X and one Y-chromosome (XY) is present in males.
- In males, during spermatogenesis, two types of gametes are produced, i.e. 50% of the total sperms carry the X-chromosomes, while the rest 50% carry Y-chromosomes besides autosomes.
- Females produce only one type of ovum with an X-chromosome.
- In case, the ovum gets fertilised with a sperm carrying X-chromosome, the zygote develops into a female (XX). If ovum gets fertilised with Y-chromosome carrying sperm, the zygote develops into a male (XY).

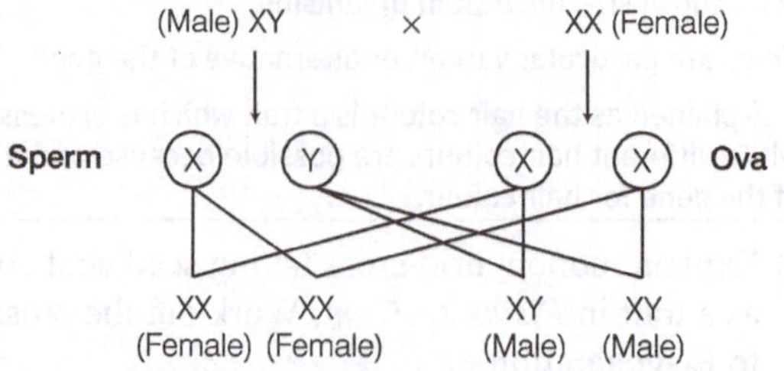

Figure 4.5 Sex-determination in human beings

- Hence, the genetic make up of sperm, which fertilises the ovum, determines the sex of a child.
- There are 50% chances of having male and 50% chances of having female in each pregnancy. So, woman should not be blamed for the sex of a child.

Sex-Determination in Honeybee

- It is known as **haplo-diploidy method** in which an unfertilised egg develops into a male (Arrhenotoky), while fertilised egg develops into female.
- This type of sex-determination is also seen in certain insects like honeybees, ants, etc.

Mutation

It is a phenomenon which causes alteration of DNA sequences resulting in changes in the genotype and the phenotype of an organism. It leads to variation in DNA in addition to recombination.

- Loss (deletion) or gain (insertion/ duplication) of a segment of DNA, results in alteration in chromosomes. As genes are located on chromosomes, alteration in chromosomes results in abnormalities. These are known as **chromosomal alterations**, which are common in cancer cells.
- Mutations also occur due to the change in a single base pair of DNA. These are called **point mutations,** e.g. sickle-cell anaemia.
- Deletions and insertions of base pairs of DNA, causes **frameshift mutations**.
- There are many physical and chemical factors that induce mutation, which are called **mutagens**, e.g. UV radiation is a mutagen.

Pedigree Analysis

It is an analysis of traits in several generations of a family. In this analysis, the inheritance of a particular trait is represented in the family tree over generations.

- Pedigree study provides a strong tool in human genetics, which is utilised to trace the inheritance of a specific trait, abnormality or disease.
- Pedigree analysis is performed for human population because Mendel's monohybrid and dihybrid cross with purelines are not possible in human.
- The symbols used in pedigree analysis are given below

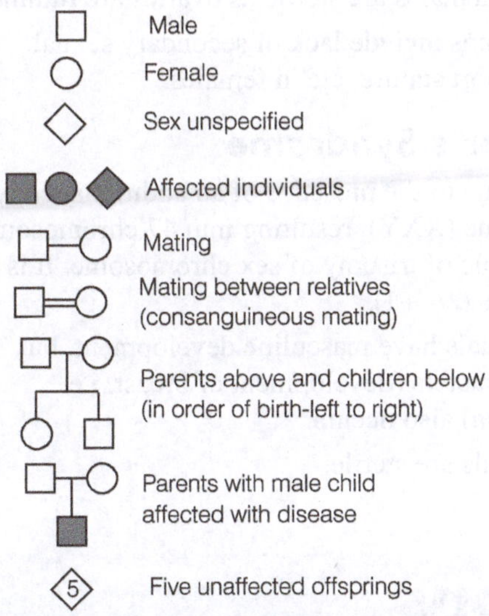

Genetic Disorders

A number of disorders in human beings are associated with the inheritance of changed or altered genes or chromosomes. These are called **genetic disorders**. These can be divided into following types

Mendelian Disorders

These are mainly determined by the alteration or mutation in the single gene. Here, chromosome number and their structure do not change. These disorders are transmitted in next generation according to the principle of inheritance and can be studied through pedigree analysis.

They may be dominant or recessive. It means Mendelian disorders are inherited according to Mendel's law of inheritance. Some common Mendelian disorders are as follows

Haemophilia

It is a sex-linked recessive disease. This means that it is transmitted from an unaffected carrier female to some of the male offsprings.

- In this disease, a single protein that is a part of cascade of proteins involved in the clotting of blood is affected.
- Due to this, in an affected individual, a small cut results in non-stop bleeding.
- The heterozygous female (carrier) may transmit the disease to sons. The possibility of a female becoming haemophilic is extremely rare because mother of such a female offspring has to be at least carrier and father should be haemophilic. In haemophilia, male is never a carrier because it is a X-linked recessive disease and male has only one X-chromosome. So, even a single allele will make a male haemophilic.
- The family pedigree of queen Victoria shows a number of haemophilic descendents as she was a carrier of the disease.

Colour Blindness

It is a recessive sex-linked trait in which eyes fail to distinguish between red and green colours.

- The recessive allele is carried on X-chromosomes.
- In female, it appears only when both the sex chromosomes carry the gene (X^cX^c).
- The females function as carriers in the presence of a single recessive gene (XX^c).
- In males, the defect may appear in the presence of a single recessive gene (X^cY) because Y-chromosome does not carry any gene for colour vision.
- Haemophilia and colour blindness show ***criss-cross* inheritance pattern.** In this inheritance sex-linked characters are transmitted from father to daughter or from mother to son.

Thalassemia

It is an autosomal-linked recessive disease, which occurs due to either mutation or deletion of genes. It results in reduced rate of synthesis of one of the globin chains of haemoglobin.

- Haemoglobin consists of an α and a β-protein. If body does not produce enough of either of these two proteins, the RBCs are not formed properly and cannot carry sufficient oxygen.
- Anaemia is the main feature of this disease.

Chromosomal Disorders

These are caused by the absence or excess or abnormal arrangement of one or more chromosomes. These disorders do not follow Mendel's law of inheritance.

All these chromosomal disorders can be easily studied *via* the analysis of **karyotype**, i.e. an organised profile of an individual's chromosomes according to their shape, size and number.

The causes of chromosomal disorders are discused below

Failure of segregation of chromatids during cell division resulting in the gain or loss of chromosome(s) is called aneuploidy, e.g. Down's syndrome.

Failure of cytokinesis after telophase stage resulting in an increase in the whole set of chromosomes is called polyploidy. It is often seen in plants.

Some examples of chromosomal disorders are as follows

Down's Syndrome

It occurs due to the presence of an additional copy of the chromosome number 21. This condition is called trisomy of 21. It is an example of autosomal trisomy. Here, total number of chromosomes becomes 47 as there is an extra copy of chromosome number 21.

The disorder was first described by Langdon Down (1866).

Affected individuals are short statured with small round head, furrowed tongue and partially open mouth.

Palm is broad with characteristic palm crease.

Physical, psychomotor and mental development is retarded.

Turner's Syndrome

It is a disorder caused due to the absence of one X-chromosome. In this case, the number of chromosomes is 45 with XO genotype. So, it is an example of sex chromosomal monosomy. It is represented as $(2n-1)$.

The affected females are sterile as ovaries are rudimentary.

Other symptoms include lack of secondary sexual characters, short stature, etc in females.

Klinefelter's Syndrome

It is caused due to the presence of an additional copy of X-chromosome (XXY), resulting into 47 chromosomes. So, it is an example of trisomy of sex chromosome. It is represented as $(2n+1)$.

Male individuals have masculine development, but feminine characters (development of breast, i.e. gynaecomastia) also occurs.

The individuals are sterile.

PYQs Previous Years' Questions

1 Mark Questions

Multiple Choice Questions

1. Select the incorrect match from the following. **CBSE 2024 (Set-I)**

	Human karyotype	Characters
(a)	45+XX	Broad palm with characteristic palm crease
(b)	44+XXY	Overall feminine development
(c)	44+XO	Sterile females as ovaries are rudimentary
(d)	44+XY	Normal male

Ans. (c) Option (c) is incorrect as

Sterile females with rudimentary ovaries are seen in females with Turner's syndrome with karyotype of **45 + XO** (absence of one of the X-chromosome).

2. A person with trisomy of 21st chromosome shows **CBSE 2024 (Set-II)**

(i) furrowed tongue
(ii) characteristic palm crease
(iii) rudimentary ovaries
(iv) gynaecomastia

Select the correct option, from the choices given below

(a) (ii) and (iv) (b) (i), (ii) and (iv)
(c) (ii) and (iii) (d) (i) and (ii)

Ans. (d) A person with trisomy of 21st chromosome is said to be suffering from Down's syndrome. This syndrome is characterised by short statured individuals with small round head, furrowed tongue, partially open mouth, broad palm with palm crease, etc.

3. Study the pedigree chart of a family showing the inheritance pattern of a certain disorder. Select the option that correctly identifies the nature of the trait depicted in the pedigree chart. **CBSE 2024 (Set-II)**

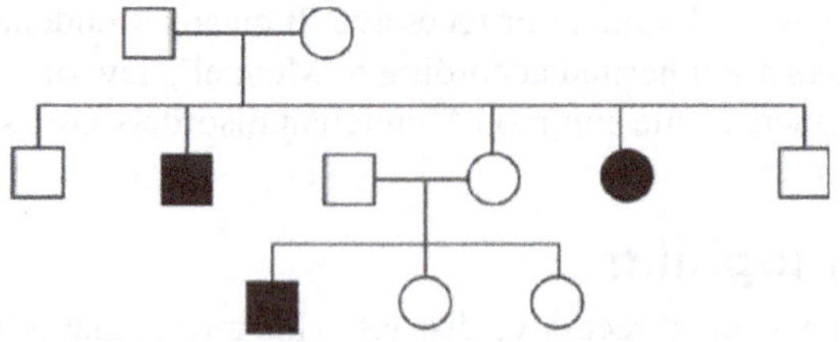

(a) Dominant X-linked
(b) Recessive X-linked
(c) Autosomal dominant
(d) Autosomal recessive

Ans. (d) The given disorder depicted in the pedigree chart is autosomal recessive. The reason behind this inference is
(i) trait is skipping generation;
(ii) trait appearing in both the sexes with equal frequency;
(iii) affected offsprings are born to unaffected parents.

4. What should be the genotype of the indicated member? **CBSE SQP 2024**

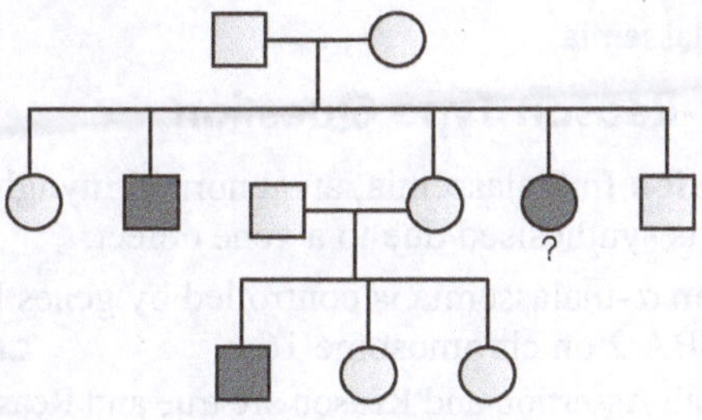

(a) AA (b) Aa
(c) XY (d) aa

Ans. (d) aa

5. Which of the following amino acid substitution is responsible for causing sickle-cell anaemia? **CBSE SQP 2021-22 Term-I**
(a) Valine is substituted by glutamic acid in the α-globin chain at the sixth position
(b) Valine is substituted by glutamic acid in the β-globin chain at seventh position
(c) Glutamic acid is substituted by valine in the α-globin chain at the sixth position
(d) Glutamic acid is substituted by valine in the β-globin chain at the sixth position

Ans. (d) Glutamic acid is substituted by valine in the β-globin chain at the sixth position.

6. Which of the following combination of chromosome numbers represents the correct sex-determination pattern in honeybees? **CBSE SQP 2021-22 Term-I**
(a) Male 32, Female 16
(b) Male 16, Female 32
(c) Male 31, Female 32
(d) Female 32, Male 31

Ans. (b) Male 16, Female 32.

7. Rajesh and Mahesh have defective haemoglobin due to genetic disorders. Rajesh has too few globin molecules while Mahesh has incorrectly functioning globin molecules. Identify the disorder they are suffering from **CBSE SQP 2021-22 Term-I**

	Rajesh	Mahesh
(a)	Sickle-cell anaemia–an autosome linked recessive trait	Thalassemia – an autosome linked dominant trait
(b)	Thalassemia–an autosome linked recessive blood disorder	Sickle-cell anaemia – an autosome linked recessive trait
(c)	Sickle-cell anaemia – an autosome linked recessive trait	Thalassemia – an autosome linked recessive blood disorder
(d)	Thalassemia – an autosome linked recessive blood disorder	Sickle-cell anaemia – an autosome linked dominant trait

Ans. (b) Rajesh, Thalassemia - an autosome linked recessive blood disorder.
Mahesh, Sickle-cell anaemia - an autosome linked recessive trait.

8.

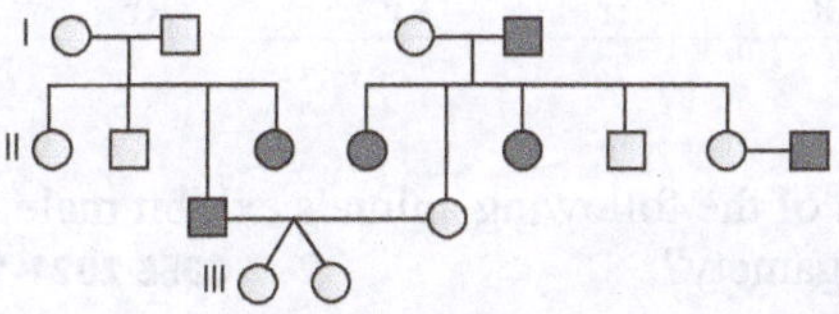

What is pattern of inheritance in the above pedigree chart? **CBSE SQP 2021-22 Term-I**
(a) Autosomal dominant (b) Autosomal recessive
(c) Sex-linked dominant (d) Sex-linked recessive

Ans. (b) Autosomal recessive.

9. A couple has two daughters. What is the probability that the third child will also be a female? **CBSE SQP 2021-22 Term-I**
(a) 25% (b) 50% (c) 75% (d) 100%

Ans. (b) 50%

10. Placed below is a karyotype of a human being.

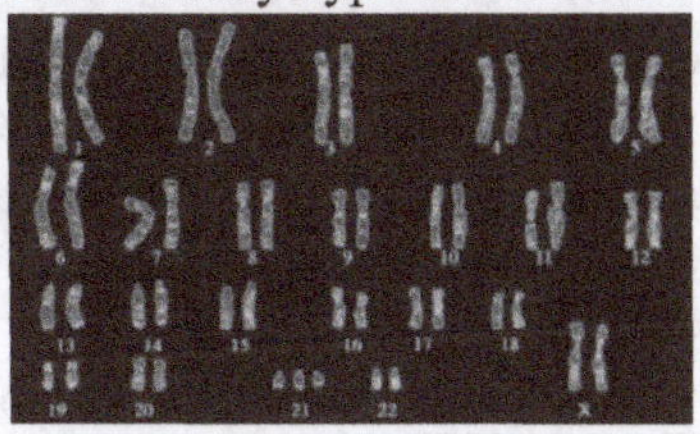

On the basis of the karyotype, which of the following conclusions can be drawn? **CBSE SQP 2021-22 Term-I**

(a) Normal human female
(b) Person is suffering from colour blindness
(c) Affected individual is a female with Down's syndrome
(d) Affected individual is a female with Turner's syndrome

Ans. (c) Affected individual is a female with Down's syndrome.

11. In humans rolling of tongue is an autosomal dominant trait (R). In a family both the parents have the trait of rolling tongue, but their daughter does not show the trait whereas the sons have the trait of rolling of tongue. **CBSE 2021-22 Term-I**

The genotypes of the family would be

	Mother	Father	Daughter	Son
(a)	Rr	Rr	rr	rr
(b)	Rr	Rr	rr	RR
(c)	rr	Rr	RR	rr
(d)	RR	rr	Rr	Rr

Ans. (b)

12. Which of the following animals exhibit male heterogamety? **CBSE 2021-22 Term-I**

(i) Fruit fly (ii) Fowl
(iii) Human (iv) Honeybee

(a) (i) and (iii) (b) (ii) and (iv)
(c) (ii) and (iii) (d) (i) and (iv)

Ans. (a) (i) and (iii)

13. Select the incorrect pair. **CBSE 2021-22 Term-I**

(a) Polygenic inheritance : Haemophilia
(b) Linkage : *Drosophila*
(c) Incomplete dominance : *Antirrhinum*
(d) Pleiotropy : Phenylketonuria

Ans. (a) Polygenic inheritance : Haemophilia

14. The correct statement with respect to thalassemia in human is **CBSE 2021-22 Term-I**

(a) α-thalassemia is controlled by a single gene HBB
(b) the gene for α-thalassemia is located on chromosome-16
(c) β-thalassemia is controlled by two closely linked gene HBA-1 and HBA-2
(d) in β-thalassemia the production of α-globin chain is affected

Ans. (b) the gene for α-thalassemia is located on chromosome-16

15. The cause of Klinefelter's syndrome in humans is **CBSE 2021-22 Term-I**

(a) absence of Y-chromosome
(b) absence of X-chromosome
(c) extra copy of an autosome
(d) extra copy of an X-chromosome

Ans. (d) extra copy of an X-chromosome

16. The autosomal disorder/disease in humans is **Delhi 2020**

(a) colour blindness (b) thalassemia
(c) haemophilia (d) Turner's syndrome

Ans. (b) thalassemia

Assertion-Reason Type Question

17. Assertion In thalassemia, an abnormal myoglobin chain is synthesised due to a gene defect.

Reason α-thalassemia is controlled by genes HBA1 and HBA 2 on chromosome 16. **CBSE 2023**

(a) Both Assertion and Reason are true and Reason is the correct explanation of Assertion
(b) Both Assertion and Reason are true and Reason is not the correct explanation of Assertion
(c) Assertion is true, but Reason is false
(d) Assertion is false, but Reason is true

Ans. (d) Assertion is false, but Reason is true.

Alpha thalassemia is caused by the mutalions in the HBA 1 and HBA 2 genes located on chromosome 16, which leads to reduce or absent synthesis of α-globin chains resulting in the formation of abnormal haemoglobin molecules.

Very Short Answer Type Questions

18. Differentiate between aneuploidy and polyploidy. **CBSE SQP 2020-21 Term-I**

Ans. Differences between aneuploidy and polyploidy are

Aneuploidy	Polyploidy
Chromosomal abnormality in which one or more chromosomes are gained or lost.	Entire extra set of chromosomes is added.
Commonly occurs in humans.	Commonly seen in plants.
e.g. trisomy, tetrasomy	e.g. triploidy, tetraploidy

19. Write the sex of a human having XXY chromosomes with 22 pairs of autosomes. Name the disorder this human suffers from. **CBSE 2018C**

Ans. The sex of a human having XXY chromosomes with 22 pairs of autosomes is male. (½)

The disorder from which this human is suffering is Klinefelter's syndrome. (½)

20. State the fate of a pair of autosome during gamete formation. **Delhi 2017**

Ans. During gamete formation, the homologous pair of autosomes gets separated from each other and moves to different gametes, so that each gamete receives haploid set of chromosomes.

21. Give an example of a sex-linked recessive disorder in humans. **Delhi 2016C**

Ans. Haemophilia is a sex-linked recessive disorder in humans.

22. Give an example of an organism that exhibits haplo-diploidy sex-determination system. **Delhi 2016C**

Ans. Haplo-diploidy sex-determination system is seen in honeybees.

23. Give one example of organism exhibiting female heterogamety. **Outside Delhi 2016C**

Or Write the chromosomal basis of sex-determination in birds. **Delhi 2016C**

Or Explain the mechanism of sex-determination in birds. **Delhi 2015**

Ans. Female heterogamety is exhibited by birds. They have ZW-ZZ type of sex-determination mechanism. In this type, the male is homogametic and the female is heterogametic. Therefore, there are two types of eggs, i.e. with Z and with W and only one type of sperms, i.e. each with Z.

When egg with Z-chromosome is fertilised by a sperm with Z-chromosome, a zygote with ZZ-chromosomes (male) is formed. Similarly when egg with W-chromosome is fertilised by a sperm with Z-chromosome, a zygote with ZW-chromosomes (female) is formed.

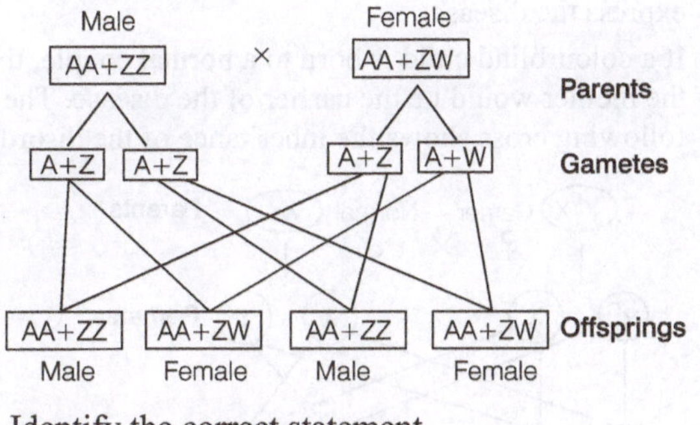

24. Identify the correct statement.

(i) Females of many birds have a pair of dissimilar ZW-chromosomes, while the males possess a pair of similar ZZ-chromosomes.

(ii) Females of many birds have a pair of similar ZZ-chromosomes, while the males possess a pair of dissimilar ZW-chromosomes. **All India 2014C**

Ans. The correct statement is

(i) Females of many birds have a pair of dissimilar ZW-chromosomes, while the males possess a pair of similar ZZ-chromosomes.

2 Marks Questions

25. Karyotype of a child shows trisomy of chromosome number 21. Identify the disorder and state the symptoms which are likely to be exhibited in this case. **CBSE SQP 2021**

Ans. 21 trisomy causes Down's syndrome in humans. It is caused due to the non-disjunction of chromosomes during cell division. **(1)**

Symptoms The affected individual is short statured with small round head, has furrowed tongue, partially open mouth, palm is broad with characteristic palm crease, physical psychomotor and mental development is retarded. **(1)**

26. State what are Mendelian disorders. Both thalassemia and colour blindness categorised as Mendelian disorders. Justify. **All India 2020**

Ans. The disorders that occur due to alternation in a single gene are called Mendelian disorders.

Both thalassemia and colour blindness are classified as Mendelian disorders.

- Colour blindness is a sex-linked recessive disorder due to defect in either red or green cone cells of the eye. This results in failure to discriminate between these colours. **(1)**
- Thalassemia is an autosomal-linked recessive disorder resulting from mutation or deletion in either the α or β-chains of haemoglobin. **(1)**

27. Write the genotypes of the parents of a child suffering from thalassemia. State the cause of this disease. **All India 2019**

Ans. The genotypes of the parents of a child suffering from thalassemia are as follows

Mother $\rightarrow Th^{B}\ Th^{B+}$

Father $\rightarrow Th^{B}\ Th^{B+}$ **(1)**

Thalassemia is an autosomal-linked recessive disease, which results in reduced rate of synthesis of one of the globin chains of haemoglobin. The disease is controlled by a single pair of allele, Th^{B} and Th^{B+}. Th^{B} codes for normal B-protein and Th^{B+} codes for an abnormal B-protein. Only homozygous individuals for Th^{B+} ($Th^{B+}\ Th^{B+}$) show the diseased phenotype. **(1)**

28. Name a disorder a human suffers from as a result of monosomy of the sex chromosome. Give the karyotype and write the symptoms. **All India 2019**

Ans. Monosomy of the sex chromosome in humans results in Turner's syndrome.

The number of chromosomes is 45 (44 + XO). **(1)**

Symptoms are as follows

- The affected females are sterile as ovaries are rudimentary.
- Other symptoms include lack of secondary sexual characters, short stature, etc. **(1)**

29. During a cytological study conducted on the chromosomes of the insects, it was observed that only 50% of the sperms had a specific structure after spermatogenesis. Name the structure and write its significance in sex-determination of insects. **CBSE SQP 2018**

Ans. In insects (e.g. grasshopper, cockroach) XX-XO type of sex-determination is observed. Males have only one X-chromosome and produce two type of sperms, i.e. 50% have X-chromosome (as observed during cytological study) and 50% without X-chromosome.

During sex-determination eggs fertilised by sperms having an X-chromosome become females (XX) and those fertilised by sperms that do not have X-chromosome become males (XO).

30. A haemophilic father can never pass the gene for haemophilia to his son. Explain. **CBSE 2018**

Or A cross between a normal couple resulted in a son who was haemophilic and a normal daughter. In course of time, when the daughter was married to a normal man, to their surprise, the grandson was also haemophilic.

(i) Represent this cross in the form of a pedigree chart. Give the genotypes of the daughter and her husband.

(ii) Write the conclusion you draw from the inheritance pattern of this disease. **Delhi 2014**

Ans. (i)

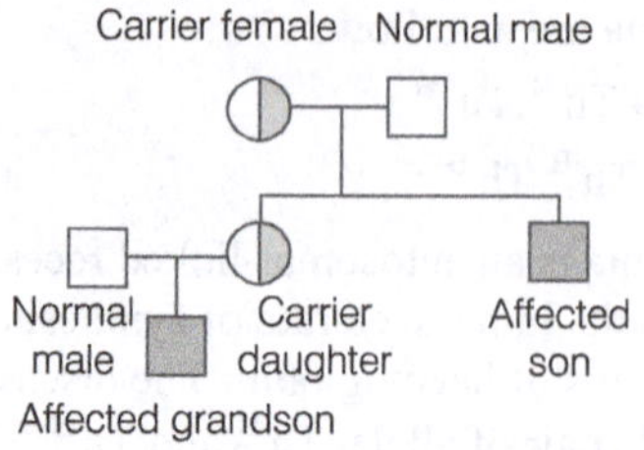

Genotypes of daughter and her husband are X^hX and XY, respectively. **(1)**

(ii) Haemophilia is a sex-linked recessive disease. It is transmitted from the carrier female to her sons. From the above pedigree chart, it can be observed that the disease is being transmitted from the carrier female to her daughter (carrier) and son (affected).

The carrier daughter transmits this disease to the grandson. This pattern of inheritance is called *criss-cross* inheritance. **(1)**

31. Is haemophilia in humans a sex-linked or autosomal disorder? Work out a cross in support of your answer. **Outside Delhi 2016C**

Ans. Haemophilia is a sex-linked disorder and more specifically it is X-linked disorder. **(1)**

If normal parents give rise to a haemophilic child, then their genotypes should be

Father — XY (normal)

Mother — XX^h (carrier/heterozygous non-haemophilic)

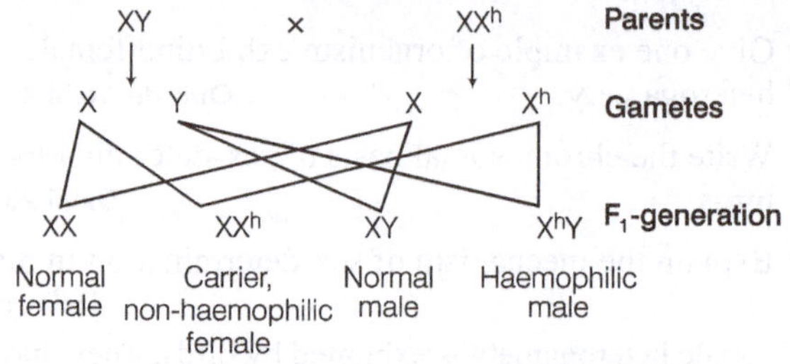

(1)

32. A couple with normal vision bears a colourblind child. Work out the cross to show how it is possible and mention the sex of the affected child. **Delhi 2016**

Or A colourblind child is born to a normal couple. Work out a cross to show how it is possible? Mention the sex of this child. **Delhi 2014**

Ans. Colour blindness is a sex-linked disease which results in the defect in either red or green cone cells of eyes. The gene for this disorder is present on the X-chromosome. Hence, it is carried by normal females that do not express the disease.

If a colourblind child is born to a normal couple, then the mother would be the carrier of the disease. The following cross shows the inheritance of the disorder

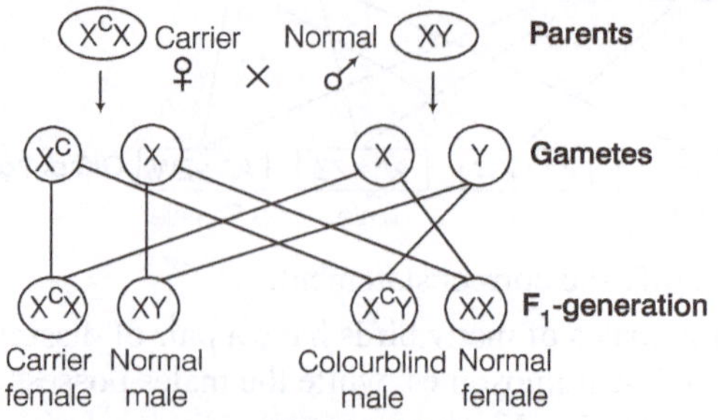

Thus, the sex of colourblind child would be male.

33. Differentiate between male and female heterogamety. **Delhi 2015**

Ans. Differences between male and female heterogamety are

Male heterogamety	Female heterogamety
Male produces two different types of gametes.	Female produces two different types of gametes.
e.g. human male produces gametes with either X or Y–chromosomes.	e.g. female birds produce gametes with either Z or W type chromosomes.

34. Why is the possibility of a human female suffering from haemophilia rare? Explain. **Foreign 2014; All India 2012, 2013, 2014C**

Ans. Haemophilia is an X-linked recessive disease. Therefore, the females having haemophilic allele on single X-chromosome do not produce haemophilic phenotype. Females suffer from this disease only if the father is haemophilic and the mother is at least the carrier of disease. Such condition is rare and hence, the human females are rarely haemophilic.

35. Identify *a*, *b*, *c*, *d*, *e* and *f* in the table given below

Syndrome	Cause	Characteristics of affected individual	Sex Male/ Female/ Both
Down's	Trisomy of 21	*a* (i) (ii)	*b*
c	XXY	Overall masculine development	*d*
Turner's	45 with XO	*e* (i) (ii)	*f*

All India 2014

Ans. (a) (i) Short stature individuals with round head and furrowed tongue.
(ii) Slow mental development.
(b) Both
(c) Klinefelter's syndrome
(d) Male
(e) (i) Rudimentary ovaries.
(ii) Lack of secondary sexual characters.
(f) Female

36. Women are often blamed for producing female children. Consequently, they are ill-treated and ostracised. How will you address this issue scientifically, if you were to conduct an awareness programme to highlight the values involved? **Delhi 2014**

Or Explain why it is scientifically incorrect to blame the mother for bearing a female child? **Delhi 2013C**

Or Do you agree to the perception in our society that the woman is responsible for the gender? Substantiate your answer scientifically. **All India 2011C**

Ans. Women are not responsible for determining the sex of a child. Moreover, it is not appropriate to ill-treat a woman for giving birth to a girl child, as both males and females are equally important for the balance of nature and continuity of species. All human beings have 23 pairs of chromosomes. A human sperm (haploid) has 22 autosomes and one of the two types of sex chromosomes, i.e. either X or Y. On the contrary, human females have 22 autosomes and one type of sex chromosome, i.e. X-chromosome.

The sex of an individual is determined by the type of the sex chromosome (X or Y) contained in the sperm that fuses with the ovum. **(1)**

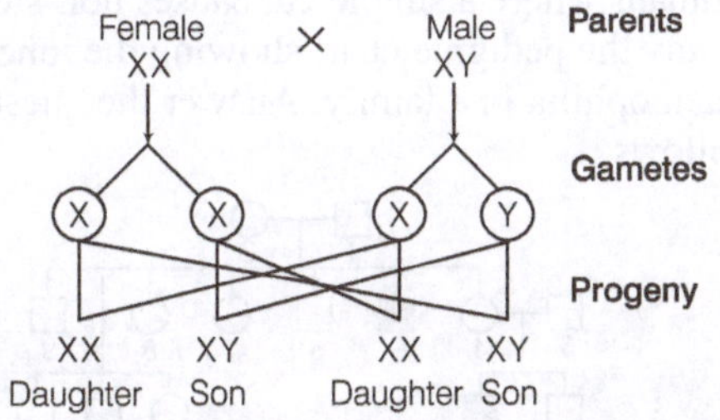

If the fertilising sperm has an X-chromosome, then the baby would be a female and if a sperm with Y-chromosome fuses with the ovum, it will develop into a male child. Thus, males are responsible for the determination of the sex of a child. **(1)**

37. Write the types of sex-determination mechanisms the following crosses show. Give an example of each type.
(i) Female XX with male XO.
(ii) Female ZW with male ZZ. **Delhi 2014**

Ans. (i) The type of sex-determination mechanism shown in female XX and male XO is called male heterogamety. In this case, males are heterogametic with half of the male gametes carrying X-chromosome while the other half being devoid of it, e.g. grasshoppers. **(1)**

(ii) The type of sex-determination mechanism is female heterogamety because female produces two different types of gametes, i.e. Z and W while males are ZZ type, e.g. birds. **(1)**

38. (i) Colour blindness in humans is a sex-linked trait. Explain with the help of a cross.

(ii) In human beings, the sex of the child is determined by the father and not by the mother. Explain.

All India 2014C

Ans. (i) Refer to answer no. 32. **(1)**

(ii) Refer to answer no. 36. **(1)**

39.

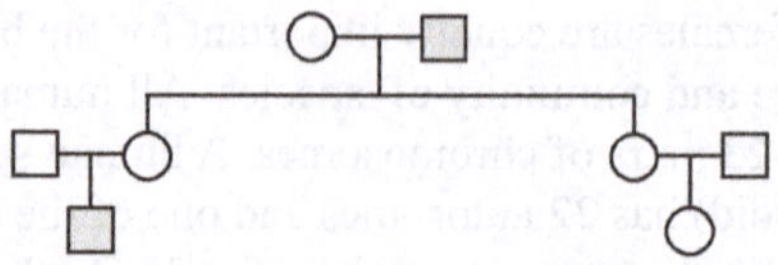

This is the pedigree of a family tracing the movement of the gene for haemophilia. Explain the pattern of inheritance of the disease in the family.

Delhi 2013C

Or Haemophilia is a sex-linked inheritance condition in humans where a simple cut causes non-stop bleeding. Study the pedigree chart showing the inheritance of haemophilia in a family. Answer the questions that follows.

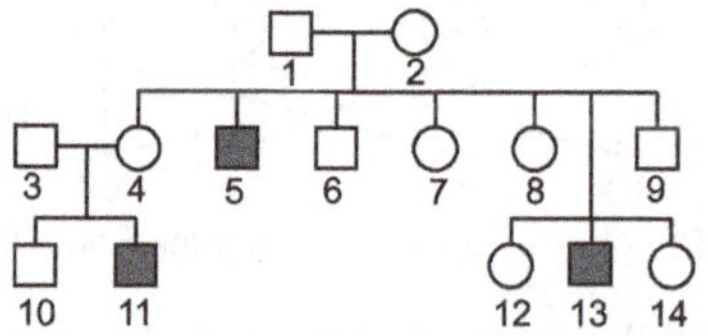

Give reasons, which explain that haemophilia is (i) sex-linked (ii) caused by X-linked gene. **Foreign 2011**

Ans. The pedigree of a family given in the question depicts that mother is normal (XX), while father is haemophilic (X^hY). As haemophilia is a sex-linked disease, F_1-generation will produce 50% carrier daughters and 50% normal sons. In F_2-generation, both carrier daughters got married to a normal man and produced 25% diseased (X^hY) and 25% normal son (XY) and 25% carrier (X^CX) and 25% normal daughter (XX). **(2)**

Or (i) (a) It is X-linked trait which is transmitted from an unaffected carrier female to some of the male offsprings.

(b) Females rarely become haemophilic as in this cases, the mother has to be at least a carrier and father should be haemophilic. **(1)**

(ii) Gene for haemophilia is X-linked or present on X-chromosome because male receives this gene from mother.

(a) So, a carrier female transmits it to her son.

(b) Disease appears more in males because they have only one X-chromosome. **(1)**

3 Marks Questions

40. Given below is a picture that shows the magnified blood smear of a patient under a microscope.

CBSE 2024 (Set-I)

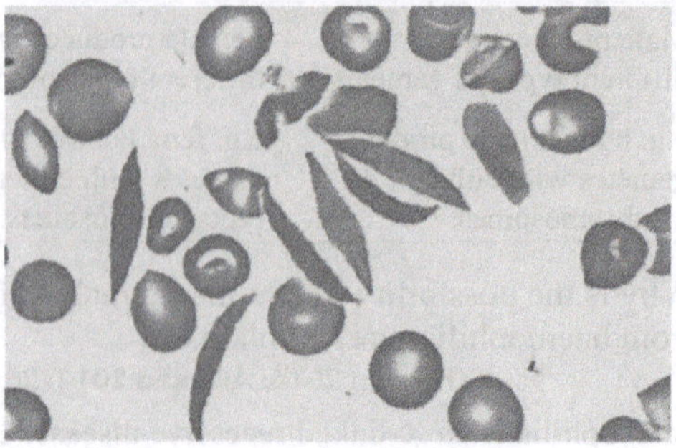

(i) Name the disease the blood smear is indicative of. Write the symptoms of the disease and its cause.

(ii) Explain the inheritance pattern of the disease with the help of a suitable cross.

Ans. (i) The given blood smear shows sickle shaped RBCs and thus, is indicative of diseases called sickle-cell anaemia.

Symptoms Biconcave disc to elongated sickle like RBC, severe anaemia, shortness of breath, etc.

Cause Substitution of glutamic acid (Glu) by valine (Val) at sixth position of beta globin chain of haemoglobin molecule. **(1)**

(ii) Sickle-cell anaemia is an autosomal recessive trait that can be transmitted from the parent to the offspring, when both partners are carrier for the gene (heterozygous). This disease is controlled by a single pair of allele Hb^A and Hb^s, where Hb stands for haemoglobin, Hb^s represents the normal genotype of blood. Only homozygous individual for Hb^s ($Hb^S Hb^S$) show the diseased phenotype. The heterozygous individuals are carriers ($Hb^A Hb^S$).

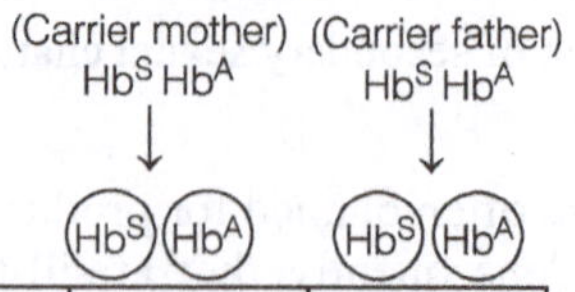

♀ \ ♂	Hb^S	Hb^A
Hb^S	$Hb^S Hb^S$ (Affected)	$Hb^S Hb^A$ (Carrier)
Hb^A	$Hb^S Hb^A$ (Carrier)	$Hb^A Hb^A$ (Normal)

Outcome : 1 Affected : 2 Carriers : 1 Normal **(2)**

41. Study the given pedigree chart and answer the questions that follow

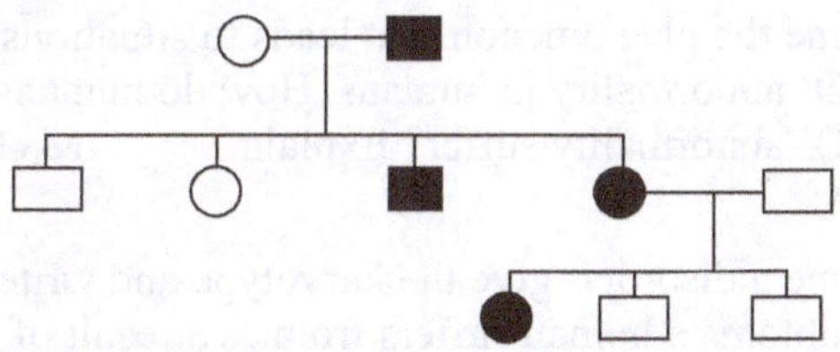

(i) Is the trait recessive or dominant?

(ii) Is the trait sex-linked or autosomal?

(iii) Give the genotypes of the parents shown in generation-I and their third child shown in generation-II and the first grandchild shown in generation-III. **CBSE SQP 2019**

Ans. (i) The given trait is dominant as it is getting expressed in all generation. (1)

(ii) The trait is autosomal because the male and female progeny of 2nd generation is equally affected by the disease or trait. (1)

(iii) If 'A' is the dominant allele for the trait and 'a' is the recessive allele, the genotype of parents shown in generation-I, 'Aa' for affected male and 'aa' for normal female.

Genotype of 3rd child in generation II is 'Aa' (affected male child) whereas, genotype of 1st grand child in gerneration 3 is 'Aa' (affected female). (1)

42. Haemophilia is a sex-linked recessive disorder of humans. The pedigree chart given below shows the inheritance of haemophilia in one family. Study the pattern of inheritance and answer the questions given below.

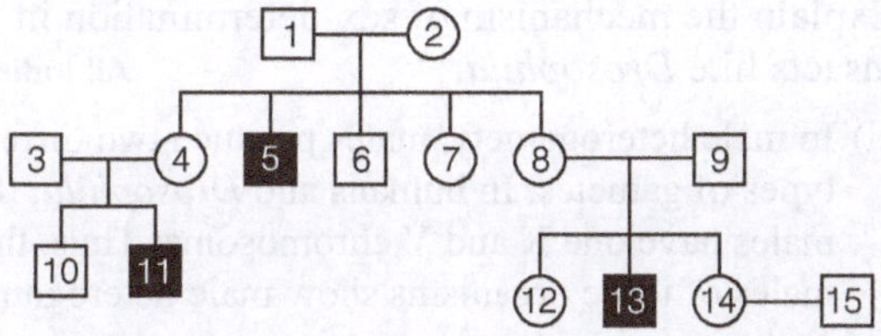

(i) Give all the possible genotypes of the members 4, 5 and 6 in the pedigree chart.

(ii) A blood test shows that the individual 14 is a carrier of haemophilia. The member numbered 15 has recently married the member numbered 14. What is the probability that their first child will be a haemophilic male ? Show with the help of Punnett square. **CBSE SQP 2019**

Ans. (i) Let XX denote female, and XY denote male.

The genotype of 4 : XX^h, it shows that the female is a carrier of haemophilia.

The genotype of 5 : X^hY, it shows a haemophilia affected male as X^h is expressed dominantly over gene Y.

The genotype of 6 : XY, it shows a healthy male. (1½)

(ii) As individual 14 is a female carrier of haemophilia (X^hX), married to the member number 15 a healthy male (XY). the probability of their first child being a haemophilic male is 25%. It can be show with the help of Punnett square as,

♂ \ ♀	X^h	X
X	X^hX	XX
Y	X^hY	XY

(1½)

43. Explain the mechanism of sex-determination in birds. How does it differ from that of human beings? **CBSE 2018**

Or Differentiate between 'ZZ' and 'XY' type of sex-determination mechanisms. **Delhi 2015**

Or Explain the sex-determination mechanism in humans. How is it different in birds? **All India 2010**

Ans. Differences between XY and ZZ types of sex-determination are

XY type sex-determination (In humans)	ZZ type sex-determination (In birds)
Females are homogametic, while males are heterogametic.	Females are heterogametic, while males are homogametic.
Female produces egg with X-chromosomes only, while male produces sperms with either X or Y-chromosomes.	Female produces eggs with either Z or W-chromosomes, while male produces sperm with Z-chromosomes.
e.g. humans, *Drosophila*	e.g. fish, birds, etc.

Sex-determination in humans Refer to answer no. 36.

Sex-determination in birds Refer to answer no. 20.

44. During a medical investigation, an infant was found to possess an extra chromosome 21. Describe the symptoms the child is likely to develop later in the life. **Delhi 2017**

Or Explain how trisomy of 21st chromosome occurs in humans. List any four characteristic features in an individual suffering from it. **Foreign 2012**

Or Name the genetic disorder caused by trisomy of 21st chromosome in a human. Write the diagnostic features of the disorder. **Delhi 2011C**

Ans. An additional copy of chromosome number 21 (trisomy of chromosome number 21) in humans results in Down's syndrome. **(1)**

Following characteristic symptoms are likely to develop in the child suffering from Down's syndrome

(i) Short statured with small, round head.
(ii) Furrowed tongue and partially open mouth.
(iii) Broad palm with characteristics palm crease.
(iv) Slow mental, physical and psychomotor development. **(2)**

45. Both haemophilia and thalassemia are blood related disorders in humans. Write their causes and the difference between the two. Name the category of genetic disorder they both come under. **All India 2017**

Ans. Haemophilia and thalassemia both are Mendelian or gene related human disorders.

Cause of haemophilia It is caused due to the absence of antihaemophilic globulin and plasma thromboplastin factor.

Cause of thalassemia It is caused due to mutation or deletion of the genes controlling the formation of globin chains (α and β) of haemoglobin.

Differences between haemophilia and thalassemia are

Haemophilia	Thalassemia
Influence on single trait.	Influence on multiple traits.
Inheritance is *criss-cross*.	Inheritance is straight from both the parents to all the offsprings.

Category of genetic disorder

Haemophilia – Sex-linked disease
Thalassemia – Autosomal recessive disease **(1 × 3)**

46. Which chromosomes carry the mutant genes causing thalassemia in humans? What are the problems caused by these mutant genes? **Delhi 2015**

Ans. Thalassemia is an autosomal-linked recessive disease, which occurs due to either mutation or deletion of genes, resulting in reduced rate of synthesis of one of the globin chains of haemoglobin. It is associated with the mutation in chromosome 11 or 16 which code for β-chain and α - chain of haemoglobin, respectively. Haemoglobin is the oxygen carrying component of the Red Blood Cells (RBCs). It consists of two different proteins, an α and a β. If the body does not produce enough of either of these two proteins, the red blood cells do not form properly and cannot carry sufficient oxygen.

This results in anaemia that begins in early childhood and lasts throughout the life. **(1 + 2)**

47. Name the phenomenon that leads to situations like 'XO' abnormality in humans. How do humans with 'XO' abnormality suffer? Explain. **Foreign 2012**

Or

Name a disorder, give the karyotype and write the symptoms a human suffers from as a result of monosomy of the sex chromosome. **Foreign 2021**

Or

(i) Name the genetic disorder in a human female having 44 + XO karyotype. Mention the diagnostic features of this disorder.
(ii) Explain the cause of such chromosomal disorder. **Delhi 2011C**

Ans. XO abnormality or monosomy of X-chromosome represents chromosomal disorder called Turner's syndrome. **(1)**

Non-disjunction is responsible for this chromosomal disorder. It is the phenomenon of failure of segregation of the members of homologous pairs of the chromosomes. Such disorder occurs due to the absence of one X-chromosome, i.e. 45 with XO (karyotype). The affected individual has underdeveloped feminine characters. Females are sterile and ovaries are rudimentary. **(2)**

48. (i) Why are *Drosophila* said to show male heterogamety? Explain.
(ii) Explain female heterogamety with the help of an example. **All India 2010**

Or

Explain the mechanism of sex-determination in insects like *Drosophila*. **All India 2010**

Ans. (i) In male heterogamety, males produce two different types of gametes. In humans and *Drosophila*, the males have one X and Y chromosome. Thus, the males of these organisms show male heterogamety as they produce two types of gametes.

- Either with or without X-chromosome.
- Some gametes with X-chromosome and some with Y-chromosome. **(1½)**

(ii) In some organisms, females produce two different types of gametes. This is termed as female heterogamety. In birds and some reptiles, female has two different sex chromosomes (one Z and one W-chromosome) whereas male has a pair of same chromosome (a pair of Z-chromosome). **(1½)**

5 Marks Questions

49. (i) How does a chromosomal disorder differ from a Mendelian disorder?

(ii) Name any two chromosomal aberration-associated disorders.

(iii) List the characteristics of the disorders mentioned above that help in their diagnosis. **Delhi 2020**

Ans. (i) Differences between chromosomal disorders and Mendelian disorders are

Chromosomal disorders	Mendelian disorders
These are caused due to the absence or excess of one or more chromosomes or abnormal arrangement of one/more chromosomes.	These are due to alteration in a single gene.
They are not transmitted as the affected individual is sterile.	They are transmitted to generations through Mendelian principles of inheritance.
e.g. Down's syndrome, Turner's syndrome.	e.g. colour blindness, thalassemia.

(2)

(ii) **Chromosomal disorders** Down's syndrome and Klinefelter's syndrome.

(iii) **Down's syndrome** The affected individual is short statured with small round head, furrowed tongue and partially open mouth. Physical, psychomotor and mental development is also retarded.

Klinefelter's syndrome It occurs in males, which show overall muscular development, but feminine development also occurs. Such individuals are sterile. (3)

50. Aneuploidy of chromosomes in human beings results in certain disorders. Draw out the possibilities of the karyotype in common disorders of this kind in human beings and its consequences in individuals. **CBSE SQP 2018-19**

Ans. Aneuploidy refers to the failure of segregation of chromatids during cell division cycle resulting in the gain or loss of chromosomes, e.g. Down's syndrome, Turner's syndrome. (2)

Down's syndrome it occurs due to the presence of an aditional copy of the chromosome number 21.

This condition is called trisomy of 21. Affected individuals are short statured with a small round head, furrowed tongue and partially open mouth. Physical psychomotor and mental development is retarded.

Karyotype with 23 pairs of autosomes and 1 pair of sex chromosomes i.e., 47 chromosomes.

Turner's Syndrome It occurs due to the absence of one of the X-chromosomes. This condition is called monosomy of the sex chromosome. Affected females are sterile as ovaries are rudimentary lack of secondary sexual characters. Short stature, webbed neck, etc., are also observed.

Karyotype with 45 number of chromosomes, i.e. 44 + XO. (3)

51. (i) Why are thalassemia and haemophilia categorised as Mendelian disorders? Write the symptoms of these diseases. Explain their pattern of inheritance in humans.

(ii) Write the genotypes of the normal parents producing a haemophilic son. **All India 2015**

Ans. (i) Thalassemia and haemophilia are categorised as Mendelian disorders because these disorders are due to alteration in a single gene. Also, they are transmitted to offspring through Mendelian principles of inheritance. (1)

Symptoms and pattern of inheritance are given below

(a) **Thalassemia** It is an autosome-linked recessive blood disorder characterised by defect in α, β or δ-chain resulting in abnormal Hb molecule.

Symptom includes anaemia, fatigue, dark urine and weakness.

Inheritance Two mutant alleles (one from each parent) must be inherited for an individual to be affected, i.e. homozygous. Heterozygous are carriers and may pass the mutant allele to their children. (1)

(b) **Haemophilia** It is a sex-linked recessive disorder whose gene is located on X-chromosome.

Symptom Prolonged clotting time and internal bleeding, even in a minor injury.

Inheritance The gene is present on X-chromosome, so it is inherited by males as they have a single X-chromosome. Affected males are said to be hemizygous. Females have two X-chromosomes, thus their possibility of being affected is rare as the mother of such female has to be at least carrier and father should be haemophilic. (1)

(ii) Genotypes of the normal parents producing a haemophilic son are X^cX (carrier mother) and XY (father).

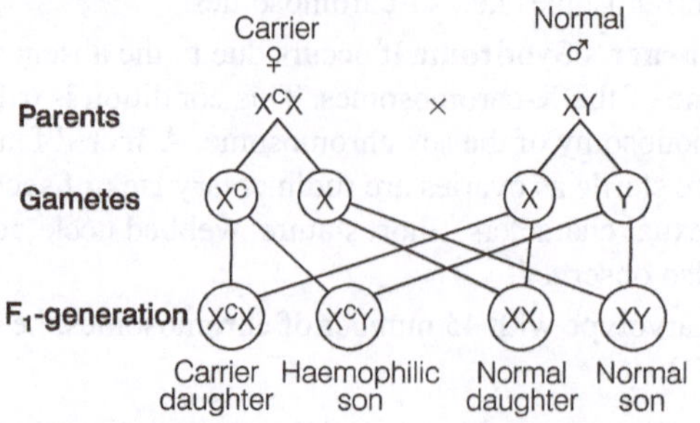

(2)

52. (i) Why are colour blindness and thalassemia categorised as Mendelian disorders? Write the symptoms of these diseases seen in people suffering from them.

(ii) About 8% of human male population suffers from colour blindness whereas only about 0.4% of human female population suffers from this disease. Write an explanation to show how it is possible? **All India 2015**

Ans. (i) Thalassemia and colour blindness are categorised as Mendelian disorder because these disorders arise due to alternations or mutation in a single gene. These are transmitted through Mendelian principles of inheritance.

Symptoms of thalassemia include
(a) yellow skin
(b) dark urine
(c) bone deformities
(d) anaemia

Symptoms of colour blindness include
(a) Difficulty in identifying brightness of different colours.
(b) Inability to differentiate between shades of colour like red and green. (3)

(ii) Colour blindness is an X-linked recessive trait which shows transmission from carrier female progeny. In males, the defect can appear in heterozygous condition beacause males possess only one X-chromosome whereas in females, it appears in homozygous condition only, which is very rare. Thus, it is more common in males than in females. (2)

Case Based/Source Based/Passage Based Questions (Based on Complete Chapter)

1. Read the following and answer any four questions given below

Sickle-cell anaemia is a genetic disorder where the body produces an abnormal haemoglobin called haemoglobin S. Red blood cells are normally flexible and round, but when the haemoglobin is defective, blood cells take on a 'sickle' or crescent shape. Sickle-cell anaemia is caused by mutations in a gene called HBB.

It is an inherited blood disorder that occurs if both the maternal and paternal copies of the HBB gene are defective. In other words, if an individual receives just one copy of the defective HBB gene, either from mother or father, then the individual has no sickle-cell anaemia, but has what is called 'sickle-cell trait'.

People with sickle-cell trait usually do not have any symptoms or problems but they can pass the mutated gene on to their children. There are three inheritance scenarios that can lead to a child having sickle-cell anaemia.

Both parents have sickle-cell trait.

One parent has sickle-cell anaemia and the other has sickle-cell trait.

Both parents have sickle-cell anaemia.

CBSE SQP 2021-22

(i) Sickle-cell anaemia is a/ an ...... disease.
(a) X-linked
(b) autosomal dominant
(c) autosomal recessive
(d) Y-linked

(ii) If both parents have sickle-cell trait, then there is .... of the child having sickle-cell anaemia.
(a) 25 % risk (b) 50 % risk
(c) 75% risk (d) No risk

(iii) If both parents have sickle-cell trait, then there is .... of the child having sickle-cell trait.
(a) 25 % risk (b) 50 % risk
(c) 75% risk (d) No risk

(iv) If one parent has sickle-cell anaemia and the other has sickle-cell trait, there is .... that their children will have sickle-cell anaemia and .... will have sickle-cell trait.
(a) 25 % risk, 75% risk
(b) 50% risk, 50% risk
(c) 75% risk, 25% risk
(d) No risk

(v)

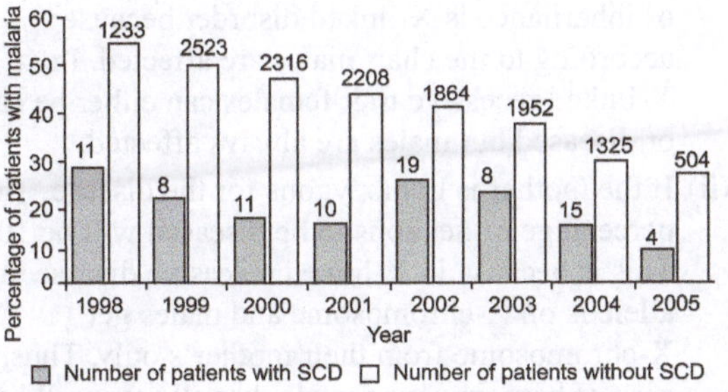

The following statements are drawn as conclusions from the above data (Kenya).

I. Patients with SCD (Sickle-Cell Disease) are less likely to be infected with malaria.
II. Patients with SCD (Sickle-Cell Disease) are more likely to be infected with malaria.
III. Over the years, the percentage of people infected with malaria has been decreasing.
IV. Year 2000 saw the largest percentage difference between malaria patients with and without SCD.

Choose from below the correct alternative.
(a) Only I is true (b) I and IV are true
(c) III and II are true (d) I and III are true

Ans. (i)-(c), (ii)-(a), (iii)-(b), (iv)-(b), (v)-(d)

2. Read the following and answer the questions given below

Codominance is the phenomenon in which two alleles express themselves independently when they are present together in an organism. In other words, in this phenomenon the offsprings shows resemblance to both the parents.

(i) Which of the following is an example of codominance?
(a) Starch grain (b) Flower colour
(c) Phenylketonuria (d) ABO blood group

(ii) Out the following the dominant allele is
(a) I^A (b) I^B
(c) I^A and I^B (d) i

(iii) The total number of genotypes of the human ABO blood types are
(a) 4 (b) 5
(c) 6 (d) 8

(iv) If the alleles from parent has blood groups I^A and I^B, respectively. What will be the possible blood group of the offspring?
(a) A (b) B
(c) AB (d) O

(v) ABO blood group is also an example of
(a) dominance (b) segregation
(c) incomplete dominance (d) multiple alleles

Ans. (i)-(d), (ii)-(c), (iii)-(c), (iv)-(c), (v)-(d)

3. Read the following and answer the questions given below

The chromosome number is fixed for all normal organisms leading to species specification whereas any abnormality in the chromosome number of an organism results into abnormal individuals. For example, in humans 46 is the fixed number of chromosomes both in male and female.

In male, it is '44 + XY' and in female, it is '44 + XX' Thus, the human male is heterogametic, in other words produces two different types of gametes one with '22 + X' chromosomes and the other with '22 + Y' chromosomes respectively. Human female, on the other hand is homogametic, i.e. produces only one type of gamete with '22 + X' chromosomes only.

Sometimes an error may occur during meiosis of cell cycle, where the sister chromatids fail to segregate called nondisjunction, leading to the production of abnormal gametes with altered chromosome number. On fertilisation such gametes develop into abnormal individuals. **CBSE 2023**

(i) State what is aneuploidy?

(ii) If during spermatogenesis, the chromatids of sex chromosomes fail to segregate during meiosis, write only the different types of gametes with altered chromosome number that could possibly be produced.

(iii) A normal human sperm (22 + Y) fertilises an ovum with karyotype '22 + XX'. Name the disorder the offspring, thus produced would suffer from and write any two symptoms of the disorder.

Or (iii) Name a best known and most common autosomal aneuploid abnormality in human and write any two symptoms.

Ans. (i) Aneuploidy is defined as the condition of abnormal number of chromosomes in a cell. It may occur due to extra or less number of chromosomes. **(1)**

(ii) The different types of gametes with altered chromosome number that could be produced is 22+0, 22+XY. **(1)**

(iii) The offspring will suffer form Klinefelter's syndrome.

The common symptoms are

(i) males with feminine characteristics.

(ii) decreased facial and body hair. **(2)**

Or

(iii) Down's syndrome (or trisomy) is the most common autosomal aneuploid abnormality in human. In down's syndrome there is a presence of an extra chromosome.

Symptoms

The two common symptoms are

(a) Individuals are short statured with small, round head and furrowed tongue and partially open mouth.

(b) Palm is broad and characteristic palm crease. **(2)**

4. Study the pedigree chart given below and answer the questions that follow. **CBSE SQP 2023**

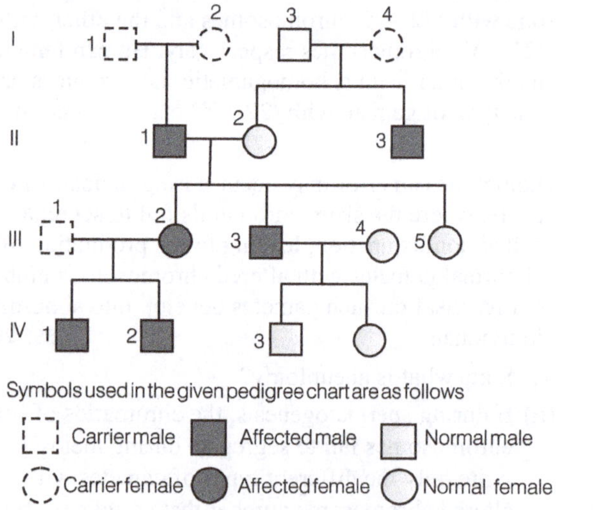

(i) On the basis of the inheritance pattern exhibited in this pedigree chart, what conclusion can you draw about the pattern of inheritance?

(ii) If the female is homozygous for the affected trait in this pedigree chart, then what percentage of her sons will be affected ?

(iii) Give the genotype of offsprings 1, 2, 3 and 4 in III generation.

Or (iii) In this type of inheritance pattern, out of male and female children which one has less probability of receiving the trait from the parents. Give a reason.

Ans. (i) On the basis of the given pedigree chart, the patten of inheritance is X-linked disorder because according to the chart males are affected. In X-linked recessive trait females can either be carrier or diseased but males are always affected. **(1)**

(ii) If the mother is homozygous for the disease. The percentage of her sons to be diseased will be 100%. This is because in X-linked recessive disease the allele is on X-chromosome and males get X-chromosome from their mother's only. Thus, in case of homozygous female, her all sons will be affected. **(1)**

(iii) Genotype of the required individuals are as follows
1. XY, 2. $\underline{X}\,\underline{X}$, 3. $\underline{X}Y$, 4. XX **(2)**

Or (iii) The possibility of the female getting the trait is less. The female will get the trait only if the mother is at least a carrier and the father is affected. **(2)**

5. Read the following and answer the questions given below

Prateek was rushed to a nearby hospital after an accident, which had caused too much blood loss. The hospital failed to supply O negative blood for transfusion. Asif, who was attending a patient there, heard about the situation and agreed to donate blood as he had the same blood group. Prateek's mother initially refused but was later convinced by her daughter's view.

(i) Why cannot O positive blood be transfused into Prateek's body?

(ii) Write the genotype of blood group O.

(iii) What gene controls ABO blood groups?

Ans. (i) O^+ blood group contains antigen for Rh-factor. Rh^- blood lacks the antigen, so if the two blood mix, it will lead to clotting and thus, death of the patient. **(2)**

(ii) ii **(1)**

(iii) ABO blood groups are controlled by the gene I. **(1)**

CHAPTER TEST

01 Mark Questions

Multiple Choice Questions

1 Gregor J Mendel, regarded as 'Father of Genetics' performed his experiment on which plant?
(a) *Psidium guajava*
(b) *Pisum sativum*
(c) *Oenothera lamarckiana*
(d) *Lathyrus sativus*

2 Mendel formulated the law of purity of gametes on the basis of
(a) dihybrid cross (b) test cross
(c) monohybrid cross (d) back cross

3 Two independent pairs of genes, which interact to produce a new trait together, but each dominant gene alone produces its own trait are called
(a) supplementary genes
(b) complementary genes
(c) epistatic genes
(d) duplicate genes

4 Which one of the following conditions correctly describes the manner of determining the sex in the given example?
(a) XY condition in humans determines male sex
(b) XO condition in humans as found in Turner's syndrome, determines female sex
(c) Homozygous sex chromosomes (XX) produce male in *Drosophila*
(d) Homozygous sex chromosomes (ZZ) determine female sex in birds

5 A normal-visioned man whose father was colourblind, marries a woman whose father was also colourblind. They have their first child as a daughter. What are the chances that this child would be colourblind?
(a) 100% (b) 0%
(c) 25% (d) 50%

6 A human female with Turner's syndrome
(a) has 45 chromosomes with XO
(b) has one additional X-chromosome
(c) exhibits male characters
(d) is able to produce children with normal husband

Assertion-Reason Type Questions

Direction (Q. Nos. 7-10) *In each of the questions below, a statement of **Assertion** is given followed by corresponding statement of **Reason**. Of the statements mark the correct answer as*

(a) If both Assertion and Reason are true and Reason is the correct explanation of Assertion
(b) If both Assertion and Reason are true, but Reason is not the correct explanation of Assertion
(c) If Assertion is true, but Reason is false
(d) If both Assertion and Reason are false

7 **Assertion** In four O'clock plant, a cross between homozygous white flower and homozygous red flower produces pink flowers.

Reason In these plants, the flower colour is determined by three alleles.

8 **Assertion** It is not possible for human parents heterozygous for skin colour to have darker or lighter children than themselves.

Reason Human skin colour is controlled by a single pair of alleles.

9 **Assertion** The non-allelic genes for red hair and freckles are usually inherited together.

Reason The genes for red hair and freckles lie close together in same chromosome.

10 **Assertion** Frequency of crossing over is higher than observed frequency of recombination of traits in the offspring.

Reason More than one cross over may occur simultaneously between the same chromatids.

2/3 Marks Questions

11 A progeny of F_1 is crossed with the homozygous recessive parent. What is this cross called? Work out how is it useful?

12 Differentiate betwen multiple allelism and pleiotropy with the help of an example each.

13 How are dominance, co-dominance and incomplete dominance patterns of inheritance different from each other?

14 Why are human females rarely haemophilic? Explain. How do haemophilic patients suffer?

15 Write a short note on autosomal recessive traits.

16 Klinefelter's syndrome is not seen in human females give reason.

05 Marks Questions

17 Give the differences between the linkage and crossing over.

18 Write the schemetic representation of dihybrid cross and mention the result.

19 Explain the process of sex-determination in birds.

20 Write notes on any two of the following

(i) Down's syndrome

(ii) Turner's syndrome

(iii) Thalassemia

Answers

1. (b)	**2.** (c)	**3.** (a)	**4.** (a)	**5.** (b)
6. (a)	**7.** (c)	**8.** (d)	**9.** (a)	**10.** (a)

05 Molecular Basis of Inheritance

TREND ANALYSIS 3 YEARS

Average No. of Questions Across all Sets

Topic	Types of Questions	2024	2023	2020
TOPIC 01 The DNA and RNA World	1 Mark	1	0	1
	2 Marks	0	0	0
	3 Marks	0	0	2
	4 Marks (Case Based)	0	0	0
	5 Marks	1	0	1
TOPIC 02 Genetic Code, Human Genome Project and DNA Fingerprinting	1 Mark	1	1	0
	2 Marks	0	0	1
	3 Marks	1	1	1
	4 Marks (Case Based)	0	0	0
	5 Marks	0	3	1

TOPIC 1

The DNA and RNA World

The DNA World

Over the years after **Mendel,** the nature of the genetic material was investigated. It resulted in the realisation that DNA is the genetic material in majority of organisms. Whereas RNA acts as a genetic material in some viruses.

Deoxyribonucleic Acid (DNA) and Ribonucleic Acid (RNA) are the two types of nucleic acid found in living systems. Nucleic acids are polymers of nucleotides (or a pair of nucleotide called **base pairs**).

For example, bacteriophage $\phi \times 174$ has 5386 nucleotides, bacteriophage λ has 48502 bp, *E. coli* has 4.6×10^6 bp and haploid content of human DNA has 3.3×10^9 bp.

Structure of Polynucleotide Chain

- A nucleotide has three parts, i.e. a nitrogenous base, a pentose sugar (deoxyribose in DNA and ribose in RNA) and a phosphate group.
- Nitrogenous bases can be **purines,** i.e. adenine and guanine or **pyrimidines,** i.e. cytosine, uracil and thymine. Uracil is present in RNA at the place of thymine (5-methyl uracil).
- A nitrogenous base is linked to the first carbon of pentose sugar through N-glycosidic linkage to form a nucleoside, e.g. adenosine, guanosine, etc.
- Two nucleotides are linked through $3' \rightarrow 5'$ phosphodiester linkage to form a dinucleotide.

- Several nucleotides can be joined to form a polynucleotide chain. In this polynucleotide chain, at one end free phosphate group is present which is known as **5′ end**, while at one end free OH group is present, which is known as **3′ end**.
- The backbone in a polynucleotide chain is formed of sugar and phosphates.
- The nitrogenous bases linked to sugar moiety project from the backbone.
- In case of RNA, every nucleotide residue has an additional N— OH group present at 2′-position in the ribose.

Discoveries Related to Structure of DNA

(i) **Friedrich Miescher** (1869), first identified DNA as an acidic substance present in the nucleus and named it as '**nuclein**'. It was later named as nucleic acid by **Altman** (1899).

(ii) **Levene** (1910) found that DNA contains phosphoric acid as well as deoxyribose sugar. He also found that four types of nucleotides are present in DNA.

(iii) **Erwin Chargaff** proposed that for a double-stranded DNA, the ratio between adenine (A), thymine (T) and guanine (G), cytosine (C) are constant and equals to one.

$$\frac{A+T}{C+G}=1$$

(iv) **James Watson** and **Francis Crick** (1953) proposed a very simple double helix model for the structure of DNA. This was based on X-ray diffraction data, produced by **Maurice Wilkins** and **Rosalind Franklin** in the same year.

Salient Features of Double Helix Structure of DNA

- The long polymer of deoxyribonucleotides is known as a **DNA**. It is made up of two polynucleotide chains.
- The two chains have anti-parallel polarity, i.e. $5' \rightarrow 3'$ for one, $3' \rightarrow 5'$ for another.
- The nitrogenous bases can be considered as steps of the coiled helix. Bases in two strands are paired through hydrogen bonds (H-bonds).
  Adenine forms two hydrogen bonds with thymine on opposite strand. Guanine bonds with cytosine by three H-bonds. Due to this, purine always comes opposite to a pyrimidine. This forms a uniform distance between the two strands of the helix.
- The two chains are coiled in a right-handed fashion. The pitch of the helix is 3.4 nm and there are roughly 10 bp in each turn. Due to this, the distance between a base pair in a helix is about 0.34 nm.
- The plane of one base pair stacks over the other in double helix. This confers stability to the helical structure in addition to H-bonds.
- Diameter of DNA double helix is 20 Å.
- The length of a DNA double helix is about 2.2 metres in humans (6.6×10^9 bp $\times 0.34 \times 10^{-9}$ m / bp). Therefore, it needs special packaging in a cell.

Packaging of DNA Helix

- **In prokaryotic cells** such as *E. coli,* the DNA (being negatively charged) is held with some proteins (positive charge) in a region called as **nucleoid**. The DNA in nucleoid is organised in large loops held by proteins. The length of DNA in *E. coli* is around 1.36 mm.
- **In eukaryotes**, there is a set of positively charged proteins called **histones**. These are rich in basic amino acid residues, lysines and arginines (both positive).
- The 5 types of histone proteins are H_1, H_2A, H_2B, H_3 and H_4. These are organised to form a unit of 8 molecules called **histone octamer** or **nu-body**.
- The negatively charged DNA is wrapped around the positively charged histone octamer to form a structure called **nucleosome**. Two nucleosomes are connected to each other with the help of linker DNA, on which H_1 histone is present. So, H_1 is also known as **linker histone**.
- A typical nucleosome contains 200 bp of DNA helix. Nucleosomes are the repeating unit of a structure called **chromatin** (i.e. thread-like stained structure) in the nucleus. Under electron microscope, the nucleosomes in chromatin can be seen as beads-on-string.

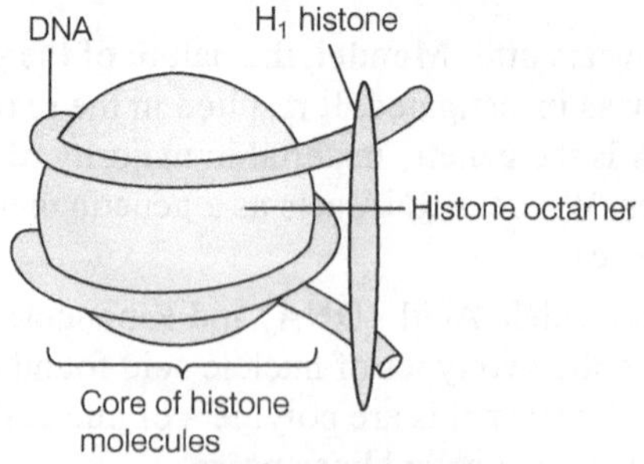

Figure 5.1 A nucleosome

- The packaging of chromatin at higher level requires additional set of proteins, which are collectively called **Non-Histone Chromosomal** (NHC) **proteins**.

- In a nucleus, some regions of chromatin are loosely packed (stains light) and are called **euchromatin** (transcriptionally active chromatin). While in some regions, chromatin is densely packed (stains dark) and are called as **heterochromatin** (transcriptionally inactive chromatin).

The Search for Genetic Material

Transforming Principle

- **Frederick Griffith** (1928) carried out a series of experiments with *Streptococcus pneumoniae* (bacterium causing pneumonia).
- According to him, when the bacteria are grown on a culture plate, some produce smooth (S) shiny colonies (S), while others produce rough (R) colonies.
- This is because the S-strain bacteria have a mucous (polysaccharide) coat, while R-strain does not. So, S-strain was infectious, while R-strain was non-infectious.
- Griffith infected two groups of mice with S-strain and R-strain, respectively. Mice infected with S-strain (virulent) died from pneumonia, but mice infected with R-strain did not develop pneumonia.

$$\text{S-strain} \xrightarrow{\text{Injection}} \text{Mice} \longrightarrow \text{Mice die}$$

$$\text{R-strain} \xrightarrow{\text{Injection}} \text{Mice} \longrightarrow \text{Mice live}$$

- In an another set of experiment, Griffith killed bacteria by heating. He observed that on injecting heat-killed S-strain bacteria, the mice remained alive. On injecting mixture of heat-killed S and live R bacteria, the mice died.

$$\underset{\text{(Heat-killed)}}{\text{S-strain}} \xrightarrow{\text{Injection}} \text{Mice} \longrightarrow \text{Mice live}$$

$$\underset{\text{(Heat-killed)}}{\text{S-strain}} + \underset{\text{(Live)}}{\text{R-strain}} \xrightarrow{\text{Injection}} \text{Mice} \longrightarrow \text{Mice die}$$

- He recovered both living S-bacteria and R-bacteria from dead mice and concluded that the 'R-strain bacteria' had been transformed by the heat-killed S-strain bacteria. Some transforming material had transferred from heat-killed S-strain to R-strain, which enabled the R-strain to synthesise a smooth polysaccharide coat and became virulent.
- Later he concluded that this must had happen due to the transfer of the genetic material. However, biochemical nature of genetic material was not defined from his experiments.

Biochemical Nature of Transforming Principle

- **Oswald Avery, Colin MacLeod** and **Maclyn McCarty** (1933-44), worked to determine the biochemical nature of transforming principle in Griffith's experiment.
- They purified biochemicals such as proteins, RNA and DNA, etc., from heat-killed S-cells and discovered that DNA alone from S-bacteria caused the transformation of R-bacteria.
- They also discovered that protease, i.e. protein digesting enzyme and RNases, i.e. RNA-digesting enzymes did not affect transformation.
- DNA digesting enzyme (DNase) cause inhibition of transformation indicating that DNA caused transformation.
- They concluded that DNA is the hereditary material. But, still all the biologists were not convinced.

DNA is the Genetic Material

Alfred Hershey and **Martha Chase** (1952) gave unequivocal proof that DNA is the genetic material.

DNA is the genetic material

[Viral DNA labelled]	**[Viral coat labelled]**
DNA labelled with ^{32}P.	Protein coat labelled with ^{35}S.
↓	↓
Viruses have infected bacteria.	Viruses have infected bacteria.
↓	↓
Blender separates viral coats from bacteria.	Blender separates viral coats from bacteria.
↓	↓
Viral replication occurs.	Viral replication occurs.
↓	↓
Radioactivity within bacterial DNA.	Radioactivity within viral coats.
↓	↓
Radioactive DNA enters from phage to bacteria indicating that DNA acts as genetic material.	Radioactive protein did not enter from virus to bacteria indicating that protein does not act as genetic material.
(a)	(b)

Figure 5.2 The Hershey and Chase's experiment

Properties of Genetic Material (DNA *Versus* RNA)

- Hershey-Chase experiment established that DNA is the genetic material.
- In some viruses, RNA was also reported as genetic material, e.g. tobacco mosaic viruses, QB bacteriophage, etc.
- **Characteristics of a Genetic Material**
  - It should be able to replicate.
  - It should be chemically and structurally stable.
  - It should provide scope for slow changes (mutation) that are required for evolution.
  - It should be able to express itself in the form of 'Mendelian characters'.

Differences between DNA and RNA

DNA	RNA
It is double-stranded with exception of some viruses.	It is generally single-stranded.
It is the genetic material in all living organisms.	It is the genetic material in some viruses only.
The sugar is deoxyribose.	The sugar is ribose.
Nitrogenous bases present are adenine, guanine, thymine and cytosine.	Nitrogenous bases present are adenine, guanine, cytosine and uracil.
It is chemically less reactive and structurally more stable.	It is chemically more reactive and structurally less stable.
It usually occurs inside the nucleus and in some cell organelles.	Small amount of RNA occurs inside the nucleus. Most of it is found in the cytoplasm.

RNA World

- The first genetic material to be discovered was RNA. There are evidences to prove that essential life processes, such as metabolism, translation, splicing, etc., have evolved around RNA.
- There are some important biochemical reactions in living systems that are catalysed by RNA catalysts and not by protein enzymes.
- DNA has evolved from RNA with chemical modifications that made it more stable, because RNA being a catalyst was reactive and hence unstable.

Types of RNA

The three types of RNAs needed to synthesise a protein in a cell are as follows

(i) ***m*RNA** (messenger RNA) provides the template for transcription.

(ii) ***t*RNA** (transfer RNA) brings amino acids and reads the genetic code.

(iii) ***r*RNA** (ribosomal RNA) plays structural and catalytic role during translation.

Central Dogma

Francis Crick proposed the central dogma in molecular biology, which states that genetic information flows from DNA to RNA and then to proteins.

DNA ⟶ RNA ⟶ Protein

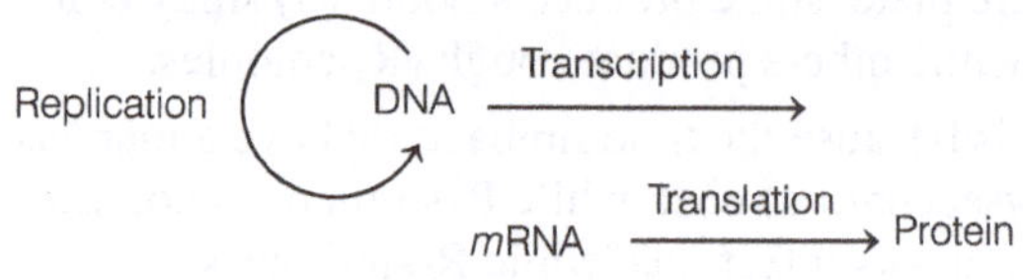

Figure 5.3 Central dogma

In some viruses, the flow of information is in reverse direction, i.e. from RNA to DNA. This process is known as **reverse transcription**. An enzyme is very important for this process known as reverse transcriptase.

Replication

The scheme for replication of DNA is termed as **semi-conservative DNA replication**. It was proposed by **Watson** and **Crick** (1953). According to it

- the two strands would separate and act as a template for the synthesis of new complementary strands.
- after replication, each DNA molecule would have one parental and one newly synthesised strand.
- the basis of semi-conservative method of replication is complementarity between nitrogenous bases.

The Experimental Proof

Matthew Meselson and Franklin Stahl performed the following experiments to prove semi-conservative mode of DNA replication in 1958. The steps of this experiment are as follows

- *E. coli* was grown on a medium containing $^{15}NH_4Cl$ as the only nitrogen source for many generations. ^{15}N (heavy isotope of nitrogen) got incorporated into newly synthesised DNA (and other nitrogen containing compounds).

- This heavy DNA molecule could be distinguished from the normal DNA by centrifugation in a cesium chloride (CsCl) density gradient.
- They then transferred the cells into a medium with normal $^{14}NH_4Cl$ and took samples at various definite intervals. As the cells multiplied and extracted, the DNA remained as double-stranded helices.
- The DNA that was extracted from the culture after the first generation (after 20 min), i.e. after the transfer from ^{15}N to ^{14}N medium, had a hybrid or intermediate density.
- It means one strand of DNA had ^{15}N, while another strand had ^{14}N. DNA extracted from the culture after second generation (after 40 min) was composed of equal amount of hybrid DNA and light (N^{14}) DNA, i.e. one DNA molecule was of $^{15}N\,^{14}N$, while another DNA molecule was of $^{14}N\,^{14}N$. So, it explains semi-conservative method of DNA replication.

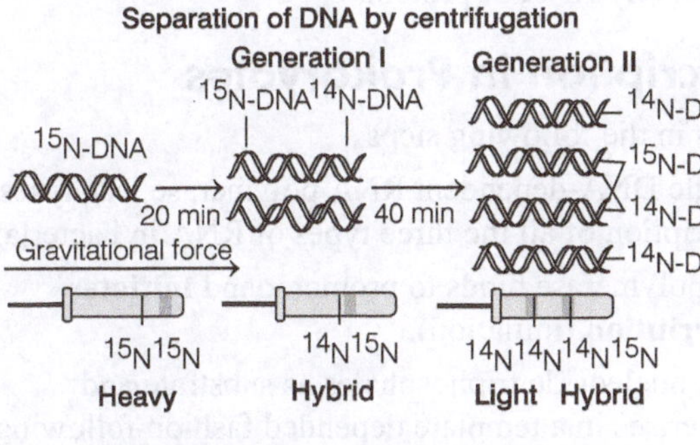

Figure 5.4 Meselson and Stahl's experiment

- Very similar experiments were carried out by **Taylor** and colleagues on *Vicia faba* (faba beans) using radioactive thymidine and the same results were obtained as in earlier experiments, i.e. DNA replicates semi-conservatively.

Machinery and Enzymes of DNA Replication

DNA replication takes place in the S-phase of cell cycle. It requires a set of catalysts or enzymes.

- The main enzyme is **DNA-dependent DNA polymerase**, since it uses a DNA template to catalyse the polymerisation of deoxynucleotides.
- Many enzymes are also required in addition to DNA-dependent DNA polymerase, such as helicase, topoisomerase, SSB, ligase, etc.
- Both the strands of DNA get separated by the activity of enzyme **helicase**. So, it causes unwinding of DNA.
- **Topoisomerase** enzyme removes tension from uncoiled DNA strand.
- **SSB protein** stabilises uncoiled DNA strand, so that it cannot coil again.

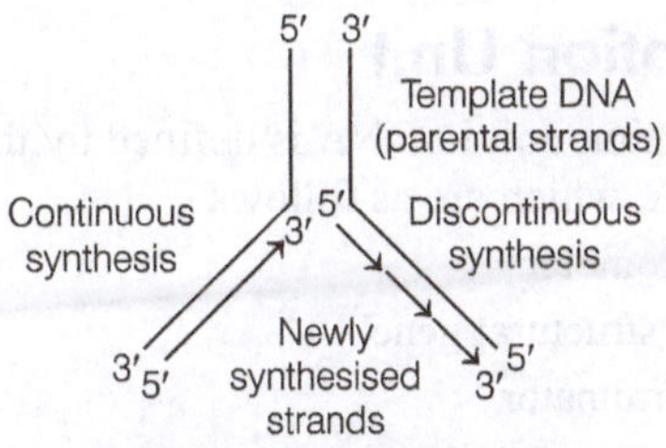

Figure 5.5 Replication fork of DNA

Process of DNA Replication

- Replication is an energy expensive process, **deoxyribonucleoside Triphosphates** (*d*NTPs) serve the dual purpose of acting as a substrate and providing energy (from two terminal phosphates).
- In a long DNA molecule, replication takes place within a small opening of the DNA helix, known as **replication fork**.
- DNA-dependent DNA polymerases catalyse polymerisation only in one direction, i.e. 5′→3′.
- Due to this, on one strand called the **leading strand** with polarity 3′→5′, replication is **continuous**. While on the other strand called the **lagging strand** with polarity 5′ → 3′ replication is **discontinuous**, i.e. in small fragments called **Okazaki fragments**. The fragments synthesised are joined by DNA ligase.
- Replication begins at a definite region in a *E. coli*, DNA molecule known as **origin of replication** *(ori)*, which has recognition site for DNA polymerase and also provides site for attachment of **RNA primer**.

Transcription

- It is the process of copying genetic information from one strand of the DNA into RNA.
- The principle of complementarity governs the process of transcription, except the adenosine now forms base pair with uracil instead of thymine.
- In transcription, only a segment of DNA is duplicated and only one of the strands is copied into RNA. Both the strands are not copied because
  (i) If both the strands code for RNA, two different RNA molecules and two different proteins would be

formed, hence complicating the genetic information transfer machinery.

(ii) Since, two RNA produced would be complementary to each other, they would form a double-stranded RNA without translation, making the process of transcription futile.

Transcription Unit

- A transcription unit in DNA is defined by three regions in the DNA, which are as follows
  - (i) A promoter
  - (ii) The structural gene
  - (iii) A terminator
- The two strands of DNA have opposite polarity and the DNA-dependent RNA polymerase also catalyses the polymerisation in only one direction, that is $5' \rightarrow 3'$ direction.
- The strand that has the polarity $3' \rightarrow 5'$ acts as a template and is referred to as **template strand**. The other strand, which has the polarity $5' \rightarrow 3'$ and the sequence same as RNA (T at the place of U) is displaced during transcription. This strand is called as **coding strand**.

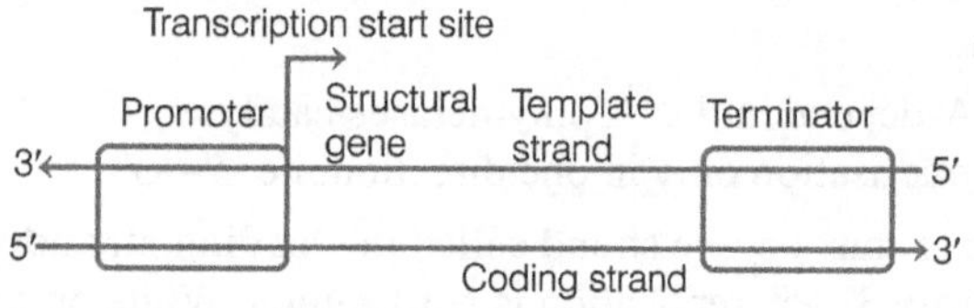

Figure 5.6 Schematic structure of a transcription unit

Note All the reference point while defining a transcription unit is made with coding strand (5′–3′).

- The **promoter** and **terminator** flank the **structural gene** in a transcription unit.
- The **promoter** is located towards 5′ end (upstream) of the structural gene.
- It is the DNA sequence that provides binding site for RNA polymerase and also the presence of promoter defines the template and coding strands. By switching its position with terminator, the definition of coding and template strands could be reversed.
- The **terminator** is located towards 3′ end (downstream) of the coding strand and it usually defines the end of the process of transcription.
- There are additional regulatory sequences that may be present further upstream or downstream to the promoter.

Transcription Unit and the Gene

- Genes are located on the chromosomes. A gene can be defined as the **functional unit of inheritance**.
- A **cistron** is a segment of DNA that codes for a polypeptide.
- The structural gene in a transcription unit could be **monocistronic** (mostly in eukaryotes) or **polycistronic** (mostly in bacteria or prokaryotes).
- In monocistronic gene, only one cistron is present in one transcription unit, while in polycistronic gene, many cistrones are present. In eukaryotes, monocistronic gene is splitted.
- The coding sequences or expressed sequences are defined as **exons**. Exons appear in mature or processed RNA. The exons are interrupted by **introns**, i.e. the non-coding sequences.
- Introns or intervening sequences do not appear in mature or processed RNA.
- Sometimes, the regulatory sequences are loosely defined as regulatory genes, even though these sequences do not code for any RNA or protein.

Transcription in Prokaryotes

It occurs in the following steps

- A single DNA-dependent RNA polymerase catalyses the transcription of all the three types of RNA in bacteria.
- RNA polymerase binds to promoter and **initiates transcription** (initiation).
- It uses nucleoside triphosphates as substrate and polymerises in a template depended fashion following the rule of complementarity.
- It also facilitates opening of the helix and continues elongation.
- Once the polymerase reaches the terminator region, the nascent RNA and RNA polymerase falls off. This results in **termination of transcription**.
- RNA polymerase is only capable of catalysing the process of **elongation**. It associates transiently with **initiation factor** (σ) and **terminator factor** (ρ), to initiate and terminate the process of transcription, respectively.
- In other words, RNA polymerase can identify promoter only when σ factor is attached on the promoter. Similarly

it terminates the process of transcription when a ρ factor is attached on the terminator. Thus, catalysing all the three steps.

- In bacteria, since the *m*RNA does not require any processing to become active and also since transcription and translation take place in the same compartment, many times the translation can begin much before the *m*RNA is fully transcribed. As a result, transcription and translation can be coupled in bacteria.

Transcription in Eukaryotes

There are some additional complexities in eukaryotes compared to than prokaryotes which are as follows

- There are at least three RNA polymerases in the nucleus in addition to the RNA polymerase.
- The **RNA polymerase-I** transcribes *r*RNAs (28S, 18S and 5.8S). **RNA polymerase-II** transcribes precursor of *m*RNA, the heterogenous nuclear RNA (*hn*RNA). **RNA polymerase-III** is responsible for the transcription of *t*RNA, 5*sr*RNA and *sn*RNAs (small nuclear RNAs).
- Another complexity is that, the primary transcripts contain both the exons and the introns and are non-functional. Hence, it is subjected to a process called **splicing**. In this process, introns are removed and exons are joined in a definite order.
- *hn*RNA undergoes additional processing called **capping** and **tailing**. In capping, an unusual nucleotide is added to the 5′ end of *hn*RNA. In tailing adenylate residues (200-300) are added at 3′ end in a template.

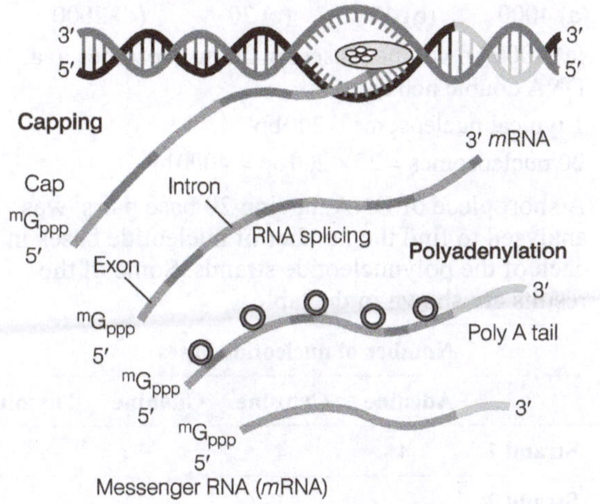

Figure 5.7 Process of transcription in eukaryotes

- Capping and tailing protect the *m*RNA from degradation by the activity of digestive enzymes present in the cytoplasm. The fully processed *hn*RNA, is called ***m*RNA**, that is transported out of the nucleus for translation process.
- Significance of these complexities are
  - The split gene arrangements represent an ancient feature of genome.
  - The presence of introns is reminescent of antiquity.
  - The process of splicing represents the dominance of RNA world.

PYQs Previous Years' Questions

1 Mark Questions

Multiple Choice Questions

1. The type of bond represented by the dotted line '.........' in a schematic polynucleotide chain is **CBSE 2024 (Set-I)**

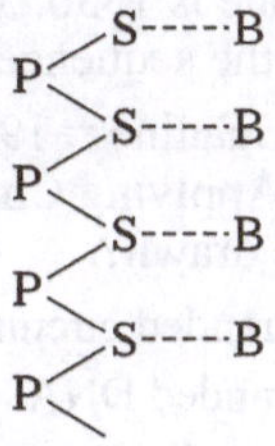

(a) hydrogen bond (b) peptide bond
(c) N-glycosidic linkage (d) phosphodiester bond

Ans. (c) A nitrogenous base (B) is linked to the OH of 1'C pentose sugar (S) through a N - glycosidic linkage.

2. If the sequence of nitrogen bases of the coding strand in a transcription unit is 5′ -ATGAATG-3′, the sequence of bases in its RNA transcription would be **CBSE 2024 (Set-II)**

(a) 5′-AUGAAUG-3′ (b) 5′-UACUUAC-3′
(c) 5′-CAUUCAU-3′ (d) 5′-GUAAGUA-3′

Ans. (a) If the coding strand in a transcription unit is 5′-ATGAATG-3′ then the RNA strand will be 5′-AUGAAUG-3′.

5′-ATGAATG-3′ Coding strand
3′-TACTTAC-5′ Template strand
5′-AUGAAUG-3′ RNA strand

3. How many base pairs will be there in 20 nucleosomes in a DNA double helix? **CBSE 2024 (Set-II)**

(a) 4000 (b) 40 (c) 20 (d) 2000

Ans. (a) 4000 bp will be present in 20 nucleosomes in a DNA double helix.

1 typical nucleosome = 200 bp

20 nucleosomes = 20×200 bp = 4000 bp

4. A short piece of DNA, having 20 base pairs, was analysed to find the number of nucleotide bases in each of the polynucleotide strands. Some of the results are shown in the table.

	Number of nucleotide bases			
	Adenine	Cytosine	Guanine	Thymine
Strand 1	4	4		
Strand 2		5		

How many nucleotides containing adenine were present in strand 2? **CBSE SQP 2024**

(a) 2 (b) 4 (c) 5 (d) 7

Ans. (d) 7

5. Which of the following amino acid residues will constitute the histone core? **CBSE SQP 2023**

(a) Lysine and arginine

(b) Asparagine and arginine

(c) Glutamine and lysine

(d) Asparagine and glutamine

Ans. (a) Histones are positively charged proteins that help in coiling of DNA. The basic amino acids that make up the histone proteins are arginine and lysine.

6. The main reason for the presence of both a leading and a lagging strand during DNA replication is **CBSE SQP 2021-22 Term-I**

(a) DNA polymerase can read only in the direction of 3′ to 5′

(b) DNA polymerase can only synthesise one strand at a time

(c) Only one strand is available to be read at any given time

(d) These are not enough RNA primers to have both strands be synthesised simultaneously

Ans. (a) DNA polymerase can read only in the direction of 3′ to 5′.

7. Which of the following is correct about mature RNA in eukaryotes? **CBSE SQP 2021-22 Term-I**

(a) Exons and introns do not appear in the mature RNA

(b) Exons appear, but introns do not appear in the mature RNA

(c) Introns appear, but exons do not appear in the mature RNA

(d) Both exons and introns appear in the mature RNA

Ans. (b) Exons appear, but introns do not appear in the mature RNA

8. The promoter site and the terminator site for transcription are located at **CBSE SQP 2021-22 Term-I**

(a) 3′ (downstream) end and 5′ (upstream) end, respectively of the transcription unit

(b) 5′ (upstream) end and 3′ (downstream) end, respectively of the transcription unit

(c) the 5′ (upstream) end of the transcription unit

(d) the 3′ (downstream) end of the transcription unit

Ans. (b) 5′ (upstream) end and 3′ (downstream) end, respectively of the transcription unit

9. Which of the following criteria must a molecule fulfill to act as a genetic material? **CBSE SQP 2021-22 Term-I**

(i) It should not be able to generate its replica.

(ii) It should chemically and structurally be stable.

(iii) It should not allow slow mutation.

(iv) It should be able to express itself in the form of Mendelian characters.

(a) (i) and (ii) (b) (ii) and (iii)

(c) (iii) and (iv) (d) (ii) and (iv)

Ans. (d) (ii) and (iv)

10. Oswald Avery, Colin MacLeod and Maclyn McCarty used enzymes to purify biochemicals such as proteins, DNA and RNA from the heat-killed S cells to see which ones could transform live R cells into S cells in Griffith's experiment. They observed that **CBSE SQP 2021-22 Term-I**

(a) Proteases and RNases affected transformation

(b) DNase inhibited transformation

(c) Proteases and lipases affected transformation

(d) RNases inhibited transformation

Ans. (b) DNase inhibited transformation

11. Total number of nucleotide sequences of DNA that codes for a hormone is 1530. The proportion of different bases in the sequence is found to be Adenine = 34%, Guanine = 19%, Cytosine = 23%, Thymine = 19%. Applying Chargaff's rule, what conclusion can be drawn? **CBSE SQP 2021-22 Term-I**

(a) It is a double-stranded circular DNA

(b) It is a single-stranded DNA

(c) It is a double-stranded linear DNA

(d) It is a single-stranded DNA coiled on histones

Ans. (b) It is a single-stranded DNA

12. A stretch of an euchromatin has 200 nucleosomes. How many bp will there be in the stretch and what would be the length of the typical euchromatin? **CBSE SQP 2021-22 Term-I**

(a) 20,000 bp and $13,000 \times 10^{-9}$ m
(b) 10,000 bp and $10,000 \times 10^{-9}$ m
(c) 40,000 bp and $13,600 \times 10^{-9}$ m
(d) 40,000 bp and $13,900 \times 10^{-9}$ m

Ans. (c) 40,000 bp and $13,600 \times 10^{-9}$ m

13. Observe structures *A* and *B* given below. Which of the following statements are correct? **CBSE SQP 2021-22 Term-I**

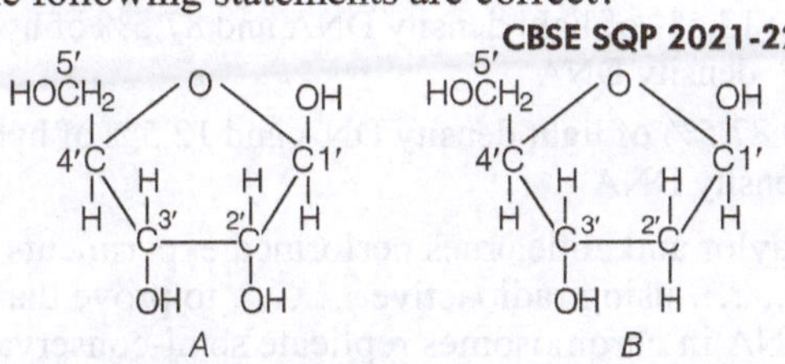

(a) *A* is having 2′—OH group which makes it less reactive and structurally stable, whereas *B* is having 2′—H group which makes it more reactive and unstable
(b) *A* is having 2′—OH group which makes it more reactive and structurally unstable, whereas *B* is having 2′—H group which makes it less reactive and structurally stable
(c) *A* and *B* both have —OH groups which make it more reactive and structurally stable
(d) *A* and *B* both are having —OH groups which make it less reactive and structurally stable

Ans. (b) *A* is having 2′—OH group which makes it more reactive and structurally unstable, whereas *B* is having 2′—H group which makes it less reactive and structurally stable

14. Two important RNA processing events lead to specialised end sequences in most human *m*RNAs, ...(i)... at the 5′ end and ...(ii)... at the 3′ end. At the 5′ end, the most distinctive specialised end nucleotide, ...(iii)... is added and a sequence of about 200 ...(iv)... is added to the 3′ end. **CBSE SQP 2021-22 Term-I**

(a) (i) initiator codon, (ii) promoter, (iii) terminator codon, (iv) release factors
(b) (i) promoter, (ii) elongation, (iii) regulation, (iv) termination
(c) (i) capping, (ii) polyadenylation, (iii) $^{m}G_{ppp}$, (iv) poly-A
(d) (i) repressor, (ii) co-repressor, (iii) operon, (iv) release factors

Ans. (c) (i) capping, (ii) polyadenylation, (iii) $^{m}G_{ppp}$, (iv) poly-A

15. Origin of replication of DNA in *E. coli* is shown below, identify the labelled parts (i), (ii), (iii) and (iv). **CBSE SQP 2021-22 Term-I**

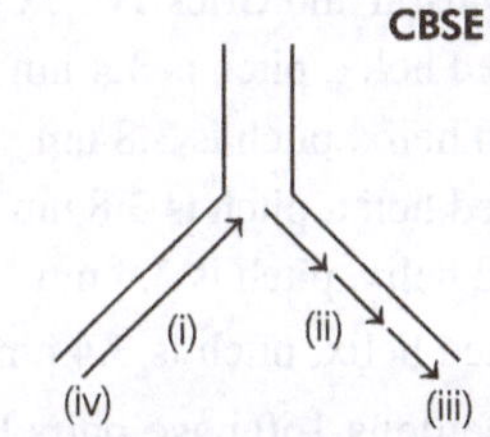

(a) (i) Discontinuous synthesis, (ii) Continuous synthesis, (iii) 3′ end, (iv) 5′ end
(b) (i) Continuous synthesis, (ii) Discontinuous synthesis, (iii) 5′ end, (iv) 3′ end
(c) (i) Discontinuous synthesis, (ii) Continuous synthesis, (iii) 5′ end, (iv) 3′ end
(d) (i) Continuous synthesis, (ii) Discontinuous synthesis, (iii) 3′ end, (iv) 5′ end

Ans. (d) (i) Continuous synthesis, (ii) Discontinuous synthesis, (iii) 3′ end, (iv) 5′ end

16. Transcription unit is represented in the diagram given below. **CBSE SQP 2021-22 Term-I**

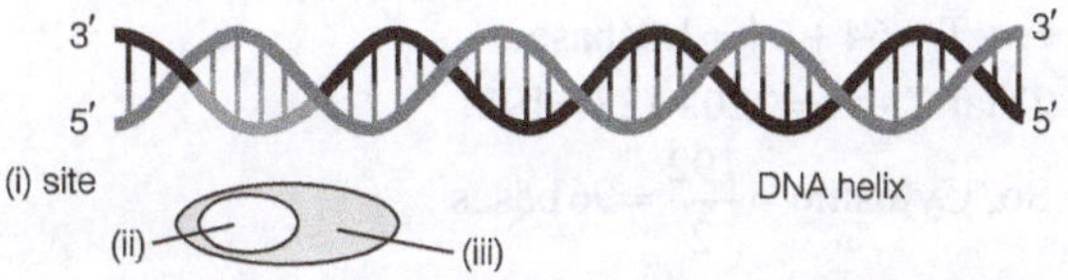

Identify site (i), factor (ii) and enzyme (iii) responsible for carrying out the process.

(a) (i) Promoter site, (ii) Rho factor, (iii) RNA polymerase
(b) (i) Terminator site, (ii) Sigma factor, (iii) RNA polymerase
(c) (i) Promoter site, (ii) Sigma factor, (iii) RNA polymerase
(d) (i) Promoter site, (ii) Sigma factor, (iii) DNA polymerase

Ans. (c) (i) Promoter site, (ii) Sigma factor, (iii) RNA polymerase

17. In order to form a dinucleotide during DNA synthesis which functional group at 3′ must be free? **CBSE SQP 2021-22 Term-I**

(a) Methyl group
(b) Phosphate group
(c) Carboxylic acid
(d) Hydroxyl

Ans. (d) Hydroxyl

18. In a cell, DNA transcription is halted when **CBSE SQP 2021-22 Term-I**

(a) RNA polymerase falls off of the DNA
(b) The end of the DNA is reached
(c) When a rho site is reached
(d) When a stop codon is reached

Ans. (c) When a rho site is reached

19. The correct feature of double-helical structure of DNA as given by Watson and Crick is **CBSE 2021-22 Term-I**

(a) right-handed helix, pitch is 3.4 nm
(b) left-handed helix, pitch is 3.8 nm
(c) right-handed helix, pitch is 3.8 nm
(d) left-handed helix, pitch is 3.4 nm

Ans. (a) right-handed helix, pitch is 3.4 nm

20. A DNA molecule is 160 base pairs long. If it has 20% adenine, how many cytosine bases are present in this DNA molecule? **CBSE 2021-22 Term-I**

(a) 48 (b) 64
(c) 96 (d) 192

Ans. (c) No. of base pairs $= 160$

Bases $= 160 \times 2 = 320$

Adenine $= 20\%$

As $A = T$

So, Thymine $= 20\%$

Adenine $= \frac{20}{100} \times 320 = 64$ bases

So, Thymine $= 64$ base

$A + T = 64 + 64 = 128$ base

Total $C + G = 320 - 128 = 192$

So, Cytosine $= \frac{192}{2} = 96$ bases

21. Study the given diagrammatic representation of Griffith's experiment to demonstrate transformation in bacteria.

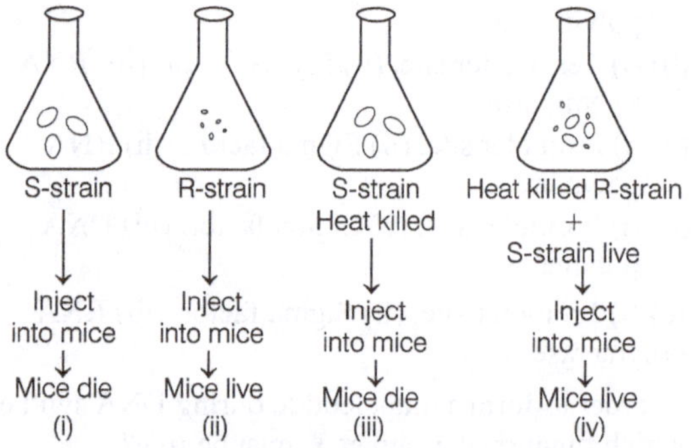

Select the option which is incorrectly representing the experiment. **CBSE 2021-22 Term-I**

(a) (i) and (iii) (b) (ii) and (iii)
(c) (iii) and (iv) (d) (ii) and (iv)

Ans. (c) (iii) and (iv)

22. The reactive hydroxyl group in the nucleotide of RNA is **CBSE 2021-22 Term-I**

(a) 5′ OH (b) 4′ OH (c) 3′ OH (d) 2′ OH

Ans. (d) 2′ OH

23. If *E. coli* were allowed to grow in the culture medium for 80 minutes by Matthew Meselson and Franklin Stahl in their experiments, the proportion of light and hybrid density DNA molecule would have been **CBSE 2021-22 Term-I**

(a) 87.5% of light density DNA and 12.5% of hybrid density DNA
(b) 75.0% of light density DNA and 25% of hybrid density DNA
(c) 50% of light density DNA and 50% of hybrid density DNA
(d) 12.5% of light density DNA and 87.5% of hybrid density DNA

Ans. (a) 87.5% of light density DNA and 12.5% of hybrid density DNA

24. Taylor and colleagues performed experiments on .... using radioactive .... to prove that the DNA in chromosomes replicate semi-conservatively. **CBSE 2021-22 Term-I**

(a) *Vicia faba*, uridine
(b) *E. coli*, uridine
(c) *Vicia faba*, thymidine
(d) *E. coli*, thymidine

Ans. (c) *Vicia faba*, thymidine

25. Histone proteins that help in forming the nucleosomes in the nucleus are rich in basic amino acids such as **CBSE 2021-22 Term-I**

(a) arginine and tyrosine (b) lysine and histidine
(c) arginine and lysine (d) histidine and tryptophan

Ans. (c) arginine and lysine

26. A diagrammatic illustration of the process of transcription by RNA polymerase-II in eukaryote is given below. Choose the most appropriate statement with respect to the fate of the precursor of *m*RNA transcribed that will be **CBSE 2021-22 Term-I**

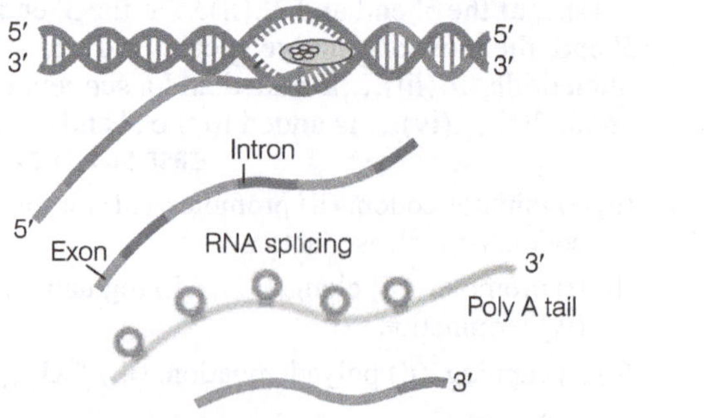

(a) Translation will take place once the precursor of *m*RNA leaves the nucleus
(b) Translation on *m*RNA will not take place once the precursor of *m*RNA leaves the nucleus

(c) Translation will take place in the nucleus
(d) The precursor of *m*RNA has to be processed further in next step before being translated

Ans. (d) The precursor of *m*RNA has to be processed further in next step before being translated

27. A region of coding strand of DNA has the following nucleotide sequence

5′ – TACGCCG – 3′

The sequence of bases on *m*RNA transcribed by this would be **CBSE 2021-22 Term-I**

(a) 5′ – UACGCCG – 3′ (b) 3′ – UACGCCG – 3′
(c) 5′ – ATGCGGC – 3′ (d) ′3 – ATGCGGC – 3′

Ans. (a) 5′ – UACGCCG – 3′

28. Charging of *t*RNA during translation is necessary for **CBSE 2021-22 Term-I**

(a) binding of anticodons of *t*RNA to the respective codons of *m*RNA
(b) peptide bond formation between two amino acids
(c) movement of ribosomes from codon to codon
(d) binding of ribosomes to the *m*RNA

Ans. (b) peptide bond formation between two amino acids

29. A template strand in a bacterial DNA has the given base sequence

5′ – AGGTTTAACG – 3′

What would be the RNA sequence transcribed from this template strand? **CBSE 2021-22 Term-I**

(a) 5′ – CGUUAAACCU – 3′
(b) 5′ – AGGUUUAACG – 3′
(c) 5′ – TCCAAATTGC – 3′
(d) 5′ – AGGTTTAACG – 3′

Ans. (b) 5′ – AGGUUUAACG – 3′

30. In a bacterium when RNA-polymerase binds to the promoter on a transcription unit during transcription, it **All India 2020**

(a) terminates the process
(b) helps remove introns
(c) initiates the process
(d) inactivates the exons

Ans. (c) initiates the process

31. If Meselson and Stahl's experiment is continued for sixth generations in bacteria, the ratio of heavy strands $^{15}N/^{15}N$: hybrid $^{15}N/^{14}N$: light $^{14}N/^{14}N$ containing DNA in the sixth generation would be

(a) 1 : 1 : 1 (b) 0 : 1 : 7
(c) 0 : 1 : 15 (d) 0 : 1 : 31

Ans. (d) If Meselson and Stahl's experiment is continued for sixth generation in bacteria the ratio of $^{15}N/^{15}N$: hybrid $^{15}N/^{14}N$: light $^{14}N/^{14}N$ would be 0 : 1 : 31.

Assertion-Reason Type Questions

Direction *(Q. Nos. 32-35) consist of two statements Assertion (A) and Reason (R). Answer these questions selecting the appropriate option given below.*

(a) Both Assertion and Reason are true and Reason is the correct explanation of Assertion.
(b) Both Assertion and Reason are true, but Reason is not the correct explanation of Assertion.
(c) Assertion is true, but Reason is false
(d) Assertion is false, but Reason is true

32. **Assertion** In molecular diagnosis, single stranded DNA or RNA tagged with radioactive molecule is called a probe.

Reason A probe always searches and hybridises with its complementary DNA in a clone of cells. **CBSE 2024 (Set-II)**

Ans. (a) Both A and R are true and R is the correct explanation of A.

A single stranded DNA or RNA, tagged with a radioactive molecule called probe is allowed to hybridise to its complementary DNA in a clone of cells followed by detection using autoradiography.

33. **Assertion** The sugar phosphate backbone of two chains in DNA double helix show anti-parallel polarity.

Reason The phosphodiester bonds in one strand go from a 3′ carbon of one nucleotide to a 5′ carbon of adjacent nucleotide, whereas those in complementary strand go *vice versa*. **CBSE 2024 (Set-II)**

Ans. (a) Both A and R are true and R is the correct explanation of A.

The backbone of a DNA strand is built up of alternate deoxyribose sugar and phosphate group. The phosphate group is connected to carbon 5 of the sugar residue of its own nucleotide and carbon 3 of the sugar residue of the next nucleotide by $3' \rightarrow 5'$ phosphodiester bonds. The two DNA chains are antiparallel, i.e. they run in opposite direction. In one chain, the direction is $5' \rightarrow 3'$, while in the opposite one, it is $3' \rightarrow 5'$.

34. **Assertion** Ribosomal RNA is synthesized in the nucleus of the cell.

Reason It is translated with the enzyme RNA polymerase-III. **CBSE SQP 2024**

Ans. (c) A is true, but R is false and R can be correct as *r*RNA transcribed by RNA polymerase-I.

35. **Assertion** Primary transcripts in eukaryotes are non-functional.

Reason Methyl guanosine triphosphate is attached to 5′ end of *hn*RNA. **CBSE SQP 2021**

Ans. (b)

Very Short Answer Type Questions

36. Write the dual purpose served by deoxyribonucleoside triphosphates in polymerisation. **CBSE 2018**

Ans. Deoxyribonucleoside Triphosphates (*d*NTPs) serve the dual purpose of
(i) acting as a substrate. (½)
(ii) providing energy (from two terminal phosphates).(½)

37. Why does *hn*RNA undergo splicing? Where does splicing occur in the cell? **Delhi 2015C**

Ans. *hn*RNA undergoes splicing to remove non-coding sequences, i.e. introns and joins exons. Splicing occurs in the nucleus of the cell. (½ + ½)

38. Name the enzyme that transcribes *hn*RNA in eukaryotes. **Delhi 2015C**

Or Write the function of RNA polymerase-II. **Foreign 2015**

Ans. The RNA polymerase-II transcribes the precursor of *m*RNA, i.e. the heterogeneous nuclear RNA (*hn*RNA).

39. Why is RNA more reactive in comparison to DNA? **Delhi 2015C**

Ans. The —OH group in the ribose of RNA at 3′ end makes the molecule more reactive, compared with DNA. RNA is also not stable under alkaline conditions.

40. Name the negatively charged and positively charged components of a nucleosome. **Delhi 2015C**

Or Name the positively charged protein around which the negatively charged DNA wrapped. **All India 2012C**

Ans. Histone proteins forming an octamer is the positively charged component and the DNA helix is the negatively charged component of nucleosome.

41. What is cistron? **All India 2015**

Ans. The segment of DNA coding for a polypeptide is known as cistron.

42. Name the transcriptionally active region of chromatin in a nucleus. **Delhi 2015**

Ans. Euchromatin (lightly stained) is the transcriptionally active region of chromatin in a nucleus.

43. What will happen if DNA replication is not followed by cell division in a eukaryotic cell? **All India 2014C**

Ans. If cell division is not followed after DNA replication then replicated chromosomes (DNA) would not be distributed to daughter nuclei. A repeated replication of DNA without any cell division results in the accumulation of DNA inside the cell. This would increase the volume of the cell nucleus, thereby causing cell expansion. Further, it will lead to polyploidy.

44. Why is it not possible for an alien DNA to become part of chromosome anywhere along its length and replicate normally? **All India 2014**

Ans. An alien DNA cannot become a part of chromosome anywhere along its length and replicate normally due to the absence of origin of replication where the replication process is initiated.

45. Name the enzyme and state its property that is responsible for continuous and discontinuous replication of the two strands of a DNA molecule. **Delhi 2013**

Ans. **DNA-dependent DNA polymerase** This enzyme can polymerise deoxynucleotides in $5' \rightarrow 3'$ direction only. Due to this, replication of DNA is continuous in one strand with polarity $3' \rightarrow 5'$ while discontinuous in another polarity $5' \rightarrow 3'$.

46. Name the enzyme that joins the small fragment of DNA of a lagging strand during DNA replication. **Delhi 2013C**

Ans. DNA ligase joins the small fragment of DNA of a lagging strand during DNA replication.

47. Which one of an intron and an exon is the reminiscent of antiquity? **All India 2013C**

Ans. Intron is considered to be the reminiscent of antiquity because these are non-coding sequences.

2 Marks Questions

48. If the base adenine constitutes 31% of an isolated DNA fragment, then write what will be the expected percentage of the base cytosine in it. Explain how did you arrive at the answer given. **CBSE 2024 (Set-II)**

Ans. If the adenine (A) constitutes 31% of an isolated DNA fragment, then the expected percentage of the base cytosine (C) will be 19%. We can calculate this using Chargaff's rule which says in DNA, A = T and G = C and the ratio of pyrimidine and purine bases is 1 : 1.

So, $A + T + C + G = 100\%$

[$A = T = 31\%$, $G = C = x$ (let)]

$$31\% + 31\% + x + x = 100\%$$
$$62\% + 2x = 100\%$$
$$2x = 38\%$$
$$x = 19\%$$

Thus, G = C = 19%

49. Carefully examine structures *A* and *B* of pentose sugar given below. Which one of the two is more reactive? Give reasons. **CBSE SQP 2020**

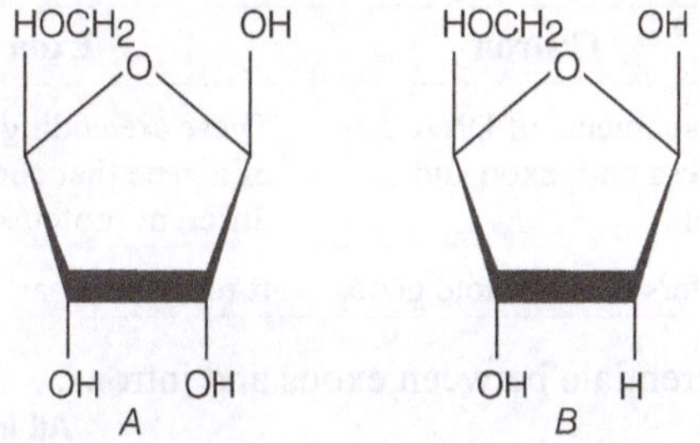

Ans. Structure *A* represents ribose sugar and structure *B* represents deoxyribose sugar.

Structure *A*, i.e. ribose sugar present in every nucleotide of RNA is more reactive making RNA highly reactive, labile and easily degradable compared to DNA.

50. What is an origin of replication in a chromosome? State its function. **Delhi 2019**

Ans. Replication does not initiate randomly at any place in DNA (chromosome). So, there is a definite region in DNA (chromosome) termed as origin of replication. It is the place from where DNA replication originates. It helps in propagation of a piece of DNA, during recombinant DNA procedures. (1 + 1)

51. Although a prokaryotic cell has no defined nucleus, yet DNA is not scattered throughout the cell. Explain. **CBSE 2018**

Ans. Prokaryotes lack a defined nucleus. However, the DNA is not scattered throughout the cell. This is due to the fact that the negatively charged DNA is held with some positively charged proteins in nucleoid or the middle region.

In this region, the DNA is organised in large loops held by proteins.

52. Describe the structure of a nucleosome. **Delhi 2017**

Or

Draw a labelled diagram of a nucleosome. Where is it found in a cell? **Foreign 2014; All India 2012**

Or

How do histones acquire positive charge? **Delhi 2011**

Ans. Nucleosome is a complex of negatively charged DNA wrapped around the positively charged histone octamer (unit of 8 molecules of histone). It is found in the nucleus of the cell.

It is made up of four types of proteins; H_2A, H_2B, H_3 and H_4 occurring in pairs. The histone proteins acquire positive charge due to the abundance of amino acid residues, i.e. lysine and arginines. Both these amino acids carry positive charges in their side chains. A typical nucleosome consists of 200 base pairs of DNA helix. A labelled diagram of nucleosome shown below

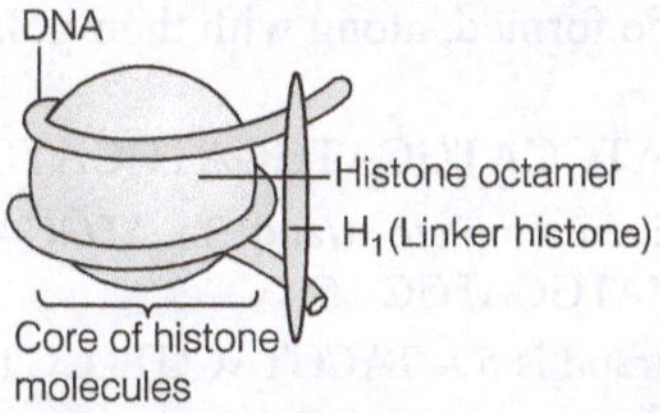

53. Discuss the role of enzyme DNA ligase plays during DNA replication. **All India 2016**

Ans. DNA ligase facilitates the joining of Okazaki fragments in lagging DNA strands together by catalysing the formation of phosphodiester bond. It also plays a role in repairing single-strand breaks in duplex DNA.

54. In a typical nucleus, some regions of chromatin are stained light and others dark. Explain why is it so and what is its significance. **Outside Delhi 2016C**

Ans. In a typical nucleus, some regions of chromatin are stained light because of loose packing of chromatin and some regions of chromatin are stained dark because chromatin is densely packed. Euchromatin is transcriptionally active chromatin (lightly stained) while heterochromatin (darkly stained) is transcriptionally inactive. (1 + 1)

55. Explain the two factors responsible for conferring stability to double helix structure of DNA. **All India 2014**

Ans. Two factors responsible for conferring stability to double helix structure of DNA are

(i) Stacking of one base pair over other. (1)

(ii) H-bonds between nitrogenous bases. (1)

56. State the difference between the structural genes in a transcription unit of prokaryotes and eukaryotes. **All India 2014**

Ans. Prokaryotic structural genes are continuous and are without any non-coding region, while eukaryotic structural genes contain exons (coding DNA) and introns (non-coding DNA).

57. Show DNA replication with the help of a diagram only. **All India 2014C; Delhi 2012**

Ans. The replication fork of DNA formed during DNA replication.

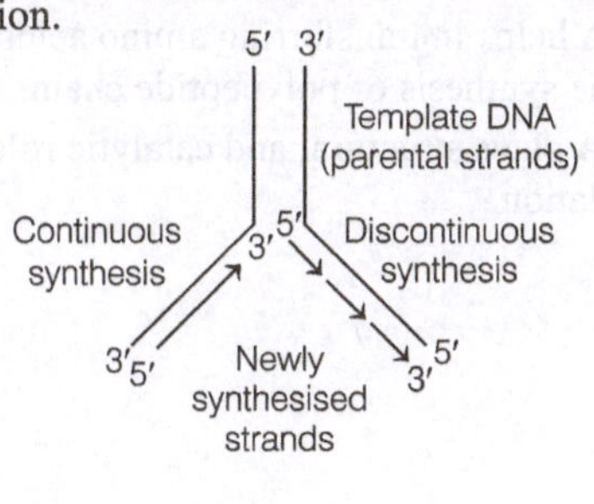

58. A template strand is given below. Write down the corresponding coding strand and the *m*RNA strand that can be formed, along with their polarity. **Foreign 2014**

3′– ATGCATGCATGCATGCATGCATGC–5′

Ans. For the given template strand 3′– ATGCATGCAT GCATGCATGCATGC– 5′

Coding strand is 5′ – TACGTACGTACGTACGTACG TACG – 3′ **(1)**

and *m*RNA strand is 5′– UACGUACGUACGUACGU ACGUACG – 3′ **(1)**

59. Draw a schematic diagram of a part of double-stranded dinucleotide DNA chain having all the four nitrogenous bases showing the correct polarity. **Delhi 2012**

Ans. Schematic diagram of a double-stranded dinucleotide DNA chain having all the four nitrogenous bases (A,T, G, C) with polarity.

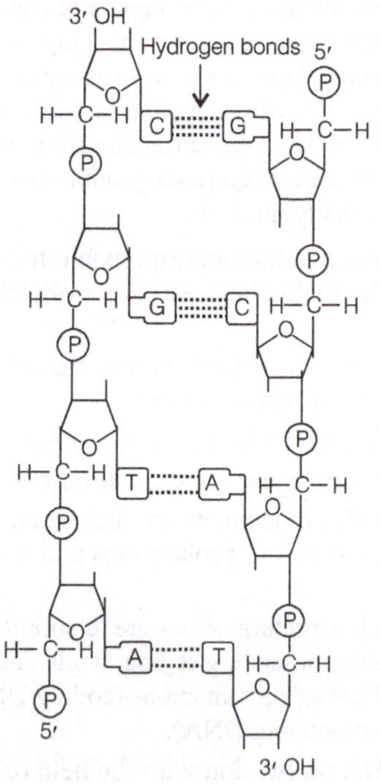

60. State the functions of the following in a prokaryote

(i) *t*RNA (ii) *r*RNA **All India 2012**

Ans. (i) ***t*RNA** helps in transferring amino acids to ribosome for the synthesis of polypeptide chain. **(1)**

(ii) ***r*RNA** plays structural and catalytic role during translation. **(1)**

61. Differentiate between a cistron and an exon. **All India 2012C**

Ans. Differences between cistron and exon are as follows

Cistron	Exon
It is segments of DNA that possess both exon and intron.	These are coding regions of a gene that code for different proteins.
It refers to the whole gene.	It refers to a part of gene.

62. Differentiate between exons and introns. **All India 2012C**

Ans. Differences between exons and introns are as follows

Exons	Introns
Regions of a gene which become part of *m*RNA.	Regions of a gene which do not form part of *m*RNA.
Code for the different proteins and hence called coding sequence.	Removed during the processing of *m*RNA because they are non-coding sequences.

63. State the dual role of deoxyribonucleoside triphosphates during DNA replication. **Delhi 2011**

Ans. (i) The deoxyribonucleoside triphosphates are the building blocks for the DNA strand (polynucleotide chain), i.e. they act as substrates. **(1)**

(ii) These also serve as energy source as ATP and GTP because of the presence of high energy terminal phosphate groups. **(1)**

64. Answer the questions based on the dinucleotide shown below.

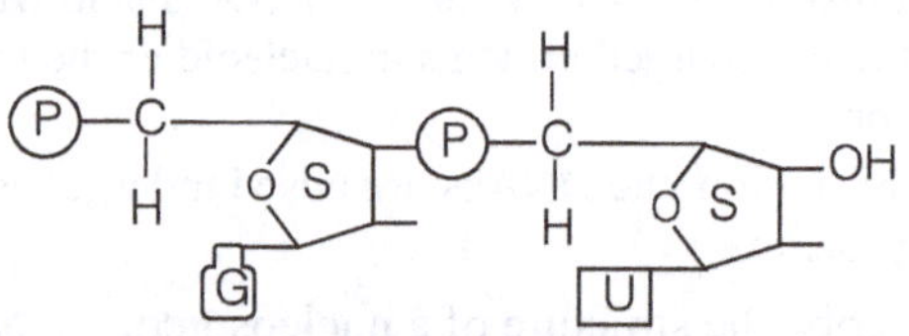

(i) Name the type of sugar guanine base is attached to.

(ii) Name the linkage connecting the two nucleotides.

(iii) Identify the 3′ end of the dinucleotide. Give a reason for your answer. **All India 2010C**

Ans. (i) Pentose sugar or deoxyribose sugar. **(½)**

(ii) Two nucleotides are linked through 3′–5′ phosphodiester linkage to form a dinucleotide. **(½)**

(iii) The ribose sugar has a free 3′—OH group which is referred to as 3′ end of the polynucleotide chain. **(1)**

65. Make a labelled diagram of an RNA dinucleotide showing its $3' \rightarrow 5'$ polarity. **All India 2010C**

Ans. RNA dinucleotide.

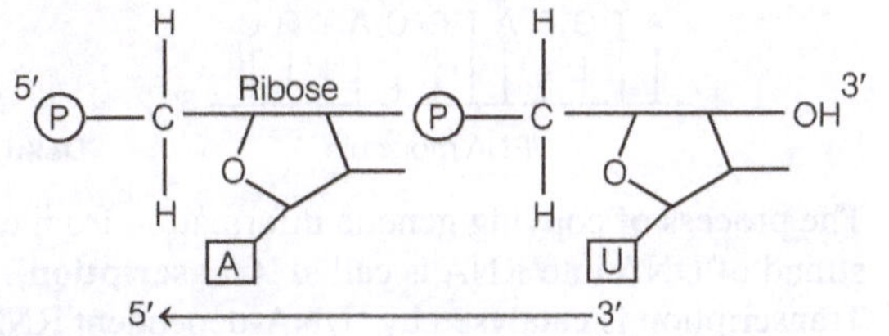

3 Marks Questions

66. (i) Why does DNA replication occur within a replication fork and not in its entire length simultaneously?

(ii) "DNA replication is continuous and discontinuous on the two strands within the replication fork". Explain with the help of a schematic representation. **CBSE 2024 (Set-II)**

Ans. (i) DNA replication occurs within a small opening of DNA helix called replication fork and not in its entire length simultaneously as

(a) It requires a high amount of energy due to large size of DNA.

(b) Polymerisation takes place only in one direction, i.e. $5' \rightarrow 3'$.

(ii) During the process of DNA replication, the replication on one strand (with polarity $3' \rightarrow 5'$) occurs continuously. The strand is known as the leading daughter strand. On the other hand, replication occurs discontinuously on the other strand (with polarity $5' \rightarrow 3'$).

Small fragments of DNA are created. These fragments known as the Okazaki fragments. This strand is known as the lagging daughter strand.

Thus, the replication occurs through a small opening called replication fork and is continuous in one direction and discontinuous in other direction. This is known as the semi-discontinuous mode of replication.

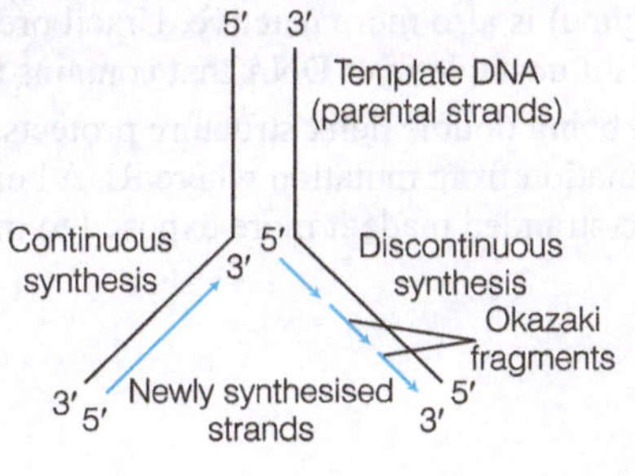

67. Explain the discovery made by Hershey and Chase using radioactive sulphur and phosphorus in their experiment. **Delhi 2020**

Ans. Refer to text on page no. 135 (DNA is the genetic material).

68. Describe the experiment where Matthew Meselson and Franklin Stahl used heavy isotope of nitrogen. **Delhi 2020**

Or Describe the experiment that helped demonstrate the semi-conservative mode of DNA replication. **All India 2016**

Or How was a heavy isotope of nitrogen used to provide experimental evidence to semi-conservative mode of DNA replication? **Foreign 2015**

Ans. **Matthew Meselson** and **Franklin Stahl** conducted an experiment with *Escherichia coli* (1958) as follows

(i) They grew many generations of *E. coli* in a medium that contained $^{15}NH_4Cl$ (^{15}N is the heavy isotope of nitrogen) as the only source of nitrogen. The result was that ^{15}N was incorporated into the newly synthesised DNA.

Upon centrifugation in a cesium chloride (CsCl) density gradient, this heavy DNA molecule could be distinguished from the normal DNA.

(ii) The cells were then transferred into a medium containing normal $^{14}NH_4Cl$.

(iii) At definite time intervals, as the cells multiplied, samples were taken and the DNA which remained as double-stranded helices were extracted.

(iv) The samples were separated independently on CsCl gradient to measure the densities of DNA.

(v) The DNA obtained from the culture, one generation after the transfer from ^{15}N to ^{14}N medium had a hybrid or intermediate density.

(vi) The DNA obtained from the culture after another generation (generation II), was composed of equal amounts of hybrid DNA and light DNA.

Separation of DNA by centrifugation

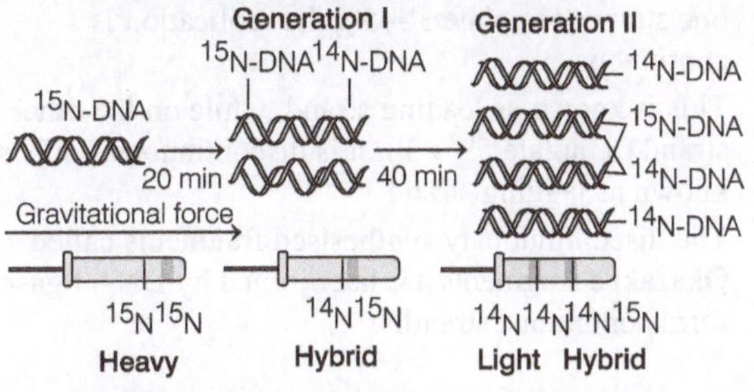

Thus, Meselson and Stahl concluded that the DNA replication is semi-conservative, i.e. out of the two strands of DNA one is the parental strand, while another is newly synthesised.

69. Answer the following questions based on Meselson and Stahl's experiment on *E. coli*.

(i) Write the name of the chemical substance used as the only source of nitrogen in the experiment.

(ii) Why did they allow the synthesis of the light and the heavy DNA molecules in the organism?

(iii) How did they distinguish the heavy DNA molecules from the light DNA molecules?

(iv) Write the conclusion the scientists arrived at the end of the experiment. **All India 2019, 11**

Ans. (i) NH_4Cl (Ammonium chloride) with N^{15} atom. (½)

(ii) It is done to show that after one generation *E. coli* with ^{15}N-DNA in a medium of ^{14}N, has DNA of intermediate density between the light and heavy DNAs.

It shows that out of the two strands, only one strand is synthesised newly, using the ^{14}N-nitrogen source in the medium. (½)

(iii) The heavy and light DNA molecules can be differentiated by centrifugation in a cesium chloride (CsCl) density gradient.

The ^{15}N-DNA was heavier than ^{14}N-DNA and the hybrid $^{15}N-^{14}N$-DNA was intermediate between the two newly form DNA strands. (1)

(iv) Scientists concluded that the DNA replication is semi-conservative, i.e. of the two strands of DNA, one is the parental strand, while the other is newly synthesised. (1)

70. Explain the mechanism of DNA replication with the help of a replication fork. What role does the enzyme DNA-ligase play in a replication fork? **Delhi 2019**

Ans. Replication in DNA strand occurs within a small opening of the DNA helix, known as replication fork.

For figure, refer to answer no. 57.

DNA polymerases catalyse polymerisation only in one direction, i.e. 5' → 3'. It creates additional complications at the replicating fork. Consequently, on one strand (template 3'→5'), the replication is continuous.

This is known as leading strand, while on the other strand (template 5' → 3'), it is discontinuous. This is known as lagging strand.

The discontinuously synthesised fragments called Okazaki a fragments are later joined by DNA ligase to form continuous strand.

71. Construct and label a transcription unit from which the RNA segment given below has been transcribed. Write the complete name of the enzyme that transcribed this RNA.

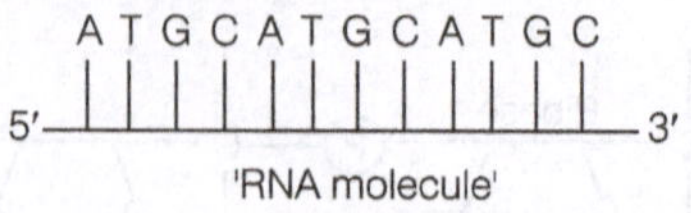

Delhi 2019

Ans. The process of copying genetic information from one strand of DNA into RNA is called '**transcription**'. Transcription is catalysed by 'DNA-dependent RNA polymerase'.

The RNA molecule given in question should be

As RNA have uracil in place of thymine.

For given RNA, the transcription unit will be

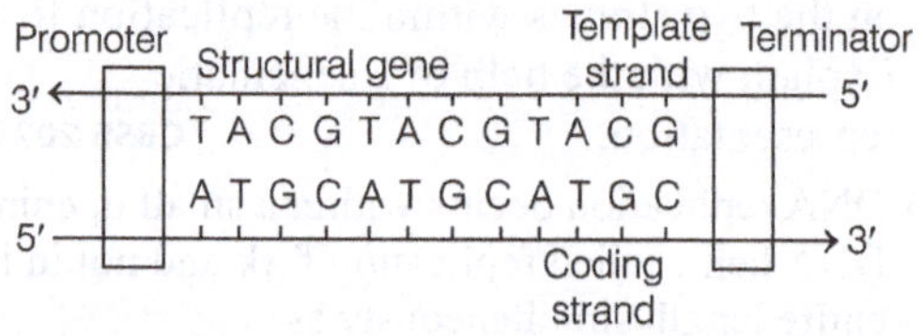

Common Mistakes Students usually get confused between template strand and coding strand.

Template strand serve as template for the synthesis of a complementary RNA transcript.

Coding strand is identical to RNA transcripts in sequence, but thymine (T) base is replaced with the uracil (U) base.

72. Why is DNA molecule considered as a better hereditary material than RNA molecule? **CBSE 2018C**

Or Why is DNA a better genetic material when compared to RNA? **Delhi 2015C**

Or Why is DNA considered a better hereditary material than RNA? **Foreign 2012**

Ans. DNA is considered a better genetic material when compared to RNA because of its high stability and low reactivity. RNA being more reactive, is labile and easily degradable.

The high reactivity of RNA is contributed by the 2'–OH group in the nucleotides. RNA as a catalyst (e.g. ribozyme) is also more reactive. Uracil present in RNA makes it unstable over DNA that contains thymine.

DNA being double helix structure protects the genetic information from mutation where RNA being single-stranded made it more exposed to mutation.

73. Name the three polymerases found in eukaryotic cells and mention their functions. **CBSE 2018C**

Ans. Three types of RNA polymerases are found in eukaryotic cells and their functions are as follows

(i) RNA polymerase-I transcribes *r*RNAs.

(ii) RNA polymerase-II transcribes the precursor of *m*RNA called *hn*RNA.

(iii) RNA polymerase-III transcribes *t*RNA, 5*sr*RNA and *sn*RNAs. **(1 × 3)**

74. Explain the post-transcriptional modifications the *hn*RNA undergoes in eukaryotic. **CBSE 2018C**

Ans. Refer to text on page no. 139.

75. Study the diagram given below. Name the linkage *X*, *Y*, *Z* and the respective molecules formed by them. **Delhi 2016C**

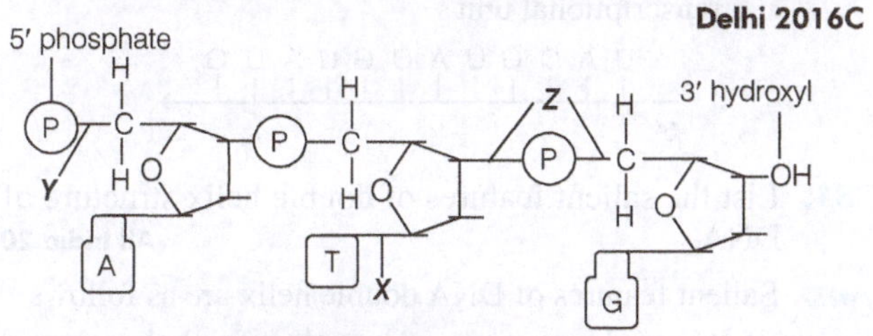

A polynucleotide chain

Ans. X : N-glycosidic linkage. It forms nucleoside.

Y : Phosphoester linkage. It forms nucleotide.

Z : 3′–5′ phosphodiester linkage. It forms polynucleotide. **(1 × 3)**

76. (i) Differentiate between a template strand and coding strand of DNA.

(ii) Name the source of energy for the replication of DNA. **Delhi 2015C**

Ans. (i) Differences between template strand and coding strand are

Template strand	Coding strand
It has 3′ – 5′ polarity.	It has 5′ – 3′ polarity.
It gets transcribed.	It does not get transcribed.
Its sequence is complementary to *m*RNA formed.	Its sequence is same as *m*RNA except, it contains 'T' instead of 'U'.

(1½)

(ii) The source of energy for the replication of DNA are the deoxyribonucleoside triphosphates that have two terminal high energy phosphates. **(1½)**

77. (i) A DNA segment has a total of 1000 nucleotides, out of which 240 of them are adenine containing nucleotides. How many pyrimidine bases this DNA segment possesses?

(ii) Draw a diagrammatic sketch of a portion of DNA segment to support your answer. **Delhi 2015**

Or (i) A DNA segment has a total of 1500 nucleotides, out of which 410 are guanine containing nucleotides. How many pyrimidine bases this segment possesses?

(ii) Draw a diagrammatic sketch of a portion of DNA segment to support your answer. **All India 2015**

Or (i) A DNA segment has a total of 2000 nucleotides, out of which 520 are adenine containing nucleotides. How many purine bases this DNA segment possesses?

(ii) Draw a diagrammatic sketch of a portion of DNA segment to support your answer. **Delhi 2014**

Ans. (i) According to Chargaff's rule, ratio of purines to pyrimidines is equal,

i.e. $A + G = C + T$

The number of adenine (A) is equal to the number of thymine (T).

$A = 240$ (given)

Therefore, $T = 240$

Also, the number of guanine (G) is equal to cytosine (C). Total number of nucleotides are 1000.

Thus, $G + C = 1000 - [A + T]$

$G + C = 1000 - 480 = 520$

Hence, $G = 260, C = 260$

The number of pyrimidine bases,

i.e. $C + T = 240 + 260 = 500$ **(1½)**

(ii) Diagrammatic sketch of portion of DNA segment

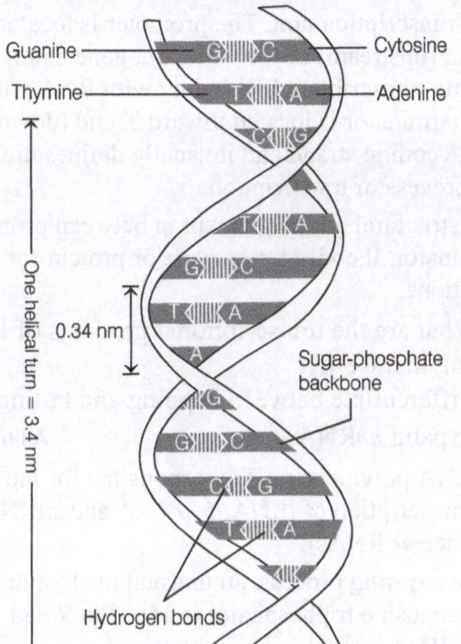

(1½)

Or (i) Given, $G = 410$

therefore, $C = 410$

$$A + T = 1500 - (G + C) = 1500 - 820 = 680$$

Hence, $A = 340; T = 340$

The number of pyrimidine bases, i.e.

$$C + T = 410 + 340 = 750$$ **(1)**

(ii) Refer to above figure. **(2)**

Or (i) Given, $A = 520$

therefore, $T = 520$

$$A + T = 520 + 520 = 1040$$

Total number of nucleotides = 2000

$$G + C = 2000 - 1040 = 960$$

$$G = 960/2 = 450$$

Hence, total number of purine bases are

$\Rightarrow A + G = 520 + 480 = 1000$ **(1)**

(ii) Refer to above figure. **(2)**

78. With the help of a schematic diagram, explain the location and role of the following in a transcription unit.

Promoter, structural gene, terminator. **All India 2014C**

Ans. Structure of a transcription unit

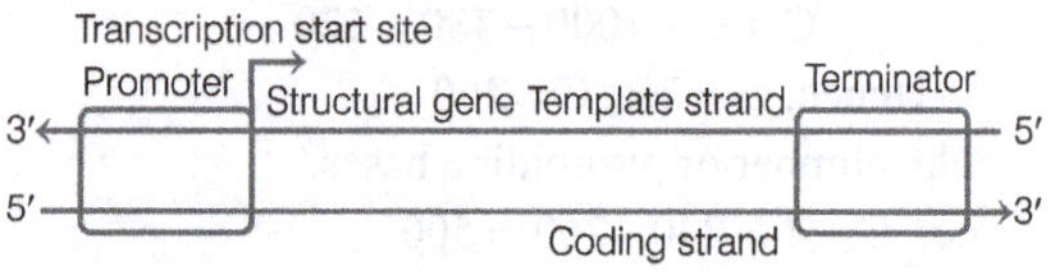

(1)

The promoter and terminator flank the structural gene in a transcription unit. The promoter is located towards 5′ end (upstream) of the structural gene and it helps to initiate transcription by binding with RNA polymerase. The terminator is located toward 3′ end (downstream) of the coding strand and it usually defines the end of the process of transcription.

The structural gene is present in between promoter and terminator. It codes for enzyme or protein for structural functions. **(2)**

79. (i) What are the transcriptional products of RNA polymerase-III?

(ii) Differentiate between capping and tailing.

(iii) Expand *hn*RNA. **All India 2014C**

Ans. (i) RNA polymerase-III is responsible for the transcription of *t*RNA, 5 *sr*RNA and *sn*RNAs (small nuclear RNAs). **(1)**

(ii) In **capping** process, an unusual nucleotide (methyl guanosine triphosphate) is added to 5′ end of *hn*RNA.

In **tailing** process, 200-300 adenylate residues are added at 3′ end of *hn*RNA. **(1)**

(iii) *hn*RNA is heterogeneous nuclear RNA. **(1)**

80. (i) Construct a complete transcription unit with promoter and terminator on the basis of hypothetical template strand given below.

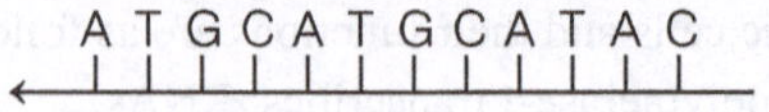

(ii) Write the RNA strand transcribed from the above transcription unit along with its polarity. **Delhi 2012**

Ans. (i) Transcription unit

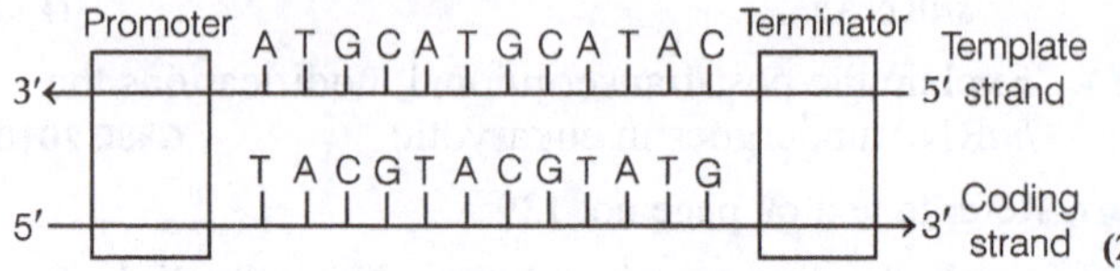

(2)

(ii) RNA strand transcribed from the above transcriptional unit

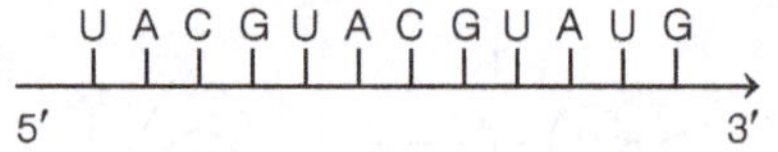

(1)

81. List the salient features of double helix structure of DNA. **All India 2012**

Ans. Salient features of DNA double helix are as follows

(i) It is made up of two polynucleotide chains containing the backbone of sugar-phosphate from which the bases project inside.

(ii) The two chains have anti-parallel polarity, i.e. one of them is $5' \rightarrow 3'$, the other has $3' \rightarrow 5'$ polarity.

(iii) The bases in two strands are paired through hydrogen bond (H—bonds) forming base pairs (bp). Adenine pairs through two hydrogen bonds with thymine on opposite strand and *vice-versa*. In the same way, guanine is bonded with cytosine through three H—bonds. Due to which, purine always comes opposite to a pyrimidine.

(iv) The two chains are coiled in a right-handed fashion. The pitch of the helix is 3.4 nm and there are roughly 10 bp in each turn. Consequently, the distance between base pair in a helix is about 0.34 nm.

(v) The plane of one base pair stacks over the other in double helix. This confers stability to the helical structure.

82. How is *hn*RNA processed to form *m*RNA? **Foreign 2012**

Ans. The precursor of *m*RNA transcribed by RNA polymerase-II is called heterogeneous nuclear RNA (*hn*RNA). It undergoes following processing to form nascent *m*RNA **(1)**

(i) **Splicing** In this process, the non-coding introns are removed and coding sequences called exons are joined in a definite order. This is required because primary transcript contains both introns and exons. **(½)**

(ii) **Capping** Refer to answer no. 79. (½)

(iii) **Tailing** Refer to answer no. 79. (½)

(iv) The fully processed *m*RNA is released from the nucleus into cytoplasm for translation. (½)

83. The base sequence in one of the strands of DNA is TAGCATGAT.

(i) Give the base sequence of the complementary strand.

(ii) How are these base pairs held together in a DNA molecule?

(iii) Explain the base complementarity rule. Name the scientist who framed this rule. **Delhi 2011**

Ans. (i) ATCGTACTA. (½)

(ii) Base pairs are held together by weak hydrogen bonds, adenine pairs with thymine by two H–bonds and guanine pairs with cytosine through three H–bonds. (1)

(iii) **Base complementarity rule** For a double-stranded DNA, this rule states that the ratio between adenine and thymine and guanine and cytosine are constant and equal to one.

Erwin Chargaff framed this rule. (1½)

84. Why do you see two different types of replicating strands in the given DNA replication fork? Explain. Name these strands. **Delhi 2011**

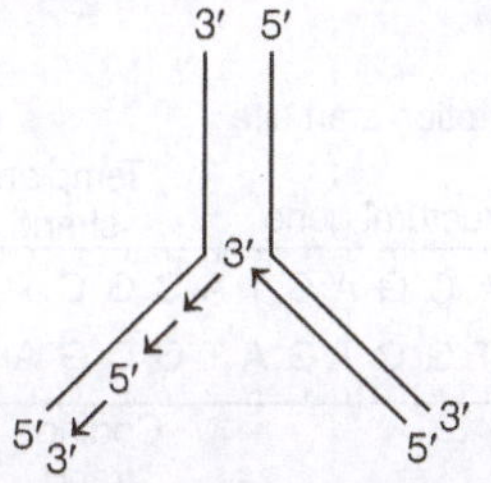

Ans. Two different types of parent strands function as template strands.

On the template strand with 3′ → 5′ polarity, the new strand is synthesised as a continuous strand because the enzyme DNA polymerase can carry out polymerisation of the nucleotides only in 5′ → 3′ direction. This is called continuous synthesis and the strand is called **leading strand.**

On the template strand with 5′ → 3′ polarity, the new strand is synthesised from the point of replication fork in short stretches called Okazaki fragments and this strand is called **lagging strand.** Okazaki fragments are later joined by DNA ligases to form a continuous strand.

85. Monocistronic structural genes in eukaryotes have interrupted coding sequences. Explain. How are they different in prokaryotes? **Delhi 2011C**

Ans. Monocistronic structural genes in eukaryotes have interrupted coding sequences due to the presence of introns, i.e. non-coding sequences. (1)

Differences between monocistronic structural gene in prokaryotes and in eukaryotes are

Structural gene in prokaryotes	Structural gene in eukaryotes
Consists of only coding sequences.	Consists of both coding and non-coding sequences.
Information is continuous as only exons are present.	Information is split due to the presence of introns in between exons.
There is no need of splicing.	Splicing is required to make functional *m*RNA.

(2)

86. Explain the role of ^{35}S and ^{32}P in the experiments conducted by Hershey and Chase. **All India 2010C**

Ans. Hershey and Chase used ^{35}S and ^{32}P in their culture medium. These are radioactive sulphur and phosphorus, respectively. These two components were used to detect whether the genetic material is DNA or protein.

Role of ^{32}P and ^{35}S

Viruses grown on medium with ^{32}S, had non-radioactive genetic material and radioactive protein as sulphur is not present in DNA but found in protein.

While those grown on ^{32}P had radioactive genetic material because DNA contains phosphorus, but proteins does not contain it. Thus, it was established that DNA is the genetic material.

87. Describe the initiation process of transcription in bacteria. **Delhi 2010**

Ans. **Initiation process of transcription in bacteria** RNA polymerase becomes associated transiently to an initiation factor sigma (σ) and binds to specific sequence on DNA called promoter to initiate transcription.

A single DNA-dependent RNA polymerase catalyses the transcription of all the three types of RNA.

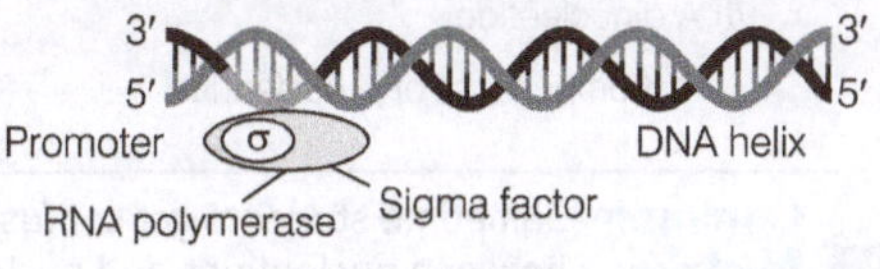

Initiation process

88. Describe the elongation process of transcription in bacteria. **Delhi 2010**

Ans. **Elongation process of transcription in bacteria** RNA polymerase facilitates opening of the DNA helix after binding to promoter. It uses ribonucleoside triphosphates as substrate and polymerises the nucleotides in a template dependent fashion following complementarity.

The process continues till RNA polymerase reaches the terminator region on the DNA strand.

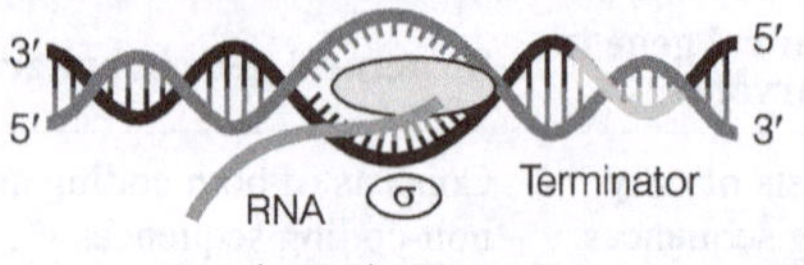

Elongation process

89. Describe the termination process of transcription in bacteria. **Delhi 2010**

Ans. Termination occurs when RNA polymerase reaches the terminator region and the nascent RNA falls off. The RNA polymerase being transiently associated with termination factor rho (ρ) also falls off the transcription unit.

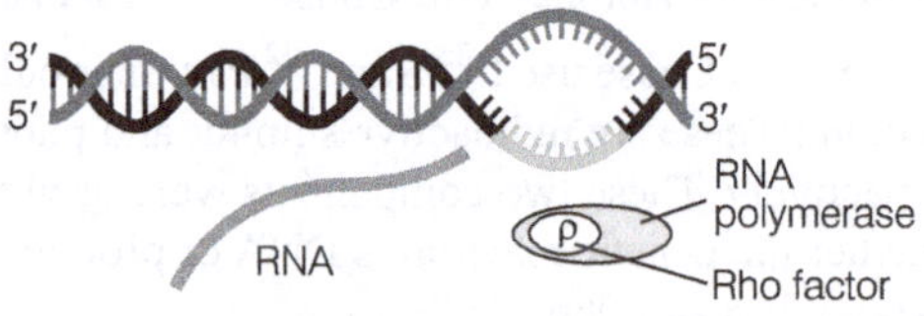

Termination process

90. Draw a schematic representation of a dinucleotide. Label the following

(i) The component of a nucleotide

(ii) 5′ end

(iii) N-glycosidic linkage

(iv) Phosphodiester linkage **Foreign 2010**

Ans. Schematic representation of a dinucleotide.

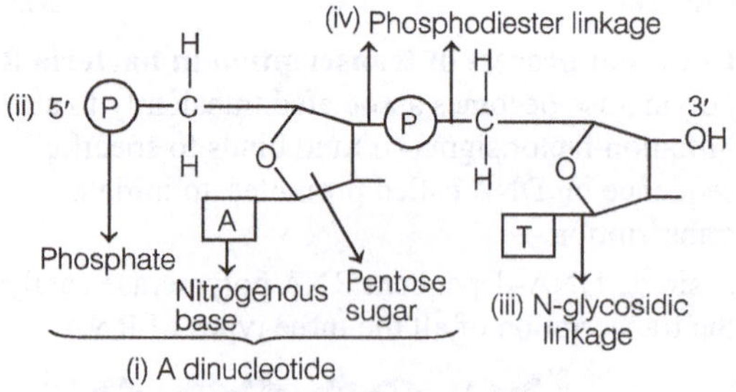

Components of a nucleotide

Common Mistakes Sometime students get confused between nucleotides and nucleosides, let us clear this confusion now.

Nucleosides Pentose sugar + Base

Nucleotides Pentose sugar + Base + Phosphate group

91. Describe the role of RNA polymerases in transcription in bacteria and in eukaryotes. **Foreign 2010**

Ans. In bacteria, there is a single DNA-dependent RNA polymerase, which catalyses the formation of *m*RNA, *t*RNA and *r*RNA. **(1)**

In eukaryotes, there are three types of RNA polymerases, which show division of labour.

These are as follows

(i) RNA polymerase-I transcribes *r*RNAs, (28S, 18S and 5.8S).

(ii) RNA polymerase-II transcribes the precursor of *m*RNA called *hn*RNA.

(iii) RNA polymerase-III transcribes *t*RNA, 5 *sr*RNA and *sn*RNA. **(2)**

5 Marks Questions

92. (i) Construct a transcription unit with a coding strand given below with proper labelling.

A T G C T G A T G C G A

(ii) When does a coding strand become a template strand?

(iii) Why does a double-helix DNA molecule transcribe into a single-stranded RNA molecule? **CBSE 2024 (Set-I)**

Ans. (i)

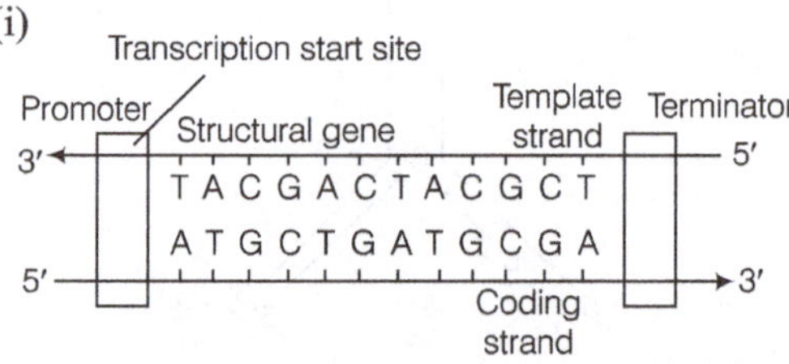

(2)

(ii) A coding strand becomes a template strand if the positions of promoter and terminator get exchanged. So, the position of promoter and terminator defines the template and coding strand. **(1)**

(iii) A double-helix DNA molecule transcribe into a single-stranded RNA molecule because only one strand is transcribed to code for RNA. If both strands act as template, they would code for two RNA molecules. having different sequences and if these RNA molecules code for proteins, then the proteins will have different sequence of amino acid. Therefore, one segment of DNA would be coding for two different proteins.

If two RNA molecules are produced simultaneously, they would be complementary to each other and hence would form a double strand RNA. Therefore, RNA would not be translated into protein. **(2)**

93. (i) Why did Hershey and Chase use '^{35}S' and '^{32}P' in their experiment ? Explain.

(ii) State the importance of (1) blending and (2) centrifugation in their experiment.

(iii) Write the conclusion they arrived at the end of their experiment. **CBSE 2024 (Set-II)**

Ans. (i) Hershey and Chase used radioactive ^{32}P to label the DNA because phosphorous was present only in DNA and not in proteins. They used ^{35}S to label the proteins because sulphur was present only in proteins and not in DNA. Using these radioactive isotopes, they were able to determine that only the DNA of the bacteriophage, not the protein, enters the bacterial cell during infection. **(1)**

(ii) Importance of blending and centrifugation during Hershey-Chase experiment was

1. **Blending** It allowed for the physical separation of bacteriophage protein coats from bacterial cells after viral infection. This step insured that only the viral DNA or RNA (depending on the phage used) entered the bacterial cells, facilitating the subsequent analysis of the genetic material's role in viral replication and infection.
2. **Centrifugation** It enabled the separation of bacteriophage protein coats from bacterial cells and their contents. By subjecting the bacteriophage infected bacterial suspension to centrifugation, the heavier bacterial cells and their contents (including any viral DNA or RNA) were pelleted to the bottom of the tube, while the lighter protein coats remained in the supernatant. **(2)**

(iii) At the end of their experiment, Hershey and Chase concluded that DNA, not protein, is the genetic material responsible for heredity and inheritance. Viruses with radioactive DNA transferred its DNA to the bacteria, but the radioactive proteins in other viruses did not get transferred. **(2)**

94. Observe the segment of *m*RNA given below. **CBSE SQP 2023**

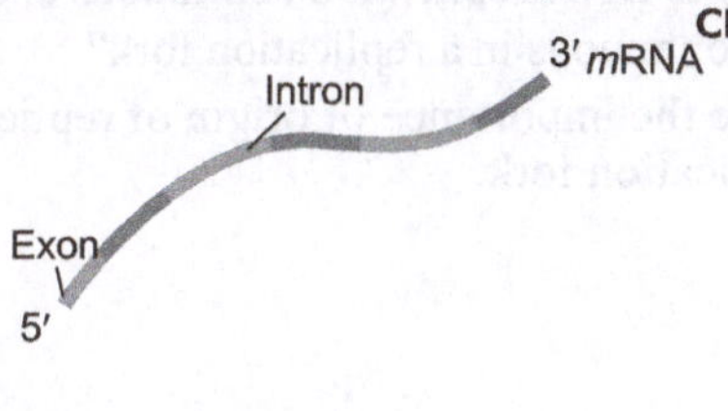

(i) Explain and illustrate the steps involved to make fully processed *hn*RNA.

(ii) Gene encoding RNA polymerase-I and III have been affected by mutation in a cell. Explain its impact on the synthesis of polypeptide, stating reasons.

Ans. (i) The *hn*RNA undergoes processes called capping and tailing followed by splicing. In capping, an unusual nucleotide is added to the 5′-end of *hn*RNA methyl guanosine triphosphate. In tailing, adenylate residues (about 200–300) are added at 3′-end in a template independent manner. Now the *hn*RNA undergoes a process where the introns are removed and exons are joined to form *m*RNA called splicing.

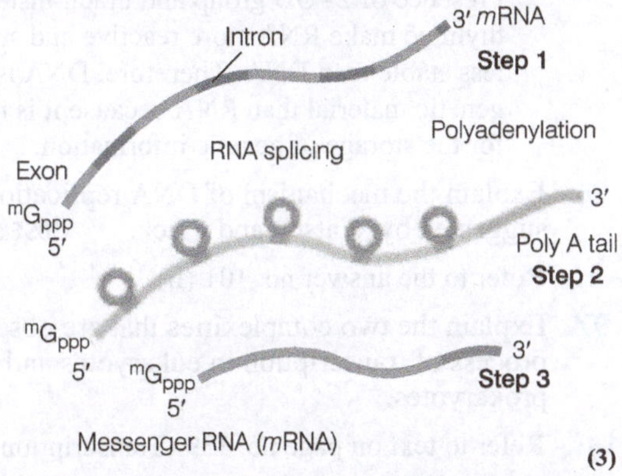

(3)

(ii) The process of translation will not happen, thus the polypeptide synthesis is stopped/ hampered.

The reason for the above is

RNA polymerase-I transcribes *r*RNAs which is the cellular factory for protein synthesis.

RNA polymerase-III helps in transcription of *t*RNA which is the adaptor molecule/ that transfers amino acids to the site of protein synthesis. **(2)**

95. Evaluate the suitability of DNA and RNA as genetic material and justify the suitability of the one that is preferred as an ideal genetic material. **CBSE SQP 2021-22**

Ans. Genetic material primarily helps to carry genetic information from one generation to another. It also acts as a source of evolution and acts as the raw material for the accumulation of variations.

Both DNA and RNA act as genetic material that can be evaluated by the following properties

(i) **It should be able to generate its replica** (Replication) As per the rule of base pairing and complementarity, both the nucleic acids (DNA and RNA) have the ability to direct their duplications.

(ii) **It should be able to express itself in the form of 'Mendelian characters'** RNA can directly code for the synthesis of proteins, hence can easily express the characters. DNA, however is dependent on RNA for synthesis of proteins. The protein synthesising machinery has evolved around RNA.

(iii) **It should provide the scope for slow changes** (mutation) **that are required for evolution** Both DNA and RNA are able to mutate. Infact, RNA being unstable, mutates at a faster rate. Consequently, viruses having RNA genome and having shorter lifespan mutate and evolve faster.

(iv) **The genetic material should be chemically and structurally stable** It is enough not to change with different stages of life cycle, age or with change in physiology of the organism.

Presence of 2′–OH group and uracil instead of thymine make RNA more reactive and structurally less stable than DNA. Therefore, DNA is a better genetic material than RNA because it is more stable for the storage of genetic information.

96. Explain the mechanism of DNA replication as suggested by Watson and Crick. **CBSE SQP 2021-22**

Ans. Refer to the answer no. 101 (ii).

97. Explain the two complexities that are observed in the process of transcription in eukaryotes and not in prokaryotes. **Delhi 2020**

Ans. Refer to text on page no. 139 (Transcription in eukaryotes).

98. (i) State the 'central dogma' as proposed by Francis Crick.

(ii) Explain, how the biochemical characterisation (nature) of 'transforming principle' was determined, which was not defined from Griffith's experiments. **CBSE 2018**

Ans. (i) **Central dogma** It states that there is one way or unidirectional flow of information from master copy DNA to working copy RNA (transcription) and from working copy RNA to building plan of polypeptide chain (translation).

$$\text{DNA} \xrightarrow{\text{Transcription}} m\text{RNA} \xrightarrow{\text{Translation}} \text{Polypeptide Chain (protein)}$$

Central dogma of molecular biology was proposed by **Crick** (1958). It can also be written as follows

$$\text{DNA} \xrightarrow{\text{Replication}} \text{DNA} \xrightarrow{\text{Transcription}} m\text{RNA} \xrightarrow{\text{Translation}} \text{Polypeptide}$$

Exception Reverse transcription is an exception to central dogma. The discovery of 'RNA-dependent DNA polymerase' gave the concept of central dogma reverse or teminism. It suggested that information flow can also take place from RNA to DNA.

$$\text{DNA} \underset{\text{Reverse transcription}}{\overset{\text{Transcription}}{\rightleftarrows}} m\text{RNA} \xrightarrow{\text{Translation}} \text{Polypeptide}$$

During this, transcription or RNA synthesis occurs over DNA and translation or protein synthesis occurs over ribosomes. In eukaryotes, these two processes are separated in time and space. This protects DNA from respiratory enzymes and RNA's degradation from nucleases. **(2½)**

(ii) Various experiments were conducted to prove that DNA is the genetic material. Griffith did his experiment and concluded that some substance causes transformation. However, he did not tell the substance that had caused the transformation.

Biochemical characterisation of transforming principle Three scientists Avery, MacLeod and McCarty revealed that the chemical nature of the transforming substance was DNA. They showed that DNA isolated from S-strain could itself confer the pathogenic properties to R-strain.

This fact suggested that DNA possesses the genetic properties.

The outline of the experiment is given below

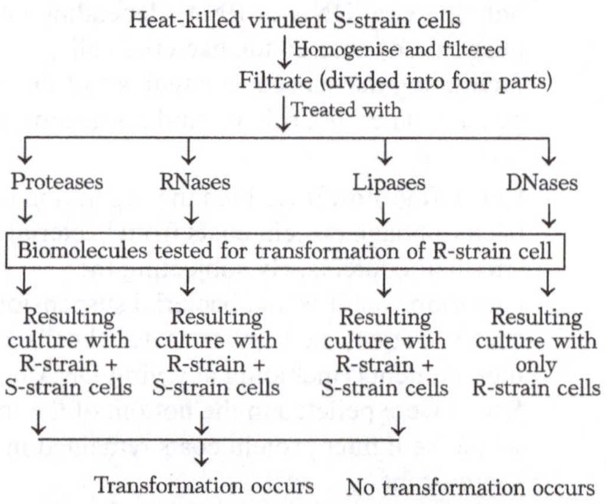

Summary of Avery, MacLeod and McCarty experiment, which demonstrates that DNA is the transforming

Thus, on the basis of their experiment, they concluded that DNA is the hereditary material. **(2½)**

99. (i) Why does DNA replication occur in small replication forks and not in its entire length?

(ii) Why is DNA replication continuous and discontinuous in a replication fork?

(iii) State the importance of origin of replication in a replication fork. **CBSE 2018C**

KEY idea

Leading strand Continuous synthesis towards growing replication fork in 5′⟶ 3′ direction.

Lagging strand Discontinuous synthesis opposite to the growing replication fork (short segments) in 3′⟶ 5′ direction.

Ans. (i) DNA replication occurs in small replication fork and not in its entire length because whole DNA cannot be opened in one stretch due to high energy requirement. **(1)**

(ii) DNA replication is continuous and discontinuous in a replication fork because the enzyme DNA polymerase can carry out polymerisation of the nucleotides only in 5′⟶3′, direction. On the template strand with 3′ ⟶5′ polarity, DNA replication is continuous. On the template strand with polarity 5′ ⟶ 3′, the DNA replication occurs in short stretches and is called discontinuous. **(2)**

(iii) Replication of DNA does not initiate randomly and DNA polymerases on their own cannot initiate replication. So, there is a need of specific sequence, called origin of replication from which the replication starts. DNA polymerase binds to it and continues the process. **(2)**

100. Answer the following questions based on Hershey and Chase's experiments.

(i) Name the kind of virus they worked with and why?

(ii) Why did they use two types of culture media to grow viruses in? Explain.

(iii) What was the need for using a blender and later a centrifuge during their experiments?

(iv) State the conclusion drawn by them after the experiments. **All India 2016**

Or How did Hershey and Chase established that DNA is transferred from virus to bacteria? **Delhi 2015**

Or Describe the Hershey and Chase's experiment. Write the conclusion drawn by the scientists after their experiment. **All India 2014**

Or Name the scientists, who proved experimentally that DNA is the genetic material. Describe their experiment. **Delhi 2014**

Or (i) Describe Hershey and Chase's experiment.

(ii) Write the aim of the experiment.

Delhi 2010C; All India 2010

Ans. (i) They worked with bacteriophage, i.e. viruses that infect bacteria. These viruses were used because during infection they transfer their genetic material into bacteria. **(½ + ½)**

(ii) They used two types of culture media, containing ^{35}S and ^{32}P, so as to compare that which one out of DNA and protein gets transferred from virus to bacteria and acts as genetic material. **(2)**

(iii) A blender and centrifuge was used to open up the bacterial cells and viral particles, so that genetic material could be exposed. **(1)**

(iv) The conclusion drawn by them after the experiment was that the DNA is the genetic material. **(1)**

Or Alfred Hershey and Martha Chase (1952) established that DNA is transferred from viruses that infect bacteria. In their experiment, bacteriophages (viruses that infect bacteria) were used.

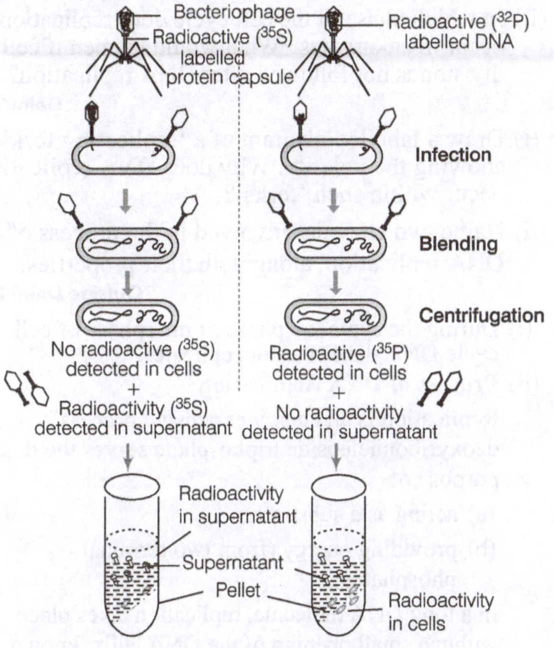

The Hershey-Chase experiment **(2)**

They grew some viruses on a medium that contained radioactive phosphorus (^{32}P) and some others on medium containing radioactive sulphur (^{35}S). Viruses grown in the presence of radioactive phosphorus contained radioactive DNA, but no radioactive protein because DNA contains phosphorus, but protein does not. In the same way, viruses grown on radioactive sulphur contained radioactive protein, but not radioactive DNA because DNA does not contain sulphur. Radioactive phages were allowed to attach to *E. coli* bacteria. As the infection proceeded, viral coats were removed from the bacteria by agitating them in a blender. The virus particles were separated from the bacteria by spinning them in a centrifuge.

Bacteria which were infected with viruses that had radioactive DNA were radioactive, indicating that DNA was the material that passed from the virus to the bacteria. Bacteria that were infected with viruses that had radioactive proteins were not radioactive. This indicated that the proteins did not enter the bacteria from viruses. It proved that DNA is the genetic material that is passed from virus to bacteria. **(3)**

101. (i) Name the stage in the cell cycle where DNA replication occurs.

(ii) Explain the mechanism of DNA replication. Highlight the role of enzymes in the process.

(iii) Why is DNA replication said to be semi-conservative? **All India 2016**

Or (i) Explain the process of DNA replication with the help of a schematic diagram.

(ii) In which phase of the cell cycle does replication occur in eukaryotes? What would happen if cell division is not followed after DNA replication? **Delhi 2014**

Or (i) Draw a labelled diagram of a 'replicating fork' showing the polarity. Why does DNA replication occur within such 'forks'?

(ii) Name two enzymes involved in the process of DNA replication, along with their properties. **Outside Delhi 2015**

Ans. (i) During the synthetic phase of interphase of cell cycle DNA duplicates or replicates. **(1)**

(ii) **Process of DNA Replication**

Replication is an energy expensive process, deoxyribonucleoside triphosphate serves the dual purpose of

(a) acting as a substrate.

(b) providing energy (from two terminal phosphates).

In a long DNA molecule, replication takes place within a small opening of the DNA helix, known as replication fork because whole DNA does not open in one stretch due to high energy requirement.

DNA-dependent DNA polymerases catalyse polymerisation only in one direction, i.e. $5' \rightarrow 3'$. This brings additional complications at the replication fork.

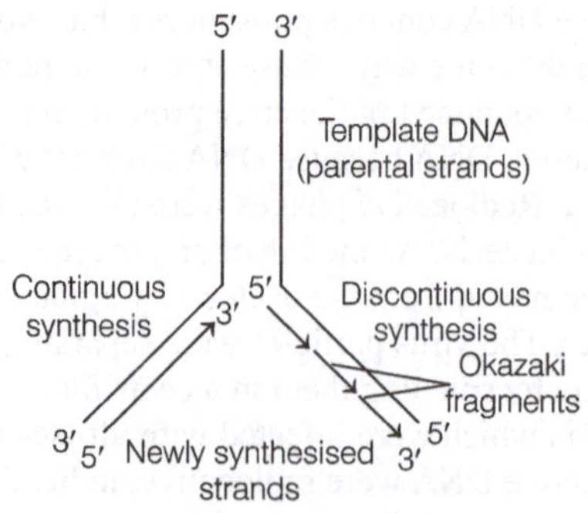

Replicating fork of DNA

On one strand (template with polarity $3' \rightarrow 5'$), replication is **continuous**, while on the $5' \rightarrow 3'$ strand, replication is **discontinuous**. Thus, the fragments synthesised are discontinuous and later joined by the enzyme **DNA ligase**.

The DNA polymerases cannot initiate replication process on their own and replication does not initiate randomly anywhere in DNA.

It begins at definite regions in a DNA molecule known as **origin of replication** (*ori*).

Enzymes for DNA Replication

The process of replication requires a set of catalysts (enzymes) as given below

(a) **DNA-dependent DNA polymerase** It is the main enzyme which uses a DNA template to catalyse the polymerisation of deoxynucleotides.

The average rate of polymerisation is 2000 bp (base pairs) per second approximately. These enzymes are highly efficient as they have to catalyse polymerisation of a large number of nucleotides in a very short time.These polymerases act very fast, catalyse the replication process with high degree of accuracy as any mistake would result in mutations.

(b) **Helicase** It unwinds the DNA strand, i.e. separates the two strands from one point for the formation of a replication fork.

(c) **DNA ligase** It facilitates the joining of DNA strands together by catalysing the formation of phosphodiester bond. It plays a role in repairing single strand breaks in duplex DNA. **(3)**

(iii) It is said to be semi-conservative because in newly synthesised DNA, one strand is parental and one is new, so it conserves the one strand. DNA replication is followed by cell division. In case the latter fails to occur, polyploidy may occur. **(1)**

102. List the criteria of a molecule that can act as genetic material must fulfill. Which one of the criteria is best fulfilled by DNA or by RNA thus making one of them a better genetic material than the other? Explain. **All India 2016**

Ans. From the Hershey and Chase experiment, the fact was established that DNA acts as genetic material. But later studies revealed that in some viruses (e.g. Tobacco Mosaic Viruses, QB bacteriophage, etc.) RNA is the genetic material.

Following are the criteria that a molecule must fulfill to act as a genetic material

(i) It should be able to replicate.

(ii) It should be chemically and structurally stable.

(iii) It should provide the scope for slow changes (mutation), which are required for evolution.

(iv) It should be able to express itself in the form of 'Mendelian characters'. **(2)**

According to these criteria, both DNA and RNA have the ability to direct their duplications (because of the rule of base pairing and complementarity).

So, both the nucleic acids (DNA and RNA) have the

ability to direct their duplications, whereas the other molecules in the living system, fail to fulfill first criteria itself, e.g. protein. The most important criteria of genetic material is the stability as the genetic material should not change with the different stages of life cycle, age or with change in the physiology of an organism.

Both DNA and RNA have the ability to mutate. Since, RNA is unstable, it mutates at a faster rate. That is why, those viruses, which have RNA genome and a shorter lifespan, undergo mutation and thus evolve rapidly.

DNA is dependant on RNA for protein synthesis, whereas RNA directly codes for protein synthesis. This proves that both RNA and DNA act as genetic material, but DNA being more stable is preferred for the storage of genetic information. **(3)**

103. Describe Meselson and Stahl's experiment that was carried in 1958 on *E. coli*. Write the conclusion they arrived at after the experiment. **All India 2016**

Or (i) What is central dogma? Who proposed it?

(ii) Describe Meselson and Stahl's experiment to prove that the DNA replication is semi-conservative. **Outside Delhi 2015C**

Or 'DNA replication is semi-conservative'. Name the scientists who proposed it and who proved it. How was it proved experimentally? **All India 2014C**

Or Describe Meselson and Stahl's experiment and write the conclusion they arrived at. **Foreign 2014; Delhi 2012**

Ans. Refer to text on page no. 136-137.

Or **Central dogma** Francis Crick proposed the central dogma in molecular biology, which states that the genetic information flows from DNA → RNA → Proteins.

$$\text{DNA} \xrightarrow{\text{Transcription}} m\text{RNA} \xrightarrow{\text{Translation}} \text{Protein}$$

104. (i) How are the following formed and involved in DNA packaging in the nucleus of a cell?

(a) Histone octamer (b) Nucleosome

(c) Chromatin

(ii) Differentiate between euchromatin and heterochromatin. **All India 2016**

Ans. (i) (a) **Histone octamer** Histones are the proteins that are rich in basic amino acids, i.e. lysine and arginine. Both these amino acids carry positive charges in their side chains. So, histones are a set of positively charged, basic proteins (histones + protamine). A histone octamer is formed by the organisation of two molecules each of H_2A, H_2B, H_3 and H_4 histones, so as to make a unit of 8 molecules. It helps to package DNA into nucleosome. **(1)**

(b) **Nucleosome** The negatively charged DNA is wrapped around the positively charged histone octamer, forming a structure known as nucleosome.

It forms the fundamental repeating units of eukaryotic chromatin. It is used to pack the large eukaryotic genome into the nucleus. **(1)**

(c) **Chromatin** One nucleosome contains 200 base pairs of DNA helix, approximately.

Nucleosomes are the repeating unit of chromatin, which are thread-like stained (coloured) bodies present in nucleus.

The nucleosomes in chromatin look like 'beads-on-string' when observed under an electron microscope.

The chromatin is further packed to form a solenoid structure of 30 mm diameter and further supercoiling tends to form a looped structure called chromatin fibre and then chromatid. This further coils and condenses at metaphase stage to form the chromosomes. **(1)**

(ii) Differences between euchromatin and heterochromatin are as follows

Euchromatin	Heterochromatin
It is lightly stained region.	It is darkly stained region of the chromatin (chromosome).
It is loosely coiled region and thus has less DNA.	It is the compactly coiled region and thus has more DNA.
It is transcriptionally active and is transcribed into *m*RNA.	It is transcriptionally inert and cannot be transcribed into *m*RNA due to very tight coiling.

(2)

105. (i) Explain with the help of Griffith's experiment how the search for genetic material was conducted and what was the conclusion drawn?

(ii) How did MacLeod, McCarty and Avery establish the biochemical nature of the so called 'genetic material' identified by Griffith in his experiment? **Delhi 2016C**

Or (i) Describe the series of experiments of F Griffith. Comment on the significance of the results obtained.

(ii) State the contribution of MacLeod, McCarty and Avery. **All India 2016, 2010**

Or (i) Describe the experiment which demonstrated the existence of transforming principle.

(ii) How was the biochemical nature of this transforming principle determined by Avery, MacLeod and McCarty? **Foreign 2015**

Or (i) Describe the various steps of Griffith's experiment that led to the conclusion of the 'transforming principle'.

(ii) How did the chemical nature of the 'transforming principle' get established? **All India 2014**

Or (i) Write the conclusion drawn by Griffith at the end of his experiment with *Streptococcus pneumoniae*.

(ii) How did O. Avery, C. MacLeod and M. McCarty prove that DNA was the genetic material? Explain. **All India 2013**

Or Describe Frederick Griffith's experiment on *Streptococcus pneumoniae*. Discuss the conclusion he arrived at. **All India 2012**

Ans. (i) **Griffith Experiments**

It took a long time to discover and prove that DNA acts as a genetic material. By 1926, the question to determine the mechanism for genetic inheritance had reached the molecular level.

Transforming Principle

Frederick Griffith in 1928, carried out a series of experiments with *Streptococcus pneumoniae* (a bacterium that causes pneumonia).

He observed that when these bacteria (*Streptococcus pneumoniae*) were grown on a culture plate, some of them produced smooth, shiny colonies (S-type), whereas the others produced rough colonies (R-type). This difference in appearance of colonies (smooth/rough) was due to the presence or absence of mucus (polysaccharide) coat.

In his experiments, he first infected two separate groups of mice as follows

S-strain (virulent strain) → Inject into mice → Mice die.

R-strain (non-virulent strain) → Inject into mice → Mice live.

S-strain (heat-killed) → Inject into mice → Mice live.

S-strain (heat-killed) + R-strain (live) → Inject into mice → Mice die.

Griffith concluded that the live R-strain bacteria, had been transformed by the heat-killed S-strain bacteria. He concluded that, there was some '**transforming** agent that was transferred from the heat-killed S-strain, which helped the R-strain bacteria to synthesise a smooth **polysaccharide coat** and thus become virulent.

He concluded that must be due to the transfer of the genetic material. However, he was not able to define the biochemical nature of genetic material from his experiments. (3)

(ii) **Contributions of MacLeod, McCarty and Avery**

These scientists worked to determine the chemical nature of transforming principle of Griffith's experiments. They discovered that protein digesting enzymes (proteases) and RNA-digesting enzymes (RNase) did not affect transformation. Digestion with DNase did inhibit transformation suggesting that DNA was responsible for the transformation. (2)

106. (i) Describe the process of trancription in bacteria.

(ii) Explain the processing the *hn*RNA needs to undergo before becoming functional *m*RNA in eukaryotes. **Outside Delhi 2016**

Or Describe the process of transcription in bacterium. **All India 2014C**

Ans. (i) The process of transcription in prokaryotes consists of three steps

(a) **Initiation** Refer to answer no. 87.

(b) **Elongation** Refer to answer no. 88.

(c) **Termination** Refer to answer no. 89. (2)

(ii) In eukaryotes, the primary transcript is often larger than the functional RNA, called heterogeneous nuclear RNA or *hn*RNA. Post-transcription processing is necessary to convert primary transcript of different types of RNAs into functional RNAs.

The processing includes

(a) **Cleavage** Larger RNA precursors are cleaved to form smaller RNAs.

(b) **Splicing** Eukaryotic transcripts possess extra segments called introns which are non-functional. They do not appear in mature or processed RNA. The functional coding sequences are called exons. Splicing is the removal of introns and fusion of exons in a definite order to form functional RNAs.

(c) **Terminal additions** (capping and tailing) Capping includes addition of an unusual nucleotide to 5′ end of *hn*RNA. These unusual segments are CCA segment in *t*RNA and cap nucleotides at 5′ end of *m*RNA. In tailing, poly-A segment (200-300 residues) are added at 3′ end of *m*RNA. Cap is formed by the modification of GTP into 7-methyl guanosine or 7 mG.

(d) **Nucleotide modifications** They are most common in *t*RNA-methylation (i.e. methyl cytosine, methyl guanosine), deamination (e.g. inosine form adenine), dihydrouracil, pseudouracil, etc. (3)

Concept Enhancer **Promoter**: located towards 5′ end (upstream) and helps to initiate transcription. **Terminator**: located towards 3′ end (downstream) and helps to end the process of transcription.

TOPIC 2

Genetic Code, Human Genome Project and DNA Fingerprinting

Genetic Code

It is a sequence of three nucleotides present on *m*RNA, which codes for a specific amino acid during translation.

It is the relationship between the sequences of nucleotides on *m*RNA and the sequences of amino acids in the polypeptide chain.

Deciphering the Code

(i) **George Gamow** a physicist suggested that the genetic code should be made up of three nucleotides. He stated that since there are only four bases and if they have to code for 20 amino acids, the code should constitute a combination of bases. But, a permutation combination of 4^3 $(4 \times 4 \times 4)$ would generate 64 codons, i.e. many more codons than required.

(ii) **Har Gobind Khorana** could synthesise RNA molecules with defined combinations of bases (homopolymers and copolymers).

(iii) **Marshall Nirenberg** made cell-free system for protein synthesis and finally the code was deciphered.

(iv) **Severo Ochoa enzyme** (polynucleotide phosphorylase) was also helpful in polymerising RNA with defined sequences in a template independent manner (enzyme synthesis of RNA).

(v) All of these investigations, finally helped to make a checker-board for genetic code as given below

First position	Second position: U	C	A	G	Third position
U	UUU Phe	UCU Ser	UAU Tyr	UGU Cys	U
U	UUC Phe	UCC Ser	UAC Tyr	UGC Cys	C
U	UUA Leu	UCA Ser	UAA Stop	UGA Stop	A
U	UUG Leu	UCG Ser	UAG Stop	UGG Trp	G
C	CUU Leu	CCU Pro	CAU His	CGU Arg	U
C	CUC Leu	CCC Pro	CAC His	CGC Arg	C
C	CUA Leu	CCA Pro	CAA Gln	CGA Arg	A
C	CUG Leu	CCG Pro	CAG Gln	CGG Arg	G
A	AUU Ile	ACU Thr	AAU Asn	AGU Ser	U
A	AUC Ile	ACC Thr	AAC Asn	AGC Ser	C
A	AUA Ile	ACA Thr	AAA Lys	AGA Arg	A
A	AUG Met	ACG Thr	AAG Lys	AGG Arg	G
G	GUU Val	GCU Ala	GAU Asp	GGU Gly	U
G	GUC Val	GCC Ala	GAC Asp	GGC Gly	C
G	GUA Val	GCA Ala	GAA Glu	GGA Gly	A
G	GUG Val	GCG Ala	GAG Glu	GGG Gly	G

Figure 5.8 Codons for the various amino acids

Salient Features of Genetic Code

These are as follows

- A codon is a triplet. Out of 64 codons, 61 codons code for amino acids and 3 codons do not code for any amino acids. Hence, they function as **stop codons** (UAA, UAG and UGA).
- One codon codes for only one amino acid, hence it is **unambiguous** and **specific**.
- Some amino acids are coded by more than one codon, hence the **code is degenerate**.
- The codon is read in *m*RNA in a contiguous fashion. There are no punctuations.
- The code is nearly **universal**. For example, from bacteria to human, UUU would code for phenylalanine (Phe). Some exceptions are found in mitochondrial codons and in some protozoans.
- **AUG** has dual functions. It codes for **methionine** (met) and also acts as **initiator codon**.

Mutations

The sudden inheritable change in the genetic material is defined as mutation.

It can be of following types

(i) **Point mutation** occurs due to change in single base pair. It results in sickle-cell anaemia (change of single base pair at the sixth position resulting in the change of amino acid residue glutamate to valine).

(ii) **Frameshift mutation** occurs where addition/insertion or deletion of one or two bases changes the reading frame from the site of mutation. It results in a protein with a different set of amino acids. Insertion or deletion of three of its multiples of bases do not alter the reading frame, but due to this, one or more amino acids coded in the protein get translated.

Translation

- It is the process of polymerisation of amino acids to form a polypeptide.
- The order and sequence of amino acids are defined by the sequence of bases in the *m*RNA.

- The amino acids are joined by a bond, which is known as a **peptide bond**. This process requires energy.
- The process of translation requires the following components– *m*RNA, ribosome, amino acids as raw material, ATP, adapter molecule-*t*RNA and aminoacyl *t*RNA synthetase enzyme for charging of *t*RNA.

*t*RNA-The Adapter Molecule

- **Francis Crick** postulated the presence of an adapter molecule that would read the code and bind to specific amino acids. This molecule is called ***t*RNA**. It may also be called as ***s*RNA**, i.e. soluble RNA as it is soluble in water.
- Clover leaf model shows *t*RNA has an anticodon loop that has bases complementary to the code. It also has an amino acid acceptor end, which helps it to bind to amino acids. It also possesses an enzyme site and a ribosome site.
- *t*RNAs are specific for each amino acid.

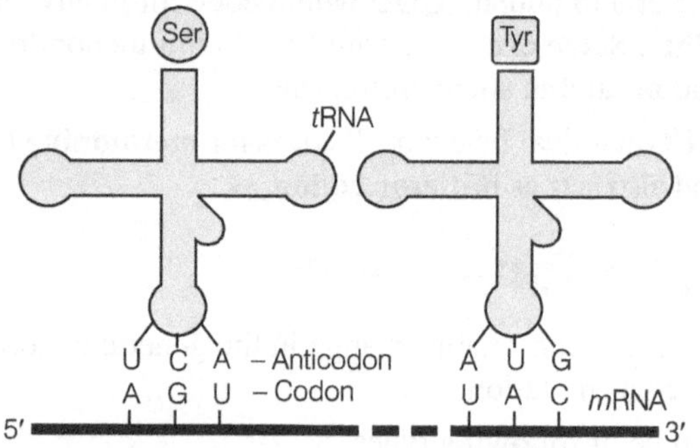

Figure 5.9 *t*RNA-the adapter molecule

For initiation, there is specific *t*RNA called initiator *t*RNA. There is no *t*RNA for stop codons.

- The secondary structure of *t*RNA looks like a clover-leaf. In actual structure, it is a compact molecule that appears like inverted L.

Phases of Translation

Phases of translation are as follows

1. Activation of Amino Acids

It occurs in the presence of ATP and link to their cognate *t*RNA, in the presence of aminoacyl *t*RNA synthase enzyme. It is known as **charging of *t*RNA** or **aminoacylation of *t*RNA**. If two such charged *t*RNAs are brought closer, the formation of peptide bond between them would occur energetically in the presence of a catalyst.

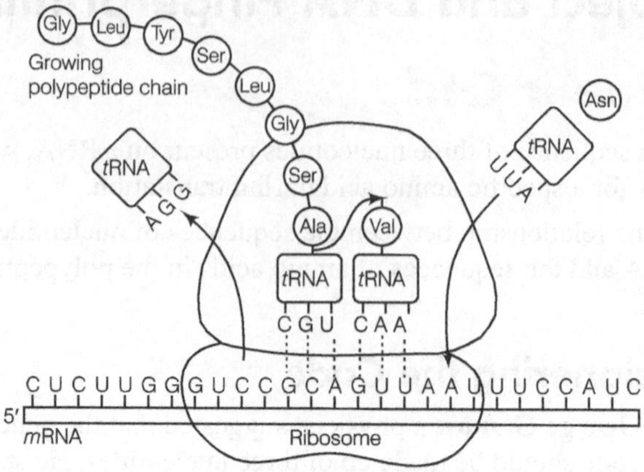

Figure 5.10 Translation

2. Initiation of Polypeptide Synthesis

- It occurs in ribosomes which is known as the **cellular factory for protein synthesis.**
- Ribosome consists of structural RNAs and about 80 different proteins.
- In its inactive state, it exists as two separated subunits, i.e. a large and a small subunit.
- There are two sites in the large subunit, i.e. the **P-site** and **A-site** for subsequent binding of amino acids.
- The small subunit (with the *t*RNA) attaches to the large subunit in such a way that the initiation codon (AUG) comes to the P-site.
- An *m*RNA also has some additional sequences that are not translated. These are referred to as **Untranslated Regions** (UTR). They are present at both 5′ end (before start codon) and at 3′ end (after stop codon) for efficient translation process.

3. Elongation of Polypeptide Chain

- It occurs when a second *t*RNA charged with an appropriate amino acid binds to the A-site of the ribosome.
- A peptide bond (CO—NH) forms between the carboxyl group of methionine and the amino group of the second amino acid.
  The reaction is catalysed by the enzyme **peptidyl transferase**.

- The complexes consisting of an amino acid linked to *t*RNA, sequentially bind to the appropriate codon in *m*RNA by forming complementary base pairs with the *t*RNA anticodon.
- The ribosome moves from codon to codon along the *m*RNA in $5' \rightarrow 3'$ direction. Amino acids are added one by one, translated into polypeptide sequences dictated by DNA and represented by *m*RNA.

4. Termination of Polypeptide Synthesis

It occur when a **release factor** binds to the stop codon. As a result, the polypeptide synthesis or elongation process stops, releasing the complete polypeptide from the ribosome.

Regulation of Gene Expression

It occurs at various levels and results in the formation of a polypeptide.

- **In prokaryotes,** gene expression is regulated by the rate of initiation of transcription.
- **In eukaryotes,** regulation is achieved at four levels
  - (i) Transcriptional level (formation of primary transcript).
  - (ii) Processing levels (regulation of splicing).
  - (iii) Transport of *m*RNA from nucleus to the cytoplasm.
  - (iv) Translational level.
    - In a transcriptional unit, the activity of RNA polymerase at a given promoter is in turn regulated by the interaction with accessory proteins.
    - In many cases, the accessibility to promoter regions of prokaryotic DNA is regulated by the interaction of proteins with sequences, termed as **operators.**
    - The sequences of the operator bind a repressor protein. Each operon has its specific operator and specific repressor. For example, *lac* operon interacts with *lac* repressor only.

Lac Operon

- **Francois Jacob** and **Jacque Monod** in 1961 were the first to propose the concept of a transcriptionally regulated system, where a polycistronic structural gene is regulated by a common promoter and regulatory genes.
- Such an arrangement is referred as an **operon,** e.g. *lac* (lactose) operon, *trp* (tryptophan) operon, *ara* (arabinose) operon, *his* (histidine) operon and *val* (valine) operon, etc.
- Let us take the example of *lac* operon. Its structure consists of various genes as follows
- One regulatory gene (the *i* gene), which codes for the repressor of the *lac* operon. The term *i* refers to the word inhibitor.
- Three structural genes are
  - *z* **gene** codes for β-galactosidase (β-gal), that helps in the hydrolysis of disaccharide into its monomeric units, i.e. lactose into galactose and glucose.
  - *y* **gene** codes for permease, that increases the permeability of the cell to β-galactosides.
  - *a* **gene** codes for a transacetylase.
- An inducer, i.e. lactose here which is the substrate for the enzyme β-galactosidase.
- If lactose is provided as the carbon source in the growth medium then in the absence of the preferred carbon source such as glucose, the lactose is transported into the cells by the action of enzyme permease. The lactose then induces the operon.

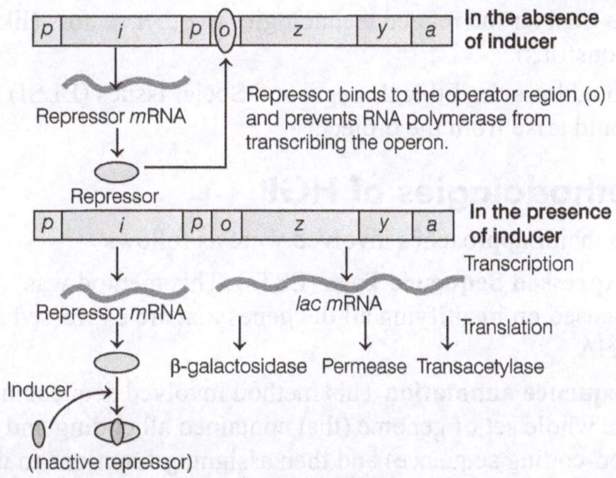

Figure 5.11 *Lac* operon

- The *i* gene synthesises the repressor of the operon. Repressor binds to the operator region of the operon, preventing RNA polymerase from transcribing the operon. However, when inducer such as lactose or allolactose is present, it binds with the repressor and inactivates it. Now, that the repressor is inactivated, RNA polymerase is allowed access to the promoter and transcription proceeds.
- Regulation of *lac* operon by repressor is referred to as **negative regulation.** *Lac* operon can work under the control of **positive regulation** also.

Human Genome Project (HGP)

- In 1990, a mega project was started to determine the nucleotide sequence of the entire human nuclear genome. It was called as Human Genome Project (HGP).
- In addition, HGP was also entrusted to elucidate the genomes of several other model organisms, e.g. *E. coli*, *Saccharomyces cerevisiae* (yeast), roundworm and mouse. It was closely associated with the rapid development of a new area in biology called **bioinformatics**.

Goals of HGP

Important goals of HGP were

- To identify all the approximately 20,000-25,000 genes in human DNA.
- To determine the sequences of the 3 billion chemical base pairs that constitute human DNA.
- To store this information in databases in digital format.
- To improve the tools required for data analysis.
- To transfer the related technologies to other sectors (like industries).
- To address the Ethical, Legal and Social Issues (ELSI) that could arise from the project.

Methodologies of HGP

Two major approaches involved were as follows

- **Expressed Sequence Tags** (ESTs) This method was focused on identifying all the genes that are expressed as RNA.
- **Sequence annotation** This method involved sequencing the whole set of genome (that contained all coding and non-coding sequence) and then assigning functions to the different regions in the sequence.

Sequencing of Genome

- For the process of sequencing, the entire DNA from a cell is isolated and broken into relatively smaller fragment.
- DNA fragments are cloned in a suitable host, (such as bacteria and yeast) using specialised vectors such as **BAC** (Bacterial Artificial Chromosome) and **YAC** (Yeast Artificial Chromosome).
- Fragments of DNA are then sequenced by automated DNA sequencers, which work on the principle of a method developed by Frederick Sanger.
- These sequences were arranged accordingly on the basis of overlapping regions of DNA fragments and were then aligned using special computer programmes.
- At last, the genetic and physical maps of the genome were constructed by collecting information about certain repetitive DNA sequences and DNA polymorphism.

Salient Features/Observations of Human Genome

- There are 3164.7 million nucleotide bases in the human genome.
- In an average gene, there are 3000 bases. The largest known human gene is **Dystrophin** (2.4 million bases).
- Total number of genes in human genome are estimated at 30,000. Almost, all (99.9%) of the nucleotide bases are exactly same in every human individual.
- For over 50% of the discovered genes, the functions are unknown.
- Less than 2% of the genome codes for proteins.
- Repeated sequences are stretches of DNA sequences, which are repeated many times (some times 100-1000 times). These have no direct coding functions, but help in understanding chromosome structure, dynamics and evolution.
- **Chromosome-1** has the maximum number of genes (2968) and **Chromosome-Y** has the least number of genes (231).
- There are about 1.4 million locations in human genome, where single-base DNA differences occur (SNPs or Single Nucleotide Polymorphisms). This information is helpful in finding chromosomal locations for disease-associated sequences and tracing human history.

Applications and Future Challenges

- Its knowledge is helpful in research involving biological systems including human biology.
- All the genes in a genome, e.g. all the transcripts in a particular tissue/organ/tumour, can be studied.

Rice Genome Project

- Rice (*Oryza sativa*) is one of the most important crops in the world. The rice genome is well mapped and it is the smallest of the major cereal crop genomes (400-430 Mb).

- The International Rice Genome Sequencing Project (IRGSP) started in September 1997. The IRGSP has evolved to include 11 nations.
- The recent interim IRGSP meeting at Clemson University in South Carolina was held on September 19 and 20, 2000. It was the longest rice genome meeting till today and was attended by more than 70 scientist and administrators from India, USA, Japan, China, Thailand, Korea, Taiwan, Brazil, France and Canada.
- Till date, 98 PACs/BACs corresponding to 12 Mb of sequence have been completed and released to DNA Data Bank of Japan.

DNA Fingerprinting

- It also called **DNA typing** or **DNA profiling** and is a technique of determining nucleotide sequences of certain areas of DNA which are unique to each individual.
- It uses satellite DNA as probe showing high degree of polymorphism and called it **Variable Number of Tandem Repeats** (VNTRs). It was discovered by **Alec Jeffreys** in 1985.
- The technique has the following steps
  - **DNA isolation** DNA is extracted from the cells in a high speed centrifuge.
  - **Amplification** Many copies of the extracted DNA can be made by the use of Polymerase Chain Reaction (PCR).
  - **Digestion** of DNA by restriction endonucleases.
  - **Separation** of DNA fragments by electrophoresis.
  - **Blotting-transfer** of the separated DNA fragments to synthetic membranes like nylon or nitrocellulose (Southern blotting).
  - **Hybridisation** with the help of a radiolabelled VNTR probe. These proteins target a specific nucleotide sequence that is complementary to them.
  - **Autoradiography** Detection of hybridised DNA fragments by autoradiography.

Applications of DNA Fingerprinting

- It helps to settle paternity or maternity disputes.
- It is used to identify perpetrators of sexual assault cases.
- It is used identify racial groups.

PYQs Previous Years' Questions

1 Mark Questions

Multiple Choice Questions

1. Listed below are some amino acids and their corresponding *m*RNA codons. **CBSE 2024 (Set-I)**

Amino acid	*m*RNA codons
Phenylalanine	UUU
Lysine	AAG
Arginine	CGA
Alanine	GCA

Select the DNA sequence that would code for the following polypeptide sequence.

Polypeptide : Alanine - Arginine - Lysine - Phenylalanine

(a) CGT GCT TTC AAA (b) CGT GCT TTC TTT
(c) CGU GCU UUC AAA (d) CGU GCU UUC TTT

Ans. (a) Polypeptide sequence :

Alanine - Arginine - Lysine - Phenylalanine
*m*RNA : GCA - CGA - AAG - UUU
DNA : CGT - GCT - TTC - AAA

2. Match the following genes of the *lac* operon listed in column A with their respective products listed in column 'B'. **CBSE 2024 (Set-I)**

A (Genes)	B (Products)
A. '*i*' gene	1. β-galactosidase
B. '*z*' gene	2. *Lac* permease
C. '*a*' gene	3. Repressor
D. '*y*' gene	4. Transacetylase

Select the correct option.

	A	B	C	D
(a)	1	3	2	4
(b)	3	1	2	4
(c)	3	1	4	2
(d)	3	4	1	2

Ans. (c) Correct matching order is as follows

(A) '*i*' gene—(3) repressor
(B) '*z*' gene—(1) β-galactosidase
(C) '*a*' gene—(4) transacetylase
(D) '*y*' gene—(2) *lac* permease

3. What is the smallest part of a DNA molecule that can be changed by a point mutation? **CBSE SQP 2024**

(a) Oligonucleotide (b) Codon
(b) Gene (d) Nucleotide

Ans. (d) Nucleotide

4. Given below is a sequence of bases in *m*RNA of a bacterial cell. Identify the amino acid that would be incorporated at codon position 3′ and codon position 5′ during the process of its translation. **CBSE 2023**

3′ AUCAGGUUUGUGAUGGUACGA 5′

(a) Phenylalanine, methionine (b) Cysteine glycine
(c) Alanine, proline (d) Serine, valine

Ans. (a) Phenylalanine, methionine

5. In *E. coli*, the *lac* operon gets switched on when **CBSE SQP 2021-22 Term-I**

(a) lactose is present and it binds to the repressor
(b) repressor binds to operator
(c) RNA polymerase binds to the operator
(d) lactose is present and it binds to RNA polymerase

Ans. (a) lactose is present and it binds to the repressor

6. Short stretches of DNA used to identify complementary sequence in a sample are called **CBSE SQP 2021-22 Term-I**

(a) probes (b) markers
(c) VNTRs (d) primers

Ans. (a) probes

7.

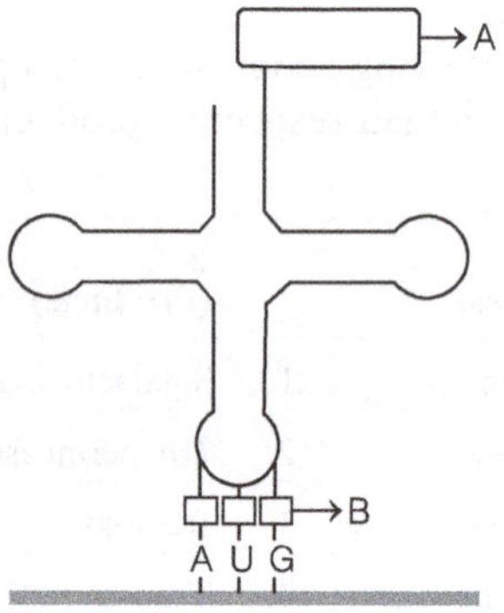

AUG on the *m*RNA will result in the activation of which of the following RNA having correct combination of amino acids? **CBSE SQP 2021-22 Term-I**

	Site *A*	Site *B*
(a)	UAC	Methionine
(b)	Methionine	UAC
(c)	Methionine	AUG
(d)	AUG	Methionine

Ans. (b) AUG codes for methionine and the complementary codon of AUG will be UAC.

8. What are minisatellites? **CBSE SQP 2021-22 Term-I**

(a) 10-40 bp sized small sequences within the genes
(b) Short coding repetitive region on the eukaryotic genome
(c) Short non-coding repetitive sequence forming large portion of eukaryotic genome
(d) Regions of coding strands of the DNA

Ans. (c) Short non-coding repetitive sequence forming large portion of eukaryotic genome

9. There was a mixup at the hospital after a fire accident in the nursery division. Which of these children belong to the parents? **CBSE SQP 2021-22 Term-I**

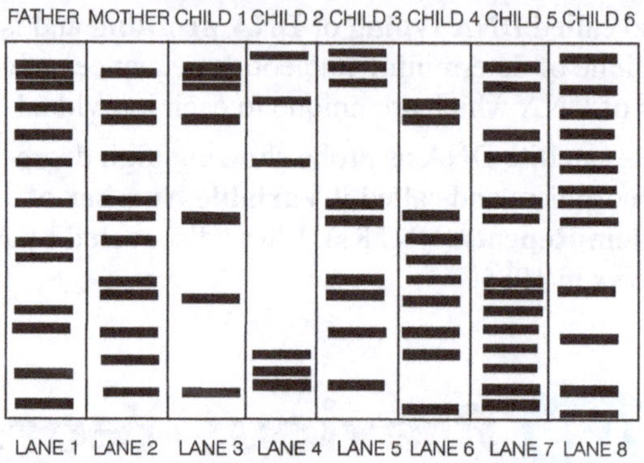

(a) All of the children (b) Children 2, 3 and 6
(c) Children 1 and 3 (d) Children 2 and 4

Ans.(c) Children 1 and 3

10. On the ribosome, *m*RNA binds ...... and two sites in the ...... for subsequent amino acids to bind to be close enough to each other for the formation of a peptide bond. **CBSE SQP 2021-22 Term-I**

(a) between the subunits; on the large subunit
(b) to the large subunit; on the small subunit
(c) to the small subunit; on the large subunit
(d) to the small subunit; between the subunits

Ans. (c) To the small subunit: on the large subunit.

11. The DNA fingerprinting pattern of child is **CBSE SQP 2021-22 Term-I**

(a) exactly similar to that of both the parents
(b) 100% similar to the father's DNA print
(c) 100% similar to the mother's DNA print
(d) 50% bands similar to father and rest similar to mother

Ans. (d) The DNA fingerprinting pattern of child is 50% band similar to father and rest similar to mother.

12. Which cellular process is shown below? **CBSE SQP 2021-22 Term-I**

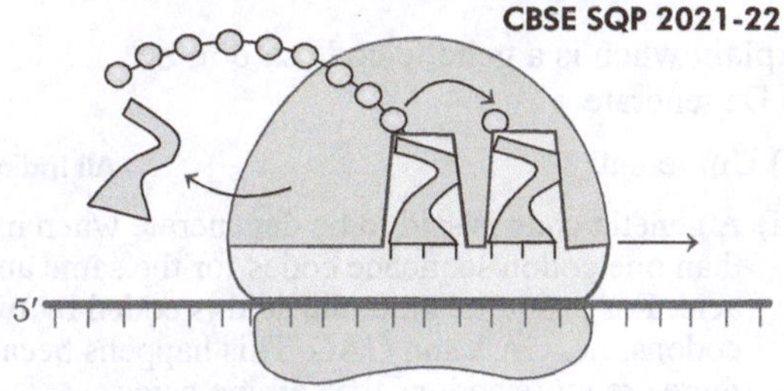

(a) DNA replication
(b) Translation - Initiation
(c) Translation - Elongation
(d) Translation - Termination

Ans. (c) The given diagram represents elongation phase of translation.

13. Which of the following are correct statements for a *t*RNA molecule? **CBSE SQP 2021-22 Term-I**

(i) It is an adapter molecule.
(ii) Previously called as *s*RNA (soluble RNA).
(iii) *t*RNA has a codon loop that has bases complementary to the code.
(iv) It also has an amino acid acceptor end to which it binds to amino acids.
(v) It is non-specific for each amino acid.

(a) (i), (ii) and (iii) (b) (ii), (iii) and (iv)
(c) (i), (ii) and (iv) (d) (i), (iv) and (v)

Ans. (c) The correct statement for *t*RNA molecule are (i), (ii) and (iv).

14. A codon is a 'triplet of bases' was suggested by **CBSE 2021-22 Term-I**

(a) Marshall Nirenberg (b) Har Gobind Khorana
(c) George Gamow (d) Francis Crick

Ans. (c) George Gamow

15. Identify the correct pair of codon with its corresponding pair of amino acid. **CBSE 2021-22 Term-I**

(a) UAA : Leucine (b) UGA : Serine
(c) AUG : Histidine (d) UUU : Phenylalanine

Ans. (d) UUU : Phenylalanine

16. In the presence of allolactose, the *lac* repressor in the operon of *E. coli* **CBSE 2021-22 Term-I**

(a) binds to the operator
(b) cannot bind to the operator
(c) binds to the promoter
(d) binds to the regulator

Ans. (b) cannot bind to the operator

17. Select the important goals of HGP from the given options. **CBSE 2021-22 Term-I**

(i) Store the information for data analysis.
(ii) Cloning and amplification of human DNA.
(iii) Identify all the genes present in human DNA.
(iv) Use of DNA information to trace human history.

(a) (i) and (ii)
(b) (ii) and (iii)
(c) (i) and (iii)
(d) (ii) and (v)

Ans. (c) (i) and (iii)

Assertion-Reason Type Question

18. **Assertion** (A) An organism with lethal mutation may not even develop beyond the zygote stage.

Reason (R) All types of gene mutations are lethal. **CBSE SQP 2021-22**

(a) Both Assertion and Reason are true and Reason is the correct explanationof Assertion
(b) Both Assertion and Reason are true, but Reason is not the correct explanation of Assertion
(c) Assertion is true, but Reason is false
(d) Assertion is false, but Reason is true

Ans. (c) Lethal mutations affect the physiology and morphology of organisms and thus the organisms with such mutations fail to develop beyond zygote stage.

All types of gene mutations are not always lethal. Some of them are even beneficial or benign.

One such example of beneficial mutation is antibiotic resistance in bacteria. Thus, A is true, but R is false.

Very Short Answer Type Questions

19. Predict the effect, if the codon UAU coding for an amino acid at the 25th position of a polypeptide of 50 amino acids, is mutated to UAA. **CBSE SQP 2022**

Ans. If the codon at 25th position is mutated to UAA, a polypeptide of 24 amino acids will be formed as UAA is a stop codon.

20. Name the technique by which gene expression can be controlled with the help of RNA molecule. **CBSE SQP 2019**

Ans. RNA interference is the technique by which gene expression can be controlled with the help of RNA molecule.

21. Name one amino acid, which is coded by only one codon. **CBSE 2018C**

Ans. Methionine.

22. Give an example of a codon having dual function. **All India 2016**

Ans. AUG is a codon with dual functions. It codes for the amino acid methionine (met) and also acts as an initiator codon of polypeptide synthesis during protein synthesis.

23. Write the two specific codons that a translational unit of *m*RNA is flanked by one on either sides. **Outside Delhi 2015C**

Ans. Two specific codons that are flanked on either sides of *m*RNA in a translation unit are

(i) Start codon (AUG)

(ii) Stop codon (UAG or UAA or UAA). (½ + ½)

24. How does a degenerate code differ from an unambiguous one? **Foreign 2015**

Ans. When some amino acids are coded by more than one codon, the code is said to be degenerate. (½)

On the other hand, when one codon codes for only one amino acid, it is called unambiguous. (½)

25. How is repetitive/satellite DNA separated from bulk genomic DNA for various genetic experiments? **Delhi 2014**

Ans. Satellite DNA is separated from bulk genomic DNA by density-gradient centrifugation technique.

26. State which human chromosome has

(i) the maximum number of genes and

(ii) the one which has the least number of genes. **Foreign 2014, 2011**

Ans. (i) Chromosome 1 (2968 genes). (½)

(ii) Chromosome Y (231 genes) (½)

27. Which one of the two subunits of ribosome encounters an *m*RNA? **Delhi 2013C**

Ans. Smaller subunit.

28. Mention the contribution of genetic maps in human genome project. **All India 2011**

Ans. Genetic maps are used as a starting point in the sequencing of whole genome.

29. Mention any two ways in which Single Nucleotide Polymorphisms (SNPs) identified in human genome, can bring out revolutionary changes in biological and medical sciences. **All India 2011**

Ans. (i) By tracing human history. (½)

(ii) By finding chromosomal locations for disease associated sequences. (½)

2 Marks Questions

30. Explain when is a genetic code said to be

(i) Degenerate

(ii) Universal **All India 2020**

Ans. (i) A genetic code is said to be degenerate when more than one codon sequence codes for the same amino acid. For example, glutamic acid is coded by two codons, i.e. GAA and GAG. This happens because there are more codons than amino acids. (1)

(ii) A genetic code is universal because one specific codon codes for same amino acid in almost all organisms. For example, AUG is a start codon in bacterial as well as in other organisms and codes for methionine. (1)

31. Why does the *lac* operon shut down sometime after the addition of lactose in the medium where *E. coli* was growing? Why low level expression of *lac* operon is always required? **CBSE SQP 2019**

Ans. After addition of lactose, complete breakdown of lactose to glucose and galactose takes place. Therefore, there is no more lactose to bind to the repressor protein and the *lac* operon shuts down.

A very low level of expression of *lac* operon has to be present in the cell and time, otherwise lactose cannot enter the cells.

32. Differentiate between the genetic codes given below

(i) Unambiguous and universal

(ii) Degenerate and initiator **All India 2017**

Ans. (i) Difference between unambiguous and universal genetic codes is

Unambiguous	Universal
In genetic code, one codon codes for only one amino acid, hence it is unambiguous.	The genetic code is universal, i.e. each codon codes for same amino acid in all organisms.

(1)

(ii) Difference between degenerate and initiator codes is

Degenerate	Initiator
Some amino acids are coded by more than one codon, hence the code is degenerate, e.g. serine, leucine, arginine are encoded by 6 codons.	These codons act as start signal for translation, e.g. AUG acts as initiator codon and it codes for methionine.

(1)

33. Following are the features of genetic codes. What does each one indicate?
Stop codon, Unambiguous codon, Degenerate codon, Universal codon. **All India 2016**

Ans. (i) **Stop codon** does not code for any amino acids, e.g. UGA.

(ii) **Unambiguous codon** codes for only one amino acid, e.g. CCG codes for proline.

(iii) **Degenerate codon** Genetic code is described as degenerate when a single amino acid is coded by more than one codon, e.g. serine is coded by 6 codons.

(iv) **Universal codons** codes for the same amino acid in all organisms (except in mitochondria and few protozoan). **(½ × 4)**

34. What is aminoacylation? State its significance. **All India 2016**

Or Explain aminoacylation of *t*RNA. **All India 2014C**

Ans. Aminoacylation or charging of *t*RNA is a process in which amino acids get activated in the presence of ATP and get linked to their cognate *t*RNA. **(1)**

Significance of aminoacylation The charged *t*RNA carries amino acids to the site of protein synthesis. If two charged *t*RNAs are brought close to each other, the formation of peptide bond is favoured energetically. **(1)**

35. State the functions of ribozyme and release factor in protein synthesis, respectively. **Outside Delhi 2015C**

Ans. **Ribozyme** in bacteria is 23S *r*RNA, that acts as an enzyme for the formation of a peptide bond between two amino acids. **(1)**

Release factor binds to the stop condon (UAA) to terminate translation and release the complete polypeptide. **(1)**

36. How would *lac* operon operate in *E. coli* growing in a culture medium, where lactose is present as source of sugar? **All India 2014C**

Ans. When lactose is present in a medium having *E. coli*, it will act as a substrate for enzyme β-galactosidase and switches on the operon. Hence, it is also termed as an inducer. It inactivates repressor by binding to it and allows RNA polymerase access to the promoter.

37. Where does peptide bond formation occur in a bacterial ribosome and how? **Foreign 2014**

Ans. A peptide bond is formed between carboxyl group (— COOH) of amino acid at P-site and amino group (— NH) of amino acid at A-site. It is formed by the enzyme peptidyl transferase in a bacterial ribosome. **(1 + 1)**

38. (i) Name the scientist who suggested that the genetic code should be made of a combination of three nucleotides.

(ii) Explain the basis on which he arrived at this conclusion. **Delhi 2014**

Ans. (i) George Gamow suggested that the genetic code should be made of a combination of three nucleotides. **(1)**

(ii) George stated that a codon must be of three bases in order to code for 20 amino acids, since there are only four bases (i.e. 4^3 or $4 \times 4 \times 4 = 64$) which code for 20 amino acids. **(1)**

39. Why is charging of *t*RNA necessary during translation process? **All India 2014C**

Ans. Amino acids are activated in the presence of ATP and linked to their cognate *t*RNA. This is called charging of *t*RNA (aminoacylation).

The process is required as the formation of peptide bond between the amino acids is favoured energetically, when they are brought together.

Activation of amino acids by ATP provides the energy for the formation of peptide bond.

40. One of the salient features of the genetic code is that it is nearly universal from bacteria to humans. Mention two exceptions to this rule. Why are some codes said to be degenerated? **Foreign 2014**

Ans. Genetic code is nearly universal except in mitochondrial codons and in some protozoans. Some amino acids are coded by more than one codon, hence some codes are said to be degenerated. **(1 + 1)**

41. Draw a schematic diagram of *lac* operon in its switched off position. Label the following

(i) Structural genes

(ii) Repressor bound to its correct positions

(iii) Promoter gene

(iv) Regulatory gene **Foreign 2012**

Ans.

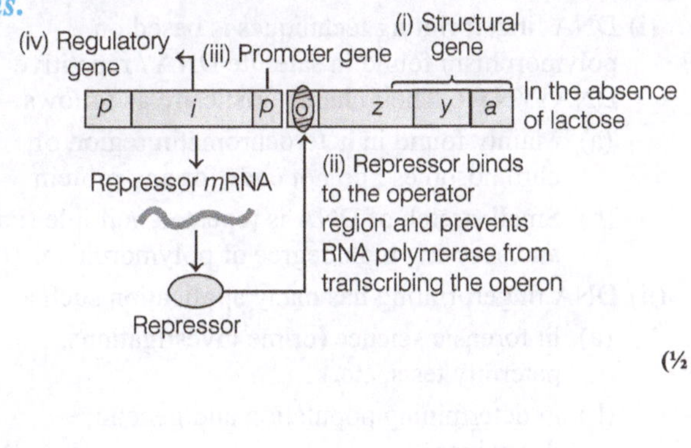

(½ × 4)

42. Write the full form of VNTR. How is VNTR different from probe? **All India 2011**

Ans. VNTR—Variable Number Tandem Repeat. **(1)**

Difference between VNTR and Probe is

VNTR	Probe
It is a class of satellite DNA, where a small sequence is arranged tandemly in many copy numbers.	It is a radiolabelled VNTR, used for hybridisation with DNA segments in question.

(1)

43. (i) Differentiate between unambiguous and degenerate codons.

(ii) Write two functions of the codon AUG. **All India 2010C**

Ans. (i) Differences between unambiguous and degenerate codons are

Unambiguous	Degenerate
No ambiguity for a particular codon. For example, GGA is an ambiguous codon, it codes for glycine as well as glutamic acid.	Code is degenerate for a particular amino acid.
A particular codon will always code for the same amino acid, where it is found.	One amino acid is coded by more than one codon, e.g. phenylalanine has two codons, i.e. UUU and UUC.

(1)

(ii) Refer to answer no. 20 **(1)**

3 Marks Questions

44. (i) Name and write two characteristics of the type of DNA that forms the basis of DNA fingerprinting technique.

(ii) Mention any two applications of this technique. **CBSE 2024 (Set-I)**

Ans. (i) DNA fingerprinting techniques is based on polymorphism found in satellite DNA / repetitive DNA /VNTR. Their characteristic are as follows -

(a) Mainly found in heterochromatin region of chromosomes ; do not code for any protein.

(b) Small stretch of DNA is repeated multiple times and showing high degree of polymorphism. **(1½)**

(ii) DNA fingerprinting has many application such as

(a) in forensic science (crime investigations, paternity tests, etc.)

(b) in determining population and genetic diversities. **(1½)**

45. Human Genome Project (HGP) was a megaproject launched in the year 1990 with some important goals. **CBSE 2023**

(i) Enlist any four prime goals of HGP.

(ii) Name any one common non-human animal model organism which has also been sequenced thereafter.

Ans. (i) Refer to text on page no. 162. **(2)**

(ii) One common non-human animal model organism which has also been sequenced there after is *Caenorhabitis elegans* (a free-living non-pathogenic nematode). **(1)**

46. (i) Identify the polarity of *X* to *X′* in the diagram below and mention how many more amino acids are expected to be added to this polypeptide chain.

(ii) Mention the codon and anticodon for alanine.

(iii) Why are some untranslated sequences of bases seen in *m*RNA coding for a polypeptide? Where exactly are they present on *m*RNA? **CBSE SQP 2023**

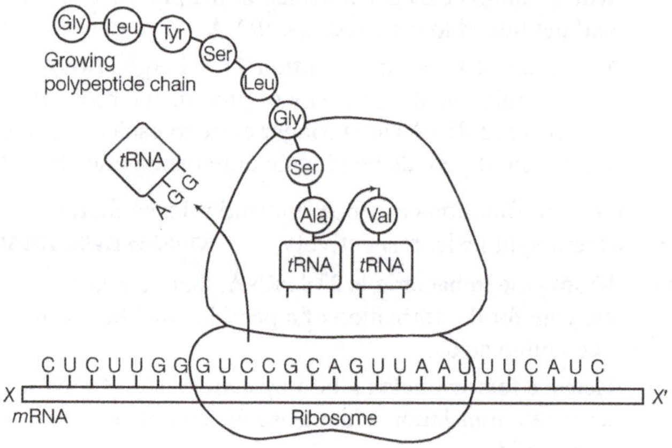

Ans. (i) The polarity of *X* to *X′* is 5′ ⟶ 3′

No more amino acids will be added to this polypeptide chain. **(1)**

(ii) Codon for alanine is GCA, while anticodon is CGU. **(1)**

(iii) The untranslated regions are required for an efficient translation process. They are present before the initiation codon at the 5′- end and after the stop/termination codon, at the 3′- end. **(1)**

47. (i) Study the table given below and identify (a), (b), (c) and (d).

Amino acid	Phe	Val
DNA code in gene	AAA	CAC
Codon in *m*RNA	(a)	(b)
Anticodon in *t*RNA	(c)	(d)

(ii) A polypeptide consists of 14 different amino acids.

(a) How many base pairs must be there in the processed *m*RNA that codes for this polypeptide?

(b) How many different types of *t*RNA are needed for the synthesis of this polypeptide? **CBSE SQP 2020**

Ans. (i) (a) UUU (b) GUG (c)AAA (d) CAC (1)

(ii) (a) An amino acid is coded by a codon (containing 3 bases).

Thus, a polypeptide containing 14 different amino acids has $= 14 \times 3 = 42$ base pairs.

(b) 14 different types of *t*RNA are needed for the synthesis of polypeptide. (2)

48. What are 'SNPs'? Where are they located in a human cell ? State any two ways the discovery of SNPs can be of important to humans. **All India 2020**

Ans. SNPs stand for Single Nucleotide Polymorphisms. They represent genetic variations that have been identified in about 1.4 million locations in DNA between the genes.

Two ways in which discovery of SNPs is important to humans are

(i) SNPs can revolutionise the process of tracing human history.

(ii) They can help in predicting an individual's response to certain drugs, susceptibility to environmental factors, etc.

49. 'A very small sample of tissue or even a drop of blood can help determine paternity'. Provide a scientific explanation to substantiate how it is possible. **All India 2019**

Ans. DNA fingerprinting is the basis of paternity testing in case of disputes. This technique is used to distinguish between individuals of same species by using their DNA sample.

The DNA is isolated from the cells and further amplified to produce many copies by using polymerase chain reaction. This amplified DNA is further processed to detect the presence of similarities between the parent and child. Because, the DNA from sample can be amplified to produce many copies in DNA fingerprinting, only a very small sample of tissue or even a drop of blood can help to determine paternity.

50. Expand 'BAC' and 'YAC'. What are they and what is the purpose for which they are used? **All India 2019, 13**

Ans. BAC — Bacterial Artificial Chromosome

YAC — Yeast Artificial Chromosome. (1)

'BAC' and 'YAC' are the two type of vectors involved in cloning. YAC uses a specific region of yeast chromosome, while BAC uses a specific region of *E. coli* chromosome. (2)

51. (i) Expand VNTR and describe its role in DNA fingerprinting.

(ii) List any two applications of DNA fingerprinting technique. **CBSE 2018**

Ans. (i) The expanded form of VNTR is Variable Number of Tandem Repeats. These are short nucleotide repeats in the DNA.

These are highly specific for individuals. No two individuals have the same VNTR.

Role of VNTR in fingerprinting VNTRs are used as probe markers in the identification of DNA of different individuals because no two individuals can have the same VNTRs (except in case of monozygotic twins). (1½)

(ii) Applications of DNA Fingerprinting

(a) The technique of DNA Fingerprinting can identify the real genetic mother, father and offspring.

(b) DNA fingerprinting is very useful in the detection of crime and legal pursuits. (1½)

52. (i) List the two methodologies which were involved in human genome project. Mention how they were used.

(ii) Expand 'YAC' and mention what was it used for. **All India 2017**

Ans. (i) Two major methodologies involved in HGP are as follows

(a) **Expressed Sequence Tags** (ESTs) This method focuses on identifying all the genes that are expressed as RNA.

(b) **Sequence annotation** This method involves the sequencing of whole set of genome (that contained all coding and non-coding sequence) and then assigning functions to the different regions in the sequence. (1 × 2)

(ii) YAC stands for Yeast Artificial Chromosome. These were used as vectors in which fragments of whole DNA of human were inserted and cloned. (1)

53. A number of passengers were severely burnt beyond recognition during a train accident. Name and describe a modern technique that can help handover the dead to their relatives. **Delhi 2017**

Or Following the collision of two trains a large number of passengers are killed. A majority of them are beyond recognition. Authorities want to handover the dead to their relatives. Name a modern scientific method and write the procedure that would help in the identification of kinship. **Delhi 2015**

Or Following a severe accident, many charred-disfigured bodies are recovered from the site making the identification of the dead very difficult. Name and explain the technique that would help the authorities to establish the identity of the dead to be able to handover the dead to their respective relatives. **All India 2014C**

Or In a maternity clinic, for some reasons the authorities are not able to handover the two newborns to their respective real parents. Name and describe the technique that you would suggest to sort out the matter. **All India 2013**

Ans. The technique that can help in the identification of victims is DNA fingerprinting which is used to distinguish between individuals of same species by using their DNA sample. The chemical structure of DNA is same in everyone (99.9%) except the order of base pairs, i.e. only 0.1% of DNA makes every individual unique.

DNA fingerprinting exploits the highly variable tandem repeating sequences, i.e. VNTRs for profiling. These VNTRs are highly conserved among members of the same species. (1)

Technique

This technique is carried out in following steps

(i) **DNA isolation** DNA is extracted from the cells in a high speed centrifuge.

(ii) **Amplification** Many copies of the extracted DNA can be made by the use of polymerase chain reaction.

(iii) **Digestion** of DNA by restriction endonucleases.

(iv) **Separation** of DNA fragments by electrophoresis.

(v) **Blotting** Transfer of separated DNA fragments to synthetic membranes (like nylon or nitrocellulose).

(vi) **Hybridisation** with the help of a radio-labelled VNTR probe (small segments of DNA which help to detect the presence of a gene in a long DNA sequence). These probes target a specific nucleotide sequence that is complementary to them.

(vii) **Autoradiography** Detection of hybridised DNA fragments by autoradiography.

The presence of similarities between the victims and their relatives determines their association on the basis of which dead bodies or newborns can be identified and handed over to their families. (2)

54. (i) What do 'Y' and 'B' stand for in 'YAC' and 'BAC' used in Human Genome Project (HGP)? Mention their role in the project.

(ii) Write the percentage of the total human genome that codes for proteins and the percentage of discovered genes whose functions are known as observed during HGP.

(iii) Expand SNPs identified by scientists in HGP. **All India 2016**

Ans. (i) Y stands for yeast in the word YAC (Yeast Artificial Chromosome) and B stands for bacteria in the word BAC (Bacterial Artificial Chromosome). These are used as vectors in cloning of DNA. (½ + ½)

(ii) Less than 2% of the total human genome codes for protein, functions of 50 % of discovered genes are not known. (½ + ½)

(iii) SNPs stands for Single Nucleotide Polymorphisms. (1)

55. (i) How many codons code for amino acids and how many are unable to do so?

(ii) Why are codes said to be

(a) degenerate and

(b) unambiguous? **Delhi 2016C**

Or

(i) How many codons code for amino acids and how many do not?

(ii) Explain the following giving one example of each.

(a) Unambiguous and specific codon

(b) Degeneration codon

(c) Universal codon

(d) Initiator codon **All India 2010C**

Ans. (i) Out of 64 codons, 61 code for amino acids and rest 3 codons do not code for any amino acids. These function as stop codons. (½ + ½)

(ii) (a) **Unambiguous and specific codon** These code for only one amino acid. Thus, making the genetic code unambiguous and specific, e.g. UUU. (½)

(b) Some amino acids are coded by more than one codon, so the code is **degenerate**, e.g. serine is coded by 6 codons. (½)

(c) Codon is nearly **universal**. Some exceptions to the rule are mitochondrial codon and in some protozoans, e.g. UUU. (½)

(d) **Initiator codon** AUG has dual function. It codes for methionine and also acts as initiator. (½)

56. Write any three goals of human genome project.
Outside Delhi 2016C

Ans. Refer to text on page no. 162.

57. What is mutation? Explain with the help of an example how does a point mutation affect the genetic code. Name another type of mutation.
Outside Delhi 2016C

Ans. A mutation is a sudden, stable, inheritable change in genetic material. A classical example of point mutation is a change of single base pair in the gene for β-globin chain that results in the change of amino acid residue glutamate to valine in a cell of a person suffering from sickle-cell anaemia. It is a genetic disease.
The other type of mutation includes frameshift insertion or deletion mutation.
The insertion or deletion of one or more bases may change the reading frame from the point of insertion or deletion. Insertion or deletion of three or its multiple bases inserts or deletes one or multiple codon, hence one or multiple amino acid may be formed in polypeptide. **(1 × 3)**

58. Explain the significance of satellite DNA in DNA fingerprinting technique. **All India 2015**

Ans. **Significance of satellite DNA in DNA fingerprinting**
A DNA satellite is a region that consists of short DNA sequences repeated many times. The variation between individuals in the lengths of their DNA satellites forms the basis of DNA fingerprinting. **(1)**
DNA satellites are of two types, i.e. **microsatellites** and **minisatellites**. The characteristic that makes them useful for identification is that they are highly **polymorphic**. The length of each satellite in DNA is inherited. **(1)**
The length of satellite regions is highly variable between people. These form small peaks during density gradient centrifugation and thus are invaluable for identification purposes. **(1)**

59. Describe how the *lac* operon operates, both in the presence and the absence of an inducer in *E. coli*.
All India 2014

Ans. *Lac* operon is made up of one regulatory gene *i* and three structural genes (*z, y, a*).
Its function in the presence and the absence of inducer is as follows
(i) **When inducer** (lactose) **is absent,** *i* gene regulates and produces repressor *m*RNA. The repressor protein binds to the operator region of operon and as a result it prevents RNA polymerase to bind to the operon. The operon is switched off in this situation. **(1½)**
(ii) **When inducer** (lactose) **is present,** lactose acts as an inducer and binds to the repressor. Thus, forming an inactive repressor.
The repressor fails to bind the operator region. The RNA polymerase binds to the operator and transcripts *lac m*RNA.
*Lac m*RNA is known to be polycistronic which produces all three enzymes, i.e. β-galactosidase, permease and transacetylase required for the hydrolysis of lactose. Operon is switched on in this situation. **(1½)**

60. Explain the process of translation. **All India 2014C**

Ans. Translation is the process of polymerisation of amino acids to form a polypeptide with the help of *m*RNA, *t*RNA and ribosomes and many enzymes involved in the process. **(1)**
The different phases of translation are
(i) **Activation of amino acids** refer to text on page no. 160.
(ii) **Initiation of polypeptide synthesis** refer to text on page no. 160.
(iii) **Elongation of polypeptide chain** refer to text on page no. 160-161.
(iv) **Termination of polypeptide synthesis** refer to text on page no. 161. **(2)**

61. (i) Which human chromosome has
(a) maximum number of genes and
(b) which one has fewest genes?
(ii) Write the scientific importance of single nucleotide polymorphism identified in human genome. **All India 2014C**

Ans. (i) Refer to answer no. 26. **(½ + ½)**
(ii) Scientists have identified about 1.4 million locations, where single base DNA differences or Single Nucleotide Polymorphisms (SNPs) occur in humans. Since, these sequences have high degree of polymorphism they form the basis of DNA fingerprinting. **(2)**

62. (i) Name the scientist who postulated the presence of an adapter molecule that can assist in protein synthesis.
(ii) Describe its structure with the help of a diagram. Mention its role in protein synthesis. **Foreign 2014**

Ans. (i) Francis Crick proposed the presence of an adapter molecule, i.e. *t*RNA which could read the code and bind to the specific amino acids, thus assisting in protein synthesis. **(1)**

(ii) A clover leaf structure of *t*RNA

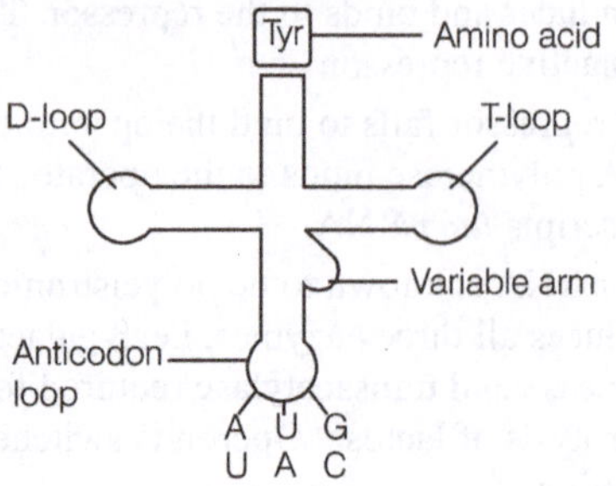

A *t*RNA functions as carrier of amino acids and participates in protein synthesis. **(1 + 1)**

63. (i) Explain DNA polymorphism as the basis of genetic mapping of human genome.
(ii) State the role of VNTR in DNA fingerprinting.
All India 2013

Ans. (i) DNA polymorphism exhibited by certain repetitive DNA sequences is used to construct genetic and physical maps of the genome which are used in human genome project. **(1½)**

(ii) Variable Number of Tandem Repeats (VNTRs) belong to a class of satellite DNA called as minisatellite. VNTRs are used as probes in DNA fingerprinting. **(1½)**

64. Given below are the sequences of nucleoside in a particular *m*RNA and amino acids coded by it.

UUUAUGUUCGAGUUAGUGUAA

Phe – Met – Phe – Glu – Leu – Val

Write the properties of genetic codes that can be and that cannot be correlated from the above given data.
Delhi 2013C, 2010C

Ans. UUUAUGUUCGAGUUAGUGUAA

Phe – Met – Phe – Glu – Leu – Val

According to the sequence given above

(i) Codon is triplet.

(ii) Genetic code is specific and unambiguous.
For example, AUG – Codes for methionine (Met)
GAG – Codes for glutamine (Glu)
UUA – Codes for leucine (Leu)

(iii) Codon is degenerate, i.e. same amino acids are coded by more than one code.
For example, UUU and UUC, both codes for phenylalanine (Phe).

(iv) Code is read without punctuation.

(v) UAA acts as a terminating code.
Thus, all properties of codon are satisfied from the above given data except the one that mostly AUG work as an initiating codon.

65. How are the structural genes activated in *lac* operon in *E. coli* ?
All India 2012

Ans. *Lac* operon consists of

(i) an operator, which controls all structural genes as a unit

(ii) a regulatory gene (*i* gene)

(iii) three structural genes (*z, y, a*), which code for enzymes and

(iv) a promoter, where RNA polymerase binds for transcription.

The regulatory gene codes for a repressor protein that has high affinity for the operator region and which prevents RNA polymerase from transcribing the structural genes, i.e. the *lac* operon is switched off or inactive. **(1)**

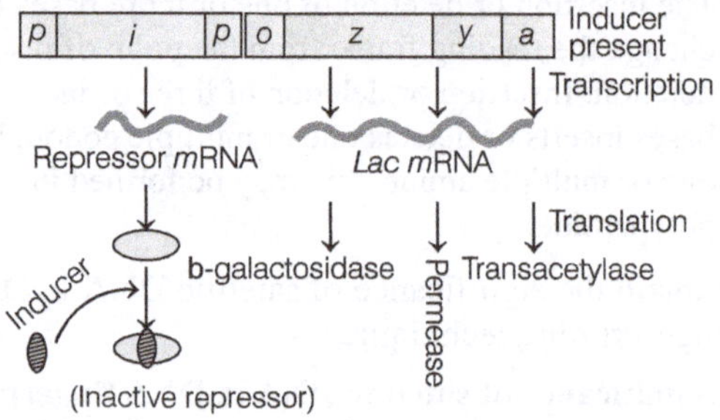

Lac operon of *E. coli* **(1)**

***Lac* operon in the presence of inducer** When inducer (lactose) is added, it binds with repressor protein and inactivates it. This allows RNA polymerase to have access to the promoter and transcription proceeds *via* the activation of structural genes. **(1)**

66. (i) Name the scientist who called *t*RNA an adapter molecule.
(ii) Draw a clover leaf structure of *t*RNA showing the following
(a) Tyrosine attached to its amino acid site.
(b) Anticodon for this amino acid in its correct site (codon for tyrosine is UAC).
(iii) What does the actual structure of *t*RNA look like?
All India 2011

Ans. (i) Francis Crick. **(1)**

(ii) Refer to answer no. 62 (ii). **(1)**

(iii) The actual structure of *t*RNA looks like an inverted L. **(1)**

67. A considerable amount of lactose is added to the growth medium of *E. coli*. How is the *lac* operon switched on in the bacteria? Mention the state of the operon when lactose is digested. **All India 2010**

Ans. In *lac* operon, when lactose is added, it enters the cell wall with the help of permease, a small amount of which is already present in cell. Lactose binds itself to active repressor and changes its structure. The repressor now fails to bind to the operator.

Then, RNA polymerase starts transcription of operon by binding to promoter site-P. All the three enzymes for lactose metabolism are synthesised.

After some time, when whole of lactose is consumed, there is no inducer present to bind to the repressor. Due to this, the repressor becomes active again, attaches itself to the operator and finally switches off the operon.

68. (i) Why is *t*RNA called an adapter?

(ii) Draw and label a secondary structure of *t*RNA. How does the actual structure of *t*RNA look like?

All India 2010C

Ans. (i) *t*RNA binds to a specific amino acid and it also reads the codon of the amino acid bound to it through its anticodon. So, it is called an adapter molecule. **(1)**

(ii)

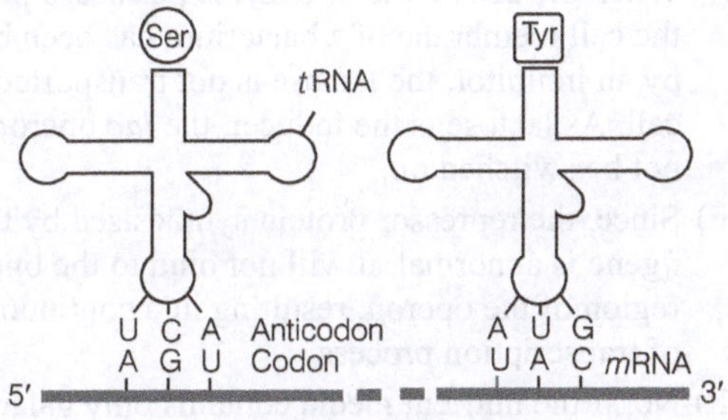

Secondary structure of *t*RNA **(1)**

In actual structure, the *t*RNA is a compact molecule, that looks like an inverted L. **(1)**

69. The following is the flowchart highlighting the steps in DNA fingerprinting technique. Identify *a, b, c, d, e* and *f*.

Isolation of DNA from blood cells
↓
Cutting of DNA by '*a*'
↓
Separation of DNA fragments by electrophoresis using '*b*'
↓
Transfer (blotting) of fragments to '*c*' membrane
↓
DNA splits into single strand
↓
Introduction of labelled '*d*' probe
↓
'*e*' of single strands with probe
↓
Detection of banding pattern by '*f*'

Delhi 2010C

Ans. *a* – Restriction endonuclease
b – Electric field
c – Nitrocellulose or Nylon
d – VNTR
e – Hybridisation
f – Autoradiography **(½ × 6)**

5 Marks Questions

70. Given below is a stretch of DNA showing the coding strand of a structural gene of a transcription unit?

5′—ATG ACC GTA TTT TCT GTA GTG CCC GTA CTT CAG GCA TAA—3′ **CBSE SQP 2024**

(i) Write the corresponding template strand and the *m*RNA strand that will be transcribed, along with its polarity.

(ii) If GUA of the transcribed *m*RNA is an intron, depict the sequence involved in the formation of *m*RNA /the mature processed *hn*RNA strand.

(a) In a bacterium (b) In humans

(iii) Upon translation, how many amino acids will the resulting polypeptide have? Justify.

Ans. 5′—ATG ACC GTA TTT TCT GTA GTG CCC GTA CTT CAG GCA TAA—3′ = Coding

(i) 3′—TAC TGG CAT AAA AGA CAT CAC GGG CAT GAA GTC CGT ATT—5′= Template

5′— AUG ACC GUA UUU UCU GUA GUG CCC GUA CUU CAG GCA UAA—3′ **(1)**

(ii) (a) **In a bacterium**

5′—AUG ACC GUA UUU UCU GUA GUG CCC GUA CUU CAG GCA UAA—3′

(b) **In humans**

5′-*m*GpppAUG ACC UUU UCU GUG CCC CUU CAG GCA UAA- Poly A tail—3′ **(2)**

(iii) 9 amino acids in the polypeptide because UAA is stop/terminator codon and does not code for any amino acid. **(1)**

71. (i) Explain the process of aminoacylation of *t*RNA and its role in the process of translation.

(ii) How does initiation of the translation process occur in prokaryotes? Explain.

(iii) Where are the untranslated regions located on *m*RNA and why? **CBSE 2023**

Ans. (i) Activation of amino acids and formation of AA-*t*RNA complex is the first step of translation. In the presence of an enzyme *t*RNA synthetase, the amino acid (AA) molecule is activated and then each amino acid is attached to the specific *t*RNA molecule at 3′ / CCA end to form aminoacyl- *t*RNA complex. The reaction needs ATP. This process is called charging of *t*RNA or aminoacylation of *t*RNA. **(2)**

(ii) During initiation of translation process the smaller ribosomal subunit attaches to the 5′end of *m*RNA to form a complex. Downstream to this *m*RNA lies the AUG initiator codon, which initiates the process of translation.

The initiation *t*RNA joins the initiation codon by its anticodon through H-bonds. Now the binding of large subunit of ribosome with its smaller subunit completes the translation -initiation-complex. At this stage, the initiator *t*RNA lies at the P-site (aminoacyl *t*RNA site) of the ribosome and the A-site (peptidyl *t*RNA site) is vacant to let another charged *t*RNA to enter. **(2)**

(iii) *m*RNA has some additional sequences that are not translated and are referred to as untranslated regions (UTRs). The UTRs are present at both the 5′-end (before the start codon) and the 3′-end (after the stop codon). They are required for an efficient translation process. **(1)**

72. Name and describe the steps involved in the technique widely used in forensics that serves as the basis of paternity testing in case of disputes. **CBSE 2023**

Ans. The technique widely used in forensics that serves as the basis of paternity testing in case of dispute is DNA fingerprinting. It is a quick way to compare the DNA sequence of any two individuals.

The steps involved in this technique are as follows

(i) **DNA isolation** DNA is extracted from the cells in a high speed centrifuge.

(ii) **Amplification** Many copies of the extracted DNA can be made by the use of polymerase chain reaction.

(iii) **Digestion** of DNA by restriction endonucleases.

(iv) **Separation** of DNA fragments by gel electrophoresis.

(v) **Southern blotting** Transfer of separated DNA fragments to synthetic membranes (like nylon or nitrocellulose).

(vi) **Hybridisation** with the help of a radio-labelled VNTR probe (small segments of DNA which help to detect the presence of a gene in a long DNA sequence). These probes target a specific nucleotide sequence that is complementary to them.

(vii) **Autoradiography** Detection of hybridised DNA fragments by autoradiography.

Overall, DNA fingerprinting is a highly accurate and reliable technique for determining paternity. This is because, it is widely used in forensic investigations and legal disputes.

73. Study the schematic representation of the genes involved in the *lac* operon given below and answer the questions that follow

p	i	p	o	z	y	a

(i) The active site of enzyme permease present in the cell membrane of a bacterium has been blocked by an inhibitor, how will it affect the *lac* operon?

(ii) The protein produced by the *i* gene has become abnormal due to unknown reasons. Explain its impact on lactose metabolism stating the reason.

(iii) If the nutrient medium for the bacteria contains only galactose; will operon be expressed? Justify your answer. **CBSE SQP 2023**

Ans. (i) When the active site of enzyme permease present in the cell membrane of a bacterium has been blocked by an inhibitor, the lactose is not transported into the cell. As lactose is the inducer, the *lac* operon will not be switched on. **(2)**

(ii) Since, the repressor protein synthesised by the *i* gene is abnormal, it will not bind to the operator region of the operon, resulting in a continuous state of transcription process. **(2)**

(iii) No, if the nutrient media contains only galactose, operon will not be expressed, because galactose is not an inducer, it is a product of lactose metabolism. **(1)**

74. (i) How and why is charging of *t*RNA essential in the process of translation?

(ii) State the function of ribosome as a catalyst in bacteria during the process of translation.

(iii) Explain the process of binding of ribosomal units to *m*RNA during protein synthesis. **CBSE 2023**

Ans. (i) Transfer RNA (*t*RNA) is an essential link between the genetic codes and proteins. During the process of translation, *t*RNA is charged with its cognate amino acid and delivers it to the ribosome, thus serving as a substrate for protein synthesis. **(1½)**

(ii) Ribosome acts as the site where protein synthesis takes place from individual amino acids. It is made up of two subunits. The smaller subunit comes in contact with *m*RNA and forms a protein synthesising complex whereas the larger subunit acts as an amino acid binding site. It also acts as a catalyst and forms peptide bond. For example, 23S *r*RNA in bacteria acts as a ribozyme. **(2)**

(iii) Initiation of protein synthesis includes binding of *m*RNA to the smaller of two ribosomal subunits and to the initiating aminoacyl-*t*RNA. The large ribosomal subunit then binds to form an initiation complex to facilitate binding of charged *t*RNA during elongation of polypeptide chain. **(1½)**

75. (i) List any four major goals of human genome project.

(ii) Write any four ways the knowledge from HGP is of significance for humans.

(iii) Expand BAC and mention its importance.

All India 2020

Ans. (i) Goals of Human Genome Project (HGP) are as follows

(a) To identify all the genes (approximately 20000-25000) in human DNA.

(b) To determine the sequences of the 3 billion chemical base pairs that constitute human DNA.

(c) To store this information in database in digital format.

(d) To improve the tools required for data analysis. **(2)**

(ii) Knowledge from HGP is significant for humans in following ways

(a) The knowledge about effects of the DNA variations among individuals can lead to discovery of new ways in diagnosis, treatment and prevention of various diseases affecting mankind.

(b) It can help in learning about DNA sequences of non-human organisms that can lead to an understanding of their natural capabilities.

(c) Its knowledge is helpful in research involving biological systems including human biology.

(d) The knowledge will make the study of interactions between various genes possible. **(2)**

(iii) BAC is Bacterial Artificial Chromosome. These are bacterial cloning vector based on F-factor of *E. coli* which can clone upto 300-350 kb of DNA fragments. These vectors have been utilised in sequencing of genome in HGP. **(1)**

76. Summarise the process by which the sequence of DNA bases in human genome project was determined using the method developed by Frederick Sanger. Name a free living non-pathogenic nematode whose DNA has been sequenced. **CBSE SQP 2020**

Ans. For human genome project, the DNA fragments were sequenced using automated DNA sequencer that worked on the principle of a method developed by F Sanger. In which the sequences were arranged based on some overlapping regions present in them. This required generation of overlapping fragments for sequencing. Alignment of these sequences was humanly not possible. Therefore, specialised computer based programmes were developed.

These sequences were subsequently annotated and were assigned to each chromosome. **(4)**

The sequence of chromosome 1 was completed only in May 2006. *Caenorhabditis elegans* is a free-living non-pathogenic nematode whose DNA has been completely sequenced. **(1)**

77. Study the schematic representation of the genes involved in the *lac* operon given below and answer the questions that follow

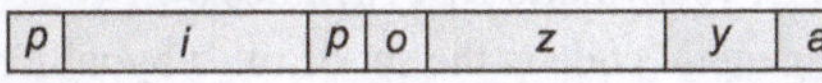

(i) Identify and name the regulatory gene in this operon. Explain its role in 'switching off' the operon.

(ii) Why is *lac* operon's regulation referred to as negative regulation?

(iii) Name the inducer molecule and the products of the genes *z* and *y* of the operon. Write the function of these gene products.

All India 2019, Foreign 2010, Delhi 2010

Ans. (i) *i* gene–regulatory gene.

It codes for the repressor protein of the operon, which is synthesised constitutively.

The repressor has the affinity for the operator gene. It binds to the operator and prevents the RNA polymerase from transcribing the structural genes. **(2)**

(ii) When repressor binds to the operator, the operon is switched off and transcription is stopped. So, it is called negative regulation. **(1)**

(iii) Lactose is an inducer molecule.

Gene '*z*' codes for β-galactosidase, which is responsible for the hydrolysis of lactose into galactose and glucose.

'*y*' gene codes for permease. It increases the permeability of the cell to lactose. **(2)**

78. (i) Write the contributions of the following scientists in deciphering the genetic code.

George Gamow, Har Gobind Khorana, Marshall Nirenberg, Severo Ochoa.

(ii) State the importance of genetic code in protein biosynthesis. **Delhi 2019**

Ans. (i) **George Gamow** coined the term genetic code and argued that since there are only four bases and if they have to code for 20 amino acids, the code should constitute a contribution of bases. He suggested that in order to code for all the amino acids the genetic code should be made up of 3 nucleotides.

Har Gobind Khorana developed a chemical method for the synthesis of RNA molecule with defined base combinations (homopolymers and copolymers).

Marshall Nirenberg put forward a cell-free system for protein synthesis that helps in deciphering the code.

Severo Ochoa showed that the polynucleotide phosphorylase also helped in polymerising RNA with defined sequences in a template independent manner (enzymatic RNA synthesis). (4)

(ii) The genetic code is the set of rules by which information encoded in genetic material is translated into proteins by living cells. The genetic code is nearly universal language that encodes directions for cells.

Their arrangement as codons, stores the blueprint for amino acid chain. This chain in turn forms proteins which regulate the biological process in every living beings. (1)

79. What is an operon? Explain the functioning of operon when in an open state. **CBSE 2018 C**

Ans. For operon and functioning of operon, refer to text on page no. 161.

80. Which methodology is used while sequencing the total DNA from a cell? Explain it in detail. **CBSE SQP 2018**

Ans. The Human Genome Project (HGP) is used to sequencing of DNA. For sequencing of DNA, it contains following steps

- Isolate the total content of DNA of a cell by sequence annotation method. (1)
- Convert DNA into random fragments of smaller size by using endonuclease enzymes and clone the DNA in suitable host by using specialised vectors. (1)
- The pieces of DNA are amplified by the Polymerase Chain Reaction (PCR). (1)
- The fragments are sequenced by automated DNA sequences. These are then arranged based on some overlapping regions (present in them). (1)
- Specialised computer based programmes are developed for the alignment of these sequences and these sequences are subsequently annotated and assigned to each chromosome. (1)

81. (i) Explain the role of regulatory gene, operator, promoter and structural genes in *lac* operon when *E. coli* is growing in a culture medium with the source of energy as lactose.

(ii) Mention what would happen if lactose is withdrawn from the culture medium. **Delhi 2016C**

Ans. (i) When many genes are regulated by a single promoter then this arrangement of genes is known as operon.

The various components of an operon are

(a) **Structural genes** Fragments of DNA, which transcribe *m*RNA for polypeptide synthesis.

(b) **Promoter gene** Sequence of DNA, where RNA polymerase binds and initiates transcription.

(c) **Operator** Sequence of DNA adjacent to promoter, where specific repressor protein binds.

(d) **Regulator gene** codes for the repressor protein that binds to the operator and suppresses its activity, hence transcription does not occur. Also, represented as '*i*' gene. (3)

(ii) If lactose is withdrawn from the culture medium, the repressor of the operon is synthesised from the *i* gene. This repressor protein binds to the operator region of operon and prevents RNA polymerase from transcribing the operon. (2)

82. (i) Write any two different levels at which regulation of gene expression could be exerted in eukaryotes.

(ii) Give a labelled schematic representation of '*lac* operon' in its 'switched off' position. **All India 2016**

Ans. (i) The different levels at which regulation of gene expression can be exerted in eukaryotes are following

(a) Transcriptional level (formation of primary transcript).

(b) Processing level (regulation of splicing). (3)

(ii) *Lac* operon in switched off position

When lactose is absent '*i* ' gene regulates and produces repressor *m*RNA in the absence of lactose, which blocks transcription. The repressor protein binds to the operator region of the operon and as a result prevents RNA polymerase from binding to the operon. The operon will be switched off in this situation. (2)

83. (i) How is DNA fingerprinting done? Name any two types of human samples which can be used for DNA fingerprinting. Explain the process sequentially.

(ii) Mention any two situations when the technique is useful. **Outside Delhi 2016C**

Ans. (i) Refer to answer no. 53. **(3)**

Samples that can be used for DNA fingerprinting are nails, blood, hair, skin, etc. **(1)**

(ii) The technique is useful in the following situations

(a) Paternity testing in case of disputes.

(b) In determining population and genetic diversities. **(1)**

84. How do *m*RNA, *t*RNA and ribosomes help in the process of translation? **All India 2015**

Or Name the major types of RNAs and explain their role in the process of protein synthesis in a prokaryote. **Foreign 2014**

Or Explain the process of protein synthesis from processed *m*RNA. **CBSE SQP 2018**

Ans. **Translation** is the process of polymerisation of amino acids to form a polypeptide. The role of *m*RNA, *t*RNA and ribosomes in the process is described below

(i) **Role of *m*RNA** The order and sequence of amino acids are defined by the sequence of bases in the *m*RNA. It stores the genetic information from DNA. The amino acids are joined by a bond, which is known as a peptide bond.

This process requires energy. *m*RNA also possesses untranslated sequences called Untranslated Regions (UTR) at both 5' end and 3' end. They help in efficient translation.

(ii) **Role of *t*RNA** It acts as an adaptor molecule. Activation of amino acids occurs in the presence of ATP and activated amino acids get linked to their cognate *t*RNA, i.e. charging of *t*RNA or aminoacylation of *t*RNA.

If two such charged *t*RNAs are brought closer, the formation of peptide bond between them would occur energetically in the presence of a catalyst.

(iii) **Role of *r*RNA** It is formed in nucleolus and it forms 80% of total RNA present inside the cell.

It is also the most stable type of RNA. It is associated with structural organisation of ribosomes (*r*RNA forms about 60% of weight of ribosomes), which are seats of protein synthesis.

(iv) **Role of ribosomes** Initiation of polypeptide synthesis occurs in ribosomes (cellular factory for protein synthesis).

Ribosome consists of structural RNAs and about 80 different proteins.

In its inactive state, it exists as two subunits, i.e. a large and a small subunit. When the small subunit encounters an *m*RNA, the process of translation of the *m*RNA to protein begins.

There are two sites in the large subunit, i.e. the **P-site** and **A-site** for subsequent amino acids to bind to and thus be close enough to each other for the formation of a peptide bond.

The small subunit (with the *t*RNA) attaches to the large subunit in such a way that the initiation codon (AUG) comes to the P-site.

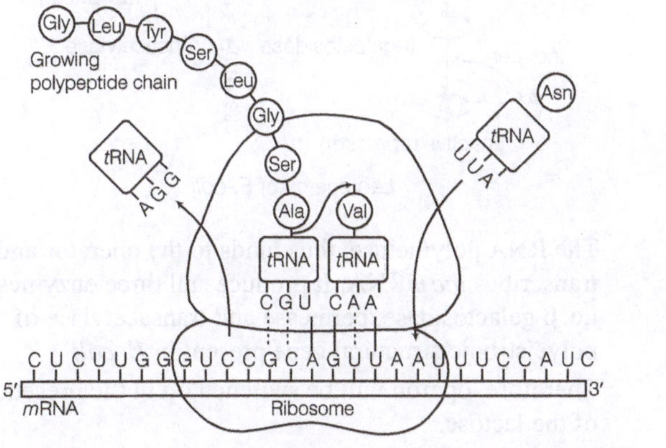

Translation

Concept Enhancer Proteins are made only when they are needed in the cell for cellular functions, that is why the mRNA codes for any protein has a stop codon which results in the termination of protein chain synthesis.

85. Sketch a schematic diagram of *lac* operon in switched on position. How is the operon switched off ? Explain. **Outside Delhi 2015C**

Ans. Refer to fig 5.11 on page no. 161 and answer no. 82 (ii).

86. (i) Write the specific features of the genetic code AUG.

(ii) Genetic codes can be universal and degenerate. Write about them, giving one example of each.

(iii) Explain aminoacylation of the *t*RNA. **All India 2013**

Ans. (i) Refer to answer no. 22.

(ii) Refer to answer no. 55 (ii).

(iii) Refer to answer no. 34.

87. Given below is the schematic representation of *lac* operon of *E. coli*. Explain the functioning of this operon when lactose is provided in the growth medium of the bacteria.

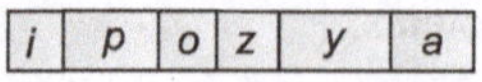

Delhi 2013C

Ans. Lactose in the *lac* operon regulates operon, by switching on and off. If lactose is present in the medium, it acts as an inducer here and the substrate for the enzyme β-galactosidase. It binds to the repressor and forms an inactive repressor, which fails to bind to the operator region of the operon.

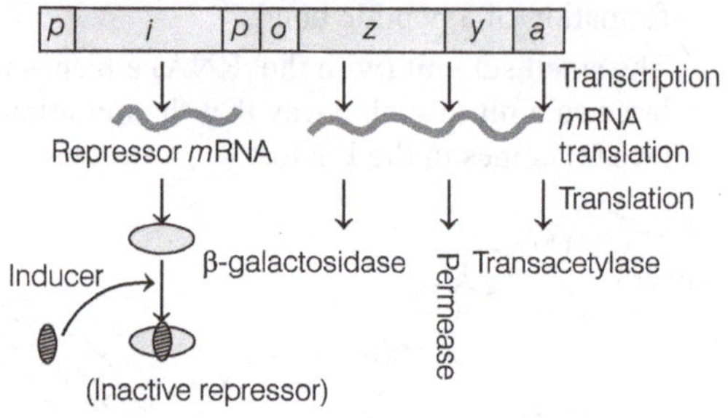

Lac operon of *E. coli*

The RNA polymerase, thus binds to the operator and transcribes *lac m*RNA. It produces all three enzymes, i.e. β-galactosidase, permease and transacetylase of polycistronic structural gene present in *E. coli*

Therefore, operon will be switched on in the presence of the lactose.

Miscellaneous Questions

3 Marks Question

1. (i) Name the enzyme responsible for transcription of *t*RNA and the amino acid, the initiator *t*RNA gets linked with.

(ii) Explain the role of initiator *t*RNA in initiation of protein synthesis. **Delhi 2012**

Ans. (i) RNA polymerase transcribes *t*RNA and the amino acid, the initiator *t*RNA gets linked with is methionine. **(1)**

(ii) The initiator *t*RNA binds the amino acid methionine at its amino acid acceptor site.

It has anticodon loop, which has anticodon for methionine, i.e. UAC. It recognises the start codon (AUG) at P-site and binds to it according to complementarity of bases. **(2)**

5 Marks Questions

2. (i) Describe the process of aminoacylation.

(ii) 'Process of transcription and translation are coupled in prokaryotes, but not in eukaryotes'. Explain. **All India 2019**

Ans. (i) Refer to answer no. 34. **(1)**

(ii) In bacteria, both processes occur in cytoplasm as there is no nucleus. In eukaryotes, transcription occurs in nucleus, while translation occurs in the cytoplasm. **(1)**

Complexities in Eukaryotic Transcription

Eukaryotes have additional complexities in gene expression than prokaryotes as mentioned in gene expression below

(a) There are at least three RNA polymerases in the nucleus other than the RNA polymerase in organelles. The **RNA polymerase-I** transcribes *r*RNAs (28S, 18S and 5.8S). **RNA polymerase-III** is responsible for the transcription of *t*RNA, 5*sr*RNA and *sn*RNAs (small nuclear RNAs).

RNA polymerase-II transcribes precursor of *m*RNA, the heterogeneous nuclear RNA (*hn*RNA).

(b) Another complexity is that, the primary transcripts contain both the exons and the introns and are non-functional. Hence, it is subjected to a process called **splicing**. In this process, introns are removed and exons are joined in a definite order.

(c) *hn*RNA undergoes additional processing called **capping** and **tailing**. In capping, an unusual nucleotide is added to the 5′ end of *hn*RNA.

In tailing, adenylate residues (200-300) are added at 3′ end in a template. Capping and tailing protect the *m*RNA from degradation by the activity of digestive enzymes present in the cytoplasm.

It is the fully processed *hn*RNA, now called *m*RNA, that is transported out of the nucleus for translation process.

Complexities in Translation in Eukaryotes

- The *m*RNA formed in nucleus has to be transported to the cytoplasm.
- Transcription and translation cannot be coupled in eukaryotes. **(3)**

3. (i) Describe the structure and function of a *t*RNA molecule. Why is it referred to as an adapter molecule?
(ii) Explain the process of splicing of *hn*RNA in a eukaryotic cell. **All India 2017**

Ans. (i) **Structure of *t*RNA**
The secondary structure of *t*RNA looks like a clover-leaf.

- All *t*RNA molecules have a guanine residue at its 5′ end.
- At its 3′ end an unpaired CCA sequence is present. Amino acids get attached to this end during translation.
- *t*RNA has an anticodon loop, an amino acid acceptor arm and a ribosome site.
- The anticodon loop has bases complementary to the code. Amino acid acceptor end binds to amino acids.

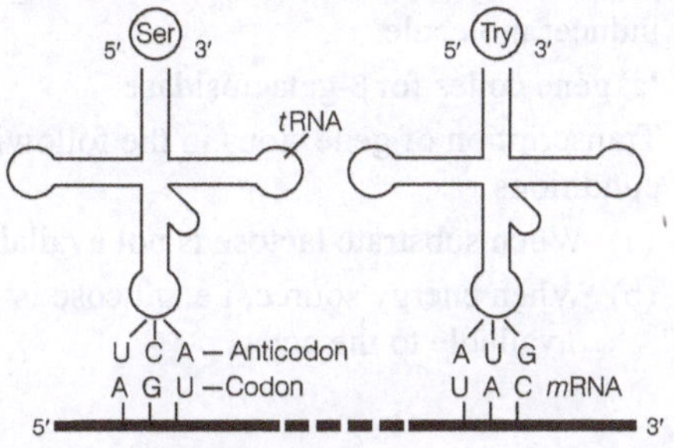

*t*RNA-the adapter molecule

Function of *t*RNA The function of *t*RNA is to align the required amino acids according to the nucleotide sequence of *m*RNA.
*t*RNA is also called the **adapter molecule** because on one hand it can read the code and on the other hand it can bind to specific amino acid. It acts as intermediate molecule between triplet code of *m*RNA and amino acid sequence of polypeptide chain. **(3)**

(ii) **Splicing of *hn*RNA** Eukaryotic transcripts possess extra segments called introns or intervening sequences or non-coding sequences. They do not appear in mature or processed RNA. The functional coding sequences are called **exons**. Splicing is removal of introns and fusion of exons to form functional RNAs. A complex called spliceosome is formed between 5′ end (GU) and 3′ end (AG) of intron. Energy is obtained from ATP. It removes the introns. The adjacent exons are brought together. The ends are sealed by RNA ligase. **(2)**

Case Based/Source Based/Passage Based Questions (Based on Complete Chapter)

1. Read the following and answer the questions given below

The process of copying genetic information from one strand of the DNA into RNA is called transcription. Also, the process or transcription is governed by the principle of complementarity, except the adenosine now forms base pair with uracil instead of thymine, unlike replication, which once set in the total DNA of an organism gets duplicated in transcription only a segment of DNA or only of the two strands is copied into RNA.

(i) Which of the following are the regions of transcription unit?
(a) Promoter (b) Structural genes
(c) Terminator (d) All of these

(ii) Which enzyme catalyses polymerisation in transcription?
(a) DNA-dependent DNA polymerase
(b) DNA-dependent RNA polymerase
(c) Helicase
(d) Gyrase

(iii) Which of the following diagram is correct.
(a)
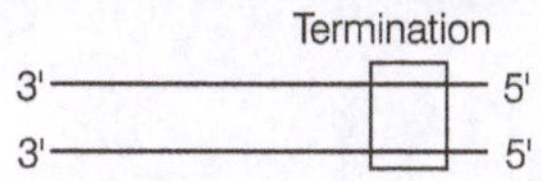

(b)
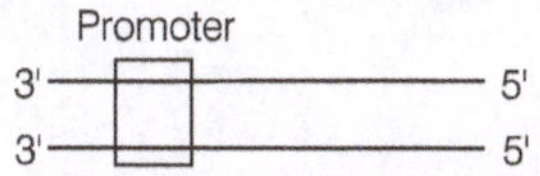

(c)
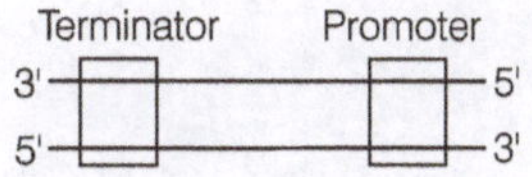

(d)
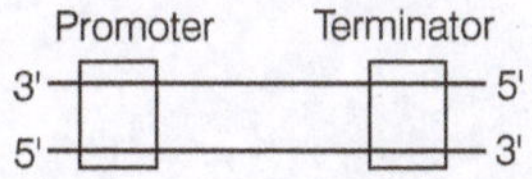

(iv) The terminator is located at
(a) 5′ end (b) 3′ end
(c) Both 5′ end and 3′ end (d) None of these

(v) The strand with 5′ ⟶ 3′ polarity is
(a) coding strand (b) template strand
(c) non-coding strand (d) replicating strand

Ans. (i)-(d), (ii)-(b), (iii)-(d), (iv)-(b), (v)-(a)

2.

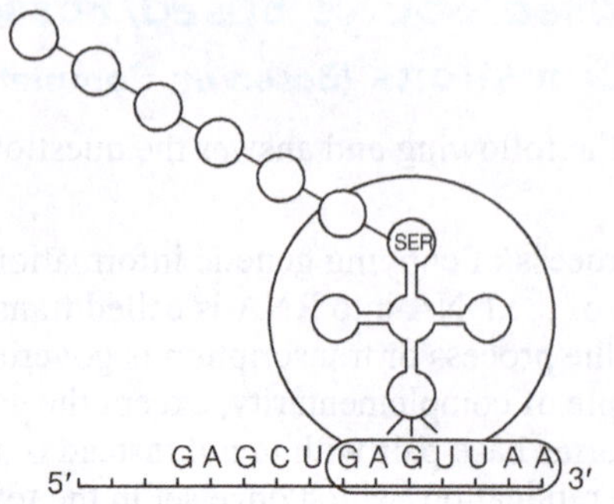

Study the figure given above and answer the following questions.

(i) Mention the DNA sequence coding for serine.

(ii) Write the anticodon of *t*RNA for the same amino acid.

(iii) Why are some untranslated sequence of bases seen in *m*RNA coding for a polypeptide? Where exactly are they present on *m*RNA?

Ans. (i) AGU **(1)**

(ii) Anticodon is UCA. **(1)**

(ii) The untranslated regions are required for efficient translation process.

They are present before the initiation codon at the 5′ end and after the stop/termination codon at the 3′ end. **(2)**

3. Study the figure given below and answer the following questions.

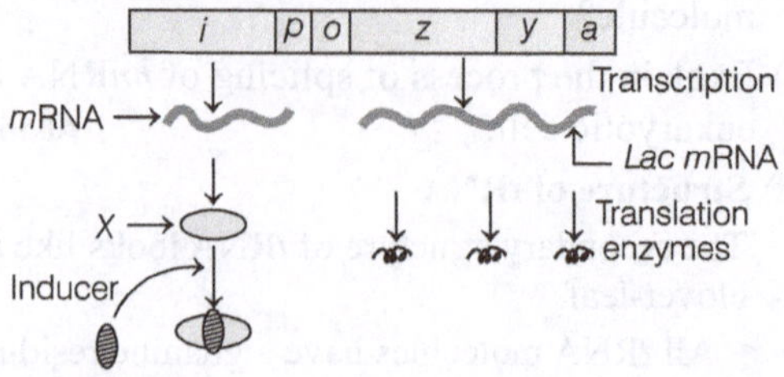

(i) Identify the molecule '*X*' synthesised by '*i*' gene. How does this molecule get inactivated?

(ii) Identify the structural gene that codes for β-galactosidase.

(iii) When does the transcription of this gene get stopped?

Ans. (i) Molecule '*X*' synthesised by '*i*' gene is a repressor protein. It gets inactivated on combining with an inducer molecule. **(1)**

(ii) '*z*' gene codes for β-galactosidase. **(1)**

(iii) Transcription of gene stops in the following conditions

(a) When substrate lactose is not available.

(b) When energy source, i.e. glucose is available to the cells. **(2)**

CHAPTER TEST

01 Mark Questions

Multiple Choice Questions

1 DNA is better genetic material than RNA because DNA
(a) has reactive 2′ OH group
(b) mutates at a faster rate
(c) is less reactive
(d) has uracil instead of thymine

2 Which of the following Chargaff's rules is incorrect?
(a) The DNA molecule has equal A—T and G—C base pairs
(b) Purines (A+ G) are always equal to pyrimidines (T + C)
(c) The amount of A is always equal to that of T and the amount of G is always equal to that of C
(d) The base ratio A+ T / G+ C varies for a given species

3 What would happen if in a gene encoding a polypeptide of 50 amino acids 25th (UAC) is mutated to UAA?
(a) A polypeptide of 49 amino acids will be formed
(b) A polypeptide of 25 amino acids will be formed
(c) A polypeptide of 24 amino acids will be formed
(d) Two polypeptides of 24 and 25 amino acids will be formed

4 ……… stabilises the chain in the single-stranded form to reduce the energy needed to unwind the DNA helix.
(a) Topoisomerase (b) Helicase
(c) SSB protein (d) Gyrase

5 Select the incorrect statements from the following.
I. Jacob and Monod proposed operon hypothesis for regulations of gene action.
II. Operon is segment of DNA that comprises of one structural gene, operator gene, promoter gene and regulator gene.
III. Inducible operon is switched on when inducer is present.
IV. Repressible operon is switched on when co-repressor is present.
(a) I and II (b) II and IV
(c) II, III and IV (d) None of these

Assertion-Reason Type Questions

Direction (Q. Nos. 6-9) *In the questions given below two statements an **Assertion** and a **Reason** are given. Give the appropriate response as*
(a) If both Assertion and Reason are true and Reason is the correct explanation of Assertion
(b) If both Assertion and Reason are true, but Reason is not the correct explanation of Assertion
(c) If Assertion is true, but Reason is false
(d) If Assertion is false, but Reason is true

6 **Assertion** Amber codon is a termination codon.
Reason If in an *m*RNA, a termination codon is present, the protein synthesis stops abruptly whether the protein synthesis is complete or not.

7 **Assertion** Only sense strand of DNA is copied into *m*RNA.
Reason The antisense strand plays a role in replication.

8 **Assertion** For replication of DNA, a small RNA chain is required as a primer.
Reason DNA polymerase cannot initiate synthesis of a new DNA strand.

9 **Assertion** A monocistronic *m*RNA can produce several types of polypeptide chains.
Reason The terminator codon is present on the *m*RNA.

2/3 Marks Questions

10 Differentiate between leading and lagging strand.

11 Discuss the role of enzyme DNA ligase during DNA replication.

12 It is established that RNA is the first genetic material. Explain giving three reasons.

13 Describe the initiation process of transcription in bacteria.

14 Give any three features of genetic code.

15 Retroviruses do not follow central dogma. Comment.

16 Explain the significance of satellite DNA in DNA fingerprinting technique.

05 Marks Questions

17 How did Hershey and Chase establish that DNA is transfered from virus to bacteria?

18 Explain the process of DNA replication with the help of schematic diagram.

19 Briefly describe any two of the following.

(i) Translation (ii) *Lac* operon

(iii) Genetic code

20 Briefly describe the technique employed in DNA fingerprinting.

21 Observe the representation of genes involved in the *lac* operon given below.

(i) Identify the region where the repressor protein will attach normally.

(ii) Under certain conditions repressor is unable to attach at this site. Explain.

(iii) If repressor fails to attach to the site what products will be formed by *z*, *y* and *a*?

(iv) Analyse why this kind of regulation is called negative regulation.

22 Refer to the below mentioned flow diagram and answer the questions that follows

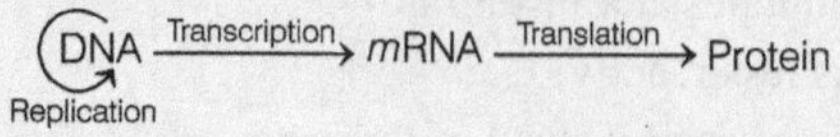

(i) What information is derived from the above mentioned flow diagram?

(ii) Who proposed this concept?

(iii) Is there any exception to this concept? If yes, describe it.

Answers

1. (c)	**2.** (d)	**3.** (c)	**4.** (c)	**5.** (b)
6. (a)	**7.** (d)	**8.** (c)	**9.** (b)	

06 Evolution

TREND ANALYSIS 3 YEARS

Average No. of Questions Across all Sets

	Types of Questions	2024	2023	2020
TOPIC 01 The Origin of Life and Evidences of Evolution	1 Mark	0	0	0
	2 Marks	0	0	0
	3 Marks	1	2	1
	4 Marks (Case Based)	0	0	0
	5 Marks	0	0	0
TOPIC 02 Theories of Evolution and Biological Evolution	1 Mark	0	1	0
	2 Marks	1	0	0
	3 Marks	0	1	1
	4 Marks	0	0	0
	5 Marks (Case Based)	0	0	0

TOPIC 1

The Origin of Life and Evidences of Evolution

The study of history of life forms on earth is called **evolutionary biology**. **Evolution** is a process that results in heritable changes in the genotype, which spread over many generations, leading to the diversity of organisms on earth. In simple words, evolution is the sequence of gradual changes from simple life forms to complex life forms over million of years.

Origin of Life

It is considered a unique event in the history of our universe.

Origin of Universe

- It is about **20 billion** years old. It contains huge galaxies.
- **Galaxies** contain stars, clouds of gas and dust.
- The origin of universe is explained by **Big Bang theory** given by **Abbe Lemaitre** in 1931.
- The Big Bang theory states that the universe arose from a huge explosion. As the universe expanded, temperature came down and hydrogen and helium were formed later. The galaxies were then formed due to the condensation of gases under gravitation.

Origin of Earth

- There was no atmosphere on the early earth. It was supposed to be formed about 4.5 billion years back in the solar system of the milkyway galaxy.
- Water vapour, methane, carbon dioxide and ammonia released from molten masses covered the surface of early earth.

- UV-rays from the sun broke up the water molecules into hydrogen and oxygen and the lighter hydrogen escaped.
- Oxygen combined with ammonia and methane to form water, carbon dioxide and other compounds.
- Subsequently ozone layer formed. As the earth cooled, water vapour fell as rain to fill the depressions and formed oceans.
- Life appeared 500 million (about 4 billion years back) years after the formation of earth.

Theories of Origin of Life

Various theories of origin of life were given by different thinkers and scientists. These are as follows

(i) **Theory of special creation** states that God created life by his divine act of creation. It was proposed by Father **Suarez.**

(ii) **Theory of panspermia/cosmozoic creation** states that the spores or panspermia came from the outer space and developed into living forms. It was given by **Arrhenius.**

(iii) **Theory of spontaneous generation** states that life originated from decaying and rotting matter like straw, mud, etc. This theory is also known as **theory of abiogenesis** or **autobiogenesis.**

- **Louis Pasteur** rejected the theory of spontaneous generation by swan-neck flask experiment. He demonstrated that life came from pre-existing life.
- In his experiment, he kept killed yeast cells in pre-sterilised flask and in another flask open into air. The life did not evolve in the former, but new living organisms evolved in the second flask.

(iv) **Theory of chemical evolution** or **Oparin-Haldane theory** states that life originated from pre-existing non-living organic molecules and that the formation of life was preceded by chemical evolution.

The conditions on the earth that favoured chemical evolution were very high temperature, volcanic storms and reducing atmosphere that contained CH_4, NH_3, water vapour, etc.

Experimental Evidence of Chemical Evolution

Miller's experiment provided experimental evidence for chemical evolution.

- The experiment was carried out by **SL Miller** and **HC Urey** in 1953.
- They took a closed flask containing CH_4, H_2, NH_3 in the ratio of 2 : 2 : 1 and water vapour at 800°C and created an electric discharge. These conditions were similar to those in primitive atmosphere.
- After a week, formation of amino acids was observed. Complex molecules like sugars, nitrogen bases, pigments and fats were seen in the flask by other scientists.
- Miller and Urey supported the idea of abiogenesis followed by chemical evolution. Analysis of the meteorite also revealed the presence of similar compounds.
- The concept of chemical evolution of life was more or less accepted.

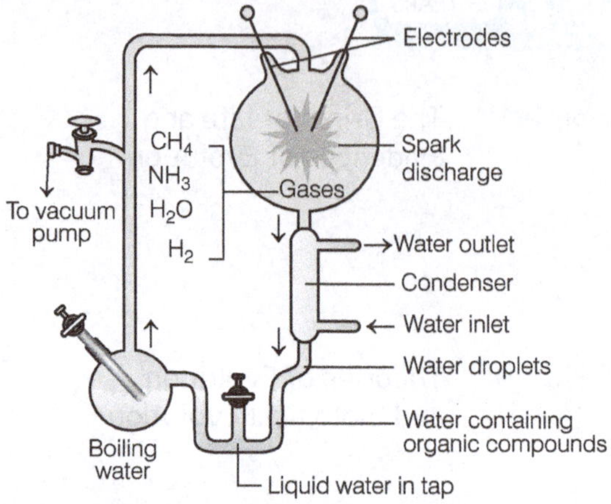

Figure 6.1 Diagrammatic representation of Miller-Urey's experiment

Origin of First Cell

- First non-cellular life forms originated 3 billion years ago. These molecules were like RNA, protein and polysaccharides inside a self-replicating metabolic capsule which later reproduced its molecules.
- Cellular life form first evolved about 2000 million years ago. These were single-celled and formed in aquatic environment.
- This form of abiogenesis, i.e. the first form of life arose slowly through evolutionary forces from non-living molecules, was accepted by many scientists.

Evidences of Evolution

Evidences that suggest that evolution had occurred on earth are derived from

(i) Palaeontology
(ii) Embryology
(iii) Comparative anatomy and morphology
(iv) Biochemical/Physiology
(v) Biogeography

Palaeontological Evidences

- Palaeontology is the study of fossils. The fossils are the remains of past organisms preserved in **sedimentary rocks.**
- Different aged rock sediments contain fossils of different life forms, which died during the formation of particular sediment.
- Some organisms appear similar to modern organisms. They represent extinct organisms like dinosaurs.
- A study of fossils in different sedimentary layers indicates the geological period in which they existed.
- The study showed that life forms varied over time and certain life forms are restricted to certain geological time scale. Hence, new forms of life have evolved at different times in the history of earth.

Embryological Evidences

The study of comparative embryology shows common patterns of development among different species.

- The principles of embryonic development were given by **von Baer**.
- **Ernst Haeckel** propounded **the theory of recapitulation** or **biogenetic law**, which stated that an individual organism in its development (ontogeny) tends to repeat the stages passed through by its ancestors (phylogeny), i.e. ontogeny recapitulates phylogeny.
- This means that the life history of an animal reflects its evolutionary history.
  For example, during the life history, frog's tadpole larva resembles fishes, hence the latter are considered as the ancestors of amphibians. The presence of gill clefts in all vertebrate embryos including human provides a strong embryological evidence.

Comparative Anatomy and Morphological Evidences

These studies highlight the similarities and differences among the organisms of today and those that existed years ago. The evidences of evolution based on comparative study of external and internal structure are as follows

Homology

- In an organism, the homology indicates common ancestry.
- The organs with same structural design and origin, but perform different functions are called **homologous organs**. For example, forelimbs of some animals like whales, bats and cheetah have similar anatomical structure, such as humerus, radius, ulna, carpals, metacarpals and phalanges. But, these forelimbs perform different functions in these animals. Other examples of homology are vertebrate heart and brain.

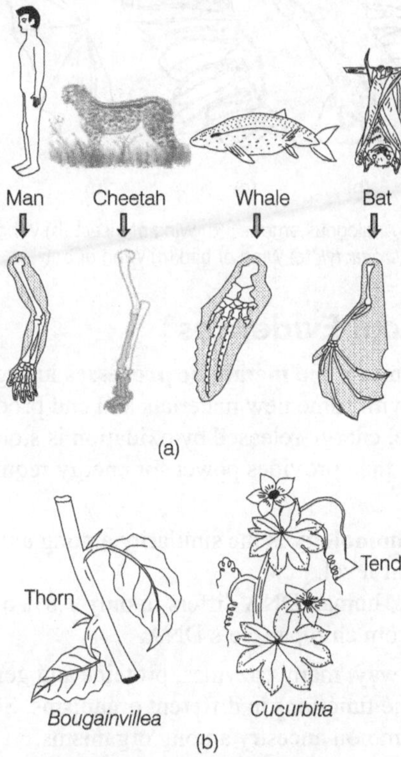

Figure 6.2 Homologous organs : (a) In animals (forelimb), (b) In plants (thorn and tendril)

- In plants, thorns and tendrils of *Bougainvillea* and *Cucurbita* represent homology.
- Homology is based on **divergent evolution,** i.e. the same structure developed along different directions due to adaptations to different needs.

Analogy

- It refers to a situation exactly opposite to homology.
- Organs which are anatomically different, but functionally similar are called **analogous organs**. For example, wings of butterfly and birds. In both organisms, wings perform same function, but they have different origin and structure.
- Analogous organs are formed as a result of **convergent evolution**. It is the evolution in which different structures evolve to perform same function and hence have similarity.
- Other examples of analogy are eyes of *Octopus* and mammals; flippers of penguins and dolphins.

- In plants, sweet potato (root modification) and potato (stem modification) are analogous structures.

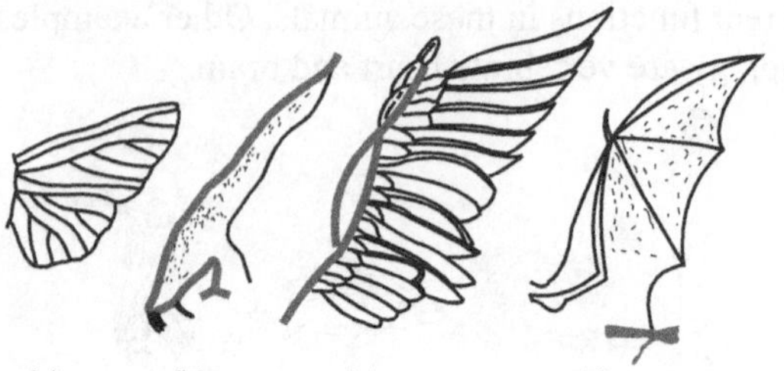

Figure 6.3 Analogous organs : (a) Wing of insect (b) Wing of *Pterodactyl* (c) Wing of bird (d) Wing of bat

Biochemical Evidences

- These account for the **metabolic processes** in organisms, are similar with some new materials and end products. For example, energy released by oxidation is stored in ATP, which then provides power for energy requiring processes.
- **Molecular homology** is the similarity among animals at the molecular level.
  For example, human DNA differs in only 1.8% of its base pairs from chimpanzee's DNA.
- In the same way, many enzymes, proteins and genes perform same functions in different organisms. So, it indicates common ancestry among organisms.

Biogeographical Evidences

These evidences are derived from the species which are restricted to a region and develop unique features. Also, many species present in far separated regions show similarity in their ancestry.

This can be explained with the help of following processes

Adaptive Radiation

It is an evolutionary process in which an ancestral stock gives rise to new species that are adapted to new habitats and new ways of life. In other words, adaptive radiation is the evolution of organisms, starting from a point which then radiates or spreads to other habitats. Examples are

(i) **Darwin's finches** These were small black birds, which Darwin observed in **Galapagos Islands.**
- He observed many varieties of finches in the same Island.
- All varieties of finches had evolved from original seed-eating finches.
- There was alternation in beaks enabling some to become insectivorous and some vegetarian.
  All these varieties evolved from original species due to different type of food available at different Islands.

Figure 6.4 Varieties of beaks of finches that Darwin found in Galapagos Islands

(ii) **Marsupials of Australia** A number of marsupials (mammals with pouch), different from each other, evolved from an ancestral stock, all within the Australian Island continent.

Convergent Evolution

It is the occurrence of more than one adaptive radiation in an isolated geographical area with different habitats. Examples of adaptive convergence or convergent evolution are Australian marsupials and placental mammals in North America.

Convergent Evolution of Australian Marsupials and Placental Mammals

Australian marsupial	Placental mammal
Marsupial mole	Mole
Numbat (banded anteater)	Anteater
Marsupial mouse	Mouse
Spotted cuscus	Lemur
Flying phalanger (sugar glider)	Flying squirrel
Tasmanian tiger cat	Bobcat
Tasmanian wolf	Wolf

PYQs Previous Years' Questions

1 Mark Questions

Multiple Choice Question

1. Evolutionary convergence is the development of a **CBSE SQP 2023**
   (a) common set of functions in groups of different ancestry
   (b) dissimilar set of functions in closely related groups
   (c) common set of structures in closely related groups
   (d) dissimilar set of functions in unrelated groups

Ans. (a) common set of functions in groups of different ancestry

Very Short Answer Type Questions

2. State the two principal outcomes of the experiments conducted by Louis Pasteur on origin of life. **Delhi 2019**

Ans. Louis Pasteur's experiments demonstrated that life comes only from pre-existing life. He showed that in swan-neck pre-sterilised flasks, life did not evolve from 'killed yeast' while in another flask open to air, new living organisms arose from 'killed yeast.'

3. State two postulates of Oparin and Haldane's theory with reference to the origin of life. **All India 2017**

Or Write the hypothetical proposals put forth by Oparin and Haldane. **Foreign 2015**

Ans. Oparin and Haldane proposed the following postulates with reference to origin of life.
(i) The first form of life came from pre-existing non-living organic molecules. (½)
(ii) The conditions on earth favouring chemical evolution were high temperature, volcanic storms and reducing atmosphere. (½)

4. Why are analogous structures a result of convergent evolution? **All India 2014**

Ans. When two species have structures that are similar in function, but differ in origin and anatomy, they are called analogous structures. These structures develop in different species which move from different areas to a common habitat where they adapt themselves accordingly, therefore it is called convergent evolution.

5. Name the type of evolution that has resulted in the development of structures like wings of butterfly and bird. What are such structures called? **Delhi 2014C**

Ans. Convergent evolution has resulted in the development of structures like wings of butterfly and birds. Such structures are called analogous organs.

6. Write the term used for resemblance of varieties of placental mammals to corresponding marsupials in Australia. **Delhi 2013C**

Ans. Adaptive radiation occurring through parallel evolution results in the resemblance of placental mammals to marsupials in Australia.

7. Identify the examples of convergent evolution from the following
   (i) Flippers of penguins and dolphins
   (ii) Eyes of *Octopus* and mammals
   (iii) Vertebrate brains **Delhi 2013**

Ans. (i) and (ii) are the examples of analogous organs representing convergent evolution.
Vertebrate brains are the example of divergent evolution.

8. Identify the examples of homologous structures from the following **Delhi 2013**
   (i) Vertebrate hearts
   (ii) Thorns in *Bougainvillea* and tendrils of *Cucurbita*.
   (iii) Food storage organs in sweet potato and potato.

Ans. Homologous organs are derived through divergent evolution, thus indicating common ancestry.
Examples of homology are
(i) Vertebrate heart and brain.
(ii) In plants, thorns and tendrils of *Bougainvillea* and *Cucurbita* represent homology.
(iii) Food storage organs, i.e. tubers in sweet potato and potato are analogous organs.

9. State the significance of the study of fossils in evolution. **Delhi 2012**

Ans. Fossils help us to know the morphological details of the organisms that were present in the past and relate them to the organisms of the present for better understanding of the process of evolution. We can also trace the time at which the particular organism existed.

10. State the significance of biochemical similarities among diverse organisms in evolution. **Delhi 2012**

Ans. Similarities in biochemicals such as DNA, help in deriving the line of evolution. Organisms with more similar DNA sequences are considered close relatives that might have evolved from the same ancestor.

11. Write the similarity between the wings of a butterfly and the wings of a bat. What do you infer from the above, with reference to evolution? **Delhi 2012**

Or Comment on the similarity between the wings of a cockroach and the wings of a bird. What do you infer from the above, with reference to evolution? **All India 2012**

Or Comment on the similarity between the flippers of dolphins and penguins, with reference to evolution. **Foreign 2012**

Ans. Similarity between the wings of butterfly and bat or cockroach and bird or flippers of dolphins and penguins is that they perform similar functions, but they are dissimilar in their basic structure and development. They are thus analogous organs. With reference to evolution, it can be inferred that these are formed as a result of convergent evolution.

12. Name the scientist who disproved spontaneous generation theory. **Delhi 2010**

Ans. Louis Pasteur disproved the spontaneous generation theory through his swan-neck flask experiment.

2 Marks Questions

13. (i) Identify the following pairs as homologous or analogous organs.
(a) Sweet potato and potato.
(b) Eye of *Octopus* and eye of mammals.
(c) Thorns of *Bougainvillea* and tendrils of *Cucurbita*.
(d) Forelimbs of bat and whale.
(ii) State the kind of evolution they represent. **All India 2015**

Or (i) Select the homologous structures from the combinations given below.
(a) Forelimbs of whale and bat.
(b) Tuber of potato and sweet potato.
(c) Eyes of *Octopus* and mammals.
(d) Thorns of *Bougainvillea* and tendrils of *Cucurbita*.
(ii) State the kind of evolution they represent. **All India 2015**

Or Select two pairs from the following which exhibit divergent evolution. Give reasons for your answer.
(i) Forelimbs of cheetah and mammals.
(ii) Flippers of dolphins and penguins.
(iii) Wings of butterflies and birds.
(iv) Forelimbs of whales and mammals. **All India 2015**

Or Write about the ancestry and evolution of bat, horse and human on the basis of a comparative study of their forelimbs. What are these limbs categorised as? **Delhi 2013C**

Ans. (i) The given pairs are identified as
(a) Analogous organs. (b) Analogous organs.
(c) Homologous organs. (d) Homologous organs.
(ii) (c) and (d) represent divergent evolution while (a) and (b) represent convergent evolution.

Or (i) (a) Forelimbs of whales and bats and (d) thorns of *Bougainvillea* and tendrils of *Cucurbita* are homologous organs.
(ii) Both these structures represent divergent evolution, i.e. sharing common ancestry, organs with same fundamental structure but different functions.

Or Divergent evolution is represented by (i) and (ii).

Or All mammals, i.e. whales, cheetah, bat, horse and human share similarities in the pattern of bones of forelimbs. These forelimbs though perform different functions, but have similar anatomical structure, i.e. all of them have humerus, radius, ulna, carpals, metacarpals and phalanges in their forelimbs. Hence, the same structure is developed along different directions due to the adaptations to different needs in these animals. This is called divergent evolution and these structures are homologous.

Common Mistakes Students get confused about the relation between these four terms; homologous organs, analogous organs, convergent evolution and divergent evolution.

These can be explained as

Homologous organs are formed as a result of divergent evolution, whereas analogous organs are formed as a result of convergent evolution.

14. Explain with the help of an example the type of evolution homology is based on. **Delhi 2015C**

Or Divergent evolution leads to homologous structures. Explain with the help of an example. **All India 2011C**

Ans. Divergent evolution is a process, where the same structure develops along different directions in different organisms due to adaptations to different needs. Divergent evolution leads to the development of homologous structures, as they all have similar anatomical structure and origin, but perform different functions. **(1)**

For example, the thorns of *Bougainvillea* and tendrils of *Cucurbita* are homologous organs as both of them are modified axillary buds, which perform different functions. **(1)**

15. (i) Explain adaptive radiation with the help of suitable example.
(ii) Cite an example where more than one adaptive radiation have occurred in an isolated geographical area.

Name the type of evolution your example depicts and state why is it so named? **All India 2014**

Ans. (i) The process of evolution of different species in a given geographical area starting from a point and literally radiating to other areas or habitat is called adaptive radiation, e.g. alterations in beaks of finches on Galapagos Islands. (1)

(ii) An example where more than one adaptive radiations have occurred in an isolated geographical area is Australian marsupials and placental mammals.

The above cited example depicts convergent evolution as these marsupials show development of similar adaptive functional structures in unrelated groups of organisms. (1)

16. What was proposed by Oparin and Haldane on origin of life? How did SL Miller's experiment support their proposal? **Foreign 2014**

Or

Mention the contribution of SL Miller's experiment to origin of life. **Delhi 2010**

Ans. Oparin and Haldane proposed that life originated on earth spontaneously from non-living matter, i.e. organic molecules.

SL Miller conducted an experiment, which provided experimental evidence for chemical evolution. He created conditions similar to primitive atmosphere, in the laboratory such as high temperature, reducing atmosphere consisting of CH_4, NH_3, etc.

When he created an electric discharge in the flask containing all the above stated components at 800°C, organic molecules, e.g. amino acids were formed.

Results indicated that the first non-cellular forms of life were created about 3 billion years ago. This also supports the hypothesis that life could have originated from organic matter.

17. List the two main propositions of Oparin and Haldane. **All India 2013**

Ans. Two main propositions of Oparin and Haldane were

(i) The primitive atmosphere was reducing, i.e. free oxygen was absent. (1)

(ii) There was high temperature, high methane, ammonia and hydrogen gas in the atmosphere. (1)

18. How do palaeontological evidences support evolution of organisms on earth? **All India 2013C**

Ans. Palaeontology is the study of past life based on fossil records. The study of fossils reveals the type of life forms occurring in the past and highlights the course of evolution of living organisms. The distribution of fossils in the sedimentary rocks of different ages fully supports the concept of evolution. It shows that structure of wing becomes more and more complex as we proceed from earliest to recent times. From the fossil records it has been concluded that evolution has taken place from the simple to complex forms in a gradual manner.

19. Write the Oparin and Haldane's hypothesis about the origin of life on earth. How does meteorite analysis favour this hypothesis? **All India 2013**

Ans. Oparin-Haldane theory states that origin of life is the result of a long series of physiochemical changes, brought about first by chemical evolution and then by biological evolution. (1)

Analysis of meteorites also revealed the presence of similar compounds as found in the primitive atmosphere, indicating the occurrence of similar processes elsewhere in space. (1)

20. Convergent evolution leads to analogous structures. Explain with the help of an example. **All India 2011C**

> **KEY idea**
> Different structure + Same function = Analogous organs and convergent evolution.

Ans. Convergent evolution is a process of evolution, where anatomically dissimilar structures in different organisms perform similar functions. It leads to the formation of analogous structures in different groups of organisms as they perform similar function, but are anatomically different. (1)

Examples, potato (stem modification) and sweet potato (root modification), flippers of penguins and dolphins. (1)

21. Why are wings of butterfly and birds said to be analogous organs? Name the type of evolution the analogous organs are a result of. **Foreign 2010**

Ans. Refer to answer no. 11.

3 Marks Questions

22. (i) Explain the significance of the experiment carried out by SL Miller. Name the scientists whose hypothesis prompted him to carry out this experiment.
(ii) How does meteorite analysis favour this hypothesis? **CBSE 2024 (Set-I)**

Ans. (i) SL Miller performed an experiment to demonstrate that UV radiations or electrical discharges or a combination of these can produce complex organic compounds from a mixture of CH_4, NH_3, H_2 and water vapour (H_2O) at 800°C. He observed the formation of amino acids, sugars, pigments, nitrogen bases and fats in the flask. This theory supported the theory of abiogenesis followed by chemical evolution.

Scientists whose hypothesis prompted him to carry out this experiment were Oparin and Haldane who gave the theory that the first form of life came from pre-existing, non-living organic molecules (e.g. RNA, protein, etc). **(2½)**

(ii) Analysis of meteorite content also revealed similar compounds indicating that similar processes are occurring elsewhere in space. **(½)**

23. Explain how did the experiment conducted by SL Miller substantiate that life evolved from pre-existing non-living organic molecules. **CBSE 2023**

Ans. Refer to the answer no. 37 (second paragraph).

24. Mention Darwin's observations made on finches during his visit to Galapagos Islands. Write the explanations given by Darwin on his observations. **CBSE 2023, 2021-22**

Or Explain adaptive radiation with the help of a suitable example. **Delhi 2015**

Or What do you infer from the resemblance between flying squirrel and flying phalanger with reference to their evolution. **Delhi 2015, 2015C**

Or Explain adaptive radiation and convergent evolution by taking example of some of Australian marsupials and Australian placental mammals. **Foreign 2010**

Or Australian marsupials and placental mammals are suitable examples of adaptive radiation and convergent evolution. Explain by giving reasons. **All India 2010C**

Ans. Adaptive radiation is the process of evolution of different species in a given geographical area starting from a point and radiating to other habitats.

Darwin went to Galapagos Islands and observed that there were many varieties of finches in the same Island. All the varieties evolved on the island itself. Darwin suggested that after originating from a common ancestral seed eating stock, the finches must have radiated to different geographical areas and undergone adaptive changes in their beaks, thus enabling some to become insectivorous while the other remained herbivore and ate seeds.

Or Many Australian marsupials, each different from the other, e.g. kangaroo, sugar glider, etc., evolved from a common ancestral stock, but all within the Australian Island continent.

When more than one adaptive radiation occur in an isolated geographical area, it can be called as convergent evolution. Australian placental mammals also show adaptive radiation in evolving into varieties of such placental mammals, each one of which appears similar to a corresponding marsupial, e.g. placental wolf and Tasmanian wolf, anteater and numbat, flying squirrel and flying phalanger, etc.

25. Mention and explain the type of evolution the thorns of *Bougainvillea* and tendrils of *Cucurbita* are a result of. Write a similar example from animal kingdom. **Delhi 2020**

Ans. Refer to text on page no. 185 (Homology).

26.

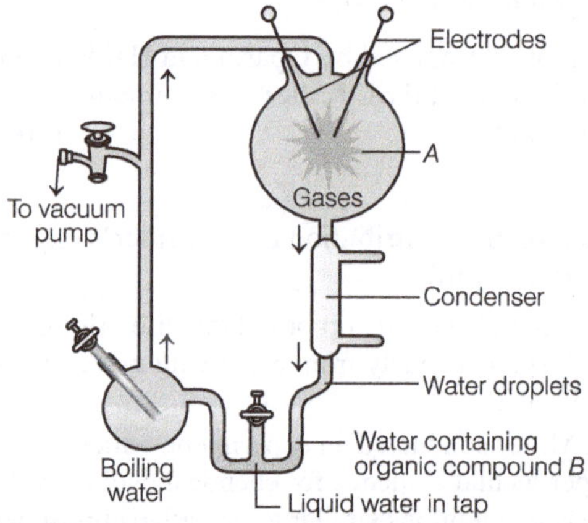

(i) State the hypothesis which SL Miller tried to prove in the laboratory with the help of the setup given above.

(ii) Name the organic compound observed by him in the liquid water at the end of his experiment.

(iii) A scientist stimulated a similar setup and added CH_4, NH_3 and water vapour at 800°C. Mention the important component that is missing in his experiment. **CBSE SQP 2019**

Ans. (i) **Chemical evolution** First form of life originated from pre-existing non-living organic molecules. **(1)**

(ii) SL Miller observed amino acids in the liquid water at the end of his experiment. **(1)**

(iii) H_2 is missing in his experiment. **(1)**

27. Given below is a diagrammatic representation of the experimental setup used by SL Miller for his experiment.

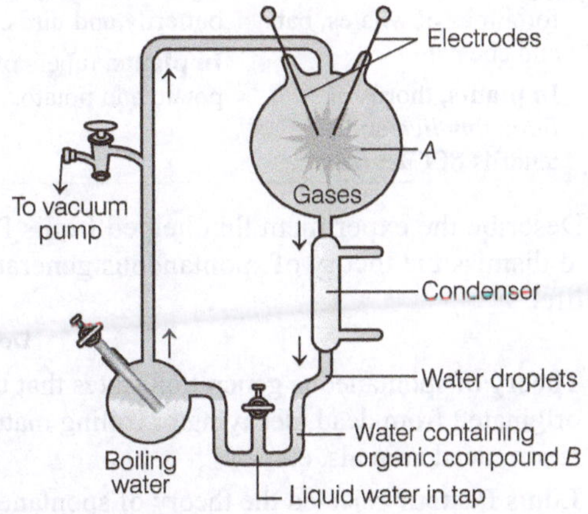

(i) Write the names of different gases contained and the conditions set for the reaction in the flask *A*.
(ii) State the type of organic molecule he collected in the water at *B*.
(iii) Write the conclusion he arrived at. **Delhi 2013C, Foreign 2011**

Ans. (i) Gases were methane, ammonia, hydrogen and water vapour. In '*A*' flask electric discharge was created using electrodes. **(1)**

(ii) The organic molecules collected in water at '*B*' were amino acids. **(1)**

(iii) He concluded that life could have come from pre-existing non-living organic molecules and their formation was preceded by chemical evolution. **(1)**

28. (i) Differentiate between analogous and homologous structures.
(ii) Select and write analogous structures from the list given below.
(a) Wings of butterfly and birds.
(b) Vertebrate hearts.
(c) Tendrils of *Bougainvillea* and *Cucurbita*.
(d) Tubers of sweet potato and potato. **CBSE 2018**

Ans. (i) Differences between analogous structure and homologous structure are

Analogous structures	Homologous structures
These have different basic plan and origin.	These have similar basic plan and origin.
These are adapted to perform same functions.	These are adapted to perform different functions.
These confirm convergent evolution, e.g. eye of *Octopus* and man.	These confirm divergent evolution, e.g. limbs of man and whale.

(2)

(ii) Analogous organs
(a) Wings of butterfly and birds.
(b) Tubers of sweet potato and potato. **(1)**

29. (i) Name the different gases contained in the flask used as an experimental setup by SL Miller.
(ii) On the basis of composition of gases in this experiment, what was the condition in the flask?
(iii) Write the conclusion drawn from this experiment. **CBSE SQP 2018**

Ans. (i) The different gases in the flask used as experimental setup by SL Miller were methane (CH_4), ammonia (NH_3), hydrogen (H_2) and water vapour. **(1)**

(ii) On the basis of composition of gases, the condition in the flask was anaerobic or anoxygenic. **(1)**

(iii) Urey and Miller conducted an experiment to prove theory of biogenesis and observed formation of amino acids. This experiment supported that life has come from pre-existing non-living organic molecules. **(1)**

30. Refer to the figure given below and answer the questions that follows

Wolf Tasmanian wolf

(i) Explain the process by which Tasmanian wolf evolved.
(ii) Name the process that has resulted in evolution of wolf and another animal such as Tasmanian wolf.
(iii) Compare and contrast the two animals shown. **CBSE SQP 2018**

Ans. (i) The Tasmanian wolf has evolved by the process of **adaptive radiation**. It is the process of evolution of different species in a given geographical area starting from a point and literally radiating to other geographical areas (habitats). **(1)**

(ii) The other related animals like placental wolf and Tasmanian wolf marsupials have evolved by the process of **convergent evolution**. **(1)**

(iii) The wolf is a placental animal, whereas Tasmanian wolf is a marsupial mammal. **(1)**

31. How do homologous organs represent divergent evolution? Explain with the help of a suitable example. **Delhi 2016**

Ans. **Homologous organs as divergent evolution**

Homology is the relation among the organs of different groups of organisms, that show similarity in the basic structure and embryonic development, but have different functions.

Homology in organs indicates common ancestry.

It is based on divergent evolution. When due to different needs, some structures develop differently, the condition is called **divergent evolution.** This results in the formation of **homologous organs.**

Examples of homology in plants and animals are as follows

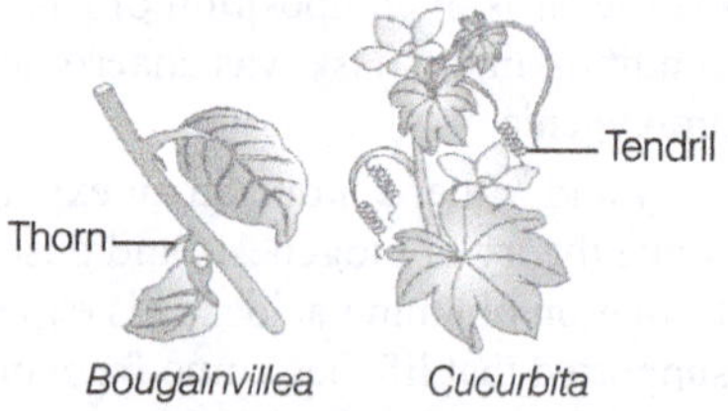

Thorns of *Bougainvillea* and tendrils of *Cucurbita*

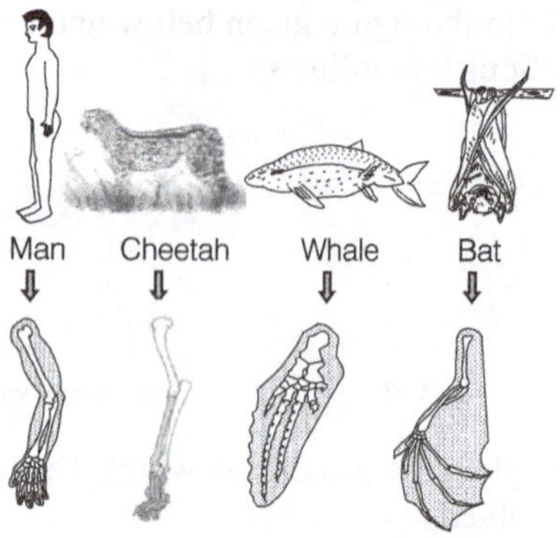

Forelimbs of animals like whale, bat, cheetah and man

32. Differentiate between homology and analogy. Give one example of each. **All India 2016**

Or Differentiate between divergent and convergent evolution. Give one example of each. **Outside Delhi 2016**

Ans. Differences between homology and analogy are

Homology/Divergent evolution	Analogy/Convergent evolution
Homology is based on divergent evolution.	Analogy is based on convergent evolution.
Structures are anatomically similar, but functionally different.	Structures are anatomically different but functionally similar.
e.g. **in animals,** forelimbs of whales, bats and cheetah. **In plants,** thorns of *Bougainvillea* and tendrils of *Cucurbita.*	e.g. **in animals,** wings of butterfly and birds. **In plants,** tubers of sweet potato and potato.

33. Describe the experiment that helped Louis Pasteur to dismiss the theory of spontaneous generation of life. **Delhi 2016C**

Ans. Theory of spontaneous generation states that the life originated from dead, decaying or rolling matters like storm, dead animals, etc.

Louis Pasteur rejected the theory of spontaneous generation and demonstrated that life had evolved from pre-existing life. In his experiment, he kept killed yeast cells in presterilised flask and in another flask open into air. The life did not evolve in the former, but new living organisms evolved in the another flask.

Concept Enhancer Redi in 1668 and Spallanzani in 1765 work separately and rejected the theory of spontaneous generation. They believe that life comes from pre-existing life.

34. Explain convergent evolution with the help of two examples. **Foreign 2015**

Ans. Refer to answer no. 20.

35. Explain the interpretation of Charles Darwin who observed a variety of small black birds on Galapagos Islands. **Delhi 2015**

Ans. Darwin found the variations in the beaks of small black birds on Galapagos Island due to their adaptation to different food habits. **(1)**

Darwin explained

(i) All the varieties must have evolved within the same Island itself. The original finches were seed-eating. From them, some arose with altered beaks as insectivorous and some as vegetarian finches.

(ii) This process of evolution of different species in a given geographical area starting from a point and radiating to other habitats is called adaptive radiation. **(2)**

36. How does the study of fossils support evolution? Explain. **Delhi 2015C**

Ans. Refer to answer no. 18.

37. State the theory of biogenesis. How does Miller's experiment support this theory? **Delhi 2012**

Or State the views of Oparin and Haldane on evolution. How does SL Miller's experiment support their views? **Delhi 2011C**

Ans. The theory of biogenesis was proposed by Oparin and Haldane. It states that life could have come from pre-existing non-living organic molecules (e.g. RNA, protein, etc.) and the formation of life forms was preceded by chemical evolution, i.e. formation of diverse organic molecules from inorganic constituents.

In 1953, Urey and Miller conducted an experiment to prove this theory. They created the conditions of primitive earth, i.e. high temperature, volcanic storms, reducing atmosphere containing CH_4, NH_3, etc., at laboratory scale.

They then stimulated electric discharge in a closed flask containing above stated components at 800°C. They observed the formation of amino acids.

In similar experiments, they observed the formation of sugars, nitrogenous bases, pigments and fats. These small organic molecules are the building blocks for proteins and other components.

Hence, this experiment supported that life came from pre-existing non-living organic molecules.

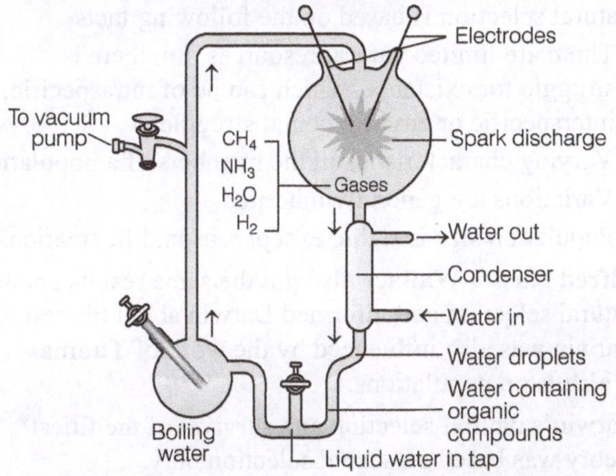

Diagrammatic representation of Miller-Urey experiment

Concept Enhancer The ratio of methane, ammonia and hydrogen taken in the large flask was 2 : 1 : 2.

5 Marks Questions

38. (i) Differentiate between analogy and homology giving one example each of plant and animal, respectively.

(ii) How are they considered as an evidence in support of evolution? **All India 2016**

Ans. (i) Refer to answer no. 32. **(3)**

(ii) Homology and analogy show the similarities and differences among the organisms of today and those existed years ago. These evidences come from the comparative study of external and internal structures.

These can be determined by the following types

Homology in organs indicates common ancestry. It is based on divergent evolution. When due to different needs, some morphologically similar structures develop differently, to perform different functions, the condition is called divergent evolution. This results in the formation of homologous organs.

Analogy had developed due to the convergent evolution where different structures evolved for the same function and have morphologically dissimilar structures. These are called analogous organs. **(2)**

39. (i) List any four evidences of evolution.

(ii) Explain any one of the evidences that helps to understand the concept of evolution. **Delhi 2016C**

Ans. (i) Evidences of evolution are derived from

(a) Palaeontology (Fossils)

(b) Comparative anatomy and morphology, i.e. homology and analogy

(c) Biochemical/Physiology

(d) Biogeography

(e) Embryology **(2)**

(ii) **Comparative anatomy** and **morphological evidences** show the similarities and differences among the organisms of today and those that existed years ago.

The evidences come from comparative study of external and internal structures.

(a) • The organs with same structural design and origin, but different functions are called **homologous organs**.
Examples are forelimbs of some animals like whales, bats and cheetah have similar anatomical structure, such as humerus, radius, ulna, carpals, metacarpals and phalanges.

• **Homology** in organ indicates common ancestry.

• Homology is based on divergent evolution. The same structures developed along different directions due to the adaptations to different needs. The condition is called **divergent evolution**.

(b) • Organs which are anatomically different, but functionally similar are called **analogous organs**. For example, wings of butterfly and birds. In both, wings perform same function, but they have different origin and structure.

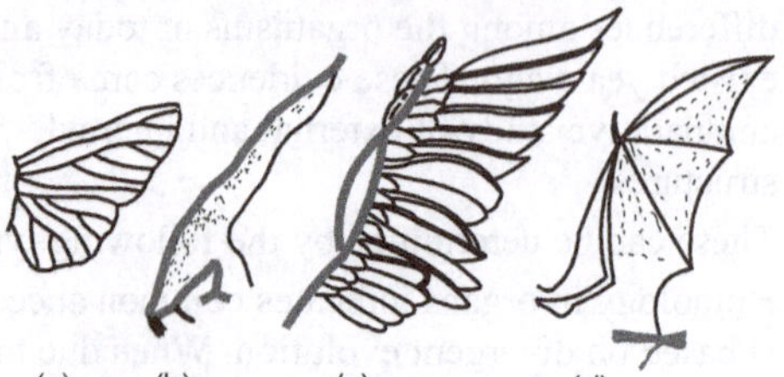

Analogous organs (a) Wing of insect (b) Wing of *Pterodactyl* (c) Wing of bird (d) Wing of bat

- **Analogy** refers to a situation exactly opposite to homology.
- Analogous organs are a result of **convergent evolution**. It can be said that above organisms had different structures, but they came in the same environment and evolved to perform same function. In plants, sweet potato (root modification) and potato (stem modification) are analogous organs. **(3)**

40. (i) How does the study of fossils help to understand evolution?

(ii) How did SL Miller provide an experimental evidence in favour of Oparin and Haldane's hypothesis? Explain. **Delhi 2016C**

Ans. (i) Refer to text on page 185 (Palaeontological evidences).

(ii) Refer to answer no. 37.

TOPIC 2

Theories of Evolution and Biological Evolution

Theories of Evolution

The important theories related to biological evolution are

Darwinism : (Theory of Natural Selection)

It was explained by Charles Robert Darwin in his book, *'Origin of Species by means of Natural Selection'*. It was based on his observations during a sea voyage around the world in ship **HMS Beagle**.

The two key concepts of Darwinism are

- **Branching descent** (adaptive radiation) and
- **Natural selection.**

According to this theory,

- There has been gradual evolution of life forms with new forms arising at different periods of history.
- Population of all organisms have variations in characteristics, which help them to adapt better to environment.
  It means individuals of a population are never same.
- Some of these characteristics enable individuals to survive better in natural conditions and reproduce. This is called **survival of the fittest**.
  The organisms which adapt well in the environment are selected by nature and thus survive more in nature. This is called **natural selection**. It means that fit individual has more chances to reproduce.
- Adaptability is inherited and fitness is the end result of the ability to adapt and get selected by nature.
- Natural selection is based on the following facts
  - There are limited natural resources. So, there is struggle for existence, which can be of intraspecific, interspecific or environmental struggle.
  - Varying characteristics in the members of a population.
  - Variations are generally inherited.
  - Population size is stable except seasonal fluctuation.
- **Alfred Russel Wallace** also got the same results about natural selection and informed Darwin about his results. Darwin was also influenced by the work of **Thomas Malthus** on populations.
- Darwin's natural selection and survival of the fittest theory was based on sexual selection only.
- At last, he proposed that natural selection leads to the formation of a new species, i.e. speciation.

Examples of Natural Selection

These are as follows

Industrial Melanism

There are two varieties of moth, white-winged and dark-winged.

- Before industrial revolution in England, in 1850s, white-winged moths were more in number than dark-winged moths. It was because on light background white-winged moth were not visible, while dark-winged moth could be eaten by predators very easily.

- After industrialisation in 1920, dark-winged moths became more than white-winged moths.
- This is because during industrialisation, tree trunks became dark due to the deposition of dust and soot particles produced as a result of air pollution.

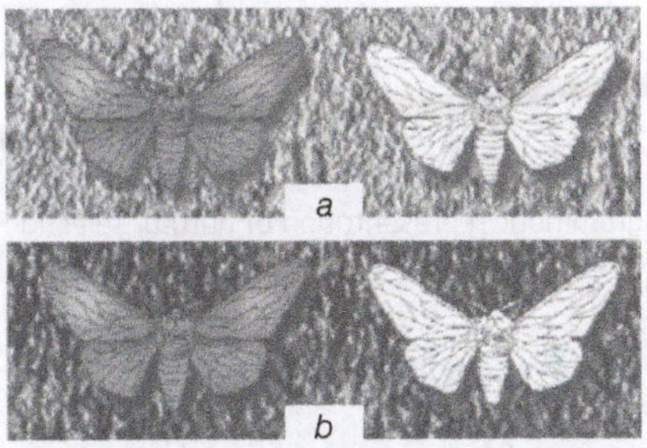

Figure 6.5 Showing white-winged moth and dark-winged moth (melanised) on a tree trunk (a) in unpolluted area (b) in polluted area

- Hence, white-winged moths could be easily detected and eaten up by the predators as they fail to camouflage but dark-winged moths were able to escape predation.
- So, nature selected only those moths which were better suited. However, none of them was eradicated completely.

Chemical Resistance

- The excess use of herbicides and pesticides leads to resistant varieties of microbes in very less time.
- A colony of bacteria growing on a medium has built-in variations in terms of ability to use a feed component. A change in medium composition selects a part of population that can survive in new condition. After some time, this variant population outgrows the other and evolves as new species.

Mutation Theory of Evolution

The mutation theory was put forth by **Hugo de Vries** based on his work on evening primrose.

- It states that evolution occurs by sudden large differences in the population, i.e. mutation and not by minor changes as stated by Darwin.
- The mutation caused speciation and de Vries called it **saltation** or **single step large mutation.**
- Mutations are random and directionless, while variations are small and directional as per Darwin.
- According to Darwin, evolution is slow and continuous process, while de Vries said it is a single-step process, which occurs due to the discontinuous variations.

Modern Synthetic Theory of Evolution

With progress in genetics, the sources of variation were explained and Darwin's theory was modified.

Now, the most accepted theory of evolution is known as **modern synthetic theory of evolution**, designated by **Huxley** in 1942 in which the origin of species is based on the interaction of genetic variation in a population, natural selection and reproductive isolation by various means such as migration hybridisation chance, etc.

Theory of Inheritance of Acquired Characters-Lamarckism

- Lamarck proposed that the evolution of life forms had occurred by the use and disuse of organs.
- He gave the example of giraffes, which initially did not have long necks. But, due to sudden disappearance of surface vegetation, they had to stretch their neck in order to reach the leaves on tall trees.
- So, they got adapted to their surroundings by elongating their necks. By passing this acquired character to succeeding generations, over the years, they came to acquire long necks.

Hardy-Weinberg Principle

This principle states that allele frequencies in a population are stable and are constant from generation to generation, i.e. gene pool is constant. It occurs when population is large and there is random mating among members of the population. This is called **genetic equilibrium** or **Hardy-Weinberg equilibrium.**

According to this principle,

- Sum total of all allelic frequencies is 1. It can be expressed by the following equation

$$p^2 + 2pq + q^2 = 1$$

where, p and q are individual frequencies of different alleles. The above equation is a binomial expansion of

$(p+q)^2$. When frequency measured differs from expected values, the difference indicates the extent of evolutionary change.

- Any fluctuation in genetic equilibrium leads to evolution.

Factors Affecting Hardy-Weinberg Equilibrium

The factors that affect Hardy-Weinberg equilibrium are given below

(i) **Gene migration or Gene flow** Due to migration, new genes or alleles are added to the new population and these are lost from the old population, in turn, changing the frequencies of both the populations.

There would be a gene flow if this gene migration occurs multiple times. So, gene flow changes the frequency of alleles in a population.

(ii) **Genetic drift** The changes occurring in frequencies of alleles by chance are called genetic drift. Sometimes due to the changes in allele frequency in new population, some different species are formed.

This is called **founder effect** and the original drifted population is called **founder**.

(iii) **Mutations** These occur randomly and at very slow rates. They lead to new phenotypes and due to considerable genetic variations, speciation occurs.

(iv) **Genetic recombination** During gametogenesis, crossing over in meiosis leads to the formation of new combination of genes.

(v) **Natural selection** It occurs due to the inheritance of variations, which leads to the survival of the fittest.

So, if above five factors are absent in a population it means there is no evolution occurring in that population. Such condition leads to the following effects

- **Stabilisation** Large number of individuals acquire mean character value.
- **Directional change** Large number of individuals acquire value other than mean character value. It means natural selection is taking place in one direction.
- **Disruption** More individuals acquire peripheral character value at both ends of the distribution curve. Here, natural selection is taking place in two different directions.

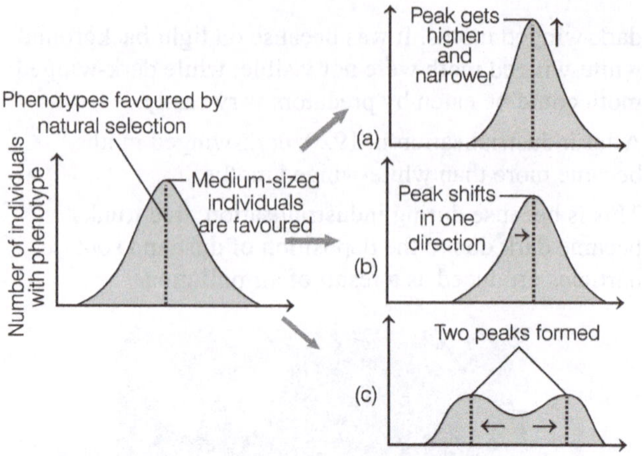

Figure 6.6 Diagrammatic representation of natural selection on different traits (a) Stabilising (b) Directional and (c) Disruptive

Human Evolution

The various stages of human evolution is as shown below

Various Stages of Human Evolution

Human ancestors/Origin period	Characteristics
Dryopithecus (20-25 mya)	More ape-like, arms and legs of same length, large brain and ate soft fruits and leaves.
Ramapithecus (14-15 mya)	More man-like, walked erect and teeth like modern man.
Australopithecus (3-4 mya)	Man-like primates, tall, walked straight, ate fruits, hunted with stone weapons, having brain capacity 400-600cc. Fossils found in Tanzania and Ethiopia.
Homo habilis (2 mya)	First humans-like being (hominid), brain capacity 650-800cc, herbivores and fossils found in East Africa.
Homo erectus (Java man) (1.5 mya)	Brain capacity 900cc, food was meat. Fossils found in Java in 1891.
Homo sapiens neanderthalensis (primitive man) (100000-40000 years ago)	Brain size 1400cc, used hides to protect body and bodies were buried after death. Fossils found in East and Central Asia.
Homo sapiens sapiens (modern man) (75000-10000 years ago)	Started agriculture, 10, 000 years back, human settlement started, prehistoric cave art developed.

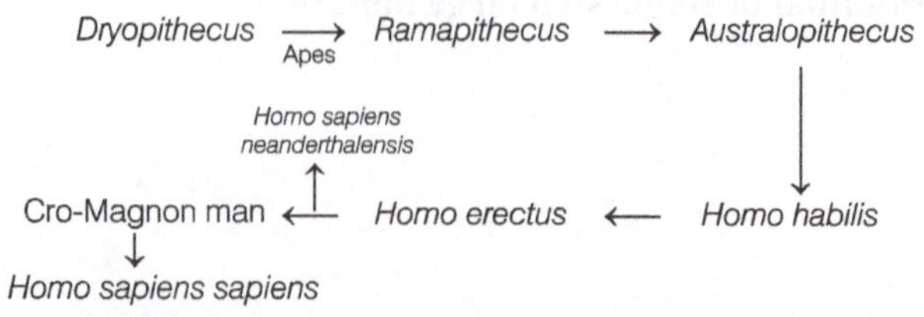

PYQs Previous Years' Questions

1 Mark Questions

Multiple Choice Questions

1. Single step large mutation leading to speciation is also called **CBSE 2024 (Set-II)**

   (a) founder effect (b) saltation
   (c) branching descent (d) natural selection

Ans. (b) According to Hugo de Vries, mutation caused speciation and called it saltation (single step large mutation).

2. Variations caused due to mutations are **CBSE SQP 2024**

   (a) random and directionless
   (b) random and directional
   (c) random and small
   (d) random, small and directiongal

Ans. (a) random and directionless

3. At which stage during evolution did human use hides to protect their bodies and buried their dead? **CBSE 2023**

   (a) *Homo habilis* (b) Neanderthal man
   (c) Java man (d) *Homo erectus*

Ans. (b) Neanderthal man

Very Short Answer Type Questions

4. According to the Hardy-Weinberg principle, the allele frequency of a population remains constant. How do you interpret the change of frequency of alleles in a population? **All India 2019**

Ans. According to Hardy-Weinberg principle, the change in frequency of alleles in a population shows the extent of evolutionary change.

5. How did Charles Darwin express fitness ? **Delhi 2019**

Or What is 'fitness of an individual' according to Darwin? **Delhi 2017**

Ans. According to Darwin, fitness of an individual is the ability of an organism to reproduce successfully and leave a large number of progenies under a particular set of selection pressures.

6. Write the names of the following.

   (i) A 15 mya primate that was ape-like.
   (ii) A 2 mya primate that lived in East African grasslands. **CBSE 2018**

Ans. (i) *Dryopithecus* (ii) *Australopithecus* (½ + ½)

7. What role does an individual organism play as per Darwin's theory of natural selection? **Delhi 2017**

Ans. According to the Darwin's theory of natural selection, the role of an individual organism is to pass on the necessary variations, changes or mutations from present generation to the next generation, that has been selected by the nature.

8. Write the probable differences in eating habits of *Homo habilis* and *Homo erectus*. **Foreign 2016**

Ans. The probable differences in eating habit of *Homo habilis* and *Homo erectus* are as follows

Homo habilis They did not eat meat.

Homo erectus They probably ate meat.

9. According to Hugo de Vries what is saltation? **All India 2016**

Or What is 'saltation' according to Hugo de Vries? **Delhi 2014**

Ans. Mutation theory of Hugo de Vries states that the evolution occurs due to the single-step large mutations occurring in a population. This is called saltation and it leads to new species formation or speciation.

10. State a reason for the increased population of dark coloured moths coinciding with the loss of lichens (on tree bark) during industrialisation period in England. **Delhi 2015**

Ans. The increase in dark population of moths was due to industrial melanism.

After industrialisation, dark-winged moths became more in number than white-winged moths. This is because tree trunks covered by lichens became dark due to the air pollution during industrialisation. White-winged moths fail to camouflage and thus decreased in number, whereas dark-winged moths were able to escape predation.

11. Write the basis of origin of variations in organisms as described by Hugo de Vries. **All India 2013C**

Ans. Mutations are the basis of origin of variations in an organism according to Hugo de Vries.

12. Mention how is mutation theory of Hugo de Vries different from Darwin's theory of natural selection. **Foreign 2011**

Ans. **Hugo de Vries theory** It states that evolution occurs due to single step large mutations called saltation, whereas **Darwin's theory** states that the speciation occurs gradually through a number of generations, with the accumulation of minor variations.

13. List the two characteristics of mutation that help in explaining evolution. **Delhi 2011C**

Ans. According to mutation theory of evolution
(i) Mutations are random, inheritable and appear in all conceivable directions. (½)
(ii) Same type of mutations can appear in the number of individuals of a species. (½)

14. When does a species become founder to cause founder effect? **Foreign 2010**

Ans. Founders effect occurs due to the change in allele frequency of a population. When the change in the allele frequency is very different in the new sample of population, that they become a different species, the original drifted population becomes founder and the effect is called founder effect.

15.
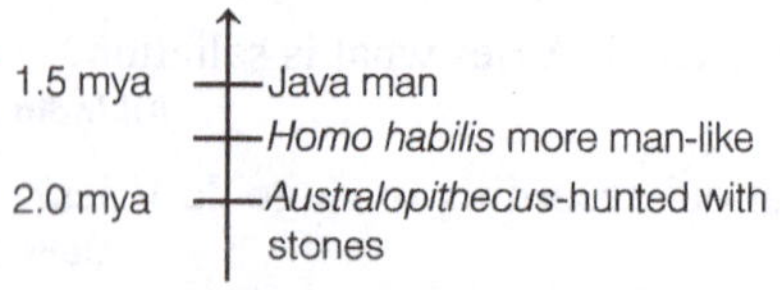

Study the ladder of human evolution given above and answer the following questions.
(i) Where did *Australopithecus* evolve?
(ii) Write the scientific name of Java man. **Delhi 2010C**

Ans. (i) *Australopithecus* evolved in East African grasslands. (½)
(ii) Java man – *Homo erectus*. (½)

2 Marks Questions

16. Observe the picture given below. Name the naturalist and write the explanation given by him that evolution of life forms had occurred on the basis of this example. **CBSE 2024 (Set-I)**

Ans. The given figure shows example of giraffes given by French naturalist **Lamarck**. Who explained his theory of evolution as
Evolution of life forms had occurred, but driven by use and disuse of organs. He gave the examples of giraffes who in attempt to forage leaves on tall trees had to adapt by elongation of their necks. As they passed on this acquired character of elongated neck to succeeding generations, giraffes, slowly, over the years, came to acquire long necks.

17. How would the gene flow or genetic drift affect the population in which either of them happen to take place ? **Delhi 2019**

Ans. If gene flow or genetic drift takes place in a population, the effect would be
(i) **Gene flow/Gene migration** Due to migration, new genes or alleles are added to the population and are lost from the old population, thus changing the frequencies of alleles in both populations. When migration occurs multiple times it is termed as gene flow. (1)
(ii) **Genetic drift** Changes occurring in allele frequencies by chance is called genetic drift. Due to changes in allele frequency in new population, some different species are formed. This is called founder effect and the original population is called founder. (1)

18. With the help of an algebraic equation, how did Hardy-Weinberg explain that in a given population the frequency of occurrence of alleles of a gene is supposed to remain the same through generations. **CBSE 2018**

Ans. **Hardy-Weinberg's principle** states that allele frequencies in a population are stable. They remain constant from generation to generation. The gene pool also remains constant. This is called genetic equilibrium.
Thus, according to this principle, the sum total of all the allelic frequencies in a population is always 1. Suppose in a diploid individual, p and q represent the frequency of allele A and allele a, respectively. The probability that an allele A with a frequency of P appears on both the chromosomes of a diploid organism in the p^2 . Similarly of aa is q^2, of Aa is $2pq$. Hence,
$p^2 + 2pq + q^2 = 1$
The difference measured in the expected values of frequencies, indicates the extent of evolutionary change.

19. Name the first human-like hominid. Mention his food habit and brain capacity. **All India 2015C**

Ans. *Homo habilis* were the first human-like hominid. They probably did not consume meat and their brain capacity was about 650-850 cc.

20. Explain how natural selection operates in nature by taking an example of white-winged and dark-winged moths of England. **All India 2014C**

Ans. In England, prior to industrialisation, the tree trunks were covered with white lichens hence, white moths could survive and were protected from predators due to white colour. On the other hand, black moths (a dark-winged moths) could be easily identified due to their dark colour and declined in number due to predation.

However, as industrialisation progressed, the lichens were replaced by soot and dust particles and dark coloured moths were benefitted due to camouflage, while white-winged moths could be easily eaten up by the predators being easily identifiable. Thus, only the dark-winged moths who were able to fit and survive, i.e. adapted well in conditions, reproduced well in nature. Thus, natural selection operates in nature by selecting the fittest characters of organisms.

3 Marks Questions

21. The graphs below show three types of natural selection. The shaded areas marked with arrows show the individuals in the population which are not selected. The dotted vertical lines show the statistical means.

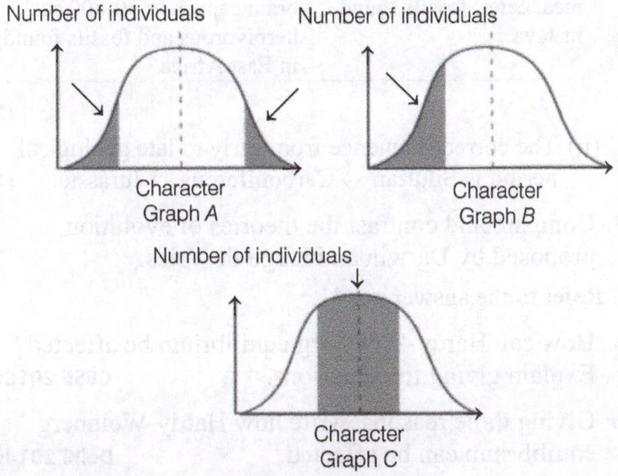

(i) What names are given to the types of selection shown in graphs *A*, *B* and *C*?

(ii) After the selection has operated for several generations in the above populations indicated as graph *A*, *B* and *C*, graphically illustrate the probable results. **CBSE SQP 2024**

Ans. (i) *A* -Stabilising, *B* - Directional, *C* - Disruptive. (1½)

(ii) Graph *A* – Stabilising
Graph *B* – Directional
Graph *C* – Disruptive

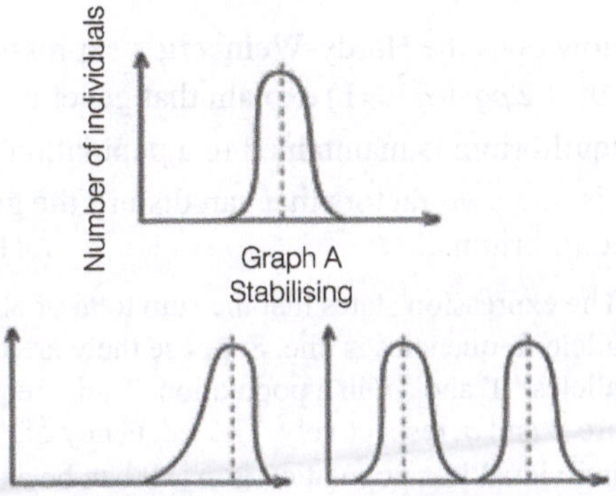

- Stabilising selection meaning a non-extreme trait is favoured instead of one of the two extreme traits.
- Directional selection mean that an extreme phenotype (character or traits) is favoured over other phenotypes and this causes the allele frequency to shift over time in favour of the extreme phenotype.
- Disruptive selection favours both extreme traits in a population. (1½)

22. Industrial melanism in England after 1850 is an excellent example of natural selection. Explain how? **CBSE 2023**

Ans. Industrial melanism in England after 1850 is an excellent example of natural selection. It is because, before industrialisation the air quality of England was good due to which lichens were able to grow on tree barks. They were white in colour. Hence, moths living on tree bark evolved with time to have a more white population due to less melanin production.

This reduced the number of black moths in the population. This was an adaptation to hide from predators.

With time as industrialisation grew the air quality reduced. This eliminated the lichens from the region. Now the dark brown to black colour of tree bark was exposed. Due to this, the moth population evolved to have more melanin giving them black color. This reduced the number of white moths in the population. This was an adaptation to hide from predators' attacks. In short, evolving with the situation gave moths' population a benefit due to natural selection.

23. (i) How is Hardy-Weinberg's expression '$(p^2 + 2pq + q^2) = 1$' derived?

(ii) List any two factors that can disturb the genetic equilibrium. **CBSE SQP 2023**

Or (i) How does the Hardy-Weinberg's expression ($p^2+2pq+q^2=1$) explain that genetic equilibrium is maintained in a population?

(ii) List any two factors that can disturb the genetic equilibrium. **All India 2010**

Ans. (i) The expression states that the sum total of all the allele frequencies is one. Suppose there are two alleles '*A*' and '*a*' in a population. Their frequencies are p and q, respectively. The frequency of '*AA*' individual in a population is p^2. It can be explained that the probability that an allele '*A*' with a frequency p appears on both the chromosomes of a diploid individual is simply the product of the probabilities, i.e. p^2. In the same way, the frequency for *aa* is q^2 and for *Aa* it is $2pq$.

$$p^2+2\,pq+q^2=1$$

where, p^2 represents the frequency of homozygous dominant genotype, $2\,pq$ represents the frequency of the heterozygous genotype and q^2 represents the frequency of homozygous recessive. **(1½)**

(ii) Genetic equilibrium is distributed by the factors like gene migration, genetic drift, mutation and gene combinations during gamete formation. Refer to text on page no. 196. **(1½)**

24. Hardy-Weinberg principle is stated in the following algebraic equation

$$p^2+2pq+q^2=1.$$

(i) State what do 'p' and 'q' denote in the equation.

(ii) State Hardy-Weinberg's principle as indicated in the equation.

(iii) What would you interpret if the value of '1' in the equation gets deviated ? **Delhi 2020**

Ans. (i) The equation $p^2+2pq+q^2=1$, mathematically represents the Hardy-Weinberg's principle. It is used to calculate the genetic variation of a population at equilibrium. In this equation,

$p=$ frequency of allele *A*.

$q=$ frequency of allele *a*.

$p^2=$ frequency of *AA* (homozygous) individuals in a population.

$q^2=$ frequency of *aa* (homozygous) individuals.

$2pq=$ frequency of *Aa* (heterozygous) individuals. **(1)**

(ii) Hardy-Weinberg's principle states that allele frequencies in a population are stable and remain constant from generation to generation, i.e. gene pool remains constant. **(1)**

(iii) Hardy-Weinberg's equation is used to measure the difference in frequencies of observed genotype measured from the frequencies predicted.

Any deviation in the value of 1 in Hardy-Weinberg's equation would show evolutionary changes. **(1)**

25. Explain the phenomenon of evolution by natural selection as supported by the variations observed in white-winged and dark-winged moth populations in England between 1850-1920. **All India 2019**

Ans. Refer to answer no. 20.

26. (i) Write two differences between *Homo erectus* and *Homo habilis*.

(ii) Rearrange the following from early to late geological periods : Carboniferous, Silurian, Jurassic. **Delhi 2019**

Ans. (i) Differences between *Homo erectus* and *Homo habilis* are

Homo erectus	*Homo habilis*
Origin period is 1.5 mya	Origin period is 1.2–1.5 mya
Brain capacity 900 cc, meat eater, fossils found in Java.	First human like beings, brain capacity 650-800 cc, herbivorous and fossils found in East Africa.

(2)

(ii) The correct sequence from early to late geological period is Silurian → Carboniferous → Jurassic. **(1)**

27. Compare and contrast the theories of evolution proposed by Darwin and Hugo de Vries.

Ans. Refer to the answer no. 41.

28. How can Hardy-Weinberg equilibrium be affected? Explain giving three reasons. **CBSE 2018C**

Or Giving three reasons, write how Hardy-Weinberg equilibrium can be affected. **Delhi 2014C**

Ans. Refer to text on page no. 196.

29. Write the characteristics of *Ramapithecus*, *Dryopithecus* and Neanderthal man. **All India 2017**

Ans. **Characteristics of *Ramapithecus***

- *Ramapithecus* survived about 14-15 million years ago during late Miocene to Pliocene.
- *Ramapithecus* walked erect on its hindlegs.
- They were similar to ape, which lived on the tree tops, but also walked on the ground.
- They ate hard nuts and seeds like modern man. Their jaws and teeth were similar to humans. **(1)**

Characteristics of *Dryopithecus*

- They lived about 25 million years ago during Miocene period.
- Legs and heels indicate that *Dryopithecus* was of a semi-erect posture and Knuckle walker.
- *Dryopithecus* was arboreal and herbivorous, who ate soft fruits and leaves.
- *Dryopithecus* had large canines and incisors. **(1)**

Characteristics of Neanderthal man

- Neanderthal man existed in the late Pleistocene period.
- Neanderthal walked upright with bipedal movement.
- The face was slightly prognathous and had low brows, receding jaws and high domed heads.
- The cranial capacity of Neanderthal man was about 1300-1600 cc and of average 1450 cc. Their jaws were deep with no chin and skull bones were thick. **(1)**

30. $p^2 + 2pq + q^2 = 1$. Explain this algebraic equation on the basis of Hardy-Weinberg's principle. **Delhi 2017**

Ans. The equation $p^2 + 2pq + q^2 = 1$, mathematically represents the Hardy-Weinberg's principle. It is used to calculate the genetic variations among a population at equilibrium.

Principle It states that allele frequencies in a population are stable and remain constant from generation to generation.
In this equation,
p – frequency of allele A.
q – frequency of allele a.
p^2 – frequency of AA (homozygous) individuals in a population.
q^2 – frequency of aa (homozygous) individuals.
$2pq$ – frequency of Aa (heterozygous) individuals.
Also, the sum total of all the allelic frequencies is equal to 1. If the p and q allele frequencies are known, then the frequencies of three genotypes can be calculated using the Hardy-Weinberg's equation. This equation can be used to measure the differences in frequencies of observed genotype measured from the frequencies predicted by the equation. The disturbance in genetic equilibrium results in evolution, thus the presence of any difference indicates the extent of evolutionary change.

31. How did industrialisation play a role in natural selection of light and dark coloured moth in England? **Delhi 2015C**

Or Explain the increase in the numbers of melanic (dark-winged) moths in the urban areas of post-industrialisation period in England. **Delhi 2012**

Ans. Refer to answer no. 20.

32. Since the origin of life on earth, there were five episodes of mass extinction of species.

(i) How is the sixth extinction presently in progress, different from the previous episodes?
(ii) Who is mainly responsible for the sixth extinction?
(iii) List any four points that can help to overcome this disaster. **All India 2014 C**

Ans. (i) Sixth extinction is different from previous episodes in the following ways

(a) It takes place rapidly, due to the reduction in number of species per unit area per unit time.
(b) In contrast to previous episodes which were naturally driven, sixth extinction is accelerated by human activities such as deforestation, industrialisation, etc. **(1)**

(ii) Human activities that ultimately lead to global warming and disruption of environmental and ecological balance are responsible for sixth extinction. **(1)**

(iii) The four measures that can be implemented to overcome this disaster are

(a) Afforestation.
(b) Reduction in overexploitation of natural resources.
(c) Conservation of species and their natural habitats to minimise their losses.
(d) Creating awareness among people regarding global warming and its consequences. **(1)**

33. Describe the three different ways by which natural selection can affect the frequency of a heritable trait in a population. **Foreign 2014**

Or

Explain the three ways in which natural selection operates on different traits in nature. **All India 2011C**

Ans. The three different ways by which natural selection can affect the frequency of a heritable trait in a population are

(i) **Stabilisation** It results in more number of individuals acquiring the mean character value, i.e. variation is much reduced. **(1)**

(ii) **Directional change** It results in more individuals acquiring value other than mean character value, i.e. the peak shifts towards one direction.

(iii) **Disruption** In this, more individuals acquire peripheral character value at both ends of the distribution curve, i.e. two peaks are formed at periphery. **(1)**

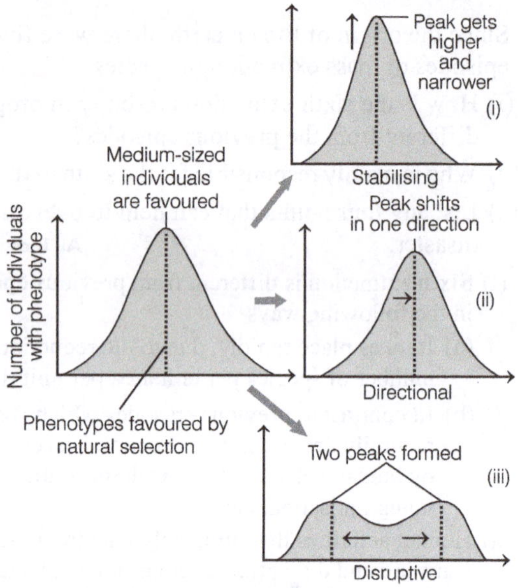

Diagrammatic representation of natural selection on different traits: (a) Stabilising (b) Directional (c) Disruptive **(1)**

34. According to Darwinian theory, the rate of appearance of new forms is linked to their life cycles. Explain. **All India 2014C**

Ans. Darwin's theory states that the fitness of an organism is measured by its reproductive ability. The appearance of new forms is linked to the lifespan of an organism.

The greater lifespan of an individual indicates that the more it can reproduce and hence greater new forms would appear. This can be observed in the development of dark-winged moths due to industrial melanism.

Refer to answer no. 20.

35. Branching descent and natural selection are the two key concepts of Darwinian theory of evolution. Explain each concept with the help of a suitable example. **All India 2011**

Ans. The two key concepts of Darwinian theory of natural selection are as follows

Branching Descent

(i) Members of a population vary in characteristics, even though they look superficially similar. Most of these variations are heritable.

(ii) Accumulation of variations over a period of time through a number of generations leads to change in population characteristics. **(1½)**

e.g. evolution of marsupials of Australia derived from a common ancestor.

Natural selection Nature selects those individuals who are fit in the environment. Fitness according to Darwin is reproductive fitness.

Those who adapt better to the habitat reproduce more and their progeny consists of more fit individuals, who are selected by nature, e.g. industrial melanism. **(1½)**

5 Marks Questions

36.

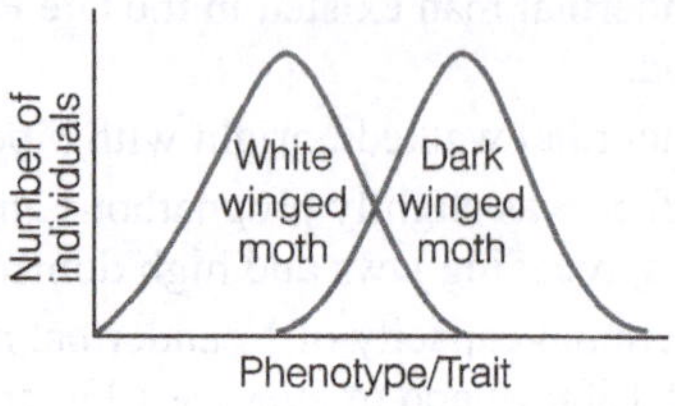

Natural selection operates in different ways in nature.

(i) Identify the type of natural selection depicted in the graph above.

(ii) In England after industrialisation, the population of dark winged moths were more favoured than white winged moth. Explain.

(iii) Anthropogenic action can enhance the rate of evolution. Explain with the help of an example. **CBSE 2024 (Set-II)**

Ans. (i) The type of natural selection depicted in the given graph is directional selection. It is due to environment favouring one phenotype (here black winged moth) more than another (here, white winged moth). **(1)**

(ii) Before industrialisation, there were more white-winged moths on trees than dark-winged or melanised moths. But after industrialisation, it reversed as the predators could now spot a month against a contrasting background.

During post industrialisation period, the tree trunk became dark due to industrial smoke and soots. Due to this site, white-winged moth did not survive due to predators, dark winged or melanised survived. Thus, dark winged moths were more favoured than white winged moth. **(2)**

(iii) Anthropogenic actions, i.e. human activities has led to the evolution of a number of new species in a short time scale. This hasten the process of evolution, e.g.

- Excess use of herbicides and pesticides in crop production has resulted in selection of resistant varieties of pests in a much lesser time scale.
- Use of antibiotics or drugs against microbes leads to resistant organism in lesser time scale.

- **Industrial melanism** After industrialisation, in England, dark-winged moth population got favoured over earlier favoured white-winged moth population. (2)

37. (i) How does Hardy-Weinberg equation explain genetic equilibrium?

(ii) Describe how this equilibrium gets disturbed which may lead to founder effect. **All India 2019, Foreign 2012**

Or (i) Describe Hardy-Weinberg principle.

(ii) List any four factors, which affect genetic equilibrium.

(iii) Describe founder effect. **Foreign 2014**

Ans. (i) According to Hardy-Weinberg principle, the allele frequencies in a population are stable and are constant from generation to generation. (1)

(ii) The four factors that affect genetic equilibrium are

(a) Gene migration

(b) Genetic drift

(c) Mutation and recombination

(d) Natural selection (2)

(iii) Whenever the gene migration occurs multiple times, it leads to some changes, that may sometimes result in change in allele frequency (at random or by chance).

This difference in allele frequency leads to a new sample of population in such a way that they evolve into a different species. Such populations are called founders and the effect generated is called founder effect. (2)

38. (i) Explain Darwinian theory of evolution with the help of one suitable example. State the two key concepts of theory.

(ii) Mention any three characteristics of Neanderthal man that lived in near East and Central Asia. **Delhi 2014**

Ans. (i) **Darwinian theory of Evolution/Darwin's theory of Natural Selection**

(a) All the populations have built in variations for each character, which help them to adapt better to the environment.

(b) The characteristics, which enable some populations to survive better in natural conditions (climate, food, physical factors) would outbreed others (survival of the fittest).

(c) The population, which better fits in an environment is selected by nature and survives more (natural selection).

(d) Adaptability is inherited and fitness is the end result of ability to adapt and get selected by nature.

The two key concepts of Darwinian theory are

- Branching descent and
- Natural selection

(For details, refer to answer no. 35). (3½)

(ii) The three characteristics of Neanderthal man that lived in near East and Central Asia are

(a) Walked upright with bipedal movement.

(b) Cranial capacity was around 1300-1600 cc.

(c) Face slightly prognathous and jaws were deep with no chin. (1½)

39. How does the process of natural selection affect Hardy-Weinberg equilibrium? Explain. List the other four factors that disturb the equilibrium. **All India 2013**

Ans. **Natural selection** affects Hardy-Weinberg equilibrium in the following ways

(i) It is a process in which heritable variations help in the survival of an organism, enabling it to reproduce and give rise to a large number of offsprings.

(ii) There may be change in the frequency of genes and alleles in the future generations.

(iii) It leads to the formation of new species.

Hardy-Weinberg law states that allelic frequencies in a population are stable and remain constant from generation to generation, but natural selection allows only one allele to adapt to changing conditions.

For other factors affecting Hardy-Weinberg equilibrium, refer to text on page no. 196.

40. (i) Name the primates that lived about 15 million years ago. List their characteristic features.

(ii) (a) Where was the man-like animal found?

(b) Write the order in which Neanderthals, *Homo habilis* and *Homo erectus* appeared on the earth. State the brain capacity of each of them.

(c) When did modern man *Homo sapiens* appear on this planet? **Delhi 2011**

Ans. (i) *Dryopithecus* and *Ramapithecus* are the primates that lived about 15 million years ago.

Their characteristics are

(a) They were hairy.

(b) They walked like gorillas and chimpanzees. *Dryopithecus* was more ape-like, while *Ramapithecus* was more man-like. (2)

(ii) (a) The man-like animal was found in East African grasslands. **(1)**

(b) They appeared in the following order *Homo habilis* → *Homo erectus* → Neanderthal. They had brain capacities of 650-800 cc, 900 cc and 1450 cc, respectively. **(1)**

(c) During ice age between 75000-10000 years ago, modern man *Homo sapiens* appeared on this planet. **(1)**

41. Explain the salient features of Hugo de Vries theory of mutation. How is Darwin's theory of natural selection different from it? Explain. **Delhi 2011**

Ans. Hugo de Vries explained that new species arise from pre-existing ones in a single generation by a sudden appearance of marked differences called mutations. He believed that it is mutation, which causes evolution. **(2)**

The differences between de Vries theory and Darwin theory are as follows

de Vries theory	Darwin theory
Evolution resulted from mutation.	Evolution resulted from variations.
Evolution was sudden.	Evolution was gradual.
Mutations are random and directionless.	Variations are small and directional.

(3)

Miscellaneous Questions

5 Marks Quetsions

1. (i) How do the observations made during moth collection in pre and post-industrialised era in England support evolution by natural selection?

(ii) Explain the phenomenon that is well-represented by Darwin's finches other than natural selection. **Delhi 2017**

Ans. (i) Natural selection is the key concept of Darwin's theory of evolution which was explained by Charles Robert Darwin. According to this theory, population of all organisms exhibit variations in characteristics, which help them to adapt better to environment. It means that individuals of a population are never same.

Some of these characteristics, enable individuals to survive better in natural conditions and reproduce. This is called as the survival of the fittest.

The organisms which adapt well in the environment are selected by nature and thus survive more in nature.

This is called natural selection. From the description given below, we can figure out that how the observations made during moth collection in pre and post-industrialised era in England supported the idea of evolution by natural selection.

Industrial melanism There are two varieties of moth, white-winged and dark-winged.

(a) **Before industrial revolution in England,** white-winged moths were more in number than dark-winged moths, because there was less pollution, which led to light trunk of trees due to the presence of lichen on them. So, on light background white-winged moths were not visible, while dark-winged moths could be eaten by predators very easily.

(b) **After industrialisation**, dark-winged moths became more than white-winged moths.

This is because during industrialisation, tree trunks covered by white lichens became dark due to air pollution (dust and soot particles). So, now white-winged moths could be detected easily. Due to this, white-winged moths could be easily eaten up by the predators as they fail to camouflage. Whereas dark-winged moths escape predation. So, nature selected only those moths which were better suited. However, none of them eradicated completely. **(2½)**

(ii) The phenomenon well-represented by Darwin's finches other than natural selection is adaptive radiation.

Adaptive Radiation

HF Osborn (1898) developed the concept of adaptive radiation or divergent evolution. It involves the development of different functional structures from a common ancestral form.

When a group of organisms shares **homologous structures**, which are specialised to perform a variety of different functions, it shows **adaptive radiation**. This represents the evolution of new forms in several directions from the common ancestral type (divergence).

The **significance** of adaptive radiation is that it suggests the existence of divergent evolution based on the modification of homologous structures.

The examples of divergent evolution are as follows

(a) **Darwin's finches of Galapagos Islands** had common ancestors. Later on, their beaks modified according to their feeding habits.

(b) **Australian marsupials and limbs of mammals** are also good examples of adaptive radiation. **(2½)**

2. (i) How did Darwin explain adaptive radiation? Give another example exhibiting adaptive radiation.
(ii) Name the scientist who influenced Darwin and how? **All India 2016**

Ans. (i) Refer to answer no. 24 of Topic 1. **(3)**
(ii) Darwin was influenced by Thomas Robert Malthus, a British economist. He put forward a theory of human population growth. He wrote the book '*On Essay on the Principles of Population*'. **(2)**

3. (i) Explain the observations and the conclusion drawn by Darwin during his visit to Galapagos Islands.
(ii) Write the two key concepts of Darwin's theory of natural selection. **Delhi 2016**

Ans. (i) Refer to answer no. 24 of Topic 1.
(ii) Refer to answer no. 35 of Topic 2.

Case Based/Source Based/Passage Based Questions (Based on Complete Chapter)

1. Stanley Miller and Harold Urey in the 1953 performed an experiment for demonstrating that ultraviolet radiations on electrical discharges or a combination of these can produce complex organic compounds from a mixture of CH_4, NH_3, H_2 and water vapour (H_2O) at 800ºC.

(i) The CH_4, NH_3 and H_2 were taken in the closed flask in the ratio
(a) 2 : 2 : 2 (b) 2 : 1 : 2
(c) 1 : 2 : 1 (d) 1 : 1 : 2

(ii) The Miller and Urey experiment supported the theory of
(a) Biogenesis (b) Mutation
(c) Abiogenesis (d) Embryology

(iii) All the conditions were set similar to those of the
(a) natural atmosphere
(b) current atmosphere
(c) primitive atmosphere
(d) Both (a) and (b)

(iv) What complex molecules were observed by the scientist in the flask?
(a) Sugar (b) Pigments
(c) Fats (d) All of these

(v) The theory of abiogenesis was supported by
(a) Louis Pasteur (b) Darwin
(c) van Helmont (d) Urey

Ans. (i)-(b), (ii)-(c), (iii)-(c), (iv)-(d), (v)-(c)

2. Study the picture given below and answer the following questions.

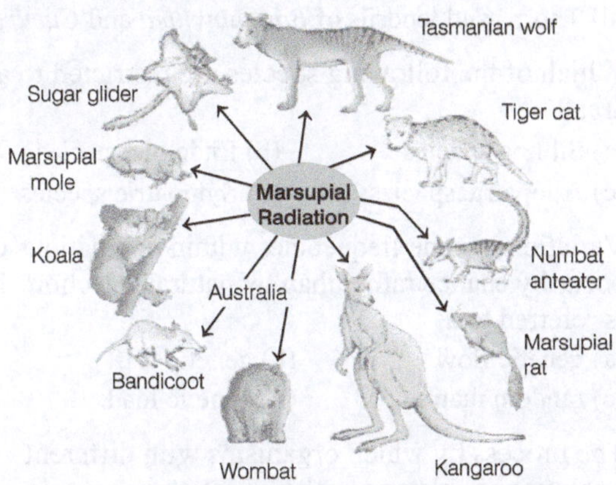

(i) Mention the specific geographical region where these organisms are found.
(ii) Name and explain the phenomenon that has resulted in the evolution of such diverse species in the region.
(iii) Explain giving reasons the existence of placental wolf and Tasmanian wolf sharing the similar habitat.

Ans. (i) Australia **(1)**
(ii) Adaptive radiation is the phenomenon in which different species are evolved in a given geographical area starting from a point and literally radiating to other habitats in that area. **(1)**
(iii) Tasmanian wolf and placental wolf share similar habitat, but in different continents. These animals had common ancestry. They also reveal adaptive radiation. **(2)**

CHAPTER TEST

01 Mark Questions

Multiple Choice Questions

1 Which one among the following is an example for homology?

(a) Eyes of *Octopus* and mammals
(b) Wings of butterfly and birds
(c) Flippers of penguins and dolphins
(d) Thorns and tendrils of *Bougainvillea* and *Cucurbita*

2 Which of the following species are restricted to an area?

(a) Sibling species (b) Endemic species
(c) Allopatric species (d) Sympatric species

3 Variation in gene frequencies within populations can occur by chance rather than by natural selection. This is referred to as

(a) genetic flow (b) genetic drift
(c) random mating (d) genetic load

4 The process by which organisms with different evolutionary history evolve similar phenotypic adaptations in response to a common environmental challenge, is called

(a) natural selection (b) convergent evolution
(c) non-random evolution (d) adaptive radiation

5 The primate, which existed 15 million years ago, among these was

(a) *Homo habilis* (b) *Australopithecus*
(c) *Ramapithecus* (d) *Homo erectus*

6 What was the most significant trend in the evolution of modern man (*Homo sapiens*) from his ancestors?

(a) Shortening of jaws
(b) Binocular vision
(c) Increasing cranial capacity
(d) Upright posture

Assertion-Reason Type Questions

Direction (Q. Nos. 7-10) *Read the **Assertion** and **Reason** carefully to mark the correct option out of the choices given below*

(a) If both Assertion and Reason are true and Reason is the correct explanation of Assertion
(b) If both Assertion and Reason are true, but Reason is not the correct explanation of Assertion
(c) If Assertion is true, but Reason is false
(d) If both Assertion and Reason are false

7 **Assertion** Darwin held that small favourable variations formed raw material for evolution.
Reason Darwin did not study the factors which produce variations.

8 **Assertion** Isolation does not allow inbreeding among otherwise potential mates.
Reason This preserves variations leading to speciation.

9 **Assertion** Pre-existing gene mutation forms the basis of adaptation.
Reason In a changed environment, hidden mutation may express resulting in adaptation and hence survival of the organism.

10 **Assertion** Natural selection really means differential reproduction.
Reason Some members of a population have traits which enable them to grow up and reproduce at a higher rate.

2/3 Marks Questions

11 What are homologous organs? How do they help in providing evidences for organic evolution?

12 How does palaeontological evidence support the theory of organic evolution?

13 Give an account of Darwin's finches.

14 How is Darwin's concept of evolution different from that of Hugo de Vries?

15 List any three drawbacks of Darwinism.

16 Mention three features of the Neranderthal man.

05 Marks Questions

17 State the modification of forelimbs in animals as an example of homology.

18 Marsupials and Australian placental mammals exhibit convergent evolution explain how?

19 What do you mean by natural selection? Explain evolution of species by this theory.

20 Write the characteristics any two of the following.

(i) *Ramapithecus* (ii) Neanderthal man
(iii) *Homo habilis*

Answers

1.	(d)	**2.**	(b)	**3.**	(b)	**4.**	(b)	**5.**	(c)
6.	(c)	**7.**	(b)	**8.**	(c)	**9.**	(a)	**10.**	(a)

07 Human Health and Diseases

TREND ANALYSIS 3 YEARS

Average No. of Questions Across all Sets

Topic	Types of Questions	2024	2023	2020
TOPIC 01 Health, Common Diseases in Humans and Immunity	1 Mark	1	4	0
	2 Marks	1	3	2
	3 Marks	1	2	4
	4 Marks (Case Based)	0	1	0
	5 Marks	1	0	1
TOPIC 02 Adolescence and Drug/Alcohol Abuse	1 Mark	0	0	0
	2 Marks	0	0	1
	3 Marks	0	0	1
	4 Marks (Case Based)	0	0	0
	5 Marks	0	0	0

TOPIC 1

Health, Common Diseases in Humans and Immunity

Health

- It is defined as a state of complete physical, mental and social well-being.
- Awareness about diseases and their effects on different body functions, vaccination against infectious diseases, proper disposal of wastes, control of vectors, maintenance of hygienic food and water resources are necessary for achieving good health.
- The factors which affect human health are
  - (i) Genetic disorders
  - (ii) Infections
  - (iii) Lifestyle (including personal hygenic, balanced diet and regular exercise)

Disease

It involves adversely affected functioning of one or more organs or systems of the body. Diseases can be broadly divided into the following two categories depending on the modes of transmission

(i) **Non-infectious diseases** which do not transmit from one person to another. They may occur due to hereditary factors, deficiencies, etc., e.g. cancer, diabetes, etc.

(ii) **Infectious diseases** which can easily transmit from one affected person to another healthy person. These diseases are usually caused by certain organisms (pathogens) like bacteria, viruses, fungi, etc., e.g. AIDS, common cold, etc.

Common Infectious Diseases

Based on the types of pathogen infectious diseases can be divided into certain categories

Bacterial Diseases

(i) **Typhoid** It is caused by bacterium *Salmonella typhi*.

- *S. typhi* enters the small intestine through food and water contaminated with them and migrates to other organs through blood.
- Intestinal perforation and death may occur in severe cases.
- **Symptoms** are high fever (39-40°C), weakness, stomach pain, constipation, headache and loss of appetite.
- **Widal test** is a confirmation test for typhoid.
- **Mary Mallon** nick named Typhoid Mary was a cook by profession and was a typhoid carrier, who spread typhoid for several years through the food she prepared.

(ii) **Pneumonia** The disease is caused by *Streptococcus pneumoniae* and *Haemophilus influenzae.*

- These bacteria infect alveoli of the lungs. The alveoli get filled with fluid, causing decrease in respiratory efficiency of the lungs.
- Pneumonia spreads by inhaling droplets/aerosol from infected individuals or even by sharing glasses and utensils with patients.
- **Symptoms** of pneumonia are fever, chills, cough, headache, increased pulse and respiratory rates, etc.
- In severe cases, the lips and finger nails may turn grey to bluish in colour.

(iii) **Dysentery**, **plague**, **diphtheria**, etc., are some other examples of bacterial diseases.

Viral Diseases

(i) **Common cold** It occurs due to a group of viruses called **rhinoviruses**.

- These viruses infect the nose and respiratory passage, but not the lungs.
- Common cold is characterised by nasal congestion and discharge, sore throat, hoarseness, cough, headache, tiredness, etc., which generally last for 3-7 days.
- The infection occurs due to droplets releasing from cough or sneezes of an infected person, either inhaled directly or transmitted through contaminated objects such as pens, books, cups, computer's keyboard or mouse, etc.

(ii) **Polio, dengue, chikungunya, mumps** and **measles,** etc., are some other examples of viral diseases.

Protozoan Diseases

(i) **Amoebiasis** (amoebic dysentery) It is caused by an intestinal endoparasite, *Entamoeba histolytica*, which is found in the large intestine of humans.

- Carrier of pathogen is housefly. It transmits the parasite from faeces of infected person to the food, thereby contaminating it.
- Infection takes place mainly through the contaminated food and water.
- **Symptoms** are abdominal pain, constipation, cramps, faeces with excess mucus and blood clots.

(ii) **Kala-azar**, **sleeping sickness**, **ascariasis**, etc., are some other protozoan diseases.

(iii) **Malaria** It is caused by a protozoan, *Plasmodium* sp. (*P. vivax*, *P. malariae* and *P. falciparum*).

- *P. falciparum* causes most serious kind of malaria, i.e. malignant malaria, which can be fatal.
- Female *Anopheles* mosquito is the vector of *Plasmodium*, which transfers the sporozoites (infectious form) in human body through the bite.
- **Antimalarial drugs** used for the treatment of malaria are **quinine** and **chloroquine**.
- Malaria can be prevented by killing mosquitoes by spraying DDT, BHC, etc., and using insect repellents, mosquito nets, etc.

- Life cycle of *Plasmodium* is given in the figure below

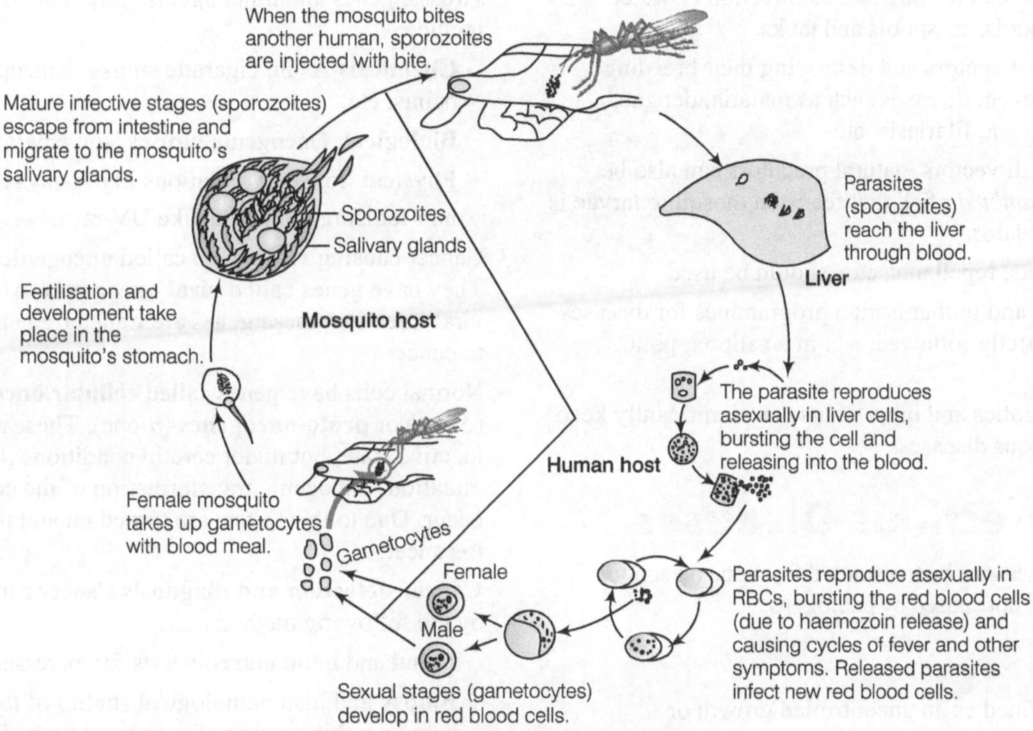

Figure 7.1 Stages in the life cycle of *Plasmodium*

Fungal Disease

Ringworm is caused by many fungi of genera *Microsporum, Trichophyton* and *Epidermophyton.*

- Infection occurs through contact with an infected person or from soil and through the use of towels, clothes, combs, etc., of an infected person.
- Heat and moisture help these fungi to grow in regions like skin folds as in groin or between the toes.
- **Symptoms** of ringworm include appearance of dry, scaly lesions on various parts of the body such as skin, nails and scalp accompanied by intense itching.

Helminthic Diseases

(i) **Ascariasis** It is caused by an intestinal endoparasite, *Ascaris lumbricoides,* commonly called as **roundworm.**

- Infection occurs as the eggs of the parasite are excreted along with the faeces of infected person, which contaminate water, soil, plants, etc. Infection reaches further to normal person *via* contaminated sources. Eggs of the parasite develop into larva, which spreads in the body along with the blood flow.
- **Symptoms** include diseases like abdominal pain, indigestion, muscular pain, fever, anaemia due to internal bleeding, nausea, headache and blockage of intestinal passage.

(ii) **Filariasis/Elephantiasis** This is caused by filarial worms, *Wuchereria bancrofti* and *Wuchereria malayi*. It is a chronic inflammation of the organs.

- *Culex* mosquito (female) is the vector.
- Genital organs also get affected leading to their deformation.
- **Symptoms** include inflammation of organs, in which they live for many years, normally affect lymph vessels of lower limbs resulting in swelling. This condition is called elephantiasis.

Common Preventive Measures

These include

- Maintenance of personal and public hygiene is important.
- Personal hygiene includes keeping the body clean, consumption of clean drinking water, food, vegetables, fruits, etc.

- Public hygiene includes proper disposal of waste, excreta, periodic cleaning and disinfection of water reservoirs, pools, cesspools and tanks.
- Eradication of vectors and destroying their breeding sites, can prevent diseases such as malaria, dengue, chikungunya and filariasis, etc.
- In order to kill vectors, natural predators can also be used, e.g. *Gambusia* fish that feeds on mosquito larvae is a natural predator.
- Mosquito nets, repellants, etc., should be used.
- Vaccination and immunisation programmes for diseases should be strictly followed, e.g. in smallpox, polio, diphtheria.
- Use of antibiotics and other drugs can significantly keep away infectious diseases.

Non-Infectious Diseases

These diseases cannot be transmitted from one person to another and are not caused by pathogens.

Cancer

- It can be defined as an uncontrolled growth or proliferation of cells without any differentiation.
- The cancer cells divide repeatedly with uncontrolled cell divisions. They do not require extracellular growth factors. The newly formed cancer cells are known as **neoplastic cells.**
- Cancer cells have lost the property of **contact inhibition** shown by normal cells, in which contact with other cells inhibit their uncontrolled growth.
  The repeated division of cancerous cells, form a large mass of cells called **tumours.**
- Cancer cells move from tumour to new sites through blood and form secondary tumour. This invasion of cancer cells from one part to other parts *via* body fluids is called **metastasis.**
- Tumours are of two types

Benign tumour	Malignant tumour
It is non-cancerous.	It is cancerous.
It does not show metastasis.	It shows metastasis and invades other body parts.
Growth stops after reaching a certain size.	Growth occurs indefinitely.
Less fatal.	Highly fatal.

- **Causes of cancer** It include certain cancer causing viruses, genes and other agents (carcinogens). They may include
  - **Chemicals** As in cigaratte smoke, benzopyrene, dyes, paints, etc.
  - **Biological** Oncogenic viruses, some parasites, etc.
  - **Physical** Ionising radiations like X-rays and γ-rays, non-ionising radiations like UV-rays.
- Cancer causing viruses are called **oncogenic viruses.** They have genes called **viral oncogenes.** At the time of viral infection, these genes are transferred and can lead to cancer.
- Normal cells have genes called **cellular oncogenes** (*c*-onc) or **proto-oncogenes** (*p*-onc). These are present in inactive state, but under certain conditions (like mutation) oncogenic transformation of the cells may occur. Due to this, *c*-onc are turned on and they can lead to cancer.
- **Cancer detection and diagnosis** Cancer can be detected by the following methods
  - **Blood** and **bone marrow** tests for increased cell counts.
  - **Biopsy** and histopathological studies of the tissue. In biopsy, a thin section of suspected tissue is studied for cell abnormality.
  - **Monoclonal antibodies** against cancer-specific antigens are also used for cancer detection. These antibodies bind to agents which are released by cancerous cells in the body.
  - Techniques like Radiography, CT and MRI.
  - **Techniques of molecular biology** can be used to detect cancerous genes in individuals with inherited susceptibility to certain cancers.

Treatment of Cancer

It involves following methods

(i) **Surgery** Tumours are removed by surgery to check further spread of cancer cells.

(ii) **Radiation therapy** Tumour cells are irradiated by lethal doses of radiation, such as cobalt 60 while taking care to protect the surrounding normal cells.

(iii) **Chemotherapy** Several chemotherapeutic drugs are used to kill cancer cells. But, their side effects like hair loss, anaemia, etc., are also reported.
Most cancers are treated by the combination of the above three.

(iv) **Immunotherapy** Biological modifiers like α-interferons are used to activate the immune system and help in destroying the tumour.

Immunity

It is the ability of an organism to resist or defend itself from the development of a disease. It is of the following types, as shown below

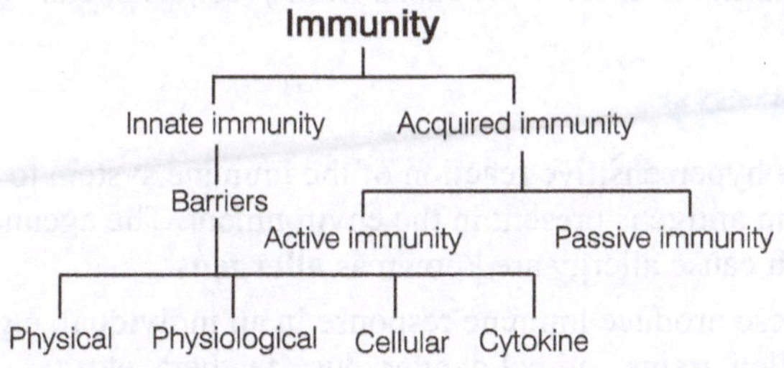

Innate Immunity

It is present since birth and is inherited from the parents. It is non-specific. It consists of following types of barriers

(i) **Physical barriers** prevent entry of micro organisms in the body, e.g. skin, mucus coating of the epithelium lining the respiratory, gastrointestinal and urogenital tracts. Mucus traps the microbes entering our body.

(ii) **Physiological barriers** prevent microbial growth in the body, e.g. acid in the stomach, lysozyme in saliva of mouth and tears from eyes.

(iii) **Cellular barriers** phagocytose and destroy microbes. For example, some leucocytes (WBCs) like Polymorphonuclear Leukocytes (PMNL or Neutrophils), monocytes and natural killer cells (type of lymphocytes) in the blood as well as macrophages in tissues.

(iv) **Cytokine barriers** are virus-infected cells, which secrete proteins called **interferons**. They protect non-infected cells from further viral infection.

Acquired Immunity

- It is not present from birth and develops during an individual's lifetime.
- It is pathogen **specific**, can differentiate between self and non-self cells and characterised by **memory**.
- When it encounters a pathogen for the first time, it produces a response called **primary response**, which is of low intensity and takes time.
- Further encounter with same pathogen produces highly intensified **secondary** or **anamnestic response** due to the memory of first encounter.

Cells of Immune Response

Immune responses are produced by two types of lymphocytes

(i) **B-lymphocytes or B-cells** produce an army of proteins (in response to pathogens) called **antibodies** in blood. B-lymphocytes are formed in bone marrow and their maturation also takes place in bone marrow.

(ii) **T-lymphocytes or T-cells** help B-cells to produce antibodies, but they themselves do not secrete these antibodies.

T-lymphocytes are formed in bone marrow, but their maturation take place in thymus gland.

On the basis of type of immune response, acquired immunity is of following two types

(i) **Humoral immune response or Antibody-Mediated Immunity** (AMI) It is mediated by antibodies present in the body fluid (humours) like blood and lymph. When a pathogen enters in body, the B-cells encounter them and produce different types of antibodies, which are released in the blood.

(ii) **Cell-mediated immune response or Cell-Mediated Immunity** (CMI) It is mediated by T-lymphocytes. Here, antibodies are not produced by T-lymphocytes instead they recognise the non-self cells.

The graft rejection during organ transplantation occurs, because of the ability of T-lymphocytes to differentiate between self and non-self, due to the cell-mediated immunity.

That is why blood group and tissue matching are essential before organ transplantation.

On the basis of trigger, acquired immunity is of following two types

Immunity

Active immunity	**Passive immunity**
• Develops due to contact with pathogen or its antigen.	• Develops when readymade antibodies are injected into the body.
• Slow but long lasting.	• Fast but lasts for only few days.
• No or few side effects.	• May cause side effects.
• Takes time to elicit response, e.g. immunity developed by vaccination.	• Effective when immune response has to be faster, e.g. injections of tetanus, colostrum secreted by mother during initial days of lactation, etc.

Antibodies

These are immunoglobulin molecules (Ig), which show up in response to foreign molecules known as antigens.

- Each antibody molecule has four peptide chains, i.e. two small chains called **light** (L) **chains** and two longer chains called **heavy** (H) **chains**.
- An antibody is represented as H_2L_2. These chains are connected by disulphide bonds. Hence, an antibody appears like a Y-shaped structure.

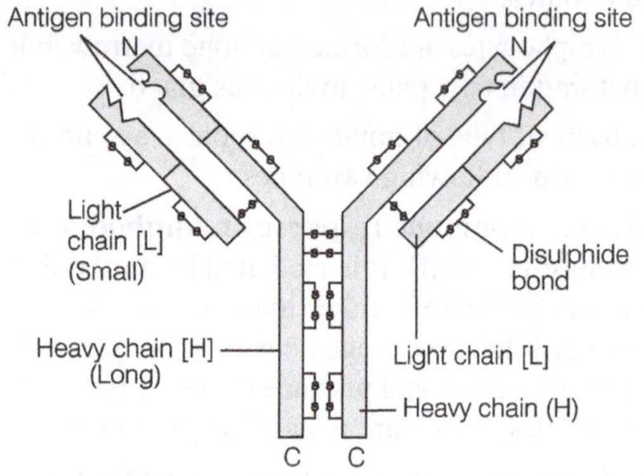

Figure 7.2 Structure of an antibody molecule

- Human body produces different types of antibodies. They include IgA, IgM, IgE, IgG, etc. IgG can cross the mother's placenta.
- Colostrum contains IgA antibody. IgA protects the infant in its initial days from microbes and infection.

Vaccination and Immunisation

- The principles of vaccination and immunisation are based on the property of memory of immune system.
- **Vaccination** is the process of introduction of weakened or inactivated pathogens or proteins (vaccine) into a person to provide protection against a disease.
- **Immunisation** is a process by which the body produces antibodies against the vaccine (primary response) and develops the ability to neutralise pathogens during actual infection (secondary response), i.e. the body becomes immune to that antigen or infection.
- **Vaccine** generates memory B and T-cells that recognise the pathogens on subsequent exposure and produce an intense immune response.
- In case of requirement of quick immune response like tetanus infection, preformed antibodies are injected into the patient. Even in the cases of snake bite, preformed antibodies or antitoxin is injected. This is called **passive immunisation**.
- **Recombinant DNA technology** has produced antigenic polypeptides of pathogen in bacteria or yeast. This allowed large scale production of vaccine, e.g. hepatitis-B vaccine produced from yeast cells, etc.

Allergy

It is a hypersensitive reaction of the immune system to certain antigens present in the environment. The agents which cause allergy are known as **allergens**.

- These produce immune response in an individual, e.g. pollen grains, animal dander, dust, feathers, etc.
- IgE antibodies are produced in response to allergens. IgE binds to allergen and then both bind on mast cell.
- This binding causes the release of chemicals like **histamine** and **serotonin** from the mast cells. These chemicals cause inflammatory reaction in the body.
- Symptoms of allergy are sneezing, watery eyes, running nose, difficulty in breathing, etc.
- Antihistamine, adrenaline and steroids are taken to reduce the symptoms of allergy.
- Modern day lifestyle has resulted into more sensitivity to allergens; e.g. asthma due to the sensitivity to environment is common these days.

Autoimmunity

It is an abnormal immune response, in which immune system of the body starts rejecting its own body cell or self-cells and molecules. The diseases caused due to the autoimmunity are called **autoimmune diseases**, e.g. rheumatoid arthritis, type-I diabetes, etc. Autoimmunity is caused due to genetic or unknown reason.

Human Immune System

This system includes (i) lymphoid organs, (ii) immune cells, (iii) soluble molecules like antibodies and (iv) lymphoid tissues.

Lymphoid Organs

These are the organs where origin, maturation and proliferation of lymphocytes occur. They are of following two types

Primary Lymphoid Organs

These are the sites where lymphocytes differentiate and mature to become antigen-sensitive, e.g. bone marrow and thymus.

- In **bone marrow**, all blood cells including lymphocytes are produced and B-lymphocytes mature.
- **Thymus** is a lobed organ, located near the heart and beneath the breast bone. It reduces in size as the age of an individual increases. T-lymphocytes develop and mature in thymus.

Secondary Lymphoid Organs

These provide the sites where lymphocytes interact with the antigen and proliferate to become effector cells, e.g. spleen, lymph nodes, tonsils, Peyer's patches of small intestine and appendix.

- **Spleen** is a large, bean-shaped organ which contains lymphocytes and phagocytes.
  It acts as a filtre to trap blood-borne microbes and contains a large pool of erythrocytes. So, it is known as **blood bank of body**.
- **Lymph nodes** are small solid structures along the lymphatic system. Their function is to trap microorganisms or other antigens that enter the lymph and tissue fluid.
- **Mucosal Associated Lymphoid Tissue** (MALT) is formed of the masses of lymphoid tissue, located within the lining of mucosa of respiratory, digestive and urogenital tracts.
  About 50% of lymphoid tissue in human body is formed by MALT.

Acquired Immuno Deficiency Syndrome (AIDS)

- AIDS was first reported in 1981 in USA. Here, syndrome means group of symptoms.
- The causative agent is **Human Immunodeficiency Virus** (HIV).
- The virus belongs to a group of viruses called **retrovirus**. It has RNA genome enclosed in an envelope.

This RNA is *ss*RNA which forms DNA *via* reverse transcription process using enzyme reverse transcriptase.

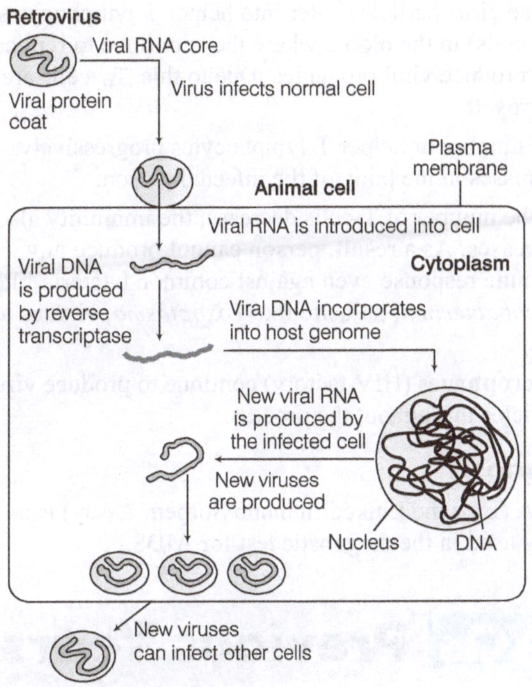

Figure 7.3 Replication of retrovirus

Transmission of HIV

HIV is transmitted by

- Sexual contact with infected person.
- Transfusion of contaminated blood and blood products.
- Sharing infected needles.
- Infected mother to unborn child through placenta.

Note Infected cell can survive, while viruses are being replicated and released.

People who are susceptible to infection are

- Drug addicts, who take intravenous drug injections.
- Individuals who are involved with multiple sexual partners.
- Individuals who require repeated blood transfusion.
- Children born to HIV positive mother.

Modes of HIV Infection

- Virus enters the macrophages, after entering into the body of a person.
- RNA gets replicated to form viral DNA by enzyme reverse transcriptase. This process is known as **reverse transcription**.

- Viral DNA gets incorporated into the host cell DNA and directs the infected cells to produce virus particles.
- These virus particles enter into helper T-lymphocytes (T_H cells) in the blood, where they continue to replicate and produce viral progenies. Due to this, T_H cells are destroyed.
- The number of helper T-lymphocytes progressively decreases in the body of the infected person.
- As the number of T-cells decrease, the immunity also decreases. As a result, person cannot produce any immune response even against common bacteria like *Mycobacterium*, parasite like *Toxoplasma*, viruses and fungi.
- **Macrophages** (HIV factory) continue to produce virus particles throughout the process.

Diagnosis

ELISA (Enzyme Linked Immuno Sorbent Assay) is a widely used in the diagnostic test for AIDS.

Treatment

Treatment with anti-retroviral drugs is only partially effective. They can only prolong the life of patient, but cannot prevent death.

Prevention of AIDS

Certain preventive measures that can prevent HIV infections are

- National AIDS Control Organisation (NACO) setup in 1991 and other NGOs educate people about AIDS.
- Role of WHO in preventing HIV infection
  - Ensure use of disposable syringes and needles.
  - Ensure that blood banks are safe from HIV.
  - Free distribution of condoms.
  - Prevention of drug abuse.
- Discouraging unsafe sex and encouraging regular check-up for HIV in susceptible populations.

PYQs Previous Years' Questions

1 Mark Questions

Multiple Choice Questions

1. In which of the following conditions/diseases is there a substantial increase in the activity of mast cells observed in the human body? **CBSE 2024 (Set-I)**

(a) Typhoid (b) Allergy
(c) Ascariasis (d) AIDS

Ans. (b) In allergy, release of the chemicals like histamine and serotonin from the mast cell (thus, its increased activity) is observed in the human body.

2. Interferons are proteins secreted by **CBSE 2024 (Set-II)**

(a) RBC (b) WBC
(c) Bacteria infected cell (d) Virus infected cell

Ans. (d) Interferons are part of cytokine barriers that help in providing innate immunity. They are proteins secreted by virus-infected cells and protect non-infected cells from further viral infection.

3. The decrease in the T-lymphocytes count in human blood will result in **CBSE 2023**

(a) decrease in antigens (b) increase in antibodies
(c) decrease in antibodies (d) increase in antigens

Ans. (b) increase in antibodies

4. Select the pathogen mismatched with the symptoms of disease caused by it from the given below **CBSE 2023**

(a) *Entamoeba histolytica* : Constipation, abdominal pain
(b) *Epidermophyton*: Dry scaly, lesions on nail
(c) *Wuchereria bancrofti* : Chronic inflammation of lymphatic vessels of lower limb
(d) *Haemophilus influenzae* : Blockage of the intestinal passage

Ans. (d) *Haemophilus influenzae* : Blockage of the intestinal passage

5. Tetanus antitoxin (tetanus toxoid) when injected into the human body it immediately provides **CBSE 2023**

(a) innate immunity (b) passive immunity
(c) autoimmunity (d) active immunity

Ans. (b) passive immunity

6. Interferons are proteins. In humans they are secreted by **CBSE 2023**

(a) thymus gland (b) B-lymphocytes
(c) viral infected cells (d) tonsils

Ans. (c) viral infected cells

7. *Apis mellifera* are killer bees possessing toxic bee venom. Identify the treatment and the type of immunity developed from the given table to treat a person against the venom of this bee. **CBSE SQP 2023**

Remedy	Immunity
(a) Inactivated proteins	Active
(b) Proteins of the venom	Passive
(c) Preformed antibodies	Passive
(d) Dead microorganisms	Active

Ans. (c) Preformed antibodies Passive

8. Interferons are most effective in making non-infected cells resistant against the spread of which of the following diseases in humans? **CBSE SQP 2023**

(a) Ascariasis (b) Ringworm
(c) Amoebiasis (d) AIDS

Ans. (d) AIDS

9. Transplantation of tissues/organs to save certain patients often fails due to rejection of such tissues/organs in the patient's body. Which type of immune response is responsible for such rejection? **CBSE SQP 2019**

(a) Auto-immune response
(b) Humoral immune response
(c) Physiological immune response
(d) Cell-mediated immune response

Ans. (d) Cell-mediated immune response

10. Which of the following are the correct reasons for Rheumatoid arthritis? **CBSE SQP 2019**

(i) Lymphocytes become more active.
(ii) Body attacks self cells.
(iii) More antibodies are produced in the body.
(iv) The ability to differentiate pathogens or foreign molecules from self cells is lost.

Choose the correct answer from the options given below.

(a) i and ii (b) iii and iv
(c) i and iii (d) ii and iv

Ans. (d) ii and iv

Asertion-Reason Type Question

11. **Assertion** (A) AIDS is a syndrome caused by HIV.

Reason (R) HIV is a virus that damages the immune system with DNA as its genetic material.

CBSE 2024 (Set-II)

(a) Both Assertion and Reason are true and Reason is the correct explanation of Assertion.
(b) Both Assertion and Reason are true, but Reason is not the correct explanation of Assertion.
(c) Assertion is true, but Reason is false
(d) Assertion is false, but Reason is true

Ans. (c) A is true, but R is false. R can be corrected as HIV is a virus that damages the immune system in human with *ss*RNA as its genetic material.

Very Short Answer Type Questions

12. State the functions of mast cells in allergy response. **All India 2019**

Ans. The function of mast cell in allergy response is that it releases histamin which causes inflammatory reactions in the body.

13. State the function of interferons. **All India 2019**

Ans. Interferons protect non-infected cells from the other virus infected cells by releasing cytokine barriers.

14. How do monocytes act as a cellular barrier in humans to provide innate immunity? **CBSE 2018 C**

Or In what way is monocyte a cellular barrier with reference to immunity? **Delhi 2015**

Ans. Monocytes phagocytose and destroy microbes present in the blood to provide innate immunity.

15. How do cytokine barriers provide immunity in humans? **CBSE 2018**

Or How do cytokinin barriers help in evading viral infections? **Delhi 2015**

Or How do interferons protect us? **All India 2012**

Ans. Cytokine barriers include interferons, which are secreted by virus infected cells. They provide protection to non-infected cells from further same viral infection.

16. Name two diseases whose spread can be controlled by the eradication of *Aedes* mosquito. **2018**

Ans. Dengue fever and chikungunya are two diseases, whose spread can be controlled by the eradication of *Aedes* mosquito. (½+ ½)

17. Suggest a method to ensure an anamnestic response in humans. **Delhi 2017**

Ans. Anamnestic response is a quick and intense response, which occurs when an individual encounters a particular antigen for the second time. It is aided by the memory of primary response stored in B-cells. By the administration of a dead or attenuated pathogen in the body of person, a secondary immune response can be ensured due to the presence of memory cells in the body.

18. Retroviruses have no DNA. However, the DNA of the infected host cell does possess viral DNA. How is it possible? **All India 2015**

Ans. Retroviruses have RNA as their genetic material. After getting into the body of a person, the virus enters the macrophages. Here, RNA is replicated to form viral DNA by using enzyme reverse transcriptase. The viral

DNA now, gets incorporated into the host cell's DNA and directs the infected cells to produce viruses.

19. Indiscriminate diagnostic practices using X-rays, etc., should be avoided. Give one reason. **Delhi 2015**

Ans. Indiscriminate diagnostic practices using X-rays should be avoided, because there are several potential risks from exposure to ionising radiations, e.g. cancer can be developed in later stages of life, various tissues can also get affected leading to cataract, hair loss, etc.

20. Name any two types of cells that act as 'cellular barriers' to provide innate immunity in humans. **Delhi 2014**

Ans. Cellular barriers include certain types of leucocytes of our body such as polymorphonuclear leucocytes, monocytes and natural killer in the blood as well as macrophages in tissues. These can phagocytose and destroy microbes and provide innate immunity to humans. (½ + ½)

21. Why is *Gambusia* introduced into drains and ponds? **All India 2014**

Ans. *Gambusia* is a fish that feeds upon mosquito larvae. Thus, it is introduced in drains and ponds to destroy disease vectors.

22. Why is secondary immune response more intense than the primary immune response in humans? **All India 2014**

Or

When does a human body elicit an anamnestic response? **All India 2013; Delhi 2011C**

Ans. The secondary or anamnestic immune response is based on the memory of primary response, i.e. first encounter with an antigen. Due to this, the second generated immune response is more fast and has higher affinity for antigen and therefore, it is more intense than primary immune response in humans.

23. How does haemozoin affect the human body when released in blood during malarial infection? **Foreign 2014**

Ans. The release of toxic haemozoin by the ruptured RBCs during malarial infection results in recurrence of high fever and chill every 3-4 days.

24. What is an autoimmune disease? Give an example. **Foreign 2014**

Ans. The abnormal response of an immune system, in which it fails to recognise 'self' and 'non-self' and starts destroying its own cells and molecules is called **autoimmune disease**. Rheumatoid arthritis is an example of autoimmune disease, which destroys articular cartilage and fusing bones. (½ + ½)

25. State two different roles of spleen in the human body. **All India 2012**

Ans. The two different roles of spleen in human body are

(i) Spleen acts as a filtre to trap blood-borne microorganisms.

(ii) It is a large reservoir of erythrocytes. (½ + ½)

26. Why do pollen grains of some flower trigger sneezing in some people? **Foreign 2012**

Ans. Pollen grains are allergens that cause allergy in some people due to release of chemicals like histamine and serotonin from mast cells. These trigger the inflammatory responses in body, such as sneezing, wheezing, etc.

2 Marks Questions

27. A farmer while working on his farm was bitten by a poisonous snake. He was rushed to a nearby health centre where the doctor gave him an injection to save his life.

(i) What did the doctor inject and why?

(ii) Name the kind of immunity provided by this injection. **CBSE 2024 (Set-I)**

Ans. (i) The doctor injected anti-venom into the farmer's body as it contains preformed antibodies against the snake venom. These ready-made antibodies are directly given to protect the body against foreign agents. (1½)

(ii) When ready-made antibodies are provided by a patient to fight against foreign antigen, it is called passive immunity. (½)

28. The graph given below indicates the administration of the first (*L*) and second dose (*M*) of a vaccine. The corresponding response of the body is indicated by *X* and *Y*. Interpret the graph and explain the reason for such a response shown by the body.

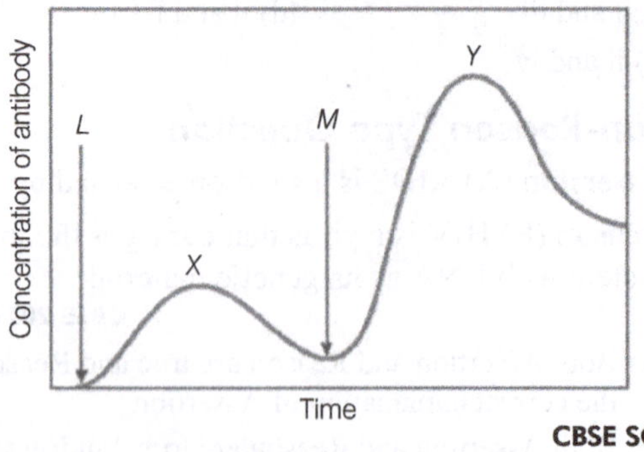

CBSE SQP 2024

Ans. On administration of the first dose of the vaccine (*L*), the body shows a response of low intensity (*X*) as the immune system comes in contact with the antigenic protein of the weakened/inactivated pathogen for the first time. This is called primary immune response. (1)

On subsequent encounter with the same antigenic protein in the second dose (*M*), the body elicits a highly intensified secondary response (*Y*). Because of the memory of the first contact with the antigen, the secondary immune response is faster and stronger, leading to more effective pathogen elimination in comparison to the primary immune response. (1)

29. Immunotherapy these days is one of the most efficient way of treatment of cancer. The therapy involved activates the immune system and destroys the tumour. **CBSE 2023**

(i) Write an example of one such biological response modifier used in immunotherapy.

(ii) Why do patients need such substances if immune system is already working in body?

(iii) State what is 'Contact inhibition'.

Ans. (i) One such example of a biological response modifier used in immunotherapy is α-interferon. (½)

(ii) Patients need substances like α-interferons in the body to activate the immune system and help in destroying the tumour. (1)

(iii) Contact inhibition is the condition when contact with other cells prevents the uncontrolled growth of the cells. It is shown by the normal cells. (½)

30. Name any two techniques used to detect the cancer of internal organs and write about any one of them. **CBSE 2023**

Ans. Biopsy and radiography are two techniques used to detect the cancer of internal organs. (1)

In biopsy, a thin section of suspected tissue is studied for cell abnormality. (1)

31. Why a malignant tumour is considered to be more damaging than benign tumour? Explain. **CBSE 2023**

Ans. Malignant tumour is cancerous and spread to the other organs of the body (metastasis) with a rapid growth rate whereas, benign tumour is non-cancerous and remains confined to affected organs in the body.

Therefore, benign tumour causes limited damage as compared to the malignant tumour.

32. During a field trip, one of your friend in the group suddenly became unwell, she started sneezing and had trouble in breathing. **CBSE SQP 2023**

Name and explain the term associated with such sudden responses. What would the doctor recommend for relief?

Ans. (i) The sudden response was due to allergy. It can be defined as the exaggerated response of the immune system to certain substances (or allergens) present in the environment. (1)

(ii) In order to reduce the symptoms, the doctor would recommend either antihistamines or adrenaline. (1)

33. How does human immunodeficiency virus cause immunodeficiency in the human body? **All India 2021-22 Term-II**

Ans. HIV virus enters the macrophages after entering into the host body. RNA gets replicated to form viral DNA, with the help of an enzyme reverse transcriptase. Viral DNA gets incorporated into the host cell DNA and stimulates the production of virus particles. These particles enter the T-lymphocytes and eventually destroy them with a decrease in number of T-lymphocytes, the immunity of an individual also decreases.

34. What are interferons? State their role in the treatment of cancer. **All India 2021-22 Term-II**

Ans. Interferons are a group of signaling proteins released by the host cells in response to the presence of several pathogens like viruses, bacteria, etc. Interferons mediate and regulate different aspects of cancer cells behaviour including proliferation and metastatic spreading. They play a key role in activating cellular immunity and increase host defence. (1 + 1)

35. 'Epithelial lining of our intestine is considered as secondary lymphoid organ'. Justify the statement. **Delhi 2021-22 Term-II**

Ans. Lymphoid organs are the organs where origin, maturation and proliferation of lymphocytes occur. They are of two types

(i) Primary lymphoid organs (1)

(ii) Secondary lymphoid organs

Epithelial lining is considered as secondary lymphoid organ as it provides the site of lymphocyte antigen interaction. (1)

36. Explain giving two reasons, how immune response by 'vaccine' is different from that by 'antitoxin' in humans. **All India 2021-22 Term-II**

Ans. Immune response by vaccine is different from that by antitoxin in humans in two ways

(i) Vaccines give long term protection unlike antitoxins.

(ii) Vaccines can either destroy, kill or render a pathogen inactive, whereas antitoxins render a toxic substance harmless. (1 + 1)

37. A boy developed some allergic reactions when he straight entered into his air conditioned room after a game of football outside his house. Write any two symptoms that could be noticed in such condition. How does our body combat such conditions? **Delhi 2021-22 Term-II**

Ans. Two symptoms that the boy could develop in such a situation are

(i) sneezing (ii) running nose

Allergens produce immune response in an individual. As a result, IgE antibodies are released in our body which bind to allergens and then both bind to mast cells. This binding causes the release of chemicals like histamine and serotonin from mast cells which cause reactions in our body.

In order to reduce such reactions, antihistamines are usually taken.

38. Humans have innate immunity for protection against pathogens that may enter the gut along with food. What are the two barriers that protect the body from such pathogens? **CBSE SQP 2021-22 Term-II**

Ans. Two barriers that protect the body from pathogens entering the gut of humans with food are

(i) **Physical barrier** mucus coating of epithelium lining the gastrointestinal tract helps in trapping microbes entering our body.

(ii) **Physiological barriers** Acid in the stomach, saliva in the mouth prevent microbial growth. (1+1)

39. Name the types of acquired immune responses and the special types of lymphocytes involved in providing them. **Delhi 2020**

Ans. Refer to text on page no. 211 (Acquired immunity).

40. Name one air-borne and a water-borne diseases in humans. List one specific symptom of each one of them. **All India 2020**

Ans. Air-borne disease is common cold. Its specific symptom is nasal congestion and discharge. Water-borne disease is typhoid. Its specific symptom is sustained high fever (39-40°C).

41. Differentiate between the roles of B-lymphocytes and T-lymphocytes in generating immune responses. **Delhi 2019**

Ans. For B and T-lymphocytes, refer to text on page no. 211.

42. Principle of vaccination is based on the property of 'memory' of the immune system. Taking one suitable example, justify the statement. **Delhi 2019**

Ans. For vaccination, refer to text on page no. 212.

43. The figure given below represents a molecule present in the body of a mammal.

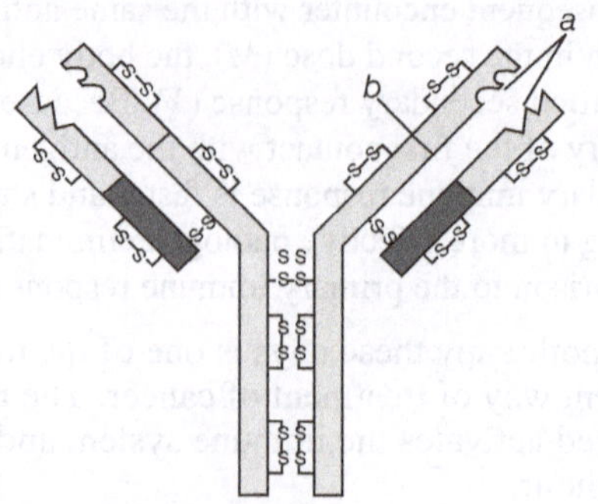

(i) Name the parts labelled '*a*' and '*b*' in the molecule shown above.

(ii) Name the type of cells that produce this molecule.

Ans. (i) The parts labelled '*a*' and '*b*' in the given diagram are 'Antigen binding site' and 'Heavy chain', respectively.

(ii) B-lymphocytes are the type of cells that produce this molecule (antibody). (1 + 1)

44. Explain the impact of removal of thymus gland on the immune system of a human body. **CBSE SQP 2018-19**

Ans. The thymus provides microenviroments for the development and maturation of T-lymphocytes. Due to the removal of thymus gland, T-cell maturation will not take place and cell-mediated immunity will decrease. Therefore, the immunity will be reduced.

45. Why is the structure of an antibody molecule represented as H_2L_2 ? Name any two types of antibodies produced in a human body. **CBSE 2018C**

Ans. For structure of antibody molecule refer to text on page no. 212 (Antibodies).

46. Mention one application for each of the following

(i) Passive immunisation

(ii) Antihistamine

(iii) Colostrum

(iv) Cytokine-barrier **All India 2017**

Ans. Applications of given components are as follows

(i) **Passive immunisation** provides a faster immune response.

(ii) **Antihistamine** is used to reduce the symptoms of allergy, such as sneezing, watery eyes, rashes, running nose, etc.

(iii) **Colostrum** consists of antibodies (e.g. IgA) that provide immunity to an infant against infections.

(iv) **Cytokine barrier** produces interferons and protects non-infected cells from further viral infection. (½ × 4)

47. Name the cells HIV (Human Immunodeficiency Virus) gains entry into after infecting the human body. Explain the events that occur in these cells. **All India 2016**

Or How do macrophages in the human body act as HIV factory? **All India 2010**

Or Name the cells that act as HIV factory in humans when infected by HIV. Explain the events that occur in the infected cell.

Ans. After infecting the human body, the HIV gains entry into macrophages.

Events occurring in these cells are as follows

(i) RNA genome of the virus replicates to form viral DNA by enzyme reverse transcriptase.

(ii) Viral DNA gets incorporated into the macrophage DNA and directs the infected cells to produce new viruses.

(iii) Macrophages continue to produce virus particles and thus called **HIV factory**.

48. Name the causative organism of the disease amoebiasis. List three symptoms of the disease. **All India 2016**

Or (i) Name the protozoan parasite that causes amoebic dysentery in humans.

(ii) Mention two diagnostic symptoms of the disease.

(iii) How is this disease transmitted to others? **All India 2016, Delhi 2012**

Ans. Refer to text on page no. 208.

49. (i) Name any two causative organisms responsible for ringworm.

(ii) State any two symptoms of the disease. **Delhi 2016C**

Ans. (i) Causative organisms responsible for ringworm are *Microsporum*, *Epidermophyton* and *Trichophyton* (all fungi). (1)

(ii) Two symptoms of the disease are

(a) Intense itching

(b) Appearance of dry, scaly lesions on various body parts. (1)

50. (i) Name any two helminths which are known pathogenic to human.

(ii) List any two symptoms of the diseases caused by any one of them. **Delhi 2016**

Or List the symptoms of ascariasis. How does a healthy person acquire this infection? **All India 2014**

Ans. (i) Helminths worms, known pathogenic to humans are

(a) *Ascaris*, the roundworm.

(b) *Wuchereria*, the filarial worm. (1)

(ii) *Ascaris* is an intestinal parasite that causes ascariasis. Symptoms of ascariasis are internal bleeding, muscular pain, fever, anaemia and blockage in intestinal passage.

A healthy person acquires this infection through consumption of water, vegetables or fruits contaminated with the eggs of parasite *Ascaris*. (1)

51. Name any two secondary lymphoid organs in a human body and state the function of any of them. **Delhi 2016C**

Ans. Secondary lymphoid organs provide the site for interaction of lymphocytes with the antigen, which then proliferate to become effector cells, e.g. spleen, tonsils and lymph nodes. (1)

Lymph nodes help to trap antigens entering the tissue fluid, whereas spleen trap the blood-borne microbes. (1)

52. How are oncogenic viruses different from proto-oncogenes?

Ans. **Oncogenic viruses** The cancer causing viruses which have viral genes or oncogenes are called oncogenic viruses. (1)

Proto-oncogenes These genes are present in normal cells, which when activated under certain conditions could lead to oncogenic transformation of the cells, thus leading to cancer. (1)

53. (i) Which organ of the human body is initially affected when bitten by an infected female *Anopheles*? Name the stage of the parasite that infects this organ.

(ii) Explain the events that are responsible for chill and high fever in the patient. **Delhi 2016C**

Ans. (i) **Liver** is initially affected by the sporozoites stage due to the bite of female *Anopheles*. (1)

(ii) Rupture of RBC and release of haemozoin is responsible for chill and high fever. (1)

54. Name an allergen and write the response of human body when exposed to it. **Delhi 2014C**

Ans. The allergen can be pollen grains, spores or dust particles. (½)

When the allergens are inhaled or enter body system, they stimulate body to produce IgE antibodies and trigger an antiallergic reaction. The chemicals such as histamine and serotonin are released from mast cells in response to allergen, thereby causing dilation of blood vessels. These chemicals also elicit inflammatory response that may result in sneezing, watery eyes, running nose, etc. (1½)

55. Differentiate between active and passive immunity. **Delhi 2014C**

Ans. Differences between active and passive immunity are

Active immunity	Passive immunity
Develops when body's own cells produce antibodies in response to infection or vaccine.	Develops when antibodies produced in other organisms are injected or administered into a person to counteract antigen.
Slow in response, but long lasting effects, e.g. immunity developed by vaccination.	Provides immediate relief, but short lived, e.g, injection of tetanus.

56. How does a vaccine for a particular disease immunise the human body against that disease? **Delhi 2013C**

Ans. During vaccination for a particular disease, an antigen or antigenic protein or weak pathogen, which is in inactive form is introduced into the body to induce mild immune response.

The vaccine generates antibodies that neutralise the toxin/pathogen and produces memory-B or T-cells, which recognise the pathogen in the subsequent encounters and produce antibodies.

57. Why is a person with cuts and bruises following an accident administered tetanus antitoxin? Give reasons. **All India 2013**

Or Why does a doctor administer tetanus antitoxin and not a tetanus vaccine to a child injured in a roadside accident with a bleeding wound? **All India 2010**

Ans. A person with cuts and bruises following an accident is administered tetanus antitoxin, because this toxin contains performed antibodies against the pathogen *Clostridium tetani*. This inactivates the pathogen and provides passive immunity.

Also, tetanus antitoxin provide instant response unlike tetanus vaccine, which take time to develop immunity.

58. A patient showed symptoms of sustained high fever, stomach pain and constipation, but no blood clot in stools. Name the disease and its pathogen. Write the diagnostic test for the disease. How does the disease get transmitted? **Delhi 2013C**

Ans. The symptoms, such as constant high fever, stomach pain and constipation, weakness and headache are shown in typhoid.

Its causative agent is a bacterium called *Salmonella typhi*. **Widal test** is used for its diagnosis.

Typhoid is transmitted through contaminated food and water. (½ × 4)

59. A student on a school picnic to a park on a windy day started sneezing and having difficulty in breathing on reaching the park. The teacher enquired whether the student was allergic to something.

(i) What is an allergy?

(ii) Write the two unique characteristics of the system involved in the response observed in the student. **Delhi 2013**

Ans. (i) Allergy is a hypersensitive response to a foreign substance coming in contact with or entering the body, e.g. sneezing, watery eyes, etc. **(1)**

(ii) It is due to the release of histamine and serotonin by the mast cells. **(1)**

60. A young boy when brought a pet dog home started to complain of watery eyes and running nose. The symptoms disappeared when the boy was kept away from the pet.

(i) Name the type of antibody and the chemicals responsible for such a response in the boy.

(ii) Mention the name of any one drug that could be given to the boy for immediate relief from such a response. **Delhi 2013**

Ans. (i) In case of allergy, IgE antibodies are involved. Histamine and serotonin are responsible for such responses. **(1)**

(ii) Antihistamine could be given for immediate relief. **(1)**

61. (i) Highlight the role of thymus as a lymphoid organs.

(ii) Name the cells that are released from the above mentioned gland. Mention, how they help in immunity? **Delhi 2012**

Ans. (i) Thymus is a primary lymphoid organ of the immune system. Here, immature lymphocytes get differentiated into antigen-sensitive T-lymphocytes. **(1)**

(ii) T-lymphocytes are released from thymus, after their maturation gets completed. They themselves do not produce antibodies, but help B-cells to produce them. They are also responsible for Cell Mediated Immune (CMI) response. **(1)**

62. Name the parasite that causes filariasis in humans. Mention its two diagnostic symptoms. How is this transmitted to others? **Delhi 2012**

Ans. *Wuchereria* (*W. bancrofti* and *W. malayi*) is the filarial worm that causes filariasis in humans. (½)

Diagnostic Symptoms

(i) The presence of nematodes in lymph vessels causes collection of fluid. It may lead to swelling in arms, breasts, legs and genital region.

(ii) Inflammation of lower limbs results in deformities. **(1)**

It is transmitted to a healthy person through the bite of the female mosquito vector, *Culex*. **(½)**

63. Name and explain the two types of immune responses in humans. **All India 2012**

Ans. Immune responses are of two types

(i) **Primary response** The reaction of the body's immune system to the first attack of microbe (antigen) is called primary immune response. It is slow and less intense. **(1)**

(ii) **Secondary response** The reaction of the body's immune system to any subsequent infection of the same microbe is termed as secondary immune response. It is fast and intense. **(1)**

64. Name the two special types of lymphocytes in humans. How do they differ in their roles in immune response? **All India 2012**

Ans. Two special types of lymphocytes in humans are

(i) B-lymphocytes or B-cells

(ii) T-lymphocytes or T-cells

Differences between B and T-lymphocytes are

B-lymphocytes	T-lymphocytes
They produce antibodies against antigen.	They stimulate B-cells to produce antibodies.
They do not respond to organ transplant.	They react to organ transplant.

(1+1)

65. (i) Name the group of virus responsible for causing AIDS in humans. Why are these virus so, named?

(ii) List any two ways of transmission of HIV infection in humans other than sexual contact? **All India 2012**

Ans. (i) Retrovirus is the group of viruses causing AIDS in humans. They contain RNA as genetic material and with the help of the enzyme reverse transcriptase, they make viral DNA using RNA as a template. Thus, they are called **retrovirus**. **(1)**

(ii) (a) By sharing infected needles.

(b) By transfusion of blood contaminated with HIV. **(1)**

66. Why is an antibody represented as H_2L_2? **Foreign 2012**

Ans. Antibody is represented as H_2L_2 because each antibody molecule has four peptide chains, i.e. two small light (L) chains and two longer heavy (H) chains.

67. Name the different types of cells providing cellular barrier responsible for innate immunity in humans. **Foreign 2012**

Ans. For cellular barrier as innate immunity, refer to page no. 211.

68. List any two emergent circumstances, when a medical doctor would recommend injection of a preformed antibody into the body of a patient and why? **Delhi 2011C**

Ans. In case of snake bite and in tetanus infection, preformed antibodies help in providing quick immune response.

69. List the two types of immunity a human baby is born with. Explain the differences between the two types. **All India 2011**

Ans. Two types of immunity with which human baby is born include

(i) **Innate immunity** It is inherited type of immunity. It protects an organism from birth throughout the life. It is not specific to particular pathogen and consists of four types of barriers namely physical, physiological, cellular and cytokine. **(1)**

(ii) **Natural passive immunity** It is passively transferred from mother to foetus through placenta, e.g. IgG antibodies can cross placental barrier to reach the foetus. **(1)**

70. How is an allergic reaction caused by an allergen? Name the drug that can reduce the symptoms of allergy? **All India 2011C**

Ans. An allergic reaction is caused by allergens as these can produce IgE type of antibodies. These antibodies cause the release of histamine and serotonin like chemicals from mast cells, which cause allergic reactions. The use of drugs like antihistamine, adrenaline and steroids quickly reduce the symptoms of allergy. **(1 + 1)**

71. Name the two types of immunity in a human body. Why are cell-mediated and humoral immunities so called? **Delhi 2011**

Ans. Types of immunity system in humans are

(i) Innate immunity and acquired immunity are two main types of immunities in human body. **(1)**

(ii) Cell mediated immunity is so called as it is mediated by specialised cells, the T-lymphocytes that recognise self and non-self cells. Humoral immunity is so called because it is mediated by antibodies, which are found circulating in body fluid (humour), e.g. blood. **(1)**

72. Write the scientific names of the causal organisms of elephantiasis and ringworm in humans. Mention the body parts affected by them. **Delhi 2011**

Ans. (i) **Elephantiasis** is caused by *Wuchereria bancrofti* and *W. malayi*. These affect lower limbs and genital organs. **(1)**

(ii) **Ringworm** is caused by *Microsporum*, *Trichophyton* and *Epidermophyton*. They affect the skin, nails and scalp. **(1)**

73. Identify *A, D, E* and *F* in the diagram of an antibody molecule given below. **Delhi 2011**

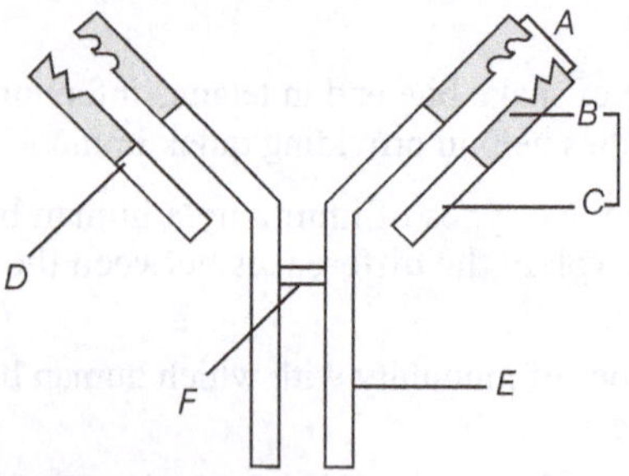

Ans. *A*–Antigen binding region, *D*–Light chain, *E*–Heavy chain, *F*–Disulphide bond/bridge (½ × 4)

74. Name the host and the site, where the following occur in the life cycle of a malarial parasite.

(i) Formation of gametocytes.

(ii) Fusion of gametocytes. **Delhi 2010**

Ans. (i) Formation of gametocytes occurs in the erythrocytes (RBCs) of human beings. (1)

(ii) Fusion of gametocytes occurs in the intestine of mosquito. (1)

75. Define the term health. Mention any two ways of maintaining it. **All India 2010**

Ans. Health can be defined as a state of complete physical, mental and social well-being. It can be maintained by taking balanced diet, maintaining personal hygiene, regular exercise/yoga, vaccination against infectious diseases, etc. (1 + 1)

76. Identify *A, B, C* and *D* in the following table.

Name of the human diseases	Name of the causal bacterial virus	Specific organ or its part affected
Typhoid	*Salmonella typhi*	*A*
Common cold	*B*	*C*
Pneumonia	*Streptococcus pneumoniae*	*D*

Foreign 2010

Ans. A – Small intestine, *B* – Rhinovirus

C – Nose, respiratory passage

D – Alveoli of lungs. (½ × 4)

77. The barriers in the innate immunity are given in the following table. Identify *A, B, C* and *D*.

Types of barrier	Barriers
Physical	Skin, *A*
Physiological	*B*, in the eye
C	Interferon
Cellular	WBC, *D*

Delhi 2010C

Ans. *A*–Epithelium lining,

B–Tears,

C–Cytokine

D–Polymorphonuclear leucocytes.

78. (i) How does a vaccine affect immunity?

(ii) How can we get immunisation against tetanus? **All India 2010**

Ans. (i) In vaccination, a preparation of antigenic proteins of pathogen or inactivated/ weakened pathogen (vaccine) are introduced into the body. The antibodies produced in the body against these antigens would neutralise the pathogenic agents during actual infection. The vaccines also generate memory-B and T-cells. (1)

(ii) Preformed antibodies for tetanus are directly injected to acquire quick immune response. This is called passive immunisation against tetanus. (1)

79. Why do normal cells not show cancerous growth? **All India 2010**

Ans. Normal cells do not show cancerous growth as

(i) Their growth and division are regulated by certain regulatory mechanisms. (1)

(ii) They show the property of contact inhibition, by virtue of which contact with other cells inhibit their uncontrolled growth. (1)

80. State the effect of carcinogens on human body. Name the carcinogenic ionising and non-ionising radiations. Mention their carcinogenic effects. **All India 2010C**

Ans. Carcinogens can transform normal cell into cancerous cells. (½)

Carcinogenic ionising radiations are X-rays and gamma rays. Carcinogenic non-ionising radiations are UV-rays. (1)

These radiations cause changes in base sequences, i.e. mutations that lead to transformation of normal cells into cancerous cell. (½)

81. (i) Explain the property that prevents normal cells from becoming cancerous.

(ii) All normal cells have inherent characteristic of becoming cancerous. Explain.

Ans. (i) Refer to text on page no. 210.

(ii) All normal cells have cellular oncogenes (*c*-onc) or proto-oncogenes. When activated under certain conditions, such genes could lead to oncogenic transformation of cells, i.e. they may become cancerous. (1 + 1)

3 Marks Questions

82. Identify *A, B, C, D, E* and *F* in the table given below **CBSE 2024 (Set-I)**

Name of human disease	Causative organism	Symptoms
Pneumonia	*Streptococcus*	*A*
Typhoid	*B*	High fever, weakness headache, stomach pain
Common cold	Rhino virus	*C*
Ringworm	*D*	Dry scaly lesions on body parts, redness, itching
Ascariasis	*Ascaris*	*E*
F	*Entamoeba histolytica*	Constipation, cramps, stools with mucus and blood clots

Ans. Completed table is given as follows

Name of human diseases	Causative organisms	Symptoms
Pneumonia	*Streptococcus*	(*A*) Chills, fever, cough, headache, lips and fingers turning bluish.
Typhoid	*Salmonella typhi* (*B*)	High fever, weakness, headache, stomach pain.
Common cold	*Rhinovirus*	(*C*) Nasal congestion and discharge, sore throat, hoarseness, cough, headache, tiredness, etc.
Ringworm	*Microsporum, Trichophyton* and *Epidermophyton* (*D*)	Dry scaly lesion on body parts, redness, itching.
Ascariasis	*Ascaris*	(*E*) Inernal bleeding muscular pain, fever anaemia and blockage of intestinal passage
Amoebiasis (*F*)	*Entamoeba histolytica*	Constipation, cramps, stools with mucus and blood clots.

83. *Plasmodium* protozoan needs both a mosquito and a human host for its continuity? Explain. **CBSE 2023**

Ans. *Plasmodium* protozoan is a digentic endoparasite because it completes its life cycle in two host.

Its primary host, where it completes its asexual cycle is the man. Its vector, or secondary host, is a female *Anopheles* mosquito, with it completes its sexual cycle. Refer to answer no. 86 (i) for life cycle of malaria parasite.

84. We all must work towards maintaining good health because 'health is wealth'. Enlist any six ways of achieving good health. **CBSE 2023**

Ans. The six important ways of achieving good health are given below

(i) Eat healthy
(ii) Regular exercise
(iii) Personal hygiene
(iv) Proper waste disposal
(v) Keep the surroundings clean
(vi) Do not consume harmful substances like alcohol and drugs. (½ × 6)

85. Highlight the structural importance of an antibody molecule with a diagram. Name the four types of antibodies found to give a humoral immune response, mentioning the functions of two of them you have studied. **CBSE SQP 2023**

Ans. An antibody molecule consists of four polypeptide chains, two long called heavy (H) chains while other two short called light (L) chains. Both are arranged in the shape of Y. Hence, the antibody is represented as H_2L_2. The four types of antibodies found to give a humoral immune response are IgA, IgM, IgE,IgG.

Functions of two antibodies are

IgA – Secreted in lactating mother to protect their infant.

IgE – Secreted to protect from allergens.

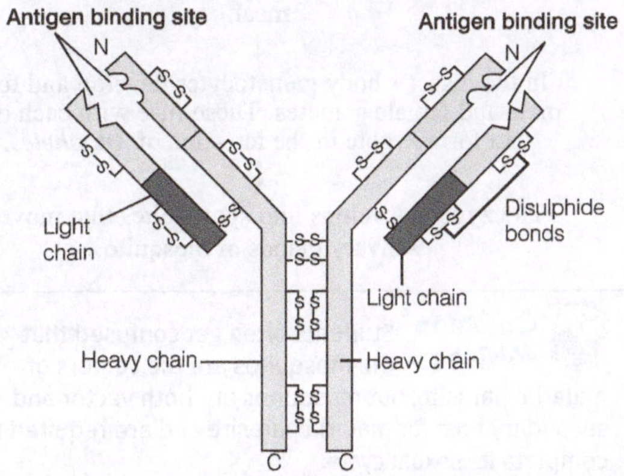

86. (i) Explain the life cycle of *Plasmodium* starting from its entry in the body of female *Anopheles* till the completion of its life cycle in humans.

(ii) Explain the cause of periodic recurrence of chill and high fever during malarial attack in humans. **CBSE SQP 2023**

Ans. (i) When a female *Anopheles* mosquito bites an infected person, the parasites enter the mosquito's body as gametocytes. It leads to fertilisation and development in the gut of the mosquito. It undergoes further development to form sporozoites that are stored in salivary glands until their transfer to human body. In the human body the sporozoites reach the liver and reproduce asexually, bursting the cells and releasing them into the RBCs as gametocytes.

(ii) The rupture of RBCs releases a toxic substance called haemozoin, which is responsible for the chill and high fever during malaria attack in humans.

Or

Life Cycle of Malarial Parasite (*Plasmodium*) in Human Body

Sporozoites are injected into body by infected female *Anopheles* mosquito

↓

Parasites (sporozoites) reach liver through blood

↓

Parasites reproduce asexually in liver cells and come out into blood by bursting of liver cells

↓

They enter red blood cells

↓

Parasits reproduce asexually in red blood cells and by bursting them release haemozoin, which causes cycles of fever, chill and shivering

↓

Released parasite enters new red blood cells and infect them

↓

Some continue asexual reproduction and others enter sexual stage and form gametocytes in RBCs, which are picked by *Anopheles* mosquito along their blood meal.

↓

In the insect's body gametocytes develop and form male and female gametes. These fuse with each other to form zygote in the intestine of *Anopheles*.

↓

The zygote develops into sporozoites that move to salivary glands of mosquito.

Common Mistakes Students often get confused that the mosquitos are the vectors of malarial parasite, but mosquitos are both vector and secondary host for malaria parasite and are required to complete its sexual cycle.

87. A patient complains of suffering from constipation, stomach ache, stool with blood clots and excess mucus. The physician diagnosed it as amoebiasis, after stool test.

(i) Write the scientific name of the microbe identified in the stool sample.

(ii) How do you think, the patient must have contracted it?

(iii) Write your suggestions to the patient to avoid infection in future. **Delhi 2021-22 Term-II**

Ans. (i) *Entamoeba histolytica*

(ii) The patient would have contraced it through contaminated food and water.

(iii) In order to avoid such an infection, the patient must take care to avoid uncovered food as the infection spreads through houseflies. **(1 × 3)**

88. (i) Explain the roles of (a) primary and (b) secondary lymphoid organs that are responsible for developing defence to combat the action of pathogens/foreign antigens which enter our body.

(ii) Doctors generally advise not to undergo surgery of tonsils. Why? **All India 2021-22 Term-II**

Ans. (i) Refer to text on page no. 213.

(ii) Doctors generally advise not to undergo surgery of tonsils because getting the tonsils removed leads to an increased rate of upper respiratory infections as tonsils possess more WBCs which help in killing germs. Removing tonsils would lead to higher infection rate.

89. (i) Write the complete name of the diagnostic test for AIDS. Explain the principle it works on.

(ii) Name the type of genetic material present in AIDS causing pathogen. **Delhi 2021-22 Term-II**

Ans. (i) There are several methods for the diagnosis of HIV infection like Enzyme Linked Immuno Sorbent Assay (ELISA), PCR test, Western blotting, etc. Out of these, ELISA and Western blotting are widely used tests. ELISA is based on the principle of antigen antibody interaction. Infection by pathogen can be detected by the presence of antigens like proteins and glycoproteins or by detecting the antibodies produced against the pathogen.

(ii) Genetic material present in AIDS causing pathogen is *ss*RNA. **(2 + 1)**

90. (i) Explain the property of contact inhibition and its effect on normal human cells and cancerous cells.
(ii) Why are biological modifiers like α-interferon required for cancer treatment? How do they act to treat the disease? **Dehli 2021-22 Term-II**

Ans. (i) In normal cells, the cell growth and differentiation is highly controlled and regulated as they show the property of contact inhibition. By virtue of this property, contact with other cells, stop the uncontrolled cell growth.
Cancerous cells do not have this property, thus such cells continue to divide, producing a mass of cells called tumour.
As a result of lack of contact inhibition, the cancerous cells damage the surrounding cells as they make them starve for nutrients. (1½)
(ii) Biological modifiers like α-interferons are a group of signaling proteins released by the host cells as a response to the presence of pathogens like viruses, bacteria, etc.
These regulate the different aspects of cancer cell's behaviour keeping a check on their spread. This further leads to their controlled growth. Interferons also play a key role in activating cellular immunity of the host organism and increase host defence. (1½)

91. Recognition of an antigenic protein of a pathogen or exposure to a pathogen occurs during many types of immune responses, including active immunity and induced active immunity. Specify the types of responses elicited when human beings get encountered by a pathogen. **CBSE SQP 2021-22 Term-II**

Ans. When human beings get encountered by a pathogen, two types of immune response are elicited,
Refer to the answer no. 63 for the types of responses elicited.

Common Mistakes Commonly students get confused that antigens are pathogen only, but antigens are substances that are part of the pathogen or are present alone or with any other foreign particles.

92. How do normal cells get transformed into cancerous neoplastic cells? Elaborate giving three examples of inducing agent. **CBSE SQP 2021-22 Term II**

Ans. Transformation of normal cells into cancerous neoplastic cells may be induced by following physical, chemical or biological agents causing DNA damage.
Physical Ionising radiations like X-rays and gamma-rays, non-ionising radiation Ultraviolet rays.
Chemical As in cigarette smoke benzopyrene, dyes, paints, etc.
Biological Oncogenic viruses, some parasites, etc.

93. A person is suffering from a high-grade fever. Which symptoms will help to identify if he/she is suffering from typhoid, pneumonia or malaria?

Ans. If a person suffering from a sustained high fever, i.e. body temperature (39°C to 40°C), stomach pain, weakness, constipation, headache, loss of appetite, the person suffers from typhoid.
If the person has fever chills and headache with lips and nails turning gray to bluish the person has pneumonia.
The person has malaria if he has chills and fever recurring every three to four days.

94. (i) Write the specific symptoms of pneumonia and amoebiasis.
(ii) Mention their mode of spread in a population. **Delhi 2020**

Ans. Refer to text on page no. 208.

95. Compare the symptoms of ascariasis, amoebiasis and elephantiasis. **Delhi 2020**

Ans. Comparison between the symptoms of ascariasis, amoebiasis and elephantiasis.

Ascariasis	Amoebiasis	Elephantiasis
Caused by *Ascaris lumbricoides.*	Caused by *Entamoeba histolytica.*	Caused by *Wuchereria bancrofti.*
Symptoms include abdominal pain, indigestion, muscular pain, fever, anaemia, nausea, headache and blockage of intestinal passage.	Symptoms are abdominal pain, constipation, cramps, faeces with excess mucus and blood clots.	Symptoms include inflammation of organs in which they live for many years, normally affect lymph vessels of lower limbs resulting in swelling of feet and genitals, hence called elephantiasis.

96. Study the diagram showing the entry of HIV into the human body and the processes that are followed. **All India 2020**

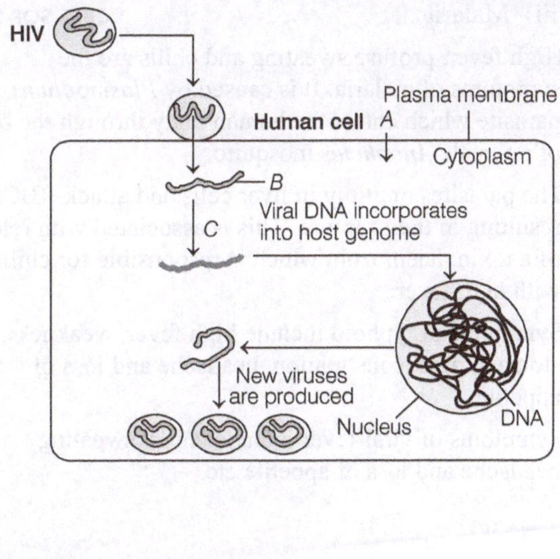

(i) Name the human cell '*A*' HIV enters into.

(ii) Mention the genetic material '*B*' HIV releases into the cell.

(iii) Identify enzyme '*C*'.

Ans. (i) HIV enters into macrophages (*A*) of human body.

(ii) Viral RNA (*B*) is the genetic material released by HIV into affected cell.

(iii) Enzyme reverse transcriptase (*C*) helps in replication of the genome of the virus in host cell. (1 × 3)

97. Following a road accident four injured persons were brought to a nearby clinic. The doctor immediately injected them with tetanus antitoxin. **All India 2020**

(i) What is tetanus antitoxin ?

(ii) Why were the injured immediately injected with this antitoxin ?

(iii) Name the kind of immunity this injection provided.

Ans. (i) Tetanus antitoxin is a preparation containing antibodies to the toxin produced by tetanus bacterium *Clostridium tetani.* (1)

(ii) The injured persons were immediately injected with tetanus antitoxin for preventing any infection and septic. Antitoxins neutralise the toxin produced by bacteria. (1)

(iii) Tetanus antitoxin represents artificial passive immunisation where quick response is generated in the body. (1)

98. A 17-year old boy is suffering from high fever with profuse sweating and chills. Choose the correct option from the following diseases which explains these symptoms and rule out the rest with adequate reasons.

(i) Typhoid

(ii) Viral fever

(iii) Malaria **CBSE SQP 2019**

Ans. High fever, profuse sweating and chills are the symptoms of malaria. It is caused by *Plasmodium* parasite which enters the human body through the bite of a female *Anopheles* mosquito.

The parasites multiply in liver cells and attack RBCs resulting in their rapture. This is associated with release of a toxin, haemozoin which is responsible for chills with high fever. (2)

Symptoms of typhoid include high fever, weakness, stomach pain, constipation, headache and loss of appetite (½)

Symptoms of viral fever include chills, sweating headache and loss of appetite etc. (½)

99. Your classmate complains of headache and cough. The doctor confirms that he is suffering from pneumonia and not common cold, on the basis of certain symptoms. List these symptoms. Mention any two precautions to be followed to prevent the spread of this disease. **CBSE SQP 2018**

Ans. The symptoms of pneumonia are

(i) High fever (ii) Grey/blue lips

(iii) Grey/blue nails. (1)

In common cold, these symptoms are not observed. Instead there is congestion/sore throat/hoarseness in common cold. (1)

The disease spread can be prevented by taking the following precautions

(i) Cover the nose when coming near to the patient.

(ii) Avoid personal goods/clothes used by patient to avoid the physical contact with the bacteria of pneumonia. (1)

100. Name a human disease, its causal organism, symptoms (any three) and vector spread by intake of water and food contaminated by human faecal matter. **All India 2017**

Or A patient is down with amoebiasis. List the symptoms that confirm this infection. Name the causative pathogen. **Delhi 2015C**

Ans. **Amoebiasis** is a disease spread by intake of water and food contaminated by human faecal matter.

Causal organism *Entamoeba histolytica.*

Symptoms

- Abdominal pain
- Constipation with cramps
- Faeces with excess mucus (1 × 3)

Vector or carrier of pathogen is housefly.

101. (i) What precaution(s) would you recommend to a patient requiring repeated blood transfusion?

(ii) If the advise is not followed by the patient there is an apprehension that the patient might contract a disease that would destroy the immune system of his/her body. Explain with the help of schematic diagram only how the immune system would get affected and destroyed. **Delhi 2017**

Ans. (i) Repeated blood transfusion may result in contracting diseases like AIDS. The recipient must ensure that the donor's blood is being screened for HIV and other pathogens. Also, he should make sure that doctors are using fresh needles. (1)

(ii) In the absence of such measures, the patient can get infected by HIV (Human Immunodeficiency Virus), which causes AIDS. It is a threatening disorder that weakens the immune system by attacking helper T-cells in the body. A schematic diagram showing the cycle of proliferation and effects of retrovirus (HIV) in infected person is as follows

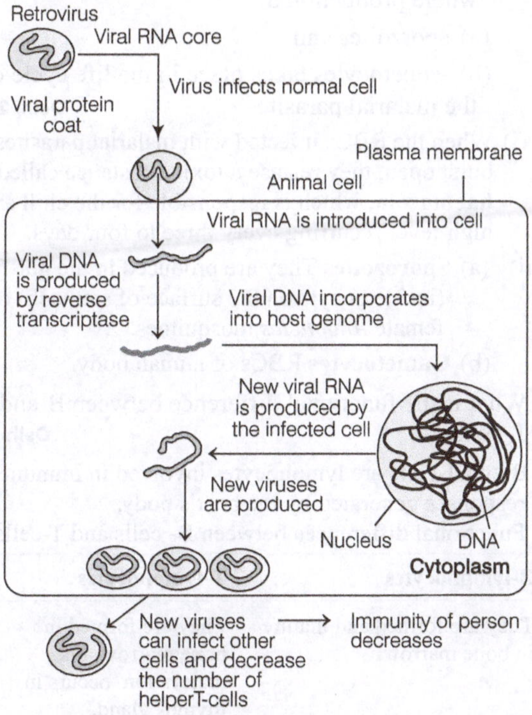

(2)

102. (i) It is generally observed that the children who had suffered from chickenpox in their childhood may not contract the same disease in their adulthood.
Explain giving reasons the basis of such an immunity in an individual. Name this kind of immunity.
(ii) What are interferons? Mention their role. **Foreign 2016**

Ans. (i) A child who had suffered from chickenpox in childhood may not contract disease in his/her adulthood. It is because during the first encounter with pathogen (chickenpox) specific antibodies (by humoral immune response) are produced to counter the attack.
During this attack, memory cells are also produced. Due to this, on subsequent exposure to the same pathogen, the immune response is more rapid and intense. That is why, second exposure to the chickenpox does not cause disease. It is known as acquired immunity of the body. (2)

(ii) Interferons are special kind of proteins secreted by virus infected cells. These protect the healthy cells from the virus attacks. (½ + ½)

103. Certain attributes of innate immunity are given in the table below. Identify *A*, *B*, *C*, *D*, *E* and *F* respectively in it.

	Types of barrier	Example of the barrier	Function
(i)	*A*	*B*	Prevent microbial growth
(ii)	*C*	Polymorpho nuclear leucocytes	*D*
(iii)	Cytokine	*E*	*F*

Delhi 2016C

Ans. (i) *A* – Physiological
B – Lysozyme in saliva (1)
(ii) *C* – Cellular
D – Phagocytose and destroy microbes (1)
(iii) *E* – Interferons
F – Prevention of viral infections (1)

104. State the three characteristics of acquired immunity. List the different ways by which it can be attained by humans. **Delhi 2016C**

Ans. The characteristics of acquired immunity are
(i) It is pathogen specific.
(ii) It is characterised by memory.
(iii) Responses can be characterised as a primary response (of low intensity) and secondary response. (1)

Acquired immunity can be attained by humans in the following ways
(i) **Active immunity** The antibodies are produced in the host body as a response to foreign entities, i.e. on living microbes or other proteins. The onset of response is slow.
(ii) **Passive immunity** The readymade antibodies are directly introduced to protect the body against foreign agents. (2)

105. How are primary and secondary immune responses carried out in the human body? Explain. **Delhi 2016C**

Ans. The primary response is the first response of immune system to a newly introduced foreign agent, while a second intensified immune response to same foreign agent is the secondary or anamnestic response. Immune responses are produced by two types of lymphocytes
(i) **B-lymphocytes** produce an army of proteins in response to pathogens, i.e. antibodies in the blood. The different types of antibodies secreted are IgA, IgM, IgE and IgG.
This response generated *via* antibodies of the immune system is also called the humoral immune response.

(ii) **T-lymphocytes** are the mediators of the Cell-Mediated Immunity (CMI). The cell-mediated immune response is responsible for the graft rejection.

106. (i) HIV and hepatitis-B are STDs. Mention the two other ways by which they can be transmitted to a healthy person.

(ii) Why is early detection of STD essential? What can it lead to otherwise? Explain. **Delhi 2016C**

Ans. (i) STDs like AIDS and hepatitis-B can be transmitted to a healthy person in the following ways

(a) Unsafe blood transfusion.

(b) From infected mother to foetus through lactation. **(1½)**

(ii) Early detection of STD is essential for timely cure. Otherwise this can lead to Pelvic Inflammatory Diseases (PIDs), abortions or even cancer of the reproductive tract. **(1½)**

Concept Enhancer STDs/STIs have a profound impact on sexual and reproductive health worldwide. STIs like herpes, syphilis, etc. can increase the risk of HIV infection.

107. A youth in his twenties met with an accident and succumbed to the injuries. His parents agreed to donate his organs. List any two essential clinical steps to be undertaken before any organ transplant. Why is the transplant rejected sometimes? What views would you share with your health club members to promote organ donation? **Delhi 2016C**

KEY idea
Organ transplant rejection is based on cell-mediated immune response.

Ans. Organ transplantation involves the removal of damaged/injured tissues or organs from the body of a person and their substitution by similar tissues/organs from a donor. Tissue matching, blood group matching are essential clinical steps before undertaking any graft/transplant. Transplantation may result in the rejection of transplanted organs as the immune system recognises the protein in the transplanted tissue or organs as foreign and initiates cellular immunity.

We should raise and promote awareness about organ donation, about need of organ and tissue donors. There are lakhs of people waiting for organ donation and many people die daily while waiting for transplant. Organs and tissues from one donor can save upto 40-50% lives. So, we should encourage and get registered for organ donation to save many lives.

108. (i) State what happens in the human body when malarial parasites infected RBCs burst to release the parasites in the blood.

(ii) Mention the specific sites in the host body, where production of

(a) sporzoites and

(b) gametocytes takes place in the life cycle of the malarial parasites. **Delhi 2015C**

Ans. (i) When the RBCs infected with malarial parasites burst open, they release a toxic substance called **haemozoin**, which is responsible for the chill and high fever recurring every three to four days. **(1)**

(ii) (a) **Sporozoites** They are produced in the gut (inside oocyte on the surface of stomach) of the female *Anopheles* mosquitoes.

(b) **Gametocytes** RBCs of human body. **(2)**

109. What is the functional difference between B-and T-cells. **Delhi 2015**

Ans. B-and T-cells are lymphocytes involved in immune responses generated by the host's body.
Functional differences between B- cells and T-cells are

B-lymphocytes	T-lymphocytes
They are formed and mature in bone marrow.	They are formed in bone marrow, but maturation occurs in thymus gland.
They produce antibody against antigen. The immune response produced is called humoral or antibody mediated immunity.	They directly attach the antigen or direct B-cells to produce antibodies. They produce cell-mediated immune response.
They do not respond to organ transplantation.	They respond to organ transplantation.

110. Mention any two human diseases caused by round worms. Name their causative agents and their mode of transmission into the human body. **All India 2015C**

Ans. Roundworms are nematodes, that cause helminthic disease in humans.

Two human diseases caused by roundworms are

(i) **Ascariasis** It is caused by intestinal endoparasite of humans, *Ascaris lumbricoides*. Infection occurs through contaminated vegetables, fruits and water. **(1½)**

(ii) **Filariasis** It is caused by filarial worms, *Wuchereria bancrofti* and *W. malayi*. It is transmitted by the bite of female *Culex* mosquito. **(1½)**

111. At what stage is *Plasmodium* picked up by the female *Anopheles*? Describe the life cycle of the parasite in this insect. **Delhi 2015C**

Ans. Female *Anopheles* picks up *Plasmodium* at gametocyte stage from human body.

Inside mosquito's body, the gametocytes develop to form male and female gametes. These gametes fuse and form zygote, which further divides to form many sporozoites in the intestine of mosquito. These sporozoites later move into salivary glands. See text on page no. 209.

112. (i) Differentiate between benign and malignant tumours.

(ii) Why is colostrum a boon to the newborn baby? **Delhi 2015C**

Ans. (i) Differences between benign and malignant tumours are

Benign tumour	Malignant tumour
Tumour remains confined to the affected organ.	The tumour spreads to other organs of the body.
The rate of tumour growth is usually slow.	Rate of tumour growth is usually rapid.
These tumours cause limited damage.	These tumours have neoplastic cells that migrate to other sites of the body and start a new tumour wherever they land. This property is called metastasis.
It is non-cancerous.	It is cancerous.

(1½)

(ii) The milk produced during the initial few days of lactation is called **colostrum**, which contains IgA antibodies. These are essential to develop resistance in newborn babies as they provide passive immunity.

Thus, breastfeeding during the initial period of infant growth is recommended by doctors for bringing up a healthy baby. **(1½)**

113. A heavily bleeding and bruised road accident victim was brought to a nursing home. The doctor immediately gave him an injection to protect him against a deadly disease.

(i) Write what did the doctor inject into the patient's body?

(ii) How do you think this injection would protect the patient against the disease?

(iii) Name the disease against which this injection was given and the kind of immunity it provides. **All India 2015**

Ans. (i) The doctor must have injected the tetanus antitoxin or preformed antibodies into the patient. **(1)**

(ii) The antitoxin injected into the patient's body has preformed antibodies which neutralise the pathogen and thus protect the patient from disease. **(1)**

(iii) The disease is tetanus, which is caused by bacterium *Clostridium tetani*. It may enter the skin through a cut or puncture wound. Once bacteria is under the skin, it makes a toxin that causes severe and painful muscle spasms, which can even be fatal. The injection provides passive immunity. **(1)**

114. Community service department of your school plans a visit to a slum near the school with an objective to educate the slum dwellers with respect to health and hygiene.

(i) Why is there a need to organise such visits?

(ii) Write the steps you will highlight, as a member of this department, in your interactions with them to enable them to lead a healthy life. **All India 2014**

Ans. (i) The community service department of schools plans a visit to a slum to educate people about health, hygiene and nutrition. These, people are always at risk of acquiring infections due to poor hygiene. Therefore, there is always a need to organise visits to slums so, as to educate and create awareness among them regarding the importance of hygiene. **(1½)**

(ii) The points to be highlighted while interacting with the slum people may be

- Importance of cleanliness and hygiene of body as well as surroundings.
- Awareness and prevention of infectious diseases. Use of public facilities, i.e. toiletries.
- Consumption of properly cooked and hygienic food and water.
- Administration of vaccines to newborn children, so as to prevent diseases. **(1½)**

115. (i) Name and explain giving reason, the type of immunity provided to the newborn by the colostrum and vaccinations.

(ii) Name the type of antibody

(a) present in colostrum.

(b) produced in response to allergens in human body. **Foreign 2014**

Ans. (i) The immunity provided by the colostrum is called the passive immunity. In this, antibodies such as IgA pass through colostrum to infants and provides immunity against infection.

Whereas, immunity provided by the vaccination is called active immunity. Vaccines are administered to the human body which results in generation of antibodies and specialised lymphocytes. (2)

(ii) (a) The type of antibody present in colostrum is IgA.

(b) IgE is produced in response to allergens in human body. (1)

116. (i) Name the causative organisms for the following diseases

(a) Elephantiasis (b) Ringworm

(c) Amoebiasis

(ii) How can public hygiene help to control such diseases? **Delhi 2014C**

Ans. (i) The causative agents or organisms for the following diseases are

(a) Elephantiasis- *Wuchereria bancrofti*

(b) Ringworm- *Microsporum*

(c) Amoebiasis-*Entamoeba histolytica* (1½)

(ii) Maintenance of public hygiene includes

- keeping body and surroundings clean.
- consumption of clean drinking water, fruits and vegetables, etc.
- proper disposal of waste and excreta.
- regular cleaning and disinfection of tanks and other water reservoirs, etc.

All the above measures help to control the increase in vectors of infectious diseases and their breeding places. Thus, there would be reduced chances of transmission of infectious diseases. (1½)

117. Study a part of the life cycle of malarial parasite given below. Answer the questions that follows.

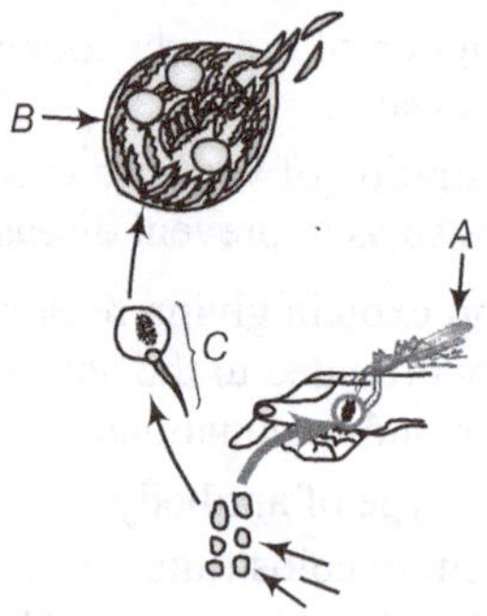

(i) Mention the role of *A* in the life cycle of the malarial parasite.

(ii) Name the event *C* and the organ where this event occurs.

(iii) Identify the organ *B* and name the cells being released from it. **Delhi 2012**

Ans. (i) *A* is female *Anopheles* mosquito. Such mosquitoes act as vectors and transmit the disease from infected to healthy individuals. (1)

(ii) The event *C* is fertilisation. It occurs in the intestinal wall of mosquito. (1)

(iii) *B* is salivary glands of mosquito, sporozoites cells are released from it. (1)

118. Study the diagram showing replication of HIV in humans and answer the following questions accordingly.

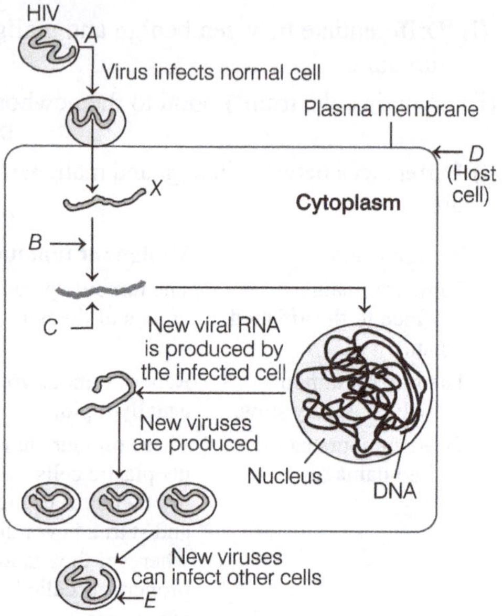

(i) Write the chemical nature of the coat *A*.

(ii) Name the enzyme *B* acting on *X* to produce molecule *C*. Name *C*.

(iii) Mention the name of the host cell *D* the HIV attacks first, when it enters into the human body.

(iv) Name the two different cells the new viruses *E* subsequently attack. **All India 2011**

Ans. (i) *A* – Protein coat (½)

(ii) *B* – Reverse transcriptase, *X*-viral RNA

C – Viral DNA (1)

(iii) *D* – Macrophages (animal or human cell) (½)

(iv) *E* – Macrophages and helper T-cells. (1)

119. (i) Name the causative agent of typhoid in humans.

(ii) Name the test administered to confirm the disease.

(iii) How does the pathogen gain entry into the human body? Write the diagnostic symptoms and mention the body organ that gets affected in severe cases? **All India 2011**

Ans. (i) *Salmonella typhi*. (½)

(ii) Widal test. (½)

(iii) Pathogens enter the human body through contaminated food and water. (1)

Diagnostic symptoms include high fever, weakness, stomach pain. The body organ affected is small intestine. (1)

120. An antibody molecule is represented as H_2L_2. Explain. **Delhi 2010**

Ans. For antibody H_2L_2, refer to text on page no. 212

Refer to figure 7.2. on page no. 212.

121. (i) All human beings have cellular oncogenes, but only few suffer from cancer disease. Give reasons.

(ii) How is a malignant tumour different from a benign tumour? **Foreign 2010**

Ans. (i) All cells have cellular oncogenes (c-onc) or proto-oncogene, but only few suffer from cancer disease because these genes code for certain growth factors. Under certain conditions, they get activated and lead to oncogenic transformation causing cancer. This transformation is induced by physical, chemical and biological factors called carcinogens. (1½)

(ii) For differences between benign and malignant tumours, refer to answer no. 112 (i). (1½)

5 Marks Questions

122. (i) Name and explain the property present in normal cells but is lost in cancer cells.

(ii) All normal human cells have genes that may become cancerous under certain conditions. Name them and explain how.

(iii) State the role of the following techniques in detection and diagnosis of cancer.

(1) Biopsy and histopathology

(2) Magnetic resonance imaging **CBSE 2024 (Set-I)**

Ans. (i) Normal cells in our body show a property called 'contact inhibition' that cancerous cells lack, contact inhibition is the property that prevents the uncontrolled proliferation of cells when they are in contact with other neighbouring cells. Cancerous cells have lost this property which leads to masses of cell called tumours. (1½)

(ii) Proto-oncogenes are genes that are present in normal human cells which, when activated under certain conditions, could lead to oncogenic transformation of the cells. Transformation of normal cells into cancerous cells may be induced by carcinogens (cancer causing agents) that may be physical, chemical or biological. (1)

(iii) 1. In biopsy, a piece or the suspected tissue is cut into thin sections and their is studied and examined under microscope (histopathological studies) by a pathologists. (1)

2. MRI uses strong magnetic fields and non-ionising radiations to accurately detect pathological and physiological changes in the living tissue. (1½)

123. Explain the role of primary and secondary lymphoid organs with the help of suitable examples. **CBSE SQP 2023**

Ans. Refer to text on page no. 213 (Lymphoid organs).

124. With the help of a flowchart illustrate how an infected animal cell can survive while viruses are being replicated or released. **CBSE SQP 2023**

Ans. Refer to figure 7.3 page no. 213.

125. Identify and name the disease in which the patient's cells lose the property of contact inhibition. State its possible causes and explain any three methods to accurately detect the pathological and physiological changes that take place due to the disease in living tissues. **CBSE SQP 2021**

Ans. The patient's cells lose the property of contact inhibition in one of the serious and complicated disease called cancer. (1)

It is characterised by the uncontrollable growth of cells leading to the formation of masses of cells called tumour.

The latter could be benign or malignant, depending upon its potential to invade new tissues or organs in body.

Possible causes of cancer Cancer could be caused due to physical, chemical or biological agents as follows

(i) **Physical causes** These generally include environmental factors like exposure to X-rays, gamma rays and UV-rays that can cause DNA damage, leading to neoplastic transformation.

(ii) **Chemical causes** Chemical carcinogens include nicotine in tobacco that can cause lung cancer.

(iii) **Biological causes** These include cancer causing oncogenic virus that contains viral oncogenes. It also includes the transformation of normal proto-oncogenes to oncogenic genes, thus leading to condition called cancer. (4)

126. A patient had tested positive to ELISA test. Identify the disease and the pathogen responsible, give reasons for the reduced/ weak immunity of the patient and trace the path, spread and effects of this pathogen in the human body. **CBSE SQP 2021**

Ans. Positive ELISA test signifies that the person is suffering from Aquired Immuno Deficiency Syndrome (AIDS). It is caused by the pathogen called Human Immuno deficiency Virus (HIV) which is a retrovirus having an envelope enclosing RNA genome.

The person suffering from AIDS has reduced or weak immunity because HIV potentially decreases the number of T-helper lymphocytes in body. Due to this, the person becomes highly susceptible to various diseases that could have been otherwise overcome, e.g. bacterial infections (especially mycobacterial infection), viral, fungal and parasitic infections. The path, spread and effect of HIV in human body is explained below

After getting into the body of the person, the virus enters into macrophages where RNA genome of the virus replicates to form viral DNA with the help of the enzyme reverse transcriptase. This viral DNA gets incorporated into host cell's DNA and directs the infected cells to produce virus particles.

The macrophages continue to produce virus and in this way, act like a HIV factory.

Simultaneously, HIV enters into helper T-lymphocytes (TH), replicate and produce progeny viruses.

The progeny viruses are released in the blood and attack other helper T-lymphocytes. This process is repeated and leads to a progressive decrease in the number of helper T-lymphocytes in the body of the infected person.

During this period, the person suffers from bouts of fever, diarrhoea and weight loss.

127. (i) How do normal cell become cancerous?

(ii) Cancer can be treated successfully only if detected at an early stage. How do the following help in detecting cancer ? **Delhi 2020**

(a) Biopsy (b) Histopathology

(c) MRI

(iii) Name any two methods that can possibly cure cancer.

Ans. (i) Normal cells have genes called **cellular oncogenes** (c-onc) or **proto-oncogenes**, which are present in inactive state. Also 'contact inhibition' exhibited by normal cells prevents their uncontrolled proliferation when they are in contact with other neighbouring cells. Thus, due to certain conditions like mutation, oncogenes are turned on is makes the cells to lose the property of contact inhibition and they continue to divide despite being in contact with other cell, which leads to masses of cells called tumours and lead to cancer. **(1½)**

(ii) Cancer can be detected by the following methods

(a) **Biopsy** In this, a suspected tissue is studied by cutting it into thin sections and staining it for cell examination.

(b) **Histopathology** It is the study of diseased cells and tissues taken from the body during biopsy by using a microscope.

(c) **MRI** (Magnetic Resonance Imaging) It uses strong magnetic fields and non-ionising radiations to accurately detect pathological and physiological changes in the living tissue. **(1½)**

(iii) **Treatment of cancer** Refer to text on page no. 210 and 211. **(2)**

128. (i) If a patient is advised anti-retroviral drug, name the possible infection he/ she is likely to be suffering from. Name the causative organism.

(ii) How do vaccines prevent subsequent microbial infection by the same pathogen?

(iii) How does a cancerous cell differ from a normal cell?

(iv) Many microbial pathogens enter the gut of humans along with food. Name the physiological barrier that protects the body from such pathogens. **CBSE SQP 2020**

Ans. (i) If a patient is advised anti-retroviral drug, he could be suffering from AIDS. It is caused by the Human Immunodeficiency Virus. **(1)**

(ii) Vaccines prevent microbial infections by initiating production of antibodies against antigens to neutralise the pathogenic agents during later actual infection. The vaccines also generate memory B-cells that recognise the pathogen quickly on subsequent exposure. **(1½)**

(iii) Normal cells show a property called contact inhibition by virtue of which contact with other cells inhibits their uncontrolled growth.

Cancer cells appear to have lost this property. These cells grow very rapidly, invading and damaging the surrounding normal tissues. Cells sloughed from such tumours reach distant sites through blood and wherever they get lodged in the body, they start a new tumour there. This property is metastasis. **(1½)**

(iv) **Physiological barriers** Acid in the stomach and saliva in the mouth. **(1)**

129. (i) Cancer is one of the most dreaded diseases. Explain 'contact inhibition' and 'metastasis' with respect to disease.

(ii) Name the group of genes that have been identified in normal cells that could lead to cancer. How do these genes cause cancer?

(iii) Name any two techniques that are useful in detecting cancers of internal organs.

(iv) Why are cancer patients often given α-interferon as part of the treatment?

Delhi 2014

Ans. (i) **Contact inhibition** is the property exhibited by normal cells. It prevents their uncontrolled proliferation when they are in contact with other neighbouring cells. But cancerous cells seem to have lost this property and continue to divide despite being in contact with other cells, which leads to masses of cells called tumours.

Metastasis is the property exhibited by malignant tumours in which cancer cells grow rapidly, invade neighbouring tissues and are capable of reaching distant sites through blood and lymph thus, spreading malignant tumours to other organs or parts of body.

These two properties make 'cancer' one of the dreaded diseases. **(2)**

(ii) The group of genes called cellular oncogenes or proto-oncogenes in normal cells could lead to cancer. These genes are present in inactivated or suppressed form. Some factors, i.e. physical, chemical or biological called carcinogens are capable of activating these oncogenes and thus, transforming normal cells into cancerous one. **(1)**

(iii) The two techniques useful in detecting cancers of internal organs, are CT (Computed Tomography) and MRI (Magnetic Resonance Imaging). **(1)**

(iv) As tumour cells are capable of avoiding recognition and destruction by immune system, the cancer patients are given α-interferons, which are biological response modifiers. They help in activating the immune system and destroy tumours. **(1)**

130. A person in your colony has recently been diagnosed with AIDS. People/residents in the colony want him to leave the colony for the fear of spread of AIDS.

(i) Write your view on the situation, giving reasons.

(ii) List the possible preventive measures that you would suggest to the residents of your locality in a meeting organised by you so that they understand the situation.

(iii) Write the symptoms and the causative agent of AIDS.

All India 2013

Ans. (i) AIDS is not contagious, i.e. it does not spread by shaking hand, talking and use of common utensils. So, there is no need of fear to live with the AIDS patient. **(1)**

(ii) Some preventive and safe steps to be suggested are

(a) Taking out HIV affected blood from blood bank, ensuring the use of only disposable needles and syringes in all public and private hospitals and clinics.

(b) Free distribution of condoms in public.

(c) Advocating safe sex and promoting regular check-up for HIV in population. **(2)**

(iii) AIDS is caused by Human Immuno deficiency Virus (HIV), a retrovirus. This virus attacks on T-helper cells, thus destroying the immune system.

The common symptoms of AIDS are weakness, fever, weight loss, regular illness, etc. **(2)**

Concept Enhancer HIV remains a major global public health issues claiming lives in million. There is no cure for HIV infection. However antiretroviral drugs stop virus from replicating in the body.

TOPIC 2

Adolescence and Drug/Alcohol Abuse

Drugs and Alcohol

- When the substances like drugs and alcohol are taken for the purpose other than medical, or taken in amount or frequencies that disturb the physical, physiological or psychological functions of person consuming it, is called **drug abuse** and **alcohol abuse**, respectively.
- Statistics show that the use of drugs and alcohol has been on a rise especially among the youth.
- Proper education and guidance would help youth to safe guard themselves against these dangerous behaviour patterns and follow healthy life styles.
- Majority of drugs are obtained from flowering plants and some from fungi. Drugs, which are commonly abused belong to the following categories
  - Opioids
  - Cannabinoids
  - Coca alkaloids or Cocaine

Other drugs include
  - Hallucinogens
  - Tobacco

Opioids

These are the drugs, which bind to the specific opioid receptors present in our central nervous system and gastrointestinal tract.

Heroin is a common opioid also called as **smack**. It is chemically diacetylmorphine, which is white, odourless, bitter crystalline compound.

- Heroin is obtained from acetylation of **morphine**. The latter is extracted from the latex of **poppy plant** *(Papaver somniferum)*.
- It is taken by snorting and injection.
- Heroin is a depressant, which slows down the body functions.
- Morphine is an effective sedative, analgesic and pain killer.

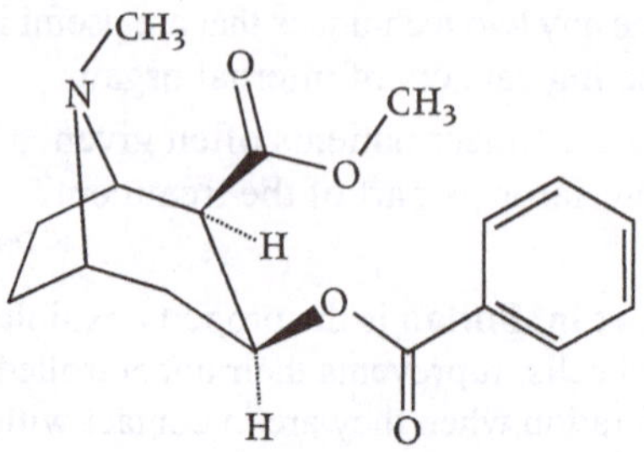

Figure 7.4 Chemical structure of morphine

Cannabinoids

These are a group of chemicals, which interact with cannabinoid receptors present mainly in the brain.

- Natural cannabinoids are obtained from the inflorescences of plant *Cannabis sativa*.
- Leaves, flower tops, resins of *C. sativa* in various combinations produce hashish, charas, marijuana and ganja.
- These are inhaled or ingested orally.
- These drugs affect cardiovascular system of the body.

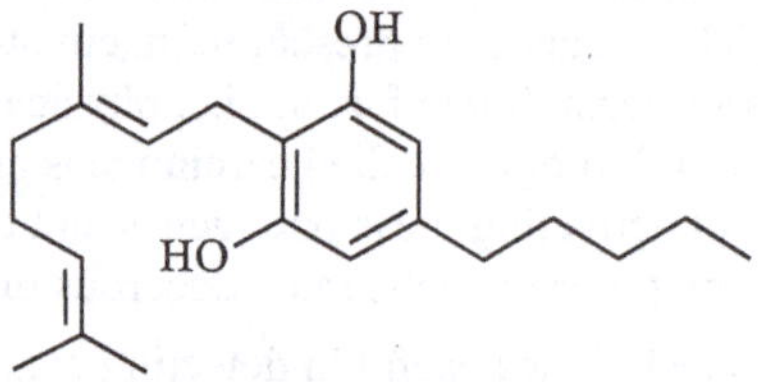

Figure 7.5 Chemical structure of cannabinoid molecule

Coca Alkaloids or Cocaine

It has a potent stimulating action on central nervous system, producing a sense of euphoria and increased energy.

- Cocaine is derived from the leaves and young branches of a South American plant called *Erythroxylum coca*.
- Its mode of intake is sniffing and snorting.
- It is a strong stimulant. When taken in high doses, it causes headache, convulsions, hallucination and death due to cardiovascular or respiratory failure.
- Commonly called **coke** or **crack**.

Hallucinogens

These are **psychedelic drugs**, because of their effect on the cerebrum and sense organs.

- These are obtained from the plants like *Atropa belladonna* and *Datura* sp.
- Lysergic Acid Diethylamide (LSD) is derived from the fungus *Claviceps purpurea*.
- Effect of these drugs occurs on thoughts, feelings and perceptions of an individual. Medically, these are prescribed to cope with depression and insomnia.
- Drugs like barbiturates, amphetamines, benzodiazepines that are used to treat depression and insomnia are also abused.

Tobacco

It contains nicotine (an alkaloid) which stimulates the adrenal gland to release adrenaline and noradrenaline, which in turn increases the blood pressure and heart rate.

- It is obtained from tobacco plant.
- Its mode of intake is smoking, chewing or as a snuff.
- Tobacco can induce lung cancer, bronchitis, emphysema, coronary heart disease, throat cancer, oral cancer and cancer of urinary bladder, etc.
- Smoking of tobacco leads to increase in carbon monoxide content of blood and reduces the concentration of haem-bound oxygen. This leads to oxygen deficiency in the body.

Alcohol

It has an anaesthetic effect on nervous system, affecting cerebrum, cerebellum and other parts.

- It is taken orally.
- Effect of alcohol is euphoria, peptic ulcer, gastric carcinoma, hepatitis, liver failure, liver cell carcinoma, etc.

Adolescence and Alcohol/ Drug Abuse

- Adolescence is a period during which a child becomes mature in terms of his/her attitudes and beliefs for independent participation in the society.
- Age between 12-18 years of age is called **adolescent period.**
- Adolescence is accompanied by several biological and behavioural changes. It is a vulnerable phase of mental and psychological development of an individual.
- In this age, urge to use drugs or alcohol occurs out of curosity or experimentation, which later turns to addiction.
- Adolescents take drugs/alcohol due to
  - Social pressure
  - Curiosity and need of adventure, excitement and experiments.
  - Avoid stress, depression and frustration.
  - Overcome hardships.
  - Avoid unsupportive family structure.

Addiction

- It is a psychological attachment to certain effects – such as euphoria and a temporary feeling of well-being associated with drugs and alcohol.
- These drive people to take them without need or even, when it becomes self-destructive.
- With repeated uses, the tolerance level increases.
- Consequently, receptors respond only to higher doses leading to greater intake and addiction.
- In the absence of any guidance or counselling, the person gets addicted and become dependent on their use.

Dependence

The tendency of the body to manifest a characteristic and unpleasant **withdrawal syndrome**, if regular dose of drugs/alcohol is discontinued abruptly is known as dependence on drug/alcohol

- Withdrawal symptoms are characterised by anxiety, shakiness, nausea and sweating.
- Sometimes, withdrawal symptoms can be so, severe that they may be life threatening.
- It leads the patient to ignore all social norms in order to get sufficient funds to fulfil his/her needs. These result in social adjustment problems.

Effects of Drug and Alcohol Abuse

Drug and alcohol affect the body in following

(i) **Alcohol affects** nervous system in following ways

- Loss of thinking power and self-control.
- Loss of emotional control and moral sense.
- Visual problems, staggering and incoherence in speech occurs.
- Neuritis may occur due to the inflammation of axon of neurons.

(ii) **Drugs exert** following effects on males
- Acne
- Aggressiveness
- Reduction in size of testes
- Sperm production lowers
- Premature baldness
- Enlargement of prostate gland

(iii) **Drug's effects** females in following ways
- Aggressiveness
- Masculinisation (features like males)
- Mood swings
- Depression
- Irregularities in menstrual cycles
- Excessive growth of facial and body hairs

(iv) Serious effects of drug and alcohol abuse in adolescents are
- Academic performance decreases.
- The absence from school/college.
- Isolation, fatigue, depression and aggressiveness occur in behaviour.
- No coordination with family members and friends.
- Weight fluctuates frequently.
- Intravenous drug intake leads to risk of AIDS and hepatitis-B.
- Alcohol intake may turn into heavy drinking habits later in life.
- Excess use of drugs and alcohol damage the nervous system and liver (cirrhosis).
- In females, drug and alcoholism affect foetus seriously.

Prevention and Control

Drugs/alcohol addiction can be prevented and controlled by the following ways
- Avoid undue peer pressure.
- Avoid disappointments and failures in life.
- Discuss and seek help of parents and elders.
- Discourage friends to take drugs/alcohol.
- Take medical help whenever required.

PYQs Previous Years' Questions

1 Mark Questions

Assertion-Reason Type Question

1. **Assertion** Smoking can raise blood pressure and increase heart rate.

   Reason Nicotine stimulates adrenal glands to release adrenaline and nor-adrenaline into the blood circulation, both of which raise blood pressure and increase heart rate. **CBSE SQP 2023**

   (a) Both Assertion and Reason are true and Reason is the correct explanation of Assertion

   (b) Both Assertion and Reason are true, but Reason is not the correct explanatio of Assertion

   (c) Assertion is true, but Reason is false

   (d) Assertion is false, but Reason is true

Ans. (a) Both Assertion and Reason are true and Reason is the correct explanation of Assertion.

Very Short Answer Type Questions

2. Mention the useful as well as the harmful drug obtained from the latex of poppy plant. **Delhi 2013**

Ans. Morphine is obtained from latex of poppy plant. It is useful as an analgesic. Heroin formed after acetylation of morphine is harmful as it is a depressant.

3. How does smoking tobacco in human lead to oxygen deficiency in their body? **Delhi 2012**

Ans. Smoking increases carbon monoxide (CO) content in blood and reduces the concentration of haem-bound oxygen. This causes oxygen deficiency in the body.

2 Marks Questions

4. (i) Write the scientific name of the plant from where natural cannabinoids are obtained.

   (ii) Mention the parts of the plant that are used for extracting the drug.

   (iii) How does the drug affect human body? **Delhi 2021-22 Term-II**

Ans. (i) *Cannabis sativa* (hemp). (½)

(ii) Flower tops and resins of *Cannabis* are used in various combinations for producing hashish, charas, ganja, etc. (½)

(iii) These drugs affect the cardiovascular system of the body other negative effects include nausea and vomiting, diarrhoea, throat irritation, etc. (1)

5. Identify the compound chemical structure as shown below. State any three of its physical properties.

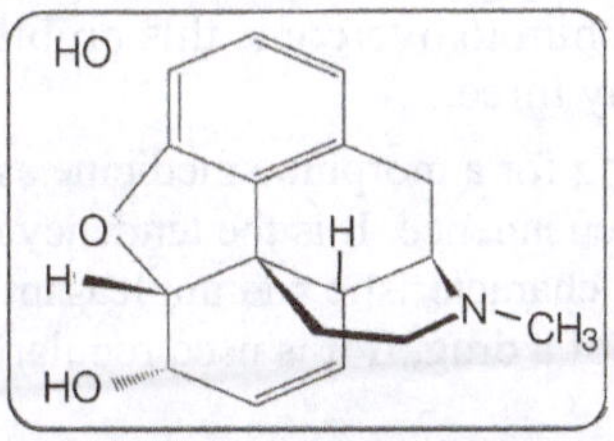

Ans. The compound shown by the given chemical structure is identified as morphine. It is a white odourless, bitter crystalline compound.

6. Differentiate between opioids and cannabinoids on the basis of their
   (i) specific receptor site in human body.
   (ii) mode of action in human body. **All India 2020**

Ans. Differences between opioids and cannabinoids

		Opioids	Cannabinoids
(i)	Specific receptor site	These drugs binds to specific opioid receptors present in our CNS and Gastro Intestinal Tract (GIT).	These drugs interact with cannabinoid receptors present in the brain.
(ii)	Mode of action	Opioids are used for pain relief and depressants. They slow down respiratory activity, digestion and other body functions.	These drugs affect the cardiovascular system and are known as mood altering drugs.

(1 + 1)

7. (i) Name the source plant of heroin drug. How is it obtained from the plant? **CBSE 2018C**
   (ii) Write the effects of heroin on the human body. **CBSE 2018 C**

Ans. (i) Heroin is obtained from *Papaver somniferum*. It is extracted from the latex of the plant. (1)
(ii) Heroin is a depressant and slows down body function. (1)

8. Why are adolescents especially advised not to smoke? How does smoking affect the functioning of the body? **Outside Delhi 2016C**

Ans. Adolescents are advised not to smoke for the following reasons
(i) Smoking paves way for hard drugs.
(ii) Smoking is associated with increased incidences of cancers of lung, throat and bronchitis and emphysema. It also increases carbon monoxide content in blood and reduces the concentration of haem-bound oxygen. (1 + 1)

9. Name two drugs obtained from poppy plant. 'These drugs are medically useful, but are often abused'. Taking the mentioned examples justify by giving reasons. **Delhi 2016 C**

Or

How are morphine and heroin related? Mention the effect each one of them has on the human body? **All India 2014C**

Ans. Both morphine and heroin are extracted from the latex of plant *Papaver somniferum.*
Heroin is actually obtained by the acetylation of morphine. Thus, both heroin and morphine are related. (1)
Both morphine and heroin act as an effective sedatives and pain killer, while heroin acts as depressant and slows down body functions. (1)

10. What happens to an individual when a regular dose of drugs/alcohol is abruptly discontinued? What characteristics manifest in the individual under such a situation? **Outside Delhi 2016C**

Or

What is 'withdrawal syndrome'? List any two symptoms it is characterised by. **Foreign 2014**

Ans. If the regular dose of drug or alcohol in an addicted person is discontinued abruptly, the body exhibits certain characteristics and unpleasant symptoms called 'withdrawal syndrome'. (1)
The 'withdrawal syndrome' is characterised by symptoms like anxiety, nausea and excessive sweating, etc. (1)

11. Write the scientific name of the source plant of the drugs-marijuana and hashish and mention their effects on human body. **Delhi 2014C**

Or

Name the plant source of ganja. How does it affect the body of the abuser? **All India 2012**

Ans. The scientific name of source plant of drugs marijuana, hashish and ganja is *Cannabis sativa.* (1)
These drugs usually affect the cardiovascular system of a human body. (1)

12. Name the plant source of the drug popularly called smack. How does it affect the body of the abuser? **Delhi 2012**

Or

Name the opioid drug and its source plant. How does the drug affect the human body? **All India 2010**

Ans. Smack is obtained from *Papaver somniferum* (poppy plant). (1)

Drugs effects

(i) It binds to specific opioid receptors present in our central nervous system and gastro-intestinal tract.

(ii) It is a depressant that slows down the body functions. (1)

13. Identify *A, B, C* and *D* in the following table

Scientific name of the source plants	Drugs	Harmful effects/Human body part affected
Papaver somniferum	*A*	Depressant/ slows body function
Cannabis sativa	Cannabinoids	*B*
Erythroxylum coca	*C*	*D*

Delhi 2012C

Ans. *A* – Heroin, *B* – Cardiovascular system
C – Cocaine, *D* – Central nervous system

14. Why is tobacco smoking associated with rise in blood pressure and emphysema (oxygen deficiency in the body)? Explain. **All India 2011**

Ans. The nicotine present in tobacco stimulates adrenal glands to secrete adrenaline and nor-adrenaline. Both these hormones increase blood pressure and heart rates. (1)

Smoking is associated with increased incidence of lung cancers. It increases carbon monoxide level of the blood, which competes with oxygen for transport. As the concentration of haem-bound oxygen decreases, there is oxygen deficiency in the body. It also increases the craving for hard drugs. (1)

3 Marks Questions

15. Study the table given below. Identify *A, B, C, D, E* and *F* in the table. **Delhi 2020**

Name of the drugs	Scientific name of source plants	Effect on human organ/system
Opioids	'*A*'	'*B*'
'*C*'	*Cannabis sativa*	'*D*'
Cocaine	'*E*'	*F*

Ans. *A* – *Papaver somniferum*

B – Depressant (slows down the body functions); effective sedative, analgesic and pain killer.

C – Cannabinoids

D – Mental retardation, lung infection, lung cancer.

E – *Erythroxylum coca*

F – Damage to blood vessels, increased heart rate, even leads to death.

16. A doctor prescribed morphine as a sedative and pain killer to your cousin, who had undergone surgery. Even after recovery, he craved for the prescribed medicine. What do you conclude about his condition?

After appraising yourself, what measures will you suggest to him to overcome this problem? Briefly explain any three.

Ans. This craving for a morphine medicine as pain killer is the drug dependence. It is the tendency of body to manifest a characteristic and unpleasant withdrawal syndrome of a drug, if it is used regularly for some time. (1½)

I will suggest following measures to my cousin

(i) Counselling about the consequences and their remedial measures.

(ii) Seeking professional and medical help immediately.

(iii) Seeking help from family and friends to overcome withdrawal symptoms. (1½)

17. Why is there a fear amongst the guardians that their adolescent wards may get trapped in drug/alcohol abuse? **All India 2017**

Ans. There is always a fear amongst guardians that their adolescents may get trapped in drug/alcohol abuse due to the following reasons

(i) Adolescence is accompanied by several biological and behavioural changes. It is a vulnerable phase of mental and psychological development of an individual in which an individual may get addicted to alcohol/drugs very easily. (1)

(ii) In this age, the first use of drugs or alcohol may be out of curiosity or experimentation, which later on turns to addiction. (1)

(iii) Adolescents usually take drugs due to social pressure, need of adventure, excitement to avoid stress, depression and frustration. (1)

18. Explain 'addiction' and 'dependence' in respect of drug/alcohol abuse in youth. **All India 2017**

Ans. **Addiction** is a psychological attachment to certain effects such as euphoria and a temporary feeling of well-being associated with drugs and alcohol. These drive people to take them without need or even when it becomes self-destructive. In the absence of any guidance or counselling, the person gets addicted and becomes dependent on their use. (1½)

Dependence on drug/alcohol is the tendency of the body to manifest a characteristic and unpleasant **withdrawal syndrome**, if regular dose of drugs/alcohol is discontinued abruptly. Withdrawal symptoms are characterised by anxiety, shakiness, nausea and sweating. Sometimes, it can be so severe that they may be life threatening. (1½)

19. Prior a sports event blood and urine samples of sports persons are collected for drug tests.

(i) Why is there a need to conduct such tests?

(ii) Name the drugs the authorities usually look for.

(iii) Write the generic names of two plants from which these drugs are obtained. **Delhi 2016**

Ans. (i) It is necessary to conduct these tests as sports-persons often take drugs to increase their performance. (1)

(ii) Cocaine and morphine are the drugs the authorities usually look for. (1)

(iii) Morphine is extracted from the latex of poppy plant *Papaver somniferum*. Cocaine is obtained from the coca plant *Erythroxylum coca*. (1)

20. A team of students is preparing to participate in the interschool sports meet. During a practice session you find some vials with labels of certain cannabinoids.

(i) Will you report to the authorities? Why?

(ii) Name a plant from which such chemicals are obtained.

(iii) Write the effect of these chemicals on human body. **Delhi 2015**

Ans. (i) Yes, I will report it to the authorities, because cannabinoids are classified as drugs and taking them without medical supervision is illegal. (1)

(ii) Cannabinoids are obtained from various parts of plant *Cannabis sativa*. (1)

(iii) **Effect** The cannabinoids interact with cannabinoid receptors in the brain and affect the cardiovascular system of the body. (1)

21. Do you support 'dope test' being conducted on sports persons participating in a prestigious athletic meet? Give three reasons in support of your answer. **All India 2014C**

Ans. Yes, the 'dope test' should be conducted on sports persons participating in a prestigious athletic meet. This is done to find out if any participant has taken any kind of performance enhancing drugs. (1)

The use of drugs in sports should be banned as

(i) they increase muscle strength.

(ii) promote aggressiveness.

(iii) increase athletic performance. (1½)

Because of above reasons, use of such drugs, e.g. steroids, analgesics, diuretics should be banned for participants as it would be unfair on the part of other participants (not consuming such drugs). (½)

22. 'Prevention is better than cure' is an apt slogan to safeguard adolescents from drug abuse. List any 6 steps that could be taken in this regard. **All India 2013C**

Ans. Six steps that could be taken to prevent adolescents from drug alcohol abuse are as follows

(i) A child should not be pushed unduly to perform beyond his/her limits in studies, sports or any other activities.

(ii) Educating and counselling him/her to face problems and stresses and accept disappointments and failures as part of life.

(iii) Parents and teachers can identify the danger signs and take appropriate steps to diagnose the malady and underlying causes.

(iv) Help should be taken from qualified psychologists and psychiatrists.

(v) Parents and teacher should become more supportive.

(vi) Help of close friends and relatives can also be taken.

Case Based/Source Based/Passage Based Questions (Based on Complete Chapter)

1. Read the following passage and answer the questions that follow

"Mosquitoes are drastically affecting the human health in almost all the developing tropical countries. Different species of mosquitoes cause very fatal diseases so much so that many humans loose their life and if they survive, are unable to put in productive hours to sustain their life. With the result the health index of the country goes down"

(i) Name the form in which *Plasmodium* gains entry into (a) human body (b) the female *Anopheles* body.

(ii) Why do the symptoms of malaria not appear in a person immediately after being bitten by an infected female *Anopheles*? Give one reason. Explain when and how do the symptoms of the disease would appear?

Or (ii) Explain the events which occur within a female *Anopheles* mosquito after it has sucked blood from a malaria patient.

(iii) Name a species of mosquito other than female *Anopheles* and the disease, for which it carries the pathogen. **CBSE 2024 (Set-II)**

Ans. (i) *Plasmodium* is a protozoan that causes malaria. It gains entry into human body and the female *Anopheles* body in different forms.

(a) In human body-sporozoites form

(b) In the female *Anopheles* body-gametocytes form. **(1)**

(ii) Symptoms of malaria like chills and fever are only visible after the release of haemozoin that takes place after a few days of infection. Thus, no symptoms appear in a person immediately after being bitten by female *Anopheles* mosquito.

Symptoms of malaria would appear after the sporozoites (parasite) multiply in the liver cells and attack RBCs and burst them. This cause the release of toxin, haemozoin which will cause fever and chills recurring every three to four days. **(2)**

Or

(ii) The events which occur in the female *Anopheles* mosquito after it sucked blood from a malarial patient are as follows

(a) Female *Anopheles* mosquito takes up gametocytes (sexual stage of *Plasmodium*) with blood meal.

↓

(b) Fertilisation and development of gametocytes take place in the mosquito's gut.

↓

(c) Mature infective stages (sporozoites) escape from gut and migrate to the mosquito's salivary glands.

↓

(d) When the mosquito bites another human, sporozoites are injected with bite.

↓

(e) Parasite (sporozoites) reach the lives through blood.

↓

(f) The parasite reproduces asexually in liver cells, bursting the cell and releasing into the blood.

↓

(g) Parasites reproduce asexually in red blood cells, bursting the RBCs and causing cycles of fever and other symptoms. Released parasites infect new RBCs.

↓

(h) Sexual stages (gametocytes) develop in RBCs.

↓

Cycle continues **(2)**

(iii) Name of mosquito-*Aedes*

Diseases caused-Dengue and chikungunya

Carrying pathogen-Virus **(1)**

2. Read the following and answer the questions given below

An immunity is an individual's ability to resist or defend itself from the development of a disease. The immunity can be either natural or acquired in nature. The natural immunity is non-specific in nature and consists of various barriers such as physical, physiological, cellular, cytokine, etc. While the acquired one is adapted by coming in contact with the environment.

(i) What type of response generated when any antigen encounters our body for the first time?
(a) Secondary response
(b) Primary response
(c) Both (a) and (b)
(d) None of the above

(ii) Which of the following lymphocytes are produced by the cells of immune response?
(a) A-lymphocyte
(b) B-lymphocyte
(c) T-lymphocyte
(d) Both (b) and (c)

(iii) Interferons is an example of
(a) physical barrier
(b) physiological barrier
(c) cellular barrier
(d) cytokine barrier

(iv) Monocytes and natural killer cells are the type of
(a) RBCs
(b) platelets
(c) lymphocytes
(d) Non-lymphocytes

(v) The secondary response is also known as
(a) anamnestic response
(b) non-specific response
(c) specific response
(d) virtual response

Ans. (i)-(b), (ii)-(d), (iii)-(d), (iv)-(a), (v)-(a)

3. When a microorganism invades a host, a definite sequence of events usually occur leading to infection and disease, causing suffering to the host. This process is called pathogenesis. Once a microorganism overcomes the defense system of the host, development of the disease follows a certain sequence of events as shown in the graph. Study the graph given for the sequence of events leading to appearance of a disease and answer the questions that follow.

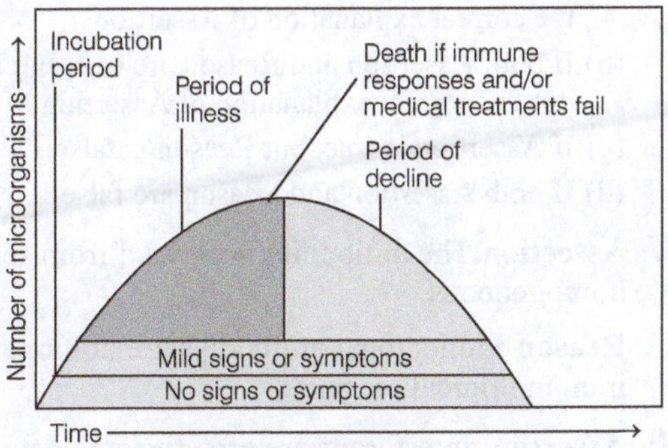

(i) In which period, according to the graph there are maximum chances of a person transmitting a disease / infection and why?

(ii) Study the graph and write what is an incubation period.
Name a sexually transmitted disease that can be easily transmitted during this period.
Name the specific type of lymphocytes that are attacked by the pathogen of this disease.

Or

(ii) Draw a schematic labelled diagram of an antibody. **CBSE 2023**

Ans. (i) According to the graph, the period during which there are maximum chances of a person transmitting a disease is period of illness, as in this period person suffering from this disease will show mild symptoms or no symptoms leading to the transmission of disease or during the period of illness the person suffering from the disease will show more symptom leading to transmission of the disease. **(2)**

(ii) The incubation period is the time period between the initial infection and the onset of symptoms. An example of a sexually transmitted disease that can be easily transmitted during this period is HIV.
The specific type of lymphocytes that are attacked by the pathogen of this disease are the $CD4^+$ T-lymphocytes **(2)**

Or (ii)

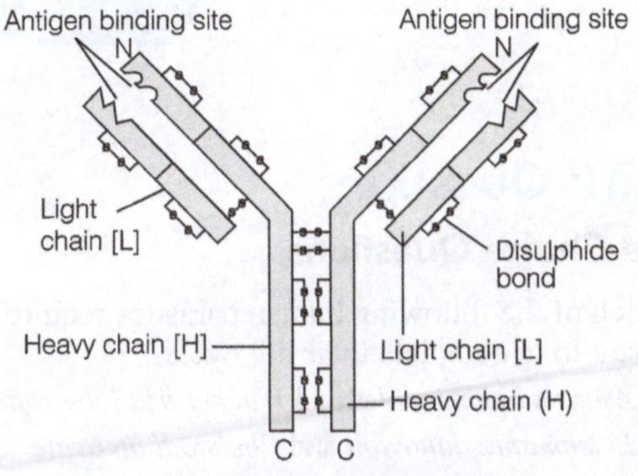

Diagram of an antibody molecule **(2)**

4. The data below shows the concentration of nicotine smoked by a smoker taking 10 puffs/ minute.

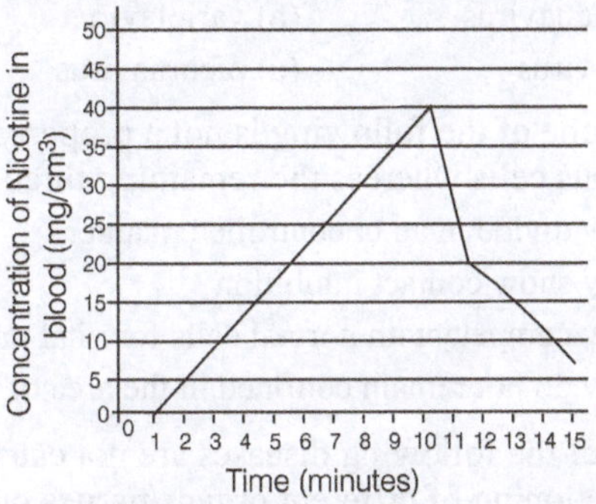

(i) With reference to the above graph explain the concentration of nicotine in blood at 10 minutes.

(ii) How will this affect the concentration of carbon monoxide and haem bound oxygen at 10 minutes?

(iii) How does cigarette smoking result in high blood pressure and increase in heart rate?

Or (iii) How does cigarette smoking result in lung cancer and emphysema? **CBSE SQP 2023**

Ans. (i) Concentration of nicotine is maximum at 10 minutes. It increases steadily in the blood to reach 45mg/cm^3. **(1)**

(ii) The concentration of CO will increase resulting in reduced concentration of haem bound oxygen. **(1)**

(iii) Nicotine results in stimulating the adrenal gland which results in release of adrenaline / nor - adrenaline in the blood resulting in increase of blood pressure and heart rate. **(2)**

Or (iii) Chemical carcinogens present in tobacco smoke are the major cause of lung cancer.
The cigarette smoke irritates the air passages of the lungs causing them to produce mucus which causes cough, resulting in enlarging air spaces (or losing their elasticity) reduction in surface area thus difficulty in breathing causing emphysema. **(2)**

CHAPTER TEST

01 Mark Questions

Multiple Choice Questions

1 Which of the following human parasites require mosquito to complete their life cycle?

(a) *Ascaris lumbricoides* and *Wuchereria bancrofti*
(b) *Leishmania donovani* and *Plasmodium ovale*
(c) *Ascaris lumbricoides* and *Leishmania donovani*
(d) *Wuchereria bancrofti* and *Plasmodium ovale*

2 Hepatitis-B virus is

(a) hepadnavirus (b) variolavirus
(c) retrovirus (d) picornavirus

3 Which one of the following is not a property of cancerous cells whereas the remaining three are?

(a) They divide in an uncontrolled manner
(b) They show contact inhibition
(c) They compete with normal cells for vital nutrients
(d) They do not remain confined in the area of formation

4 Which of the following diseases are not caused by malfunctioning of different organs/tissues or glands?

(a) Cardiac failure (b) Kidney failure
(c) Osteoporosis (d) Diabetes

5 Which of the following statements are true for antibodies?

I. Proteins produced within plasma cells.
II. Contain two polypeptide chains.
III. The chains are joined by disulphide bonds.
IV. All antibodies are immunoglobulins.

(a) I, II and III (b) II, III and IV
(c) I, II and IV (d) I, III and IV

6 Immunity that develops in the foetus after receiving antibodies from mother's blood through placenta is

(a) naturally acquired active immunity
(b) artificially acquired active immunity
(c) naturally acquired passive immunity
(d) artificially acquired passive immunity

Assertion-Reason Type Questions

Direction (Q. Nos. 7-10) *In each of the following questions, a statement of **Assertion** is given followed by corresponding statement of **Reason**. Of the statements, mark the correct answer as*

(a) If both Assertion and Reason are true and Reason is the correct explanation of Assertion
(b) If both Assertion and Reason are true, but Reason is not the correct explanation of Assertion
(c) If Assertion is true, but Reason is false
(d) If both Assertion and Reason are false

7 **Assertion** The antibodies separated from serum are homogeneous.

Reason Monoclonal antibodies are homogeneous immunological reagents.

8 **Assertion** Interferons are effective against viruses.

Reason Proteins which can be synthesised only by genetic engineering are effective against viruses.

9 **Assertion** The most successful transplants are autografts.

Reason In autograft, antigens, encoded by Major Histocompatibility Complex (MHC) are properly matched.

10 **Assertion** In malaria, a person experiences chills and high fever recurring every three to four days.

Reason This is caused by the release of haemozoin with rupture of liver cells.

2/3 Marks Questions

11 Mention any three characteristics features of viral fever.

12 Explain any three preventive measures to control typhoid infection.

13 How does the human body protect itself from infections?

14 Enlist the basic mode of transmission of AIDS.

15 What is addiction? State any four reasons of drug addiction.

16 Briefly explain any three methods involved in the treatment of cancer.

17 In your locality, if a person is addicted to alcohol, what kind of behavioural changes do you observe in that person? Suggest measures to overcome the problem.

05 Marks Questions

18 Define metastatis. Suggest three early diagnostic symptoms of cancer.

19 Explain the adaptive immunity with emphasis on its properties, activation and its role in vaccination.

20 Briefly explain the life cycle of HIV, mention its mode of transmission and the precautionary measures that should be taken to avoid such infections.

21 What is meant by drug and alcohol abuse? Mention the effects of drug abuse in both males and females. How is today' generation more prone to getting affected by such abuses?

22 State which of the following are incorrect along with proper explanation to your answer.

(i) Alcohol precedes adolescence.

(ii) LSD is a hallucinogen.

(iii) Brown sugar is heroin.

(iv) Cocaine is obtained from *Thea sinensis*.

(v) Hallucinogens are called vision producing drugs.

23 (i) What is meant by addictive disorder?

(ii) Mention any two ways in which opiate narcotics affect human body.

(iii) Name any two opiate narcotics.

Answers

1. (d)	**2.** (a)	**3.** (b)	**4.** (d)	**5.** (d)
6. (c)	**7.** (d)	**8.** (c)	**9.** (a)	**10.** (c)

08

Microbes in Human Welfare

TREND ANALYSIS 3 YEARS

Average No. of Questions Across all Sets

Topic	Types of Questions	2024	2023	2020
TOPIC 01 Microbes in Household Products, Industrial Products and in Sewage Treatment	1 Mark	1	1	1
	2 Marks	0	0	0
	3 Marks	0	0	0
	4 Marks (Case Based)	0	0	0
	5 Marks	1	0	0
TOPIC 02 Microbes in Production of Biogas, as Biocontrol Agents and Biofertilisers	1 Mark	0	0	1
	2 Marks	1	2	0
	3 Marks	0	0	1
	4 Marks (Case Based)	0	0	0
	5 Marks	0	0	0

TOPIC 1

Microbes in Household Products, Industrial Products and in Sewage Treatment

- Microbes are the major components of biological systems on the earth. They are present everywhere, i.e. in soil, water, air, inside our body and those of other animals and plants.
- They can also be found deep inside the geysers (thermal vents with temperature around 100° C), deep in soil, under the layer of snow and in highly acidic environments.
- Microbes are so minute that they cannot be seen by naked eyes. Various types of microbes are protozoan, bacteria, fungi, virus, viroids and prions (proteinaceous infectious agents), etc.

Microbes in Household Products

The common products obtained by the use of microbes are curd, dough, toddy, cheese, etc.

Curd

- It is formed by adding small amount of curd (that contain bacteria such as *Lactobacillus* and **Lactic Acid Bacteria** (LAB) in milk.
- LAB at suitable temperature multiply and convert milk into curd, which also improves its nutritional quality by increasing the content of vitamin-B_{12}.

- During growth, LAB produce acids that coagulate and partially digest the milk proteins.
- LAB also checks disease causing microbes in the stomach.

Dough

- It is formed by the fermentation caused by bacteria.
- Dough that is used to make bread, is fermented using baker's yeast (*Saccharomyces cerevisiae*).
- Carbon dioxide (CO_2) released during the process of fermentation gives the fluffy appearance to dough.
- It is used to make foods like idli, dosa and to different types of breads.

Toddy

It is a traditional drink of Southern India. It is made by the fermentation of sap from palm trees by bacteria. It is a refreshing drink which can be used for producing vinegar, jaggery or palm sugar.

Cheese

Different varieties of cheese are made by the partial degradation of milk using different microbes.

(i) **Swiss cheese** is made by a bacterium *Propionibacterium shermanii*. The large holes in this cheese are due to the production of large amount of CO_2 by the bacterium.

(ii) **Roquefort cheese** is made by the ripening with fungi, *Penicillium roqueforti* to obtain a specific flavour. It is the best known cheese made from sheep's milk.

(iii) **Camembert cheese** employs *Penicillium camemberti* for ripening.

Other Products

Microbes are also used to ferment fish, soybean and bamboo shoots to make food.

Microbes in Industrial Products

Microbes have immense importance in many industries. The main industrial products obtained from microbes are fermented beverages, antibiotics, organic acids, alcohol, enzymes and bioactive molecules, etc. For the production of these products on industrial scale from raw material, microbes are grown in very large vessels called **fermentors**.

Fermented Beverages

These include wine, beer, whisky, brandy and rum.

- These are obtained by fermenting malted cereals and fruit juices with *Saccharomyces cerevisiae* or **Brewer's yeast** to produce ethanol on commercial scale.

$$C_6H_{12}O_6 \longrightarrow 2C_2H_5OH + 2CO_2$$

- Variety of alcoholic drinks depends on the type of raw material used for fermentation and the type of processing (with or without distillation).
- Wine and beer are produced without distillation.
- Whisky, brandy and rum are produced by the distillation of the fermented broth.

Antibiotics (*Anti*-against and *bios*-life)

These are chemical substances, which are produced by some microbes and can kill or retard the growth of other (disease causing) microbes.

- **Penicillin** was the first antibiotic discovered by **Alexander Fleming**.
- Fleming discovered penicillin while working on *Staphylococcus* bacteria. He observed a mould growing in one of his unwashed culture plates around which *Staphylococcus* could not grow. He found that it was due to a chemical produced by the mould. He named it penicillin after the mould *Penicillium notatum*.
- **Ernst Chain** and **Howard Florey** discovered full potential of this antibiotic.
- Penicillin was extensively used to treat Americans soldiers wounded during World War II. Fleming, Chain and Florey were awarded Nobel Prize in 1945 for this discovery.
- Antibiotics are also used to cure deadly diseases such as plague, whooping cough, diphtheria and leprosy.

Organic Acids

These are produced by the microbial metabolic action. Important ones are

- Citric acid – *Aspergillus niger* (fungi)
- Acetic acid – *Acetobacter aceti* (bacteria)
- Butyric acid– *Clostridium butylicum* (bacteria)
- Lactic acid – *Lactobacillus* (bacteria)

Enzymes

Enzymes used in various fields are also produced by microbes as given below

- **Lipase** is used in detergent formulations and helps in removing oily stains from the laundry.

- **Pectinases** and **proteases** are used for clarifying bottled juices because these enzymes digest the pectin fibres present in the fruit wall and juices. The bottled fruit juices bought from the market are clearer as compared to those made at home for this reason.
- **Streptokinase** is produced by the bacterium *Streptococcus*. It is modified by genetic engineering and is used as a 'clot buster' for removing clots from blood vessels of patients, who have undergone myocardial infarction leading to heart attack.

Bioactive Molecules

Bioactive molecules produced by microbes are

- **Cyclosporin-A** It is produced by the fungus *Trichoderma polysporum*. It is used as immuno-suppressive agent in organ-transplant patients. It acts by inhibiting the activation of T-cells.
- **Statins** produced by the yeast *Monascus purpureus* has been used as blood cholesterol lowering agents. These act by competitively inhibiting the enzyme responsible for the synthesis of cholesterol, e.g. pravastatin, simvastatin, etc.

Microbes in Sewage Treatment

- Sewage is the municipal wastewater containing mainly human excreta. It also contains large quantity of organic matter and pathogenic microbes.
  Therefore, before discharging into natural bodies, sewage needs to be made less polluting and this process employs the use of microbes.
- Sewage treatment is carried out in **Sewage Treatment Plants** (STPs) using heterotrophic microbes, naturally present in the sewage.
- This treatment is carried out in following two steps

Primary Treatment (Physical Treatment)

- This step involves the physical removal of large and small particles from sewage through filtration and sedimentation.
- Floating debris is removed by sequential filtration by passing the sewage water through wire mesh screens.
- After this, the grit (soil and small pebbles) is removed by sedimentation in settling tanks. The sediment is called **primary sludge** and the supernatant formed is called **primary effluent**.
- The primary effluent is then taken for secondary treatment.

Secondary Treatment (Biological Treatment)

- Primary effluent is passed into large aeration tanks with constant mechanical agitation and air supply.
- This allows vigorous growth of useful aerobic microbes into **flocs** (masses of bacteria associated with fungal filaments to form mesh-like structures).
- These microbes consume major part of organic matter in the effluent, while growing and hence reduce the **Biochemical Oxygen Demand** (BOD) of the effluent.
- When BOD of the sewage gets reduced, significantly the effluent is passed into **settling tank**.
- The bacterial flocs are allowed to settle in the tank and the sediment is called **activated sludge**.
- A small amount of activated sludge is pumped back into the aeration tank to serve as the inoculum.
- The remaining major part of the sludge is pumped into large tanks called **anaerobic sludge digesters**.
- In anaerobic sludge digesters, other kinds of bacteria, which grow anaerobically, digest the bacteria and fungi in the sludge. During this process, bacteria produce a mixture of gases, such as methane, hydrogen sulphide and the carbon dioxide, which form **biogas** (It can be used as source of energy as it is inflammable).
- The effluent from secondary treatment is generally released into natural water bodies like rivers and streams.

Biochemical Oxygen Demand (BOD)

BOD refers to the amount of the oxygen that would be consumed if all the organic matter in one litre of water is oxidised by bacteria.

- BOD measures the rate of uptake of oxygen by the microbes in a sample of water. Indirectly, it measures the organic matter present in the water.
- More BOD of water indicates more polluting potential.

River Action Plans

- Due to the increasing urbanisation, sewage is being produced in larger quantities. But the number of sewage treatment plants has not increased correspondingly.
  So, the untreated sewage is often discharged directly into the rivers leading to their pollution and increase in water borne diseases.
- The Ministry of Environment and Forests has initiated **Ganga Action Plan** and **Yamuna Action Plan** to save the major rivers of our country from pollution.
- Under these plans, building of a large number of sewage treatment plants is proposed, so that only treated sewage may be discharged in the rivers.

PYQs Previous Years' Questions

1 Mark Questions

Multiple Choice Questions

1. *Lactobacillus* that sets milk into curd is categorised as **CBSE 2024 (Set-I)**
   (a) cyanobacteria
   (b) archaebacteria
   (c) chemosynthetic bacteria
   (d) heterotrophic bacteria

Ans. (d) *Lactobacillus* is heterotrophic bacteria which convert milk into curd as they convert lactose into lactic acid.

2. During biological treatment of sewage, the masses of bacteria held together by fungal filaments to form mesh-like structures are called **CBSE 2024 (Set-II)**
   (a) primary sludge (b) flocs
   (c) activated sludge (d) anaerobic sludge

Ans. (b) In the secondary or biological treatment of sewage, the primary effluent is passed into large aeration tanks to allow vigorous growth of useful aerobic microbes into flocs. Flocs are masses of bacteria associated with fungal filaments to form mesh like structures, which help in decreasing BOD of water by decreasing its organic matter.

3. A patient was advised to have a kidney transplant. To suppress the immune reaction, the doctor would administer him **CBSE SQP 2024**
   (a) statins produced from *Monascus purpureus*
   (b) statins produced from *Streptococcus thermophilus*
   (c) cyclosporin-A produced from *Trichoderma polysporum*
   (d) cyclosporin-A produced from *Clostridium butylicum*

Ans. (c) cyclosporin-A produced from *Trichoderma polysporum*

4. Given below are the lists of the commercially important products and their source organisms. Select the option that gives the correct matches.

	List A (Bioactive products)		List B Microbes (Source organism)
A.	Cyclosporin-A	1.	*Streptococcus*
B.	Statins	2.	*Tricoderma polysporum*
C.	Streptokinase	3.	*Penicillium notatum*
D.	Penicillin	4.	*Monascus purpureus*

Codes **CBSE 2023**

	A	B	C	D
(a)	1	2	3	4
(b)	3	4	2	1
(c)	4	3	2	1
(d)	2	4	1	3

Ans. (d) A–2, B–4, C–1, D–3

5. Which of the following water samples in the table given below, will have a higher concentration of organic matter? **CBSE SQP 2023**

Water sample	Level of pollution	Value of BOD
(a)	High	High
(b)	Low	Low
(c)	Low	High
(d)	HIgh	Low

Ans. (a)

6. Large holes in Swiss cheese are due to **All India 2020**
   (a) *Propionibacterium shermanii*
   (b) *Saccharomyces cerevisiae*
   (c) *Penicillium chrysogenum*
   (d) *Acetobacter aceti*

Ans. (a) *Propionibacterium shermanii*

Very Short Answer Type Questions

7. What are 'flocs' formed during secondary treatment of sewage ? **Delhi 2019**

Ans. Flocs are masses of bacteria held together by slime and fungal filaments to form mesh-like structures. They are used during the secondary sewage treatment in the aeration tank to increase decomposition.

8. Give the scientific name of the source organism from which the first antibiotic was produced. **CBSE SQP 2019, Foreign 2014**

Ans. *Penicillium notatum* is a mold from which the first antibiotic was produced.

9. Why do we add an inoculum of curd to milk for curdling it? **Delhi 2015C**

Or Why is 'starter' added to set the milk into curd? Explain. **All India 2014C**

Or Name the nutrient that gets enhanced while curdling of milk by *Lactobacillus*? **All India 2014C**

Ans. When a small amount of curd as starter or inoculum is added to fresh milk as millions of Lactic Acid Bacteria

(LAB) present in this starter grow in milk and convert it into curd. During this process, acids are produced by LAB that coagulate and partially digest the milk protein (casein). LAB increase vitamin-B_{12} content along with other vitamins in the curd.

10. How is lactic acid bacteria beneficial to us other than helping in curdling the milk? **All India 2015C**

Ans. Two benefits of LAB are given below

(i) They improve the nutrient quality of curd by increasing the vitamin-B_{12} content. (½)

(ii) LAB also check the growth of disease causing microbes in the stomach. (½)

11. Write the scientific name of the microbe used for fermenting malted cereals and fruit juices. **Delhi 2011**

Ans. *Saccharomyces cerevisiae* also called brewer's yeast, is the microbe used for fermenting malted cereals and fruit juices.

12. Why is sewage water treated until the BOD is reduced? Give a reason. **Delhi 2010C**

Ans. The higher the BOD of sewage water, more is its polluting potential. So, the sewage water is treated, till its BOD is reduced which further indicates the reduction in the organic matter present in it.

2 Marks Questions

13. What are flocs? State their role in biological treatment of sewage. **Delhi 2021-22 Term-II**

Ans. Flocs are masses of bacteria associated with the fungal filaments to form mesh-like structures formed during the secondary treatment of sewage. They digest most of the organic material from the sludge. Thus, help in reducing the Biochemical Oxygen Demand (BOD) of the effluent. This further helps in effective treatment of sewage. (½ + 1½)

14. Mention the common bacterium found in the anaerobic sludge during sewage treatment and also in the rumen of cattle. How is this bacterium commercially useful? **All India 2021-22 Term-II**

Ans. The common bacterium found in the anaerobic sludge during sewage treatment and also in the rumen of cattle is methanogens.

These have become industrially important as their technical application lies in the production of biogas by digestion of organic substrates. Also, they find their role in the sewage treatment plants in order to filtre the wastewater. (1 + 1)

15. Different species belonging to genus-*Trichoderma* are useful to humans as well as to plants. Justify their roles by giving one instance of each. **All India 2021-22 Term-II**

Ans. Different species of the genus–*Trichoderma* are useful to both humans as well as plants. This can be understood as *Trichoderma polysporum* produces cyclosporin-A that acts as an immunosuppressive agent during organ transplant.

Apart from this, *Trichoderma* species promotes the growth of plants and limits the growth of plant pathogens, they effectively act as biofungicides, degrading other fungi.

16. Water samples were collected at points *A*, *B* and *C* in a segment of a river near a sugar factory and tested for BOD level. The BOD levels of samples *A*, *B* and *C* were 400 mg/L, 480 mg/L and 8 mg/L, respectively. What is this indicative of? Explain why the BOD level gets reduced considerably at the collection point *C*?

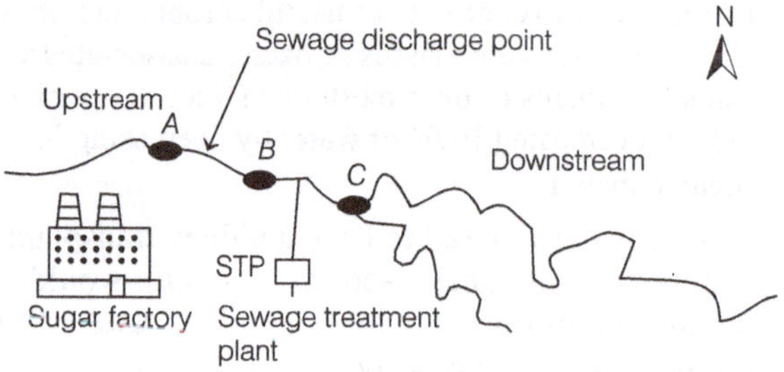

CBSE SQP 2021-22 Term-II

Ans. BOD (Biological Oxygen Demand) helps to indicate the level of pollution in a water body. In the given results, at collection points *A* and *B*, the BOD level is high due to high organic pollution caused by sugar factory and sewage discharge. (1)

At the collection point *C*, the water was released after secondary treatment where vigorous growth of useful aerobic microbes into flocs consume the major part of the organic matter present in the river water or effluent due to sugar factory and sewage discharge. (1)

17. A patient admitted in ICU was diagnosed to have suffered from myocardial infarction. The condition of coronary artery is depicted in the image below. Name two bioactive agents and their mode of action that can improve this condition.

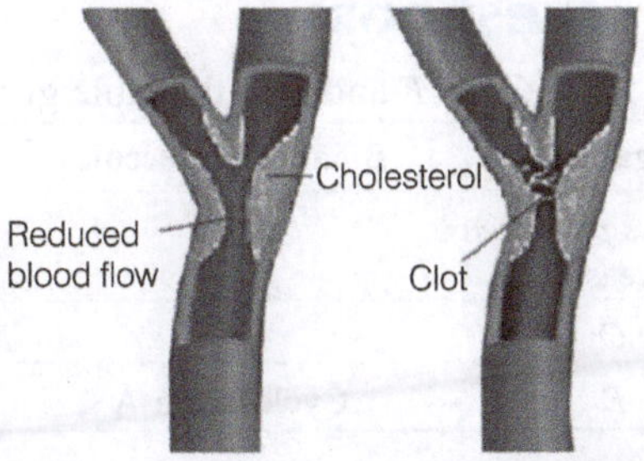

CBSE SQP 2021-22 Term-II

Ans. Two bioactive agents which can help the patient who suffered from myocardial infarction are

(i) **Streptokinase** (produced by the bacterium *Streptococcus*) It can be used as a clot buster for removing clots from the blood vessels of the patient. **(1)**

(ii) **Statins** (produced by the yeast *Monascus purpureus*) These act as blood cholesterol lowering agents. These are given because the patient diagnosis shows arteriosclerosis due to cholesterol. **(1)**

18. (i) A patient who had an organ transplant was given cyclosporin-A. Mention the microbial source and state the reason for administration of this bioactive molecule.

(ii) Bottled fruit juices bought from the market are clearer as compared to those made at home. Give reason. **CBSE SQP 2018**

Ans. (i) Cyclosporin-A is an immunosuppressant. Source—*Trichoderma polysporum* (fungus). Immunosuppressants are drugs, that are used to prevent graft rejection. Cyclosporin-A destroys T-cells mediated immune responses, while spares humoral antibody responses. **(1)**

(ii) Bottled juices of market are clearer as compared to home made juice because in these juices pectinase enzyme is added, which digest the pectin and other fibres present in juices. Pectinases are obtained commercially from *Byssochlamys fulvo*. **(1)**

19. Distinguish between the roles of flocs and anaerobic sludge digesters in sewage treatments. **Delhi 2016**

Ans. In sewage treatment, flocs consume major part of the organic matter, converting it into microbial biomass and releasing lot of minerals.

It reduces the BOD of sewage, while in anaerobic sludge digesters, many anaerobic bacteria are present, which digest the organic mass. During this digestion, methane, CO_2, etc., are produced. **(1 + 1)**

20. List the events that reduce the Biological Oxygen Demand (BOD) of a primary effluent during sewage treatment. **Delhi 2016**

> **KEY idea**
> Amount of pollution denotes the levels of BOD.

Ans. To reduce the BOD of primary effluent during sewage treatment, it is passed into large aeration tanks with constant mechanical agitation and air supply. This allows vigorous growth of aerobic microbes into flocs which consume major part of organic matter in the effluent. Hence, BOD of effluent is reduced.

21. Explain the different steps involved during primary treatment phase of sewage. **All India 2015**

Ans. **Primary treatment** of sewage involves the physical removal of large and small particles from sewage through filtration and sedimentation.

The steps involved in this process are

(i) Floating debris is removed by sequential filtration by passing through wire mesh screens.

(ii) After this, the grit (soil and small pebbles) is removed by sedimentation in settling tanks. The sediment is called **primary sludge** and the supernatant forms the **primary effluent**.

(iii) The effluent is then taken for the secondary treatment.

22. Mention a product of human welfare obtained with the help of each one of the following microbes.

(i) LAB

(ii) *Saccharomyces cerevisiae*

(iii) *Propionibacterium shermanii*

(iv) *Aspergillus niger* **Delhi 2015**

Ans.

	Microbes	Product of human welfare
(i)	LAB	Curd
(ii)	*Saccharomyces cerevisiae*	Bread and cakes
(iii)	*Propionibacterium shermanii*	Swiss cheese
(iv)	*Aspergillus niger*	Citric acid

(½ × 4)

23. Bottled fruit juices are clearer as compared to those made at home. Explain. **Foreign 2015**

Ans. Refer to answer no. 18 (ii).

24. Name two groups of organisms which constitute 'flocs'. Write their influence on the level of BOD during biological treatment of sewage. **All India 2014C**

Ans. The groups of organisms which constitute mesh-like structures called 'flocs' are bacteria and fungi. (1)

The bacterial masses associated with fungal filaments called flocs, consume the major part of organic matter present in effluent, thereby reducing the BOD of the waste significantly during biological or secondary treatment of sewage. (1)

25. Name the bacterium responsible for the large holes seen in Swiss cheese. What are these holes due to? **All India 2013**

Ans. Swiss cheese is produced by the bacterium *Propionibacterium shermanii*. The large holes in Swiss cheese are due to the production of large amount of CO_2 gas. (1 + 1)

26. Name the source of streptokinase. How does this bioactive molecule function in our body? **Delhi 2012**

Or Name the enzyme produced by *Streptococcus* bacterium. Explain its importance in medical sciences. **All India 2011**

Ans. Streptokinase enzyme is produced by the bacterium *Streptococcus*. It is modified by genetic engineering and is used as a clot buster for removing clots from the blood vessels of patients who have suffered from myocardial infarction. (1 + 1)

27. Mention the importance of lactic acid bacteria to humans other than setting milk into curd. **Delhi 2012**

Ans. (i) Lactic Acid Bacteria (LAB) are used to produce an acid called lactic acid that is an important industrial product. It is also used in beverages, meat products, confectionary, dairy products, etc. (1)

(ii) It checks the disease causing microbes in the stomach. (1)

28. Name the source of cyclosporin-A. How does this bioactive molecule function in our body? **All India 2012**

Or Name the source of statin and state its action on the human body. **Foreign 2012**

Ans. Cyclosporin-A is produced by the fungus *Trichoderma polysporum*. It is used as an immunosuppressive agent in organ-transplant patients as it suppresses the activation of T-cells in body. (1)

Statin is produced by yeast *Monascus purpureus*. It is used as blood cholesterol lowering agent. It acts by competitively inhibiting the enzyme responsible for the synthesis of cholesterol. (1)

29. How does addition of a small amount of curd to fresh milk help formation of curd? Mention a nutritional quality that gets added to the curd. **Delhi 2010**

Ans. Refer to answer no. 9.

3 Marks Questions

30. Identify *A, B, C, D, E* and *F* in the table given below.

Organisms	Bioactive molecules	Uses
Monascus purpureus (yeast)	*A*	*B*
C	*D*	Antibiotic
E	Cyclosporin-A	*F*

CBSE 2024 (Set-II), Delhi 2010C

Ans. *A*–Statins, *B*–They are used as blood cholesterol lowering agents, *C*–*Penicillium notatum*, *D*–Penicillin, *E*–*Trichoderma polysporum*, *F*–Used as an immunosuppressive agent in organ transplant patients.

31. The aeration tank of a sewage treatment plant is not functioning properly. Explain in detail the impact of this on the treatment of sewage and BOD of the effluent. **CBSE SQP 2024**

Ans.
- It will adversely affect the secondary treatment or biological treatment of sewage.
- When the aeration tank is not functional, the air will not be pumped into it.
- This will not allow the vigorous growth of useful aerobic microbes into flocs (masses of bacteria associated with fungal filaments to form mesh like structures).
- Thus, the major part of the organic matter in the effluent will not be consumed by these bacteria.
- The BOD (Biochemical Oxygen Demand) of the effluent will not be reduced. BOD refers to the amount of the oxygen that would be consumed if all the organic matter in one litre of water were oxidised by bacteria.
- The greater the BOD of wastewater, more is its polluting potential. Thus, the effluent will remain polluted with high amount of organic matter and high BOD. (½ × 3)

32. Define flocs and state their importance in biological treatment of wastewater. **CBSE SQP 2022**

Or Describe how do 'flocs' and 'activated sludge' help in sewage treatment. **Delhi 2017**

Ans. Roles of 'flocs' and 'activated sludge' in sewage treatment are as follows

Flocs These are masses of bacteria held together by slime and fungal filaments to form mesh-like structures.

These are used during the secondary sewage treatment in the aeration tank to increase the rate of decomposition.

The microbes digest a lot of organic matter, converting it into microbial biomass and releasing a lot of minerals. As a result, BOD of the sewage reduces. As the BOD of waste is reduced to 10-15% of raw sewage, it is passed into settling tank. In these tanks, flocs are allowed to undergo sedimentation.

Activated sludge The sediment of settling tank is called activated sludge. A part of it is used as inoculum in aeration tanks.

The remaining part is passed into a large tank called anaerobic sludge digester. In these tanks, anaerobic microbes are present that digest the organic mass as well as aerobic microbes of activated sludge. The remaining sludge is used as manure or compost.

33. Large quantities of sewage is generated everyday in cities and towns, which is treated in Sewage Treatment Plants (STPs) to make it less polluted. Given below is the flow diagram of one of the stages of STP.

Observe the given flow diagram and answer the questions accordingly.

Primary effluent is passed into large aeration tank

↓

Effluent passed into settling tank to form the sediment

(i) Why primary effluent is passed into large aeration tanks?

(ii) Write the technical term used for the sediment formed? Mention its significance.

(iii) Explain the final step that results in the formation of biogas in the large tank before the treated effluent is released into water bodies.

CBSE SQP 2020

Ans. (i) The primary effluent is passed into aeration tanks where it is constantly agitated mechanically and air is pumped into it. This allows vigorous growth of useful aerobic microbes into flocs (masses of bacteria associated with fungal filaments to form mesh-like structure).

(ii) The sediment formed is called activated sludge. A small part of the activated sludge is pumped back into the aeration tank to serve as the inoculum.

(iii) The final step is the digestion of the biomass and aerobic microbes by anaerobic microbes. During this digestion, bacteria produce a mixture of gases such as methane, hydrogen sulphide and carbon dioxide. **(1 × 3)**

34. State the medicinal value and the bioactive molecules produced by *Penicillium notatum, Monascus purpureus* and *Trichoderma polysporum*.

All India 2019, 2015

Ans.

Microbes	Bioactive molecules	Medicinal value
Penicillium notatum	Penicillin	Used as antibiotic against many fungal and bacterial diseases in humans and animals.
Monascus purpureus	Statins	Used as blood cholesterol lowering agent. It acts by competitively inhibiting the enzyme responsible for the synthesis of cholesterol.
Trichoderma polysporum	Cyclosporin-A	Used as immuno-suppressive agent in organ transplant patients.

35. Explain the different steps involved in the secondary treatment of sewage. **CBSE SQP 2019**

Or Secondary treatment of the sewage is also called biological treatment. Justify this statement and explain the process. **All India 2017**

Ans. The **secondary treatment** of sewage is also called biological treatment because in this treatment, sewage is subjected to biodegradation. It means that it involves the participation of microorganisms. The process of secondary treatment involves following steps

(i) Primary effluent is passed into large aeration tanks with constant mechanical agitation and air supply. This allows vigorous growth of useful aerobic microbes into **flocs** (masses of bacteria and fungi filaments).

(ii) These microbes consume major part of organic matter in the effluent, while growing. This reduces the BOD of the effluent the sediment is called **activated sludge.**

(iii) The remaining major part of the sludge is pumped into large tanks called **anaerobic sludge digesters,** where other kinds of bacteria, which grow anaerobically, digest the bacteria and the fungi in the sludge.

Now the effluent from secondary treatment is generally released into natural water bodies. **(1 + 2)**

36. The three microbes are listed below. Name the product produced by each one of them and mention their use. **CBSE 2018C**

(i) *Aspergillus niger* (ii) *Trichoderma polysporum*

(iii) *Monascus purpureus*

Ans. (i) Citric acid is produced from fungi *Aspergillus niger*.
Use Citric acid is used as a flavouring and preserving agent specially in soft drinks. (1)

(ii) Cyclosporin-A is produced by the fungus *Trichoderma polysporum*.
Use It is used as immunosuppressive agent in organ transplant patient. (1)

(iii) Statins are produced by the yeast *Monascus purpureus*.
Use It is used as blood cholesterol lowering agent. (1)

37. Make a list of three household products along with the names of the microorganisms producing them. **All India 2016**

Ans. (i) Curd : *Lactobacillus* (1)
(ii) Bread : *Saccharomyces cerevisiae* (1)
(iii) Swiss cheese : *Propionibacterium shermanii.* (1)

Concept Enhancer LAB have been used for decades even in agricultural systems to improve soils and control diseases.

38. Determination of Biological Oxygen Demand (BOD) can help in suggesting the quality of a water body. Explain. **Delhi 2015**

Ans. BOD is the amount of dissolved oxygen required for the microbial breakdown of biodegradable organic matter. (1)

Aerobic organisms use a lot of oxygen and as a result, there is a sharp decline in Dissolved Oxygen (DO) in the water body. This can cause death of fishes and other aquatic species. (1)

Determination of BOD is thus, an important parameter in determining the quality of a water body. The presence of more organic waste increases the microbial activity. Thus, decreasing the DO. BOD is higher in polluted water and lesser in clean water. (1)

39. How can sewage be used to generate biogas? Explain. **Foreign 2015**

Ans. Refer to text on page no. 246 (Secondary treatment).

40. Identify *A, B, C, D, E* and *F* in the table given below.

Scientific name of the organism	Product produced	Use in human welfare
Streptococcus	Streptokinase modified	*A*
B	Cyclosporin-A	*C*
Monascus purpureus	*D*	*E*
Lactobacillus	*F*	Sets milk into curd

Foreign 2014

Ans. The codes are identified as
A– Clot buster in patients who underwent myocardial infarction.
B– *Trichoderma polysporum*
C– Immunosuppressive agent in organ transplantation
D– Statins
E – Blood cholesterol lowering agents
F – Lactic acid

41. Mention the product and its use, produced by each of the microbes listed below
(i) *Streptococcus* (ii) *Lactobacillus*
(iii) *Saccharomyces cerevisiae* **All India 2010**

Ans. (i) ***Streptococcus*** Product is streptokinase. It is used as a clot buster for removing the clots from the blood vessels of patients suffering from myocardial infarction. (1)

(ii) ***Lactobacillus*** Product is lactic acid. It is used to convert milk into curd and improves nutrient quality of curd by enriching it with vitamin-B_{12}. (1)

(iii) ***Saccharomyces cerevisiae*** Product is ethanol and it is used in making bread and beverages. (1)

5 Marks Questions

42. Large quantities of sewage are generated every day in cities as well as in towns and are treated in Sewage Treatment Plants (STPs) to make them less polluting. Given below is the flow diagram of stages of STP.

Study the flow diagram and answer the questions that follow

Primary effluent passed into large aeration tanks
↓
Effluent passed into settling tanks to form 'sediment'

(i) (1) Why is primary effluent passed into large aeration tanks?
(2) What is the 'sediment' formed, referred to as? Mention its significance.
(3) Explain the final step in the settling tank before the treated effluent is released into water bodies.

(ii) Name any two organisms commonly used as biofertilisers, belonging to different kingdoms. Write how each one acts as a biofertiliser. **CBSE 2024 (Set-I)**

Ans. (i) 1. The primary effluent in passed into large aeration tank for aerobic digestion of effluent by flocs masses of bacteria associated with fungi in a mesh like structures to decrease its BOD by digesting the organic matter in it. (1)

2. 'Sediment' formed is referred to as activated sludge. A part of this is pumped back into the aeration tank to serve as the inoculum. (1)

3. The final step in the settling tank is anaerobic digestion by fungi and bacteria in anaerobic sludge digesters. After which, the treated effluent is generally released into natural water bodies. (1)

(ii) *Rhizobium* fixes atmospheric nitrogen into plant usable organic forms by forming symbiotic association with legumes.

Azospirillum fixes atmospheric nitrogen while free living in the soil and enriching the nitrogen content of soil. (2)

43. List the events that reduce the Biological Oxygen Demand (BOD) of a primary effluent during sewage treatment. **Delhi 2016**

Ans. Refer to text on page no. 246.

Common Mistakes Commonly students get confused that good quality of water has higher BOD, but
Higher BOD : Poor quality of water
Lower BOD : Good quality of water

44. List the events that lead to biogas production from wastewater whose BOD has been reduced significantly. **Delhi 2016**

Or

Explain the process of secondary treatment given to the primary effluent upto the point it shows significant change in the level of Biological Oxygen Demand (BOD) in it. **All India 2015**

Ans. For biogas production, refer to answer no. 20 and 35. The gases from biogas are used as a source of energy because they are inflammable.

45. (i) Name the category of microbes naturally occurring in sewage and making it less polluted during the treatment.

(ii) Explain the different steps involved in the secondary treatment of sewage. **Foreign 2014**

Ans. (i) The category of microbes naturally occurring in sewage and making it less polluted are bacteria and fungi, where in masses of bacteria get associated with filaments of fungi to form mesh-like structure called flocs. (2)

(ii) For different steps involved in secondary or biological treatment of sewage, refer to answer no. 35. (3)

TOPIC 2

Microbes in Production of Biogas, as Biocontrol Agents and Biofertilisers

Microbes in Production of Biogas

- **Biogas** is a mixture of gases (mainly methane) produced by the microbial activity and may be used as a fuel.
- Certain bacteria, which grow anaerobically on cellulosic material produce large amount of methane along with CO_2 and H_2. These bacteria are called **methanogens** (one of the common bacterium is *Methanobacterium*).
- **Methanogens** are commonly found in the anaerobic sludge during sewage treatment and are also present in the rumen (a part of stomach) of cattle.
- In rumen, methanogens help in the breakdown of cellulose anaerobically thereby releasing CO_2 and H_2. This process plays an important role in the nutrition of cattle. The excreta of cattle called **gobar**, is rich in these bacteria. Therefore, cow dung can also be used to produce biogas, commonly called **gobar gas**.

Biogas Production

- The biogas plant consists of a concrete tank (10-15 feet deep) in which bio-wastes are collected and a slurry of dung is fed.
- A floating cover is placed over the slurry, which keeps on rising as the gas is produced in the tank due to microbial activity.
- The plant has an outlet, which is connected to a pipe to supply biogas to nearby houses.
- The spent slurry is removed through another outlet and may be used as fertiliser.
- In rural areas, cattle dung is available in plenty. So, more biogas plants are built in these areas to produce biogas for cooking and lighting.
- This technology of biogas production was developed in India due to the efforts of **Indian**

Agricultural Research Institute (IARI) and **Khadi** and **Village Industries Commission** (KVIC).

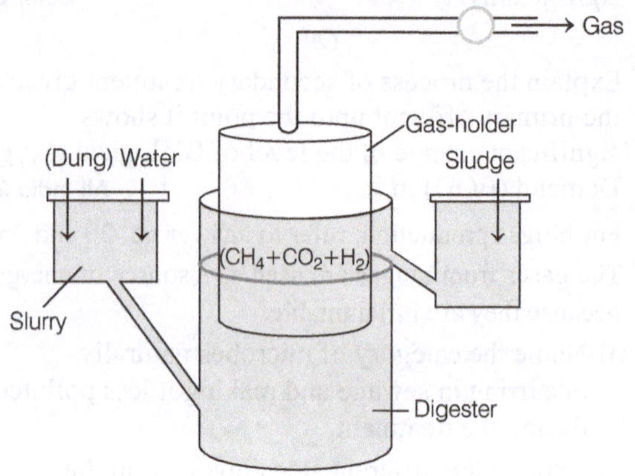

Figure 8.1 A typical biogas plant

Microbes as Biocontrol Agents

- **Biocontrol** refers to the use of biological methods for controlling the plant diseases and pests.
- The insecticides and pesticides are although useful for field output, but they are toxic and extremely harmful to humans and animals because they are polluting our environment, crop plants, etc.
- Biocontrol agriculture relies on the natural control of pests, i.e. natural predation rather than introduced chemicals. Their mode of action is contrary to the conventional farming practices which often uses chemical methods to kill both useful and harmful life forms indiscriminately.
- A key belief of the organic farmer is that biodiversity furthers health. They believe in holistic approach that seeks to develop an understanding of the webs of interaction between the myriad of organisms that constitute the field fauna and flora.
- They hold the view that the eradication of the creatures that are often described as pests is undesirable because without them, the beneficial predatory and parasitic insects would not survive.
- Some approaches for biological farming are
  - Familiarity with various life forms inhabiting the field.
  - Understanding of their life cycles, patterns of feeding and preferred habitat of predators and pests.
  - Greatly reduced dependency on toxic chemicals and pesticides by the use of biocontrol measures.
  - Instead of eradicating the pests completely, they are kept at manageable levels by a complex system of checks and balances within a living and vibrant ecosystem.

Examples of Biocontrol Agents

- Ladybird and dragonflies used to get rid of aphids and mosquitoes, respectively.
- The bacteria, *Bacillus thuringiensis* (*Bt*) is used to control butterfly catterpillars.
- The fungus, *Trichoderma* is used for the treatment of plant diseases.
  These are free-living fungi that are very common in the root ecosystems.
- Baculoviruses are pathogens that attack insects and other arthropods.
  - Majority of baculoviruses which are used as biocontrol agents belong to the genus– *Nucleopolyhedrovirus*.
  - These are species specific, narrow spectrum insecticides. Which means they do not harm non-target organisms.
  - Baculoviruses are beneficial in **Integrated Pest Management** (IPM) programme, in which beneficial insects are conserved.

Microbes as Biofertilisers

Microbes as biofertilisers enrich the nutrient (nitrogen, phosphorus, etc.) quality of the soil. The main sources of biofertilisers are bacteria, fungi and cyanobacteria.

1. Bacteria as Biofertilisers

- The nodules on the roots of leguminous plants are formed by the symbiotic association of *Rhizobium* bacteria.
  These bacteria fix atmospheric nitrogen into organic forms, which is used by the plants as nutrient.
- Other bacteria, such as *Azospirillum* and *Azotobacter*, fix atmospheric nitrogen while free-living in the soil. They enrich the nitrogen content of the soil.

2. Fungi as Biofertilisers

- Fungi form symbiotic association with plants (mycorrhiza).
- Many members of the fungus genus–*Glomus* form mycorrhiza.
- The fungal symbiont absorbs phosphorus from the soil and passes it to the plant.
- Mycorrhiza shows the following benefits

– Resistance to root borne pathogens.
– Tolerance to salinity and drought.
– Overall increase in plant growth and development.

3. Cyanobacteria as Biofertilisers

- Cyanobacteria are autotrophic microbes and many of them can fix atmospheric nitrogen.
- Examples of cyanobacteria are *Anabaena*, *Nostoc*, *Oscillatoria*, etc.
- Blue-green algae also add organic matter to the soil and increase its fertility.

Uses of Biofertilisers

A number of biofertilisers are available commercially in the market. Farmers use them in fields to replenish soil nutrients and to reduce dependence on the chemical fertilisers. These biofertilisers do not allow the pathogens to flourish and these are non-polluting.

PYQs Previous Years' Questions

1 Mark Questions

Multiple Choice Question

1. Bacteria present in rumen of a cattle digest cellulose to produce **Delhi 2020**
(a) polysaccharides (b) sucrose
(c) ethanol (d) methane

Ans. (d) methane

Very Short Answer Type Questions

2. Write any two places where methanogens can be found. **Delhi 2019**

Ans. (i) Rice fields (ii) Alimentary canal of ruminants. (½ × 2)

3. Name the type of association that the genus-*Glomus* exhibits with higher plants. **All India 2014**

Ans. The genus–*Glomus* exhibits symbiotic association with higher plants called mycorrhiza.

4. State one reason for adding blue-green algae to the agricultural soil. **Delhi 2014C**

Ans. Blue-green algae are added to agricultural soil because they add organic matter to the soil and also increase its fertility.

5. What makes the *Nucleopolyhedrovirus* a desirable biological control agent? **All India 2013C; 2012C**

Or

What is the significance of *Nucleopolyhedrovirus* in pest management?

Ans. *Nucleopolyhedrovirus*, a genus of baculoviruses is useful in controlling many insects and other arthropods. They are species specific, narrow spectrum bioinsecticide with no side- effects on plants, mammals, birds, fish and non-target insects. Therefore, they serve as an important component of integrated pest management programme in dealing with ecological sensitive areas. These properties are useful in organic farming.

6. Mention the role of cyanobacteria as biofertilisers. **All India 2012**

Ans. Cyanobacteria fix atmospheric nitrogen and increase the organic matter of the soil through their photosynthetic activity.

7. Mention two advantages of adding blue-green algae to paddy fields. **All India 2011C**

Ans. In the paddy fields, cyanobacteria such as blue-green algae fix atmospheric nitrogen to enrich the nitrogen content of soil. Therefore, the entire need of nitrogen to rice crop can be supplied by blue-green algae, leading to increase in the yield. (½+½)

8. Name any one symbiont, which serves as biofertiliser. Mention its specific role. **All India 2010C**

Ans. *Rhizobium* is a symbiotic bacteria that serves as biofertiliser. (½)
The bacteria fix the atmospheric nitrogen into organic forms, which is used by the plants as nutrients. (½)

2 Marks Questions

9. Answer the questions based on the typical biogas plant diagram given below **CBSE 2024 (Set-II)**

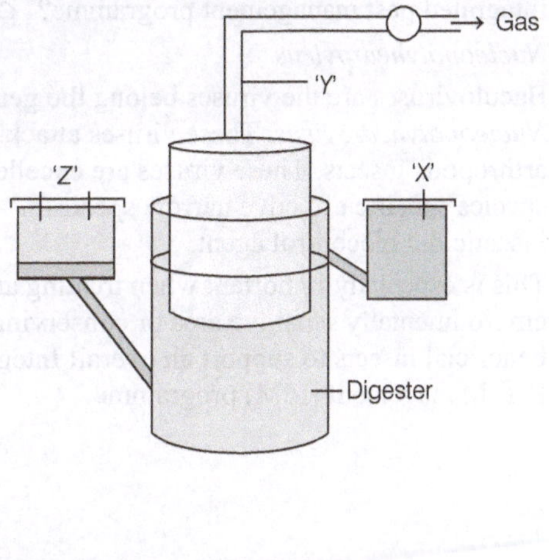

(i) Identify '*X*', '*Y*' and '*Z*'.

(ii) Why is dung preferred for the production of biogas?

Ans. (i) *X* – Sludge

Y – Gas outlet

Z – Dung + Water

(ii) Dung is preferred for the biogas production due to its large availability in rural areas, its nutrient composition and its non-polluting or eco-friendly nature, etc.

10. Why do organic farmers not recommend complete eradication of insect pests ? Explain giving reason. **CBSE 2024 (Set-I)**

Ans. Organic farmers do not recommend complete eradication of insect pests because without them, the beneficial predatory and parasitic insects which depend upon them as food or hosts would not be able to survive. The predators as well as parasites also act as biocontrol agents and help in the maintenance of ecological balance. Organic farmers believe that biodiversity furthers health. More the variety in a biodiversity, more is the sustainability it supports.

11. Certain specific bacterial spores are mixed in water and sprayed over *Brassica* crop to control butterfly caterpillars.

Name this bacterium and its mode of action on the butterfly catterpillars. **CBSE 2023**

Ans. To control butterfly caterpillars, bacteria such as *Bacillus thuringiensis* are used in the form of sprays, sachets as dry spores. These are mixed with water and are sprayed onto vulnerable plants like *Brassica* and fruit trees , where these are eaten by insects larvae. This kills the larvae due to the release of toxin in their gut, thereby eradicating the caterpillars, but leaving other insects unharmed.

12. (i) Give an example of a genus of virus used as narrow spectrum insecticidal biocontrol agent.

(ii) How does its use serve as an aid in overall integrated pest management programme? **CBSE 2023**

Ans. (i) *Nucleopolyhedrovirus.* (½)

(ii) Baculoviruses are the viruses belong the genus-*Nucleopolyhedrovirus*. These viruses attack the arthropods/insects. These viruses are excellent species specific effective narrow spectrum insecticidal biocontrol agent.

This is especially important when treating an environmentally sensitive area or conserving beneficial insects to support an overall Integrated Pest Management (IPM) programme. (1½)

13. Organic farmer use *Trichoderma* and baculovirus as biological control agents. Explain. **Delhi 2021-22 Term-II**

Ans. Biocontrol refers to the use of biological methods for controlling plant diseases and pests *Trichoderma* sp. are the most widely used fungal biocontrol agents. It used against fungal disease of pulses, cotton, maize, etc. It has moderate effects on the soil balance and does not harm the beneficial organisms. Similarly, baculoviruses attack insects and other arthropods.

They do not harm plants, fishes, birds and non-target organisms.

Thus, these are more often used in organic farming by the farmers.

14. Farmers are often suggested to use the following organisms in their cropland so as to improve the soil fertility.

(i) *Rhizobium* (ii) *Anabaena*

Explain. **Delhi 2021-22 Term-II**

Ans. Farmers are often suggested to use *Rhizobium* and *Anabaena* in their cropland so as to improve the soil fertility.

Both *Rhizobium* and *Anabaena* act as biofertilisers. These enrich the nutrient quality of the soil. *Rhizobium* is a soil-dwelling bacteria that help in fixing atmospheric nitrogen in leguminous plants and thus help the plant to grow well.

Anabaena is a cyanobacterium and adds organic matter to the soil, thus increase its fertility.

15. Name the effective biocontrol agents of several plant pathogens belonging to group of viruses. Also write about the ways they support the environment. **All India 2021-22 Term-II**

Ans. Baculoviruses are effective biocontrol agents of several plant pathogens. These belong to the genus– *Nucleopolyhedrovirus.*

These are species specific, narrow spectrum insecticides which cause no harm to plants, mammals, birds, fish and other non-target insects.

They are also beneficial in the integrated pest management programme. Thus, they support the environment.

16. Your advice is sought to improve the nitrogen content of the soil to be used for cultivation of a non-leguminous terrestrial crop.

(i) Recommend two microbes that can enrich the soil with nitrogen.

(ii) Why do leguminous crops require such enrichment of the soil ? **CBSE 2018**

Ans. (i) • *Azospirillum* • *Azotobacter* (½ × 2)

(ii) The leguminous plants have nodules in their roots. These root nodules are formed by the symbiotic association of *Rhizobium*.

These bacteria fix atmospheric nitrogen and convert it into organic form. This organic form of nitrogen is used later on by the plants nutrient. Therefore, they do not require enrichment of the soil. (1)

17. How does the application of the fungal genus–*Glomus*, to the agricultural farm increase the farm output? **Delhi 2017**

Ans. The application of *Glomus* to agricultural field increases the farm output by increasing the nutrient availability to the crops. *Glomus* develops symbiotic association called mycorrhiza with the roots of plants. It absorbs phosphorus from the soil and passes it to the plant it is associated with.

In return, it derives sugars from the host plant cells for its survival. (1)

Thus, it acts as a biofertiliser. This association has other advantages also, like

(i) Resistance to root borne pathogens

(ii) Tolerance to salinity and drought

(iii) Increase in plant growth and development. (1)

Concept Enhancer The hyphae of *Glomus* contain glomalin, a glycoprotein. This acts as a main reserve for carbon present in soil.

18. How does the application of cyanobacteria help to improve agricultural output? **Delhi 2017**

Ans. **Role of cyanobacteria in improving agricultural output** Cyanobacteria are autotrophic microbes found in aquatic and terrestrial environments. Most of these fix atmospheric nitrogen, e.g. *Anabaena, Nostoc, Oscillatoria,* etc.

In paddy fields, cyanobacteria serve as an important biofertiliser as they enrich the nitrogen content in the soil. They also add organic matter to the soil. thus, increasing the fertility.

Thus, application of cyanobacteria helps in improving agricultural output.

19. Name a genus of baculovirus. Why are they considered good biocontrol agents? **All India 2016**

Ans. A genus of baculoviruses is *Nucleopolyhedrovirus.* (1)

Refer to answer no. 5 for their role as an biocontrol agents. (1)

20. What are methanogens? Name the animals in which methanogens occur and the role they play there. **Delhi 2014**

Ans. Methanogens are the groups of anaerobic bacteria, that produce large amount of methane gas. (½)

Methanogens are found in the rumen of cattle and in the anaerobic sludge during sewage treatment. (1)

The methanogens present in the intestine of animals and humans act on cellulosic part of food and digest them, thereby releasing methane along with CO_2 and H_2. (½)

21. Explain the significant role of the genus–*Nucleopolyhedrovirus* in an ecological sensitive area. **All India 2014**

Ans. For *Nucleopolyhedrovirus*, refer to answer no. 5.

22. How do mycorrhizae act as biofertilisers? Explain. Name a genus of fungi that forms a mycorrhizal association with plants. **Delhi 2012**

Or How do plants benefit from having mycorrhizal symbiotic association? **Foreign 2010**

Ans. Fungi form symbiotic association with plants, which is called mycorrhiza. The fungal symbiont in these associations absorbs phosphorus from soil and passes it to the plant. It also provides resistance to root borne pathogens and increases plant growth. Thus, it acts as a biofertiliser. The fungi belonging to the genus–*Glomus* form mycorrhizal associations with plants.

23. How do methanogens help in producing biogas? **Delhi 2012**

Ans. Methanogens grow anaerobically on cellulosic material and produce large amount of methane along with CO_2 and H_2. Since, biogas is a mixture of methane and CO_2, methanogens help in its production.

24. Why is *Rhizobium* categorised as a symbiotic bacterium? How does it act as biofertilisers? **Delhi 2012**

Ans. The nodules on the roots of leguminous plants are formed by *Rhizobium* bacteria for their survival. These bacteria fix atmospheric nitrogen into organic form, which is used by the plant as nutrients.

Since, *Rhizobium* forms symbiotic association with leguminous plants, these are considered as symbiotic bacteria. (1)

Rhizobium fixes the atmospheric nitrogen into organic form, i.e. nitrates which can be utilised by the plant as nutrient. So, it is used as biofertilisers. (1)

25. Name a free-living and a symbiotic bacterium that serves as biofertiliser. Why are they called so? **All India 2010C**

Ans. ***Azotobacter*** is a free-living bacteria serving as a biofertiliser. These bacteria absorb free-nitrogen from the soil, air and convert it into salts of nitrogen compounds and enrich the soil nutrients.

Rhizobium is a symbiotic bacteria that lives in the root nodules of legumes and fixes atmospheric nitrogen into organic compounds and enrich the soil nutrients. (1 + 1)

3 Marks Questions

26. *Bacillus thuringiensis* plays an important role in integrated pest management strategy. Explain how, any two crops that are protected efficiently from pests. **All India 2021-22 Term-II**

Ans. Integrated Pest Management (IPM) strategy is an ecosystem based strategy which focuses on long-term prevention of pests or their damage through a combination of techniques like biological control, use of resistant varieties, etc. In other words, it is an approach to control the pest in an integrated way.

Bacillus thuringiensis plays a major role in the integrated pest management strategy. It is used to control butterfly catterpillars. Dried spores of *Bt* are mixed with water and sprayed on plants in order to protect them from various pests (specially catterpillars). It also renders non-target insects/beings unharmed. Thus, they are equally important in the IPM strategy.

Two crops that are protected effectively from pests include *Brassica* and cotton.

27. Study the picture of biogas plant given below and answer the questions that follow. **Delhi 2020**

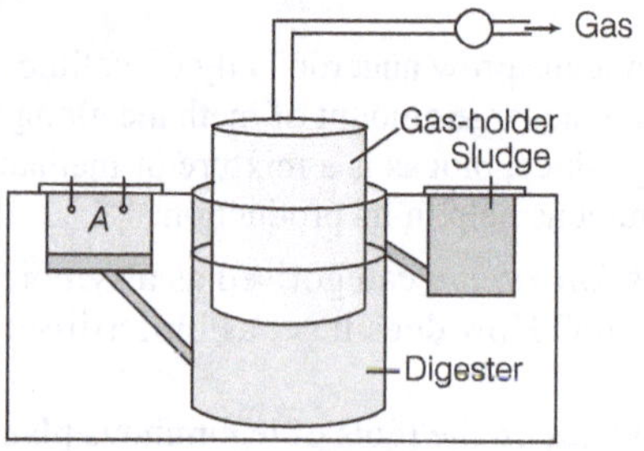

(i) Name the components gaining entry from *A* into the chamber.

(ii) Mention the group of bacteria and the condition in which they act on the component that entered *A* in the digester.

(iii) Name the components that get collected in gas holder.

Ans. (i) The dung and water are the components which gain entry from point *A* of the digestive chamber. **(1)**

(ii) Methanogens are the group of bacteria which act upon the dung matter to produce methane. The common methanogenic bacterium is *Methanobacterium.*

These bacterium need anaerobic condition to digest cellulosic material present in cattle dung. **(1)**

(iii) The components that get collected in gas holder or chamber are mainly methane gas (CH_4) along with carbon dioxide (CO_2) and hydrogen (H_2) gases used as fuel. **(1)**

28. How does the activity of each one of the following help in organic farming? **Delhi 2019**

(i) Mycorrhiza (ii) Cyanobacteria

(iii) *Rhizobium*

Ans. Refer to text on page no. 254.

29. Name the genus to which baculoviruses belong. Describe their role in the integrated pest management programmes. **All India 2019**

Or Baculoviruses are good example of biocontrol agents. Justify giving three reasons. **CBSE 2018C**

Ans. Refer to text on page no. 254.

30. Microbes can be used to decrease the use of chemical fertilisers. Explain how this can be accomplished. **CBSE SQP 2019**

Ans. **Biofertilisers** are organisms that enrich the nutrient quality of soil by enhancing the availability of nutrients to the crops. The main sources of biofertilisers are as given below

(i) **Bacteria** Nitrogen-fixing bacteria fix atmospheric nitrogen into organic form, which is used by the plants as nutrient, e.g. *Rhizobium* is a symbiotic bacterium that lives in the root nodules of legumes and fixes atmospheric nitrogen into organic compounds.

Azotobacter and *Azospirillum* are free-living bacteria, which absorb free nitrogen from the soil, air and convert it into salts of nitrogen compounds.

(ii) **Fungi** They form symbiotic association with plants, i.e. **mycorrhiza**, which absorb phosphorus from soil and passes it to the plants.

Many members of genus–*Glomus* form mycorrhiza with plant roots.

(iii) **Cyanobacteria** These are autotrophic microbes found in aquatic and terrestrial environments. Most of them fix atmospheric nitrogen, e.g. *Anabaena, Nostoc, Oscillatoria*, etc.

- In paddy fields, cyanobacteria serves as important biofertiliser.
- Blue-Green Algae (BGA) add organic matter to the soil. Thus, increasing its fertility, but still BGA are not very popularly used.

31. Cow dung and water is mixed and this slurry is fed into the biogas plant for digestion by microbes. The person performing the process shares that there is no need to provide any inoculum for it. Give reason. What is the role of microbes at the source? Under which condition will they be most active and effective? **CBSE SQP 2018**

Ans. (i) There is no need to provide inoculum because cow dung contains methanogen bacteria. **(1)**

(ii) These bacteria help in digestion of cellulose in the alimentary canal of cattles. **(1)**

(iii) These bacteria are anaerobic and can work in the absence of oxygen. So, they are active and effective in anaerobic conditions. **(1)**

Concept Enhancer Methanogens are also effectively known to decrease the concentration of organic matter in wastewater runoff.

32. (i) Organic farmers prefer biological control of diseases and pests to the use of chemicals for the same purpose. Justify.

(ii) Give an example of a bacterium, a fungus and an insect that are used as biocontrol agents.

Ans. (i) Organic farmers do not use any chemical for raising crops. They simply depend on biological control methods to control insects and pests. This way they avoid deleterious effects of chemicals on food products as well as on the environment. These chemicals get accumulated in food chain and ecosystem whereas biological control methods are safe as they do not harm any form of life. **(1½)**

(ii) Examples of biological control agents are as follows

(a) **Bacterium** *Bacillus thuringiensis* for the control of cotton bollworm.

(b) **Fungus** *Trichoderma* species for controlling fungal soil borne diseases like damping off of vegetables.

(c) **Insects** Ladybird beetle for the control of aphids. **(1½)**

33. What are methanogens? How do they help to generate biogas? **All India 2015**

Ans. Methanogens are the group of anaerobic bacteria that produce large amount of methane gas. These are found in the rumen of cattle and in the anaerobic sludge. **(1)**

Methanogens grow anaerobically on cellulosic material and produce large amount of methanogens along with CO_2, H_2. Since, biogas is the mixture of CO_2, H_2 and methane, methanogens help in its production. **(2)**

34. How are baculoviruses and *Bacillus thuringiensis* used as biocontrol agents? Why are they preferred over readily available chemical pesticides? **All India 2014C**

Ans. ***Bacillus thuringiensis*** **as Biocontrol Agent**

(i) Through genetic engineering, the gene coding for the toxic protein is introduced into crop plants, which makes them resistant to insect pests.

(ii) When they are eaten by the larvae, the toxin becomes active in the gut of larvae and kills the them.

(iii) They are available in sachets as dried spores, which have to be mixed with water and sprayed onto vulnerable plants. **(1)**

Baculoviruses uses (*Nucleopolyhedrovirus*) as biocontrol agents refer to answer no. 5. **(1)**

Biological control of pests and pathogens must be preferred over conventional use of chemical pesticides because

(i) the chemicals cause pollution to soil, ground water and agricultural products.

(ii) the chemicals are toxic and harmful to both human beings and animals.

(iii) overuse of chemical fertilisers makes soil infertile.

(iv) chemicals kill harmful as well as useful organisms indiscriminately. **(1)**

35.

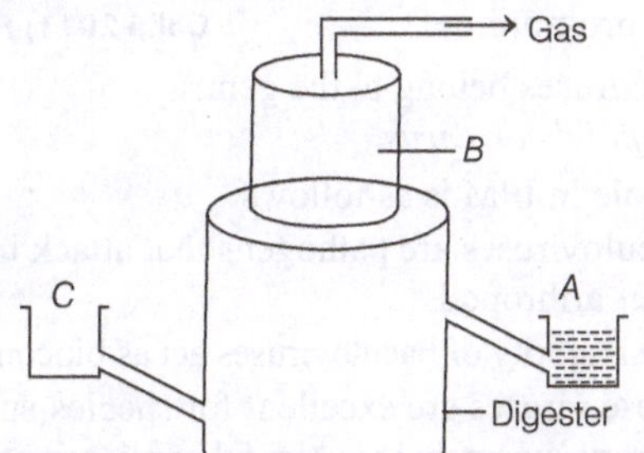

The diagram above is that of a typical biogas plant. Explain the sequence of events occurring in a biogas plant. Identify *A*, *B* and *C*. **Delhi 2011**

Ans. The sequence of events occurring in a biogas plant are as follows

(i) The biogas plant tank is fed with a slurry of dung.

(ii) A floating cover is placed over the slurry, which keeps on rising as the gas is produced in the tank due to the microbial activity.

(iii) Methanogens like *Methanobacterium* grow anaerobically on cellulosic plant material in cow dung to produce large amount of methane, CO_2 and H_2.

(iv) The plant has an outlet, which is connected by a pipe to supply biogas in nearby houses.

(v) The spent slurry is removed through another outlet and used as biofertilisers. **(1½)**

A–Sludge tank, *B*–Gas holder, *C*–Dung water **(1/2 × 3)**

36. (i) Why do farmers prefer biofertilisers to chemical fertilisers these days? Explain.

(ii) How do *Anabaena* and mycorrhiza act as biofertilisers? **Delhi 2011**

Ans. (i) A farmer relies on biofertilisers then chemical fertilisers because
(a) Chemical fertilisers significantly increase the soil pollution and reduce quality of soil, cause water pollution, when it drains into nearby water bodies, after rain.
(b) Overuse of chemical fertiliser makes the soil unfit for raising any crop. **(1)**
(ii) *Anabaena* fixes atmospheric nitrogen, thus enriching the nitrogen content of the soil, as well as the organic matter. **(1)**
In mycorrhiza, the fungal symbiont absorbs phosphorus from the soil and passes it to the plant and provides resistance to root borne diseases.
Since, they fulfill the nitrogen and phosphorus requirement, they act as biofertilisers. **(1)**

37. Name the genus to which baculoviruses belong. Describe their role in the Integrated Pest Management (IPM) programme. **Delhi 2011; Foreign 2011**

Ans. Baculoviruses belong to the genus– *Nucleopolyhedrovirus*. **(1)**
Their role in IPM is as follows
(i) Baculoviruses are pathogens that attack insects and other arthropods.
(ii) The majority of baculoviruses act as biocontrol agents.
(iii) These viruses are excellent for species-specific, narrow spectrum insecticidal applications.
(iv) They do not show negative impacts on plants, mammals, bird, fish or even non-target insects.
Therefore, they play an important role as biocontrol agent. **(2)**

38. An organic farmer relies on natural predation for controlling pests and diseases. Justify by giving reasons, why this is considered to be a holistic approach? **Foreign 2010**

Ans. Organic farming is a holistic approach that seeks to develop an understanding of the webs of interaction among the myriads of organisms that form the flora and fauna of the field.
(i) An organic farmer works to create a system, where the insects are not eradicated, but kept at manageable level by a complex system of checks and balance within a living and vibrant ecosystem. **(1)**
(ii) Organic farming states that the eradication of pests is not only possible, but also undesirable, because many beneficial predatory and parasitic insects cannot survive without them. **(1)**
(iii) The use of biocontrol methods reduces the use of chemical pesticides and thereby pollution. **(1)**

5 Marks Question

39. What are biofertilisers? Describe their role in agriculture. Why are they preferred over chemical fertilisers? **Foreign 2015**

Ans. Biofertilisers are the living organisms that promote the growth of plants by replenishing the nutrients in the soil. These include bacteria, fungi and cyanobacteria. **(1)**

Role of Biofertlisers in Agriculture

Some biofertilisers such as *Rhizobium* bacteria live in symbiotic association with plants. They live within the root nodules of leguminous plants.
These bacteria fix atmospheric nitrogen and enrich the nitrogen content of soil.
Fungi such as *Glomus* forms symbiotic association with plants (mycorrhiza) by absorbing phosphorus and passing it to plants.
Cyanobacteria such as *Nostoc* and *Anabaena* fix atmospheric nitrogen and act as biofertilisers especially in paddy fields. **(2)**
Biofertilisers are preferred over chemical fertilisers. Refer to answer no. 32 (i). **(2)**

Case Based/Source Based/Passage Based Questions (Based on Complete Chapter)

1. Read the following and answer any **four** questions from 1(i) to 1(v) given below

Ecological Indicators

The presence of dragonflies can reveal changes in the water ecosystems more quickly than studying other animals or plants. Infact from the nymph to the adult stage, the dragonfly has a significant, positive ecological impact. Dragonfly eggs are laid and hatched in or near water, so their lives impact both water and land ecosystems. Once hatched, dragonfly nymphs can breathe underwater which enables them to eat mosquito larvae, other aquatic insects and worms and even small aquatic vertebrates like tadpoles and small fish and in the air adult dragonflies capture and eat adult mosquitoes.
Community wide mosquito control programme that spray insecticides to kill adult mosquitoes also kill dragonflies. **CBSE SQP 2022**

(i) The approach to biological control includes
(a) import and release of an insect pest to a new area to provide hosts for natural enemies
(b) import and release of natural enemies from the native home of an alien insect pest that has invaded a new area

(c) preservation of natural enemies (predators and parasitoids) that are already established in an area
(d) use of insecticides to reduce alien insect pests to establish new equilibrium position

(ii) Two diseases less likely to occur in a region with plenty of dragonflies are.......
(a) yellow fever and amoebic dysentery
(b) malaria and yellow fever
(c) anthrax and typhoid
(d) cholera and typhoid

(iii) Dragonflies indicate positive ecological impact as
(a) the presence of dragonflies indicates polluted water
(b) dragonfly nymphs selectively eat mosquito larvae
(c) they help to decrease the probability of diseases spread by vectors
(d) dragonfly does not cause any harm to beneficial species

(iv) The most effective stages in the life cycle of dragonfly that eradicates mosquitoes are
(a) larvae and adult (b) caterpillar and adult
(c) nymph and adult (d) pupa and adult

(v) **Assertion** (A) Releasing dragonflies in areas where there is an outbreak of malaria diseases can be an environment friendly method of control.
Reason (R) Dragonflies are dominant species and will not allow mosquitoes to reproduce.
(a) If both A and R are true and R is the correct explanation of the A
(b) If both A and R are true, but R is not the correct explanation of A
(c) If A is true, but R is false
(d) If both A and R are false

Ans. (i)-(c), (ii)-(b), (iii)-(c), (iv)-(c), (v)-(c)

2. Read the following and answer the questions given below
Sewage is considered as the municipal wastewater that contains mainly human excreta. It has large quantity of organic matter and various pathogenic microbes. Therefore, it is mandatory to make sewage less polluting in nature before it is discharged in local or near by water bodies.

(i) The primary treatment of sewage is
(a) physical treatment
(b) chemical treatment
(c) biological treatment
(d) Both (a) and (b)

(ii) The floating debris in primary treatment is removed by
(a) filtration (b) sedimentation
(c) sequential filtration (d) floculation

(iii) Soil and pebbels are sent to .... tank after sedimentation.
(a) main tank (b) aeration tank
(c) settling tank (d) secondary tank

(iv) The masses of bacteria associated with fungal filaments forms mesh-like structure called
(a) pebble (b) flocs
(c) float (d) sediment

(v) The increased BOD has direct relationship with the
(a) pollution of water
(b) uptake of oxygen by microbes
(c) Both (a) and (b)
(d) None of the above

Ans. (i)-(a), (ii)-(c), (iii)-(c), (iv)-(b), (v)-(c)

3. During a seminar on human welfare, Dr. Hardik asserted the benefits of microorganisms in human welfare and for environment. He also mentioned the application of these microbes in sewage treatment, industrial production and as biofertilisers.

(i) Name the microbe used for fermenting malted cereals to produce ethanol.
(ii) How microbes are employed for medical purposes?
(iii) What is the role of flocs in sewage treatment?
(iv) Mention the role of *Glomus* in mycorrhiza.
(v) Name any two organisms which serve as biofertiliser in paddy fields.

Ans. (i) Brewer's yeast or *Saccharomyces cerevisiae*. (½)
(ii) Cyclosporin-A produced by the fungus *Trichoderma polysporum,* is used as an immunosuppressive agent in organ transplant patient. Statins are blood cholesterol lowering agents and these are produced by the yeast *Monascus purpureus*. (1)
(iii) Flocs are the masses of bacteria associated with fungal filaments to form mesh-like structures. These consume major part of organic matter in the effluent and thus reduces the BOD of sewage water. (1)
(iv) *Glomus* absorbs phosphorus from soil and passes it to the plant. It also helps the plants to tolerate salinity, drought and provides resistance to root borne pathogen. (1)
(v) *Anabaena* and *Nostoc*. (½)

CHAPTER TEST

01 Mark Questions

Multiple Choice Questions

1 Which microorganism is used to make butter milk?
(a) *Leuconostoc* sp. (b) *Penicillium* sp.
(c) *Lactobacillus* sp. (d) *Acetobacter* sp.

2 Which of the following microbes gives nutritional supplement, i.e. protein as a product?
(a) *Corynebacterium* (b) *Pseudomonas*
(c) *Chlorella* (d) *Acetobacter*

3 Which one of the following is used in the production of citric acid?
(a) *Aspergillus niger*
(b) *Rhizopus arrhizus*
(c) *Acetobacter*
(d) *Saccharomyces cerevisiae*

4 Which one of the following is not an example of carrying out biological control of pests/diseases using microbes?
(a) *Trichoderma* sp. against certain plant pathogens
(b) *Nucleopolyhedrovirus* against early blight in potato
(c) *Bt* cotton to increase cotton yield
(d) Ladybird beetle against aphids in mustard

5 *Monascus purpureus* is a yeast used commercially in the production of
(a) ethanol
(b) streptokinase for removing clots from the blood vessels
(c) citric acid
(d) blood cholesterol lowering statins

6 Choose the correct statement, about bioinsecticides.
I. Predator bug is used to control sugarcane leaf hopper in Hawaii.
II. *Bacillus papillae* and *Bacillus lentimorbus* mixture is called doom.
III. Boverin is a effective fungus, against citrus rust mite.
(a) Only I (b) Only II
(c) I and II (d) I and III

Assertion-Reason Type Questions

Direction (Q. Nos. 7-10) *In the questions given below two statements an **Assertion** and a **Reason** are given. Give the appropriate response as*
(a) If both Assertion and Reason are true and Reason is the correct explanation of Assertion
(b) If both Assertion and Reason are true, but Reason is not the correct explanation of Assertion
(c) If Assertion is true, but Reason is false
(d) If Assertion is false, but Reason is true

7 **Assertion** Yeast gives the bread dough puffed appearance.
Reason CO_2 is produced by microbes during their anaerobic respiration.

8 **Assertion** Secondary treatment of sewage is called biological treatment.
Reason Microorganisms are used for treating the waste during secondary treatment of sewage.

9 **Assertion** Beer and wine are called soft liquors, while gin, rum, etc., are hard liquors.
Reason Beer and wine are made without distillation.

10 **Assertion** Griseofulvin extracted from *Penicillium griseofulvum* is used for ringworm treatment.
Reason *Trichophyton, Epidermophyton,* etc., cannot grow well in the presence of *Penicillium griseofulvum.*

2/3 Marks Questions

11 In which food would you find lactic acid bacteria? Mention some of their useful applications.

12 Define BOD. What is its significance in an aquatic ecosystem?

13 What is the key difference between primary and secondary sewage treatment?

14 What are methanogens? How do they help to generate biogas?

15 How do biofertilisers enrich the fertility of the soil?

16 What is IPM? Give an example of bioinsecticides and how it helps in pest control?

17 (i) Organic farmers prefer biological control of diseases and pests to the use of chemicals for the same purpose. Justify.

(ii) Give an example of a bacterium, a fungus and an insect that are used as biocontrol agents.

05 Marks Questions

18 Explain the utility of microbes in producing household products in detail.

19 Explain the process of sewage water treatment before it can be discharged into natural water bodies. Why is this treatment essential?

20 What are biofertilisers? Name the categories of organisms used as biofertilisers with an example for each. How do they function in organic farming?

21 What is biogas? Explain its production with the help of a diagram.

22 Discuss the role of microbes as biofertilisers in detail.

23 Due to the increasing use of insecticides and pesticides in agricultural practices, government advised farmers to adopt organic farming and use of biocontrol agents. Farmers were also informed about various biocontrol agents and their target organisms.

(i) Mention the use of biocontrol agents in agriculture.

(ii) Which biocontrol agents are used to get rid of aphids and mosquitoes?

(iii) Why baculoviruses are used as biocontrol agents?

(iv) In order to control butterfly caterpillars in brassicas and fruit trees, which biocontrol agent(s) can be used?

(v) Name a free-living fungi that is commonly found in root ecosystem and used as biocontrol agent.

Answers

1. (c)	**2.** (d)	**3.** (a)	**4.** (c)	**5.** (d)
6. (c)	**7.** (a)	**8.** (a)	**9.** (a)	**10.** (b)

09

Biotechnology: Principles and Processes

TREND ANALYSIS 3 YEARS

Average No. of Questions Across all Sets

Topic	Types of Questions	2024	2023	2020
TOPIC 01 Principles of Biotechnology and Tools of Recombinant DNA Technology	1 Mark	0	1	0
	2 Marks	0	1	2
	3 Marks	1	0	2
	4 Marks (Case Based)	0	0	0
	5 Marks	0	1	0
TOPIC 02 Processes of Recombinant DNA Technology	1 Mark	1	1	0
	2 Marks	0	1	1
	3 Marks	0	0	0
	4 Marks (Case Based)	1	0	0
	5 Marks	0	1	0

TOPIC 1

Principles of Biotechnology and Tools of Recombinant DNA Technology

Biotechnology

According to the **European Federation of Biotechnology** (EFB), biotechnology is the integration of natural science and organisms, cells, parts thereof and molecular analogues for products and services. The term 'Biotechnology' was coined by **Karl Ereky** in 1919.

Principles of Biotechnology

These are based on the concept of the following techniques

(i) **Genetic engineering** It is the technique to alter the chemistry of genetic material (DNA/RNA) and to introduce these into another organisms, so as to change the phenotype or physiology of the host organism.

(ii) **Sterilisation techniques** Adequate maintenance of sterile conditions to support the growth of only desired microbes/eukaryotic cells in large quantities for manufacturing the biotechnological products like antibiotics, vaccines, enzymes, etc.

Principle of Genetic Engineering

Techniques of genetic engineering include creation of recombinant DNA, use of gene cloning and gene transfer which allow us to isolate and introduce only a set of desired genes into the target organisms precisely. In this way, we can produce a desired product (cells or protein) in huge scale with desired qualities.

The basic steps in genetic engineering can be summarised as

- **Identification** of DNA with desirable genes.
- **Introduction** of the identified DNA into a suitable host to form recombinant DNA (*r*DNA).
- **Maintenance** of introduced DNA in the host and transfer of the DNA to its progeny.
- **Extraction** of desired gene product.

Construction of First Artificial Recombinant DNA

- The first artificial recombinant DNA was synthesised by **Stanley Cohen** and **Herbert Boyer** in 1972. They isolated the antibiotic resistance gene by cutting out a piece of DNA from a plasmid of *S. typhimurium* with the help of restriction enzyme.
- The cut piece of DNA was then linked to the plasmid DNA with the enzyme **DNA ligase**. The plasmid DNA acts as **vector** to transfer the piece of DNA attached to it into the host cells.
- When this DNA was transferred into *E. coli*, it could replicate using the new host's DNA polymerase enzyme and produced multiple copies (cloning).

Tools of Recombinant DNA Technology

Genetic engineering or recombinant DNA technology can be accomplished by using following key tools

(i) Restriction enzymes
(ii) Cloning vectors
(iii) DNA ligases
(iv) Competent host organism

These are discussed in detail below

1. Restriction Enzymes

- They are also known bs **'molecular scissors'** and are used for cutting DNA at specific location.
- Two enzymes from *E. coli* that were responsible for restricting the growth of bacteriophage were isolated in 1963. One of them added methyl group to DNA and the other cut DNA into segments. The latter was called **restriction endonuclease.**
- The **first restriction endonuclease**, *Hind* II was isolated by **Smith Wilcox** and **Kelley** (1968).

Naming of Restriction Enzymes

- The first letter of enzyme is derived from the genus name and the next two letters come from the species name of the prokaryotic cell from which enzymes are extracted.
- The Roman numbers after the name shows the order in which the enzymes were isolated from the bacterial strain. For example, *Eco*RI comes from *Escherichia coli* RY13 and *Eco*RII comes from *E. coli* R 245, etc.

Classification of Restriction Enzymes

- Restriction enzymes belong to a class of enzymes called **nucleases**. These are of two types
  (i) **Exonucleases** remove nucleotides from the ends of the DNA (either 5′ or 3′) in one strand of duplex.
  (ii) **Endonucleases** make cut at specific positions within the specific sequences of DNA. These specific sequences are called **recognition sequences.**
- Each restriction endonuclease recognises a specific **palindromic nucleotide sequences** in the DNA.
- **Palindrome** in DNA is a sequence of base pairs that reads same on the two strands when the orientation of reading is kept same. For example, the following sequences read the same on the two strands in $5' \rightarrow 3'$ direction as well as $3' \rightarrow 5'$ direction.

5′— GAATTC — 3′; 3′ — CTTAAG — 5′

Mechanism of Action of Restriction Enzymes

- These enzymes cut the strand of DNA a little away from the centre of the palindrome sites and produce **sticky ends** on each strand. These are named so, because they form hydrogen bonds with their complementary cut counterparts.
- The stickiness of the ends facilitates the action of the enzyme **DNA ligase.**
- The sticky ends are complementary to each other when cut by same restriction enzyme, therefore these can be joined together (end-to-end) by using DNA ligases.

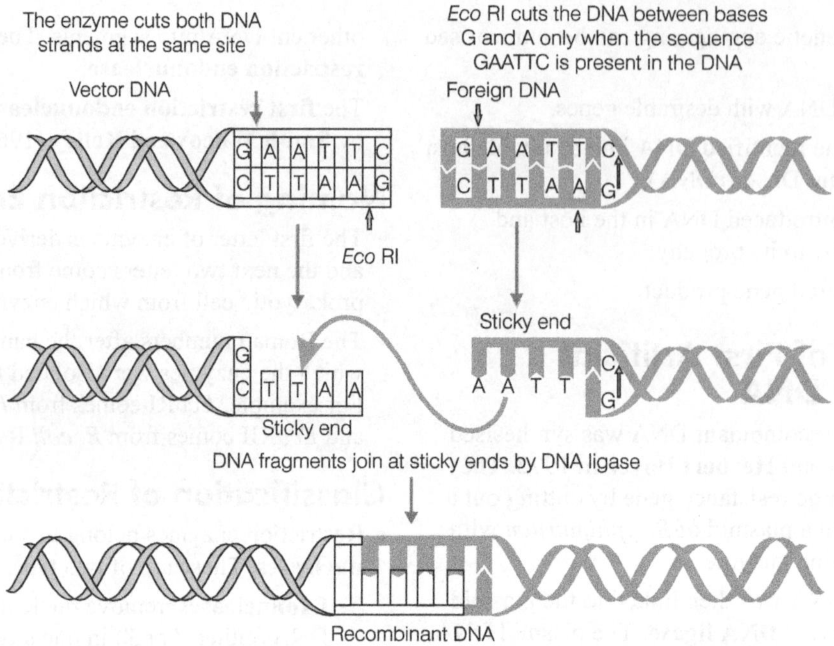

Figure 9.1 Steps in the formation of recombinant DNA by the action of restriction endonuclease enzyme-*Eco*RI

Separation and Isolation of DNA Fragments

- The cutting of DNA by restriction endonucleases results in the formation of fragments which can be separate by using a technique called **gel electrophoresis**.
- DNA fragments are negatively charged molecules and move towards the anode under an electric field through a agarose gel matrix.
- The DNA fragments separate (resolve) according to their size through the sieving effect provided by the agarose gel. The smaller the fragment size, the farther it moves.
- The separated DNA fragments can be visualised only after staining the DNA with ethidium bromide followed by their exposure to UV radiation, which are seen as bright orange coloured bands.
- These separated bands are cut out from the agarose gel and extracted from the gel piece. This is called **elution**.

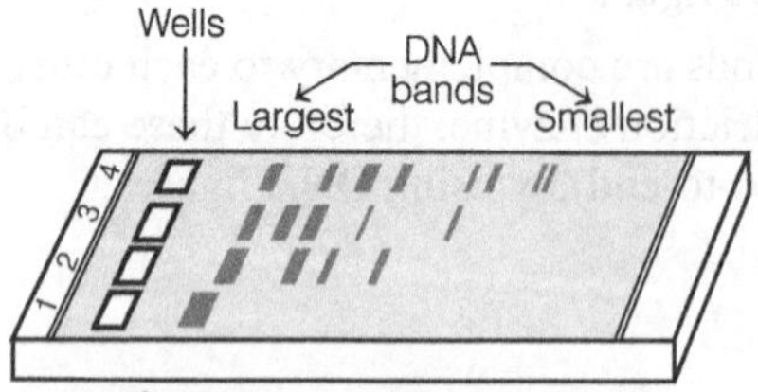

Figure 9.2 A typical agarose gel electrophoresis showing migration of undigested (lane 1) and digested set of DNA

2. Cloning Vectors

The DNA molecule that can carry a foreign DNA segment and replicate inside the host cell is called as a **vector**.

The vectors used in recombinant DNA technology include

(i) **Plasmids** Autonomously replicating circular, extrachromosomal DNA.

(ii) **Bacteriophages** Virus infecting bacteria.

(iii) **Cosmids** Hybrid vectors derived from plasmids which contain *cos* site of λ-phage.

(iv) **Ti-plasmid** The Tumour inducing (Ti) plasmid of *Agrobacterium tumefaciens* is used as a cloning vector in plant cells.

(v) **Virus** Retrovirus, adenovirus, papillomavirus are also used as cloning vectors in animals because of their ability to transform normal cells into cancerous cells.

Features of Cloning Vector

(i) **Origin of replication** (*ori*) is a sequence from where replication starts.

- Any piece of DNA when linked to this sequence can be made to replicate within the host cells.
- The sequence is also responsible for controlling the copy number of the linked DNA.

(ii) **Selectable marker** helps in identifying and eliminating non-transformants (without recombinant DNA) and selectively permitting the growth of the transformants (contain recombinant DNA).

- **Transformation** is a process through which a piece of DNA is introduced in a host bacterium.
- The genes encoding resistance to antibiotics such as ampicillin, chloramphenicol, tetracycline or kanamycin, etc., are some useful selectable markers for *E. coli*.

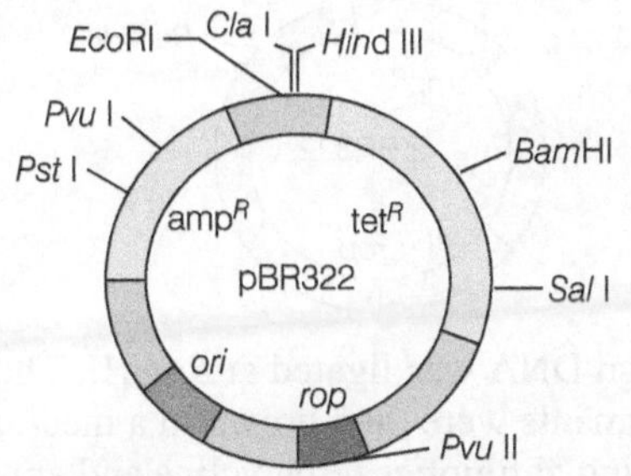

Figure 9.3 *E. coli* cloning vector pBR322 showing restriction sites (*Hind* III, *Eco* RI, *Bam* HI, *Sal* I, *Pvu* II, *Pst* I, *Cla* I), *ori* and antibiotic resistance genes (amp^R and tet^R), *rop* codes for the proteins involved in the replication of the plasmid

(iii) **Cloning sites** are required to link the alien DNA with the vector. It contains restriction sites.
- **Ligation of alien DNA** is carried out at a restriction site present in one of the two antibiotic resistance genes. For example, ligating a foreign DNA at the *Bam*HI site of tetracycline resistance gene in the vector pBR322.
  - The recombinant plasmids lose tetracycline resistance due to insertion of foreign DNA. But, it still can be selected out from non-recombinant ones by plating the transformants on ampicillin containing medium.
  - The transformants growing on ampicillin containing medium are then transferred on a medium containing tetracycline.
  - The recombinants grow on ampicillin containing medium, but not on that containing tetracycline.
  - On the other hand, the non-recombinants grow on the medium containing both the antibiotics.
- Other selectable markers can differentiate recombinants from non-recombinants on the basis of their ability to produce colour in the presence of a chromogenic substrate.
  - In this method, a recombinant DNA is inserted within the coding sequence of an enzyme β-galactosidase.
  - It results in the inactivation of gene for the enzyme β-galactosidase (insertional inactivation).
  - The bacterial colonies whose plasmids do not have an insert, produce blue colour when grown on a chromogenic substrate because of the presence of β-galactosidase enzyme. The presence of an insert in bacterial colonies does not produce any colour due to the insertional inactivation of gene producing β-galactosidase enzyme.

3. DNA Ligases (Molecular Glue)

These enzyme repair broken DNA by joining two nucleotides. It is used in genetic engineering to reverse the action of restriction enzymes, i.e. to join complementary DNA strands/ends together, e.g. T_4 DNA ligase.

4. Competent Host Organism (For Transformation with Recombinant DNA)

It is required because DNA being a hydrophilic molecule, cannot pass through cell membranes. Hence, the bacteria should be made **competent** to accept the DNA molecules. **Competency** is the ability of a cell to take up foreign DNA.

Methods to make a cell competent are as follows

(i) Chemical Method

- In this method, the cell is treated with a specific concentration of a divalent cation such as calcium to increase pore size in the cell wall.
- The cells are then incubated with recombinant DNA on ice, followed by placing them briefly at 42°C and then putting it back on ice. This is called **heat shock treatment**.
- This enables the bacteria to take up the recombinant DNA.

(ii) Physical Method

- In this method, a recombinant DNA is directly injected into the nucleus of an animal cell by **microinjection method**.
- In plants, cells are bombarded with high velocity microparticles of gold or tungsten coated with DNA. This method is called as **biolistics** or **gene gun method**.

(iii) Disarmed Pathogen Vectors

These when allowed to infect the cell, transfer the recombinant DNA into the host.

PYQs Previous Years' Questions

1 Mark Questions

Multiple Choice Questions

1. Identify the activity of endonuclease and exonuclease in the given image.

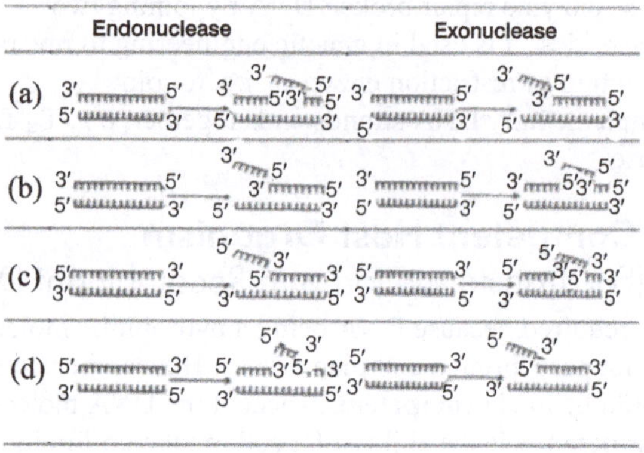

CBSE SQP 2024

Ans. (d)

2. Given below is the restriction site of a restriction endonuclease *Pst* I and the cleavage sites on a DNA molecule. **CBSE 2023**

↓
5′ C – T – G – C – A – G 3′
3′ G – A – C – G – T – C 5′
↑

Choose the option that gives the correct resultant fragments by the action of the enzyme *Pst* I.

(a) 5′C – T – G   C – A – G 3′
    3′ G – A – C – G – T   C – 5′

(b) 5′ C – T   G – C – A – G 3′
    3′ G – A – G – C   T – C 5′

(c) 5′ C – T – G – C   A – G3′
    3′ G – A – C – G   T – C 5′

(d) 5′ C – T – G – C – A   G 3′
    3′ G   A – C – G – T – C 5′

Ans. (d) 5′ C – T – G – C – A   G 3′
    3′ G   A – C – G – T – C 5′

Pst I is a type II restriction endonuclease which cleaves DNA at the recognition sequence 5′–CTGCA/G-3′ generating fragments with 3′ cohesine termini.

3. The figure below shows the structure of a plasmid.

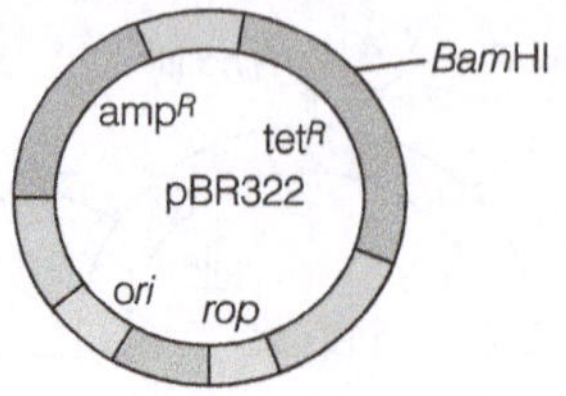

A foreign DNA was ligated at *Bam*HI. The transformants were then grown in a medium containing antibiotics tetracycline and ampicillin. Choose the correct observation for the growth of bacterial colonies from the given table.

	Medium with tetracycline	Medium with ampicillin
(a)	Growth	No growth
(b)	No growth	Growth
(c)	No growth	No growth
(d)	Growth	Growth

CBSE SQP 2023

Ans. (b) Bacterial colonies will show no growth in medium containing tetracycline, whereas growth is observed in medium containing ampicillin.

4. Name the enzymes *P* and *Q* that are involved in the processes given below.

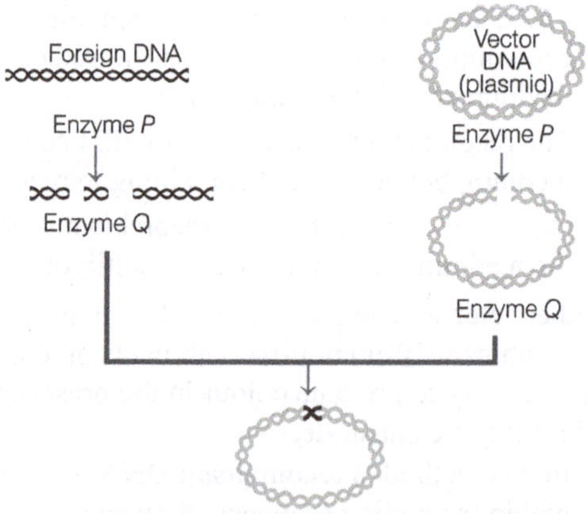

(a) Enzyme *P*–Exonuclease and Enzyme *Q*–Permease
(b) Enzyme *P*–Exonuclease and Enzyme *Q*–Ligase
(c) Enzyme *P*–Endonuclease and Enzyme *Q*–Permease
(d) Enzyme *P*–Restriction endonuclease and Enzyme *Q*–Ligase

CBSE SQP 2020

Ans. (d) *P* enzyme is restriction endonuclease and *Q* enzyme is ligase. (1)

5. A biotechnologist wanted to create a colony of *E. coli* possessing the plasmid pBR322, sensitive to tetracycline. Which one of the following restriction sites would he use to ligate a foreign DNA? **CBSE SQP 2020**

(a) *Sal* I (b) *Pvu* I (c) *Eco*RI (d) *Hind* III

Ans. (a) *Sal* I (1)

Assertion-Reason Type Questions

Direction (Q. Nos. 6-7) consist of two statements Assertion (A) and Reason (R). Answer these questions selecting the appropriate option given below

(a) Both Assertion and Reason are true and Reason is the correct explanation of Assertion
(b) Both Assertion and Reason are true, but Reason is not the correct explanation of Assertion
(c) Assertion is true, but Reason is false
(d) Assertion is false, but Reason is true

6. **Assertion** PCR is a powerful technique to identify genetic disorders.

Reason PCR can detect mutations in low amounts of DNA. **CBSE SQP 2024**

Ans. (a) Both Assertion and Reason are true and Reason is the correct explanation of Assertion

7. **Assertion** *E. coli* having pBR322 with DNA insert at *Bam*HI site cannot grow in medium containing tetracycline.

Reason Recognition site for *Bam*HI is present in tet^R region of pBR322. **CBSE SQP 2021-22**

Ans. (a) Both Assertion and Reason are true and Reason is the correct explanation of Assertion

Very Short Answer Type Questions

8. Name the commonly used vector for cloning genes into higher organisms. **CBSE SQP 2021-22**

Ans. The commonly used vectors for cloning genes into higher organisms are retrovirus, adenovirus, tobacco mosaic virus, papilloma virus, cauliflower mosaic virus, etc.

9. What is the cell that receives a recombinant gene called ? **All India 2019**

Ans. Host cell is the cell that receives a recombinant gene.

10. Write the specific point in the palindrome and the bond that is cut by *Eco*RI. **All India 2019**

Ans. Restriction endonuclease *Eco*RI cuts the DNA at the sequence known as palindromic sequence, i.e. GAATTC. The type of bond broken by *Eco*RI is phosphodiester bond between the G and A bases of the palindrome. This site is known as restriction site.

11. Write the two components of the first artificial recombinant DNA molecule constructed by Cohen and Boyer. **CBSE SQP 2018**

Or Write the two components of first artificial recombinant DNA molecule constructed by Cohen and Boyer. **Foreign 2014**

Ans. The two components of first artificial recombinant DNA molecule constructed by Cohen and Boyer are
(i) Antibiotic resistance gene (½)
(ii) Plasmid of *Salmonella typhimurium* (½)

12. Suggest a technique to a researcher who needs to separate fragments of DNA. **Delhi 2016**

Or Mention the use of gel electrophoresis in biotechnology experiments. **Outside Delhi 2016C**

Ans. Gel electrophoresis is used to separate the fragments of DNA that were cut by restriction endonucleases.

13. Name the technique that is used to alter the chemistry of genetic material (DNA, RNA) to obtain desired result. **Delhi 2016C**

Ans. The technique used to alter the chemistry of genetic material to obtain desired result is called genetic engineering.

14. Why is it not possible for an alien DNA to become part of a chromosome anywhere along its length and replicate normally? **All India 2014**

Ans. The alien DNA itself cannot multiply and replicate but requires a specific sequence for initiating its replication called origin of replication (*ori*) in a chromosome. *ori* acts as the starting point of replication as it aids in binding of DNA polymerase.

15. Mention the type of host cells suitable for the gene guns to introduce an alien DNA. **Delhi 2014**

Ans. Plant host cells are suitable for the gene guns to introduce an alien DNA.

16. Name the host cells in which microinjection technique is used to introduce an alien DNA. **Foreign 2014**

Ans. The microinjection technique is usually carried out in animal cells to inject alien DNA directly into the nucleus.

17. Name the material used as matrix in gel electrophoresis and mention its role. **All India 2014C**

Ans. The material used as matrix in gel electrophoresis is agarose. (½)
This agarose gel acts as a sieve to separate the DNA fragments according to their size. (½)

18. Write any four ways used to introduce a desired DNA segment into a bacterial cell in recombinant technology experiments. **All India 2013**

Ans. Ways to introduce desired DNA into bacterial cell are
(i) microinjection
(ii) disarmed pathogen vectors
(iii) treatment of host cell by bivalent cations such as calcium
(iv) biolistic or gene gun

19. How can retroviruses be used efficiently in biotechnology experiments inspite of them being disease causing? **All India 2013C**

Ans. Retroviruses can be used in biotechnology experiments after being disarmed, i.e. removal of virulent gene so that it is unable to cause infection in hosts they are transferred to.

20. State what happens when an alien gene is ligated at *Pvu* I site of pBR322 plasmid. **All India 2013C**

Ans. An alien gene ligated at *Pvu* I site of pBR322 plasmid cause the transformant cell to loose the ampicillin-resistance activity as amp^R gene becomes non-functional. Thus, the recombinant does not grow in the presence of ampicillin.

21. Why is 'plasmid' an important tool in biotechnology experiments? **All India 2013C**

Ans. Plasmids have the ability to replicate within bacterial cells independently of chromosomal DNA. They have high copy number, therefore an alien DNA ligated to it, will have equal copy number as that of plasmids. So, they are used as vectors in gene cloning experiments and thus act as an important tool in biotechnology.

22. State what happens when an alien gene is ligated at *Sal* I site of pBR322 plasmid. **Delhi 2013C**

Ans. When an alien gene is ligated at *Sal* I site of tetracycline resistance gene in the vector pBR322, the recombinant plasmid lose its tetracycline resistance.

23. Why do DNA fragments move towards the anode during gel electrophoresis? **Delhi 2011C**

Ans. DNA fragments are negatively charged molecules and hence they move toward the positive charged anode during gel electrophoresis.

24. Mention the uses of cloning vector in biotechnology. **Delhi 2011**

Ans. **Uses of Cloning Vector in Biotechnology**
(i) Helps in linking the foreign/alien DNA with the host's DNA. (½)
(ii) Helps in the selection of recombinants from the non-recombinants. (½)

25. Biotechnologists refer to *Agrobacterium tumefaciens* as a natural genetic engineer of plants. Give reasons to support the statement. **All India 2011**

Ans. *Agrobacterium tumefaciens* is a pathogen of several dicot plants. It is used as a natural genetic engineer because it is able to deliver a piece of its DNA (called T-DNA) to transform normal plant cells into tumour cells. It directs the tumour cells to synthesise the chemicals required by the pathogen.

26. Why is it essential to have a selectable marker in a cloning vector? **All India 2011**

Ans. Selectable marker in cloning vector helps in identifying and selecting the recombinants and eliminating the non-recombinants.

27. In the year 1963, two enzymes responsible for restricting the growth of bacteriophage in *E. coli* were isolated. How did enzymes act to restrict the growth of the bacteriophage? **All India 2011C**

Or How is the action of exonuclease different from that of endonuclease? **All India 2010**

Ans. Two enzymes responsible for restricting the growth of bacteriophage in *E. coli* are
Exonucleases Remove nucleotides from the ends of DNA.
Endonucleases Cut DNA at specific points. (½ × 2)

28. What is the host called that produces a foreign gene product? What is this product called? **Foreign 2010**

Ans. Transgenic organisms or genetically modified organisms are the host that produces a foreign gene product. Recombinant proteins are the products formed by these host cells. (½× 2)

2 Marks Questions

29. 5′ − G↓ A A T T C − 3′

3′ − C T T A A↑ G − 5′ **CBSE 2024 (Set-II)**

(i) Name the restriction enzyme that recognises the given specific sequence of bases. What are such sequence of bases referred to as?

(ii) What are the arrows in the given figure indicating? Write the result obtained thereafter.

Ans. (i) The given specific sequence, i.e. 5′-GAATTC-3′ is cut specifically by *Eco* RI restriction enzyme to form sticky ends. Such sequences are called palindrome, i.e. a sequence of base pairs in DNA that reads the same in both directions. **(1)**

(ii) Arrows in the given figure indicate restriction sites of *Eco* RI. When the DNA sequences are cut by restriction enzymes like *Eco* RI, it results in the formation of 'sticky-ends'. Results can be written as follows

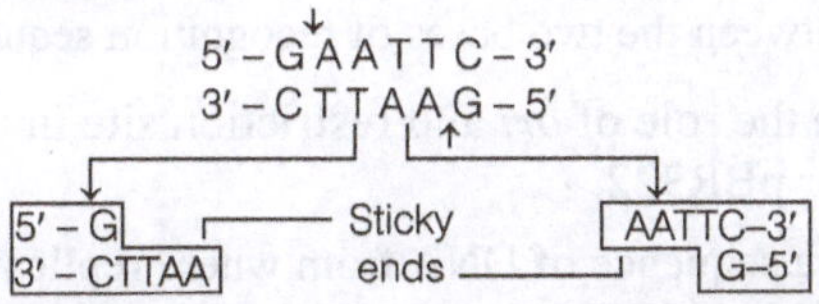

(1)

30. The image below shows the result of plating bacteria in chromogenic medium after incorporating the gene of interest in plasmid. Some plates had blue colonies; some plates had white colonies. A single bacterium extracted from plate I, II, III is shown below.

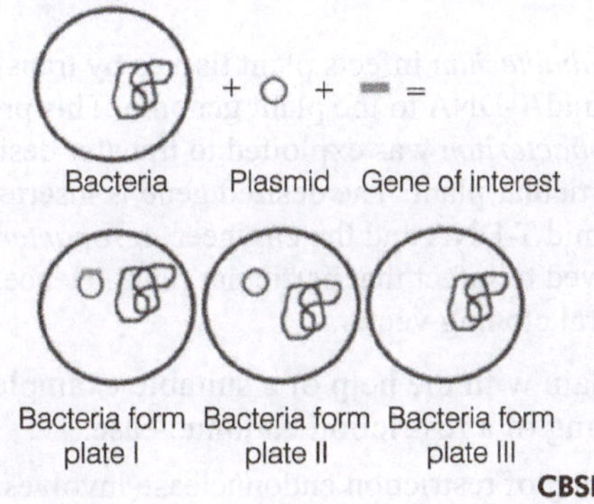

CBSE SQP 2024

On the basis of your observations

(i) Identify the plate(s) which is/are white. Give a reason.

(ii) Identify the plate(s) which is/are blue. Give a reason.

Ans. (i) **Plate I**, β-galactosidase enzyme is responsible for blue colour. Gene is inserted in the β-galactosidase site of the plasmid thereby causing insertional inactivation of the enzyme, so no blue colour is made. **(1)**

(ii) **Plate II** Gene of interest not inserted in the plasmid. So, blue colour of colonies will appear. **(½)**

Plate III No plasmid **(½)**

31. (i) State the principle involved in separation of DNA fragments using gel electrophoresis.

(ii) How are DNA fragments visualised once they are separated by gel electrophoresis? **CBSE 2023**

Ans. (i) DNA is negatively charged, therefore when an electric current is applied to the gel, DNA will migrate towards the positively charged electrode. Shorter strands of DNA move more quickly through the gel than longer strands, resulting in the fragments being arranged in order of size. **(1)**

(ii) The separated DNA fragments can be visualised only after staining the DNA with a compound known as ethidium bromide followed by exposure to UV radiation. As we cannot see pure DNA fragments in the visible light and without staining. **(1)**

32. CTTAAG

GAATTC

(i) What are such sequences called? Name the enzyme used that recognises such nucleotide sequences.

(ii) What is their significance in biotechnology? **CBSE SQP 2023**

Ans. (i) Such sequences are called palindromic sequences. The enzyme that recognises such sequences is endonuclease or restriction endonuclease. **(1)**

(ii) Significance of restriction enzyme is that these enzymes inspects the length of a DNA sequence and makes cuts at specific sequence, leaving behind sticky ends for ligation of vector and foreign DNA. **(1)**

33. Explain the method to increase the competency of the bacterial cell membrane to take up recombinant DNA. **CBSE SQP 2021-22**

Ans. DNA is a hydrophilic molecule therefore it cannot pass through the cell membrane. In order to force bacteria to take up the plasmid, the bacterial cell is made competent. For this purpose, bacterial cell is treated with specific concentration of a divalent cation like calcium. Recombinant DNA is then forced into such cells through pores in the cell wall. It is done by incubating the host cells with recombinant DNA on ice followed by placing them at 42°C (heat shock) and then putting them back on ice.

34. Explain the role of enzymes in the extraction of DNA from *Rhizopus* in its purest form. **CBSE SQP 2021-22**

Ans. The extraction of DNA from *Rhizopus* in its purest form can be done by treating the fungal cells with enzymes such as chitinase, which will dissolve the cell wall. The RNA can be removed by treatment with ribonuclease whereas proteins can be removed by treatment with protease. Other molecules can be removed by appropriate treatments thereby purifying DNA.

35. What are sticky ends? State their significance in recombination DNA technology. **CBSE SQP 2021-22**

Or How are sticky ends formed on a DNA strand? Why are they called so? **Delhi 2014**

Ans. Sticky ends are the overhanging stretches on each strand of DNA. These are formed when restriction enzymes cut the DNA strand a little away from the centre of palindrome sites, but between the same two bases on the opposite strands.

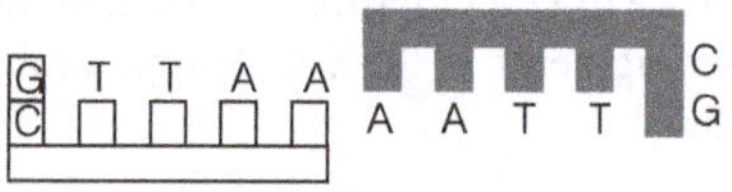

Sticky ends **(1)**

Significance of sticky ends They form hydrogen bonds with their complementary counterparts and facilitate the action of DNA ligase enzyme. **(1)**

36. Write the basis of naming the restriction endonuclease *Eco*RI. **Delhi 2020**

Ans. Refer to text on page no. 265 (Naming of restriction enzymes).

37. All cloning vectors do have a selectable marker. Describe its role in recombinant DNA technology. **All India 2020**

Ans. Refer to text on page no. 266 (Selectable marker).

38. β-galactosides enzyme is considered a better selectable marker. Justify the statement. **Delhi 2019**

Ans. Coding sequence of β-galactosidase is a better marker, as the recombinants and non-recombinants are differentiated on the basis of their ability to produce colour in the presence of a chromogenic substrate, while the selection of recombinants due to inactivation of antibiotic resistant gene is a tedous and time taking process to grow them simultaneously on two antibiotics containing media.

39. While cloning vectors, which of the two will be preferred by biotechnologists - bacteriophages or plasmids? Justify with reason. **CBSE SQP 2019**

Ans. For cloning the vectors, biotechnologists prefer bacteriophages because they have very high copy number of their genome within the bacterial cells, while plasmids have very low copy number, have only one or two copies in per cell.

40. Explain the mode of action of *Eco*RI. **Delhi 2016C**

Or What is *Eco*RI? How does *Eco*RI differ from an exonuclease? **Delhi 2015C**

Or How does a restriction nuclease function? Explain. **All India 2014**

Ans. Restriction nucleases function by inspecting the length of DNA sequence and then binding to specific recognition sequences and cutting the strands at sugar phosphate backbones.

These nucleases are of two types depending on their mode of action

(i) **Restriction exonucleases** cut sequences at terminal ends of DNA.

(ii) **Restriction endonucleases**, e.g. *Eco*RI, cut between the two bases of recognition sequence.

41. Write the role of *ori* and restriction site in a cloning vector pBR322. **Delhi 2014**

Ans. *ori* is a sequence of DNA from where replication starts. Any piece of DNA that needs to replicate in the host cell has to be linked to it. **(1)**

Restriction site is the recognition site made of palindromic sequence for restriction enzymes. **(1)**

42. State how was *Agrobacterium tumefaciens* made as a useful cloning vector to transfer DNA to plant cells. **Delhi 2014**

Ans. *Agrobacterium* infects plant tissues by transferring its plasmid T-DNA to the plant genome. This property of *Agrobacterium* was exploited to transfer desired gene to a particular plant. The desired gene is inserted in the plasmid T-DNA and the engineer *Agrobacterium* is allowed to infect that particular plant. Hence, it acts as a natural cloning vector.

43. Explain with the help of a suitable example the naming of a restriction endonuclease. **Delhi 2014**

Ans. Naming of restriction endonuclease involves the following rules

(i) The first letter of the enzyme comes from the genus and next two letters from species of the prokaryotic cell from where enzymes are extracted.

(ii) The Roman numbers following the name shows the order in which the enzymes were isolated from the bacterial strain. For example, *Eco* RI is derived from *Escherichia coli* RY 13, *Hind* II from *Haemophilus influenzae* Rd, etc.

44. How is insertional inactivation of an enzyme used as a selectable marker to differentiate recombinants from non-recombinants? **Foreign 2014**

Ans. The insertional activation of an enzyme, e.g. β-galactosidase occurs by inserting the desired gene in the coding region of enzyme. It results in inactivation of β-galactosidase gene in recombinants. Due to this, the recombinant or transformed hosts are unable to produce any colour when grown on chromogenic substrate. Thus, β-galactosidase acts as a selectable marker to differentiate recombinants from non-recombinants.

45. Explain palindromic nucleotide sequence with the help of a suitable example. **Foreign 2014**

Ans. The palindromic nucleotide sequence is the sequence of base pairs in DNA that reads the same on both the complementary strands of DNA, with same orientation of reading. For example,

5′–GAATTC–3′
3′–CTTAAG–5′

46. Why are molecular scissors called so? Write their use in biotechnology. **Foreign 2014**

Ans. Molecular scissors are so called because they cut DNA at specific sequences between base pairs.

Molecular scissors or restriction enzymes cut DNA at desired sequences and generate sticky ends that facilitate the cut DNA to join with host genome or vector DNA. They play an important role in genetic engineering or biotechnology. It is because with the help of these enzymes we can cut the desired gene and introduce into vectors for expression. (1 +1)

47. Why is making cells competent essential for biotechnology experiments? List any two ways by which this can be achieved. **Delhi 2014C**

Or

Why and how bacteria can be made 'competent'? **Delhi 2013**

Ans. Since, DNA molecules are hydrophilic, they cannot pass through cell membranes. For recombinant DNA to be integrated into vector or host genome, it is necessary for the DNA to be inserted in the cell. Therefore, making the host cells competent is necessary in biotechnology experiments. (1)

The two ways by which cells can be made competent to take up DNA are

(i) **Chemical method** The host cell is treated with a specific concentration of divalent cation, i.e. calcium increases the pore size in the cell membrane. Incubating, the cells with recombinant DNA on ice, followed by brief treatment of heat at 42°C and again putting them back on ice. (½)

(ii) **Physical method** In this method, a recombinant DNA is directly injected into the nucleus of an animal cell by micro-injection. (½)

48. How is an exonuclease functionally different from an endonuclease? Give an example of any two endonucleases other than *Sal* I. **Delhi 2013C**

Ans. **Exonucleases** are the enzymes which cleave base pairs of DNA at their terminal ends and act on single-strand of DNA or gaps in double-stranded DNA. While, **endonuclease** cleaves DNA at any point except the terminal ends and can make cut on one strand or on both the strands of double-stranded DNA, e.g. *Eco* RI and *Hin*d II. (1+1)

49. Explain the work carried out by Cohen and Boyer that contributed immensely in biotechnology. **Delhi 2012**

Ans. Stanley Cohen and Herbert Boyer constructed the first artificial recombinant DNA (*r*DNA) molecule.

They isolated the antibiotic-resistance gene by cutting out a piece of DNA from a plasmid with the help of restriction enzyme and linked it to a native plasmid of *Salmonella typhimurium* with the help of DNA ligase.

50. (i) A recombinant vector with a gene of interest inserted within the gene of β-galactosidase enzyme is introduced into a bacterium. Explain the method that would help in selection of recombinant colonies from non-recombinant colonies.

(ii) Why is this method of selection referred to as insertional inactivation? **All India 2012**

Ans. (i) The recombinant colonies can be differentiated from non-recombinant colonies by their inability to produce colour in the presence of a chromogenic substrate.

The recombinants do not produce any colour, while the non-recombinants produce a blue colour with chromogenic substrate in the medium. It occurs because of the presence of β-galactosidase in former and its absence in latter cells. (1)

(ii) The enzyme β-galactosidase becomes inactivated on insertion of recombinant DNA, within the coding sequence of enzyme. Thus, the method is called insertional inactivation. (1)

51. State the role of UV-light and ethidium bromide during gel electrophoresis of DNA fragments. **Delhi 2012C**

Ans. DNA fragments are observed only after staining with ethidium bromide followed by their exposure to UV radiation. This gives bright orange colour to DNA fragments. (1+1)

52. Explain giving reasons why an alien piece of DNA needs to be integrated to a specific sequence of host DNA for its cloning. **All India 2011**

Ans. Refer to answer no. 14.

53. List the key tools used in recombinant DNA technology. **Delhi 2011**

Ans. Key tools used in recombinant DNA technology are restriction enzymes, polymerases, ligases, cloning vectors and competent host organism or cells.

54. Explain the role of Ti-plasmids in biotechnology. **Delhi 2011**

Ans. The Ti-plasmid isolated from *Agrobacterium* is responsible for the natural transformation of plant cells into tumours. So, it is modified into a non-pathogenic vector, but still is able to deliver the DNA.

This disarmed plasmid of *Agrobacterium* is used as a vector for the transformation of plant cells, thus plays an important role in biotechnology.

55. Study the diagram given below and answer the following questions.

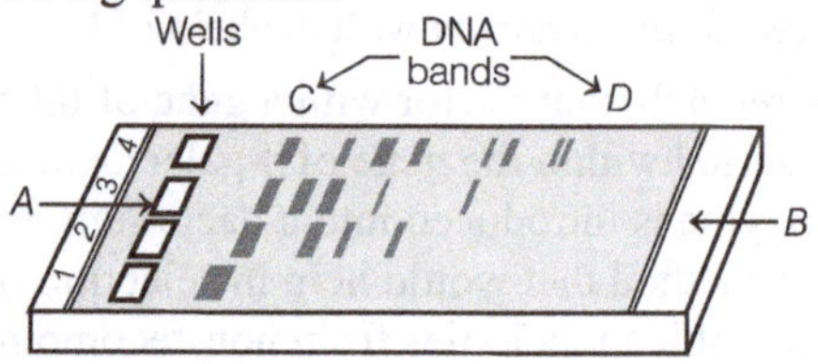

(i) Why have DNA fragments in band *D* moved farther away in comparison to those in band *C*?

(ii) Identify the anode end in the diagram.

(iii) How are these DNA fragments visualised? **Foreign 2011**

Ans. (i) In band *D*, DNA fragments are smaller than those on band *C*. The fragments separate according to their size through the sieving effect provided by the gel. So, the smaller fragments move farther away than the larger ones. **(1)**

(ii) *B* is anode end in the diagram as DNA fragments are moving towards this end. **(½)**

(iii) Gel containing DNA fragments are stained with ethidium bromide and exposed to UV radiation. Bright orange coloured bands of DNA become visible. **(½)**

56. Explain the action of the restriction endonuclease *Eco*RI. **Foreign 2010**

Or (i) Illustrate the recognition sequence of *Eco* RI and mention what such sequences are called?

(ii) How does restriction endonuclease act on a DNA molecule? **All India 2010C**

Ans. Restriction endonuclease *Eco*RI cuts the DNA strands a little away from the centre of the **palindromic sequence**, but between the same two bases, i.e. G and A, on both the strands. The site of action of enzyme in palindrome sequence GAATTC is called recognition site. **(1)**

(i) Due to this, single-stranded portions called sticky ends, overhang at the end of each strand. **(½)**

(ii) Because of the stickiness, they easily form hydrogen bonds with their complementary counterparts. **(½)**

3 Marks Questions

57. (i) Explain the convention for naming *Eco*RI.

(ii) With the help of an illustration only, show the action of *Eco*RI on a DNA polynucleotide. **CBSE 2024 (Set-I)**

Ans. (i) The convention for naming *Eco*RI is as follows

First letter, *E* → *Escherichia* (genus)

Second two letters *co* → *coli* (species)

Fourth letter, R → name of the strain

Roman number I → order of isolation of enzymers (from that strain of bacteria) **(2)**

(ii) Refer to fig. 9. 1 on page no. 266. **(1)**

58. (i) Why must a cell be made 'competent' in biotechnology experiments. How does calcium ion help in doing so?

(ii) State the role of 'biolistic gun' in biotechnology experiments. **CBSE 2024 (Set-II)**

Ans. (i) DNA is a hydrophilic molecule, so it cannot pass through cell membranes. In order to force bacteria to take up the plasmid, the bacterial cells must first be made competent. Thus, a competent host is important in biotechnological experiments.

The cells can be made competent by various methods like chemical method ($CaCl_2$ method) and physical methods (microinjection and biolistic/gene gun).

$CaCl_2$ is known to increase the efficiency of DNA uptake to produce transformed bacterial cells. The divalent Ca^{2+} ions create transient pores on the bacterial cell wall by which the entry of foreign DNA is facilitated into the bacterial cells. **(2)**

(ii) Biolistics or gene gun is an important physical method to make a host competent. In this method, DNA is introduced into plants to make competent host. Cells are bombarded with high velocity microparticles of gold or tungsten coated with DNA. **(1)**

59. Carefully observe the given picture. A mixture of DNA with fragments ranging from 200 base pairs to 2500 base pairs was electrophoresed on agarose gel with the following arrangement.

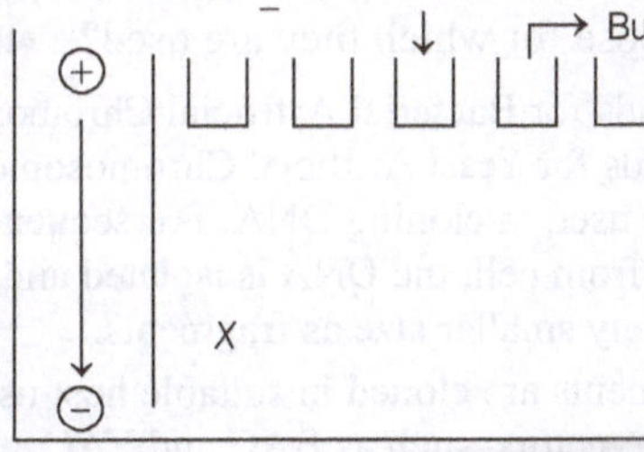

(i) What result will be obtained on staining with ethidium bromide? Explain with reason.

(ii) The above set-up was modified and a band with 250 base pairs was obtained at *X*.
What change (s) were made to the previous design to obtain a band at *X*? Why did the band appear at the position *X*? **CBSE SQP 2023**

> **KEY idea**
> DNA molecules move towards the anode (positively charged).

Ans. (i) No bands will be obtained as all DNA will be seen in the well only. DNA fragments being negatively charged will not move towards negative end/ cathode. DNA being negatively charged will remain stationed at the positive end/ anode end of the agar block. **(2)**

(ii) (a) Position of the positive terminal end/ anode and the negative terminal end/ cathode was inter-changed.

(b) The fragment with least base pairs got separated faster and move faster to the anode end. Thus, making a band appear at X. **(1)**

60. Only with the help of a labelled diagram, show the steps of formation or recombinant DNA by the action of restriction endonuclease enzyme *Eco*RI. **All India 2021-22 Term-II**

Ans. Refer to figure 9.1 on page no. 266.

61. (i) Given below is the stepwise schematic representation of the process of electrophoresis. Identify the 'alphabets' representing (a) Anode end (b) smallest/lightest DNA strand in the matrix (c) Agarose gel. **Delhi 2021-22 Term-II**

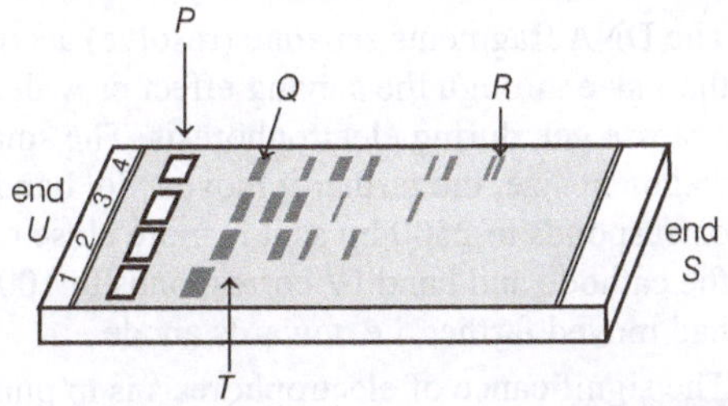

(ii) What is elution? State the importance of elution in this process.

Ans. (i) (a) Alphabet '*S*' represents anode end.

(b) Alphabet '*R*' represents smallest/lightest DNA strand.

(c) Alphabet '*T*' represents agarose gel. **(1½)**

(ii) The process of separating or cutting of DNA out from the agarose gel and extracting from the gel pieces is called elution.

Importance By the process of elution the separated DNA fragments can be stained (mainly by using a dye called EtBr) and amplified by PCR to be used in various techniques such as DNA fingerprinting, etc. **(1½)**

62. The image below depicts the result of gel electrophoresis.

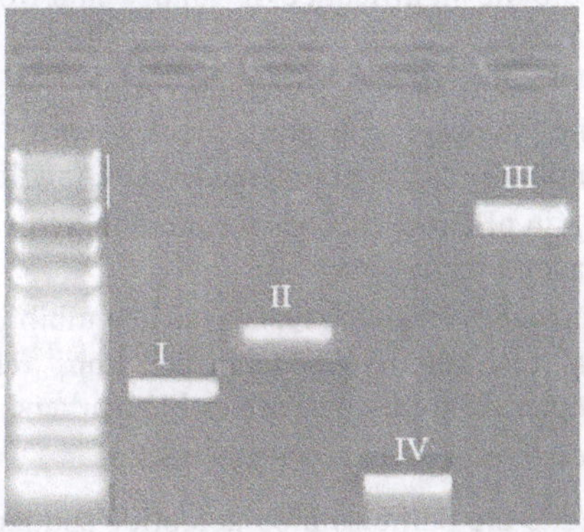

If the ladder represents sequence length upto 3000 base pairs (bp),

(i) which of the bands (I - IV) correspond to 2500 bp and 100 bp, respectively?

(ii) explain the basis of this kind of separation and also mention the significance of this process. **CBSE SQP 2021-22 Term-II**

Ans. (i) Band III corresponds to 2500 base pairs and band IV corresponds to 100 bp. **(1)**

(ii) The DNA fragments separate (resolve) according to their size through the sieving effect provided by the agarose gel, during electrophoresis. The smaller the fragment size, the farther it moves. So, band III corresponds to 2500 bp as it is more close towards the cathode and band IV corresponds to 100 bp as it had moved farther, i.e. towards anode. **(1)**

The significance of electrophoresis is to purify the DNA fragments for using in various techniques such as DNA fingerprinting, etc. **(1)**

63. Observe the diagram shown below of pBR322. Answer the questions that follows

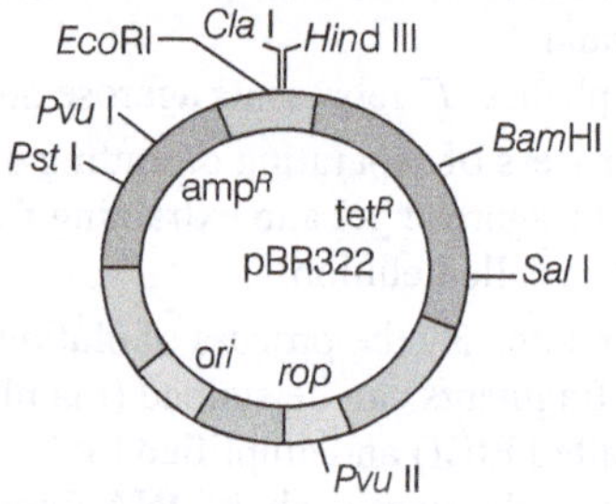

(i) What is pBR322 ?

(ii) Write the role of '*rop*'.

(iii) State the significance of 'amp^R' and 'tet^R'. **Delhi 2020**

Ans. (i) pBR322 is an *E. coli* cloning vector. This is small, autonomously replicating circular, extra chromosomal, double-stranded DNA molecule. **(1)**

(ii) *rop* in pBR322 encodes for protein involved in plasmid replication. **(1)**

(iii) The genes encoding resistance to antibiotics like tet^R resistant to tetracycline and amp^R resistant to ampicillin are used as selectable markers. **(1)**

For detail refer to text on page. no. 265.

64. (i) Write the palindromic nucleotide sequence *Eco* RI recognises.

(ii) Draw the vector DNA and a foreign DNA showing the sites where *Eco*RI has acted to form the sticky ends.

(iii) Name the enzyme that helps in forming recombinant DNA. **All India 2020**

Ans. (i) The palindromic nucleotide sequence *Eco* RI recognises is

5′ ____ GAATTC _____ 3′
3′ ____ CTTAAG _____ 5′ **(1)**

(ii) Refer to text on page no. 266. (Figure no. 9.1) **(1)**

(iii) The enzyme that helps in the formation of recombinant DNA by joining with vector DNA is DNA ligase. **(1)**

65. Expand 'BAC' and 'YAC'. What are they and what is the purpose for which they are used? **All India 2019**

Ans. 'BAC' stands for Bacterial Artificial Chromosome and 'YAC' stands for Yeast Artificial Chromosome. These are vectors used in cloning DNA. For sequencing the total DNA from cell, the DNA is isolated and converted into relatively smaller size as fragments.

DNA fragments are cloned in suitable host using specialised vectors, such as BAC and YAC.

Fragments of DNA are then sequenced by automated DNA sequencer.

66. Explain how 'sticky ends' are obtained in a DNA segment. Write their importance in DNA technology. **All India 2019**

Ans. Refer to answer no. 35.

Role of the sticky ends These are produced from hydrogen bonds with their complementary cut counterparts. The stickiness of the ends facilitates the action of the enzyme DNA ligase which helps to region the cut DNA.

67. (i) Mention the importance of gel-electrophoresis in biotechnology.

(ii) Explain the process of this technique. **All India 2019**

Ans. (i) DNA fragments formed by the use of restriction endonucleases are separated by gel-electrophoresis. **(1)**

(ii) DNA fragments are negatively charged molecules. Thus, they move towards the positive charged anode under electric field through the medium. The smaller fragments move farther in the gel as compared to larger fragments due to the sieving effect of gel. **(2)**

68. How does β-galactosidase coding sequence act as a selectable marker? Why is it a preferred selectable marker to antibiotic resistance genes? Explain. **All India 2019**

Ans. **Selectable marker** It helps in identifying or selecting transformants and eliminating non-transformants and selectively permit the growth of the transformants.

β-galactosidase acts as a selectable marker by inducing the property of insertional inactivation in transformed cells. In this process the recombinants and non-recombinants are differentiated on the basis of colour production in the presence of chromogenic substrate.

A recombinant DNA is inserted within the coding sequence of an enzyme β-galactosidase which results into inactivation of the enzyme.
Therefore, the bacterial colonies having inserted plasmid, show **no colouration** while, those without plasmid show blue colour.

69. Give reason why
(i) DNA cannot pass into a host cell through the cell membrane.
(ii) Proteases are added during isolation of DNA for genetic engineering.
(iii) Single cloning site is preferred in a vector.
All India 2019

Ans. (i) Hydrophobic molecules can diffuse through the lipid bilayer of the plasma membrane and not hydrophilic molecules. DNA being hydrophilic with the sugar-phosphate backbone, cannot pass through the cell membrane. (1)
(ii) Proteases catalyse the breakdown of proteins present in the solution to its component amino acid. If the proteins are not removed from DNA preparation then, they could interfere with any downstream treatment of DNA (such as action of restriction endonuclease, DNA ligase, etc). (1)
(iii) Single cloning sites are preferred as the the cloning of a sequence at more than one recognition sites within the vector would generate several fragments leading to complication in gene cloning. (1)

70. Describe the formation of recombinant DNA by the action of *Eco*RI. **Delhi 2019**

Or Prepare a flowchart information of recombinant DNA by the action of restriction endonuclease enzyme *Eco*RI. **Foreign 2015**

Ans. Formation of recombinant DNA

Isolation of DNA from the cell
↓
Cut with the help of *Eco*RI
↓
Generation of sticky ends
↓
Same mechanism is done with plasmid DNA
↓
Join together with DNA ligase
↓
Formation of recombinant DNA

Role of *Eco*RI in recombinant DNA (In detail) Refer to answer no. 56.

71. (i) How do DNA fragments migrate and resolve in a gel electrophoresis?
(ii) How lane 1 is different from lane 2, 3 and 4 in the gel electrophoresis set up?
(iii) How pure DNA fragments are made observable in the visible light? **CBSE SQP 2019**

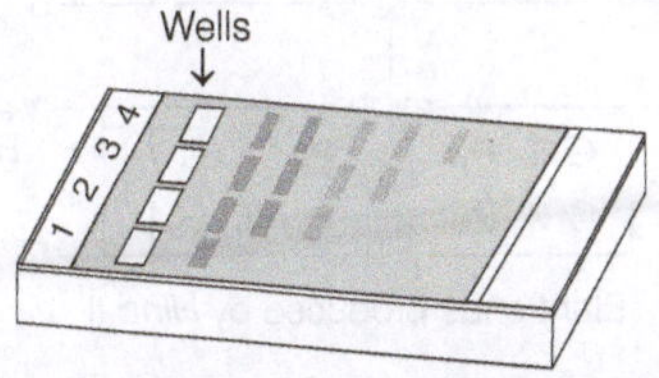

Ans. (i) DNA fragments resolve (separate) according to their size through sieving effect provided by the agarose gel. DNA fragments being negatively charged move towards the positive charged anode. Hence, the smaller the fragement size, farther it moves.
(ii) The given agarose gel electrophoresis is showing migration of undigested DNA fragments in lane 1 and digested set of DNA fragments in lane 2 to 4.
(iii) The separated DNA fragments can be visualised as bright orange coloured bands only after staining the DNA with Ethidium Bromide (EtBr) followed by their exposure to UV radiation. (1 × 3)

72. Explain the roles of the following with the help of an example each in recombinant DNA technology.
(i) Restriction enzymes
(ii) Plasmids **CBSE 2018**

Ans. (i) **The restriction enzymes** are known as molecular scissors. These enzymes belong to a large group of enzymes called nucleases, which are of following two types
(a) **Exonucleases** Those, who remove nucleotides from the ends of the DNA (either 5′ or 3′) in one strand of duplex.
(b) **Endonucleases** Those, who make cuts at specific position within the DNA. Each restriction endonuclease functions by 'inspecting' the length of a DNA sequence.

Role of restriction enzymes The restriction endonucleases are used to cut plasmid DNA as well as foreign DNA at desired sites. The foreign DNA is then inserted into plasmid DNA which takes the foreign DNA into the desired host organism.

Example The first discovered restriction enzyme is *Hind* II. It was isolated from *Haemophilus influenzae.* It always cuts DNA at 5′ GT (Pyrimidine

T or C) (Purine A or G) AC3′ and 3′CA (Purine A or G) (Pyrimidine T or C) TG5'.

It produces DNA segments with blunt ends.

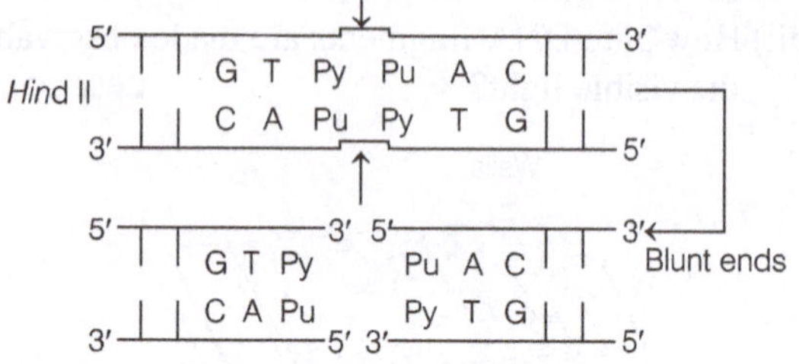

Blunt ends produced by *Hind* II

(1½)

(ii) **Plasmids** These are extrachromosomal, self-replicating, double-stranded, closed and circular DNA molecules. It is found only in bacteria and few yeast cells.

Role of plasmid in recombinant DNA technology These are used as vectors to carry the desired gene (foreign genes) into the desired host organisms.

For example, pBR322 is widely used plasmid vector. In its name p signifies plasmid, B is from **Boliver** and R is from **Rodriguez**.

Boliver and Rodriguez were two scientists who developed pBR322 in 1977. This plasmid has genes for resistance against ampicillin and tetracycline.

They have restriction sites for enzymes like *Pvu* I, *Pst* I, *Sal* I, *Bam* HI.

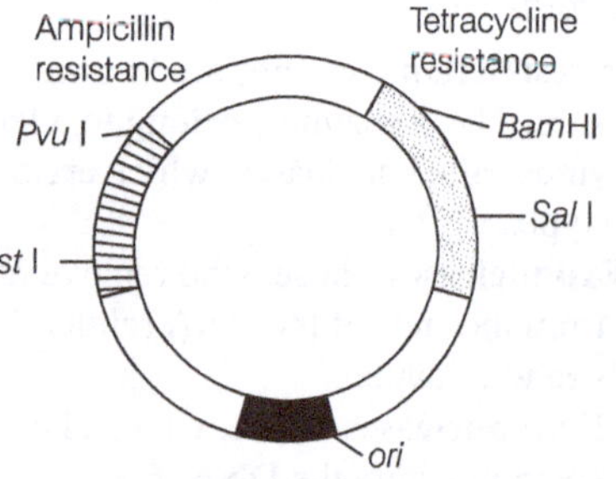

pBR322 plasmid

(1½)

73. (i) In pBR322, foreign DNA has to be introduced in tet^R region. From the restriction enzymes given below, which one should be used and why?

Pvu l, *Eco*RI, *Bam*HI

(ii) Give reasons, why the other two enzymes cannot be used. **CBSE SQP 2018**

Ans. (i) Among the given restriction enzymes, i.e. *Pvu* I, *Eco*RI and *Bam*HI, the enzyme *Bam*HI should be used as restriction enzyme because the restriction site for this enzyme is present in tet^R region. **(1½)**

(ii) The restriction site for *Pvu* l is present in amp^R region, so it cannot be used. *Eco*RI will not be used as restriction site of this enzyme is not present in selectable marker tet^R. **(1½)**

74. Given below is the diagram of agarose gel kept under UV light.

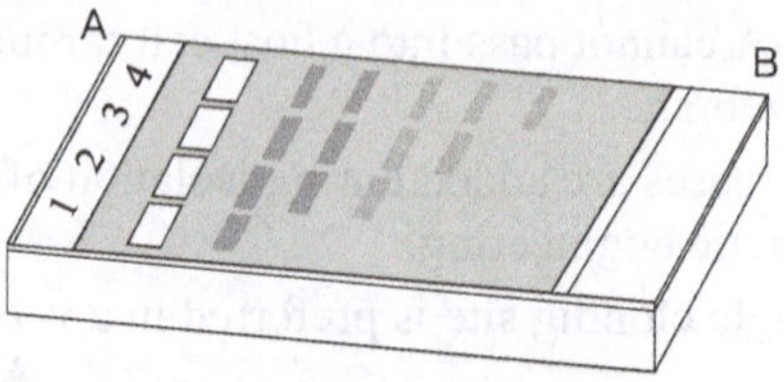

(i) Mark the positive and negative terminals.

(ii) What is the charge carried by DNA molecules and how does it help in its separation?

(iii) How are the separated DNA fragments finally isolated? **CBSE SQP 2018**

Ans. (i) *B* is the positive terminal, whereas *A* is the negative terminal of this agarose gel. **(1)**

(ii) DNA fragments are negatively charged molecules. So, they move towards the positive electrode (anode). **(1)**

(iii) The separated DNA fragments are finally isolated by the process of elution. In this, gel bands containing DNA fragments are cut and DNA is extracted from this gel piece. **(1)**

75. Explain the role(s) of the following in biotechnology

(i) Restriction endonuclease

(ii) Gel-electrophoresis

(iii) Selectable markers in pBR322 **Delhi 2017**

Ans. (i) **Restriction endonucleases** These are the bacterial enzymes that cut *ds*DNA into fragments after recognising and binding to the specific nucleotide sequences, known as recognition site. These enzymes are used to form recombinant molecules of DNA, composed of DNA from different sources. **(1)**

(ii) **Gel-electrophoresis** is the technique which allows the separation and visualisation of fragments of DNA on an agarose gel matrix.

Since, the DNA fragments are negatively charged molecules, they separate and move towards the anode (+ ve) under the influence of an electric field. DNA fragments are separated on the basis of their size through the sieving effect provided by the gel. **(1)**

(iii) **Selectable markers in pBR322** help in identification and selection of transformants.

pBR322, an *E. coli* cloning vector has two antibiotic resistance genes, i.e. for ampicillin and tetracycline, which act as selectable marker. When a foreign DNA is ligated at the site of tetracycline resistance (tet^R) gene in pBR322, the recombinant plasmid lose tetracycline resistance due to insertional inactivation of foreign DNA, but can still be selected out from non-recombinants by placing the transformants on ampicillin containing medium. (1)

76. (i) Explain the significance of palindromic nucleotide sequences in the formation of recombinant DNA.
(ii) Write the use of restriction endonuclease in the above process. **All India 2017**

Ans. (i) **Palindromic nucleotide sequences** in the DNA are group of letters that form the same words when read both forward and backward. For example, the following sequence reads the same on the two strands in 5′ → 3′ direction as well as 3′ → 5′ direction.

5′— GAATTC —3′
3′— CTTAAG —5′

Significance These sequences act as recognition sites which are recognised by specific restriction endonucleases. (2)

(ii) **Use of restriction endonuclease** During recombinant DNA formation, these enzymes recognise and make a cut at specific positions within the DNA and vector. Due to this function, restriction endonucleases are also called as molecular scissors. (1)

77. (i) Name the selectable markers in the cloning vector pBR322. Mention the role they play.
(ii) Why is the coding sequence of an enzyme β-galactosidase a preferred selectable marker in comparison to the ones named above? **All India 2016**

Ans. (i) **Selectable markers** in cloning vector pBR322 are ampicillin and tetracycline resistance gene. They help in the selection of transformants and eliminating the non-transformants. (1)

(ii) The selection of recombinants due to inactivation of resistance gene is a difficult process and requires simultaneous plating on two plates having different antibiotics.
Thus, enzyme β-galactosidase is preferred as a selectable marker as it allows to differentiate non-recombinants from recombinants easily by insertional inactivations technique. (2)

78. (i) Why must a cell be made 'competent' in biotechnology experiments? How does calcium ion help in doing so?
(ii) State the role of 'biolistic gun' in biotechnology experiments. **All India 2016**

Ans. (i) Refer to answer no. 47. (2)
(ii) Biolistic guns or gene guns are used to bombared *r*DNA loaded on gold or tungsten particles with high velocity into host cells. In this way, the *r*DNA is delivered to the desired host cells. (1)

79. How does *Agrobacterium tumefaciens* act as a suitable vector in the biotechnological experiments? Site an example where it has been successfully used as a vector. **Outside Delhi 2016C**

Ans. Refer to answer no. 42.
Agrobacterium has been used as vector to introduce a gene from Tobacco Mosaic Virus (TMV) into tobacco plants. (2 +1)

80. Describe a palindrome with the help of an example. **Delhi 2016C**

Ans. Refer to answer no. 76 (i). (3)

81. (i) Why was a bacterium used in the first instance of the construction of an artificial recombinant DNA molecule?
(ii) Name the scientists who accomplished this and how? **Delhi 2016C**

Ans. (i) A bacterium *Salmonella typhimurium* was used in the first instance of the construction of artificial recombinant DNA molecule because of the possibilities of linking a gene encoding antibiotic resistance with a native plasmid of the bacterium. This was made possible by the availability of restriction enzymes and the enzyme DNA ligase. (1)

(ii) Stanley Cohen and Herbert Boyer accomplished this in 1972 by isolating the antibiotic resistance gene by cutting out a piece of DNA from a plasmid which was responsible for conferring antibiotic resistance. The cutting of DNA at specific sites was possible with the availability of restriction enzymes. The cut DNA was linked with the plasmid DNA using the enzyme DNA ligase. The plasmid DNA acts as vector to transfer the piece of DNA attached to it. (2)

82. State the functions of the following in the cloning vector pBR322.
(i) *ori*
(ii) *rop* and
(iii) *Hind* III sites **All India 2015C**

Ans. (i) Refer to answer no. 41 (*ori*).
(ii) ***rop*** in pBR322 encodes for protein involved in plasmid replication.
(iii) ***Hind* III** is a restriction site in pBR322, where *Hind* III endonuclease makes a cut for the introduction of foreign DNA segment. (1×3)

83. Name and explain the technique used for separating DNA fragments and making them available for biotechnology experiments. **Foreign 2015; All India 2014**

Ans. DNA fragments formed by the use of restriction endonucleases are separated by gel electrophoresis. **(1)**

(i) DNA fragments are negatively charged molecules. Thus, they move towards the positive charged anode under electric field through the gel medium.

(ii) DNA fragments separate according to their size due to sieving effect of agarose gel.

(iii) The separated DNA fragments can be viewed by staining the DNA with ethidium bromide followed by exposure to UV radiation.

(iv) The separated bands of DNA are cut and extracted from gel piece. This is known as elution. **(2)**

84. Draw a schematic diagram of the *E.coli* cloning vector pBR322 and mark the following in it

(i) *ori*

(ii) *rop*

(iii) Ampicillin resistance gene

(iv) Tetracycline resistance gene

(v) Restriction site *Bam*HI

(vi) Restriction site *Eco*RI **Delhi 2015**

Or Draw a schematic sketch of pBR322 plasmid and label the following in it

(i) Any two restriction sites

(ii) *ori* and *rop* genes

(iii) An antibiotic resistant gene. **Delhi 2012**

Ans. *E. coli* cloning vector pBR322.

Refer to figure 9.3 on page no. 267.

85. (i) Draw schematic diagrams of segments of a vector and a foreign DNA with the sequence of nucleotides recognised by *Eco*RI.

(ii) Draw the vector DNA segment and foreign DNA segment after the action of *Eco* RI and label the sticky ends produced. **Delhi 2014C**

Ans. (i) Refer to figure 9.1. on page no. 266.

(ii) Refer to figure 9.1 on page no. 266.

86. What are 'cloning sites' in a cloning vector? Explain their role. Name any two such sites in pBR322. **All India 2014C**

Ans. The cloning sites contain the specific unique recognition sequence for a particular restriction enzyme, so as to link the foreign DNA with the vector DNA and thus create a recombinant DNA molecule. **(1)**

These sites are important for joining the DNA fragments of vector and alien DNA. Multiple recognition sequences for a particular restriction enzyme within a DNA or vector complicate the process of gene cloning. **(1)**

The two cloning sites in pBR322 are *Bam* HI for tetracycline resistant gene and *Pvu* I for ampicillin resistant genes. **(1)**

87. (i) Explain the basis on which the gel electrophoresis technique works.

(ii) Write any two ways the products obtained through this technique can be utilised. **Delhi 2013C**

Ans. (i) Refer to answer no. 75 (ii). **(1)**

(ii) Products obtained *via* gel electrophoresis can be utilised in following ways

(a) To construct a recombinant DNA molecule by joining them with cloning vector.

(b) For amplification of desired segment using Polymerase Chain Reaction (PCR). **(2)**

88. How are the following used in biotechnology ?

(i) Plasmid DNA

(ii) Recognition sequence

(iii) Gel electrophoresis **All India 2011C**

Ans. (i) **Plasmid DNA** It is used for constructing recombinant DNA, by ligating the alien piece of DNA with it. It is used as a cloning vector and helps in the selection of recombinants from non-recombinants. **(1)**

(ii) **Recognition sequences** These are specific base sequences of DNA, where restriction enzyme cuts the DNA. They are utilised to extract the desired gene or fragments from DNA molecules. **(1)**

(iii) **Gel electrophoresis** It is a technique, used to separate the DNA fragments according to their size through seiving effect of the gel. **(1)**

89. (i) Name the organism in which the vector shown is inserted to get the copies of the desired gene.

(ii) Mention the area labelled in the vector responsible for controlling the copy number of the inserted gene.

(iii) Name and explain the role of a selectable marker in the vector shown. **All India 2010**

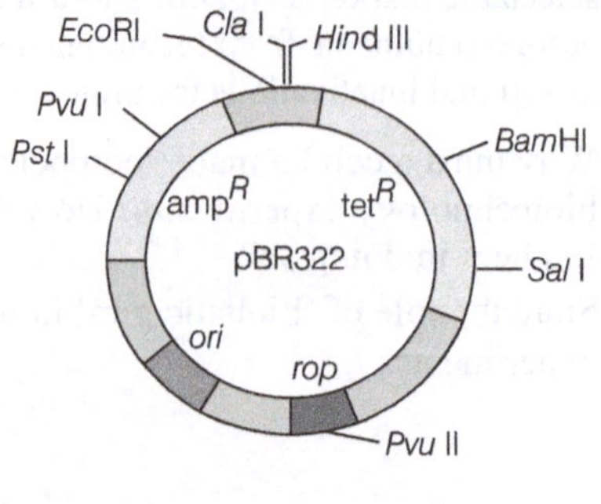

Ans. (i) *Escherichia coli (E. coli)* (½)

(ii) *ori* in the vector is responsible for controlling the copy number of inserted gene. (½)

(iii) The genes encoding resistance to antibiotics like tet^R resistant to tetracycline and amp^R resistant to ampicillin are used as selectable markers. If a foreign DNA is ligated at the *Bam*HI site of tetracycline resistance gene, the recombinant plasmids will lose the tetracycline resistance due to insertional inactivation, but transformants can be selected by growing them on ampicillin containing medium. The selectable markers help in identifying and eliminating non-transformants and selectively permitting the growth of transformants. (2)

90. (i) *Eco*RI is a restriction endonuclease. How is it named so? Explain.

(ii) Write the sequence of DNA bases that the enzyme recognises. Mention the point at which the enzyme makes a cut in the DNA segment.

Delhi 2010C

Ans. (i) Refer to answer no. 42.

(ii) Refer to answer no. 57 and 58.

Common Mistakes Students often get confused that all restriction enzymes are restriction endonucleases but it is a wrong concept. Restriction enzymes are of two types namely, exonucleases and endonucleases.
Restriction exonucleases Cut DNA from its ends.
Restriction endonucleases Cut DNA at specific sequence inside the DNA.

5 Marks Questions

91. (i) Draw a schematic diagram of the cloning vector pBR 322 and label (1) *Bam* HI site (2) gene for ampicillin resistance (3) '*ori*' (4) '*rop*' gene.

(ii) State the role of '*rop*' gene.

(iii) A cloning vector does not have a selectable marker. How will it affect the process of cloning?

(iv) Why is insertional inactivation preferred over the use of selectable markers in cloning vectors?

CBSE 2024 (Set-II)

Ans. (i) Refer to fig. 9.3 on page no. 267.

(ii) The '*rop*' gene codes for the proteins involved in the replication of the plasmid.

(iii) If the cloning vector does not have a selectable marker, the selection of the transformed cells will not be possible. Thus, the absence of a selectable marker significantly will hinder the efficiency and success of the cloning process.

(iv) Insertional inactivation is preferred over the use of selectable markers in cloning vectors because it allows for easy identification of recombinant plasmids without the need of additional selection step unlike simultaneous or duplicate plating having different antibiotics in case of selectable markers. Intsertional inactivation simplifies the cloning process and eliminate the need for antibiotic selection, making it more convnient and cost-effective.

92. (i) '*Eco*RI' has played very significant role in *r*DNA technology.

(a) Explain the convention for naming *Eco*RI.

(b) Write the recognition site and the cleavage sites of this restriction endonuclease.

(ii) What are the protruding and hanging stretches of DNA produced by these restriction enzymes called? Describe their role in formation of *r*DNA.

CBSE 2023

Ans. (i) (a) *Eco*RI comes from *Escherichia coli* RY13 strain. In *Eco*RI, '*E*' comes from the genus '*Escherichia*' and '*co*' comes from the species name '*coli*'. The genus and species names should be in italics.
The letter 'R' is derived from the name of the strain RY13. Roman numbers following the names indicate the order in which the enzymes were isolated from that strain of bacteria.

(b) *Eco*RI is a type II restriction enzyme that cuts only at the restriction site with the 5′-GAATTC-3′ sequence. It chops the DNA at a specified location, resulting in sticky ends.
*Eco*RI has a palindrome recognition site that cuts DNA following G, creating sticky ends with AATT. It is a six-nucleotide sequence with GAATTC in the 5′ to 3′ direction and CTTAAG in the 3′ to 5′ direction on the complementary strand. (3)

(ii) The protruding and hanging stretches of DNA produced by these restriction enzymes are called sticky ends. They are important in the formation of *r*DNA because they form hydrogen bonds with their complimentary cut counter parts. This stickiness of the ends facilitates the action of the enzyme DNA ligase. (2)

93. Unless the vector and source DNA are cut, fragments separated and joined, the desired recombinant vector molecule cannot be created.

(i) How are the desirable DNA sequences cut?

(ii) Explain the technique used to separate the cut fragments.

(iii) How are the resultant fragments joined to the vector DNA molecule?

Delhi 2015C

Ans. (i) The desirable DNA sequences are cut by using restriction endonuclease enzyme. These enzymes cut at specific site in palindromic sequence between same two bases on both the strands. (2)

(ii) Refer to answer no. 83. (2)

(iii) The resulting fragments are joined together with vector DNA by DNA ligase enzyme. It forms phosphodiester bonds between them. (1)

Concept Enhancer During electrophoresis of macromolecules we use agarose instead of agar because agarose is a purified version of agar. Agar contains mixture of polysaccharides and some charge which can be interfare in the separation of DNA fragments or other macromolecules.

94. (i) With the help of diagrams show the different steps in the formation of recombinant DNA by action of restriction endonuclease enzyme *Eco*RI.

(ii) Name the technique that is used for separating the fragments of DNA cut by restriction endonucleases. **All India 2011**

Ans. (i) Refer to figure 9.1 on page no. 266.

(ii) Refer to answer no. 83.

Common Mistakes Students get confused that during electrophoresis DNA fragments separate on the basis of charge but it is a wrong concept. It can be explained as since, DNA has a uniform mass/charge ratio, DNA fragments are separated by size within the agarose gel. It means smaller the fragment size, the farther it will move.

TOPIC 2

Processes of Recombinant DNA Technology

Process of recombinant DNA technology involves the following steps in sequence

1. Isolation of the Genetic Material (DNA)

It is carried out in the following steps

- DNA is enclosed within the membranes. To release DNA along with other macromolecules such as RNA, proteins, polysaccharides and lipids, bacterial cells/plant or animal tissues are treated with enzymes such as **lysozyme** (bacteria), **cellulase** (plant cells), **chitinase** (fungus).
- RNA can be removed by treating it with **ribonuclease** whereas proteins can be removed by their treatment with **protease**.
- Other molecules can be removed by appropriate treatments and ultimately purified DNA is precipitated out after the addition of **chilled ethanol**.
- Purified DNA can be seen as collection of fine threads in the suspension which can be removed by spooling.

2. Cutting of DNA at Specific Locations

It is done by using restriction enzymes. The purified DNA molecules are incubated with the specific restriction enzyme at optimum conditions for the enzyme to act.

3. Isolation of Desired DNA Fragment

It is carried out using agarose gel electrophoresis (as discussed earlier).

4. Amplification of Gene of Interest Using Polymerase Chain Reaction (PCR)

It is a technique in which multiple copies of specific DNA (gene of interest) sequence are produced *in vitro*.

The technique was developed by **Kary Mullis** in 1985 who received Nobel Prize in chemistry in 1993.

(i) **PCR Technique Requires**

- A **DNA template**, which is a double-stranded DNA that needs to be amplified.
- **Primers** are small chemically synthesised oligonucleotides of about 10-18 nucleotides that are complementary to a region of template DNA.
- **Enzyme** used is DNA *Taq* polymerase (obtained from a bacterium, *Thermus aquaticus*).
- **Deoxyribonucleotides** are required for the synthesis of new strands.
- **A thermostable** DNA polymerase (*Taq* polymerase) is used in the reaction because it can tolerate and remain active during the high temperature induced denaturation of *ds*DNA.

(ii) **Steps in PCR**

- **Denaturation** of double-stranded DNA is carried out by applying high temperature of 95°C for 15 seconds. Each separated single strand acts as a template for DNA synthesis.

- **Annealing** is carried out by two sets of primers, which are added in the reaction. They anneal to the 3′ end of each separated strand. Primers act as initiator of replication.
- **Extension** is done by DNA polymerase, by adding nucleotides complementary to the template in the reaction.
- These steps are repeated many times to obtain several copies of the desired DNA.

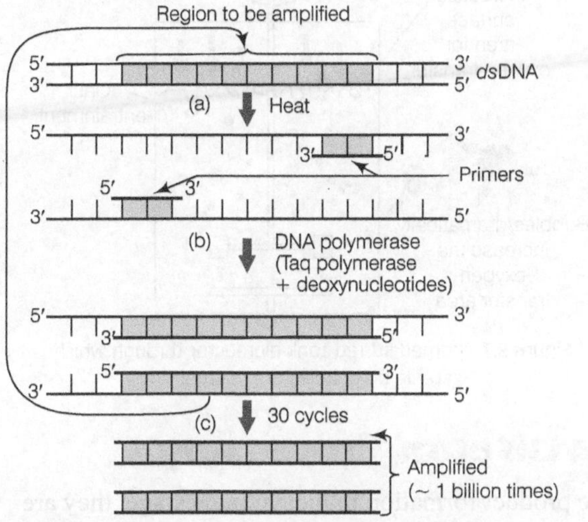

Figure 9.4 Polymerase Chain Reaction (PCR) : Each cycle has three steps (a) Denaturation (b) Primer annealing and (c) Extension of primers

5. Ligation of DNA Fragment into a Vector

It requires a vector DNA and source DNA.

- These are cut with the same endonuclease to obtain sticky ends.
- Both are then ligated by mixing vector DNA, gene of interest and enzyme **DNA ligase** to form recombinant DNA.

6. Insertion of Recombinant DNA into the Host Cell/Organism

It occurs by several methods (Heat shock, microinjection, gene gun, etc.) before which the recipient cells are made competent to receive the DNA.

7. Selection of Transformed (Recombinant) Cells

- If recombinant DNA carrying antibiotic resistance gene (e.g. ampicillin) is transferred into *E. coli* cells, the host cell is transformed into ampicillin resistant cells.
- The ampicillin resistant gene can be called a **selectable marker**. When these cells are grown on agar plates containing ampicillin, only transformants grow and others cells die.

8. Culturing the Host Cells

The cells containing the foreign gene is cultured on an appropriate medium at optimal conditions. On large scale, cells are grown in a **continuous culture system** in which fresh medium is added from one side to maintain growth phase of cells and the desired protein is collected from the other side.

9. Extraction of Desired Gene Product

Cells grown on cultures are made to express recombinant protein which is then extracted and purified by various separation methods.

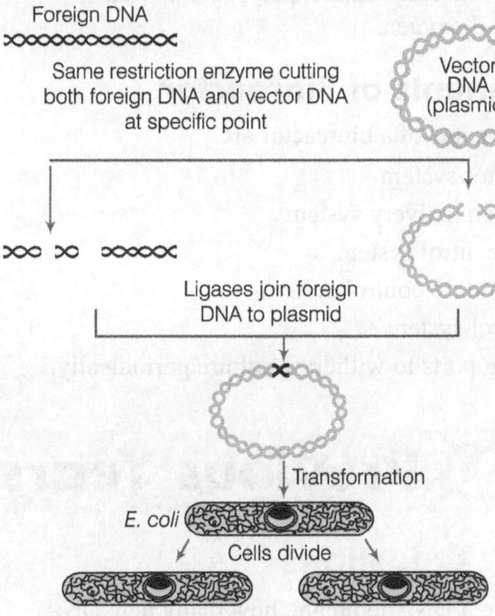

Figure 9.5 Diagrammatic representation of recombinant DNA technology

Bioreactors

These are the large volume (100-1000 L) vessels in which raw materials are biologically converted into specific products, individual enzymes, etc., using microbial, plant, animal or human cells.

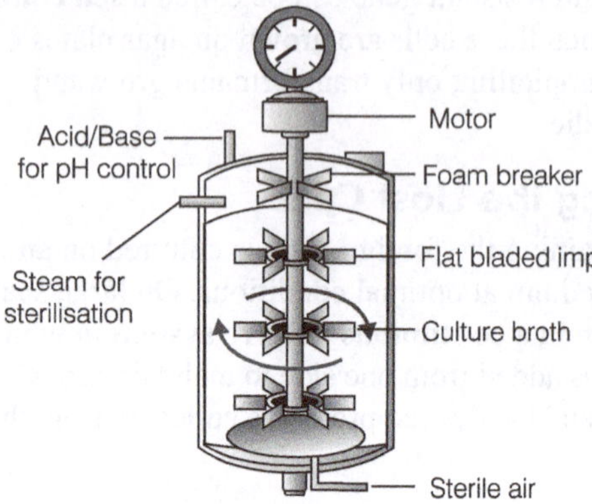

Figure 9.6 Simple stirred-tank bioreactor

It provides the optimal conditions for manufacturing the desired product quantity by providing growth conditions like temperature, pH, substrate, salts, vitamins and oxygen.

Components of Bioreactor

The components of a bioreactor are

- An agitator system
- An oxygen delivery system
- A foam control system
- A temperature control system
- pH control system
- Sampling ports to withdraw culture periodically.

Types of Bioreactor

(i) The **stirred-tank reactor** is usually cylindrical or with a curved base to facilitate the mixing of the reactor contents.
- The stirrer facilitates mixing and oxygen availability throughout the bioreactor.
- The most commonly used bioreactors are of stirring type.

(ii) In the **sparged stirred-tank bioreactor**, sterile air bubbles are sparged to increase the surface area for oxygen transfer.

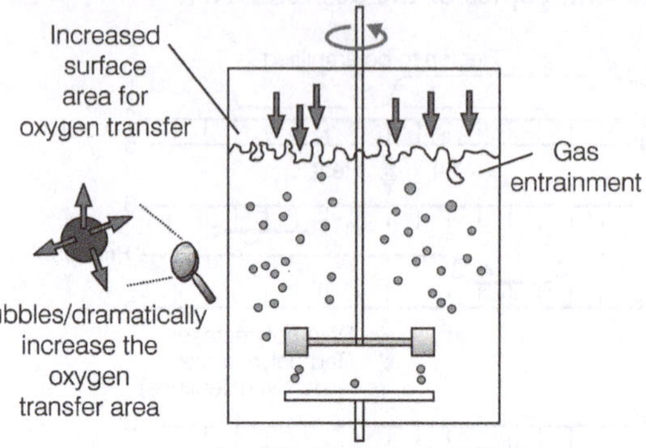

Figure 9.7 Sparged stirred-tank bioreactor through which sterile air bubbles are sparged

Downstream Processing

After the product formation in biosynthetic stage, they are subjected to a series of processes, collectively referred to as downstream processing.

These include

- Separation of desired product
- Purification of products
- Formulation with preservatives

Finally, these products undergo strict quality control testing before being marketed as a finished product.

PYQs Previous Years' Questions

1 Mark Questions

1. Using a DNA template, how many new DNA molecules would be generated after 10 cycles of amplification in PCR? **CBSE 2024 (Set-I)**

(a) 512 (b) 1024
(c) 2048 (d) 256

Ans. (b) After '*n*' number of PCR cycle, 2^n copies of DNA are produced. So, after 10 such cycle, number of DNA molecules generated would be 2^{10}, i.e. 1024 DNA molecules.

2. Which one of the following enzymes, a fungal cell should be treated with to get the DNA along with other macromolecules released from it? **CBSE 2024 (Set-II)**

(a) Isozymes (b) Cellulose
(c) Ribonuclease (d) Chitinase

Ans. (d) A fungal cell should be treated with chitinase to get the DNA along with other macromolecules such as RNA, proteins, polysaccharides and also lipids released from it. In case of bacteria, lysozyme is used and in plant cells, cellulose enzyme is used for the same purpose.

Assertion-Reason Type Question

3. **Assertion** (A) Synthetic oligonucleotide polymers are used during annealing in a PCR.

Reason (R) The primers bind to the double stranded DNA at their complementary regions. **CBSE 2023**

(a) Both Assertion and Reason are true and Reason is the correct explanation of Assertion

(b) Both Assertion and Reason are true, but Reason is not the correct explanation of Assertion

(c) Assertion is true, but Reason is false

(d) Assertion is false, but Reason is true

Ans. (a) Both Assertion and Reason are true and Reason is the correct explanation of Assertion

Very Short Answer Type Question

4. Name the enzymes that are used for the isolation of DNA from bacterial and fungal cells for recombinant DNA technology. **All India 2014; Foreign 2014**

Ans. The enzymes used for the isolation of DNA from bacterial cells is lysozyme and those from fungal cells is chitinase.

2 Marks Questions

5. Name the source of the DNA polymerase used in PCR technique. Mention why is it used? **All India 2013, 2012; Foreign 2011**

Ans. The DNA polymerase used in PCR is *Taq* polymerase which is extracted from *Thermus aquaticus*. It is a thermostable enzyme that can withstand high temperature (94°-95°C) used in the denaturation step for the separation of DNA strands. Hence, it can be used for a number of cycles of DNA amplification without being denatured. (1+1)

6. (i) Write the scientific name of the source organism of the thermostable DNA polymerase used in PCR.

(ii) State the advantage of using thermostable DNA polymerase. **CBSE 2023**

Ans. (i) *Thermus aquaticus* (1)

(ii) Refer to page 282. (1)

7. What are bioreactors? How are large volumes of cultures maintained and processed in them? **CBSE SQP 2021-22**

Ans. Bioreactors are large vessels in which raw materials are biologically converted into specific products such as enzymes using microbial, plant, animal or human cells.

A bioreactor provides the optimal conditions for achieving the desired product by providing optimum growth conditions like temperature, pH, substrate, salts, vitamins and oxygen. (1 + 1)

8. Name the two most common bioreactors and mention their importance in biotechnology. **Delhi 2020**

Ans. The two most common bioreactors are

(i) Simple stirred-tank bioreactor

(ii) Sparged stirred-tank bioreactor (1)

Importance in Biotechnology

These are used for the production of desired gene products in large quantity. (1)

9. How is a continuous culture system maintained in bioreactors and why? **Delhi 2019**

Ans. The cells can be multiplied in a continuous culture system. In this, the used medium is drained out from one side, while fresh medium is added from the other side to maintain the cells in their physiologically most active (log/exponential) phase. This type of culturing method produces a larger biomass leading to higher yields of desired products.

10. Name the type of bioreactor shown. Write the purpose for which it is used. **All India 2011**

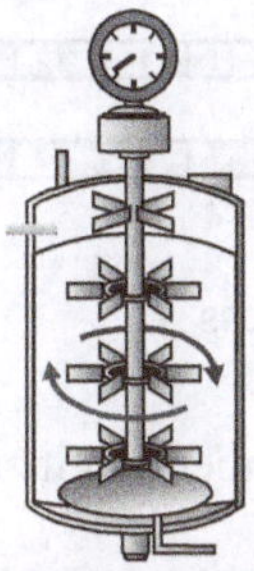

Ans. In the given figure, simple stirred-tank bioreactor is shown. (1)

Bioreactors are used to produce large quantities of the desired gene products. (½×2)

11. What is genetic engineering? List the steps in *r*DNA technology. **All India 2011**

Ans. Genetic engineering is the process of artificial synthesis, isolation, modification, combination, addition and repair of genetic material as needed. (1)

Steps of *r*DNA technology involve

(i) Isolation of genetic material.

(ii) Cutting of DNA at specific locations.

(iii) Amplification of gene of interest using PCR.

(iv) Preparation and insertion of *r*DNA into host cell.

(v) Obtaining desirable gene product. (1)

12. (i) Mention the number of primers required in each cycle of Polymerase Chain Reaction (PCR). Write the role of primers and DNA polymerase in PCR.

(ii) Give the characteristic feature and source organism of the DNA polymerase used in PCR.

All India 2010

Ans. (i) Two sets of primers are required in each cycle of polymerase chain reaction. Primers are required for the addition of nucleotides to make multiple copies of the DNA of interest. The enzyme DNA polymerase extends the primers by using the nucleotide provided in the reaction medium. **(1)**

(ii) Refer to page no. 282. **(1)**

13. A schematic representation of Polymerase Chain Reaction (PCR) upto the extension stage is given below. Answer the questions that follows.

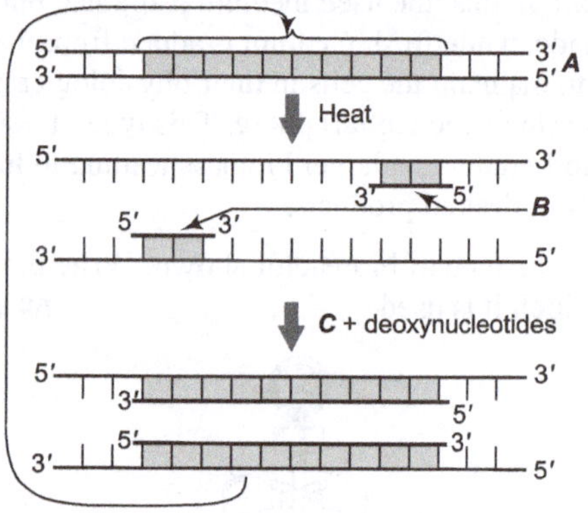

(i) Name the process *A*.

(ii) Identify *B*.

(iii) Identify *C* and mention its importance in PCR.

Foreign 2010

Ans. (i) *A*–Denaturation of the double-stranded DNA **(½)**

(ii) *B*–Primers **(½)**

(iii) *C*–DNA polymerase or *Taq* polymerase **(½)**

Importance in PCR

It extends the primers using the nucleotides provided in the reaction medium and the genomic DNA as the template. *Taq* polymerase is thermostable enzyme and it can withstand the high temperature used in denaturation step. **(½)**

14. Any recombinant DNA with a desired gene is required in billion copies for commercial use. How is the amplification done? Explain. **Delhi 2010C**

Ans. Amplification of recombinant DNA gene is done using Polymerase Chain Reaction (PCR).

It is carried out in the following steps

(i) **Denaturation** The double-stranded DNA is denatured by applying high temperature of 95°C for 15 seconds. Each separated strand acts as a template for the synthesis of new strands.

(ii) **Annealing** Two sets of primers are added, which anneal to the 3′ end of each separated strand.

(iii) **Extension** *Taq* polymerase extends the primers by adding nucleotides complementary to the template provided in the reaction medium. *Taq* polymerase is used in the reaction because it can tolerate high temperature. All these steps are repeated many times to get several copies of the desired DNA.

3 Marks Questions

15. Causative agents of HIV-AIDS and Covid-19 belong to the same group of viruses. To diagnose and amplify the genetic material for further study of Covid-19 virus, 'RT-PCR' test is carried out.

(i) What does 'RT-PCR' stand for?

(ii) Explain the various steps of PCR technique.

All India 2021-22 Term-II

Ans. (i) RT-PCR stands for Real Time Reverse Transcription Polymerase Chain Reaction.

(ii) Refer to text on page no. 282 and 283.

16. In a pathological lab, a series of steps were undertaken for finding the gene of interest. Describe the steps, or make a flowchart showing the process of amplification of this gene of interest.

CBSE SQP 2021-22 Term-II

Ans. Polymerase Chain Reaction (PCR) is a technique to obtain multiple copies of a gene of interest *in vitro*. This technique helps to amplify DNA through a simple enzymatic reaction.

The steps of PCR are as follows

Refer to the answer no. 14.

17. When the gene product is required in large amounts, the transformed bacteria with the plasmid inside the bacteria are cultured on a large scale in an industrial fermenter which then synthesises the desired protein. This product is extracted from the fermenter for commercial use.

(i) Why is the used medium drained out from one side while fresh medium is added from the other? Explain.

(ii) List any four optimum conditions for achieving the desired product in a bioreactor. **CBSE SQP 2020**

Ans. (i) To maintain the cells in their physiologically most active (log/exponential) phase, the used medium is drained out from one side while fresh medium is added from the other side. **(1½)**

(ii) Four optimum conditions required for achieving the desired product in a bioreactor are temperature, pH, substrate and oxygen. **(1½)**

18. Describe the roles of (i) high temperature, (ii) primers and (iii) bacterium. *Thermus aquaticus* in carrying the process of polymerase chain reaction. **All India 2019**

Or Describe the roles of heat, primers and the bacterium *Thermus aquaticus* in the process of PCR. **All India 2017**

Ans. **Role of Heat** In PCR (*in vitro*), the DNA strands are separated by heating at 95°C for two minutes. Heating causes the breakage of H-bonds between bases of two strands leading to its unwinding.

Role of Primers Primers are short lengths of DNA of about 20bp long that are required to start DNA polymerisation in PCR. The primers hybridise to their complementary sequence on the DNA strands at 40-50°C temperature and help in DNA polymerisation.

Role of *Thermus aquaticus* An enzyme called *Taq* polymerase is isolated from *Thermus aquaticus*. Since, this bacteria thrives in temperature as high as 95°C, this enzyme can also tolerate high temperature without undergoing denaturation. Therefore, this enzyme is used in PCR instead of normal DNA polymerase.

19. Describe the process of amplification of 'gene of interest' using PCR technique. **Delhi 2019**

Ans. Refer to answer no. 14.

20. Explain three steps involved in polymerase chain reaction.

(i) List the three steps involved in Polymerase Chain Reaction (PCR).

(ii) Name the source organism of *Taq* polymerase. Explain the specific role of this enzyme in PCR. **2018; Foreign 2014**

Ans. (i) Refer to answer no. 14.

(ii) Refer to page no. 282.

21. (i) How has the development of bioreactor helped in biotechnology?

(ii) Name the most commonly used bioreactor and describe its working. **CBSE 2018**

Ans. (i) **Bioreactors** These are the large volume vessels approximately (100-1000 L) in which raw materials are biologically converted into specific products, individual enzymes, etc., using microbial, plant, animal or human cells.

A bioreactor provides the optimal conditions for achieving the desired product by providing optimum growth conditions like temperature, pH, substrate, salts, vitamins and oxygen. These cells can also be multiplied in a **continuous culture** system.

In this, the used medium is drained out from one side while fresh medium is added from the other side to maintain the cells in their physiologically most active log/exponential phase. This type of culturing method produces a larger biomass leading to higher yields of desired products. Thus, it plays a very important role particularly in traditional biotechnology. (1½)

(ii) The most commonly used bioreactor is simple **stirred tank bioreactor**. It is usually cylindrical or with a curved base to facilitate the mixing of the reactor contents. The stirrer activity facilitates even mixing and availability of O_2 throughout the bioreactor. Alternatively air can also be bubbles into the medium. It has an agitator system, a temperature control system, a pH control system and sample ports, so that small samples can be withdrawn periodically. (1½)

22. Write the steps you would suggest to be undertaken to obtain a foreign-gene product. **Delhi 2017**

Ans. To obtain a foreign-gene product following steps should be undertaken

(i) Identification of DNA with desirable genes.

(ii) Introduction of the identified DNA into suitable host to form recombinant DNA (*r*DNA).

(iii) Maintenance of introduced DNA in particular host and gene cloning.

(iv) Transfer of the DNA (gene transfer) to its progeny.

(v) Selection of the recombinants from non-recombinants.

(vi) Expression of gene of interest by culturing recombinant cells.

(vii) Culturing of cells in bioreactors for large scale production of desired gene product.

23. Suggest and describe a technique to obtain multiple copies of a gene of interest *in vitro*. **All India 2016**

Ans. Polymerase Chain Reaction (PCR) is a technique to obtain multiple copies of a gene of interest *in vitro*. This technique amplifies DNA through a simple enzymatic reaction. This technique was developed by **Kary Mullis** in 1985.

The basic requirements of a PCR are the following

(i) DNA template

(ii) Primers

(iii) Enzyme—*Taq* polymerase

For detailed description of process, refer to answer no. 14. (3)

24. Why is *Taq* polymerase preferred in PCR? Mention the source of this enzyme. **Delhi 2015C**

Ans. Refer to answer no. 18 (iii).

25. Draw a labelled sketch of sparged stirred-tank bioreactor. Write its application. **Delhi 2015**

Ans. Sparged stirred-tank bioreactor

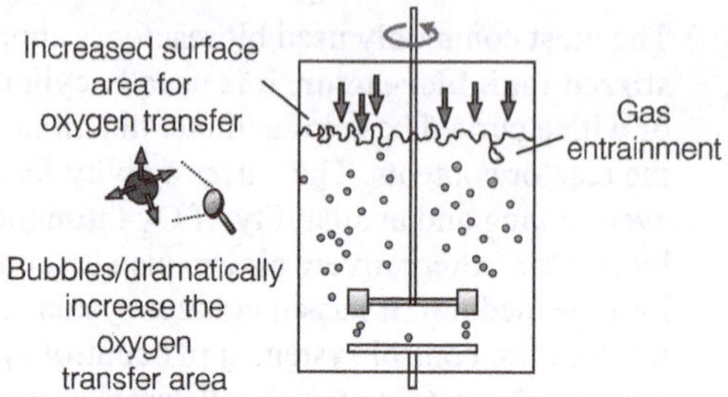

(2)

Application These bioreactors are used to produce large quantities of products, enzymes, etc., using microbial, plant, animal or human cells. (1)

26. Rearrange the following in the correct sequence to accomplish an important biotechnological reaction

(i) *In vitro* synthesis of copies of DNA of interest
(ii) Chemically synthesised oligonucleotides
(iii) Enzyme DNA polymerase
(iv) Complementary region of DNA
(v) Genomic DNA template
(vi) Nucleotides provided
(vii) Primers
(viii) Thermostable DNA polymerase (from *Thermus aquaticus*)
(ix) Denaturation of *ds*DNA. **All India 2015**

Ans. The correct sequence of reactions are

(ix) Denaturation of *ds*DNA
↓
(v) Genomic DNA template
↓
(ii) Chemically synthesised oligonucleotides
↓
(vii) Primers
↓
(iv) Complementary region of DNA
↓
(vi) Nucleotides provided
↓
(iii) Enzyme DNA polymerase
↓
(viii) Thermostable DNA polymerase (from *Thermus aquaticus*)
↓
(i) *In vitro* synthesis of copies of DNA of interest.

27. Many copies of a specific gene of interest are required to study the detailed sequencing of bases in it. Name and explain the process that can help in developing large number of copies of this gene of interest. **Foreign 2015**

Ans. PCR is the process that can help in developing large number of copies of a gene of interest. (1)

Process of PCR Refer to answer no. 14. (2)

28. (i) What is a bioreactor? How does it work?

(ii) Name two commonly used bioreactors. **Delhi 2014C**

Ans. (i) Bioreactors are large vessels in which raw materials are biologically converted into specific products by microbial plant, animal or human cells.

The bioreactors work by providing optimal conditions to process the culture as well as the production of desired product by maintaining optimum pH, temperature, oxygen and other growth conditions required. (2)

(ii) The two commonly used bioreactors are
(a) Simple stirred-tank bioreactors.
(b) Sparged stirred-tank bioreactors. (1)

Concept Enhancer Biological product(s) formed in the bioreactor cannot be used immediately because they may contain some impurities that could be harmful or interfere with its activity. This is because further processing and purification is required before using that product(s).

29. What is a bioreactor used for? Name a commonly used bioreactor and any two of its components. **All India 2014C**

Ans. Refer to answer no. 28 (i).

The components of a commonly used **stirred-tank bioreactor** are
(i) Inlet for sterile air or oxygen
(ii) Agitator system
(iii) Temperature control system
(iv) pH control system
(v) Foam control system
(vi) Sampling ports

30. Explain in sequence the process of amplification of a gene of interest using Polymerase Chain Reaction. **All India 2013C, 2012, 2012C**

Or

How is the amplification of a gene sample of interest carried out using Polymerase Chain Reaction (PCR)? **All India 2012**

Or Describe the process of gene amplification for *r*DNA technology experiments. **All India 2011C**

Ans. Refer to answer no. 14.

Refer to figure 9.4 on page no. 283.

5 Marks Questions

31. Bioreactors are the containment vehicles of any biotechnology-based production process. For large scale production and for economic reasons the final success of biotechnological process depends on the efficiency of the bioreactor.

Answer the following questions with respect to the given paragraph.

(i) List the operational guidelines that must be adhered to so as to achieve optimisation of the bioreactor system. Enlist any four.

(ii) Mention the phase of the growth we refer to in the statement 'Optimisation of growth and metabolic activity of the cells'.

(iii) Is the biological product formed in the bioreactor suitable for the intended use immediate? Give reason in support of your answer. **CBSE 2023**

Ans. (i) The operational guidelines that must be adhered to so as to achieve optimisation of the bioreactor system are

(a) monitoring and control of key parameters.

(b) optimisation of mixing and aeration.

(c) minimising contamination.

(d) maintenance and cleaning of the bioreactor. **(2)**

(ii) The phase of the growth referred to in the statement "Optimisation of growth and metabolic activity of the cells" is the exponential phase of growth. **(1)**

(iii) In many cases, further processing and purification of the biological product are required before it can be used for its intended purpose. This is because the product may contain impurities or other components that could be harmful or interfere with its activity. **(2)**

32. Oil spill is a major environmental issue. It has been found that different strains of *Pseudomonas* bacteria have genes to breakdown the four major groups of hydrocarbons in oil. Trials are underway to use different biotechnological tools to incorporate these genes and create a genetically engineered strain of *Pseudomonas* - a 'super-bug', to breakdown the four major groups of hydrocarbons in oil. Such bacteria might be sprayed onto surfaces polluted with oil to clean thin films of oil.

(i) List two advantages of using bacteria for such biotechnological studies?

(ii) For amplification of the gene of interest PCR was carried out. The PCR was run with the help of polymerase which was functional only at a very low temperature. How will this impact the efficiency of the PCR? Justify.

(iii) If such bacteria are sprayed on water bodies with oil spills, how will this have a positive or negative effect on the environment? Discuss. **CBSE SQP 2023**

Ans. (i) Bacteria can be used for such biotechnological studies because we can easily grow a large quantity of the bacteria as they have plasmids and can easily transform. **(1)**

(ii) PCR will not amplify the gene.

If the polymerase enzyme denatures at low temperature, it means that it will not be able to withstand high temperature which is essential for separating/opening/ unwinding/ denaturing DNA strand to open. Thus, subsequent step of extending the primers using the nucleotides provided in the reaction and the genomic DNA as template will not occur. **(2)**

(iii) In case such bacteria are sprayed on water bodies with oil spills, then it will have both positive and negative effects.

Positive effect Oil spills can be treated and the environment becomes better/ cleaner. Also the water becomes more potable/ safe for aquatic forms/ safe for water birds like sea gulls.

Negative effect The bacteria can mutate/ can harm other organisms/ can conjugate with other non-virulent forms and make them super bugs with detrimental effect/ unpredictable/ for a longer duration. It may reduce the dissolved oxygen and leading to mortality of aquatic organisms. **(2)**

33. (i) Describe the different steps in one complete cycle of PCR.

(ii) State the purpose of such an amplified DNA sequence. **All India 2015C**

Ans. (i) Refer to text on page no. 282-283. **(2)**

(ii) Applications of PCR technique

(a) In diagnosis of pathogens for specifc infections, like HIV

(b) To identify mutations in organisms

(c) In DNA fingerprinting

(d) Prenatal diagnosis

(e) Gene therapy **(3)**

34. If a desired gene is identified in an organism for some experiments, explain the process of the following

(i) Cutting this desired gene at specific location.

(ii) Synthesis of multiple copies of this desired gene.

All India 2011

Ans. (i) Cutting of desired gene at specific location is done by incubating the DNA with specific restriction endonuclease. Restriction enzymes recognise a particular palindromic nucleotide sequence and cuts the DNA at that site. **(1½)**

(ii) Synthesis of multiple copies of desired gene is carried out by Polymerase Chain Reaction (PCR). **(1½)**

Refer to answer no. 14. **(2)**

Miscellaneous Questions

3 Marks Questions

1. Write the function of the following in biotechnology.

Outside Delhi 2016C

(i) Polymerase chain reaction technique.

(ii) Restriction endonucleases.

(iii) Bacterium *Thermus aquaticus*.

Ans. (i) Polymerase chain reaction technique is used to prepare multiple copies of a gene of interest *in vitro* using two sets of primers and the enzyme DNA polymerase. **(1)**

(ii) Restriction endonucleases are enzymes that make cut at specific positions within the DNA. **(1)**

(iii) Bacterium *Thermus aquaticus* produces an enzyme *Taq* polymerase which is heat stable, i.e. resistant to denaturation by heat. The enzyme is used to amplify a specific DNA fragment in PCR technique. **(1)**

2. Explain the basis on which the gel electrophoresis technique works. Write any two ways the products obtained through this technique can be utilised.

Delhi 2013C

Ans. Gel electrophoresis technique works on the principle of separation of DNA fragments on the basis of their size and electric charge. **(1)**

Since, DNA is negatively charged molecule so, they can be separated according to their size when they move towards anode under an electric field through a medium or matrix (commonly used is agarose). Shorter molecules move faster towards anode and migrate farther than the longer one. **(1)**

The products obtained through this technique can be utilised in the following ways

(i) Construction of recombinant DNA by joining with cloning vectors.

(ii) Used in making multiple copies of same DNA by using PCR (Polymerase Chain Reaction). **(1)**

3. How can the following be made possible for biotechnology experiments?

(i) Isolation of DNA from bacterial cell.

(ii) Reintroduction of the recombinant DNA into a bacterial cell.

Foreign 2012

Ans. (i) Isolation of DNA from bacterial cell can be done by

(a) treating the bacterial cells with enzymes such as lysozyme to remove cell wall. **(1)**

(b) RNA associated with DNA can be removed by the treatment with ribonuclease, whereas protein can be removed by treatment with protease. Similarly other molecules (if any) are removed by appropriate treatment. **(1)**

(ii) Reintroduction of the recombinant DNA into bacterial cell can be done by the following methods

(a) The recipient bacterial cell is made 'competent' to take up the recombinant DNA by its treatment with a specific increased concentration of calcium ions.

(b) The recombinant DNA is forced into the cells by heat shock treatment, i.e. by incubating the cells with *r*DNA on ice followed by placing them at 42°C (heat shock) and then again putting them back on ice. This enables bacteria to take up *r*DNA. **(1)**

4. (i) Identify *A* and *B* illustrations in the following

(a)

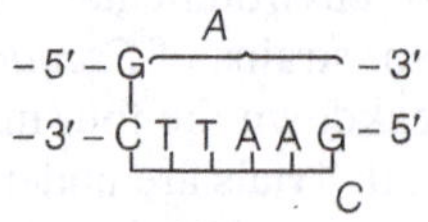

(b)

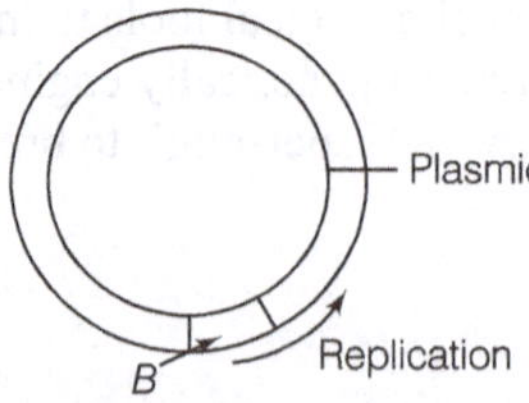

(ii) Write the term given to *A* and *C* and why?

(iii) Expand PCR. Mention its importance in biotechnology.

Delhi 2011

Ans. (i) (a) *A* is recognition or restriction site (GAATTC), which is recognised by restriction enzyme *Eco* RI.

(b) *B* is *rop* gene protein involved in the replication of plasmid coded by this gene. **(1)**

(ii) *A* and *C* are called palindromes. These are sequence of base pairs that reads same on the two strands of DNA, when orientation of reading is kept same. **(1)**

(iii) PCR is Polymerase Chain Reaction in which multiple copies of the gene of interest can be synthesised *in vitro*. Thus, PCR can be utilised to amplify a single gene or fragment into thousands of copies to be used in cloning experiments. **(1)**

Case Based/Source Based/Passage Based Questions (Based on Complete Chapter)

1. Study the diagram given below that shows the steps involved in the procedure of selecting transformed bacteria and answer the questions that follow

CBSE 2024 (Set-I)

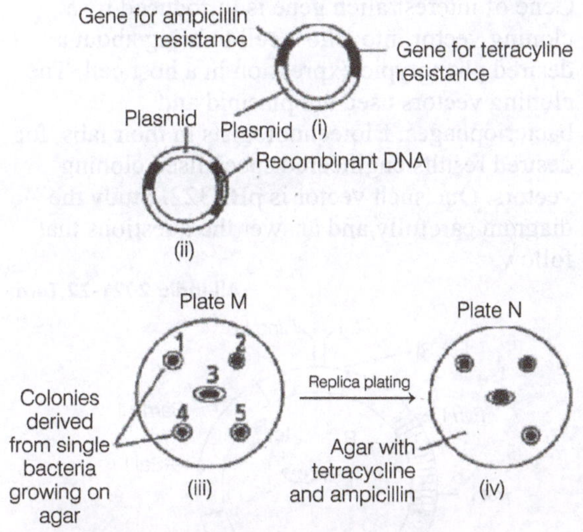

(i) Identify the colony that has got transformed. Justify your answer.

(ii) What are the sites in a plasmid called where ampicillin and tetracycline resistance genes are inserted? State their role in genetic engineering.

(iii) Name two enzymes playing an important role in genetic engineering.

Or

(iii) State the role of β-galactosidase in insertional inactivation.

Ans. (i) Colony 4 got transformed as it failed to grow on agar containing ampicillin and tetracycline. Since, it is transformed, its gene for tetracycline and ampicillin resistance became inactive, thus it lost its ability to grow in both of them (ampicillin and tetracycline). **(1)**

(ii) Selectable markers are sites where ampicillin and tetracycline resistance genes are inserted. They are very important in genetic engineering as they help in the selection of the transformants from those of the non- transformants. **(2)**

(iii) *Eco*RI, *Hind* III **(1)**

Or (iii) β - galactosidase acts as a reporter enzyme. It is produced by *lac z*, a reporter gene. In insertional inactivation, when there is inactivation of *lac z* gene due to insert , no B - galactosidase is formed and thus no blue colour in formed. Thus, giving a white coloured colonies of transformants. **(1)**

2. The structure below shows pUC18 which is similar to pBR322 in its function. However, they differ in some of their restriction sites and number of ori. The ori number for pBR322 is approximately 20.

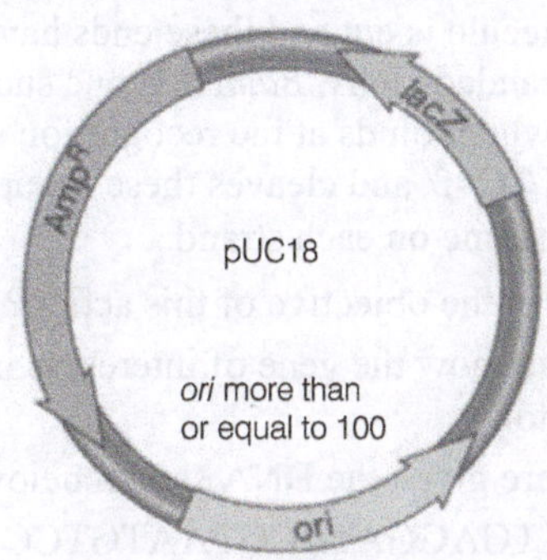

(i) How are pUC18 and pBR322 used in biotechnological studies?

Or What will be the impact if *ori* in the above structure gets damaged?

(ii) The *lac z* gene has many recognition sites. Study the segment of DNA given below and answer the questions

5′ ... ATC GTA AAG CTT CAT….3′
3′ ... TAG CAT TTC GAA GTA…5′

(a) Applying your knowledge of palindrome sequences identify and mark the possible region where the restriction enzyme *X* will act.

(b) Restriction enzyme *Y* was used to extract gene of interest from a plant. This gene needs to be inserted in the given DNA segment which has been treated with restriction enzyme X. Will there be a successful recombination? Explain with a reason.

(iii) Which one of the two (pUC18 and pBR322) would you prefer for biotechnological studies? Justify.

CBSE SQP 2024

Ans. (i) Plasmids act as vectors which can be used to insert the gene of interest from a desired organism into a host. **(1)**

Or *ori* (Origin of replication) No replication will take place resulting in no copies of linked DNA. **(1)**

(ii) (a) 5′... ATC GTA/AAG CTT /CAT...3′
3′... TAG CAT/TTC GAA /GTA...5′

Or 5′... AAG CTT ...3′
3′... TTC GAA ...5′

(b) No, as the restriction enzymes need to be the same which cut the DNA of the plasmid and the gene of interest from the plant. **(2)**

(iii) pUC18 as it has a higher copy rate. **(1)**

3. Read the following and answer the questions given below.
Some restriction enzymes break a phosphodiester bond on both the DNA strands, such that only one end of each molecule is cut and these ends have regions of single stranded DNA. *Bam*HI is one such restriction enzyme which binds at the recognition sequence, 5′-GGATCC- 3′ and cleaves these sequences just after the 5′- guanine on each strand.

(i) What is the objective of this action?

(ii) Explain how the gene of interest is introduced into a vector.

(iii) You are given the DNA shown below.
5′ATTTTGAGGATCCGTAATGTCCT 3′
3′ TAAAACTCCTAGGCATTACAGGA 5′
If this DNA was cut with *Bam*HI, how many DNA fragments would you expect? Write the sequence of these double-stranded DNA fragments with their respective polarity.

(iv) A gene M was introduced into *E. coli* cloning vector pBR322 at *Bam*HI site. What will be its impact on the recombinant plasmids? Give a possible way by which you could differentiate non-recombinant to recombinant plasmids.

CBSE SQP 2021-22 Term-II

Ans. (i) Restriction enzymes help to break phosphodiester bond on both the DNA strands. These are used in recombinant DNA technology. By this method we can recombine desired compatible ends. **(1)**

(ii) Restriction enzyme cuts the DNA of the vector and then enzyme DNA ligase ligates the gene of interest into the DNA of the vector. **(1)**

(iii) *Bam*HI recognition sequence is 5′-GGATCC-3′ and it cleaves these sequence just after the 5′-guanine. In the given sequence the restriction will work as follows

↓

5′ ATTTTGAGGATCCGTAATGTCCT 3′
3′ TAAAACTCCTAGGCATTACAGGA 5′

↓ 2 fragments

5′-ATTTGAG-3′ 5′GATCCGTAATGTCCT-3′
3′-TAAAACTCCTAG-5′ 3′- GCATTACAGGA 5′ **(1)**

(iv) *Bam*HI site will affect tetracycline antibiotic resistance gene, hence the recombinant plasmids will lose tetracycline resistance due to inactivation of the resistance gene.
Recombinants can be selected from non-recombinants by plating them into a medium containing tetracycline as the recombinants will not grow in the medium because the tetracycline resistance gene is cut. **(1+1)**

4. Gene of interest/alien gene is introduced by a cloning vector into a host cell to bring about a desired phenotypic expression in a host cell. The cloning vectors used are plasmid and bacteriophages. Biotechnologists in their labs, for desired results engineered specialised cloning vectors. One such vector is pBR322. Study the diagram carefully and answer the questions that follow.

All India 2021-22 Term-II

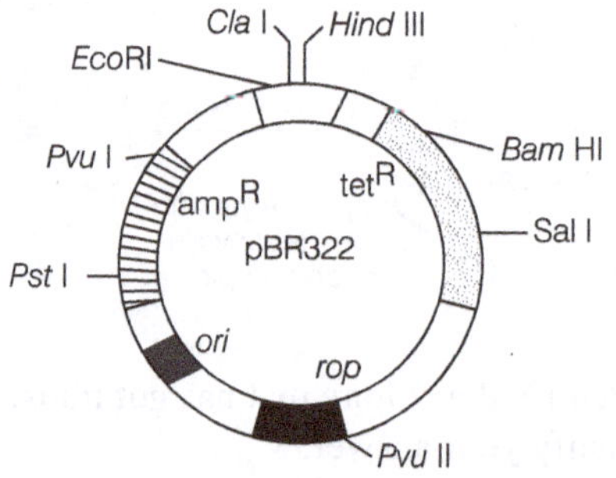

(i) What do '*Eco*RI', '*Bam* HI' and '*Hind* III' represent? State their functions.

(ii) Identify the gene you would select for the role of a selectable marker in pBR322. Explain why?

(iii) Write the property/characteristic of plasmid and bacteriophage that makes them efficient cloning vectors.

(iv) Biotechnologists always insert '*ori*' gene in their engineered cloning vector. Justify the statement.

(v) Will the experiment be successful if the alien DNA is ligated at *Hin*d III restriction site? Give reason in support of your answer.

Ans. (i) '*Eco*RI',*Bam*HI' and '*Hin*d III' are restriction enzymes which cuts the DNA either from the ends of DNA or make cut at specific positions within the DNA. **(1)**

(ii) The genes encoding resistance to antibiotics such as ampicillin, tetracycline etc. can be considered a useful selectable markers for *E. coli* cloning vector pBR322 because the *E. coli* cells do not carry resistance against any of these antibiotics. **(1)**

(iii) The property/characteristics of plasmid and bacteriophage that makes them efficient cloning vector are as follows

(a) Plasmids are small autonomously replicating usually circular, extra chromosomal double stranded DNA molecule that occurs in many bacteria and some yeasts.

(b) Bacteriophages are viruses infecting bacteria used as vector becuase of very high copy number of their genome within the bacterial cell. **(1)**

(iv) Biotechnologist always insert '*ori*' gene in their engineered cloning vector because this is the sequence from where the replication starts and any piece of DNA when, linked to this sequence can be made to replicate within the host cells. This sequence is also responsible for controlling the copy number of the linked DNA. **(1)**

(v) No, the experiment will not be successful if the alien DNA is ligated at *Hin*d III restriction site because ligation of alien DNA is carried out at a restriction site present in one of the two antibiotic resistance genes, i.e. *Bam*HI and *Sal*I for tetracycline or at *Pvu*I, *Pst*I for ampicilline. **(1)**

5. Read the following and answer the questions given below

Enzyme *taq* polymerase, is extracted from a eubacterial microorganism *Thermus aquaticus* from Yellowstone National Park in Montana, USA and isolated by Chien *et al*. (1976). *Taq* polymerase successfully replaced the DNA polymerase from *E. coli* that was being used in PCR earlier and this shift revolutionised the PCR technique.

(i) *Taq* polymerase after its discovery replaced *E. coli* DNA polymerase in PCR technique. Explain giving reasons why was the need felt for the change?

(ii) What is a primer and its importance in PCR?

(iii) Write the importance of PCR as a diagnostic tool.

Delhi 2021-22 Term-II

Ans. (i) *Taq* polymerase is isolated from a thermophilic bacterium, i.e. *Thermus aquaticus* and has a property to remain active during the high temperature induced denaturation of double-stranded DNA. Therefore, it replaced *E. coli* DNA polymerase in PCR technique. **(2)**

(ii) Refer to text on page 282. **(1)**

(iii) Refer to answer no. 33 (ii) of Topic 2. **(2)**

CHAPTER TEST

01 Mark Questions

Multiple Choice Questions

1 Who discovered recombinant DNA (*r*DNA) technology?
(a) Har Gobind Khorana
(b) James D Watson
(c) Stanely Cohen and Herbert Boyer
(d) Walter Sutton and Avery

2 The construction of the first recombinant DNA was done by using the native plasmid of
(a) *E. coli*
(b) *Salmonella typhimurium*
(c) *Bacillus thuringiensis*
(d) Yeast

3 Which of the following is not correct regarding *Eco*RI restriction endonuclease enzyme?
(a) It recognises the palindromic sequences
(b) It is isolated from *Escherichia coli* RY13
(c) It produces blunt ends
(d) Both (b) and (c)

4 Which of the following statements is incorrect about '*ori*'?
(a) It stands for origin of replication
(b) It is one of the feature of a good vector
(c) It is a RNA sequence
(d) It is linked to the foreign DNA to replicate within the host cell

5 Which vector can clone only a small fragment of DNA?
(a) Bacterial artificial chromosome
(b) Yeast artificial chromosome
(c) Plasmid
(d) Cosmid

6 An analysis of chromosomal DNA using the Southern hybridisation technique does not use
(a) electrophoresis (b) blotting
(c) autoradiography (d) PCR

Assertion-Reason Type Questions

Directions (Q. Nos. 7-10) *In the questions given below two statements: an **Assertion** and a **Reason** are given. Give the appropriate response as*
(a) If both Assertion and Reason are true and Reason is the correct explanation of Assertion
(b) If both Assertion and Reason are true, but Reason is not the correct explanation of Assertion
(c) If Assertion is true, but Reason is false
(d) If Assertion is false, but Reason is true

7 **Assertion** A genetic probe is not always helpful in the detection of specific DNA sequence.
Reason Genetic probe is a radiolabelled *c*DNA, which has complementary base sequence, of which the DNA fragment is to be detected.

8 **Assertion** Plasmids are extrachromosomal DNA.
Reason Plasmids are found in bacteria and are useful in recombinant DNA technology.

9 **Assertion** Restriction endonucleases are also called molecular scissors.
Reason When fragments generated by restriction endonucleases are mixed, they join together due to their sticky ends.

10 **Assertion** *Agrobacterium tumefaciens* is popular in genetic engineering because this bacterium is associated with the roots of all cereal and pulse crops.
Reason A gene incorporated in the bacterial Ti-plasmid gets automatically transferred to the infected crop.

2/3 Marks Questions

11 How are sticky ends formed on a DNA strand? Why are they so called?

12 Draw a schematic sketch of pBR322 plasmid and label the following in it.
(i) Any two restriction sites
(ii) *ori* and *rop* genes
(iii) An antibiotic resistant gene.

13 What modification is done on the Ti-plasmid of *Agrobacterium tumefaciens* to convert it into a cloning vector?

14 List any five growth conditions that a bioreactor should provide for obtaining the desired product?

15 Write a note on downstream processing.

16 Mention any three applications of polymerase chain reaction.

17 Refer to the following flow diagram and answer the questions that follows

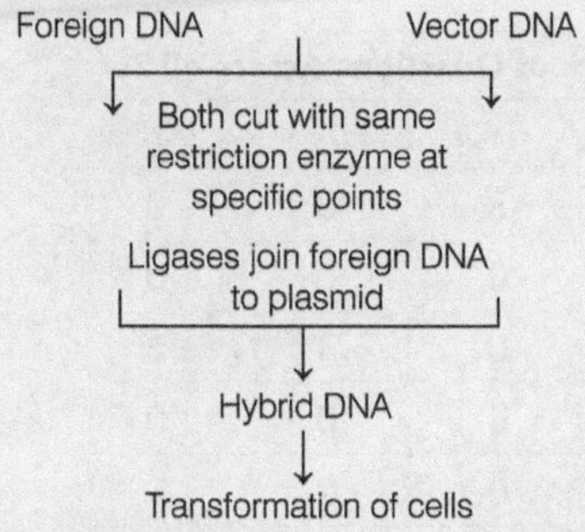

(i) A plasmid DNA and a linear DNA (both of same size) have one site for a restriction endonuclease. When cut and separated on agarose gel electrophoresis, plasmid shows one DNA band, while linear DNA shows two fragments. Justify.

(ii) How are transformed cells selected ?

18 Refer to below mentioned diagram and answer the questions that follows

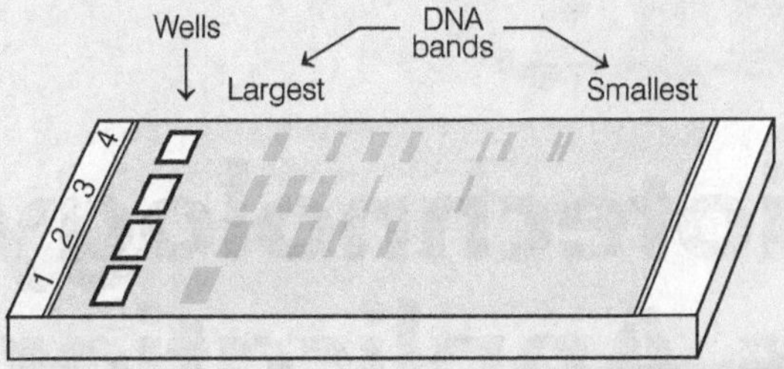

(i) What is depicted in the above diagram?

(ii) What can be understood from the lanes 1, 2, 3 and 4 ?

(iii) How are separated DNA fragments visualised ?

05 Marks Questions

19 Give an account of the blue white method of selection of recombinants.

20 What does PCR stand for? Describe the different steps of PCR.

21 What are the different types of vectors? Briefly explain.

22 Give a brief account on genetic engineering.

Answers

1.	(c)	2.	(b)	3.	(c)	4.	(c)	5.	(c)
6.	(d)	7.	(d)	8.	(b)	9.	(b)	10.	(d)

10

Biotechnology and its Applications

TREND ANALYSIS 3 YEARS

Average No. of Questions Across all Sets

Topic	Types of Questions	2024	2023	2020
TOPIC 01 Biotechnological Applications in Agriculture and Medicine	1 Mark	3	0	0
	2 Marks	0	0	0
	3 Marks	0	3	2
	4 Marks (Case Based)	0	0	0
	5 Marks	0	0	1
TOPIC 02 Transgenic Animals and Ethical Issues	1 Mark	1	0	0
	2 Marks	0	0	2
	3 Marks	1	0	0
	4 Marks (Case Based)	0	0	0
	5 Marks	0	0	0

TOPIC 1

Biotechnological Applications in Agriculture and Medicine

Biotechnology essentially deals with industrial scale production of biopharmaceuticals and other biological products. The applications of biotechnology include therapeutics, diagnostics, genetically modified crops for agriculture, processed food, bioremediation, waste treatment and energy production, etc.

Biotechnology has the following three critical research areas

- To provide the best catalyst in the form of improved organism, usually a microbe or pure enzyme.
- To create optimal conditions through engineering for a catalyst to act.
- Downstream processing technologies to purify protein/organic compounds.

Biotechnological Applications in Agriculture

Role of biotechnology in agriculture can be understood under various categories as discussed below

Food Production

Biotechnology has certain applications in agriculture which may be used for increasing food production.

Regarding this, it may involve following three aspects

- Agrochemical based agriculture.
- Organic agriculture.
- Genetically engineered crop-based agriculture.

Green Revolution

It has increased the food production due to the use of

- improved crop varieties.
- agrochemicals (fertilisers and pesticides).
- better management of agricultural practices.

Excessive use of agrochemicals such as fertilisers, insecticides or pesticides leads to pollution and degradation of environment. These are expensive also. Thus, to assure their minimum use, genetically improved crops were developed.

The traditional breeding techniques failed to keep pace with demand. So, other technologies came into light. These provided sufficiently fast and efficient systems for crop improvement. One such technique is explained below

Tissue Culture

It is a technique of regeneration of whole plant from any part of a plant by growing it on culture medium under aseptic conditions.

- The capacity of a plant cell or explant to grow into a whole plant is called **totipotency**.
- **Explant** is the part of plant, e.g. leaf, stem, embryo, etc., taken out and grown in test tube under sterile conditions in special nutrient medium.
- The method of growing or producing thousands of plants in very less time through tissue culture is called **micropropagation**.
- The **nutrient medium** on which an explant is grown must provide a carbon source such as sucrose and also inorganic salts, vitamins, amino acids and growth regulators like auxins, cytokinins, etc.
- The plants produced from tissue culture are genetically identical to the original plant from which they are grown, so they are called **somaclones**.
- Advantages of tissue culture are
  - More number of plants can be produced in a short time.
  - Disease-free plants can be developed from diseased plants.
  - Seedless plants can be multiplied.

Tissue Culture Technique

Various tissue culture techniques are as follows

Meristem Culture

- It can be done to recover healthy plants from diseased plants.
- Meristem (apical and axillary) is the only virus-free part of a virus-infected plant as meristem cells divide very fast.
- Virus-free plants can be obtained by removing the meristem and growing it *in vitro*.
- Plants developed successfully from meristem culture are banana, sugarcane, potato, etc.

Somatic Hybridisation

It is the process of fusion of protoplast of different varieties or species of plant on a suitable nutrient medium *in vitro* to develop a somatic hybrid.

Procedure

- Single cells from selected plants are isolated.
- Cell walls are digested by enzymes like pectinase and cellulase to expose the marked protoplasts.
- Naked protoplasts are isolated from the plasma membrane.
- Isolated protoplasts are fused to obtain hybrid protoplasts under sterile conditions in special nutrient medium.
- Hybrid protoplasts obtained are cultured in a suitable medium to form new plant.

  For example, Pomato is a somatic hybrid produced by the fusion of tomato and potato protoplasts.

  This plant did not have all desirable combination of characters. Hence, it is not used for commercial utilisation.

Genetically Modified Organisms (GMOs)

These are plants, animals, bacteria and fungi, whose genes have been altered by genetic manipulation. Genetic modifications in plants have lead to following

- Crops became more tolerant to abiotic stresses, such as cold, drought, salt, heat, etc.
- Reduced dependency on chemical pesticides with the development of pest resistant crops.
- Post-harvest losses are greatly reduced.

- Increased efficiency of mineral usage in plants, that helps to prevent early exhaustion of fertility of soil.
- Enhanced nutritional value of food, e.g. vitamin-A enriched rice (golden rice).
- Tailor made plants are created by using (Genetic Modification or GM) to supply alternative resources to industries, in the form of starches, fuels and pharmaceuticals.

Insect Resistant Plants

- These are genetically modified plants resistant to insects. Their use in agriculture can lead to decrease in amount of insecticide usage. Most common example of this, is *Bt* crops, e.g. *Bt* cotton, *Bt* corn, *Bt* brinjal, etc.
- In these plants, *Bt* gene that has been cloned from the strains of a bacterium, *Bacillus thuringiensis* (*Bt* is short form) is expressed. This gene provides resistance to insects and acts as a biopesticide.
- This bacterium produces an insecticidal protein that has the ability to kill certain insects including lepidopterans (tobacco, budworm and armyworm), coleopterans (beetles) and dipterans (flies and mosquitoes).
- The protein crystals are formed during a particular phase of growth of bacterium and is known as **Cry protein**.
- *Bt* toxin protein exists as inactive protoxins in bacteria. Once an insect ingests the inactive toxin, it is converted into the active form due to the alkaline pH of the gut leading to the solubilisation of crystals.
- The activated toxin binds to the surface of midgut epithelial cells and creates pores that causes cell swelling and lysis, leading to the death of the insect.
- Most *Bt* toxins are insect-group specific. The toxin is coded by a gene named *cry*, e.g. the proteins encoded by the genes *cry* IAc and *cry* IIAb control the cotton bollworms and that of *cry* IAb controls corn borer.

Pest Resistant Plants

- Several nematodes parasites a wide variety of plants and animals including human beings.
- A nematode, *Meloidogyne incognita*, infects the roots of tobacco plants and causes reduction in yield. The infestation of these nematodes can be prevented by the use of a nobel strategy called **RNA interference** (RNAi). RNAi takes place in all eukaryotic organisms as a method of cellular defence by silencing of specific *m*RNA due to complementary *ds*RNA molecule that binds to and prevents translation of the *m*RNA.
- Nematode specific-genes were introduced into host plant using *Agrobacterium* vectors. It was found that the parasite could not survive in a transgenic host expressing specific interferring RNA. The transgenic plant, therefore protected itself from the parasite.

Biotechnological Applications in Medicine

Biotechnology has made immense impact in the area of healthcare by enabling the mass production of safe and more effective therapeutic drugs. Currently, about 30 recombinant therapeutics have been approved for human use over the world. In India, 12 of these are presently being marketed.

Various contributions of biotechnological applications in medicine are listed below

Genetically Engineered Insulin

- It leads to sufficient availability of insulin for the management of adult-onset diabetes.
- When there is lack of insulin in the body, glucose is not converted into glycogen. Hence, glucose level increases in blood and secreted in the urine, this condition is known as **Type I diabetes** or **Insulin Dependent Diabetes Mellitus** (IDDM).
- Insulin used for the treatment of diabetes was earlier extracted from the pancreas of slaughtered cattle and pigs. This caused allergy or other reactions in some patients, due to an immune response elicited in their body.
- Insulin consists of two short polypeptide chains, i.e. chain-A and B, linked together by disulphide bridges. Chain-A contains 21, while chain-B contains 30 amino acids.
- In mammals, insulin is synthesised as a prohormone, i.e. it needs to be processed before it becomes fully mature and functional hormone. This prohormone contains an extra stretch called the **C-peptide** (33 amino acids). This is also known as **proinsulin**.
- **C-peptide** is not present in the mature insulin and is removed during maturation into insulin.
- **Eli Lilly** an American company in 1983, prepared two DNA sequences corresponding to A and B chains of human insulin and introduced them in the plasmids of *E. coli* to produce insulin chains.

Chains-A and B were produced separately, extracted and combined by creating disulphide bonds to form human insulin.

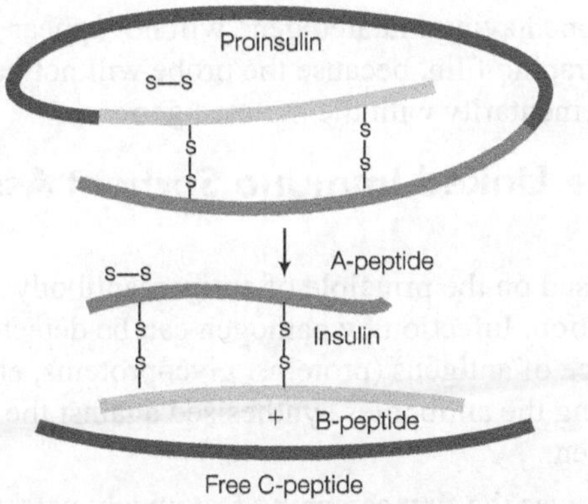

Figure 10.1 Maturation of proinsulin into insulin (simplified)

Genetically Engineered Vaccines

(Vaccine Production)

Vaccines produced through genetic engineering are called **recombinant vaccines** or '**subunit vaccines**' or '**second generation vaccines**', e.g. hepatitis-B. These are of two types

(i) **Protein vaccines** are based on the use of specific protein produced by *r*DNA.

(ii) **DNA vaccines** are based on the use of genetically engineered DNA that is injected in the body to produce an immunological response.

Stem Cell Technology

- These are undifferentiated biological cells that can differentiate into specialised cells and can divide through mitosis are called **stem cells.**
- These cells are found in multicellular organisms.
- They are mainly of two types, i.e. **embryonic stem cells,** which are isolated from the inner cell mass of blastocysts and **adult stem cells,** which exist throughout the body after embryonic development and are found inside different type of tissue such as brains.

Application

The potential applications of stem cell include organ and tissue regeneration, bone marrow transplantation, brain disease treatment, cell deficiency therapy, cardiovascular disease treatment, blood disease treatment, etc.

Gene Therapy

- It is a collection of methods that allows correction of gene defects, diagnosed in a child or embryo.
- In gene therapy, genes are inserted into a person's cells and tissues to treat a disease.
- Correction of a genetic defect involves delivery of a normal gene into the individual or embryo to take over the function or compensate for the non-functional gene.
- First gene therapy was given to a four year old girl with **Adenosine Deaminase** (ADA) **deficiency** by **M Blease** and **WF Andresco** in 1990s.
- ADA is caused due to the deletion of the gene for adenosine deaminase. This enzyme is very essential for immune system to function.
- In some children, ADA deficiency can be cured by bone marrow transplantation and enzyme replacement therapy. But of these two approaches are not completely curative.

Steps of Gene Therapy

Steps involved in gene therapy of ADA are as follows

- In first step of gene therapy, lymphocytes from the blood of the patient are grown in a culture outside the body.
- A functional ADA *c*DNA (using a retroviral vector) is then introduced into these lymphocytes. These lymphocytes are subsequently returned to the patient. These cells now produce ADA in the body.
- As these cells are not immortal, the patient requires periodic infusion of such genetically engineered lymphocytes.
- If the gene isolated from bone marrow cells producing ADA is introduced into cells at early embryonic stages, then it could be a permanent cure.

Some other diseases that can be treated by gene therapy are haemophilia, cystic fibrosis, Parkinson's disease, etc.

Molecular Diagnosis

By use of conventional methods of diagnosis (serum and urine analysis), early detection of diseases is not possible. To overcome this problem, some molecular diagnosis techniques were developed that provide early detection of diseases. These are as follows

Polymerase Chain Reaction (PCR)

- It helps in early detection of diseases or pathogens by the amplification of their nucleic acid.

- Low concentration of pathogens (bacteria, viruses, etc.) in the blood does not allow its detection, by conventional methods.
- PCR can amplify nucleic acids of such pathogens even when their concentration is very low (at a time when the symptoms of disease are not yet visible).
- For example, PCR technique can be used for detecting HIV in suspected AIDS patients, genetic mutation in suspected cancer patients and in identifying genetic disorders.

Recombinant DNA Technology

It is a modern molecular diagnostic technique. It is done in the following steps

- A single-stranded DNA or RNA tagged with a radioactive molecule called **probe** is allowed to hybridise to its complementary DNA in a clone of cells. Probes are very short fragments (15-30 bp).
- The cells are then detected by autoradiography.
- The clone having mutated gene will not appear on the photographic film, because the probe will not have complementarity with the mutated gene.

Enzyme Linked Immuno Sorbent Assay (ELISA)

- It is based on the principle of antigen-antibody interaction. Infection by pathogen can be detected by the presence of antigens (proteins, glycoproteins, etc.) or by detecting the antibodies synthesised against the pathogen.
- ELISA was the first screening test widely used for HIV because of its high sensitivity.

PYQs Previous Years' Questions

1 Mark Questions

Multiple Choice Questions

1. The specific *Bt* toxin genes which protect the cotton plants against the cotton bollworms are **CBSE 2024 (Set-I)**

(a) *cry* I Ac and *cry* II Ab

(b) *cry* I Ab and *cry* I Bc

(c) *cry* II Ac and *cry* I Ac

(d) *cry* II Ab and *cry* I Ab

Ans. (a) The specific *Bt* toxin genes which protect the cotton plants against cotton bollworms are *cry* IAc and *cry* II Ab, while *cry* IAb controls corn borer.

2. The main objective of production of pest resistant GM crops is to **CBSE SQP 2024**

(a) encourage eco-friendly pesticides

(b) reduce pesticide accumulation in food chain

(c) eliminate pests from the field without the use of manual labour

(d) retain maximum nutritional content in the crop that would be otherwise consumed by pest

Ans. (b) reduce pesticide accumulation in food chain

Assertion-Reason Type Questions

Direction (Q. Nos. 3-4) *consist of two statements Assertion (A) and Reason (R). Answer these questions selecting the appropriate option given below.*

(a) Both Assertion and Reason are true and Reason is the correct explanation of Assertion

(b) Both Assertion and Reason are true, but Reason is not the correct explanation of Assertion

(c) Assertion is true, but Reason is false

(d) Assertion is false, but Reason is true

3. **Assertion** (A) *Agrobacterium tumefaciens* is a pathogen of several monocot plants.

Reason (R) It is able to deliver a piece of DNA known as T-DNA to transform normal plant cells into a tumor. **CBSE 2024 (Set-I)**

Ans. (d) A is false, but R is true. A can be corrected as *Agrobacterium tumefaciens* is a pathogen of several dicot plants.

4. **Assertion** (A) Functional ADA cDNA genes must be inserted in the lymphocytes at the early embryonic stage in gene therapy for ADA deficiency.

Reason (R) Cells in the embryonic stage are immortal, differentiated and easy to manipulate. **CBSE 2024 (Set-I)**

Ans. (c) A is true, but R is false. R can be corrected as Cells in the embryonic stage are immortal, undifferentiated and easy to manipulate. Embryonic cells are pluripotent, i.e. they can give rise to all somatic cell types.

Very Short Answer Type Questions

5. Differentiate between proinsulin and mature insulin. **CBSE SQP 2021-22**

Ans. Differences between proinsulin and mature insulin are

Proinsulin	Mature insulin
Contains three polypeptides *viz.*, A, B and C.	Contains two polypeptides *viz.*, A and B.
Non-functional form.	Functional form.

6. Write the two specific '*cry*' genes that encode the proteins which control cotton bollworms. **All India 2019**

Ans. *cry* IAc and *cry* IIAb control cotton bollworm and *cry* I Ab controls corn borer.

7. Mention the chemical change that proinsulin undergoes, to be able to act as mature insulin. **CBSE 2018**

Ans. The C-peptide present in proinsulin is removed during its maturation.

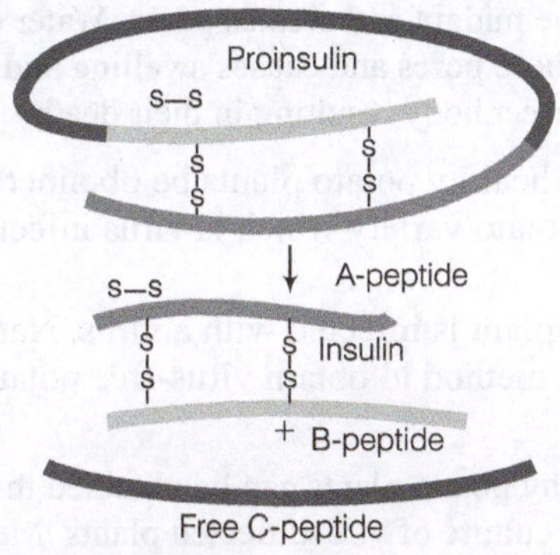

Maturation of proinsulin into insulin (simplified)

8. What are *cry* genes? In which organisms are they present? **All India 2017**

Ans. '*cry* genes' are genes found in *Bacillus thuringiensis*, a bacterium. These genes encode for protein crystals that contain a toxic insecticidal protein called *Bt* toxin. (½ + ½)

9. Suggest any two possible treatments that can be given to patient exhibiting adenosine deaminase deficiency. **Delhi 2015**

Or A boy has been diagnosed with ADA (Adenosine Deaminase) deficiency. Suggest any one possible treatment. **Delhi 2014C**

Ans. (i) Bone marrow transplantation. (½)

(ii) Gene therapy (not permanent cure). (½)

10. Why do children cured by enzyme replacement therapy for adenosine deaminase deficiency need periodic treatment? **All India 2015**

Ans. Children cured by enzyme replacement therapy for adenosine deaminase deficiency need periodic treatment because in such type of treatment genetically engineered lymphocytes are used and these cells are mortal.

11. State the role of C-peptide in human insulin. **All India 2014**

Ans. The C-peptide is an extra stretch of the peptides that connect the A and B-polypeptide chains of insulin in prohormone. During processing to release mature and functional insulin, this C-peptide is removed.

2 Marks Questions

12. (i) Name (a) one GM cereal crop having enhanced nutritional value, (b) the nutrient is rich in.

(ii) State any two benefits of genetically modified crops. **CBSE 2023**

Ans. (i) (a) A GM cereal crop with enhanced nutritional value is golden rice.

(b) It is rich in vitamin-A. (1)

(ii) For two benefits of genetically modified crops refer to answer no. 23. (1)

13. Explain the events that occur in the host cell on introduction of nematode-resistant gene into the tobacco plant by using *Agrobacterium* vectors. **CBSE SQP 2020**

Ans. The process of RNA interference (RNAi) takes place in all eukaryotic organisms as a method of cellular defence. The events that occur in the host cell on introduction of nematode-resistant gene into the tobacco plant by using *Agrobacterium* vectors are Both sense and antisense RNA are produced in the host cell. These two RNAs are complementary to each other and form a double-stranded RNA. The *ds*RNA initiates RNAi and hence a specific *m*RNA of the nematode is silenced.

14. Explain the relevance of 'totipotency' and 'somaclones' in raising healthy banana plants from virus infected banana plants. **Delhi 2019**

Or

How is it possible to recover healthy banana plants from a diseased but desirable quality of banana plant? Explain? **Foreign 2012**

Ans. The capacity to generate a whole plant from any cell/explant is called **totipotency**. By application of these methods, it is possible to achieve propagation of a large number of plants in very short duration. This method of producing thousands of plants through tissue culture is called micropropagation. Each of these plants will be genetically identical to the original plant from which they were grown also called somaclones. (1)

Meristem (axillary and apical) remains free from pathogens due to the absence of vascular supply. Thus, meristematic tissues are used in recovering healthy plants from diseased plants. Many important food plants like banana, etc., have been produced on a commercial scale using this method. (1)

15. You have obtained a high yielding variety of tomato. Name and explain the procedure that ensures retention of the desired characteristics repeatedly in large populations of future generations of the tomato crop. **CBSE 2018**

Ans. The procedure that ensures retention of the desired characteristics repeatedly in large populations of future generations of the tomato crop is **micropropagation**. (1)

Healthy explants are taken from the tomato plants and grown in sterile conditions in special nutrient medium. The tomato plants produced from tissue culture are genetically identical to the original plant from which they are grown, so they are called somaclones. Also, through micropropagation more number of tomato can be produced in a short time. (1)

16. (i) Why are the plants raised through micropropagation termed as somaclones?

(ii) Mention two advantages of this technique. **All India 2015**

Ans. (i) The method of producing thousands of plants through tissue culture is called **micropropagation**. The plants produced through micropropagation are genetically identical to the original plant from which they are grown, so they are called as **somaclones**. (1)

(ii) **Advantages of micropropagation** These are as follows

(a) More number of plants can be produced in a short time.

(b) Disease-free plants can be developed from diseased plants.

(c) Seedless plants can be multiplied. (1)

17. Name the source used to produce hepatitis-B vaccine using *r*DNA technology. **Delhi 2015C**

Ans. The source used to produce hepatitis-B vaccine by using *r*DNA technology is yeast. Recombinant DNA technology has allowed the production of antigenic polypeptides of pathogen in bacteria or yeast. Vaccines produced using this approach allows large scale production and hence greater availability for immunisation.

18. Why does *Bt* toxin not kill the bacterium that produces it, but kills the insect that ingests it? **Delhi 2014**

Or Why do the toxic insecticidal proteins secreted by *Bacillus thuringiensis* kill the insect and not the bacteria itself? **Foreign 2010**

Ans. *Bt* toxin does not kill bacteria because in bacteria it exists in inactive state. (1)

When *Bt* toxin is ingested by an insect, it gets converted into its active form due to the alkaline pH of the gut.

The activated toxin binds to the surface of the epithelial cells of the midgut and creates pores. Water enters through these pores and causes swelling and lysis of cells in insect body resulting in their death. (1)

19. How can healthy potato plants be obtained from a desired potato variety which is virus infected? Explain. **Delhi 2014**

Or A potato plant is infected with a virus. Name and explain a method to obtain virus-free potato plants from it. **CBSE 2014C**

Ans. The healthy potato plants can be obtained through meristem culture of virus infected plants. Meristematic tissues are free from virus and other infections. So, they are used as explants and cultured under *in vitro* conditions to produce new healthy plants, by micropropagation or tissue culture.

20. Explain how Eli Lilly, an American company, produced insulin by recombinant DNA technology. **Foreign 2014**

Ans. Steps involved in insulin production by Eli Lilly company are as follows

(i) DNA sequences corresponding to the two polypeptide, A and B-chains of insulin were synthesised *in vitro*.

(ii) They were introduced into plasmid DNA of *E. coli*.
(iii) This bacterium was cloned under suitable conditions.
(iv) The transgene was expressed in the form of polypeptides A and B, secreted into the medium.
(v) They were extracted and combined by creating disulphide bridge to form human insulin.

21. What do '*cry* genes' in *Bacillus thuringiensis* code for? State its importance for cotton crop. **All India 2014C**

Or Name the soil bacterium that produces a protein/chemical that is toxic to insect pests. Show with example that these are encoded by different forms of the genes. **All India 2012**

Ans. '*cry* genes' in *Bacillus thuringiensis* code for toxic insecticidal proteins called Cry proteins which are encoded by different forms of a gene called *cry* gene, e.g. *cry* IAc and *cry* II Ab control the cotton bollworm whereas *cry* IAb controls corn borer. **(1)**

Cry proteins when expressed in cotton crops through genetic engineering confer pest resistance against cotton bollworms and prevent damage. When the larva of these insects feed upon cotton plant parts, the toxin gets activated in their gut, lysing their cells and leads to death, thus making the plants pest resistant. **(1)**

22. Human insulin when synthesised in the body needs to be processed before it can act. Explain giving reasons. **Delhi 2014C**

Or Why is proinsulin so called? How is proinsulin different from functional insulin in humans? **All India 2013, 2012C**

Ans. Human insulin when initially synthesised in human body consists of three peptide chains-A, B and C. The C-peptide is an extra stretch of amino acids joining the A and B-chains. This is called proinsulin or prohormone. It undergoes processing or splicing to release the functional mature insulin that can carry out its normal functions.

During processing, the C-peptide is removed. Only A and B-chains contribute to form the functional insulin.

23. Write any two ways how genetically modified plants are found to be useful? **All India 2014C**

Ans. The genetically modified plants are found to be useful as they

(i) reduce or minimise the use of agrochemicals, i.e. fertilisers, insecticides, herbicides, etc. **(1)**

(ii) reduce post-harvest losses and enhance nutritional value of crop. **(1)**

24. (i) Mention the cause and the body system affected by ADA deficiency in humans.

(ii) Name the vector used for transferring ADA-DNA into the recipient cells in humans. Name the recipient cells. **All India 2012**

Ans. (i) For ADA deficiency, refer to answer no. 17. **(1)**

(ii) Retroviral vector is used to transfer ADA-DNA into the recipient cells of human, i.e. lymphocytes. **(1)**

25. Explain how a hereditary disease can be corrected? Give an example of the first successful attempt made towards correction of such disease. **Delhi 2011**

Ans. Hereditary disease can be corrected by gene therapy. It is a collection of methods that allows correction or replacement of defective genes. The first gene therapy was given in 1990 to a 4 years old girl with Adenosine Deaminase (ADA) deficiency. It is caused due to the deletion of gene for adenosine deaminase.

The treatment involves following steps

(i) Lymphocytes from the blood of patient are grown on culture outside the body.
(ii) A functional ADA, *c*DNA (using a retroviral vector) is then introduced into these lymphocytes.
(iii) Such genetically engineered lymphocytes are returned to the blood of patient.
(iv) Periodic infusion of such genetically engineered lymphocytes is required by the patient.

26. How does recombinant DNA technology help in detecting the presence of mutant gene in cancer patients? **All India 2011C**

Ans. A single-stranded DNA or RNA, tagged with a radioactive molecule (probe) is allowed to hybridise with its complementary DNA in a clone of cells followed by detection using autoradiography. The clone having the mutated gene will not appear on photographic film, because probe will not be complementary with mutated gene, thus helpful in detecting the presence of mutated gene in cancer patients.

27. Why is the introduction of genetically engineered lymphocytes into an ADA deficiency patient not a permanent cure? Suggest a possible permanent cure. **Delhi 2010**

Ans. The genetically engineered lymphocytes have a definite lifespan. Hence, the patient requires periodic infusion of genetically engineered lymphocytes, so the cure is not permanent. The cure can be permanent, if the gene isolated from marrow cells producing ADA is introduced into the cells at early embryonic stages. **(1 + 1)**

28. How did Eli Lilly synthesise the human insulin? Mention one difference between this insulin and the one produced by the human pancreas. **All India 2010**

Ans. (i) For insulin synthesis, refer to answer no. 20. (1)

(ii) Differences between insulin produced by *r*DNA and insulin produced by human pancreas are

Insulin produced by *r*DNA	Insulin produced by human pancreas
It has A and B-polypeptides.	It has three polypeptides. A, B and C-chains before maturing, called the prohormone.
It directly synthesises mature hormone.	It undergoes processing to form mature and functional hormone.

(1)

29. How is *Bt* cotton made to attain resistance against bollworm? **Delhi 2010C**

Ans. *Bt* toxin genes *cry* IAc and *cry* IIAb control cotton bollworms. These genes are isolated from the bacterium and are incorporated into cotton plants.
For action of *Bt* toxin, refer to answer no.18 for methodology.

3 Marks Questions

30. A farmer grew 2 varieties of corn crop in field *A* and *B*. He grew normal corn crops in field *A* and GM corn crops in field *B*. He observed corn borers attacked only in field *A*. To control it, spores of *Bt* were sprayed in field *A*.

(i) Name the gene in the spores responsible for the control of this pest.

(ii) What effect will the spores of *Bt* have on the insect pest?

(iii) How has field *B* developed resistance against this pest? **CBSE SQP 2024**

Ans. (i) *cry* I Ab (1)

(ii) The spores of *Bt* contain crystalline toxin which is inactive; for this crystalline toxin protein to become active it needs alkaline pH, which is present in insect gut. The gut lining is broken down/mid gut epithelial cells become porous/swollen resulting in cell lysis. (1)

(iii) The *Bt*-toxin gene is cloned and inserted into the plant genome by recombinant DNA technology. These genetically modified (GM) plants express the *Bt*-toxin genes and become pest-resistant in field *B*. (1)

31. Lipoprotein lipase deficiency (LPLD) is a genetic disorder in which a person has a defective gene for lipase. This leads to high triglycerides, stomach pain, fat deposits under the skin. It may eventually affect the liver, pancreas and may also cause diabetes. The disorder occurs if a child acquires defective genes from both parents (autosomal recessive). ERT (Enzyme Replacement Treatment) is one of the treatments offered to patients with LPLD. **CBSE SQP 2024**

(i) (a) What procedure is followed in ERT?

(b) What could be one possible drawback of ERT?

(ii) How can LPLD be treated using biotechnology? Elaborate.

Ans. (i) (a) Functional enzyme lipase is given to the patient by injection. (½)

(b) This procedure is not completely curative. (½)

(ii) • The disease can be treated by using gene therapy.

- Gene therapy is a collection of methods that allows correction of a gene defect that has been diagnosed in a child/embryo.
- Here genes are inserted into a person's cells and tissues to treat a disease. Correction of a genetic defect involves delivery of a normal gene into the individual or embryo to take over the function of and compensate for the non-functional gene. (2)

32. "RNA interference has been used to produce transgenic tobacco plants to protect them from the infestation by specific nematodes." Explain the novel strategy exploited by the biotechnologists. **CBSE 2023**

Ans. Refer to text 'Pest resistant plants' on page no. 298.

33. On spraying *Bacillus thuringiensis* on an infected cotton crop field the pests are killed by the toxin, however the toxin although produced by the bacteria does not effect it. Explain giving reason. **CBSE 2023**

Or Why do lepidopterans die when they feed on *Bt* cotton plant? Explain how does it happen? **Delhi 2017**

Ans. *Bt* cotton plants are the transgenic plants that express a *Bacillus thuringiensis* gene called *cry* gene.
This gene, encodes for protein crystals having insecticidal properties against insects of group Lepidoptera, Diptera and Coleoptera. Inside the bacterium, these proteins remain inactive and do not harm the bacteria. However, these inactive crystals can get activated in the alkaline pH present in the gut of insects upon ingestion.

After activation, these crystals can bind to the receptors present on the membranes of gut epithelial cells. Due to this binding, the membrane swells and pores are created on them. These pores lead to bursting of cell and soon the lepidopteran dies.

34. Eli Lilly's contribution for diabetic patients through *r*DNA technology has been over whelmingly accepted. Explain how. **CBSE 2023**

Or With the help of a story board or a flowchart only, explain all the stages of how human insulin is produced through *r*DNA technology? **All India 2021-22 Term-II**

Or Explain the various steps involved in the production of artificial insulin. **All India 2017**

Or Explain how Eli Lilly, an American company produced insulin by recombinant DNA technology? **CBSE 2018 C**

Or Recombinant DNA technology is of great importance in the field of medicine. With the help of a flowchart, show how this technology has been used in preparing genetically engineered human insulin. **Delhi 2015**

Or Explain the application of *r*DNA technology to produce insulin. **Delhi 2015C**

Ans. An American company Eli Lilly produced insulin *via* recombinant DNA technology in 1983.

Insulin production by using recombinant DNA technology is shown in flow chart below

DNA sequences corresponding to the two polypeptides, i.e. A and B-chains of insulin are synthesised *in vitro*

↓

They are introduced into plasmid DNA of *E. coli*

↓

This bacterium is cloned under suitable conditions

↓

The transgene is expressed in the form of polypeptides, i.e. A and B-chains secreted into the medium

↓

They are extracted and combined by creating disulphide bridge to form human insulin.

35. What are Cry proteins? With the help of a suitable example, explain how it acts as a biological pesticide. **Delhi 2021-22 Term-II**

Ans. Cry proteins are poisonous proteins called insecticidal proteins which are secreted in crystal form by *Bacillus thuringiensis* during a specific growth process. **(1)**

Process This toxic protein is coded by different form of a gene called *cry* gene, i.e. *cry* IAc and *cry* II Ab. Incorporating these genes in the plant through genetic engineering provides resistance against insects and acts as biological pesticides, e.g. *Bt* cotton.

It is a genetically modified crop in which the *Bt* genes are incorporated due to which when insects such as lepidopterans, coleopterans and dipterans ingest it, the inactive toxin converted into active toxin due to the alkaline pH of the gut which solubilise the crystal. After activation these crystals bind with the receptors present on the gut epithelial cells. Due to this the membrane swells and pores are created. These pores lead to bursting of cell and soon the insect dies. **(2)**

36. 'Genetically modified plants are considered to be superior to non-genetically modified plants'. Explain giving there reasons why? **All India 2021-22 Term-II**

Or What is GMO? List any five possible advantages of a GMO to a farmer. **All India 2016**

Or Why GMOs are so called ? List the different ways in which GMO plants have benefitted and have become useful to humans. **All India 2020**

Ans. The plants, bacteria, fungi and animals whose genes have been altered are called Genetically Modified Organisms (GMOs). GM plants are useful in many ways. **(1)**

Genetic modification has done the following changes to the phenotypic expression of the plants.

(i) Crops become more tolerant to abiotic stresses like cold, drought, salt and heat.

(ii) Dependence on chemical pesticides has reduced, i.e. pest-resistant crops.

(iii) Helped to reduce post-harvest losses.

(iv) Efficiency of mineral usage increased in plants, preventing early exhaustion of fertility of soil.

(v) Enhanced nutritional value of food, e.g. vitamin-A enriched rice. **(2)**

Concept Enhancer There are several GM crop plants with improved nutritional value of foods and reduce the reliance on chemical pesticides, e.g. golden rice, i.e. vitamin-A enriched rice.

37. (i) Write the difference between the proinsulin and mature insulin.

(ii) How did American company Eli Lilly produce human insulin using *r*DNA technique ? **Delhi 2020**

Ans. (i) Insulin is a hormone secreted by pancreas. It consists of two short polypeptide chains, i.e. chain-A and B, linked together by disulphide bridges. Chain-A contains 21, while chain-B contain 30 amino acids. Whereas, proinsulin contains an extra stretch called C-peptide. This C-peptide is absent in mature insulin as it is removed during maturation. **(1½)**

(ii) Refer to answer no. 20. **(1½)**

38. 'Specific *Bt* toxin gene is incorporated into cotton plant so as to control infestation of bollworm'. Mention the organism from which the gene was isolated and explain its mode of action. **CBSE SQP 2020**

Or How has the study of biotechnology helped in developing pest-resistant cotton crop? Explain. **Delhi 2016C**

Or One of the major contributions of biotechnology is to develop pest-resistant varieties of cotton plants. Explain how it has been made possible. **Foreign 2015**

Or Name the pest that destroys the cotton bolls. Explain the role of *Bacillus thuringiensis* in protecting the cotton crop against the pest to increase the yield. **All India 2013**

Or How is the *Bt* cotton plant created as a GM plant? How is it protected against bollworm infestation? **Delhi 2013C**

Or Name the genes responsible for making *Bt* cotton plants resistant to bollworm attack. How do such plants attain resistance against bollworm attacks? Explain. **Delhi 2012**

Ans. Biotechnology had helped in generating plant varieties against the pests that destroy the cotton balls, i.e. cotton bollworms and cotton borer.

Bt cotton is created by using some strains of a bacterium, *Bacillus thuringiensis* (*Bt* is short form).

(i) This bacterium produces protein that kills certain insects such as lepidopterans (tobacco budworm and armyworm), coleopterans (beetles) and dipterans (flies and mosquitoes).

(ii) *Bacillus thuringiensis* forms protein crystals during a particular phase of their growth. These crystals contain a toxic insecticidal protein.

(iii) *Bt* toxin protein exists as inactive protoxin in bacteria, but once an insect ingests this inactive toxin, it is converted into an active form due to the alkaline pH of the gut, which solubilises the crystals.

(iv) The activated toxin binds to the surface of midgut epithelial cells and creates pores that cause cell swelling and lysis leading to death of insect.

(v) Specific *Bt* toxin genes were isolated from *Bacillus thuringiensis* and incorporated into several crop plants.

(vi) Most *Bt* toxins are insect-group specific. The toxin is coded by a gene named *cry*. For example, the proteins encoded by the genes *cry* IAc and *cry* IIAb control the cotton bollworms and *cry* IAb controls corn borer. **(1/2 × 6)**

39. Name the technique and the property of plant cells that can to grow somaclones of certain desired variety of apple. Explain how somaclones of apple can be obtained in the lab, so as to get the desired variety on a large scale. **All India 2019**

Or How are somaclones cultured from explants in *in vitro* conditions? Why are somaclones so called? **All India 2019**

Ans. Micropropagation is the technique of tissue culture that can help to grow somaclones. Somaclones cultured from explants are grown in following steps

(i) The explant is grown in a petridish/test tube under sterile conditions in a special nutrient medium.

(ii) The medium must contain carbon source like sugar, inorganic salts, vitamins, minerals, amino acids, growth regulators like auxins and cytokinins.

(iii) The medium should be replaced regularly to restore nutrients in it. **(2)**

Since, all plants produced by tissue culture are genetically identical to the original plant from which they are cultured, they are called as somaclones. Three food plants produced by micropropagation are tomato, banana, apple, etc. **(1)**

40. A person is born with a weakened immune system due to deficiency of an enzyme which is a hereditary disease. Suggest a technique for complete cure for this disease. Identify the deficient enzyme and explain the technique used for its cure. **CBSE SQP 2018**

Ans. (i) The deficiency of Adenosine Deaminase (ADA) may cause the weakening of immune system. **(1)**

(ii) It can be treated by gene therapy technique. **(1)**

(iii) In this technique, the isolated lymphocytes from bone marrow of the patient are cultured first. The functional ADA gene (*c*DNA) is introduced into the cultured lymphocytes by using suitable vectors. These lymphocytes are then introduced back into bone marrow of the patient. These then start producing the enzyme needed. Permanent care is achieved by introducing ADA complementary DNA at embryonic stage. **(1)**

41. *cry*IAb is introduced in a plant to prevent infestation by corn borer.

(i) What is the resultant plant referred as?

(ii) Summarise the action of the gene introduced. **CBSE SQP 2018**

Ans. (i) Corn borer is an insect, which infests the corn plants. So, referred plant is *Bt* corn, which is obtained by the introduction of *cry* I Ab gene in this plant. **(1)**

(ii) Refer to the answer no. 33. **(2)**

42. Why is molecular diagnosis preferred over conventional methods? Name any two techniques giving one use of each. **Delhi 2016C**

Ans. Using conventional methods of diagnosis (serum and urine analysis), early detection of diseases is not possible. To overcome this problem, some molecular diagnosis techniques were developed that provide early detection of diseases.

These are as follows

(i) Polymerase Chain Reaction (PCR) helps in early detection of diseases or pathogens by the amplification of their nucleic acid. PCR can amplify nucleic acids of pathogens even when their concentration is very low.

This technique can be used for detecting HIV in suspected AIDS patients, genetic mutations in suspected cancer patients and in identifying genetic disorders. **(2)**

(ii) Enzyme Linked Immunosorbent Assay (ELISA) is based on the principle of antigen-antibody interaction. Infection by pathogen can be detected by the presence of antigens (proteins, glycoproteins, etc.) or by detecting the antibodies synthesised against the pathogen. **(1)**

43. Explain enzyme replacement therapy to treat adenosine deaminase deficiency. Mention two disadvantages of this procedure. **All India 2016**

Ans. In enzyme replacement therapy, the patient is given functional ADA (Adenosine Deaminase) by injection. **(1)**

Refer to answer no. 25 for methodology. **(1)**

Disadvantages

(i) The patient does not completely recover from the disease.

(ii) It needs periodic injections of the enzyme to the patients. **(1)**

44. People are quite apprehensive to use GM crops. Give three arguments in support of GM crops so as to convince the people in favour of such crops. **Outside Delhi 2016C**

Ans. The GMOs are the plants, animals, bacteria, etc., whose genes have been altered by genetic manipulation. They were created because

(i) The agrochemicals used in agriculture are too costly.

(ii) Excess use of chemicals in field adversely affects our environment by causing pollution. GMOs are beneficial in many ways. **(1½)**

Advantages of GMOs are as follows

(i) Enhanced tolerance against abiotic stresses, such as cold, drought, salt, heat.

(ii) Reduced dependence on chemical pesticides.

(iii) Reduced post-harvest losses.

(iv) Increased efficiency of mineral usage by plants. **(1½)**

Concept Enhancer Viruses are also used as vectors to transfer healthy genes portions of genes as they attack their hosts and introduce their genetic material into the host cell as part of their replication cycle.

45. Differentiate between somaclones and somatic hybrids. Give one example of each. **All India 2016**

Ans. The plants, which are genetically similar to the parent plant are called **somaclones**, e.g. banana, sugarcane, etc. The process of fusion of protoplast of somatic cells obtained from different varieties or species of a plant on a suitable nutrient medium *in vitro* to develop a hybrid, is known as **somatic hybridisation**.

The hybrids so produced are called **somatic hybrids,** e.g. pomato is a somatic hybrid produced by the fusion of tomato and potato protoplasts. **(2 + 1)**

46. Suggest and describe a technique through which a virus-free healthy plant can be obtained from a diseased sugarcane plant. **Delhi 2015C, All India 2014 C**

Or Scientists have succeeded in recovering healthy sugarcane plants from a diseased one.

(i) Name the part of the plant used as explant by scientists.

(ii) Describe the procedure the scientists followed to recover the healthy parts.

(iii) Name the technology used for crop improvement. **All India 2011**

Ans. The virus-free healthy sugarcane plant can be obtained through meristem culture of diseased plant; as meristematic tissues are free from viruses. They can be used as explants for micropropagation. **(1)**

Steps in Meristem Culture

(i) The shoot tip explants are grown in nutrient medium in either a test tube or a petridish, under aseptic/sterile *in vitro* conditions.

(ii) The nutrient medium should have carbon source, inorganic salts, vitamins, amino acids and growth regulators like auxin and cytokinin in proper defined ratio.

(iii) The plantlets, thus obtained are later shifted to nurseries, under observation and finally to fields. **(2)**

47. Mention the cause of ADA deficiency in humans. How has genetic engineering helped patients suffering from it? **Outside Delhi 2015C**

Or

(i) Explain the effect of deletion of the gene for ADA in an individual.

(ii) How does the gene therapy help in this case? **All India 2010C**

Ans. (i) Deletion of the gene for ADA in an individual leads to ADA deficiency disorder. Adenosine Deaminase (ADA) enzyme is crucial for immune system to function. **(1)**

(ii) Gene therapy is helpful in the treatment of ADA deficiency.

Refer to answer no. 25 for methodology. **(2)**

48. Describe any three potential applications of genetically modified plants. **All India 2015**

Ans. Potential applications of genetically modified plants are

(i) Nutritional enhancement, e.g. vitamin-A enriched rice.

(ii) Stress tolerant crops became more tolerant to abiotic stresses such as cold, drought, etc.

(iii) Creation of tailor made plants by using GM plants to supply alternative resources of industries in the form of starches, biofuels, etc. **(1 × 3)**

5 Marks Questions

49. (i) Name the nematode (scientific name) that infects the roots of tobacco plant and reduce its yield.

(ii) Name the vector that is used to introduce nematode-specific genes into the host plant (tobacco).

(iii) How do sense and anti-sense RNAs function?

(iv) Why could parasite not survive in a transgenic tobacco plant? **CBSE 2024 (Set-II)**

Ans. (i) The nematode, *Meloidegyne incognitia* infects the tobacco roots and reduces its yield. **(1)**

(ii) The vector that is used to introduced nematode-specific genes into the host plant (tobacco) is *Agrobacterium tumefaciens.* **(1)**

(iii) Sense and antisense RNA function in the following ways

1. **Sense RNA** It corresponds directly to the coding strand of DNA and carries the same sequence as the *m*RNA.
2. **Anti-sense RNA** It has a complementary sequence to the sense RNA or *m* RNA. It is synthesised to target specific *m*RNA molecules.

The two RNA's being complementary to each other formed a double stranded RNA (*ds*RNA) that initiated RNAi and thus, silences the specific target *m*RNA leading to degradation of target *m*RNA. **(1½)**

(iv) Parasites may not survive in a transgenic tobacco plant due to the expression of nematode-specific genes introduced into the plant. These genes may produce anti-sense and sense RNAs that interfere with the parasite's life cycle, development or ability to infect the plant. The transgenic plant therefore got itself protected from the parasite. Additionally, transgenic tobacco may exhibit enhanced resistance mechanism which can inhibit parasite infection and survival. **(1½)**

50. Insects in the lepidopteran group lay eggs on maize crops. The larvae on hatching feed on maize leaf and tender cob. In order to arrest the spread of three such lepidopteran pests, *Bt* maize crops were introduced in an experimental field. A study was carried out to see which of the three species of lepidopteran pests was most susceptible to *Bt* genes and its product.

The lepidopteran pests were allowed to feed on the same *Bt* maize crops grown on 5 fields (*A-E*). The graph below shows the leaf area damaged by these three pests after feeding on maize leaves for five days.

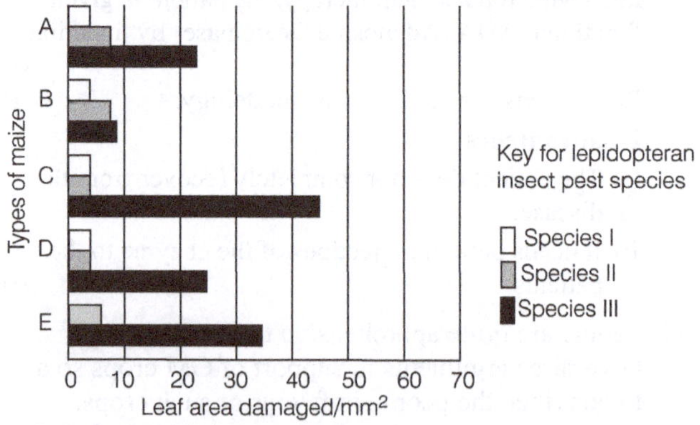

Insect gut pH was recorded as 10, 8 and 6 for species I, II and III, respectively. **CBSE SQP 2023**

(i) Evaluate the efficacy of the *Bt* crop on the feeding habits of the three species of stem borer and suggest which species is least susceptible to *Bt* toxin.

(ii) Which species is most susceptible to *Bt* maize? Explain why.

(iii) Using the given information, suggest why similar effect was not seen in the three insect species?

Ans. (i) Species III is least susceptible. (1)

(ii) Species I and II are more susceptible to *Bt* maize. This is because, the gut pH of species I and II is alkaline which convert the *Bt* toxin protoxins into an active form in the gut which solubilises the toxin crystals. The activated toxin binds to the surface of midgut epithelial cells and create pores that cause cell swelling and lysis and eventually cause death of the insect. (2)

(iii) Insect species I and II have alkaline gut pH, which solubilises the insecticidal protein crystals of protoxin and makes it active. Species III has an acidic gut pH and the protoxin continues to remain in an inactive form doing no harm to insect species III. Thus, similar effect was not seen in the three insect species. (2)

51. (i) Explain the different steps carried out in Polymerase Chain Reaction (PCR) and the specific roles of the enzymes used.

(ii) Mention application of PCR in the field of

(a) Biotechnology

(b) Diagnostics **All India 2020**

Ans. (i) Refer to text on page no. 281-282 of Ch-9.

(ii) Application of PCR in

(a) **Biotechnology** In DNA fingerprinting, where PCR is used to synthesise DNA for fingerprinting assays.

(b) **Diagnostics** PCR is used in early detection of a disease or pathogen, e.g. detect HIV in suspected AIDS patients, detect mutations in genes in suspected cancer patients, etc.

52. Explain the application of biotechnology in producing *Bt* cotton. **Delhi 2014**

Ans. For the use of biotechnology to develop *Bt* cotton, refer to answer no. 38.

Common Mistakes Commonly students get confused that *Bt* in *Bt* crops stands for Biotechnology, but instead it stands for *Bacillus thuringiensis* from which the *cry* genes were isolated.

53. (i) Name the technology that has helped scientists to propagate the desired crops on a large scale in a short duration. List the steps carried out to propagate the crops by the said technique.

(ii) How are somatic hybrids obtained? **Delhi 2014**

Ans. (i) Tissue culture is the technique that has helped scientists to propagate plants with desirable traits on a large scale, in short duration. Since, large number of plants are propagated through this culture, it is also referred to as micropropagation. The steps involved in this technique are

(a) Explants are derived from any part of plant (to be propagated), i.e. tips of carrot.

(b) Explants are grown in sterile conditions in special nutrient medium to regenerate complete plants.

(c) Nutrient media must contain a carbon source (such as sucrose), organic salts, vitamins, amino acids and phytohormones, i.e. auxin and cytokinin.

(d) Hence, propagation is achieved for a large number of plants under *in vitro* conditions.

(e) All the plants obtained by tissue culture are called somaclones, since they are genetically identical to each other as well as to their parent plant. (3)

(ii) Somatic hybrids are obtained by the method of somatic hybridisation. In this method, the naked protoplasts of cells of two plants are hybridised. Protoplasts are isolated by dissolving cell wall and fused to get a hybrid protoplast. The fused nucleus is called heterokaryon that grows further to form a a new plant. The plants thus formed are called somatic hybrids. (2)

54. (i) Name the source from which insulin was extracted earlier. Why is this insulin no more in use by diabetic people?

(ii) Explain the process of synthesis of insulin by Eli Lilly company. Name the technique used by the company.

(iii) How is the insulin produced by human body different from the insulin produced by the above mentioned company? **All India 2011**

Ans. (i) Earlier insulin was extracted from pancreas of slaughtered pigs and cattle animals.

Insulin obtained from these sources caused some allergy and some other reactions due to which it is no more in use by diabetic people. (1)

(ii) For production of human insulin by Eli Lilly company, refer to answer no. 20. (3)

(iii) For difference in insulin produced by pancreas and by using *r*DNA technology, refer to answer no. 28 (ii). (1)

TOPIC 2

Transgenic Animals and Ethical Issues

Transgenic Animals

These are animals that have had their DNA manipulated to possess and express an extra (foreign) gene. Using *r*DNA technology many transgenic rats, rabbits, pigs, sheeps, cows and fish have been produced.

Common reasons for developing transgenic animals include

Study of Normal Physiology and Development

Transgenic animals can be used to understand regulation of genes, their effect on the normal functions of the body and its development, e.g. study of growth factors.

Study of Diseases

Transgenic animals can be used for studying genes, which are responsible for causing diseases in human and their treatments, e.g. transgenic models have been developed for many diseases like cancer, cystic fibrosis, Alzheimer's disease.

Biological Products

These can be produced by introducing the portion of DNA, which codes for a particular biological product into transgenic animals.

For example,

- Human protein (α-1 antitrypsin) is used to treat emphysema.
- The first transgenic cow (1997), Rosie produced human protein enriched milk (2.4 g/L). This milk contained the human α-lactalbumin and was more nutritionally balanced for human babies than natural cow milk.

Vaccine Safety

It can be ensured by testing vaccines on transgenic mice before being used in humans, e.g. polio vaccine. It can replace the use of monkeys to test the safety of batches of the vaccine.

Chemical Safety Testing

- It is also known as toxicity/safety testing and can be done by using transgenic animals. It is similar to the procedure used for testing toxicity of drugs.
- The animals are made to carry genes, which make them more sensitive to the toxic substances than non-transgenic animals.
- When exposed to toxic substances, their effects are studied in a short time.

Ethical Issues

Some of the ethical issues regarding the applications of biotechnology are as follows

- Manipulation of living organisms by human race can be unethical and should not go unregulated. The genetic modification of organisms can have unpredictable results when such organisms are introduced into an ecosystem.
- The modification/usage of living organisms for public services (food/medicine for example) has also created problems with patents granted for the same.
- There is growing public concern that certain companies are being granted patents for the products and technologies that make use of genetic materials like plant and other biological resource that have long been developed by the farmers and indigenous people of a specific region.
- In order to control these issues, the Indian government has set-up an organisation named **Genetic Engineering Approval Committee** (GEAC), which makes decisions regarding the validity of GM research and the safety of introducing GM organisms for public services.

Biopatent

It is a set of exclusive rights granted by a government to the inventors or their assignee to prevent others from commercial use of their invention. When patent is granted for biological entities and for products derived from them, they are called **biopatents**.

Controversy Regarding Biopatent of Basmati Rice

- Rice is being used since thousands of years in Asian countries, of which 200000 varieties are in India alone.
- Basmati rice is famous for its aroma and flavour, whose 27 varieties are cultivated in India.
- An American company in 1997, got patent rights for Basmati rice through the US Patent and Trademark Office and was allowed to sell a 'new' variety of Basmati

in the US and abroad. So, other people selling Basmati rice could be restricted by the patent.

- This new variety of Basmati was derived from Indian farmer's varieties.
- Indian Basmati was crossed with semi-dwarf varieties and claimed as an invention or novelty.
- Besides Basmati rice, unauthorised attempts were made for patent of turmeric and neem (Indian traditional herbal medicines).

If attention is not paid immediately to counter these patent applications, other countries/individuals may encash our rich legacy.

Biopiracy

- It refers to the use of bioresources by multinational companies and other organisations without proper authorisation (and without any payment) from the countries and people concerned.
- The majority of industrialised nations are financially rich, but poor in biodiversity and traditional knowledge, in comparison to developing and underdeveloped countries.
- Traditional knowledge related to bioresources can be exploited to develop modern applications and to save time, efforts and expenditure.
- Due to these reasons, there has been growing realisation of the injustice, inadequate compensation and benefit sharing between developed and developing countries.
- Some nations are developing laws to prevent such unauthorised exploitation of their bioresources and traditional knowledge.
- The Indian Parliament has recently cleared the second amendment of the Indian Patents Bill. It takes consideration of such issues including patent terms, emergency provisions, research and development initiative.

PYQs Previous Years' Questions

1 Mark Questions

Very Short Answer Type Questions

1. Which one of the following transgenic animals is being used to test the safety of the polio vaccine? **CBSE 2024 (Set-I)**

(a) Sheep (b) Goat
(c) Pig (d) Mice

Ans. (d) Transgenic mice are being used to test the safety of the polio vaccine.

2. Name the first transgenic cow developed and state the improvement in the quality of the product produced by it. **CBSE SQP 2019**

Ans. Rosie was the first transgenic cow. It is important because it produces human protein enriched milk (2.4 g/L). It contained the human α-lactalbumin and was nutritionally more balanced for human babies than natural cow's milk.

3. What is biopiracy? **Delhi 2017**

Ans. Biopiracy refers to the use of bioresources by multinational companies and other organisations without proper authorisation from people and countries concerned.

4. What are transgenic animals? Give an example. **All India 2016**

Ans. Animals with manipulated DNA to possess and express the characters of an extra (foreign) gene are known as transgenic animals, e.g. transgenic rats, rabbits, pigs, etc. (½ + ½)

5. Mention two objectives of setting up GEAC by our government. **All India 2015**

Ans. GEAC is an organisation setup by the Indian government to make decisions pertaining with genetic research and experiments. The two objectives of setting up Genetic Engineering Approval Committee (GEAC) by the Indian government are

(i) To make decisions regarding the validity of GM research. (½)

(ii) To make decisions regarding the safety of introducing GM organisms for public services. (½)

2 Marks Questions

6. Why are certain animals called 'transgenic'? Give an example of such an animals that is being used for testing the vaccine safety for a specific human disease. Name the disease. **Delhi 2020**

Ans. Certain animals are called transgenic because their DNA is manipulated to possess and express an useful and extra (foreign) gene. **(1)**

Transgenic mice are being used for testing the vaccine safety for the polio disease, before being used in humans. It can replace the use of monkeys to test the safety of batches of the vaccine. **(1)**

7. What are transgenic animals ? How was the first transgenic cow found to be more useful than the normal cow, for humans? **Delhi 2020**

Ans. Transgenic animals are animals that have had their genome, i.e. DNA manipulated to possess and express a useful and extra (foreign) gene, e.g. transgenic cow, transgenic rat, etc.

The transgenic cow 'Rosie' produced human protein enriched milk (2.4 gm/L). It contained the human α-lactalbumin and was nutritionally more balanced for human babies than normal cow's milk. **(1+1)**

8. What is biopiracy? State the initiative taken by the Indian Parliament against it. **Delhi 2014**

Ans. For biopiracy, refer to answer no. 2. **(1)**

The Indian Parliament has cleared a second amendment of Indian Patents Bill as an initiative step against biopiracy. This bill considers issues including patent terms, emergency provisions as well as research and development initiative. **(1)**

9. How have transgenic animals proved to be beneficial in

(i) production of biological products?

(ii) chemical safety testing? **Delhi 2014, 2013**

Ans. (i) The transgenic animals have proved to be beneficial in the production of biological products like human protein α-1 antitrypsin (by coding genes for that protein only), for the treatment of emphysema and production of human protein (α-lactalbumin) enriched milk by transgenic cow, i.e. Rosie.

This milk was more nutritionally balanced for human babies than natural cow's milk. **(1)**

(ii) Transgenic animals are studied for testing toxicity of drugs and other chemicals, as they carry genes that make them more sensitive to toxic substances. **(1)**

3 Marks Questions

10. (i) What are transgenic animals?

(ii) Name the first transgenic cow and state its importance. **CBSE 2024 (Set-I)**

Ans. (i) Refer to page no. 310.

(ii) The first transgenic cow was named 'Rosie' Refer to page no. 310

11. The Indian government refuted the attempt by a Multinational Company (MNC) to patent the antiseptic property of curcumin derived from turmeric. Analyse the unethical practice adopted by the MNC, state its implications and suggest provisions in the Indian law to prevent such malpractices. **CBSE SQP 2019**

Ans. The use of bioresources by multinational companies and other organisations without proper authorisation from the countries and people concerned without any payment is termed as biopiracy.

The unauthorised exploitation of bioresources by MNCs results in economical loss, infringement of traditional knowledge and injustice to the concerned region and its inhabitants.

Indian Parliament has recently passed the 2nd amendment of Indian patents bill, which has empowered India to prevent unauthorised exploitation of our bio-resources and traditional knowledge by other countries. This bill also considers patent terms and initiates research development in this field.

12. (i) What are transgenic animals?

(ii) Name the transgenic animal having the largest number amongst all the existing transgenic animals.

(iii) Mention any three purposes for which these animals are produced. **CBSE 2018 C**

Ans. (i) **Transgenic animals** refer to text on page no. 310. **(1)**

(ii) Transgenic mice have the largest number (over 95%) amongst all the existing transgenic animals. **(1)**

(iii) For purpose of producing transgenic animals, refer to text on page no. 310. **(1)**

13. Biopiracy should be prevented. State why and how. **All India 2011**

Ans. Biopiracy should be prevented because

(i) The countries and people concerned are not given adequate compensatory payment. **(1)**

(ii) The countries/people also lose their right to grow and use breeding experiments to improve the other varieties of the same species. **(1)**

It may be prevented by implementing specific laws that take into consideration all the biopatents and biopiracy related issues. **(1)**

Case Based/Source Based/Passage Based Questions (Based on Complete Chapter)

1. Read the following paragraph and answer the questions that follow

There are two different farm lands, one where *Bt* cotton crop was cultivated and the other where non *Bt* cotton crop (indigenous) was cultivated. Farmers responsible for this experimental cultivation were free to use the farming practices of their choice. During the cultivation period, the data was collected with respect to the amount of pesticide use, water required for irrigation and at harvesting time, the crop productivity. Based on the data collected, a bar graph was plotted which is shown below.

All India 2021-22 Term-II

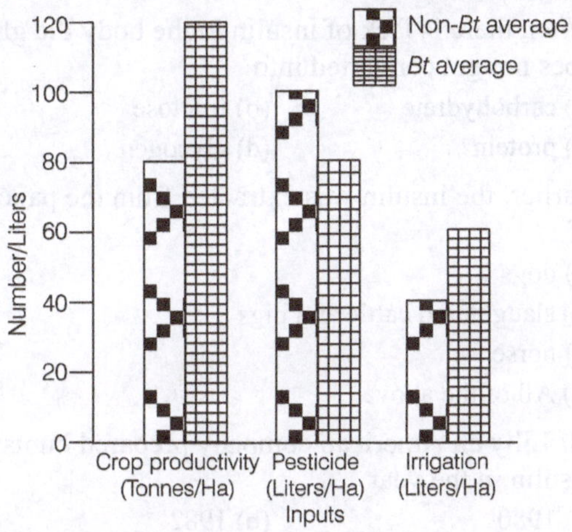

Answer the following questions

(i) Write your interpretation with reason, on the basis of the three parameters plotted in the graph.

(ii) Which one of the crops would you like to cultivate in your farm and why?

(iii) Which one out of these two crops would a farmer from Rajasthan like to cultivate and why?

Ans. (i) On comparing non-*Bt* average and *Bt* average crops, the following three inferences can be drawn.

(a) With regard to crop productivity, the number of *Bt* average crops was found to be more than that of non-*Bt* since being genetically modified, the latter were destroyed by cotton bollworms.

(b) Growing *Bt* crops require less conventional or chemical insecticides because of genetic modifications in them, whereas in non-*Bt* crops the use of pesticides is in higher amount.

(c) Genetically modified crops (*Bt* here) require more water for irrigation when compared to normal or non-*Bt* crops, since they show resistance to biotic and abiotic stress. **(2)**

(ii) It is better to cultivate *Bt* crops in our farms as they provide many advantages such as

- Better yield/high productivity
- Resistance to pests and insects
- Control of soil pollution **(2)**

(iii) A farmer from Rajasthan would like to cultivate non-*Bt* crops as it requires less water for irrigation (since Rajasthan is a state with less water availability). It, however, leads to increased crop production, thus increased income. **(1)**

2. Read the following paragraph and answer the questions that follow

Biotechnology revolves around the "gene of interest" with an objective to open various avenues for human welfare in health, medicine, pharma, agriculture, etc., using different techniques, tools and processes. One of the break throughs of biotechnology in medicine is the gene therapy.

Delhi 2021-22 Term-II

(i) Name the human disease for which the gene therapy was used for the first time.

(ii) Explain the steps of gene therapy carried to cure the disease using the lymphocytes of the patient. Why is this therapy not a permanent cure of the disease?

(iii) Write the possible permanent cure of the disease by the gene therapy that is in progress.

Ans. (i) The gene therapy was first given to a 4 years old girl with Adenosine Deaminase (ADA) deficiency. **(1)**

(ii) Refer to text on page no. 299. **(2)**

(iii) Refer to text on page no. 299. **(2)**

3. Read the following paragraph and answer the questions that follow

GM crops especially *Bt* crops are known to have higher resistance to pest attacks. To substantiate this an experimental study was conducted in 4 different farmlands growing *Bt* and non-*Bt* cotton crops. The farmlands had the same dimensions, fertility and were under similar climatic conditions. The histogram below shows the usage of pesticides on *Bt* crops and non-*Bt* crops in these farmlands.

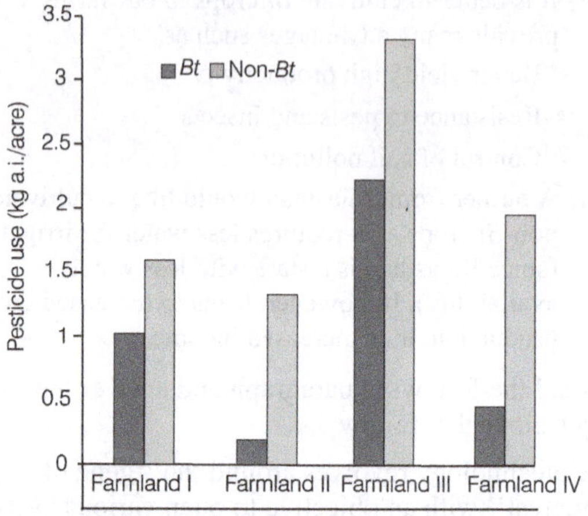

(i) Which of the above 4 farmlands has successfully applied the concepts of biotechnology to show better management practices and use of agrochemicals? If you had to cultivate, which crop would you prefer (*Bt* or non- *Bt*) and why?

(ii) Cotton bollworms were introduced in another experimental study on the above farmlands wherein no pesticide was used. Explain what effect would a *Bt* and non- *Bt* crop have on the pest. **CBSE SQP 2021-22 Term-II**

Ans. (i) From the given four farmlands, the farm land II has successfully applied the concepts of biotechnology to show better management practices and use of agrochemicals. Because their pesticide use is the least out of the four.

If we were given preference between *Bt* and non-*Bt* crops, we will cultivate *Bt*-crop.

This is because use of pesticide is highly reduced for *Bt* crop. **(1 + 1)**

(ii) If cotton bollworms were introduced in the experimental farmland, they will show following effects

(a) **Effect on *Bt* crop** In *Bt* crop, a *cry* gene has been introduced from bacterium, *Bacillus thuringiensis* (*Bt*) which causes synthesis of a toxic protein. This protein becomes active in the alkaline gut of bollworm feeding on cotton. Thus, punches holes in their gut lining, causing death of the insect.

(b) **Effect on non-*Bt* crop** A non-*Bt* crop will have no effect on the cotton bollworm. The yield of cotton will decrease and non-*Bt* crop will succumb to pest attack. **(3)**

4. Read the following paragraph and answer the questions that follow

Biotechnology had an immense impact in the area of health care too by enabling the mass production of safe and more effective therapeutic drugs. It has been estimated that currently about 30 recombinant therapeutics have been approved for human use over the world. In India alone, 12 of these are presently being marketed.

(i) When there is lack of insulin in the body the glucose does not get converted into

(a) carbohydrate (b) fructose
(c) protein (d) glycogen

(ii) Earlier, the insulin was extracted from the pancreas of

(a) dogs
(b) slaughtered cattle and pigs
(c) horse
(d) All of the above

(iii) Eli Lilly an American company prepared human insulin in the year

(a) 1980 (b) 1982
(c) 1983 (d) 1984

(iv) The type of bond found in the structure of insulin is

(a) hydrogen bond (b) covalent bond
(c) disulfide bond (d) All of these

(v) Which of the following peptide is not found in mature insulin?

(a) A-peptide (b) B-peptide
(c) C-peptide (d) Both (a) and (c)

Ans. (i)-(d), (ii)-(b), (iii)-(c), (iv)-(c), (v)-(c)

5. Read the following paragraph and answer the questions that follow

Scientists have long been altering the genes of food crops to boost food production and to make crops more pest or cold resistant. Proponents of GMO says that these crops are environmental friendly and safe to eat. However, critics claim that GM crops require increased amount of pesticides and herbicides and thus these damage the environment.

(i) Giving an example of *Bt* cotton, prove the critics point invalid.

(ii) GM crops are designed to develop natural resistance from insect and pests. Name some crop which are modified using *Bacillus thuringiensis,* except *Bt* cotton.

(iii) Name the Indian organisation which make decisions regarding the validity of GM research.

(iv) Name two Indian crops which were biopirated by some multinational companies.

Ans. (i) *Bt* cotton produces toxin proteins that kill certain insects like lepidopterans, coleopterans and dipterans. Thus, this crop does not require the application of herbicides and pesticides. **(2)**

(ii) *Bt*-tomato, *Bt*-corn, *Bt*-soyabean, etc. **(1)**

(iii) Genetic Engineering Approval Committee (GEAC).

(iv) Basmati rice, turmeric and neem. **(1)**

6. Read the following paragraph and answer the questions that follow

Anil's father is suffering from high blood sugar. Doctors had advised regular insulin injections, which were declined by the family due to objections on the process used in insulin production. The doctor explained the process now used in insulin production and its advantages.

(i) Why did the family decline the use of insulin injection despite its necessity ?

(ii) Name the process by which insulin is produced now-a-days and the organism involved.

(iii) State one similar example wherein a person born with a hereditary disease can be cured *via* corrective therapy.

(iv) What values are shown by the doctor?

Ans. (i) Earlier the insulin was produced by slaughtering of animals like pigs. They also cause allergic reactions in patients. The family declined because they were against such process and products. **(1)**

(ii) The process is recombinant DNA technology and organism used is *E. coli.* **(1)**

(iii) A person born with a hereditary disease can be cured using corrective therapy *via* gene therapy. This involves correction of gene defect. **(1)**

(iv) The doctor is responsible, aware of recent developments in science and honest towards his duty. **(1)**

CHAPTER TEST

Mark Questions

Multiple Choice Questions

1 Consumption of which one of the following foods can prevent the kind of blindness associated with vitamin-A deficiency?
(a) *Flavr Savr* tomato
(b) Canolla
(c) Golden rice
(d) *Bt* brinjal

2 *Bacillus thuringiensis* forms protein crystals which contain insecticidal protein. This protein
(a) does not kill the carrier bacterium which is itself resistant to this toxin
(b) binds with epithelial cells of midgut of the insect pest ultimately killing it
(c) is coded by several genes including the gene *cry*
(d) is activated by acid pH of the foregut of the insect pest

3 Which one of the following bacteria is used for the production of transgenic plants?
(a) *Escherichia coli*
(b) *Pseudomonas*
(c) *Staphylococcus aureus*
(d) *Agrobacterium tumefaciens*

4 The first clinical gene therapy was given for treating
(a) diabetes mellitus
(b) chickenpox
(c) rheumatoid arthritis
(d) adenosine deaminase deficiency

5 Which of the following techniques is based on the principle of antigen-antibody interaction?
(a) PCR (b) ELISA
(c) Recombinant DNA technology
(d) Gene therapy

6 Transgenic animals can be used to
(a) study normal physiology
(b) study vaccine safety
(c) to produce biological products
(d) All of the above

Assertion-Reason Type Questions

Direction (Q. Nos. 7-10) *In the questions given below two statements an* ***Assertion*** *and a* ***Reason*** *are given. Give the appropriate response as*
(a) If both A and R are true and R is the correct explanation of A
(b) If both A and R are true, but R is not the correct explanation of A
(c) If A is true, but R is false
(d) If A is false, but R is true

7 **Assertion** Restriction endonucleases are also called 'molecular scissors'.
Reason When fragments generated by restriction endonucleases are mixed, they join together due to their sticky ends.

8 **Assertion** All endonucleases cut DNA at specific sites.
Reason Endonucleases were discovered from viruses.

9 **Assertion** Use of chitinase enzyme is necessary for isolation of DNA from fungal cells.
Reason Fungal cell wall is made up of chitin and chitinase is able to digest it.

10 **Assertion** ADA deficiency disorder is caused due to the excessive synthesis of gene for adenosine deaminase.
Reason It affects the human immune system.

2/3 Marks Questions

11 Is the use *Bacillus thuringiensis* limited to cotton plant only? How is it beneficial to other crops?

12 What is RNA interference? Give any one application of RNA interference.

13 Name the source used to produce hepatitis-B vaccine using *r*DNA technology.

14 Write about the amendment passed by the Indian Parliament regarding patent issues.

15 With respect to understanding disease, discuss the importance of transgenic animal models.

16 How is DNA recombinant technology helpful in detecting the presence of mutated genes in the cancer patients?

17 Refer to the diagram given below and answer the questions that follows

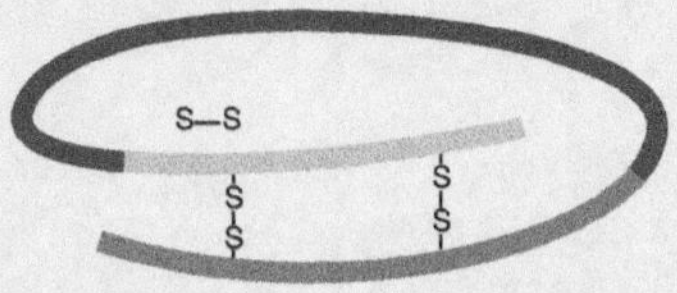

(i) Identify the structure shown above in the diagram, as pro-insulin or insulin.

(ii) What is the major difference between insulin and pro-insulin?

(iii) What is humulin?

05 Marks Questions

18 Highlight five areas, where biotechnology has influenced our lives.

19 Correct the following statement by giving reasons.

'The mature insulin molecules consists of three short polypeptides chains.'

20 Compare and contrast the advantages and disadvantages of the production of genetically modified crops. How have the GM crops affected the lives of farmers as well as others?

21 Write a self-explanatory note on biopatent.

22 (i) Which insects are killed by *Bacillus thuringiensis*?

(ii) The *Bt* binds to which cells?

(iii) In which plants *Bt* toxin is used?

23 Many proteins are secreted in their inactive form. This is also true for many toxic proteins produced by microorganisms.

Explain, how the mechanism is useful for the organism producing the toxin?

24 What is meant by the term biopesticide? Name and explain the mode of action of a popular biopesticide.

25 Correct the following statement by giving reasons.

'The mature insulin molecule consists of three short polypeptide chains'.

26 Diagrammatically represent the experimental steps in cloning and expressing a human gene (say the gene for growth hormone) into a bacterium like *E. coli*.

Answers

1. (c)	**2.** (b)	**3.** (d)	**4.** (d)	**5.** (b)
6. (d)	**7.** (b)	**8.** (c)	**9.** (a)	**10.** (d)

11

Organisms and Populations

TREND ANALYSIS 3 YEARS

Average No. of Questions Across all Sets

Topic	Types of Questions	2024	2023	2020
TOPIC 01 Population	1 Mark	0	1	0
	2 Marks	0	0	0
	3 Marks	0	0	1
	4 Marks (Case Based)	0	0	0
	5 Marks	0	0	0
TOPIC 02 Population Interactions	1 Mark	1	3	0
	2 Marks	0	2	1
	3 Marks	0	0	1
	4 Marks (Case Based)	0	0	0
	5 Marks	0	0	0

TOPIC 1

Population

Population can be defined as the total number of individuals of a species in a specific geographical area, which can interbreed under natural conditions to produce fertile offsprings and function as a unit of biotic community.

Population Attributes

There are certain characteristics of a population. Some of them are as follows

1. Population Size or Density

It is the number of individuals of a species per unit area or volume at a given time.

Population Density (*PD*)

$$= \frac{\text{Number of individuals in a region } (N)}{\text{Size of unit area in the region } (S)}$$

or $PD = \frac{N}{S}$

Although total number is the most appropriate measure of population density. In some cases, it is difficult to determine.

So, in these cases, the per cent cover or biomass is a more appropriate measure of the population size, e.g. 200 *Parthenium* plants and a single huge banyan tree. In this case, the banyan tree produces much more biomass.

2. Birth Rate or Natality

It is expressed as the number of birth per 1000 individuals of a population per year, e.g. if in a pond, there were 20 lotus plants last year and through reproduction, 8 new plants are added then,

$$\text{Birth rate} = \frac{8}{20} = 0.4 \text{ offspring per lotus per year}$$

3. Death Rate or Mortality

It is expressed as the number of deaths per 1000 individuals of a population per year, e.g. if 4 individuals in a population of 40 fruitflies died during a specified time interval (say a week).

$$\text{Death rate} = \frac{4}{40}$$

$$= 0.1 \text{ individual per fruitfly per week}$$

4. Sex Ratio

It is expressed as the number of females and males per 1000 individuals of a population in a given time, e.g. 60% females and 40% males in a population.

Age Pyramid

- When the age distribution (per cent individuals of a given age or age group) is plotted for the population in which pre-reproductive age is at base, reproductive is at middle and post-reproductive is at top, we get a pyramid called age pyramid.
- The shape of the pyramids reflects the growth status of the population that whether it is expanding (triangular-shaped), stable (bell-shaped) or declining (urn-shaped).

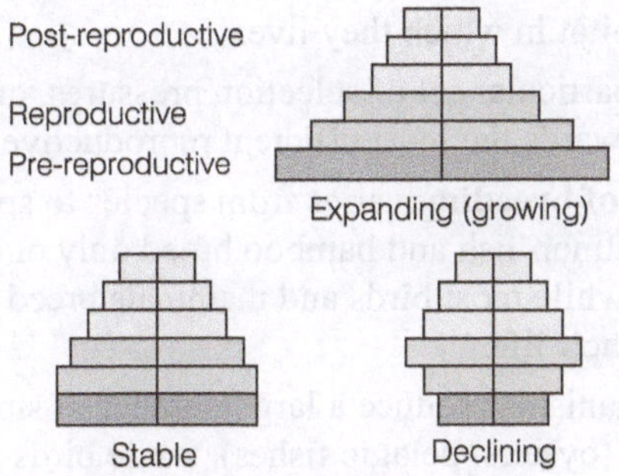

Figure 11.1 Representation of age pyramids for human population

Population Growth

- The size of a population for any species is not a static parameter.
- It keeps changing with time, depending on various factors including food availability, predation, pressure and adverse weather conditions.
- The density of a population in a given habitat during a given period fluctuates due to changes in four basic processes
  - (i) **Natality** is the number of births during a given period in the population that are added to the initial density.
  - (ii) **Mortality** is the number of deaths in the population during a given period.
  - (iii) **Immigration** is the number of individuals of the same species that have come into the habitat from elsewhere during the time period under consideration.
  - (iv) **Emigration** is the number of individuals of the population who left the habitat and moved elsewhere during a given time period.

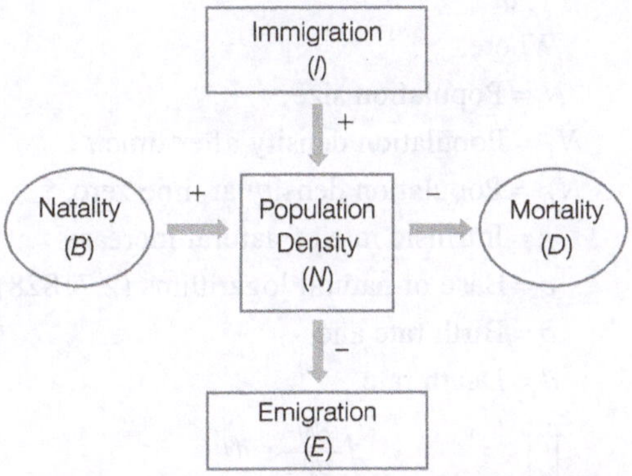

Figure 11.2 Factors influencing population density

- Population density can be given by the following equation

$$N_{t+1} = N_t + [(B + I) - (D + E)];$$

this is density at time $t + 1$.

Where, N = Population density, t = Time,
B = Birth rate, I = Immigration,
D = Death rate, E = Emigration,
N_t = Population in beginning.

The equation demonstrates that the population density will increase, if the number of births plus the number of immigrants $(B + I)$ is more than the number of deaths plus the number of emigrants $(D + E)$, otherwise it will decrease.

Growth Models

A population growth models tries to predict the population of an organism that reproduces according to fixed rules. The two models of population growth are given below

1. Exponential Growth (A-curve)

- It occurs normally when resources, i.e. food and space are unlimited.
- Equation for exponential growth can be represented as follows

$$\frac{dN}{dt} = (b - d) \times N$$

Let $(b - d) = r$, then

$$\frac{dN}{dt} = rN \quad \text{or} \quad N_t = N_0 e^{rt}$$

Where,

N = Population size,

N_t = Population density after time t

N_0 = Population density at time zero,

r = Intrinsic rate of natural increase

e = Base of natural logarithms (2.71828),

b = Birth rate and

d = Death rate

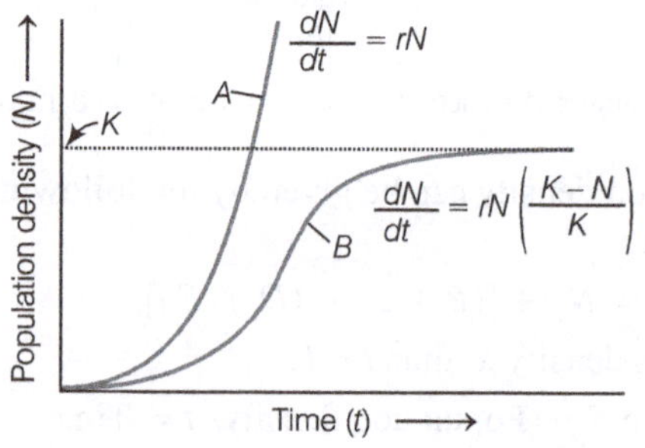

Figure 11.3 Population growth curve; *A* when responses are not limiting the growth, plot is exponential, *B* when responses are limiting the growth, plot is logistic, *K* is carrying capacity

- r is an important parameter assessing impacts of any biotic or abiotic factor on population growth.
- In exponential growth, when N in relation to time (t) is plotted on graph, the curve becomes J-shaped as shown in graph.

2. Logistic Growth (B-curve)

- It occurs when resources become limited at certain point of time, so no population can grow exponentially.
- Due to competition between individuals for limited resources, the fittest individual will survive and reproduce.
- In nature, a given habitat has enough resources to support a maximum possible number, beyond which no further growth is possible. This is called **carrying capacity** (K) of a habitat.
- A population growing in a habitat with limited resources shows initially a **lag phase**, followed by phases of **acceleration** and **deceleration** and finally an **asymptote,** when the population density reaches the carrying capacity.
- The logistic growth shows sigmoid curve and this is also called **Verhulst-Pearl logistic growth.**

It can be shown by the following equation

$$dN/dt = rN\left(\frac{K - N}{K}\right)$$

Where,

N = Population density at time t

r = Intrinsic rate of natural increase

K = Carrying capacity

- The logistic growth model is considered more realistic since, resources for growth of most animal populations are finite and become limited sooner or later.

Life History Variation

- **Darwinian fitness** (high r value) states that the populations evolve to maximise their reproductive fitness in the habitat in which they live.
- Under a particular set of selection pressures, organisms evolve towards the most efficient reproductive strategy.
- The **rate of breeding** varies from species to species, e.g. Pacific salmon fish and bamboo breed only once in their lifetime, while most birds and mammals breed many times in their life.
- Some organisms produce a large number of small-sized offspring (oysters, pelagic fishes), while birds and mammals produce a small number of large-sized offspring.
- Ecologists suggest that life history traits of organisms have evolved in relation to the constraints imposed by the abiotic and biotic components of the habitat in which they live.

PYQs Previous Years' Questions

1 Mark Questions

Multiple Choice Questions

1. Important attributes belonging to a population, but not to an individual are
 I. birth rate and death rate
 II. male and female
 III. birth and death
 IV. sex-ratio

 Select the correct option from the options given below. **CBSE 2023**

 (a) Only I (b) Only II
 (c) II and III (d) I and IV

Ans. (d) I and IV

2. Swati was growing a bacterial colony in a culture flask under ideal laboratory conditions where the resources are replenished. Which of the following equations will represent the growth in this case?

 (Where population size is *N*, birth rate is *b*, death rate is *d*, unit time period is *t* and carrying capacity is *K*). **CBSE SQP 2023**

 (a) $dN/dt = KN$ (b) $dN/dt = r\,N$
 (c) $dN/dt = r\,N(K\text{-}N/K)$ (d) $dN/dt = r\,N(K\text{+}N/K)$

Ans. (b) $dN/dt = r\,N$

Assertion-Reason Type Question

3. Given below is the age pyramid of population in one of the states in India as per 2011 census. It depicts the male population on the left hand side, female population on the right hand side, newborns towards the base and gradually increasing age groups as we move from base to the top, with the oldest population at the top. Study this pyramid and comment upon the appropriateness of the Assertion (A) and the Reason (R).

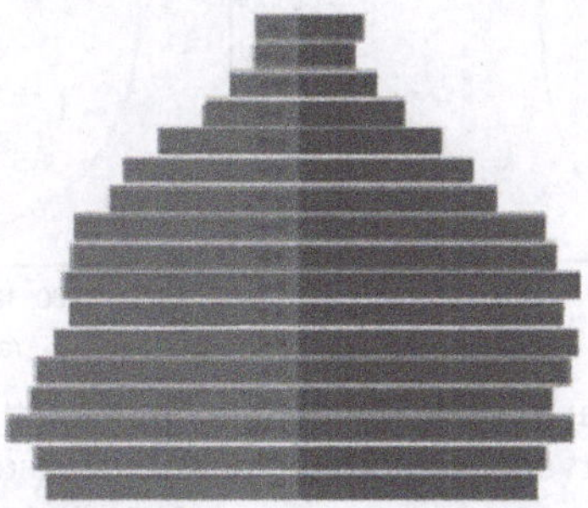

Assertion (A) It is a stable population.

Reason (R) The pre-reproductive and reproductive individuals are almost in equal numbers and the post-reproductive individuals are relatively fewer. **CBSE SQP 2023**

(a) Both Assertion and Reason are true and Reason is the correct explanation of Assertion

(b) Both Assertion and Reason are true, but Reason is not the correct explanation of Assertion

(c) Assertion is true, but Reason is false

(d) Assertion is false, but Reason is true

Ans. (a)

Very Short Answer Type Questions

4. Provide an instance where the population size of species can be estimated indirectly, without actually counting them or seeing them. **Delhi 2016C**

Ans. Tiger population in National Parks is calculated on the basis of pugmarks and faecal matter.

5. In a pond, there were 20 *Hydrilla* plants. Through reproduction, 10 new *Hydrilla* plants were added in a year. Calculate the birth rate of the population. **Delhi 2012**

> **KEY idea**
>
> Birth rate = Number of births of new individuals per unit of population per unit time.

Ans. The birth rate of *Hydrilla*

$$= \frac{\text{Number of individuals born}}{\text{Total number of individuals}}$$

$$= \frac{10}{20}$$

$= 0.5$ per *Hydrilla* plant per year.

Birth rate is 0.5 per *Hydrilla* plant or 500 per thousand/year.

6. In a pond, there were 200 frogs. 40 more were born in a year. Calculate the birth rate of the population. **Delhi 2010**

Ans. The birth rate of frog population

$$= \frac{40}{200}$$

$= 0.2$ per frog/year

or 200 per thousand/year.

2 Marks Questions

7. Observe the population growth curve and answer the questions given below **CBSE 2024**

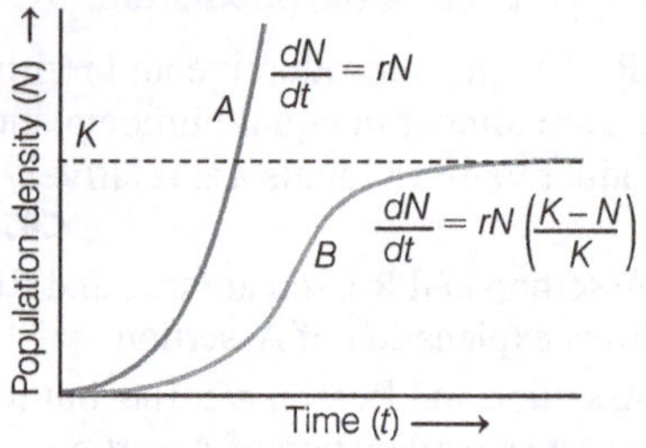

(i) State the conditions under which growth curve '*A*' and growth curve '*B*' plotted in the graph are possible.

(ii) Mention what does '*K*' in the graph represent.

Ans. (i) The growth curve '*A*' is possible when responses are not limiting the growth, i.e. unlimited resource availability is found. This type of growth curve is J-shaped and the plot is exponential.

The growth curve '*B*' is possible when responses are limiting the growth, i.e. limited resources are present. This type of growth curve is S-shaped and the plot is logistic. **(1)**

(ii) '*K*' in the graph represents the carrying capacity of an environment. **(1)**

8.

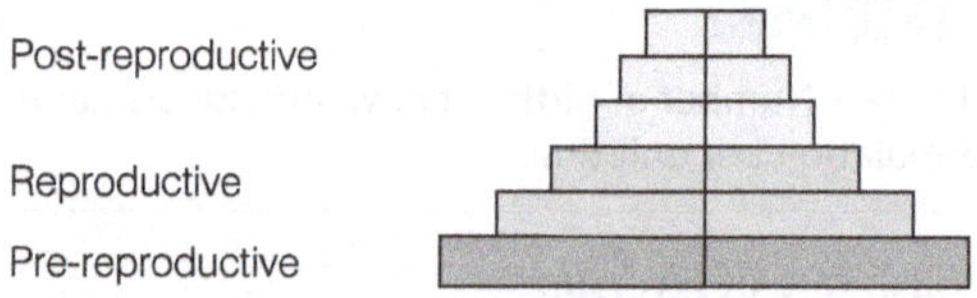

Identify the type of pyramid given above. Write the identifying feature on the basis of which you identified it. **Delhi 2021-22 Term-II**

Ans. The type of pyramid given is expanding. This type of pyramid is triangle in shape. It depicts population which have a higher percentage of pre-reproductive or younger people in the age groups.

This feature helps us in identify the pyramid correct.

9.

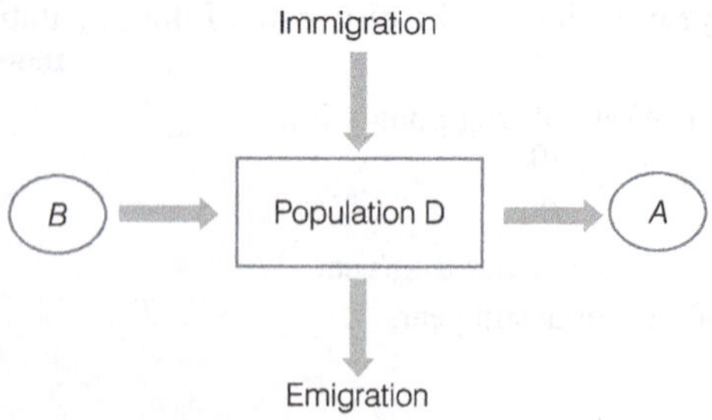

Observe the schematic representation given and answer the following questions.

(i) Identify *A* and *B*.

(ii) Calculate the growth rate of bacteria in a curd sample, where 1 million bacteria increased to two million, within a period of one hour. **Delhi 2021-22 Term-II**

Ans. (i) *A* – Mortality, *B* – Natality **(½)**

(ii) Given that number of bacteria (initially) = 10,00,000

Final number of bacteria = 20,00,000

Time taken for doubling = 60 minutes (1 hour)

Growth rate can be calculated by the formula

$$N_t = N_o \times (1+r)^t$$

Where, N_t = amount at time 't'

N_o = amount at time 0

r = growth rate

t = time passed

$\Rightarrow 20,00,000 = 10,00,000 \times (1+r)^t$

$\Rightarrow \quad 2 = (1+r)^{60} = (1+r) = (2)^{1/60}$

$r = (2)^{1/60} - 1$

$\Rightarrow \quad r = 0.0116$ **(1½)**

10. As per a recent newspaper report, a particular country showed declining population growth rate. According to you, what could be the two most possible reasons for this decline and why? **All India 2021-22 Term-II**

Ans. Growth rate refers to the percentage change of a specific variable within a specific time period. In case of declining population growth rate, the two possible reasons could be

(i) **Death rate** (mortality) Number of deaths during a given period. This affects the overall population of a country. Increasing death rate could be due to several factors like bad medical services, etc.

(ii) **Emigration** It is the number of individuals of a population who left the habitat and gone elsewhere in search of food, jobs or many other factors. **(1+1)**

11. The graphs given below, *A* and *B* represent population of elephants in two different National Parks (a hypothetical situation) at different times.

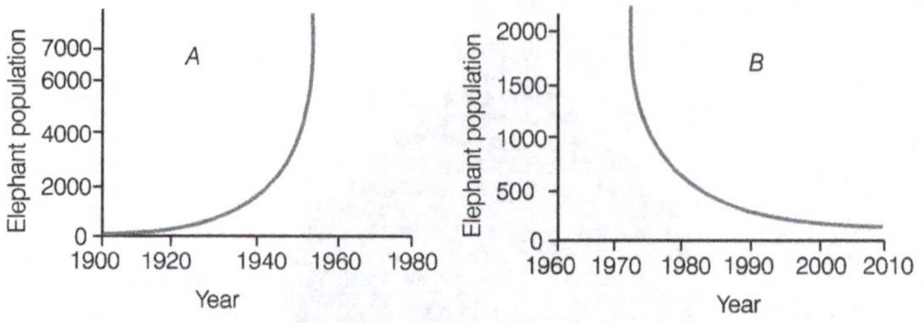

Study the graphs and comment upon the pattern of growth observed. Mention the possible reason for such patterns seen in nature. **All India 2021-22 Term-II**

Ans. In graph *A* the population of elephants shows an increase in number with increasing years or time span. In graph *B* the situation is just opposite to that shown in graph *A*. With the increasing time span, the population of elephants has shown a decline and a constant (from year 2000 to 2010). **(1)**

Possible reasons for decreasing population (graph *B*) could be

- Habitat loss and fragmentation
- Hunting and poaching

Reasons for increase in elephant population (graph *A*) could be

- Afforestation
- Ban on illegal poaching activities. **(1)**

12. Draw the labelled diagrams of stable and declining age pyramids of human population. **All India 2015C**

Ans. For stable and declining age pyramids of human population diagrams, refer to figure 11.1 on page no. 319.

13. Construct an age pyramid which reflects an expanding growth status of human population. **All India 2014**

Ans. The age pyramid geometrically represents the proportions of different age groups (pre-reproductive, reproductive and post-reproductive) in population. The triangular shape of age pyramid represents the expanding growth status of human population, because it has maximum number of individuals in pre-reproductive age group.

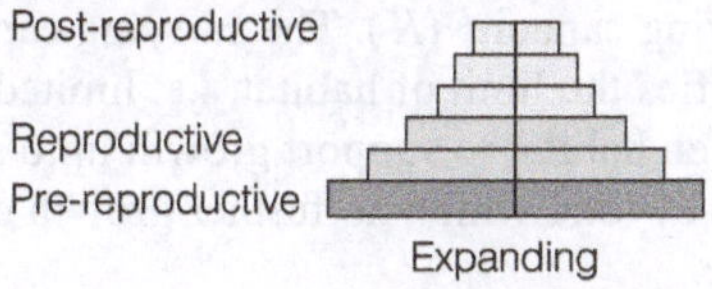

14. Construct an age pyramid which reflects a stable growth status of human population. **All India 2014**

Ans. The age pyramid that reflects a stable growth status of human population can be represented as follows

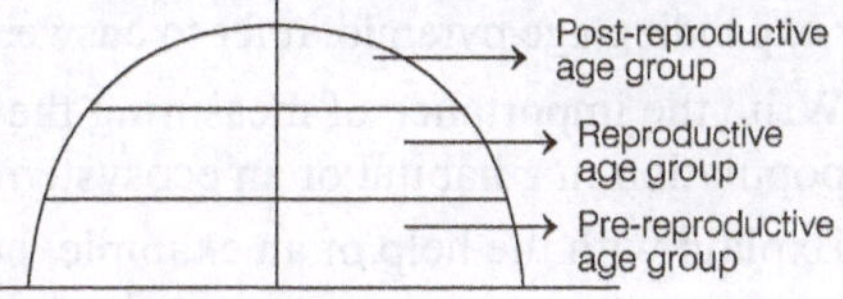

15. Explain Verhulst-Pearl logistic growth of a population. **All India 2014**

Ans. Verhulst-Pearl logistic growth is a type of population growth in which the population growing in a habitat with limited resources initially shows a lag phase, followed by exponential phase and finally a declining or stationary phase. When the growth or density of population reaches carrying capacity.

It can be explained by following equation

$$dN/dt = rN\left(\frac{K-N}{K}\right)$$

Where, N – Population density at time t

r – Intrinsic rate of natural increase

K – Carrying capacity

3 Marks Questions

16. The population of a metro city experiences fluctuations in its population density over a period of time.

(i) When does the population in a metro city tend to increase ?

(ii) When does the population in metro city tend to decline?

(iii) If 'N' is the population density at the time 't', write the population density at the time '$t+1$'. **All India 2020**

Ans. (i) The population in metro cities tend to increase when natality (rate of birth) and immigration (number of individuals of same species added to the habitat) increases. **(1)**

(ii) The population declines when the number of deaths along with the number of emigrants $(D+E)$ is more than number of births and number of immigrants $(B+I)$. **(1)**

(iii) Population density at time $(t+1)$ will be

$$N_{(t+1)} = N_t + [(B+I)-(D+E)]$$

Where

N = Population density

t = Time

B = Birth rate

I = Immigration

D = Death rate

E = Emigration **(1)**

17. Study the graph given below and answer the questions that follow

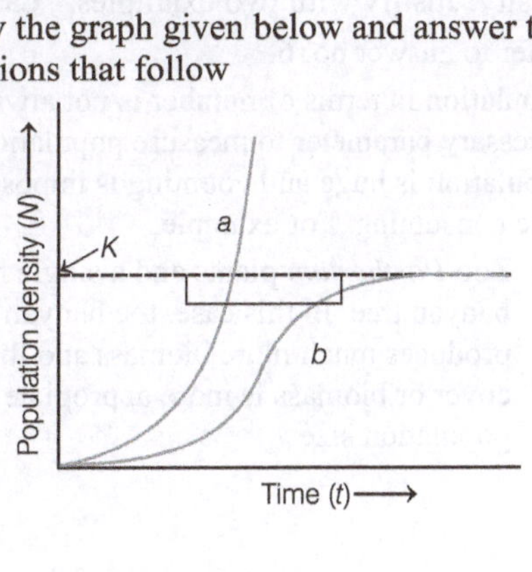

(i) The curve 'b' is described by the following equation :

$$\frac{dN}{dt} = rN\left\{\frac{K-N}{K}\right\}$$

What does 'K' stand for in this equation? Mention its significance.

(ii) Which one of the two curves is considered a more realistic one for most of the animal populations?

(iii) Which curve would depict the population of a species of deer if there are no predators in the habitat? Why is it so? **All India 2019**

> **KEY idea**
>
> a = Exponential growth or J-shaped curve.
>
> b = Logistic growth or sigmoid curve.

Ans. (i) 'K' stands for 'carrying factor'. The carrying capacity signifies the limit of habitat, i.e. limited resources in a given habitat to support growth upto a certain level beyond which no further growth can take palce. **(1)**

(ii) The curve 'b' is considered a more realistic one for most of the animal populations. It is so, becasue in the curve 'b', the sources of food and space are limited and it supports the growth curve of animal populations. **(1)**

(iii) The curve 'b' would depict the population of a species of deer, if there are no predators in the habitat. In the absence of predators, prey population will increase. Thus, the competition will increase due to the limited food and shelter resources within the prey population. **(1)**

18. (i) In a pond there were 200 frogs. 40 more were born in the year. Calculate the birth rate of the population.

(ii) Population in terms of number is not always a necessary parameter to measure population density. Justify with two examples. **CBSE SQP 2019**

Ans. (i) Refer to answer no. 6. **(1)**

(ii) Population in terms of number is not always a necessary parameter to measure population if the population is huge and counting is impossible and is time consuming. For example,

(a) Zoo *Partherium* plants and a single huge banyan tree. In this case, the banyan tree produces much more biomass and the pre cent cover or biomass is more appropiate measure of population size.

(b) The number of fishes cought per trap, in this case relative densities is a good measure of its total population density in the lake. **(2)**

19. Study the graph given below and answer the questions that follows

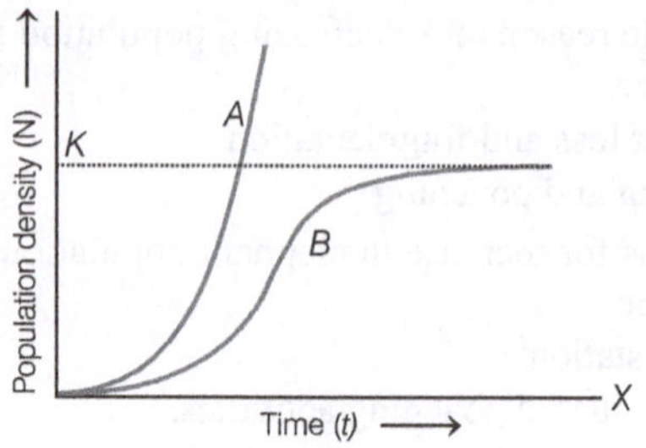

(i) Write the status of food and space in the curves A and B.

(ii) In the absence of predators, which one of the two curves would appropriately depict the prey population?

(iii) Time has been shown on X-axis and there is a parallel dotted line above it. Give the significance of this dotted line. **Delhi 2014**

Ans. (i) The status of food and space in curve A is unlimited resources, while in curve B the sources of food and space are limited. **(1)**

(ii) In the absence of predators, the curve B would appropriately depict the competition for limited food and shelter resources within the prey population. **(1)**

(iii) The dotted line in the above graph represents the carrying capacity (K). The carrying capacity signifies the limit of habitat, i.e. limited resources in a given habitat to support growth upto a certain level beyond which no further growth can take place. **(1)**

20. Construct the age pyramid which reflects growth status of human population. **All India 2014**

Or

Draw and explain expanding age pyramids of human population. Why is it so called? **All India 2014C**

Ans. For expanding age pyramid, refer to answer no. 8.

21. (i) Write the importance of measuring the size of a population in a habitat or an ecosystem.

(ii) Explain with the help of an example, how the percentage cover is a more meaningful measure of population size than mere numbers. **All India 2013**

Ans. (i) Measurement of population in a habitat determines the relative abundance of a particular species and its effect on the available resources of that particular habitat. **(1)**

(ii) The percentage cover is more meaningful measure of population size than more numbers because the relative abundance of a species is not only determined by number of individuals, but by both the relative abundance in biomass and number. **(1)**

For example, in a unit area, the number of grass species or relative abundance in number is high, but not the relative biomass, if the same area has one or two *Ficus benghalensis* tree, it is very low in relative abundance, but high in relative abundance of biomass. **(1)**

22. (i) Explain death rate in a population by taking a suitable example.

(ii) Write the other two characteristics, which only a population shows but an individual cannot.

All India 2013

Ans. (i) Death rate or Mortality is expressed as the number of deaths of individual of a population per year. For example, if 80 individuals in a laboratory population of 800 fruitfly died in a week, then death rate is

$$\frac{80}{800} = 0.1 \text{ per fruitfly/week}$$ **(2)**

(ii) Characteristics of population, not exhibited by individual are

(a) Population size or Density.

(b) Population interactions. **(1)**

23. (i) Explain birth rate in a population by taking a suitable example.

(ii) Write the other two characteristics, which only a population shows but an individual cannot.

All India 2013

Ans. (i) Due to natality or birth rate, population increases continuously. It is the production of new individuals by birth, hatching or by asexual mode, etc. It is expressed as the number of birth per 1000 individuals of a population per year. **(1)**

(ii) The characteristic, which are unique to the group (population) and are not shown by an individual are

(a) **Population dynamics** theorise to explain population growth. Size of population for any species is not a static parameter. Population growth changes during time and depends upon food availability, predation, pressure, weather and also depends upon natality, mortality, immigration and emigration.

(b) **Regulation of population** governs population density or population size. It is the number of individuals of a species per unit area or volume. **(2)**

24. (i) List any three ways of measuring population density of a habitat.

(ii) Mention the essential information that can be obtained by studying the population density of an organism. **All India 2013**

Ans. (i) Three ways of measuring population density of a habitat

A– Per cent cover for trees with larger canopy.

B– Number of fishes caught per trap (relative density).

C– Pug marks or faecal pellets for tiger census (indirect method). **(2)**

(ii) The population density tells us about the status of a species, i.e. the outcome of competition, impact of predation or effect of pesticides, etc. **(1)**

25. Study the three different age pyramids, for human population given below and answer the questions that follow.

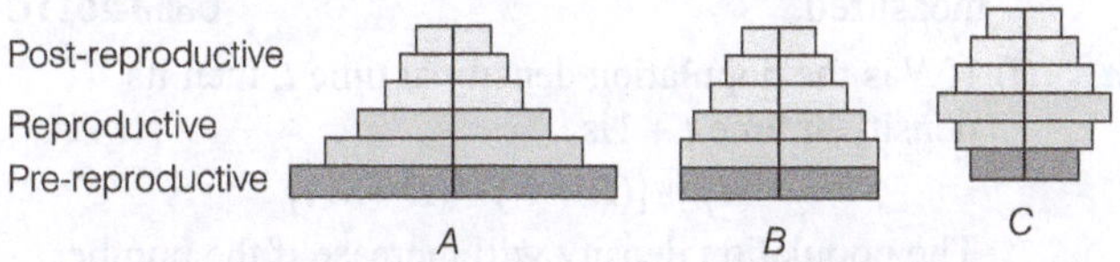

(i) Write the names given to each of these age pyramids.

(ii) Mention the one, which is ideal for human population and why. **Foreign 2011**

Ans. (i) *A* – Expanding, *B* – Stable, *C* –Declining **(1)**

(ii) Stable population is ideal for human population. It is beneficial for the survival and better living of the human population. It is helpful for planning sustainable living. **(2)**

5 Marks Questions

26. (i) Study the flow chart given below and complete the equation that follows by identifying 1, 2, 3 and 4.

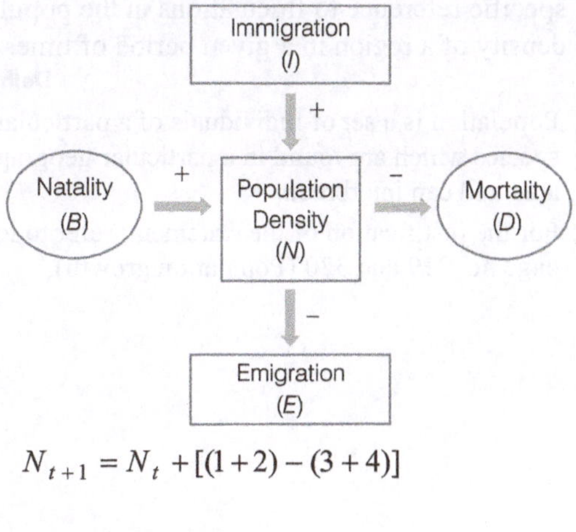

$$N_{t+1} = N_t + [(1+2) - (3+4)]$$

(ii) Mention the different ways by which the population density of different species can be measured. **All India 2019**

Or

(i) Explain the equation

$$N_{t+1} = N_t + [(B + I) - (D + E)]$$

on the basis of the flowchart given below

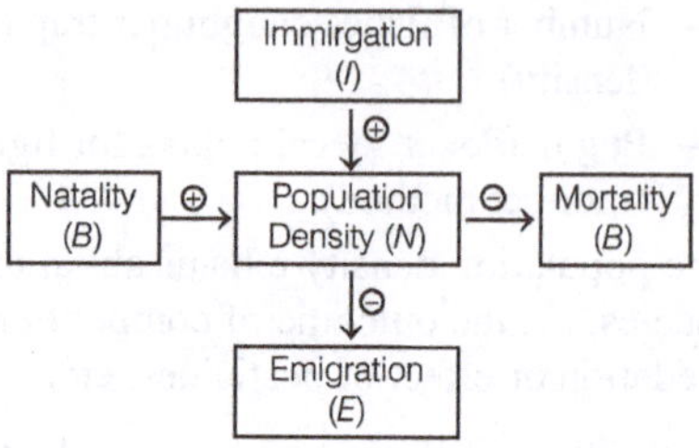

(ii) Mention the different ways by which the population density of different species can be measured. **Delhi 2011C**

Ans. (i) If N is the population density at time t, then its density at time $t+1$ is

$$N_t + [(B + I) - (D + E)]$$

The population density will increase if the number of birth and the number of immigrants, i.e. $(B+I)$ is more than the number of death and the number of emigrants, i.e. $(D+E)$. **(2)**

(ii) For different ways of measurement of population, density, refer to answer no. 24 (i). **(3)**

Common Mistakes Often students get confused between migration and immigration. So, migration is a temporary movement of animals from one place to another whereas immigration is permanent movement.

27. (i) What is 'population' according to you as a biology student?

(ii) 'The size of a population for any species is not a static parameter'. Justify the statement with specific reference to fluctuations in the population density of a region in a given period of time. **Delhi 2019**

Ans. (i) Population is a set of individuals of a particular species which are found in a particular geographical area and can interbreed. **(2)**

(ii) For the justification of the statement, refer to text on page no. 319 and 320 (Population growth). **(3)**

28. (i) Compare, giving reasons, the J-shaped and S-shaped models of population growth of a species.

(ii) Explain 'fitness of a species', as mentioned by Darwin. **All India 2017**

Ans. (i) Differences between J-shaped and S-shaped models of population growth are

J-shaped population growth	S-shaped population growth
Population growth occurs in J-shaped manner when resources are unlimited in a habitat.	Population growth occurs in S-shaped manner when resources are limited in a habitat.
A stationary or steady phase is seldom achieved.	A stationary or steady phase is reached.
Population crashes ultimately due to mass mortality.	Population seldom crashes.
The growth curve is characterised by initial lag phase followed by acceleration phase.	The growth curve initially depicts a lag phase followed by accleration phase, deceleration phase and an upper asymptote that represents the carrying capacity.
The J-shaped growth curve can be represented as 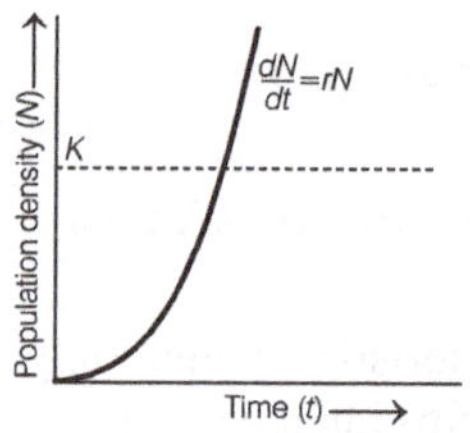	The S-shaped growth curve can be represented as 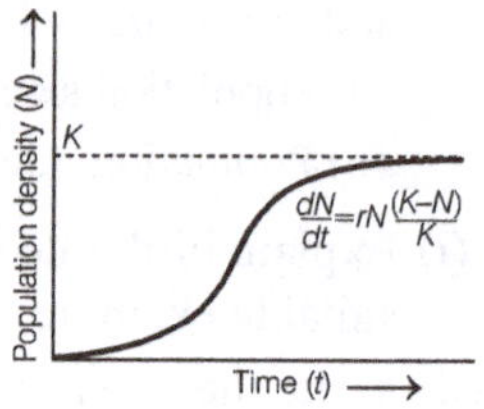

(3)

(ii) **Fitness of a species as mentioned by Darwin**

Darwinian fitness (high 'r' value) states that the population evolves to maximise its reproductive fitness in the habitat where it lives. Under a particular set of selection pressure, organisms evolve towards the most efficient reproductive strategy. The rate of breeding varies from species to species. Some species breed only once in their lifetime (Pacific salmon fish and bamboo), while some breed many times in their lifetime (birds and mammals). Some organisms produce a large number of small-sized offspring (oysters), whereas other produce a small number of large-sized offspring (birds and mammals). **(2)**

29. (i) What is an age pyramid?

(ii) Name three representative kinds of age pyramids for human population and list the characteristics for each one of them. **Delhi 2017**

Or

(i) What is an age pyramid?

(ii) Explain with the help of figures, the three different types of age pyramids represented by human population. **Delhi 2011C**

Ans. (i) **Age pyramids** When the age distribution (per cent individuals of a given age or age group) is plotted for the population, it is called age pyramid. **(1)**

(ii) Population at any given time is composed of individuals of different ages. For human population, the age pyramids generally show age distribution of males and females in a combined diagram.

The shape of the pyramids reflects the growth status of the population that whether it is **expanding** (triangular-shaped), **stable** (bell-shaped) or **declining** (urn-shaped).

(a) **Expanding or Triangular age pyramid** In this, number of pre-reproductive individuals is very large, number of age reproductive individuals is moderate, while post-reproductive individuals are fewer. This type of age pyramid shows that population is growing. This type of population growth is observed in developing countries like India, Brazil.

(b) **Stable or Bell-shaped age pyramid** In this, the number of pre-reproductive and reproductive individuals is almost equal. Post-reproductive individuals are comparatively fewer. The population size remains stable, neither growing nor diminishing. This type of population growth is observed in countries like USA, Denmark.

(c) **Declining or Urn-shaped age pyramid** The proportion of reproductive age group is higher than the individuals in pre-reproductive age group. The number of post-reproductive individuals is also sizeable. It is declining or diminishing population with negative growth. This type of population growth is observed in countries like Japan.

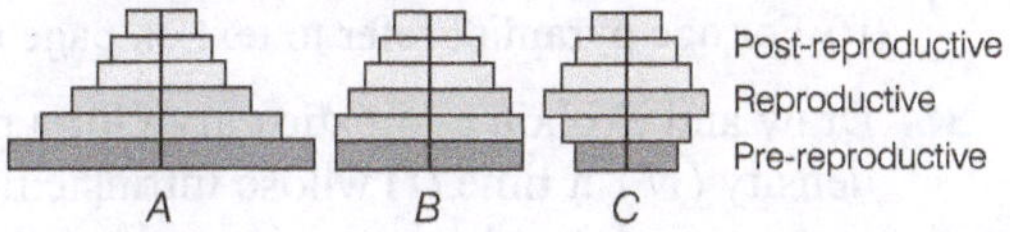

(4)

30. (i) Represent diagrammatically three kinds of age pyramids for human populations.

(ii) How does an age pyramid for human population at given point of time help the policy makers in planning for future? **Delhi 2016**

Or Analysis of age pyramids for human population can provide important inputs for long-term planning strategies. Explain. **Delhi 2015**

Ans. (i) Refer to answer no. 29 (ii). **(3)**

(ii) A policy maker works on population projection to assess future demand of food, water, energy as well as health and reproductive age. The age pyramids reflect several possible scenario of future of fertility and mortality. At given point of time, the expanding age-pyramids for human population have more pre-reproductive and reproductive population and less post-reproductive population. Thus, this type of age pyramids help the policy makers in planning for future economic growth of the country. **(2)**

31. (i) Name the two growth models that represent population growth and draw the respective growth curves they represent.

(ii) State the basis for the difference in the shape of these curves.

(iii) Which one of the curves represents the human population growth at present? Do you think such a curve is sustainable? Give reason in support of your answer. **All India 2016**

Ans. (i) The two growth models are

(a) Exponential growth curve **(1)**

(b) Logistic growth curve. **(1)**

(ii) Refer to answer no. 28 (i). **(2)**

(iii) The human population at present is represented by logistic growth curve. The logistic growth curve is sustainable because the biological factors and carrying capacity support it. **(1)**

32. (i) What is population density? Why are ecologists interested in measuring it?

(ii) Write the different ways of measuring population density. Explain any two with the help of specific examples. **All India 2016C**

Ans. (i) Population density means number of individuals present per unit area. It can be measured by determining the population size. Ecologists are interested in measuring population density for the following reasons

(a) The size of the population tells us a lot about its status in the habitat.

(b) Ecological processes such as outcome of competition with another species, the impact of a predator or the effect of pesticide application can be easily evaluated in terms of change in the population size. **(2)**

(ii) The different methods to study population size are as follows

(a) **Per cent cover or Biomass** In an area with 200 *Parthenium* plants and only one banyan tree with large canopy, the denstiy of banyan tree is small, but does not reflect its important role in the community. Here the per cent cover or biomass is more meaningful method of assessing population density.

(b) **Total number** It involves the counting of organisms in the given area.

(c) **Relative density** In this method, there is no need to count the organisms individually, e.g. the number of fishes caught per trap gives the measure of their total density in a given waterbody.

(d) **Indirect assessment** The tiger census is based on pugmarks and faecal pellets. **(3)**

33. (i) List the different attributes that a population has and not an individual organism.

(ii) What is population density? Explain any three different ways the population density can be measured, with the help of an example each.

All India 2015

Ans. (i) **Population attributes** are certain characteristics of a population. Some of them are as follows

(a) **Population size** or **Density** is the number of individuals of a species per unit area or volume.

Population Density

$$(PD) = \frac{\text{Number of individuals in a region } (N)}{\text{Number of unit area in the region } (S)}$$

$$\Rightarrow \quad PD = \frac{N}{S}$$

(b) **Birth rate** or **Natality** is expressed as the number of births per 1000 individuals of a population per year, e.g. if in a pond, there were 20 lotus plants last year and through reproduction 8 new plants are added then,

Birth rate $= \frac{8}{20} = 0.4$ offspring per lotus per year.

(c) **Death rate** or **Mortality** is expressed as the number of deaths per 1000 individuals of a population per year, i.e. if 4 individuals in a population of 40 fruitflies died during a specified time interval (say a week) then,

Death rate $= \frac{4}{40} = 0.1$ individuals per fruitfly per week.

(d) **Sex ratio** is expressed as the number of females and males per 1000 individuals of a population in a given time, e.g. 60% females and 40% males in population.

(e) **Age pyramid** When the age distribution (per cent individuals of a given age or age group) is plotted for the population, it is called **age pyramid.** **(3)**

(ii) Refer to answer no. 32. **(2)**

34. (i) Name the population growth pattern the equation $\left(\frac{dN}{dt} = rN\right)$ represents. What does '*r*' represent in the equation? Write its importance in population growth.

(ii) Explain the principle of carrying capacity by using population Verhulst-Pearl logistic growth curve.

Delhi 2014C

Ans. (i) The exponential growth pattern is represented by equation $\left(\frac{dN}{dt} = rN\right)$.

Here '*r*' represents the intrinsic factor (a rate of natural increase). This pattern results in a J-shaped curve. Any species growthing exponentially under unlimited resource conditions can reach enormous population densities. **(2½)**

(ii) The Verhulst-Pearl logistic growth curve is explained by $\frac{dN}{dt} = rN\left(\frac{K-N}{K}\right)$ where, *K* represents the carrying capacity. It can be referred to as nature's limit of natural resources that a habitat provides to its individuals of a growing population, beyond which there is no growth in that particular habitat. **(2½)**

35. (i) Explain the birth rate and death rate in the population with the help of an example each.

(ii) What is age pyramid? Draw an age pyramid of an expanding population. **All India 2011C**

Ans. (i) Refer to the answer no. 33(i) (b) and (c). **(3)**

(ii) For age pyramid, refer to text on page no. 319. **(2)**

36. Draw and explain a logistic curve for a population of density (*N*) at time (*t*) whose intrinsic rate of natural increase is (*r*) and carrying capacity (*K*). **Delhi 2010**

Ans.

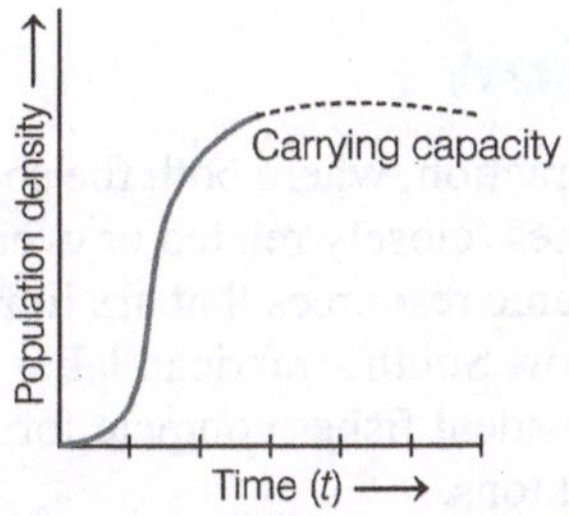

(2)

(i) Population initially shows a lag phase and then shows a phase of acceleration or exponential growth followed by phase of deceleration. (½)

(ii) Population can grow exponentially for a certain period of time and then assumes a steady state, as the resource availability becomes limited at some point of time. (½)

(iii) Every environment has resources to support a particular maximum number of individuals, called its carrying capacity. Beyond that, there is no increase in size/density of a population. (½)

(iv) A population showing logistic growth shows a sigmoid curve, when the number of individuals is plotted as a function of time. (½)

(v) Equation can be described as (½)

$$\frac{dN}{dt} = rN\left(\frac{K-N}{K}\right)$$

where, N = Population density at time t,
r = Intrinsic rate of natural increase,
K = Carrying capacity.

(vi) The model is more realistic in nature, because no population can sustain the exponential growth indefinitely. (½)

37. (i) Explain with the help of a graph the population growth curve, when resources are (*A*) limiting, (*B*) not limiting.

(ii) Nature has a carrying capacity for a species. Explain. **Foreign 2010**

Ans. (i)

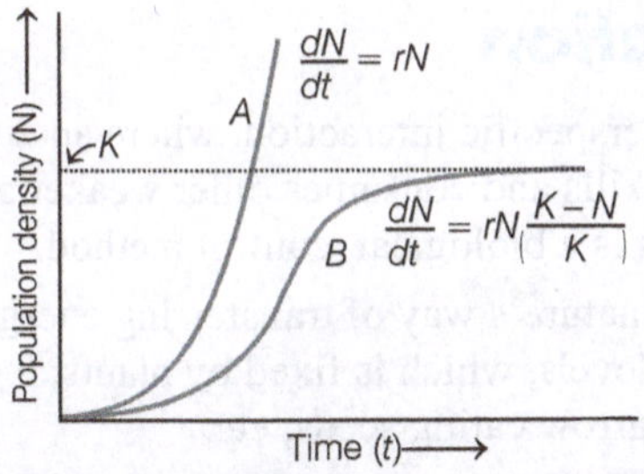

(1)

***B*-Resources are limiting** The population growth curve is sigmoid. It is represented by the equation

$$dN/dt = rN\left(\frac{K-N}{K}\right)$$

where,
N = Population density at time t,
r = Intrinsic rate of natural increase
K = Carrying capacity. (1)

***A*-Resources are unlimited** The population growth curve is J-shaped. It is represented by the equation

$$dN/dt = rN \text{ or } N_t = N_0e^{rt}$$

where,
Population density after time t,
N_0 = Population density at time zero
r = Intrinsic rate of natural increase, e = The base of natural logarithm (2.71828). (1)

(ii) The resources become limited at certain point of time. So, no population can grow exponentially. Every environment or habitat has limited resources to support a particular maximum number of individuals beyond which no further growth is possible. This is called its carrying capacity (K). (2)

TOPIC 2
Population Interactions

They explain that in nature, animals, plants and microbes cannot live in isolation, but interact in various ways to form a biological community.

(i) Interspecific interactions arise from the interaction of populations of two different species.

(ii) This interaction may be
(a) Beneficial/Positive (+)
(b) Detrimental/Harmful (–)
(c) Neutral (neither harm nor benefit) to one of the species or Both (0)

Population Interactions

Species *A*	Species *B*	Name of interaction
+	+	Mutualism
–	–	Competition
+	–	Predation
+	–	Parasitism
–	0	Amensalism
+	0	Commensalism

Some of the population interactions are as follows

Predation

It is an interspecific interaction, where an animal called **predator** kills and consumes other weaker animals called **prey**. This is a biological control method.

- It is the nature's way of transferring energy to higher trophic levels, which is fixed by plants, e.g. tiger eating a deer, sparrow eating seeds, etc.
- Important roles of predators are
  - They keep prey population under control.
  - They help in maintaining species diversity in a community by reducing the intensity of competition among prey species.
  - In the absence of predators, prey species could achieve very high population densities and cause instability. So, besides acting as 'conduits' for energy transfer across trophic levels, predators play very important role to provide population stability.
  - When certain exotic species are introduced into a geographical area, they become invasive and start spreading fast because the invaded land does not have natural predators.
- If a predator is too efficient and over exploits its prey, then the prey might become extinct. Following it, the predator will also become extinct because of the lack of food.

Defensive Measures of Prey Against Predator

Prey species have evolved various defence mechanisms to lesser the impact of predation. Some of them are

- Some species of insects and frogs are cryptically coloured (camouflaged) to avoid being detected easily by the predator. Some are poisonous and therefore avoided by the predator.
- Phytophagous insects like Monarch butterfly is highly distasteful to its predators (birds) because of a special chemical present in its body.
- Some plants have thorns or spines for defence mechanism, e.g. *Acacia*, *Cactus*.
- Some plants produce highly poisonous chemicals like cardiac glycosides, nicotine, caffeine, quinine, strychnine, opium, etc. These are actually defence mechanisms against grazers and browsers. e.g. *Calotropis*.

Competition

It is a type of interaction, where both the species suffer. It occurs when species (closely related or even unrelated), compete for the same resources that are limited, e.g. in some shallow South American lakes visiting flamingoes and resident fishes compete for their common food, i.e. zooplanktons.

In other words, competition is a process in which the fitness of one species (measured in terms of its 'r' the intrinsic rate of increase) is lower in the presence of another species.

- It may be
  - **Intraspecific** (within same species).
  - **Interspecific** (between different species).
- In interference/interspecific competition, the feeding efficiency of one species might be reduced due to the interfering and inhibitory presence of other species, although the resources (food and space) are plenty.
- **Competitive release** is a phenomenon, in which a species whose distribution is restricted to a small geographical area. Because of the presence of competitively superior species, is found to expand its distributional range dramatically when the competing species is experimentally removed.
- **Connell's elegant** field experiments showed that on the rocky sea coasts of Scotland, the larger and competitively superior barnacle *Balanus* dominates the intertidal area and excludes the smaller barnacle *Chathamalus* from that zone.
- **Gause's competitive exclusion principle** states that two closely related species competing for the same resources cannot coexist indefinitely. The competitively inferior one will be eliminated eventually (true if resources are limiting), e.g. when goats were introduced in Galapagos Islands, the Abingdon tortoise became extinct within a decade due to greater browsing efficiency of the goats.
- **Resource partitioning** states that if two species compete for the same resource, they could avoid competition by choosing, for instance, different times for feeding or different foraging patterns.

Parasitism

- It is the mode of interaction between two species in which one species (parasite) depends on the other species (host) for food and shelter and in this process, the parasite damages the host.

- Hence, one organism is benefitted (parasite), while the other is being harmed (host).
- Majority of parasites harm the host. They reduce the survival, growth and reproduction ability of the host and reduce its population density.

Adaptation in Parasites

Adaptations of a parasite are

- Parasite is host-specific in a way that both host and parasite tend to coevolve.
- Loss of unnecessary sense organs.
- The presence of adhesive organs or suckers.
- Loss of digestive system.
- High reproductive capacity.

Life Cycle of Parasites

The life cycles of parasites are often complex, involving one or two intermediate hosts or vectors to facilitate parasitisation of its primary host, e.g.

(i) **Human liver fluke** (a trematode parasite) depends on two intermediate hosts (a snail and a fish) to complete its life cycle.

(ii) **Malarial parasite** (*Plasmodium*) needs a vector (mosquito) to spread disease to other hosts.

Types of Parasites

Parasites can be of the following two types

(i) **Ectoparasites** live on the external surface of the host organism for food and shelter, e.g. the lice on humans, ticks on dogs, copepods, *Cuscuta*, etc.

(ii) **Endoparasities** live inside the hosts body at different sites like liver, kidney, lungs, etc., for food and shelter, e.g. tapeworm, liver fluke, *Plasmodium*, etc.

> **Brood parasitism** is a phenomenon in which one organism (parasite) lays its eggs in the nest of another organism, e.g. cuckoo lays its egg in crow's nest and let the host incubate them.

Commensalism

It is the interaction between two species, where one species is benefitted and the other is neither harmed nor benefitted.

Some examples of commensalism are

- An orchid growing as an epiphyte on a mango tree gets shelter and nutrition from the mango tree.
- Barnacles growing on the back of whale are benefitted by getting to move to different locations for food as well as shelter.

Mutualism

It is an interaction that confers benefits to both the interacting species. Some examples of mutualism are

- **Lichens** represent an intimate mutualistic relationship between a fungus and photosynthesising algae or cyanobacteria. Here, the fungus helps in the absorption of nutrients and provides protection, while algae prepare the food.
- **Mycorrhizae** are close mutual association between fungi and the roots of higher plants. Fungi help the plant in absorption of nutrients, while the plant provides food for the fungus.
- Plants and animals also show mutual relationship, e.g. the female wasp uses the fig fruit not only as an oviposition (egg-laying) site, but uses the developing seeds within the fruit for nourishing its larvae. The wasp pollinates the fig's inflorescence, while searching for suitable egg-laying sites. In return, fig provides the wasp some seeds as food for the developing wasp larvae.
- Not all orchids offer rewards, e.g. mediterranean orchid *Ophrys* employs 'sexual deceit' to get pollinated by a species of bee. One petal of its flower bears an uncanny resemblance to the female of the bee in size, colour and markings. The male bee is attracted and pseudocopulates with the flower.
- During this process, pollen is dusted from the flower. When the same bee pseudocopulates with another flower, it transfers pollen to it and hence, pollinates the flower. This case indicates the process of **coevolution.**

PYQs Previous Years' Questions

1 Mark Questions

Multiple Choice Questions

1. Read the four statements given below and select the option having two correct statements. **CBSE 2024 (Set-I)**

   (i) A lion eating a deer and a sparrow feeding on grains are ecologically similar in being consumers.

   (ii) Predator starfish *Pisaster* helps in maintaining species diversity of some invertebrates.

   (iii) Predators ultimately lead to extinction of prey species.

   (iv) Production of chemical nicotine and strychnine by plants are metabolic disorders.

   (a) (i) and (iii) (b) (ii) and (iv)
   (c) (i) and (ii) (d) (iii) and (iv)

Ans. (c) Statements (i) and (ii) are correct, while statements (iii) and (iv) are incorrect and they can be corrected as

- Predators generally maintain the equilibrium in the species diversity. It is only in the case when they over exploit the prey, the prey would become extinct and following it, the population of predator will also become extinct due to lack of food.
- Production of chemicals nicotine and strychnine by plants are defence mechanisms against grazers and browsers. **(1)**

2. Many copepods live on the body surface of marine fish. This relationship is an example of **CBSE 2023**

   (a) commensalism (b) parasitism
   (c) amensalism (d) mutualism

Ans. (b) parasitism

3. Interaction between clown fish living among the stinging tentacles of sea anemone is an example of **CBSE 2023**

   (a) amensalism
   (b) parasitism
   (c) mutualism
   (d) commensalism

Ans. (d) commensalism

4. A tight one-to-one relationship between many species of fig tree and certain wasps is an example of **CBSE 2023**

   (a) commensalism (b) parasitism
   (c) amensalism (d) mutualism

Ans. (d) mutualism

5. Sea anemone gets attached to the surface of the hermit crab. The kind of population interaction exhibited in this case is **CBSE SQP 2023**

   (a) amensalism (b) commensalism
   (c) mutualism (d) parasitism

Ans. (b) commensalism

Assertion-Reason Type Question

6. **Assertion** (A) In *Ophrys*, one petal of the flower bears an uncanny resemblance to the female bee.

   Reason (R) Two closely related species competing for the same resource can coexist simultaneously. **CBSE SQP 2021**

   (a) Both Assertion and Reason are true and Reason is the correct explanation of Assertion
   (b) Both Assertion and Reason are true, but Reason is not the correct explanation of Assertion
   (c) Assertion is true, but Reason is false
   (d) Assertion is false, but Reason is true

Ans. (c) In *Ophrys*, one petal of its flower resembles to the female bee in size, colour and marking. The male bee is attracted to it, pseudocopulates with flower and thus pollinate the flower.

Two closely related species competing for the same resource cannot coexist simultaneously and the competitively inferior species eliminate eventually. It is known as Gause's competitive exclusion principle. Thus, A is true, but R is false.

Very Short Answer Type Questions

7. State the type of interaction that exists between ticks and dogs. **All India 2015C**

Ans. The type of interaction that exists between ticks and dog is parasitism. Ticks are ectoparasite.

8. Name the interaction that exists between *Cuscuta* and shoe-flower plant. **Delhi 2015C**

Ans. The interaction between *Cuscuta* and shoe-flower bush is called parasitism. Here, *Cuscuta* is the parasite, which infests the shoe-flower bush and derives nutrition from it.

9. Name the type of interaction seen between fig and wasps. **All India 2015C**

Or Comment on the interaction between certain species of fig trees and wasps. **Delhi 2010C**

Ans. Mutualism is the interaction that exists between fig and wasps.

10. Name the two intermediate hosts on which the human liver fluke depends to complete its life cycle, so as to facilitate parasitisation of its primary host. **Delhi 2014**

Ans. The human liver fluke requires two intermediate hosts, i.e. freshwater snail and fish to complete its life cycle and facilitate parasitisation of its primary host. (½+½)

11. Write, what do phytophagous insects feed on? **Delhi 2012**

Ans. Phytophagous insects feed on sap mainly, but can consume the other parts of plants as well.

12. Mention the unique feature with respect to flowering and fruiting in bamboo species. **Delhi 2012**

Ans. Bamboo plants flower only once in their lifetime, generally after 50-100 years. They produce large number of fruits and then die.

13. Pollinating species of wasps show mutualism with specific fig plants. Mention the benefits the female wasps derive from the fig trees from such an interaction. **All India 2011**

Ans. The wasp uses the fig plant ovary for oviposition. It also uses the developing seeds of the fruit to nourish its larvae.

14. Why are cattle and goats not seen browsing on *Calotropis* growing in the fields? **Foreign 2011**

Ans. Cattle or goat do not graze on *Calotropis* plant because it produces poisonous cardiac glycosides.

15. Why do predators avoid eating monarch butterfly? How does the butterfly develop this protective feature? **Foreign 2010**

Ans. Predators avoid the monarch butterfly as it is highly distasteful to its predators (birds) because of a special chemical present in its body. It acquires this chemical during the caterpillar stage by feeding on a poisonous plant (milkweed).

2 Marks Questions

16. 'Cattle and goats do not browse the *Calotropis* plant.' Justify the statement giving reasons. **CBSE 2023**

Ans. Organisms to survive in the complex food web have evolved characters to support their living and prevent them from predators. One of such example is *Calotropis*. *Calotropis* plant also known as milkweed produce a chemical compound cardiac glycoside that affect the mammalian heart. It is the defence mechanism in *Calotropis* plant to keep cattle stay away from it. This is the reason cattle and goats do not feed/browse on this plant.

17. (i) Give an example of a genus of fungi that forms mycorrhizal association with plants.

(ii) How does the plant derive benefits from this association? **CBSE 2023**

Ans. (i) The fungi which belongs to genus-*Glomus* forms mycorrhiza. (1)

(ii) The symbiotic association between fungi and plants is called as mycorrhiza in which fungi absorbs phosphorus from soil which is then used by plants as nutrients. (1)

18. Why are predators considered to be 'prudent' in nature? Explain. **All India 2021-22 Term-II**

Ans. Predators are considered prudent in nature as these prey on a population in a way that the population of the organisms continues to survive and is not overexploited. In case the prey population becomes extinct, the predator population will soon finish due to lack of availability of food.

19. Define interference competition. Give one example that supports competitive exclusion occurring in nature. **CBSE SQP 2021-22**

Ans. Interference competition is the feeding efficiency of one species which might be reduced due to the interfering and inhibitory presence of the other species, even if resources (food and space) are abundant. Examples that support competitive exclusion occurring in nature are as follows

- The Abingdon tortoise became extinct within a decade after goats were introduced on the island, apparently due to the greater browsing efficiency of the goats.
- The larger and competitively superior barnacle *Balanus* dominates the intertidal area and excludes the smaller barnacle *Chathamalus* from that zone.

(any two) (1 × 2)

20. Mention how plants have developed mechanical and chemical defence against herbivores to protect themselves with the help of one example of each. **All India 2020**

Ans. Plants like animals cannot run away from their predators. Therefore, plants have developed many mechanical and chemical defences against the herbivores. For example,

(i) Thorns in *Acacia* and *Cactus* are morphological or mechanical adaptations which discourage animals by causing physical damage.

(ii) *Calotropis* produces a highly poisonous cardiac glycosides as a chemical means to discourage grazing.

21. State Gause's 'competitive exclusion principle'. How have the recent studies modified this principle? **All India 2019**

Ans. Gause's competitive exclusion principle states that two closely related species competing for the same resources cannot coexist indefinitely and the competitively inferior one will be eliminated eventually (true if resources are limiting). This principle has been modified to 'complete competitors cannot coexist' one of the primary ways niche-sharing species can coexist is the competition-colonisation trade-off. In simple terms, species that are better competitors will be specialists, whereas species that are better colonisers are more likely to be generalists.

22. What is mutualism? Mention any two examples where the organisms involved are commercially exploited in agriculture. **All India 2015**

Or Explain mutualism with the help of an example. **All India 2014**

Ans. **Mutualism** is an interaction that confers benefits to both the interacting species. Two examples where organisms involved are commercially exploited in agriculture are

(i) **Mycorrhizae** represent a close mutual association between fungi and the roots of higher plants. Fungi help the plants in absorption of nutrients, specially phosphorus, while the plants provides food for the fungus.

(ii) **Lichens** represent an intimate mutualistic relationship between a fungus and photosynthesising algae or cyanobacteria.

Here, the fungus helps in the absorption of nutrients and provides protection, while algae prepare the food.

23. Koel is clever enough to lay eggs in a crow's nest. Write the reason for this peculiar behaviour. Name the type of interaction. **All India 2015C**

Or Explain brood parasitism with the help of an example. **All India 2012**

Ans. Brood parasitism in birds is a fascinating example of parasitism in which the parasitic bird lay its eggs in the nest of its host and let the host incubate them.

During the course of evolution, the egg of the koel have evolved to resemble the host's egg (i.e. crow) in size and colour to reduce the chances of the host bird detecting the foreign eggs and ejecting them from the nest.

24. Describe the mutual relationship between fig tree and wasp and comment on the phenomenon that operates in their relationship. **All India 2014**

Ans. The relationship between fig tree and wasp shows mutualism. The wasp while searching for sites to lay its eggs, pollinates the fig's inflorescence. On the other hand, the fig not only provides shelter (fruit) for oviposition to wasp, but also allows its larvae to feed on seeds.

25. Apart from being a part of food chain, predators play other important roles. Mention any two such roles supported by examples. **Delhi 2014**

Ans. Apart from being a part of food chain, predators play important role in

(i) **Maintaining the prey population** and regulating interspecies population. **(1)**

(ii) **Indicating ecological disturbances** as predators are small in number and highly sensitive to ecological changes owing to their excessive adaptation. **(1)**

26. How does monarch butterfly defend itself from predators? Explain. **Delhi 2013C**

Ans. For defence mechanism evolved by the monarch butterfly, refer to answer no. 15.

27. Why are herbivores considered similar to predators in an ecological context? Explain. **All India 2010**

Ans. Refer to answer no. 41(i).

28. How does the floral pattern of mediterranean orchid *Ophrys* guarantee cross-pollination? **Delhi 2010**

Ans. In the flowers of *Ophrys*, one petal resembles the female of a bee species in size, colour, markings, etc. Male bee perceives it as a female and pseudocopulates with it.

During the process, the pollen grains from the anthers get dusted on the body of the bee. When the bee is attracted to another flower of this orchid species, the process is repeated and the pollen grains from the body of the bee get dusted on the stigma, thus cross-pollination is achieved.

29. How do plants benefit from having mycorrhizal symbiotic association? **Foreign 2010**

Ans. Benefits to plants having mycorrhizal symbiotic association are

(i) The fungus absorbs nutrients from the soil and passes it on to the plant.

(ii) Mycorrhiza provides resistance to root-borne pathogens.

(iii) They show increased tolerance to salinity and drought.

(iv) An overall increase occurs in plant growth and development.

30. Explain the two defence mechanisms evolved in preys to avoid overpopulation of their predator. **All India 2010C**

Ans. Defence mechanisms evolved in preys are

(i) To avoid being detected easily by the predators, some species of insects and frogs are cryptically coloured (camouflaged). **(1)**

(ii) Some plants have thorns or spines for defence mechanism, e.g. *Acacia, Cactus*. **(1)**

3 Marks Questions

31. Study the table showing the population interaction between species 'Z' and 'Y', respectively. Assign the appropriate '+'/'–' signs for '*A*', '*B*', '*D*', '*E*' and respective interactions for '*C*' and '*F*'.

Species 'Z'	Species 'Y'	Name of interaction
A	*B*	Mutualism
		C
D	*E*	Parasitism
+	0	*F*

Delhi 2020

Ans.

Species 'Z'	Species 'Y'	Name of interaction
+ (*A*)	+ (*B*)	Mutualism
–	–	Competition (*C*)
+ (*D*)	– (*E*)	Parasitism
+	0	Commensalism (*F*)

32. Mention the special adaptations evolved in parasites and why? **Delhi 2019**

Or Explain parasitism and coevolution with the help of one example of each. **All India 2016**

Ans. Coevolution is a phenomenon where many parasites have evolved to be host-specific in such a way that both the host and parasite tend to co-evolve. If the host develops special mechanism to resist the parasite, the parasite also has to evolve the mechanisms to counteract the host's resistance, e.g. bees. **(1)**

Many living organisms live as a parasite on host (plant or animals). Parasite ensures free-lodging and meals from the host and for this it evolves mechanisms to encounter and neutralise the resistance coming from host.

This can be understood by the following examples

(i) Parasites evolve special adaptations like
- loss of unnecessary sense organs.
- presence of adhesive organs like suckers.
- loss of digestive system.
- high reproductive capacity.

(ii) The host in turn evolves special mechanism for rejecting or resisting the parasite. So, when the parasite is not able to complete its life cycle on single host it finds alternative host or secondary host to complete their life cycle. Two examples are
- Liver fluke–hosts are man and snail.
- Malaria parasite–hosts are man and mosquito. **(2)**

33. Predation is usually referred to as a detrimental association. State any three positive roles that a predator plays in an ecosystem. **All India 2016**

Or

What is 'predation'? Explain with the help of suitable examples why is it required in a community with rich biodiversity. **All India 2015C**

Ans. Predation is an interspecific interaction, where an animal, called predator, kills and consumes the other weaker animal called prey.

Predation is nature's way of transferring the energy fixed by plants to higher trophic level, e.g. a tiger (predator) eating a deer (prey), a sparrow (predator) eating fruit or seed (prey), etc.

Predators are required because

(i) They keep prey population under control. This is called biological control.

(ii) They also help in maintaining species diversity in community by reducing the intensity of competition among prey species.

(iii) These act as 'conduits' for energy transfer across trophic level.

(iv) Predators also play very important role to provide population stability.

34. Name and explain the type of interaction that exists in mycorrhiza and between cattle egret and grazing cattle. **All India 2016**

Ans. Mycorrhiza is mutual association between fungi and roots of higher plants. Where the fungi help plant in the absorption of essential nutrients from the soil, while in turn it provides the fungi with energy yielding carbohydrates. Thus, both partners are benefitted. **(1½)**

The cattle egret and grazing cattle share commensalism type of relationship. The grazing cattle flush out insects from grass while grazing. So, it becomes easier for egret to catch and feed on them. In this, one partner gets benefit, while other remains unaffected. **(1½)**

35. Differentiate among mutualism, parasitism and commensalism. Provide one example for each of them. **Foreign 2015**

Ans. Differences between mutualism, parasitism and commensalism are

Mutualism	Parasitism	Commensalism
It benefits both the interacting species.	It benefits one species, while other species is harmed.	Interaction between two species, where one species is benefitted and the other is neither harmed nor benefitted.
e.g. lichens represent mutualism between fungus and algae.	e.g. *Cuscuta*, tape worm and *Plasmodium*.	e.g. an orchid growing as an epiphyte on a mango tree.

36. Describe the mutual relationship between fig tree and wasp and comment on the phenomenon that operates in their relationships. **Delhi 2014**

Ans. For relationship between fig tree and wasp, refer to answer no. 24.

37. Name the type of interaction seen in each of the following examples:

(i) *Ascaris* worm living in the intestine of human.

(ii) Wasp pollinating fig's inflorescence.

(iii) Clown fish living among the tentacles of sea anemone.

(iv) Mycorrhizae living on the roots of higher plants.

(v) Orchid growing on a branch of mango tree.

(vi) Disappearance of smaller barnacles when *Balanus* dominated in the coast of Scotland. **Delhi 2011**

Ans. (i) Parasitism (ii) Mutualism

(iii) Commensalism (iv) Mutualism

(v) Commensalism (vi) Competition

5 Marks Questions

38. Given below is a table depicting population interactions between species A and species B.

Type of interaction	Species A	Species B
(a)	(–)	(0)
(b)	(+)	(–)

Name the types of interactions (a) and (b) in the above table. Justify giving three reasons, how the type of interaction (b) is important in an ecological context. **CBSE SQP 2020**

Ans. (a) Amensalism

(b) Predation **(2)**

The above given interactions are ecologically important as

- These are nature's way of transferring energy fixed by plants to higher trophic levels/conduits for energy transfer.
- These keep prey population under control.
- The predators help in maintaining species diversity in a community, by reducing the intensity of competition among competing prey species. **(3)**

39. What is the association between the bumble bee and its favourite orchid *Ophrys*? How would extinction or change of one affect the other? **Delhi 2012**

Ans. Mutualism is an association seen between the bumble bee and the orchid *Ophrys*. In this, both species are benefitted. One petal of orchid flower bears an uncanny resemblance to the female of the bee in size, colour and markings. The male bee is attracted to what it perceives as a female and pseudocopulates with the flower. During the process, the bee gets dusted with pollen from the flower. When this same bee pseudocopulates with another flower, it transfers pollens to it and thus pollinates the flower. **(3)**

Extinction of bumble bee will definitely affect the orchid flower because these bees are the means of pollination for the flower and if they get extinct, the pollination percentage will be reduced. But, the extinction of the orchid will not affect the bumble bee population. **(2)**

40. Study the table given below and answer the questions that follows

Species A	Species B	Name of interaction
(+)	(+)	*A*
(–)	(–)	*B*
(+)	(–)	*C*
(–)	(0)	*D*

(+) = Beneficial interaction

(–) = Detrimental interaction

(0) = Neutral interaction

Identify *A, B, C* and *D* in the given table and explain any three of them with the help of an example each. **Delhi 2011C**

Ans. *A* is **mutualism**, it is an interaction, where both species derive benefit from the interaction, e.g. lichens.

B is **Competition**, it is an interaction, where both species suffer due to similar requirement of resources, that are limited, e.g. in some South American lakes, visiting flamingoes and resident species compete for the common food.

C is **predation**, it is an interaction where an animal called predator kills and consumes other weaker animals called prey, i.e. one is beneffited and other is harmed, e.g. tiger and the deer.

D is **Amensalism**, it is an interaction, where one species is harmed, while other is neither benefitted nor harmed. *Penicillium* produces the toxin penicillin which kills other pathogen, but it itself does not get affected.

(any three)

Common Mistakes Often students get confused that predation and parasitism are same interaction but,

Predation Predator kills and consume the prey.

Parasitism Parasite invade the cells of host, use resources and cause harm.

41. (i) Why are herbivores considered similar to predators in the ecological context? Explain.

(ii) Differentiate between the following interspecific interactions in a population.

(a) Mutualism and competition

(b) Commensalism and amensalism **All India 2010**

Ans. (i) Herbivores feed on plants. They are considered as predators because like them they also transfer energy across the trophic levels. Besides this, they also keep the population of their prey under control. For example, when the prickly pear cactus was introduced in Australia in early 1920, they spread rapidly causing havoc. Their population was controlled by introducing cactus-feeding predator (a moth). **(2)**

(ii) (a) Differences between mutualism and competition are

Mutualism	Competition
It benefits both the interacting species.	Both the interacting species suffer.
Two individuals may be physically or physiologically associated.	No physical association between competitors.
Lichens represent mutualism between fungus and algae, where fungus absorbs nutrition and provides protection, while algae prepares food.	In some South American lakes, visiting flamingoes and resident species compete for the common food.

(1½)

(b) Differences between commensalism and amensalism are

Commensalism	Amensalism
Interaction between two species where one species is benefitted and the other is neither harmed nor benefitted.	Interaction between two different species, in which one species is harmed and the other is neither benefitted nor harmed.
e.g. an orchid growing as an epiphyte on a mango tree benefits by getting shelter and nutrition but the mango tree is not harmed or benefitted.	e.g. *Penicillium* produces a toxin killing other microorganisms but is not affected itself.

(1½)

Case Based/Source Based/Passage Based Questions (Based on Complete Chapter)

1. Observe the graph given below.

The graph represents inter-specific interaction between two species of paramecia competing for the same resource in a culture medium. *Paramecium caudatum* and *Paramecium aurelia* were grown in separate cultures as well as in mixed cultures. It was found that each species grew in numbers according to the logistic equation.

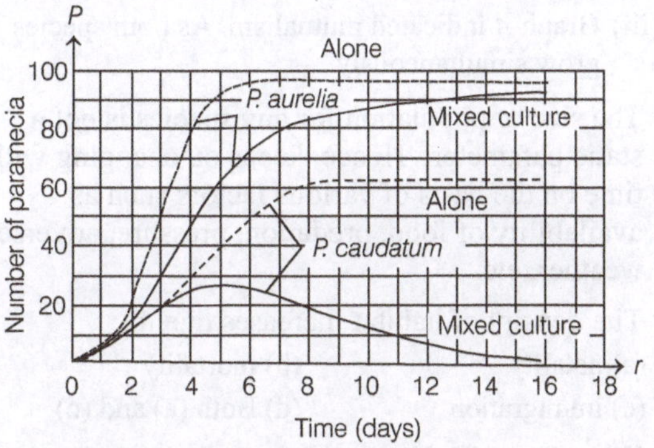

(i) Which species is competitively superior? Support it with the data provided in the graph.

(ii) State the underlying principle for the above result and name the scientist associated with this principle.

(iii) Explain the mechanism in which two or more species competing with each other can coexist.

Or (iii) Graphs *A* and *B* shown below depict interaction of two species. Which graph indicates mutualism? Give reason.

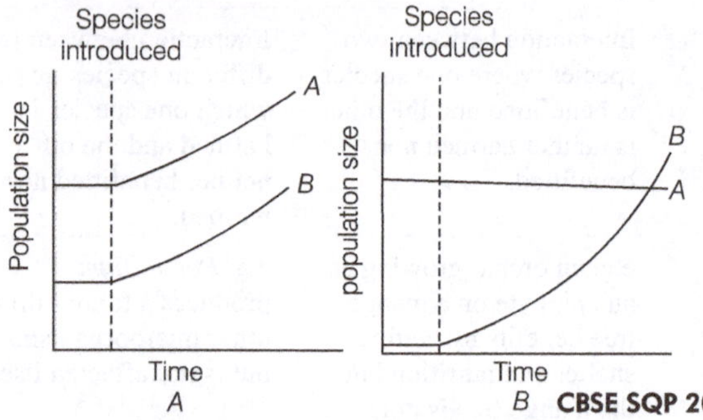

CBSE SQP 2024

Ans. (i) *P. aurelia* species is competitively superior *P. aurelia* grows in numbers more quickly than *P. caudatum* and shows more individuals in the same volume of culture/ 100 *Paramecium aurelia* in 6 days whereas 60 *P. caudatum* in 8 days. **(1)**

(ii) Competitive exclusion principle' which states that two closely related species competing for the same resources cannot coexist indefinitely and the competitively inferior one will be eliminated. GF Gause, associated with it. **(1)**

(iii) One such mechanism is 'resource partitioning'. If two species compete for the same resource, they could avoid competition by choosing different times for feeding or different foraging patterns, to avoid competition and coexist due to behavioural differences in their foraging activities. **(1)**

Or (iii) Graph *A* indicated mutualism. As both species grow simultaneously. **(1)**

2. The size of population for any species is not a static parameter. Hence, keeps on changing with time on the basis of various factors such as availability of food, predation, pressure, adverse weather, etc.

(i) The density of habitat increases due to
(a) natality (b) mortality
(c) immigration (d) Both (a) and (c)

(ii) What does '*N*' denotes in the equation below?

$$N_{t+1} = N_t\ [(B+I)-(D+E)]$$

(a) Birth rate (b) Death rate
(c) Population density (d) Population is beginning

(iii) Which one will produce more biomass?
(a) Single huge banyan tree
(b) 200 *Parthenium* plants
(c) 150 *Parthenium* plants
(d) All will produce equal biomass

(iv) The tiger census is based on
(a) Pugmarks (b) Faecal pellets
(c) Both (a) and (b) (d) None of these

(v) Exponential growth curve occurs when
(a) resources are limited
(b) resources are unlimited
(c) resources are not present at all
(d) All of the above

Ans. (i)-(d), (ii)-(c), (iii)-(a), (iv)-(c), (v)-(b)

3. Read the following and answer the questions given below

Ecology is a vast arena in biology, which is a study of organisms, their distribution and interaction with each other and the environment. To study the relationship between prey, predators, other interactions and phenomenon like competition, camouflage, mimicry, etc., it is mandatory to study the theory of population interaction. The interaction between nature, animals, plants and microbes to form a biological community is known as population interaction. These interactions can be intraspecific, i.e. existing between organisms of same population and interspecific, i.e. between members of different species.

(i) Name the association in which one species produces poisonous substance or a change in environmental conditions that is harmful to another species.

(ii) What do you mean by facultative mutualism?

(iii) Why did the Abingdon tortoise in Galapagos island become extinct?

(iv) How will the ability to camouflage benefits the prey?

Ans. (i) Amensalism is an interaction between different species, in which one species is harmed and the other is neither benefitted nor harmed, e.g. *Penicillium*, a mould secretes penicillin which kills bacteria, but the mould remains unaffected. **(1)**

(ii) Facultative mutualism is an interaction between two different species in which both are mutually benefitted, but they can live without each other. **(1)**

(iii) The Abingdon tortoise in Galapagos island became extinct due to interference competition, i.e. the feeding efficiency of species A might be reduced due to the interfering and inhibitory presence of the species B. Therefore, when goats were introduced in Galapagos island Abingdon tortoise become extinct due to greater browsing efficiency of the goats. **(1)**

(iv) Camouflage is a phenomenon of blending of an organism with the surrounding due to similar colour, marking and shape, so as to avoid the predators, e.g. leaf-like insects such as grasshopper. **(1)**

CHAPTER TEST

01 Mark Questions

Multiple Choice Questions

1 If birth rate is 100, death rate is 10 and number of individuals in population group is 1000, then what will be the percentage of natural growth rate?

(a) 0.09% (b) 9.0% (c) 0.9% (d) 90%

2 Bell-shaped age pyramid indicates that

(a) number of pre-reproductive and reproductive individual is almost equal

(b) post-reproductive individuals are comparatively fewer

(c) the population size remains stable

(d) All of the above

3

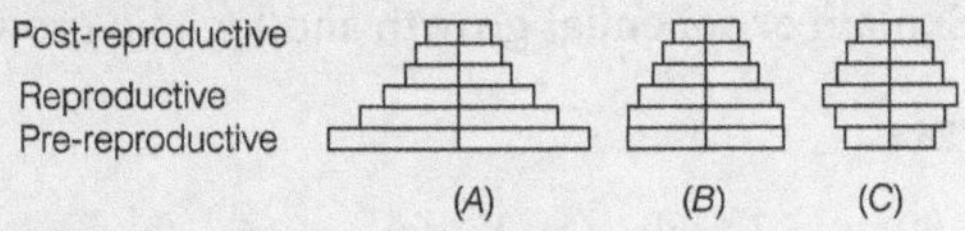

Select the correct option with respect to age pyramids.

(a) *A*–Expanding, *B*–Stable, *C*–Declining

(b) *A*–Stable, *B*–Expanding, *C*–Declining

(c) *A*–Stable, *B*–Declining, *C*–Expanding

(d) *A*–Declining, *B*–Stable, *C*–Expanding

4 The equation of sigmoid curve is

(a) $\frac{dN}{dt} = rN$ (b) $\frac{dN}{dt} = rN\left(1-\frac{N}{K}\right)$

(c) $\frac{dN}{dt} = 1-\frac{l}{K}$ (d) $\frac{dN}{dt} = \left(1-\frac{N}{K}\right)$

5 Predators also help in ...*A*... species diversity in a community, by ...*B*... the intensity of competition among competing prey species. Here, *A* and *B* can be

(a) *A*–exceeding, *B*–increasing

(b) *A*–maintaining, *B*–reducing

(c) *A*–reducing, *B*–maintaining

(d) *A*–maintaining, *B*–increasing

6 The prickly pear cactus becomes unusually abundant after its introduction in Australia because it

(a) does not have its predator

(b) formed new mycorrhizal association

(c) lost its thorns

(d) All of the above

7 Level of competition between species depends on

(a) availability of resources

(b) population density

(c) group interaction of organism

(d) All of the above

Assertion-Reason Type Questions

Direction (Q. Nos. 8-10) *In the questions given below two statements an Assertion and a Reason are given. Give the appropriate response as*

(a) If both Assertion and Reason are true and Reason is the correct explanation of Assertion

(b) If both Assertion and Reason are true, but Reason is not the correct explanation of Assertion

(c) If Assertion is true, but Reason is false

(d) If Assertion is false, but Reason is true

8 **Assertion** Predation is an interspecific interaction with a feeding strategy.

Reason Predation and prey maintain fairly stable population through time and rarely one population become abundant or scarce.

9 **Assertion** In commensalism one organism is benefitted and other is unaffected.

Reason Cattle egret bird and cattle is an example of commensalism.

10 **Assertion** Monarch butterfly are highly distasteful to predator.

Reason This is because they look ugly.

2/3 Marks Questions

11 List the methods used to estimate population size.

12 Differentiate between commensalism and mutualism by taking one example of each.

13 Explain birth rate and death rate in population with the help of an example.

14 Mention the characteristic of exponential growth.

15 Why do clown fish and sea anemone pair up? What is this relationship called?

16 A child felt stomach ache, nausea and loss of appetite. He consulted a doctor. The doctor prescribed him stool test. After the report of stool test, doctor told that he was infected with roundworm a parasite. What kind of parasite (exo or endo) is roundworm?

17 State Gause's competitive exclusion principle.

18 The given graph shows the population of a state according to the age group. Consider the graph given below and answer the following questions.

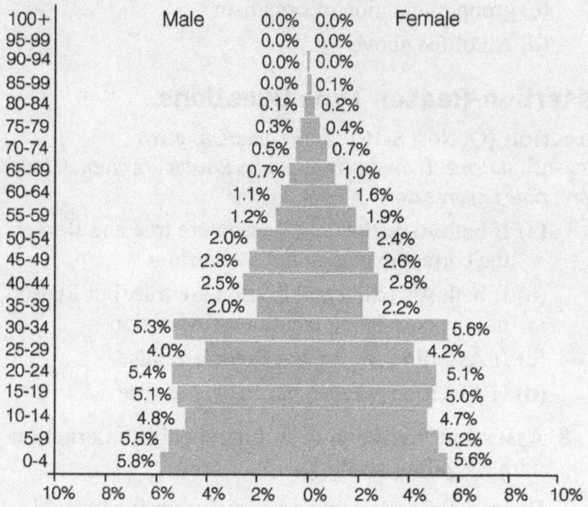

(i) What information can be inferred form the above graph?

(ii) This kind of graph is often referred to as expanding in terms of age pyramid. How far do you agree? Give reason.

(iii) What according to you can be the reason for this expanding population? State any two.

05 Marks Questions

19 Explain with the help of figures the three different type of age pyramids represented by human population.

20 Differentiate between parasitism and predation.

21 Write notes on any two

(i) Competition (ii) Mutualism

(iii) Commensalism

22 Explain exponential growth and logistic growth.

Answers

1. (b)	**2.** (d)	**3.** (a)	**4.** (b)	**5.** (b)
6. (a)	**7.** (d)	**8.** (a)	**9.** (b)	**10.** (c)

12 Ecosystem

TREND ANALYSIS 3 YEARS

Topic	Types of Questions	2024	2023	2020
TOPIC 01 Ecosystem : Structure and Function, Productivity and Decomposition	1 Mark	0	2	0
	2 Marks	0	0	2
	3 Marks	1	0	1
	4 Marks (Case Based)	0	0	0
	5 Marks	0	0	0
TOPIC 02 Energy Flow in Ecosystem	1 Mark	0	0	0
	2 Marks	0	0	1
	3 Marks	0	0	0
	4 Marks (Case Based)	0	0	0
	5 Marks	0	0	0

Average No. of Questions Across all Sets

TOPIC 1

Ecosystem : Structure and Function, Productivity and Decomposition

An ecosystem is a functional unit of nature, where living organisms interact among themselves and with the surrounding physical environment. The word 'ecosystem' was coined by **Sir AG Tansley** (1935).

The size of an ecosystem varies greatly from a small pond to a large forest or a sea.

Ecosystem can be grouped into two main categories

(i) **Terrestrial ecosystem** Forest, grassland, desert, etc.

(ii) **Aquatic ecosystem** Pond, lake, river, wetland, estuary, etc.

Crop fields and an aquarium are considered as **man-made ecosystems**, while river and forest are **natural ecosystems**.

Structure and Function of Ecosystem

- Each ecosystem consists of **biotic** (autotrophs, herbivores and carnivores) and **abiotic components** (soil, air, etc.). Their interaction with each other result in a physical structure, that is the characteristic for each type of ecosystem.
- The two important structural features of an ecosystem are
  - Identification and enumeration of plant and animal species of an ecosystem gives its **species composition**.
  - Vertical distribution of different species occupying different levels is called **stratification**.

  For example, trees occupy top vertical strata or layer of a forest, shrubs the second and herbs and grasses occupy the bottom layer.

- Major functional components of an ecosystem are
  1. Productivity
  2. Decomposition
  3. Energy flow
  4. Nutrient cycling
- To understand the concept of an aquatic ecosystem, let us take a small pond ecosystem as an example.
  A pond is a shallow waterbody in which all the above mentioned basic structural and functional components are present.
  (i) **Abiotic components** are water with all the dissolved inorganic and organic materials and soil deposited at the bottom.
  (ii) **Autotrophic components** are phytoplanktons, some algae and the floating, submerged and marginal plants. They can make their own food from inorganic substances, found at the edges.
  (iii) **Consumers** are zooplanktons, which are free-swimming and bottom dwellers. These are dependent on autotrophs for their nutrition.
  (iv) **Decomposers** are the fungi, bacteria and flagellates found abundantly in the bottom.

  Functioning of pond ecosystem occurs in following steps
  - Autotrophs convert inorganic material into organic material with the help of solar energy.
  - Heterotrophs consume autotrophs.
  - Decomposers decompose dead organic materials and mineralise it to release them back for reuse by the autotrophs.
  - The above events are repeated again and again.
  - Unidirectional movement of energy occurs towards the higher trophic levels and lost in the form of heat to the environment.

Productivity

It is the rate of biomass production. It is expressed in $g^{-2}yr^{-1}$ or (kcal m^{-2}) yr^{-1}. Productivity is of the following types

1. Primary Productivity

- The amount of biomass or organic matter produced per unit area over a time period by plants during photosynthesis is called primary productivity.
- The primary productivity can be divided into
  (i) **Gross Primary Productivity** (GPP) of an ecosystem is the rate of production of organic matter during photosynthesis. A considerable amount of GPP is utilised by plants in respiration.
  (ii) **Net Primary Productivity** (NPP) is gross primary productivity minus respiratory losses (R).
  $$NPP = GPP - R$$
  NPP is the available biomass for the consumption by heterotrophs, i.e. herbivores and decomposers.
- Annual NPP of the whole biosphere is about 170 billion tons (dry weight) of organic matter.
  Of this, despite of occupying about 70% of the surface of earth, the productivity of the oceans is only 55 billion tons. This is due to very less light availability in oceans for photosynthesis.
- Primary productivity of an ecosystem depends on
  - Plant species inhabiting a particular area.
  - Availability of nutrients in the soil.
  - Photosynthetic capacity of plants.
  - Variety of environmental factors.

2. Secondary Productivity

It is defined as the rate of formation of new organic matter by consumers.

Decomposition

- It is the process in which decomposers breakdown complex organic matter into inorganic substances like carbon dioxide, water and nutrients.
- The raw materials called **detritus** include dead plant remains such as leaves, barks, flowers and dead remains of animals body, faecal matter, etc.

Process of Decomposition

Process of decomposition occurs in the following steps
(i) **Fragmentation** is the breakdown of detritus into smaller particles by **detritivores**, e.g. earthworm, mites.
(ii) **Leaching** is the process by which water soluble inorganic nutrients go down into the soil horizon and get precipitated as unavailable salts.

(iii) **Catabolism** is the process of degradation of detritus into simple inorganic substances by bacterial and fungal enzymes.

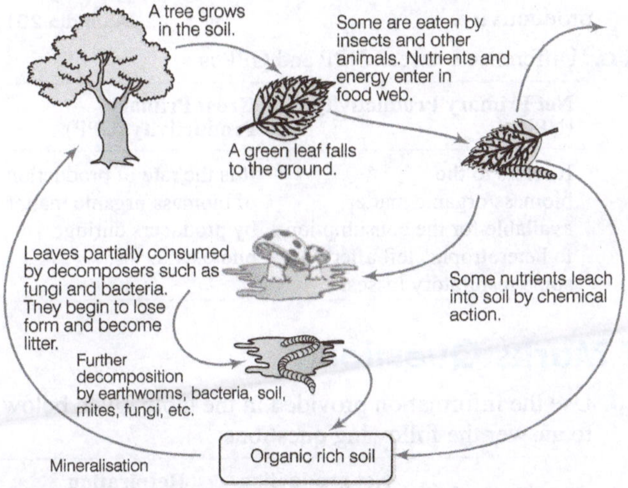

Figure 12.1 Diagrammatic representation of decomposition cycle in a terrestrial ecosystem

(iv) **Humification** is the process of accumulation of a dark coloured amorphous substance called **humus.** It is highly resistant to microbial action, undergoes decomposition at an extremely slow rate and serves as a reservoir of nutrients.

(v) **Mineralisation** is the process by which humus is further degraded by some microbes to release inorganic substances.

Factors Affecting Rate of Decomposition

Decomposition rate depends on the following

- Oxygen availability
- Chemical composition of detritus
- Climatic factors
- Temperature and soil moisture.
- Decomposition rate is slower, if detritus is rich in lignin and chitin. It is quicker, if detritus is rich in nitrogen and water soluble substances like sugars.
- Warm and moist environment speeds up decomposition, whereas low temperature and anaerobiosis inhibit decomposition and causes the formation of organic materials.

PYQs Previous Years' Questions

1 Mark Questions

Multiple Choice Questions

1. Which one of the following is not a characteristic feature of humus that formed during decomposition of detritus? **CBSE 2024 (Set-II)**
   (a) Amorphous, colloidal, dark coloured substance
   (b) Amorphous, colloidal, light coloured substance
   (c) Substance resistant to microbial action
   (d) Colloidal substance

Ans. (a) Humus is a colloidal, amorphous, dark coloured substance that is highly resistant to microbial action.

2. The primary productivity in an ecosystem is expressed as **CBSE 2023**
   (a) $gm^{-2}\ yr^{-1}$
   (b) $gm^{-2}\ yr$
   (c) $kcal\ m^{-2}\ yr^{-1}$
   (d) $kcal\ m^{-2}$

Ans. (d) $kcal\ m^{-2}$

Assertion-Reason Type Question

3. **Assertion** (A) Decomposition process is slower if detritus is rich in lignin and cutin.
   Reason (R) Decomposition is largely an oxygen requiring process. **CBSE 2023**
   (a) Both A and R are true and R is the correct explanation of A
   (b) Both A and R are true, but R is not the correct explanation of A
   (c) A is true, but R is false
   (d) A is false, but R is true

Ans. (b) Both A and R are true, but R is not the correct explanation of A

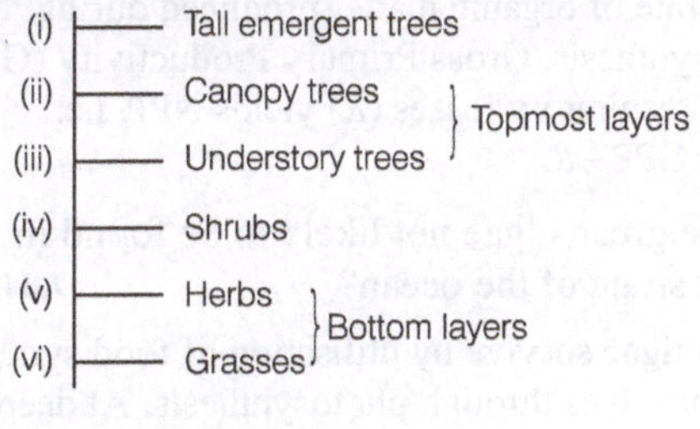

Very Short Answer Type Questions

4. How does a detritivore differ from a decomposer? Explain with an example of each. **Delhi 2015C**

Ans. Difference between detritivores and decomposers is

Detritivores	Decomposers
The organisms which feed on detritus and break them into small particles, e.g. earthworm.	The organisms which result in enzymatic breakdown of complex organic matter into inorganic substances, e.g. some bacteria and fungi.

5. How is 'stratification' represented in a forest ecosystem? **Delhi 2014**

Ans. The stratification, i.e. the vertical distribution of species at different levels in a forest ecosystem. It can be represented as

(i) Tall emergent trees
(ii) Canopy trees } Topmost layers
(iii) Understory trees
(iv) Shrubs
(v) Herbs } Bottom layers
(vi) Grasses

6. Mention any two reasons, why the primary productivity varies in different types of ecosystems. **All India 2014C**

Ans. The primary productivity varies in different types of ecosystems because

(i) It depends upon plant species (producers) of a given ecosystem and their photosynthetic capacity.

(ii) It is dependent on various environmental factors, availability of nutrients. (½+½)

7. Write the equation that helps in deriving the net primary productivity of an ecosystem. **Delhi 2013**

Or How is the net primary productivity of an ecosystem derived ? **All India 2012C**

Ans. Net Primary Productivity (NPP) is the weight of the organic matter stored by the producers which is available to heterotrophs for consumption. It is equal to the rate of organic matter produced during photosynthesis. Gross Primary Productivity (GPP) minus respiratory losses (R) yields NPP, i.e. $NPP = GPP - R$.

8. Why are green algae not likely to be found in the deepest strata of the ocean? **All India 2013**

Ans. Green algae survive by utilisation of food synthesised by themselves through photosynthesis. At deepest layer in ocean, light is absent. So, photosynthesis does not take place and hence green algae are not likely to be found in deep strata of ocean.

9. Write a difference between net and gross primary productivity. **All India 2011**

Ans. Difference between NPP and GPP is

Net Primary Productivity (NPP)	Gross Primary Productivity (GPP)
It refers to the biomass/organic matter available for the consumption to heterotrophs, left after some respiratory losses.	It is the rate of production of biomass/organic matter by producers during photosynthesis.

2 Marks Questions

10. Use the information provided in the table given below to answer the following questions:

Trophic level	Net production ($kJm^{-2}y^{-1}$)	Respiration ($kJm^{-2}y^{-1}$)
Top carnivore	50	35
Carnivores	420	378
Herbivores	4490	4041
Producers	45000	40,367

(i) Calculate the gross primary productivity.

(ii) Analyse the trend in the net production from producers to top carnivore. Give a reason for your observation. **CBSE SQP 2024**

Ans. (i) The GPP is the total amount of carbon compounds produced by photosynthesis of plants in an ecosystem in a given period of time.

$$GPP = NPP + R$$

$$\therefore \quad GPP = 45000 + 40367$$

$$= 85367 \text{ kgm}^{-2}\text{y}^{-1}$$ (1)

(ii) Net production is gradually reducing as we move from producers to consumers due to heat loss/respiration /10% law. (1)

11. Name and explain the processes earthworm and bacteria carry on detritus. **All India 2020**

Ans. Earthworm and bacteria help in breaking down the detritus (i.e. dead remains of plant and animals) into smaller particles. This process is known as decomposition. Bacteria secrete digestive enzymes to digest the organic matter externally and facilitate the cyclic exchange of materials between the biotic community and the environment, while earthworms breakdown the large detritus molecules into fine particles.

12. How is humus formed ? Mention any three characteristics of humus. **All India 2020**

Ans. Humus is a dark coloured amorphous substance formed as a result of humification, i.e. partial decomposition of detritus. (½)

Characteristics of humus are

(i) It is highly resistant to microbial action.

(ii) It undergoes decomposition at an extremely slow rate.

(iii) It serves as reservoir of nutrients due to its colloidal nature. (1½)

13. Write the relationship between productivity, gross primary productivity, net primary productivity and secondary productivity. **All India 2019**

Ans. The rate of biomass production is called productivity, expressed in term of gm^{-2} yr^{-1} for an ecosystem. It can be divided into Gross Primary Productivity (GPP) and Net Primary Productivity (NPP). GPP of an ecosystem is the rate of production of organic matter during photosynthesis. NPP is the available biomass for the consumption of heterotrophs (herbivores and decomposers). Secondary productivity is defined as the rate of formation of new organic matter by consumers i.e. NPP = GPP − *R*.

14. Describe how do oxygen and chemical composition of detritus control decomposition. **Delhi 2011**

Ans. **Effect of oxygen** The decomposition of detritus is largely an oxygen requiring process. Most of the decomposers (bacteria and fungi) are aerobic organisms. They require oxygen for their cellular activities while acting on dead organic matter. (1)

Effect of chemical composition Decomposition rate is slower, if detritus is rich in lignin and chitin. It is quicker if detritus is rich in nitrogen and water soluble substances like sugars. (1)

3 Marks Questions

15. (i) State what is primary productivity and mention its units.

(ii) Some ecologists observed that primary productivity of a place in Rajasthan was low as compared to a particular place in Kerala. Explain why. **CBSE 2024 (Set-I)**

Ans. (i) Primary productivity is the rate at which solar energy is converted into organic substances through the process of photosynthetic and chemosynthetic autotrophs. It is also referred as the production of organic compounds through the biological process of photosynthesis. Its unit is gm^{-2}yr^{-1} or (k cal m^{-2}) yr^{-1}. (1½)

(ii) Primary productivity depends on the plant species inhabiting a particular area, environmental factors, availability of nutrients and photosynthetic capacity of plants.

Primary productivity of a place in Rajasthan, i.e. an arid (dry) region has low primary productivity because of some unfavourable environmental conditions, like absence of water, high temperature and lack of vegetation.

On the other hand, Kerala, i.e., a coastal area has more primary productivity because of favourable environmental conditions like availability of water, moderate temperature and moderate amount of vegetation. (1½)

16. How would you differentiate between gross primary productivity from net primary productivity and secondary productivity of an ecosystem? **Delhi 2020**

Ans.

Gross primary productivity	Net primary productivity	Secondary productivity
It is the rate of production of biomass/organic matter by producers during photosynthesis.	It is equal to gross primary productivity minus respiration losses by the plants, which is finally available to the consumers.	It is defined as the rate of production of new organic matter by consumers over a period of time.

17. Describe the inter-relationship between productivity, gross primary productivity and net productivity. **All India 2017**

Ans. The rate of biomass production is called **productivity**. It is expressed in terms of gm^{-2} yr^{-1} or (kcal m^{-2}) yr^{-1}

Productivity of an ecosystem can be categorised as primary and secondary productivity.

Primary Productivity (PP) is the amount of biomass or organic matter produced per unit area over a time period by plants during photosynthesis. It can be divided into

- **Gross Primary Productivity** (GPP) It is the rate of production of organic matter during photosynthesis. A considerable amount of GPP is utilised by plants in respiration.
- **Net Primary Productivity** (NPP) It is the amount of energy left in the producers after utilisation of some energy for respiration. (2)

Inter-relationship between GPP and NPP

Gross primary productivity minus the respiration losses is net primary productivity. It is actually the available biomass for consumption by heterotrophs. GPP − *R* = NPP where, *R* = Respiration losses. (1)

18. Why earthworm is considered a farmer's friend? Explain humification and mineralisation occurring in a decomposition cycle. **Foreign 2015**

Ans. Earthworms are farmer's friend because these help in fragmentation of detritus and loosening of the soil. Both these processes are helpful for the decomposition of dead organic matter at a faster rate into inorganic substances like carbon dioxide, water and nutrients. These can be used by crop plants for their growth.

Humification and mineralisation occurring during decomposition cycle are as follows

Humification It is the process of accumulation of dark coloured amorphous substance called humus. Humus is highly resistant to microbial action and undergoes decomposition at very slow rate.

Mineralisation It is the process by which humus is degraded by some microbes to release inorganic substances. **(2)**

Concept Enhancer Fungi are considered an important decomposers especially in the forests. Termites and millipeds also contribute in the process of decomposition.

19. How does a detritivore differ from a decomposer? Explain with an example. **Delhi 2015C**

Ans. The differences between detritivores and decomposers are

Detritivores	Decomposers
These are soil dwelling small worm-like animals.	These are microorganisms.
These animals can ingest the food materials in their bodies.	These secrete digestive enzymes over the matter to be decomposed.
Ecologically, they cause pulverisation or fragmentation of detritus.	These organisms cause humification and mineralisation of organic matter.
e.g. earthworm.	e.g. bacteria, fungi.

20. Justify the importance of decomposer in an ecosystem. **Foreign 2015**

Ans. When a plant or animal dies, it leaves behind nutrients and energy in the organic material present in its body. Decomposers complete the decomposition process by breaking down this organic matter into NH_4, CO_2 and nutrients. This releases raw nutrients in a form, which is usable to plants again. This process resupplies nutrients to the ecosystem. When the decomposers feed on dead organisms, they leave behind nutrients. These nutrients become part of the soil.

21. (i) What is primary productivity? Why does it vary in different types of ecosystems?

(ii) State the relation between gross and net primary productivity. **Delhi 2014**

Ans. (i) For primary productivity, refer to answer no. 17. For causes of its variation in different types of ecosystems, refer to answer no. 6. **(1½)**

(ii) For relation between gross and net primary productivity, refer to answer no. 17. **(1½)**

5 Marks Questions

22. Taking the example of a lake as a simple aquatic ecosystem, interpret how various functions of this ecosystem are carried out. Make a food chain that is functional in this ecosystem. **CBSE SQP 2018**

Ans. The solar radiation is the ultimate source of energy for all ecosytems. So, aquatic ecosystem (pond) too has energy input through solar radiation. The other functional aspects of this ecosystem are as follows

- **Productivity** Aquatic ecosystem consists of phytoplanktons (unicellular plants). These are autotrophs, which convert solar radiation and other inorganic nutrients into food and thus make first trophic level. **(1)**
- **Energy flow** The unidirectional flow of energy occurs from phytoplanktons to small zooplanktons and then other carnivores of different levels. There is dissipation and loss of heat at every trophic level. **(1)**
- **Decomposition** This occurs as all the plants and animals die and their bodies are decomposed by decomposers (mainly fungi and bacteria). This process involves catabolism, fragmentation of dead organic matter, leaching of nutrients, humification and mineralisation by bacteria, fungi and flagellates, which are found in abundance at the bottom of the lake. **(1)**
- **Nutrient cycling** It occurs by the decomposition of dead organic matter to release the nutrients back to be reused by the autotrophs. **(1)**

Food chain of aquatic ecosystem

Producers → Phytoplanktons → Zooplanktons (Primary consumers) → Small fishes → Big fishes. **(1)**

23. How is detritus decomposed step-by-step by different agents and made available as nutrients to the plants? Explain. **Delhi 2013C**

Or Explain the different steps involved in the process of decomposition of detritus. **Delhi 2011C**

Or Describe the process of decomposition of detritus under the following heads fragmentation, leaching, catabolism, humification and mineralisation. **Delhi 2010**

Ans. **Detritus** It is the raw material for decomposition. It includes dead remains of plants (leaves, bark and flowers) and of animals including faecal matter.

It is largely an aerobic process, i.e. requires oxygen for its processing. Different steps involved in the process of decomposition are

(i) **Fragmentation** is the process of breaking down of detritus into smaller particles.

(ii) **Leaching** is the process by which water soluble inorganic nutrients go down into the soil horizons and get precipitated as unavailable salts.

(iii) **Catabolism** is the process of degradation of detritus into simple organic material by the action of bacterial and fungal enzymes and their further conversion into inorganic compounds.

(iv) **Humification** is a process that leads to an accumulation of a dark coloured, amorphous and colloidal substance called humus, which is highly resistant to microbial action and decomposes at a very slow rate. It serves as a reservoir of nutrients.

(v) **Mineralisation** is the process by which humus is further degraded by microbial action and releases inorganic nutrients.

TOPIC 2

Energy Flow in Ecosystem

Energy Flow

- Sun is the only source of energy for all the ecosystems on earth, except for deep sea hydrothermal vents in sea water ecosystem. Of the total incident solar radiation, less than 50% is **Photosynthetically Active Radiation** (PAR).
- Plants capture only 2-10% of the PAR and this small amount of energy sustains the entire living world.
- There is unidirectional flow of energy from the sun to producers and then to consumers. This indicates the first law of thermodynamics.
- Ecosystem needs a constant supply of energy to synthesise the molecules they require, to counteract the universal tendency towards increasing disorderliness. This indicates the second law of thermodynamics.
- In an ecosystem, major **producers** are green plants, i.e. herbaceous and woody plants. In aquatic ecosystem, the producers constitute phytoplanktons, algae and higher plants.

Food Chain

In an ecosystem, there is transfer of food from one organism to another organism, this food transfer makes a chain known as food chain.

Types of Food Chain

There are various types of food chains that operate in an ecosystem. These include

(i) **Grazing Food Chain** (GFC) starts with green plants (producer) at first trophic level.

- In an aquatic ecosystem, the GFC is the major channel for energy flow.
- Energy for food chain comes from sun.

A simple Grazing Food Chain (GFC) is depicted below

Grass (Producer) ⟶ Goat (Primary consumer) ⟶ Man (Secondary consumer)

(ii) **Detritus Food Chain** (DFC) starts with dead organic matter with decomposers called **saprophytes** at first trophic level, e.g. bacteria and fungi.

- In a terrestrial ecosystem a large fraction of energy flows through this type of food chain.
- Energy for the food chain comes from organic remain or detritus.
- Detritus food chain may be connected with the grazing food chain at various levels, forming a **food web**.

Food Web

When a number of food chains interconnect with each other forming a web-like pattern is known as food web. Various characteristics of food web include

- In a food web, one organism can hold more than one position.
- The flow of energy is very difficult to calculate.
- It is a series of branching lines.

Trophic Level

It is the specific place occupied by an organism in the food chain in an ecosystem. There are many trophic levels in nature including

- Producer (first trophic level)
- Herbivore (second trophic level)
- Carnivore (third trophic level)
- Top carnivore (fourth trophic level)
- All animals are consumers or heterotrophs. If they feed on the producers they are called **primary consumers**, e.g. insects, birds, mammals and molluscs.
- The consumers that feed on herbivores (primary consumers) are called **primary carnivores** or **secondary consumers**. The animals that eat primary carnivores are called **secondary carnivores**.

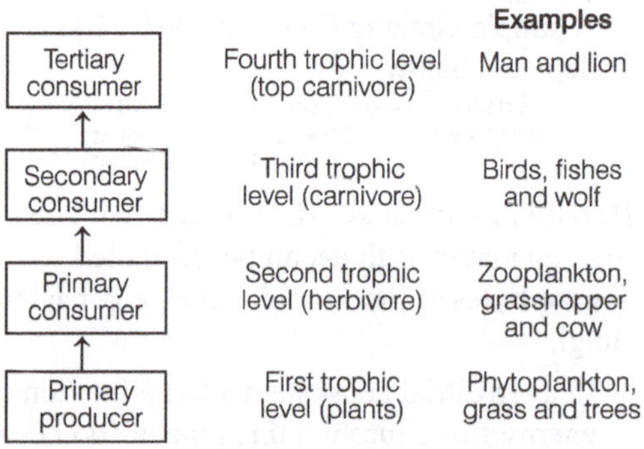

Figure 12.2 Diagrammatic representation of trophic levels in an ecosystem

It is to note that

- Amount of energy decreases at successive trophic levels.
- Organisms at each trophic level depend on those at the lower trophic level for their energy demands.

Ten Per Cent Law (10% Law)

Flow of energy through different trophic levels, i.e. from producers to top carnivores can be easily depicted on the basis of the diagram given below

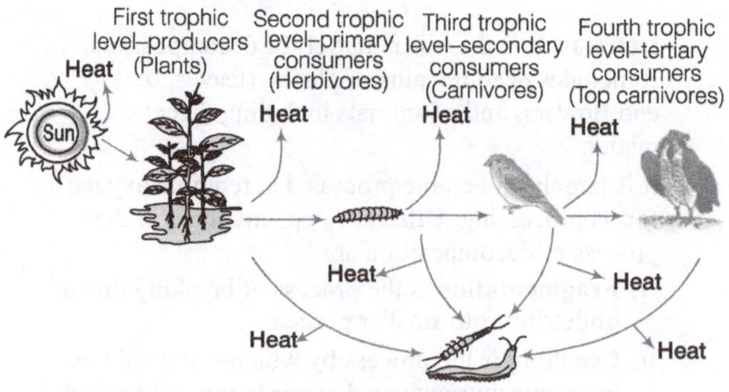

Figure 12.3 Diagrammatic representation of flow of energy through different trophic levels

- Each trophic level has a certain mass of living material at a particular time called the **standing crop**. It is measured as the mass of living organism (biomass) or the number in a unit area.
- The number of trophic levels in the grazing food chain is restricted as the transfer of energy follows **10% law**, i.e. only 10% energy is transferred to each trophic level from the lower trophic level.
- So, maximum amount of energy is lost during energy flow from one trophic level to another. In this way, top consumer gets least energy.

Ecological Pyramid

It is the graphical representation of relation between producers and consumers in terms of number, biomass and energy in the form of pyramid. In pyramid structure, the base (broader) always represents the producers or the first trophic level and the apex (narrower) represents top level consumer or last trophic level.

Types of Ecological Pyramids

(i) **Pyramid of number** represents the relationship in terms of numbers, between the producers and consumers in an ecosystem. It can be

- Upright, e.g. in grassland ecosystem
- Inverted, e.g. in tree ecosystem

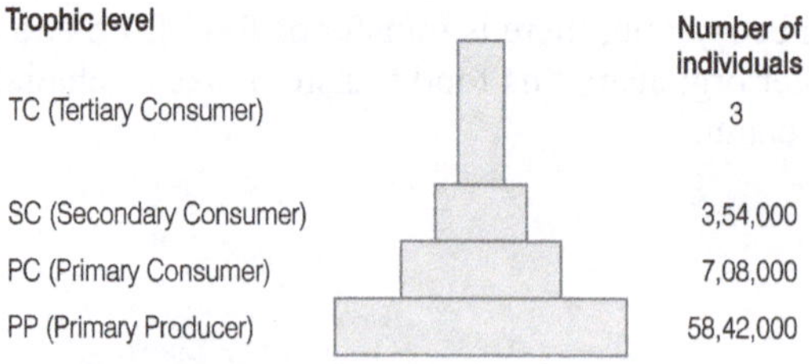

Figure 12.4 Pyramid of numbers in a grassland ecosystem. Only three top carnivores are supported in an ecosystem based on the production of nearly 6

(ii) **Pyramid of biomass** represents the relationship between producers and consumers in terms of biomass. It can be

- Upright, e.g. in grasslands ecosystem
- Inverted, e.g. in pond ecosystem

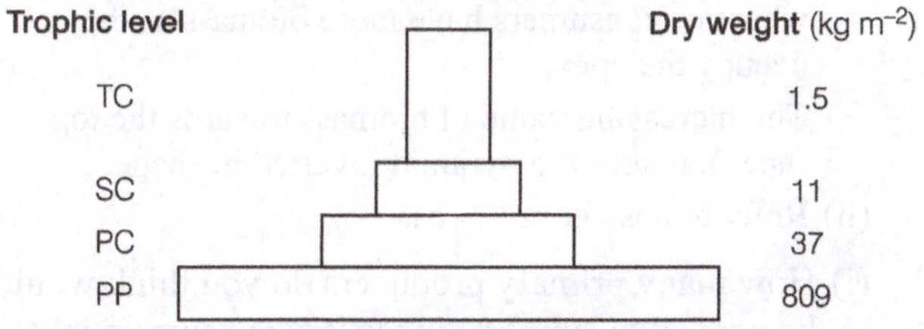

Figure 12.5 Pyramid of biomass shows a sharp decrease in biomass at higher trophic levels

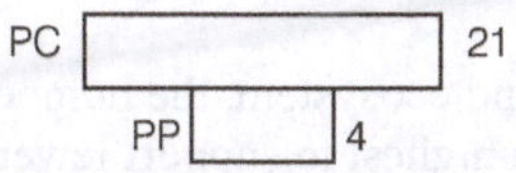

Figure 12.6 Inverted pyramid of biomass. Small standing crop of phytoplankton supports large standing crop of zooplanktons

(iii) **Pyramid of energy** states the relationship between the producers and consumers in an ecosystem in terms of flow of energy. Each bar in the energy pyramid indicates the amount of energy present at each trophic level in a given time or annually per unit area.

It is always upright because the energy is lost as heat at each step.

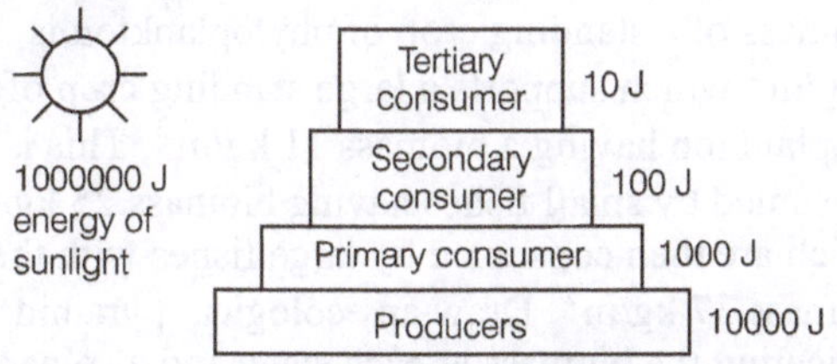

Figure 12.7 An ideal pyramid of energy. Observe that primary producers convert only 1% of the energy of the sunlight available to them into NPP

- A given species may occupy more than one trophic level in the same ecosystem at the same time, e.g. a sparrow is a primary consumer, when it eats seeds, fruit, peas and a secondary consumer, when it eats insects and worms.

Limitation of Ecological Pyramids

Ecological pyramids also have certain limitations;

- It does not take into account the same species belonging to two or more trophic levels.
- It assumes a simple food chain, which never exists in nature. It does not accommodate a food web.
- Saprophytes/decomposers are not given any position in ecological pyramids.

PYQs Previous Years Questions

1 Mark Questions

Mutiple Choice Question

1. Which of the following food chains is the major conduit for energy flow in terrestrial and aquatic ecosystems, respectively? **CBSE SQP 2023**

	Terrestrial ecosystem	Aquatic ecosystem
(a)	Grazing	Grazing
(b)	Detritus	Detritus
(c)	Detritus	Grazing
(d)	Grazing	Detritus

Ans. (c)

Very Short Answer Type Questions

2. 'Man can be a primary as well as secondary consumer'. Justify this statement. **Foreign 2015**

Ans. Man can be a primary as well as secondary consumer because man eats both plant as well as meat of other animals. So, man is herbivore as well as carnivore.

3. State what does standing crop of a trophic level represent. **Delhi 2013**

Ans. Standing crop of a trophic level represents the total mass of living material or energy content of all the organisms of a trophic level at a particular time and location.

4. What is a detritus food chain made up of ? How do they meet their energy and nutritional requirements? **All India 2013**

Ans. Detritus food chain is made up of decomposers, i.e. some bacteria and fungi. (½)

They meet their energy and nutrient requirements by degrading the dead organic matter of detritus. (½)

5. List any two ways of measuring the standing crop of a trophic level. **Foreign 2010**

Ans. Standing crop can be measured as

(i) Biomass of living organisms in a unit area. (½)

(ii) Number of living organisms in a unit area. (½)

2 Marks Questions

6. Biomass of a standing crop of phytoplankton is 4 kg/m^2 which supports a large standing crop of zooplankton having a biomass 11 kg/m^2. This is consumed by small fishes having biomass 25 kg/m^2 which are then consumed by large fishes with the biomass 37 kg/m^2. Draw an ecological pyramid indicating the biomass at each stage and also name the trophic levels. Mention whether it is an upright or inverted pyramid. **CBSE SQP 2024**

Ans.

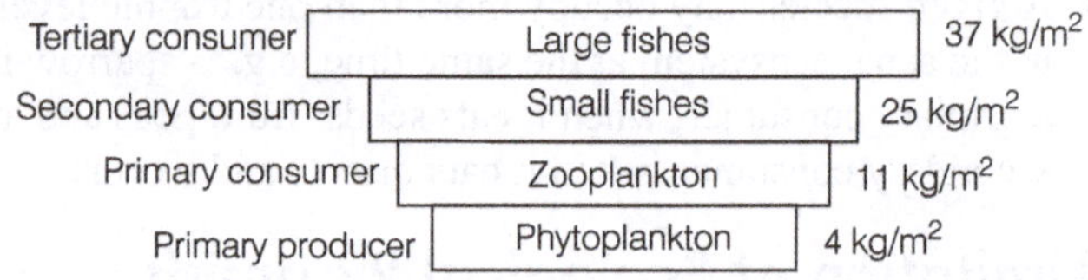

Inverted pyramid of biomass

7. (i) Draw a pyramid of numbers where a large number of insects are feeding on the leaves of a tree. What is the shape of this pyramid?

(ii) Will the pyramid of energy be also of the same shape in this situation? Give reason for your response. **CBSE SQP 2023**

Ans. (i) According to the question, pyramid of number will be as given

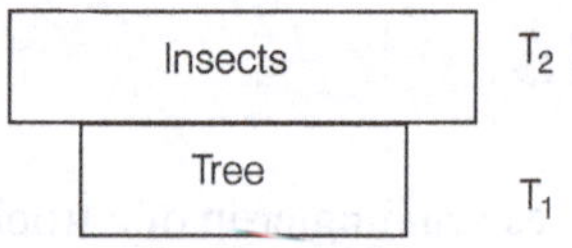

Here, T_1 and T_2 represent trophic levels 1 and 2, respectively. The shape of this pyramid will be inverted because a large number of insects feed on one tree. **(1)**

(ii) No, the pyramid of energy is always upright and never goes inverted as, during the flow of energy from one trophic level to another, some energy is always lost as heat at every trophic level. **(1)**

8. (i) Given below is a pyramid of biomass in an ecosystem where each bar represents the standing crop available in the trophic level. With the help of an example explain the conditions where this kind of pyramid is possible in nature? **CBSE SQP 2023**

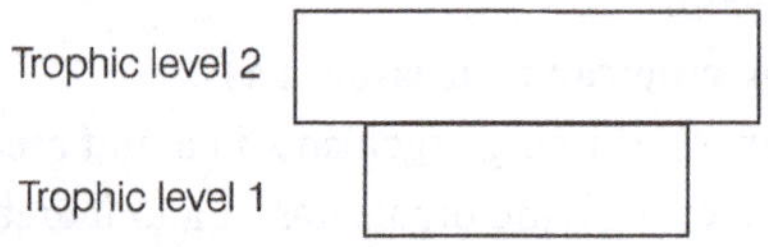

(ii) Will the pyramid of energy be also of the same shape in this situation? Give reason for your response.

Ans. (i) Inverted pyramids of biomass are seen in aquatic conditions where producers have least biomass whereas, consumers have more biomass as they occupy the apex. **(1)**

The increasing value of biomass towards the top (apex), makes the pyramid inverted in shape.

(ii) Refer to answer no. 7 (ii). **(1)**

9. (i) How many primary producers do you think would be needed to support six tertiary consumers in a grassland ecosystem ?

(ii) Draw a grassland pyramid to substantiate answer. **Delhi 2020**

Ans. (i) In grassland ecosystem, the number of producers (plants) is highest to support fewer herbivores (primary consumers) and carnivores (secondary and tertiary consumers).

Only three top carnivores are supported in an ecosystem based on the production of nearly 60 lakh plants. As mentioned above, three tertiary consumers are supported by 60 lakh plants. Six tertiary consumers will be supported by 120 lakh plants. **(1)**

(ii) Pyramid of numbers in a grassland ecosystem as shown below

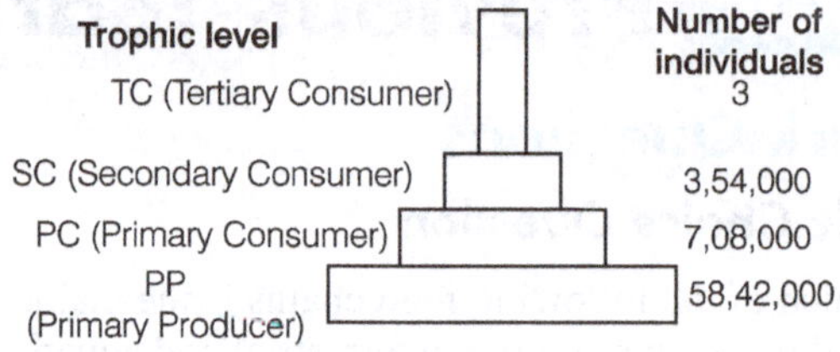

(1)

10. Construct a pyramid of biomass starting with phytoplankton. Label its three trophic levels. Is the pyramid upright or inverted? Justify your answer. **CBSE SQP 2020**

Ans.

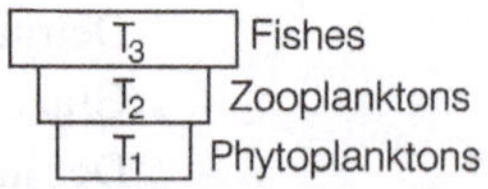

Pyramid of biomass in sea **(1)**

The pyramid of biomass in pond ecosystem is inverted because the biomass of fishes is much more than that of the zooplankton and phytoplankton. In a pond ecosystem, a small standing crop of phytoplanktons supports a large standing crop of fishes.

11. It is possible that a species may occupy more than one trophic level in the same ecosystem at the same time. Explain with the help of one example. **All India 2013**

Ans. A single species may occupy more than one trophic level at the same time in ecosystem because, the trophic level of species represents the functional level of species in the energy flow. (1)

For example, sparrow is primary consumer when it eats seeds and secondary consumer when feeds on insects and worms. The preference of food habit depends on the available food. (1)

12. Discuss the relationship between detritus food chain and grazing food chain in a terrestrial ecosystem. **All India 2012C**

Ans. The producers occupy the first trophic level in terrestrial ecosystem and thus make base of food chain. These producers (plants) are grazed upon by the grazers (herbivores). Primary carnivores prey upon herbivores and are eaten up by secondary carnivores.

The decomposers act on all dead animals/plants and return nutrients stored in them to the soil. These nutrients are again used up by the plants and cycle goes on. This way the grazing food chain and detritus food chain are linked up.

Concept Enhancer A much larger fraction of energy flows through detritus food chain than the grazing food chain in a terrestrial ecosystem.

13. Identify the type of given ecological pyramid and give one example each of pyramid of number and pyramid of biomass in such cases. **All India 2011**

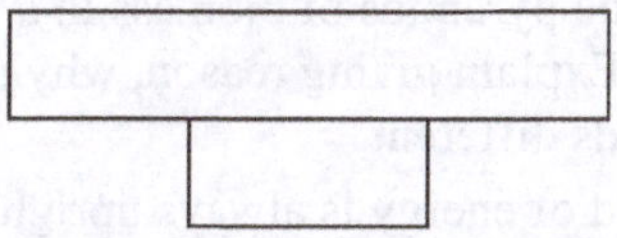

Or Explain standing crop in an ecosystem. Draw a pyramid of biomass when a small standing crop of phytoplanktons supports a large standing crop of zooplankton in the sea. **Delhi 2010**

Ans. Given ecological pyramid represents the **inverted pyramid of biomass** wherein small standing crop of phytoplanktons supports large standing crop of zooplankton.

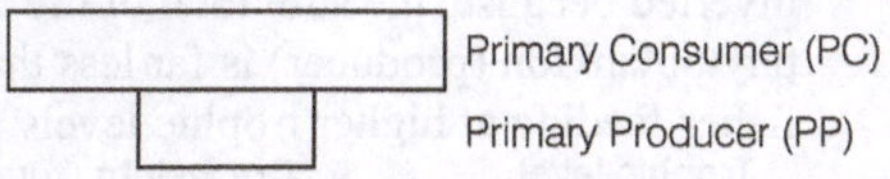

Pyramid of biomass (standing crop)

Pyramid of number is inverted in tree ecosystem and that of biomass in pond ecosystem.

Or For standing crop in an ecosystem, refer to answer no. 3.

3 Marks Questions

14. (i) How is the grazing food chain different from the detritus food chain?

(ii) "The detritus food chain may be connected to the grazing food chain at some levels in an ecosystem". Give an example in support of the statement. **CBSE 2024 (Set-II)**

Ans. (i) The differences between Grazing Food Chain (GFC) and Detritus Food Chain (DFC) are as follows

GFC	DFC
Sun is the major source of energy.	Detritus is the major source of energy.
Producers (e.g. plants and algae) occupies the first trophic level.	Detritivores feeding on the detritus occupies the first trophic level.
e.g. Grass → Goat → Man	e.g. Dead leaves → Wood louse → Black bird
Comparatively lesser amount of energy flows through this chain.	Much larger amount of energy flows through this chain.
Long-sized chain.	Small sized chain.
Much more common.	Less common.
Major energy flow path in an aquatic ecosystem.	Major conduit of energy in terrestrial ecosystem.

(1½)

(ii) The Detritus Food Chain (DFC) may be connected to the Grazing Food Chain (GFC) at same level in an ecosystem. It can be supported by the fact that certain organisms of the GFC are predators to certain animals of DFC.

For example, earthworms which are detritivores are eaten by small birds (DFC) which becomes prey to predators like vulture/kites or even small animals of the GFC. (1½)

15. (i) What does an ecological pyramid represent?

(ii) The ecological pyramids may have an 'upright' or an 'inverted' shape. Justify with the help of suitable examples. **CBSE 2024 (Set-II)**

Ans. (i) Refer to text on page no. 348.

(ii) Refer to text on page no. 349.

16. 'In a food chain, a trophic level represents a functional level, not a species'. Explain. **Delhi 2016**

Ans. In a food chain, a trophic level represents a functional level, not a species because the trophic level is a specific position of an organism in the food chain. All organisms occupy a particular place in their natural

surrounding or in a community according to their feeding relationship with other organisms.
This specific position is based on the organism's feeding relationship with other organisms and the source of their nutrition or food. (1½)
Producers occupy the first trophic level, primary consumers (herbivores) occupy the second and the secondary consumers (carnivores) occupy the third level on the basis of their function in food chain.

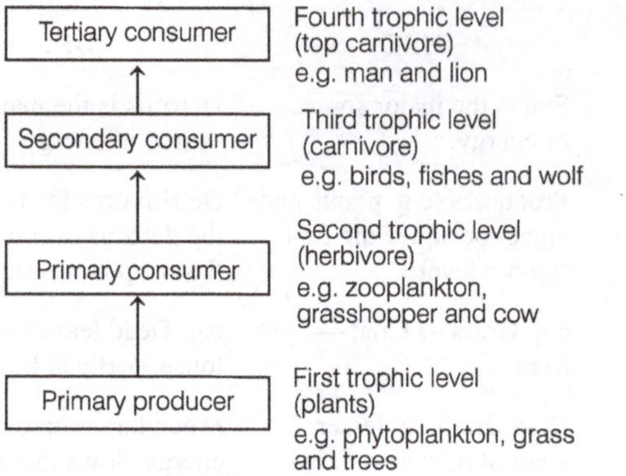

Diagrammatic representation of trophic levels in an ecosystem (1½)

17. In a botanical garden of a city there is a huge banyan tree growing on which hundreds of birds and thousands of insects live. Draw the pyramids of numbers and also biomass represented by this community. Comment giving reasons on the two different pyramids drawn. **Delhi 2016C**

Ans. Pyramid of number and pyramid of biomass showing interaction between trees, insects, birds and big birds is as follows

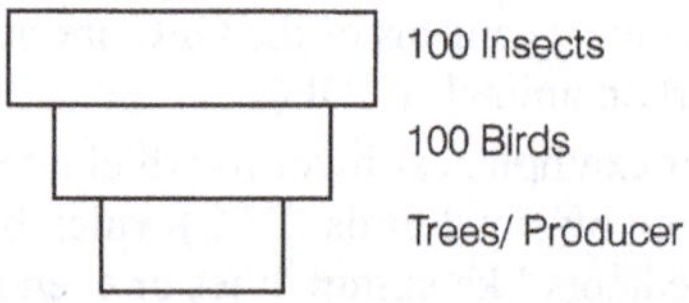

Pyramid of number (spindle-shaped)

Pyramid of number in this ecosystem is inverted as the number of insects is maximum. The number of trees and birds are less than the insects. (1½)

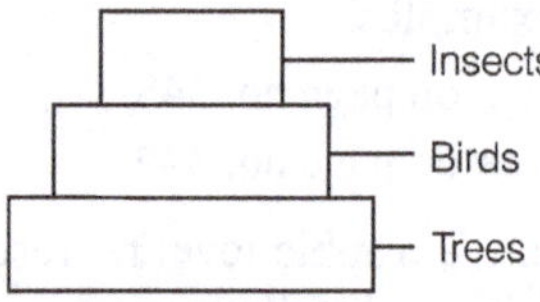

Pyramid of biomass

The pyramid of biomass in this ecosystem is upright because the biomass decreases at each trophic level. (1½)

18. Differentiate between two different types of pyramids of biomass with the help of an example. **Delhi 2013**

Ans. Pyramid of biomass refers to the relationship between producers and consumers in terms of biomass. It can be upright, e.g. in grasslands ecosystem or inverted, e.g. in pond ecosystem. (2)

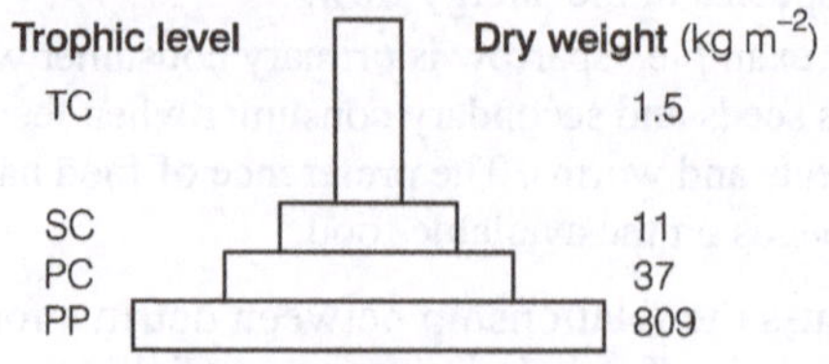

Pyramid of biomass shows a sharp decrease in biomass at higher trophic levels

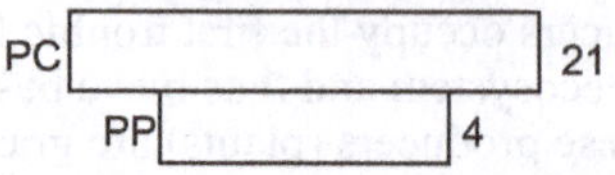

Inverted pyramid of biomass. Small standing crop of phytoplankton supports large standing crop of zooplankton (1)

5 Marks Questions

19. (i) The pyramid of energy is always upright. Explain.

(ii) Explain with the help of labelled diagrams the difference between an upright pyramid of biomass and an inverted pyramid of biomass. **All India 2019**

Or It is often said that the pyramid of energy is always upright. On the other hand, the pyramid of biomass can be both upright and inverted. Explain with the help of examples and sketches. **All India 2015**

Or (i) Draw the pyramids of biomass in a sea and in a forest. Explain giving reason, why are the two pyramids different.

(ii) Pyramid of energy is always upright. Explain. **Foreign 2010**

Ans. (i) **Pyramid of energy** It represent the total energy of the organism in each trophic level. Pyramid of energy is always upright, i.e. it can never be inverted because when enegy is transferred from a particular trophic level to the next trophic level, some energy is always lost as heat at each step. (2)

(ii) (a) **The pyramid of biomass in a sea ecosystem** is inverted because, the sum total of the weight of phytoplankton (producer) is far less than a few fishes feeding at higher trophic levels.

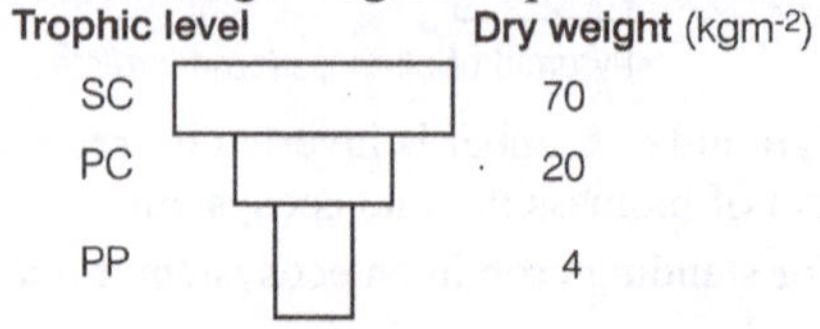

Sea ecosystem

(b) **Pyramid of biomass in a forest ecosystem** is upright because producers are more in biomass than primary consumers. Primary consumers are more than secondary consumers and secondary consumers are more than tertiary consumers (top).

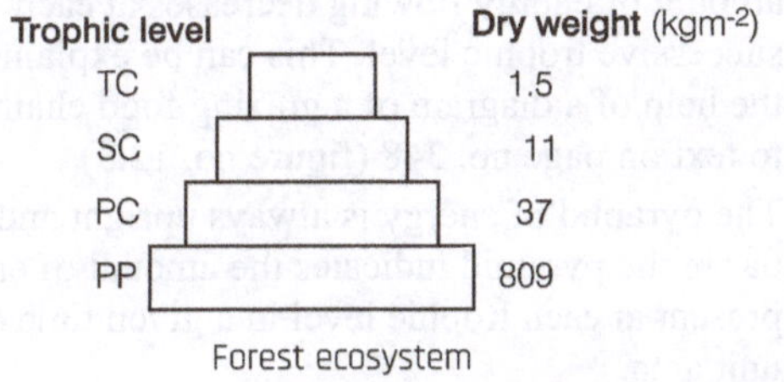

Forest ecosystem

(3)

Concept Enhancer Pyramid of energy is considered to be an ideal pyramid existing in the ecosystem. This is because the pyramid of energy it is the most accurate representation of the energy flow through a food chain as it indicates how much energy is lost at each trophic level.

20. (i) What is a trophic level in an ecosystem? What is 'standing crop' with reference to it ?

(ii) Explain the role of the 'first trophic level' in an ecosystem.

(iii) How is the detritus food chain connected with the grazing food chain in a natural ecosystem?

CBSE 2018

Ans. (i) **Trophic level** Organisms occupy a place in the natural surroundings or in a community according to their feeding relationship with the other organisms. Organisms also occupy a specific place in the food chain on the basis of their nutrition or food. It is known as trophic level.

Standing crop refers to the mass of a living material at a particular time in a trophic level. **(1½ + 1½)**

(ii) **First trophic level** consists of producers. These are autotrophs. They trap the light energy and convert it into chemical energy.

The organisms of other trophic levels, i.e. consumers, depend on them for their energy and food requirement. Thus, first trophic level plays a very important role in the ecosystem. **(1)**

(iii) **Connection between grazing food chain and detritus food chain** Grazing food chain and detritus food chain are connected to each other.

Nutrients released by decomposers of detritus food chain are utilised by plants or autotrophs of grazing food chain.

These plants in turn transfer these nutrients to other organisms. The dead remains of these organisms are source of food for the decomposers. **(1)**

21. (i) What is an ecological pyramid? Compare the pyramids of energy, biomass and number.

(ii) Write any two limitations of ecological pyramids.

All India 2017

Ans. (i) **Ecological pyramid** It is the diagrammatic illustration of connection between different trophic levels in terms of energy, biomass and number of organisms.

The base of each pyramid represents the producers or the first trophic level. Apex represents tertiary or top level consumers. In general, all pyramids are upright, but there are few exceptions.

Comparison of Different Types of Pyramids

Pyramid of energy	Pyramid of biomass	Pyramid of number
It represents total energy of the organisms in each trophic level.	It represents the total weight of the organisms in each trophic level.	It represents the total number of organisms at each trophic level.
Pyramid of energy is always upright because when energy is transferred from a particular trophic level to next, some energy is always lost.	It is upright in case of terrestrial ecosystem.	Pyramid of number is upright in most ecosystems.
It can never be inverted.	It is inverted for aquatic ecosystems.	In a tree ecosystem, pyramid of number is inverted.

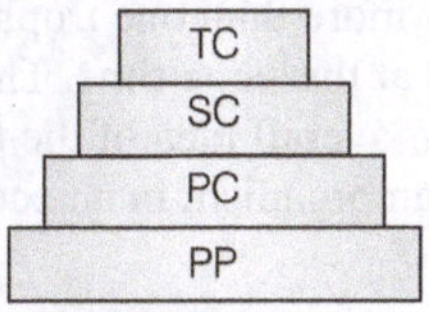

Pyramid of energy

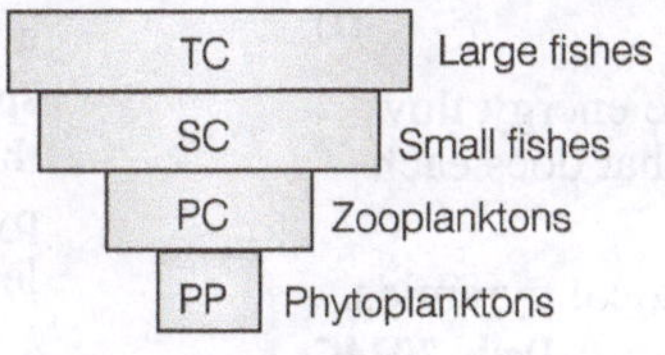

Inverted pyramid of biomass (sea)

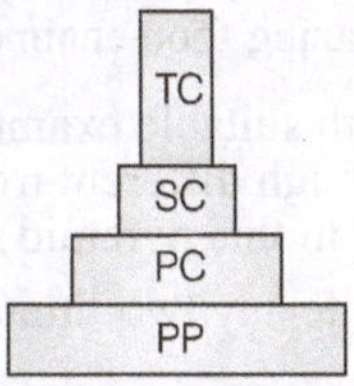

Pyramid of number in a grassland ecosystem

(3)

Note TC (Tertiary Consumer), SC (Secondary Consumer), PC (Primary Consumer), PP (Primary Producer)

(ii) **Limitations of ecological pyramids**

- It never takes into account the same species belonging to two or more trophic levels.
- Saprophytes are not given any place in ecological pyramid even though, they play an important role in ecosystem. **(2)**

Concept Enhancer Ecological pyramids are also known as Eltonian pyramids as it was developed by Charles Elton.

22. (i) Taking example of a small pond, explain how the four components of an ecosystem function as a unit.

(ii) Name the type of food chain that exists in a pond.

All India 2016

Ans. (i) Following are the four components of pond ecosystem which function as unit

(a) Abiotic (light, temperature, water).

(b) Autotrophs (producers mainly phytoplanktons).

(c) Heterotrophs (zooplankton, small fishes, big fishes).

(d) Decomposers (bacteria, fungi). **(2)**

Pond ecosystem is self-sustainable unit. Abiotic components are water, inorganic nutrients dissolved in water, light, temperature. Biotic components are producers like algae and aquatic plants. Consumers are zooplanktons, larvae, tadpole and some fishes.

Primary carnivores are water beetles, scorpions, dragonfly larvae, *Hydra* and some fishes. Decomposers include fungi, bacteria and some flagellates.

This pond system performs all the functions of an ecosystem, which are given below

(a) **Autotrophs** They convert inorganic materials with the help of solar energy.

(b) **Heterotrophs** They consume autotrophs.

(c) **Decomposers** They decompose and mineralise dead organic materials to release them back for reuse by the autotrophs. The above events are repeated again and again. **(2)**

(ii) Grazing food chain exists in a pond. **(1)**

23. (i) With suitable examples, explain the energy flow through different trophic levels. What does each bar in this pyramid represent?

(ii) Write any two limitations of ecological pyramids.

Delhi 2014C

Ans. (i) The energy flows unidirectionally from the first trophic level (producers) to last trophic level (consumers) and as the energy flows from one trophic level to another, some energy is always lost as heat into the surrounding environment. So, the amount of energy flowing decreases at each successive trophic level. This can be explained with the help of a diagram of a grazing food chain. Refer to text on page no. 348 (figure no. 12.3)

The pyramid of energy is always upright and each bar in the pyramid indicates the amount of energy present at each trophic level in a given time or per unit area. **(3)**

(ii) The limitations of ecological pyramids are

(a) It does not consider the same single species operating at two or more trophic levels.

(b) It assumes simple food chains that do not exist in nature and do not accommodate food web.

(c) Saprophytes, detritivores and decomposers are not given any place in pyramids, despite their vital role in ecosystem (any two). **(2)**

24. (i) Draw a pyramid of numbers of a situation, where a large population of insects feed upon a very big tree. The insects in turn, are eaten by small birds which in turn are fed upon by big birds.

(ii) Differentiate giving reasons, between the pyramid of biomass of the above situation and the pyramid of numbers that you have drawn.

Delhi 2012

Ans. (i) For pyramid of numbers, refer to answer no. 17. **(2½)**

(ii) For differentiation between the pyramid of biomass and pyramid of numbers of given situation, refer to answer no. 21 (i). **(2½)**

25. (i) Explain the significance of ecological pyramids with the help of an example.

(ii) Why are the pyramids referred to as upright or inverted? Explain.

All India 2012

Ans. (i) **Significance of ecological pyramids**

They graphically represent the relation between producers and consumers in order to calculate energy content, biomass and number of organisms of that trophic level. A trophic level represents only a functional level not a species as such. A given species may occupy more than one trophic level in the same ecosystem at the same time. The ecological pyramids provide an overall idea of the trophic levels occupied by an organism in an ecosystem.

Example A sparrow is a primary consumer when it eats seeds, fruits, peas and a secondary consumer when it eats insects and worms. **(2)**

(ii) **Upright pyramids** When producers are more in number and biomass than the herbivores and herbivores are more in number and biomass than the carnivores, pyramids are referred to as upright.

Energy at a lower trophic level is always more than at a higher trophic level. Pyramid of energy is referred to as always upright.

Inverted pyramids When the numbers and biomass of producers are less and consumers increase and become largest in top consumer level. Pyramid of number and biomass is referred to as inverted. **(3)**

Case Based/Source Based/Passage Based Questions (Based on Complete Chapter)

1. The diagrammatic illustration of connection between different trophic levels is given below.

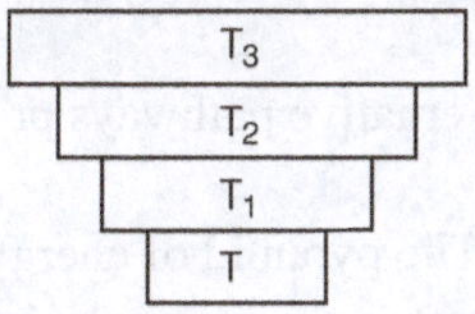

(i) Identify the type of ecological pyramid
(a) upright (b) bell-shaped (c) inverted (d) decline

(ii) What does the base of this pyramid indicate?
(a) Primary consumer (b) Producers
(c) Secondary consumer (d) Tertiary consumer

(iii) What does the apex of this pyramid indicate?
(a) Primary consumer (b) Secondary consumer
(c) Tertiary consumer (d) Producers

(iv) This type of pyramid is also observed in
(a) pyramid of number in tree ecosystem
(b) pyramid of biomass in pond ecosystem
(c) pyramid of biomass in tree ecosystem
(d) Both (a) and (b)

(v) The first trophic level in any pyramid is always occupied by
(a) producers only
(b) can be producer on primary consumers
(c) secondary consumer
(d) tertiary consumer

Ans. (i)-(c), (ii)-(b), (iii)-(c), (iv)-(d), (v)-(a)

2. Observe the diagram given below and answer the following questions.

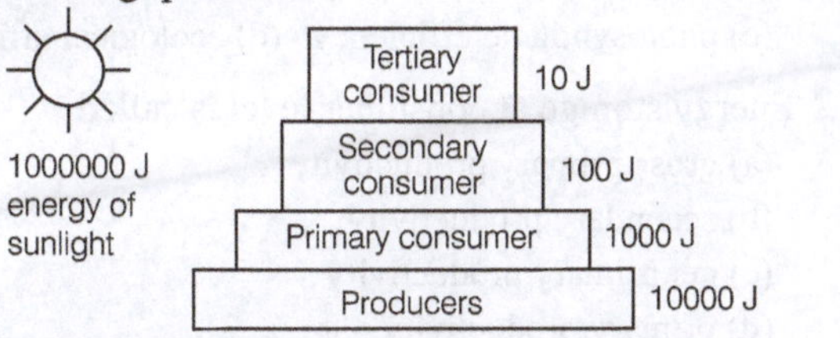

An ideal pyramid of energy. Observe that primary producers convert only 1% of the energy of the sunlight available to them into NPP

(i) Why is pyramid of energy always upright?

(ii) Can a given species occupy more than one trophic level in the same ecosystem at the same time?

(iii) State any two limitations of ecological pyramids.

Ans. (i) Pyramid of energy states the relationship between the producers and consumers in an ecosystem in terms of flow of energy. It is always upright because the energy is lost as heat at each step. **(1)**

(ii) A given species may occupy more than one trophic level in the same ecosystem at the same time, e.g. a sparrow is a primary consumer when it eats seeds, fruit, peas and a secondary consumer when it eats insects and worms. **(1)**

(iii) Ecological pyramids also have certain limitations. These are

(a) They do not take into account the same species belonging to two or more trophic levels.

(b) They assume a simple food chain, which never exists in nature. **(2)**

CHAPTER TEST

01 Mark Questions

Multiple Choice Questions

1 The percentage of energy transferred from one trophic level to the next is called

(a) net production efficiency (b) assimilation efficiency
(c) photosynthetic efficiency (d) ecological efficiency

2 Energy storage at consumer level is called

(a) gross primary productivity
(b) secondary productivity
(c) net primary productivity
(d) primary productivity

3 PAR stands for

(a) Photosynthesis Active Reaction
(b) Photosynthesis Absorb Radiation
(c) Photosynthetically Active Radiation
(d) Photosynthetically Active Reaction

4

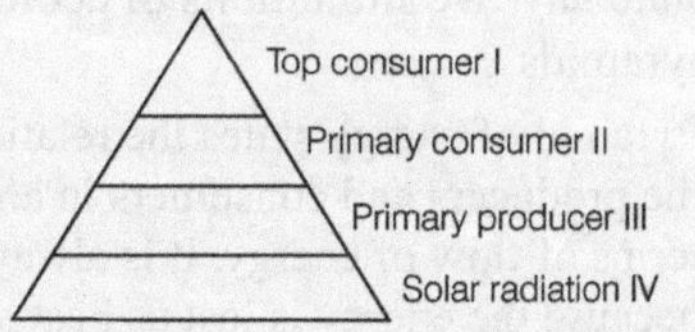

I. 10 kcal/m^2/yr II. 100 kcal/m^2/yr
III. 1000 kcal/m^2/yr IV. 10000 kcal/m^2/yr

Refer to the above diagram of energy pyramid. The ecological efficiency at primary consumer level, in comparison to that at secondary consumer level is

(a) same
(b) more
(c) less
(d) cannot be ascertained from the data

5 If a single plant species is removed from a food web, then most likely

(a) an animal species will fill the unoccupied niche
(b) other plants will produce enough food for herbivores
(c) dependent herbivores will have to find new food sources
(d) carnivores will be unaffected by the loss

6 Secondary productivity is rate of formation of new organic matter by

(a) producer (b) parasite
(c) consumer (d) decomposer

Assertion-Reason Type Questions

Direction (Q. Nos. 7-10) *In the questions given below two statements an* ***Assertion*** *and a* ***Reason*** *are given. Give the appropriate response as*

(a) If both Assertion and Reason are true and Reason is the correct explanation of Assertion
(b) If both Assertion and Reason are true, but Reason is not the correct explanation of Assertion
(c) If Assertion is true, but Reason is false
(d) If Assertion is false, but Reason is true

7 **Assertion** The rate of decomposition of detritus is reduced in the regions of high altitude.
Reason It happens due to immobilisation of nutrients.

8 **Assertion** If a particular crop is destroyed due to some diseases, the herbivores in that area do not perish.
Reason Alternative pathways provided by the food web.

9 **Assertion** The pyramid of energy is always upright.
Reason Number of autotrophs in the pyramid of energy are maximum.

10 **Assertion** Herbivores are also called as first order consumers.
Reason These obtain their food directly from plants.

2/3 Marks Questions

11 State difference between natural and artificial ecosystem.

12 Construct an ideal pyramid of energy when 1000000 J of sunlight is available. Label all its levels.

13 Distinguish between upright and inverted pyramid.

14 Describe the different classes of consumers.

05 Marks Questions

15 'The energy flow in the ecosystem follows the first and second law of thermodynamics'. Explain.

16 Describe the abiotic and biotic components of an ecosystem.

17 Organisms at a higher trophic level have less energy available. Comment.

Answers

1.	(d)	**2.**	(b)	**3.**	(c)	**4.**	(a)	**5.**	(c)
6.	(c)	**7.**	(a)	**8.**	(a)	**9.**	(c)	**10.**	(a)

13

Biodiversity and its Conservation

TREND ANALYSIS 3 YEARS

Average No. of Questions Across all Sets

	Types of Questions	2024	2023	2020
TOPIC 01 Biodiversity	1 Mark	0	3	0
	2 Marks	1	0	0
	3 Marks	0	0	0
	4 Marks (Case Based)	1	0	0
	5 Marks	0	0	0
TOPIC 02 Conservation of Biodiversity	1 Mark	0	0	0
	2 Marks	0	0	0
	3 Marks	0	1	2
	4 Marks (Case Based)	0	0	0
	5 Marks	0	0	0

TOPIC 1

Biodiversity

- It can be defined as the occurrence of different types of genes, gene pools, species, habitats and ecosystem in a given region at a given time.
- The term biodiversity was given by a sociobiologist **Edward Wilson** to describe the combined diversity at all the levels of biological organisation.
- There are more than 20,000 species of ants, 3,00,000 species of beetles, 28,000 species of fishes and nearly 20,000 species of orchids.
- The most important levels of biodiversity are as follows

1. Genetic Diversity

- It shows high diversity at gene (and chromosomal) level.
  - The genetic variation (in terms of allelic forms of the same gene) expressed by the medicinal plant *Rauwolfia vomitoria* growing in different Himalayan ranges is in terms of the potency and concentration of the active chemical (reserpine) that the plant produces.
  - India has more than 50,000 genetically different strains of rice and 1000 varieties of mango.

2. Species Diversity

It is the measure of the varieties of species and their abundant presence within a region, e.g. Western Ghats have more amphibians than Eastern Ghats. **Species richness** and **species evenness** are the two important measures of species diversity.

3. Ecological Diversity

It refers to the diversity at ecosystem level. It makes communities more productive and stable, e.g. India has a greater ecosystem diversity (in terms of variety of habitats in deserts, rainforests, mangroves, coral reefs, wetlands, estuaries and alpine meadows) than a Scandinavian country like Norway.

Global Species Diversity

It means total species present on the earth.

- According to IUCN (2004), the total number of plant and animal species is slightly more than 1.5 million.
- For many taxonomic groups, species inventories are more complete in temperate than in tropical countries.
- A more conservative and scientifically sound estimate by **Robert May**, places the global species diversity at about 7 million.
- More than 70% of all the species recorded are animals, while plants comprise no more than 22% of the total.
- Among animals, insects are most species rich taxonomic group, making about 70% of the total. It means, out of every 10 animals, 7 are insects on the earth.
- The number of fungal species in the world is more than the combined total of the species of fishes, amphibians, reptiles and mammals.
- Biologists are not sure about number of prokaryotic species because
  - conventional taxonomic methods are not suitable for identifying microbial species.
  - many species are not culturable in the lab.

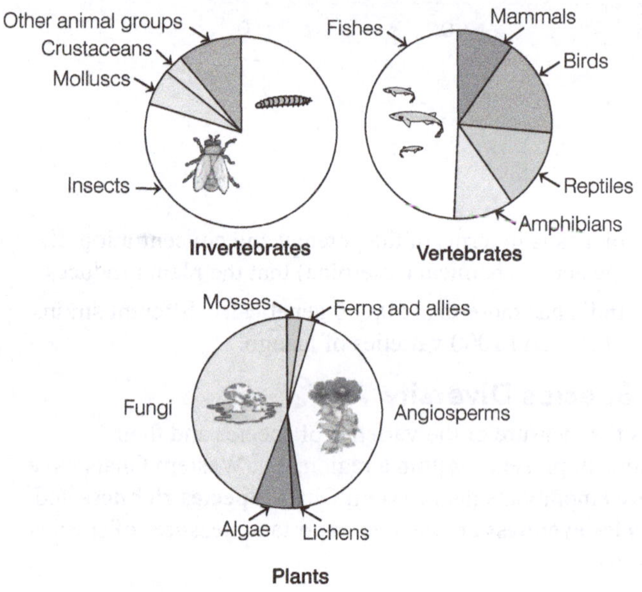

Figure 13.1 Proportionate number of species of major taxa in global biodiversity

Biodiversity in India

- Although India has only 2.4% of the world's land area, its share of the global species diversity is 8.1%. This makes India one of the 12 megadiversity countries of the world.
- About 45,000 species of plants and twice as many of animals have been recorded from India.
- According to May's global estimates, only 22% of the total species have been recorded so far. If this proportion is applied to India's diversity figures, there may be probably more than 1,00,000 plant species and more than 3,00,000 animal species yet to be discovered and described.
- A large fraction of these species faces the threat of becoming extinct even before we discover them.

Patterns of Biodiversity

The patterns indicate that the biodiversity is not uniform throughout the world because it is affected by

1. Latitudinal Gradients

- These demonstrate the decrease in species diversity as we move away from the equator towards the poles.
- Tropics (latitudinal range of 23.5°N-23.5°S) harbour more species than temperate or polar areas.
- For example, Colombia located near the equator has around 1400 species of birds, while New York at 41°N has 105 species and Greenland at 71°N has only 56 species.
- Studies indicate that the tropical areas have more biodiversity. For example,
- India with much of its land area in the tropical latitudes, has more than 1200 species of birds.
- A tropical forest in equator has upto 10 times as many species of vascular plants as a forest of equal area in a temperate region like the midwest of USA.
- Tropical Amazonian rainforest in South America has the greatest biodiversity on earth. It homes 40,000 species of plants, 3,000 of fishes, 1300 of birds, 427 of mammals, 427 of amphibians, 378 of reptiles and of more than 1,25,000 invertebrates.
- Scientists estimate that in these rainforests, there might be atleast 2 million insect species waiting to be discovered and named.

Reasons for Greater Biodiversity in Tropics

- Speciation is generally a function of time. The temperate regions were subjected to frequent glaciation in the past, but the tropics have remained undisturbed and hence had evolved more species diversity, because it had a long evolutionary time for species diversification.
- Tropical environments, unlike temperates ones, are less seasonal, relatively more constant and predictable. Such constant environments promote niche specialisation and lead to a greater species diversity.
- More solar energy is available in tropics, which contributes to higher productivity. This in turn might contribute indirectly to greater diversity.

2. Species-Area Relationships

- **Alexander von Humboldt**, a German naturalist and geographer observed that within a region, species richness increased with increasing explored area, but up to a limit.
- In fact, the relation between species richness and area for a wide variety of taxa (like angiosperm plants, birds, bats and freshwater fishes) turn out to be rectangular hyperbola.

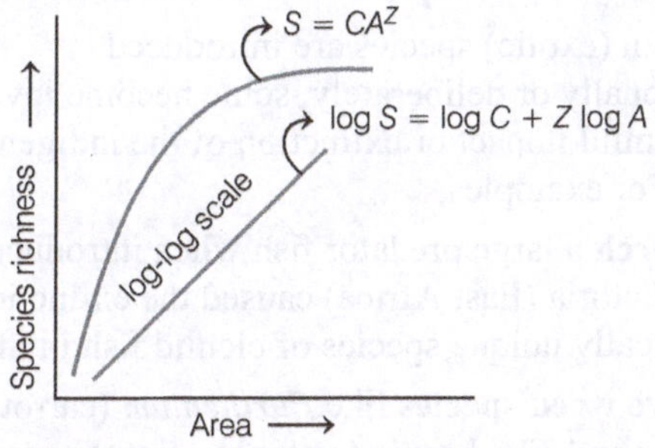

Figure 13.2 Showing species-area relationship

- On a logarithmic scale, the relationship is a straight line as given in the following equation

$$\log S = \log C + Z \log A$$

where, S = Species richness,
A = Area, C = Y-intercept,
Z = Slope of the line (regression coefficient)

- The value of Z lies in the range of 0.1-0.2 regardless of taxonomic group or the region.
- If we analyse the species-area relationship among very large areas like the entire continents, the slope of the line will be much steeper, i.e. Z values in the range of 0.6-1.2. For example, for fruit eating (frugivorous) birds and mammals in the tropical forests of different continents, the slope is found to be 1.15.

Importance of Species Diversity to the Ecosystem

These are as follows

- According to ecologists, communities with more species tend to be more stable than those with less species.
- Attributes of a stable community are as follows
  - It should not show too much variation in productivity from year-to-year.
  - It must be either resistant or resilient to occasional disturbances (natural or man-made).
  - It must be resistant to invasions by alien species.
- **David Tilman's** long term experiments on ecosystem found that plots with more species showed less year-to-year variation in total biomass. He also showed that increased diversity contributed to higher productivity.
- It is not clear how species richness contributes to the well-being of an ecosystem. But, it is enough to realise that rich biodiversity is not only essential for ecosystem health, but imperative for the survival of the human race on this planet.

Rivet Popper Hypothesis

- **Paul Ehrlich** through his rivet popper hypothesis tried to explain the importance of biodiversity for the survival of species.
- This hypothesis assumes the ecosystem to be an airplane and the species to be the rivets joining all parts together.
- If every passenger pops a rivet to take home (resulting in species extinction), it may not affect the flight safety initially (proper ecosystem functioning) but with time as more and more rivets are removed, the plane becomes dangerously weak.
- Loss of rivet on the wings (key species that drives major ecosystem functions) is a more serious threat to flight safety than loss of a few rivets on the seats or windows of the plane.

Loss of Biodiversity

It is caused by factors like over-population, urbanisation and industrialisation.

- The colonisation of tropical Pacific Islands by humans have led to the extinction of more than 2000 species of native birds.
- The IUCN Red List (2004) documents the extinction of 784 species (including 338 vertebrates, 359 invertebrates and 87 plants) in the last 500 years.
- Some latest examples of recent extinctions are Dodo (Mauritius), Quagga (Africa), Thylacine (Australia), Steller's sea cow (Russia) and three sub-species of tiger (Bali, Javan and Caspian).
- The last twenty years alone have witnessed the disappearance of 27 species.
- Presently, 12% of bird species, 23% of all mammal species, 32% of all amphibian species and 31% of all gymnosperm species in the world face the threat of extinction.
- Careful analysis of records shows that amphibians appear to be more vulnerable to extinction.
- The grim scenario of extinctions is the fact that more than 15,500 species worldwide are facing the threat of extinction.
- Presently '**sixth extinction** ' is in progress. Its species extinction rates are 100-1000 times faster than in the pre-human times. Human activities are responsible for such faster rates and if the present trend continues, nearly half of species on earth will become extinct within 100 years.

Results of Loss of Biodiversity in a Region

These are as follows

- Decline in plant production.
- Lowered resistance to environmental perturbations, such as drought.
- Increased variability in certain ecosystem processes such as plant productivity, water use, pest and disease cycles.

Causes of Loss of Biodiversity

They are also named as **The Evil Quartet**. These are as given below

1. Habitat Loss and Fragmentation

- The main cause of extinction of species is the destruction of their habitat.
- For examples,
  - Tropical rainforests once covering more than 14% of the land surface, now cover only 6% of land area and they are being destroyed fast.
  - Amazon rainforest (called lungs of the planet) is being cut and cleared for the cultivation of soybeans and for conversion to grasslands for raising beef cattle.
- When large habitats are broken up into small fragments due to various human activities, mammals and birds requiring large territories and certain animals with migratory habits are badly affected, leading to their population decline.
- The degradation of habitats by pollution also threatens the survival of many species and many have already become extinct in last 500 years.

2. Overexploitation

Overexploitation of natural resources by humans results in degradation and extinction of the resources. For example, Steller's sea cow, passenger pigeon and many marine fishes have become extinct in last 500 years.

3. Alien (Exotic) Species Invasions

When alien (exotic) species are introduced unintentionally or deliberately, some become invasive and cause harmful impact or extinction of the indigenous species. For examples,

- **Nile perch** a large predator fish when introduced in Lake Victoria (East Africa) caused the extinction of an ecologically unique species of cichlid fish in the lake.
- **Invasive weed species** like *Parthenium* (carrot grass), *Lantana* and *Eichhornia* (water hyacinth) caused environmental damage and pose threat to native species.
- The recent example is of the African cat fish (*Clarias gariepinus*), introduced for aquaculture purpose, is posing a threat to the indigenous cat fishes of Indian rivers.

4. Coextinctions

When a species becomes extinct, the plant and animal species associated with it in an obligatory manner, also become extinct.

For example, if the host species becomes extinct, all those parasites exclusively found on it will also become extinct. In plant pollinator mutualism, extinction of one results in the extinction of the other.

PYQs Previous Years' Questions

1 Mark Questions

Multiple Choice Questions

1. The IUCN Red Data List (2004) in the last 500 years documents the extinction of nearly 784 species including **CBSE 2023**
(a) 330 invertebrates (b) 338 invertebrates
(c) 359 invertebrates (d) 362 invertebrates

Ans. (c) 359 invertebrates.

2. Which one of the following groups faces maximum threat of extinction? **CBSE 2023**
(a) Gymnosperms (b) Birds
(c) Amphibian (d) Mammals

Ans. (c) Amphibian.

3. The sixth extinction in progress currently is different from all previous extinctions on earth as it is **CBSE 2023**
(a) 10-100 times faster
(b) 100-1000 times faster
(c) 100-10,000 times faster
(d) 1000-10,000 times faster

Ans. (b) 100-1000 times faster

4. The most important cause of biodiversity loss is **CBSE SQP 2020**
(a) overexploitation of economic species
(b) habitat loss and fragmentation
(c) invasive species
(d) breakdown of plant-pollinator relationships

Ans. (b) Habitat loss and fragmentation is the most important cause of biodiversity loss.

Assertion-Reason Type Questions

5. **Assertion** (A) Communities that comprise of more species tend to be more stable.
Reason (R) A higher number of species results in less year-to-year variation in total biomass. **CBSE 2024 (Set-II)**
(a) Both Assertion (A) and Reason (R) are true and Reason (R) is the correct explanation of Assertion (A)
(b) Both Assertion (A) and Reason (R) are true, but Reason (R) is not the correct explanation of Assertion (A)
(c) Assertion (A) is true, but Reason (R) is false
(d) Assertion (A) is false, but Reason (R) is true

Ans. (a) Both A and R are true and R is the correct explanation of A.
According to Tilman, communities with a higher number of species results in less year to year variation in total biomass. Thus, they do not show too much variation in productivity from year-to-year and therefore, remain stable.

6. **Assertion** (A) A community with more species is more stable than that with less species.
Reason (R) More the number of species, lesser the variation in the total biomass production year after year. **CBSE SQP 2021-22**
(a) Both Assertion and Reason are true and Reason is the correct explanation of Assertion
(b) Both Assertion and Reason are true, but Reason is not the correct explanation of Assertion
(c) Assertion is true, but Reason is false
(d) Assertion is false, but Reason is true

Ans. (a)

Very Short Answer Type Questions

7. Which of the three forests, temperate, mangroves and tropical evergreen is more vulnerable to invasion by outside animals and plants? **CBSE SQP 2021-22**

Ans. Tropical evergreen forest is more vulnerable to invasion by outside animals and plants because of the occurrence of suitable environmental conditions and highest resource availability.

8. Identify *A* and *B* in the figure given below representing proportionate number of major vertebrate taxa. **Delhi 2014**

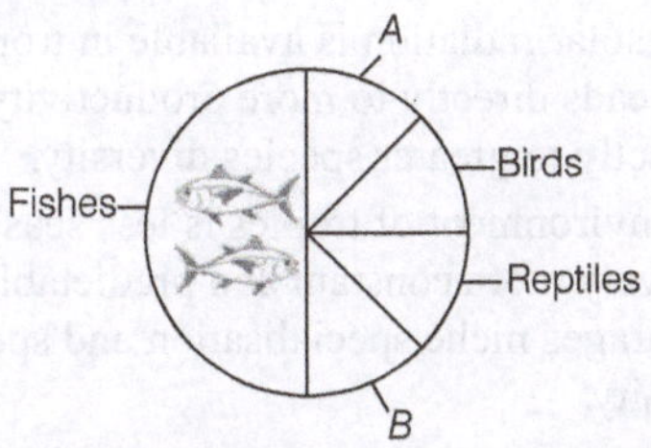

Ans. In the mentioned diagram, among the major vertebrate taxa
A represents mammals.
B represents amphibians. (½ ×2)

2 Marks Questions

9. A specific plant species was introduced into Australia in 1920 and later it became invasive spreading over millions of hectares of rangeland. **CBSE 2024 (Set-I)**

(i) Name the plant that was introduced into Australia and mention the reason for its uncontrollable growth.

(ii) State how its spread was eventually brought under control.

Ans. (i) The prickly pear cactus was introduced into Australia in the early 1920's and caused havoc by spreading rapidly into millions of hectares of rangeland due to lack of any of its natural predators in the new land. **(1)**

(ii) The invasive prickly pear cactus was brought under control by introducing a cactus feeding predator (a moth) from its natural habitat. **(1)**

10. 'The tropical regions are likely to have more biological diversity than the temperate ones'. Give two reasons to justify the statement. **CBSE SQP 2021-22**

Or Where would you expect more species biodiversity in tropics or in polar regions? Give reasons in support of your answer. **Outside Delhi 2013**

Or Giving two reasons explain why there is more species biodiversity in tropical latitudes than in temperate ones. **All India 2010**

Or Write any two hypothesis put forth by ecologists explaining the existence of greater biodiversity in tropical regions than in temperate regions. **Foreign 2010**

Ans. Biodiversity is more in tropical latitudes than in temperate or in polar regions. The reasons are as follows

(i) Speciation is a function of time. The temperate regions were subjected to frequent glaciation in the past, while the tropics have remained undisturbed and so had longer time to evolve more species diversity.

(ii) More solar radiation is available in tropical region. This leads directly to more productivity and indirectly to greater species diversity.

(iii) The environment of tropics is less seasonal and relatively more constant and predictable, which encourages niche specialisation and species diversity. **(Any two)**

11. How is an alien species invasion considered as one of the cause of biodiversity loss? Support you answer with the help of an example. **All India 2019**

Or Alien species invasions is one of the causes of biodiversity loss. Explain with the help of an example. **All India 2012C**

Or With the help of an example, explain how alien species invasion causes biodiversity loss? **Delhi 2011**

Or Alien species are a threat to native species. Justify taking examples of an animal and a plant alien species. **All India 2010**

Or Sometimes alien species affect the indigenous organisms leading to their extinction. Substantiate this statement with the help of any two examples. **Delhi 2010C**

Or What is meant by alien species invasion? Name one plant and one animal alien species that are a threat to our Indian native species. **All India 2013**

Ans. Intentional or chance introduction of exotic species into new Islands or countries by man is called alien species invasion.

Alien species become invasive, compete with the native species and cause extinction of indigenous species.

(i) Introduction of Nile perch into Lake Victoria leads to extinction of more than 200 species of cichlid fish in that lake. **(1)**

(ii) Carrot grass (*Parthenium*) and *Lantana* introduced in our country have become invasive and cause environmental damage. They pose a threat to the native species of plants in our forests. **(1)**

12. Substantiate with the help of one example that in an ecosystem, mutualists

(i) tend to coevolve and

(ii) are also one of the major causes of biodiversity loss. **Delhi 2019**

Ans. (i) In nature mutualists often co-evolve such as mediterranean orchid *Ophrys*. They employ sexual deceit to get pollinated by a species of bee. One petal of flower resembles to female bee. If female bee changes its colour pattern even slightly the success of pollination will be reduced unless orchid flower coevolves to maintain resemblance with female bee. **(1)**

(ii) Coextinction is the one of the Evil Quartet in which organism with obligatory relationship like plant pollinator mutualism will result in extinction of one partner, if other is eliminated in nature. **(1)**

13. Identify the areas labelled i, ii, iii and iv in the pie chart given below representing the biodiversity of plants showing their proportionate number of species of major taxa. **CBSE 2018C**

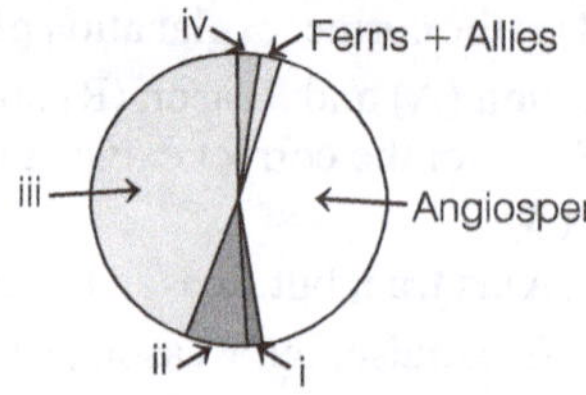

Ans. (i) Lichens
(ii) Algae
(iii) Fungi
(iv) Mosses (½ ×4)

14. Evaluate the effects of loss of biodiversity in a region. Mention any four such effects. **CBSE SQP 2018**

Ans. The biodiversity refers to the variety and variability of living organisms on earth. The consequences of loss of biodiversity could be as follows
(i) There will be an increased rate of species extinction.
(ii) There will be lowered resistance to environmental perturbations such as drought, etc.
(iii) There will be decline in the total existing number of plant/animal species.
(iv) It will affect the normal natural ecosystem functioning. (½ × 4)

15. List four causes of biodiversity loss. **Delhi 2014C**

Ans. The four causes of biodiversity loss are as follows
(i) Habitat loss and fragmentation.
(ii) Overexploitation.
(iii) Alien species invasions and
(iv) Coextinctions. (½ ×4)

16. 'Stability of a community depends on its species richness.' Write how did David Tilman show this experimentally. **Outside Delhi 2013**

Ans. The stability of a community depends on species richness. This was confirmed by David Tilman.
Through his ecology experiments Tilman showed
(i) The plots with more species showed less year-to-year variations in total biomass.
(ii) Plots with increased diversity showed higher productivity.

17. State the use of biodiversity in modern agriculture. **Outside Delhi 2011**

Ans. The use of biodiversity in agriculture is immense. It is a source of hybrids, GM plants, biopesticides, organic farming, biofertiliser, improved varieties of plants, disease resistant plants. It also promotes sustainable management of agricultural resources, conservation and farming of all wild and native varieties of plants, etc.

18. Justify with the help of an example where a deliberate attempt by humans has led to the extinction of a particular species. **Delhi 2011**

Ans. Overexploitation of natural resources or over hunting of animals has led to extinction of particular species, e.g. Steller's sea cow and passenger pigeon.
Other examples of human driven extinction include Dodo bird due to habitat fragmentation. (1 × 2)

19. The given graph shows species-area relationship. Write the equation of the curve *A* and *B* and explain.

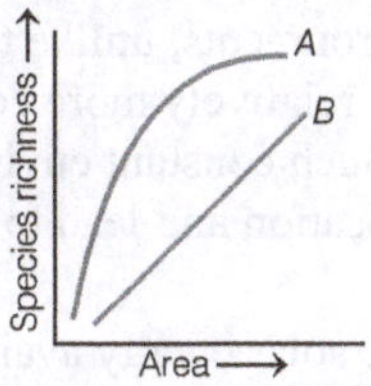

All India 2011

Ans. The equation for the curve *A* is $S = CA^Z$

B is $\log S = \log C + Z \log A$

where, *S*– Species richness, *A*–Area, *C*– *Y*-intercept, *Z*– Slope of line (regression coefficient) (1)

(i) Alexander von Humboldt observed that within a region, species richness increased with increasing explored area, but only upto a limit.
(ii) The relation between species richness and area for a wide variety of taxa like angiosperms, birds, fishes, etc., turns out to be a rectangular hyperbola. (1)

20. Explain, taking one example, the effect of coextinction on biodiversity. **Delhi 2011C**

Ans. Coextinction refers to the extinction of a species, if the plant and animal species associated with it in an obligatory relationship also gets extinct. For example, coevolved plant-pollinator mutualism as in case of *Pronuba yuccasella* and *Yucca*. If one partner is on the verge of extinction, the other partner will also get extinct.

21. How does overexploitation of beneficial species affect biodiversity? Explain with the help of one example. **Delhi 2011C**

Ans. Human beings when overexploit any plant/animal species, it affects their population size. The marine fish population around the world are declining due to overharvesting. It results in endangering the continued existence of some commercially important species. In the last 500 years, extinction of Stellar's sea cow and passenger pigeon were due to the overexploitation of these animals by humans.

3 Marks Questions

22. Tropical regions harbour more species than the temperate regions. How have biologists tried to explain this in their own ways? Explain. **CBSE 2024 (Set-II)**

Ans. Tropical regions harbour more species than the temperate regions. Biologists tried to explain this in their own ways by proposing various hypothesis, some of the important ones are
(i) Speciation is generally a function of time, unlike temperate regions subjected to frequent glaciations in the past, tropical latitudes have remainded

undisturbed for millions of years and thus, had a long evolutionary time for species diversification. **(1)**

(ii) Tropical environments, unlike temperate ones, are less seasonal, relatively more constant and predictable. Such constant environments promote niche specialisation and lead to a greater species diversity. **(1)**

(iii) There is more solar energy available in the tropics which contributes to higher productivity and which in turn might contribute indirectly to greater diversity. **(1)**

23. Give three reasons as to why the prokaryotes are not given any figures for their diversity by the ecologists. **CBSE SQP 2024**

Ans. Prokaryotic organisms diversity is not given any figures by ecologist because of following reasons

- Classification and identification of vast diversity of microbes is very difficult and cannot be efficiently done with use of currently available methods.
- For many microorganisms, it is difficult to culture them under laboratory condition.
- According to current biochemical and molecular techniques, it is estimated that microbes diversity can range in billions with microbes inhabiting diverse habitat on earth, with enormous diversity present in air, water and soil. Hence, more advanced molecular and biochemical techniques are needed to classify and identify this enormous diversity of microbes.

24. (i) There was loss of biodiversity in an ecosystem due to a new construction project in that area. What would be its impact on the ecosystem? State any three.

(ii) List any three major causes of loss of biodiversity. **CBSE SQP 2023**

Ans. (i) Refer to answer no. 14.

(ii) Refer to answer no. 15.

25. Explain the concept of ''coextinction'' by taking two examples. **Delhi 2021-22 Term-II**

Ans. Refer to text on page no. 360.

26. (i) Write the inference drawn by Alexander von Humboldt after his extensive explorations of South American jungle.

(ii) Study the graph given below.

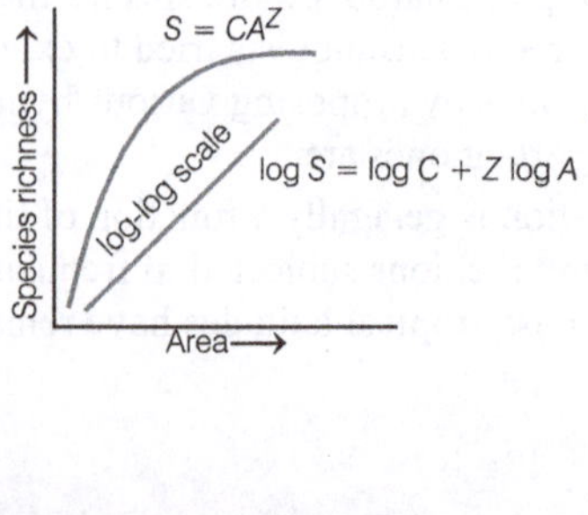

As per Alexander von Humboldt, what do the symbols *S, A, Z* and *C* in the graph stand for, in respect of a species and area relationship? **Delhi 2021-22 Term-II**

Ans. (i) German naturalist and geographer, A v Humboldt during his exploration in South American jungles made two inferences

(a) Within a region, species richness increased with increasing explored area, but only upto a limit.

(b) The relationship between species richness and area for a wide variety of taxa (angiospermic plants, birds, bats, freshwater fishes) turns out to be a rectangular hyperbola. **(1½)**

(ii) According to Humboldt, the meanings of the symbols in respect of a species and area relationship, are as follows

S – Species richness

A – Area

Z – Slope of the line (Regression coefficient)

C – Y-intercept **(1½)**

27. The graph given below shows species-area relationship of a certain region.

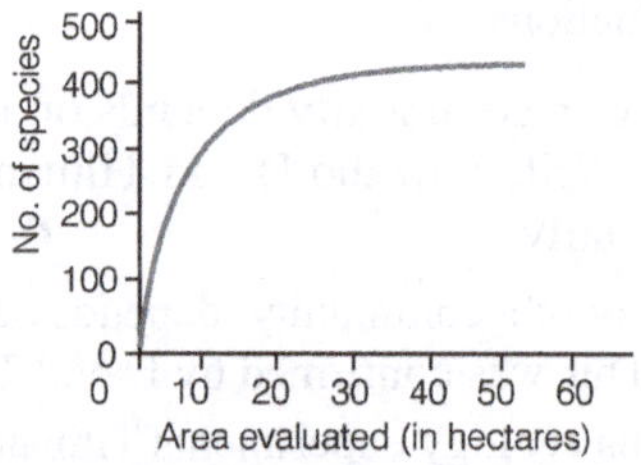

(i) Study the graph and explain what it represents.

(ii) After a while, a small area was taken for constructing a road which divided the region into two. Write the impact this construction would have on species richness of the region. **All India 2021-22 Term-II**

Ans. (i) The given graph represents species-area relationship. It shows that within an area (region), the species richness increases with the increase in explored area, but only to a certain limit. Thus, it becomes constant after a certain time period. **(2)**

(ii) If a small area is taken for constructing a road, thus dividing the region into two, the species richness will decreases. **(1)**

28. How did Dr. David Tilman relate experimentally, the stability of a community and its species richness? Explain. **All India 2021-22 Term-II**

Ans. Dr. David Tilman's long term ecosystem experiments using outdoor plots provided some tentative answers on the relation of stability of a community and its species richness. He showed that stability of a community depends on its species richness by using outdoor plots. Each plot had a different number of species. Tilman found that plots with more species showed less year to year variation in total biomass. He also showed experimentally that increased diversity contributed to higher productivity.

29. (i) 'The Evil Quartet' describes the rates of species extinction due to human activities. Explain how the population of organisms is affected by fragmentation the habitats.

(ii) Introduction of alien species has led to environmental damage and decline of indigenous species. Give any one example of how it has affected the indigenous species.

(iii) Could the extinction of Steller's sea cow and passenger pigeon be saved by man? Give reasons to support your answer.

Ans. (i) When a large habitat is broken into small fragments (fragmentation of habitat) due to various activities, mammals and birds requiring large territories and certain animals with migratory habitats are badly affected, leading to population decline. **(1)**

(ii) Introduction of alien species causes species extinction. For example, Nile perch when introduced in to lake Victoria eventually led to the extinction of an ecologically unique assemblage of more than 200 species of cichild fish. **(1)**

(iii) Yes, humans have overexploited natural resources for their greed rather than need leading to extinction of these (steller's sea cow and passenger pigeon) animals. **(1)**

30. Alien species are highly invasive and are a threat to indigenous species. Substantiate this statement with any three examples. **CBSE SQP 2019**

Or Alien species are highly invasive and are a threat to indigenous species. Substantiate this statement with any three examples. **All India 2012**

Ans. For alien species invasion, refer to answer no. 31 (iii).

Other examples include *Parthenium* (carrot grass) and *Lantana*.

31. Name and describe any three causes of biodiversity losses. **Delhi 2017**

Or Name and explain any two ways that are responsible for the loss of biodiversity. **Foreign 2014**

Ans. Causes of biodiversity losses are as follows

(i) **Habitat Loss and Fragmentation**

The main cause of extinction of species is the destruction of their habitat. For example, tropical rainforests once covering more than 14% of the land surface, now cover only 6% of land area. **(1)**

(ii) **Overexploitation** of natural resources by humans results in degradation and extinction of the resources. For example, Steller's sea cow, passenger pigeon and many marine fishes have become extinct in last 500 years. **(1)**

(iii) **Alien** (Exotic) **Species Invasions** When alien (exotic) species are introduced unintentionally or deliberately, some become invasive and cause harmful impact resulting in extinction of the indigenous species, e.g. Nile perch. **(1)**

32. Write the importance of species diversity to the ecosystem. Support your answer with the finding of Tilman. **Delhi 2016**

Ans. (i) Ecologists for many years, believe that communities with more species are more stable than those with less species. Greater species diversity ensures natural sustainability for all life forms. **(1)**

(ii) David Tilman's long term ecosystem experiments using outdoor plots provided answers to stability of a biological community and species richness in that community. Tilman found that plots with more species showed less year-to-year variation in total biomass. He also showed in his experiments that increased diversity contributed to higher productivity. **(2)**

Concept Enhancer Species diversity on earth is not uniformly distributed, but shows interesting patterns. It is generally highest in the tropics and decreases towards the poles.
For example, most of the India lies near the equator. Hence, it has rich biodiversity of approx. 1200 species of birds. New York belonging to temperate region has moderate biodiversity. Green land, Arctic region, etc, belongs to polar region which has least biodiversity.

33. Since the origin of life on earth, there were five episodes of mass extinction of species.

(i) How is the 'sixth extinction', presently in progress, different from the previous episodes?

(ii) Who is mainly responsible for 'Sixth extinction'?

(iii) List any four points that can help to overcome this disaster. **Outside Delhi 2014**

Ans. (i) The current species extinction rate is estimated to be 100-1000 times faster than in the pre-human era. **(1)**

(ii) All activities performed by human beings for survival and maintenance of their lifestyle. **(1)**

(iii) Point that can help to overcome this disaster are as follows

(a) Preventing habitat loss and fragmentation.
(b) Checking overexploitation.
(c) Preventing alien species invasion.
(d) Preventing coextinction.
(e) Conservation/protection of species. (any four) **(1)**

Concept Enhancer Earth is heading to sixth extinctions and it would be anthropogenic which will lead to serious ecological, economical and social consequence.

34. The following graph shows the species-area relationship. Answer the following questions as directed.

(i) Name the naturalist who studied the kind of relationship shown in the graph. Write the observations made by him.

(ii) Write the situations as discovered by the ecologists when the value of Z (slope of the line) lies between

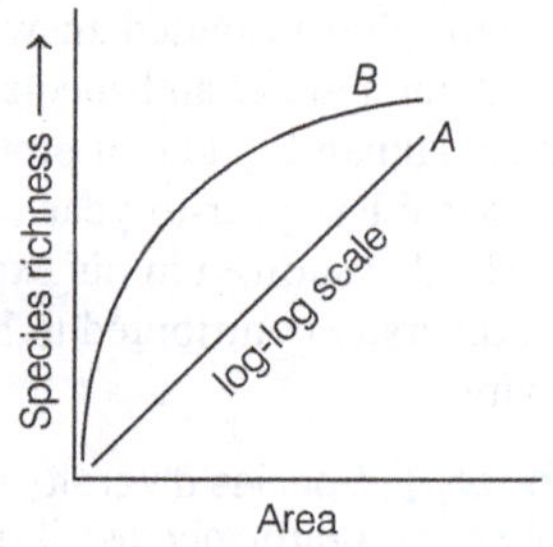

(a) 0.1 and 0.2 (b) 0.6 and 1.2

What does Z stand for?

(iii) When would the slope of the line B become steeper? **All India 2014**

Ans. (i) Alexander von Humboldt studied the relationship shown in above graph. He observed that the species richness in an area increased with an increase in exploring area, upto a certain limit only. **(1)**

(ii) (a) Ecologists have observed that when the value of Z lies between 0.1-0.2 then the species are considered for a small or average area.

(b) When the value of Z lies between 0.6-1.2, the area considered is very large. Z represents the slope of the line, i.e. regression coefficient.

(iii) The slope of the line B will become steeper when very large areas such as continents are considered for species-area relationship. **(2)**

35. Taking one example each of habitat loss and fragmentation, explain how are the two responsible for biodiversity loss. **All India 2012**

Ans. For fragmentation and habitat loss, refer to text on page no. 360. **(1)**

Habitat losses due to intentional/unintentional human activities or by natural means, results in negative impact on the biodiversity. **(1)**

36. (i) Explain the species-area relationship using the graphical representation given below.

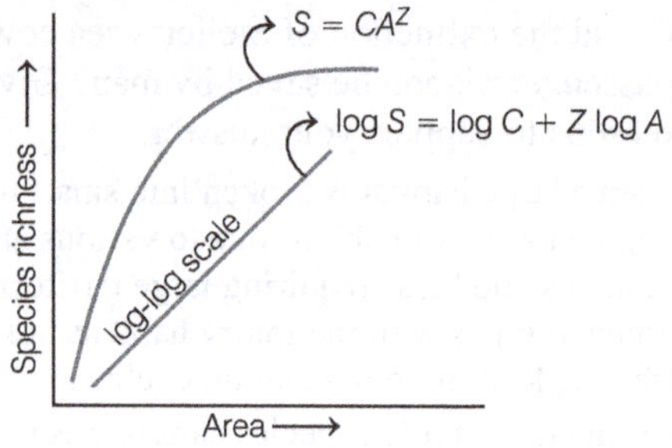

(ii) Explain giving reasons why there is greater biodiversity in tropical regions of the earth. **All India 2012C**

Ans. Refer to text on page no. 359.

37. Explain by giving example, how coextinction is one of the causes of loss of biodiversity. List the other three causes also (without description). **Foreign 2011**

Ans. **Coextinction** is one of the causes of loss of biodiversity as when a species becomes extinct, the plant and animal species associated with it in an obligatory manner, also becomes extinct. For example, **(1)**

(i) In plant pollinator mutualism, extinction of one results in the extinction of other.

(ii) If a host fish becomes extinct, the unique parasites depending on it would also become extinct.

The other causes of loss of biodiversity are

- Habitat loss fragmentation
- Overexploitation
- Invasion of alien species. **(2)**

TOPIC 2

Conservation of Biodiversity

Reasons for Conservation of Biodiversity

There are various reasons for conservation of biodiversity. These can be grouped as

1. Narrowly Utilitarian Arguments

- Humans derive several direct economic benefits from nature such as food (cereals, pulses and fruits), firewood, fibre, construction material, industrial products (tannins, lubricants, dyes, resins and perfumes) and products of medicinal utilities.
- More than 25% of drugs sold today are derived from plants and about 25,000 species of plants are used by native people as traditional medicines.
- **Bioprospecting** is exploring the molecular, genetic and species level diversity for products of economic importance.
  It helps nations endowed with rich biodiversity to reap enormous benefits.

2. Broadly Utilitarian Arguments

- Biodiversity plays a major role in many ecosystem services that are provided by nature and we cannot put an economic value on these services.
- Some of them are
  - **Production of oxygen** Amazon forest is estimated to produce 20% of the total oxygen in the atmosphere through photosynthesis.
  - **Pollination** Ecosystem provides pollinators like bees, bumblebees, birds and bats.
  - **Aesthetic pleasures** like walking through thick woods, watching spring flowers in full bloom or waking up to koel or bulbul's song in the morning.

3. Ethical Reasons

- Every species has an intrinsic value, even if it may notbe of current or any economic value to us.
- We have a moral duty to care for their well-being and pass on our biological legacy in good order to future generations.

Biodiversity Conservation Methods

The two basic approaches of biodiversity conservation are

I. *In situ* conservation (on-site conservation).

II. *Ex situ* conservation (off-site conservation).

In Situ Conservation

It involves protection of species in their natural habitat.

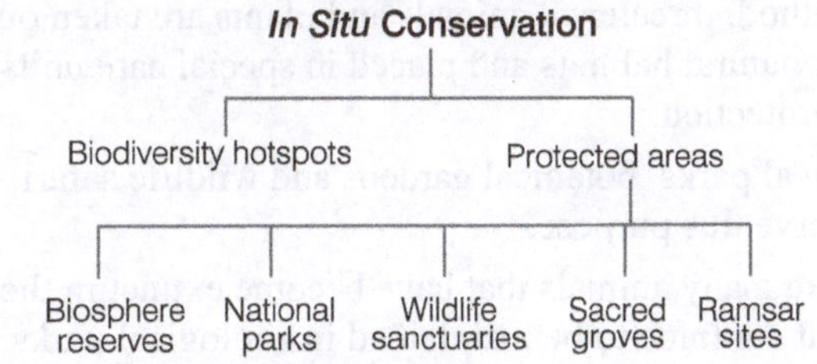

Biodiversity Hotspots

- These are the regions with high levels of species richness and high degree of endemism (i.e. species confined to that region are not found anywhere else).
- Hotspots cover less than 2% of the earth's land area.
- The total number of biodiversity hotspots in the world are 34.
- These hotspots are regions of accelerated habitat loss.
- Three hotspots which cover India's biodiversity regions are **Western Ghats** and **Sri Lanka, Indo-Burma** and **Himalaya**.
- These hotspots can reduce the ongoing mass extinctions by almost 30%.

Protected Areas

- These are ecologically unique and biodiversity rich regions. These are legally protected as **biosphere reserves, national parks** and **sanctuaries**.
- India has 14 biosphere reserves, 90 national parks and 448 wildlife sanctuaries.
- The first national park setup in India was **Jim Corbett National Park** (1936).

Sacred Groves

- These are forest areas set aside, all the trees and wildlife within it are venerated and given total protection. These are religious and cultural places, which are protected.

- Some of the sacred groves in India are
  - Western Ghat regions of Karnataka and Maharashtra.
  - Khasi and Jaintia Hills in Meghalaya.
  - Aravalli Hills of Rajasthan.
  - Sarguja, Chanda and Bastar areas of Madhya Pradesh.
  - **Ramsar sites** These are wetlands designated as internationally important under the convention on wetlands held at Ramsar Iran in 1971, for the conservation and wise use of wetlands. There are 26 Ramsar sites in India. Some are Chilka lake (Odisha), Sambhar lake (Rajasthan), etc.

Ex Situ Conservation

In this method, threatened animals and plants are taken out from their natural habitats and placed in special care units for their protection.

- Zoological parks, botanical gardens and wildlife safari parks serve this purpose.
- There are many animals that have become extinct in the wild, but continue to be maintained in zoological parks.
- **Cryopreservation** (preserving at –196°C) technique is used to preserve sperms, eggs, animal cell, tissue, seeds of different genetic strains and embryos for longer times in viable and fertile conditions in gene banks, seed banks, etc.
- *In vitro* propagation of plants is carried out by applying tissue culture method.

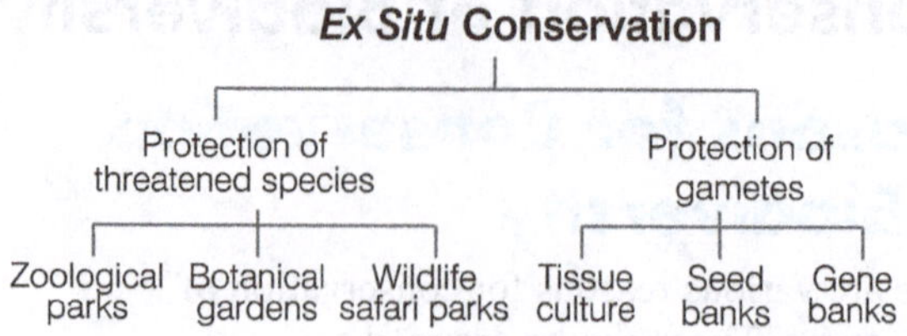

Conventions on Biodiversity

- The conservation of biodiversity is a collective responsibility of all the nations.
- Historic convention on biological diversity (The Earth Summit) was held in Rio de Janeiro in 1992. It called upon all nations to take appropriate measures for conservation of biodiversity and sustainable utilisation of its benefits.
- The **World Summit** on sustainable development was held in Johannesburg, South Africa in 2002, as a follow up in which 190 countries pledged their commitment to achieve significant reduction in the current rate of biodiversity loss at global, regional and local levels by 2010.

PYQs Previous Years' Questions

1 Mark Questions

Multiple Choice Question

1. Which of the following is an example of *ex situ* conservation? **CBSE SQP 2023**

   (a) Sacred groves (b) National park
   (c) Biosphere reserve (d) Seed bank

Ans. (d)

Very Short Answer Type Questions

2. Why Western Ghats in India have been declared as biological hotspot? **Delhi 2015**

Ans. Western Ghats have been declared as biological hotspot due to their rich biodiversity and ecological condition favoring many species of plants and animals. Many endemic species of amphibians, reptiles and fishes are found in these regions.

3. Write the importance of cryopreservation in conservation of biodiversity. **Delhi 2011**

Ans. The importance of cryopreservation in conservation of biodiversity is that gametes of threatened species can be preserved in viable and fertile conditions for long periods by cryopreservation.

2 Marks Questions

4. How are '*in situ*' and '*ex situ*' approaches of biodiversity conservation different from each other? **Delhi 2021-22 Term-II**

   Or

   Differentiate between *in situ* and *ex situ* approaches of conservation of biodiversity. **All India 2011**

Ans. Refer to the answer no. 20.

5. Explain how advanced *ex situ* conservation techniques assist in preserving threatened species of plants and animals. **CBSE SQP 2021-22**

Ans. *Ex situ* conservation involves the off-site conservation of threatened species outside their natural habitats.

- In recent years, *ex situ* conservation has evolved advanced techniques, beyond keeping the threatened species in enclosures.
- Gametes of threatened species can now be preserved in viable and fertile condition for long periods using cryopreservation techniques. Thus, eggs can be fertilised *in vitro*.
- In plants, the explants can be propagated using tissue culture methods and can be kept for long periods in seed banks.

6. Suggest two practices giving one example of each, that help to protect rare or threatened species. **All India 2017**

Ans. Practices that help to protect rare threatened species are as follows

(i) ***In situ*** (on-site) **conservation** involves protection of species in their natural habitat. It involves biosphere reserves, national parks, wildlife sanctuaries, sacred groves, etc. (1)

(ii) ***Ex situ*** (off-site) **conservation** involves placing threatened animals and plants in special care units for their protection. Zoological parks, botanical gardens and wildlife safari parks serve this purpose. (1)

7. Why are sacred groves highly protected? **All India 2016**

Ans. Sacred groves are small patches of forests with special religious importance in a particular culture.

(i) These are also mythologically important.

(ii) These are undisturbed forests without any human interventions.

(iii) These are highly protected, hence they include a number of rare, endangered and endemic species.

8. List any four techniques where the principle of *ex situ* conservation of biodiversity has been employed. **All India 2015**

Ans. Four techniques where principle of *ex situ* conservation of biodiversity has been employed are

(i) Tissue culture

(ii) Cryopreservation

(iii) Botanical gardens

(iv) Zoological parks (½ × 4)

9. Why is there a need to conserve biodiversity? **Foreign 2014**

Ans. The main reasons to conserve biodiversity are as follows

(i) **Narrowly utilitarian reasons** These are obvious reasons as human derives multiple economic benefits like food, fibre, medicinal and industrial products, etc. (1)

(ii) **Broadly utilitarian reasons** Biodiversity plays a major role in providing ecosystem services which cannot be given a price-tag, e.g. oxygen, pollination, aesthetic pleasure, etc. (1)

10. State the uses of biodiversity in modern agriculture. **All India 2011**

Ans. Uses of biodiversity in modern agriculture are

(i) Humans obtain food, fibres, medicines and many industrial products from plants.

(ii) Wild varieties of plants are used for breeding to obtain disease and pest resistant crops with many desirable traits.

(iii) By exploring molecular, genetic and species level diversity for economically important products, rich biodiversity can be obtained. (any two) (1 + 1)

11. Why certain regions have been declared as biodiversity hotspots by environmentalists of the world? Name any two hotspot regions of India. **Delhi 2010**

Ans. Certain regions are declared hotspots by the environmentalists, because these regions have very high levels of species richness and high degree of endemism. (1)

Hotspots of India are Western Ghats and Sri Lanka, Himalayas and Indo-Burma. (1)

12. White Bengal tigers are protected in special settings in zoological parks. Tiger reserves are maintained in Western Ghat.

(i) How do these two approaches differ from each other? Mention the advantages of each one.

(ii) What is the significance of cryopreservation technique? **All India 2010C**

Ans. (i) Zoological parks are man-made places where endangered species are kept and taken care of by specialised skilled persons. It helps to prevent species extinction.

Tiger reserves are natural habitats of tigers in which they are protected in natural habitat. It helps in recovering population of the species where they have developed their distinctive features. (1)

(ii) Cryopreservation is *ex situ* conservation technique in which tissues, organs, embryos, seeds gametes, pollens, etc., are stored at very low temperature of −196°C for future use. (1)

3 Marks Questions

13. "Biodiversity plays a major role in many ecosystem services that nature provides."
(i) Describe any two broadly utilatarian arguments to justify the given statement.
(ii) State one ethical reason of conserving biodiversity. **CBSE 2023**

Ans. (i) Two broadly Utilatarian Argument that biodiversity plays an important role in ecosystem services that nature provides are given below
(a) Production of oxygen , e.g. Amazon forests is called lungs of earth' as it produces 20 % of the total oxygen in the earth's atmosphere *via* photosynthesis.
(b) Pollination of flowers without which fruits and seeds are not produced is provided by pollinator layer, i.e. bees, bumble bees, birds, bats, etc. **(2)**

(ii) Every species has an intrinsic value, if it is not of any economic value to us. It is our moral duty to care for their well-being and pass on our biological legacy in good order to future generations. Moreover, many plants like tulsi and peepal have religious importance as well. **(1)**

14. 'Forests provide intangible benefits to us'. Explain by taking three different areas, how. **Delhi 2021-22 Term-II**

Ans. Forests provide us with many intangible or indirect benefits which affect national welfare, environment, resources and security. These benefits have a major influence in controlling the quality of life. Three of these benefits are
(i) **Improvement of agrosystem** Presence of trees around farmlands creates habitat for various carnivores. These carnivores feed on preys like rats and mice and thus keep their population under check. Also, the temperature, rainfall and humidity pattern is well regulated. **(1)**
(ii) **Control of flood** Forests control flood by decreasing the possibilities of soil erosion on the up hills. Through the control of soil erosion, the hills become fertile. **(1)**
(iii) **Conservation of wildlife habitat** Forests are best suited habitats for wildlife in terms of food and shelter. Clearing away of forests leads to disturbances in forest wildlife and an eventual extinction of some species in case conditions worsen. **(1)**

15. How are the advanced *ex situ* techniques helping in conserving threatened species? Give three examples. **All India 2021-22 Term-II**

Ans. *Ex situ* conservation strategy involves 'off-site' conservation. It is the method of conserving all the living species in the artful habitats which have similar resemblances to their natural habitat. The major advantage of *ex situ* conservation technique is that it allows for a more focussed approach to the protection of a species.
This type of conservation involves various techniques that help in conserving the germplasm.
(i) **Cryopreservation** This method is used for virtually indefinite storage of genetic material for a much greater time period. When compared with other *ex situ* methods. This is applicable to both plants and animals, e.g. seeds (in case of plants), sperms, eggs or embryos in case of animals. Thus, it helps in conserving diversity of nearly threatened species. **(1)**
(ii) **Seed banks** These are cold storages wherein seeds are kept under controlled temperature and humidity for storage seeds that are preserved this technique remian viable for longer duration. **(1)**
(iii) **Zoological parks** In zoological parks (zoos), wild animals are maintained in captivity and conservation of endangered and rare species can be carried out to increase their number. **(1)**

16. (i) The image shown below is of a sacred grove found in India. Explain how has human involvement helped in the preservation of these biodiversity rich regions.

(ii) Value of Z (regression coefficient) is considered for measuring the species richness of an area. If the value of Z is 0.7 for area A and 0.15 for area B, which area has higher species richness and a steeper slope? **CBSE SQP 2021-22 Term-II**

Ans. (i) India's history of religious and cultural traditions emphasised on the protection of nature. In many cultures, tracts of forest are set aside, all the trees and wildlife within are venerated and given total protection. Sacred groves in many states are the last refuges for a large number of rare and threatened plants. **(2)**

(ii) Ecologists have discovered that the value of *Z* or regression coefficient increases, the slope of the line becomes steeper in a species area relationship graph. Thus, the value of *Z* for area A is more than the value of *Z* for area *B*. Thus, area *A* will have more species richness and a steeper slope. **(1)**

17. (i) Explain the concept of endemism.

(ii) Name four regions in and around our country that are considered hotspots. **Delhi 2020**

Ans. (i) Endemism is the ecological state of a species being unique to a defined geographic location, such as an island, nation, country or other defined zone or habitat type, i.e. endemic species only in one specific geographic region, e.g. kangaroo of Australia. **(1½)**

(ii) Hotspots which cover India's biodiversity regions are **Western Ghats and Sri Lanka, Indo-Burma** and **Himalaya**. **(1½)**

18. Explain any three ways other than zoological parks, botanical gardens and wildlife safaries, by which threatened species of plants and animals are being conserved '*ex situ*'. **All India 2020**

Ans. Three other ways of *ex situ* conservation of threatened animals are

(i) **Seed banks** In this approach, the storage of different genetic strains of commercially important plants in the form of seeds is carried out. **(1)**

(ii) **Tissue culture** This method is useful in maintaining a large number of genotypes in small area, rapid multiplication of even endangered species and for hybrid rescue. Many clones of a plants are produced using the technique of micropropagation. **(1)**

(iii) **Cryopreservation** It is a method of *in vitro* conservation in liquid-N_2 at temperature of –196°C (–130°F) in a controlled freezer for vegetatively propagated crops and storing other biological materials. **(1)**

Concept Enhancer Generally students get confused that tissue culture is associated with plant only, but tissue culture technique is for both plants and animals.

19. State any two criteria for determining biodiversity hotspots. Name any two hotspots designated in India. **CBSE SQP 2020**

Ans. Two criteria for determining biodiversity hotspot are

High levels of species richness

High degree of endemism (i.e. species confined to that region and not found anywhere else).

Two **biodiversity hotspots** in India include Western Ghats and Indo-Burma.

20. Differentiate between *in situ* and *ex situ* approaches for conserving biodiversity. Give an example for each. **CBSE SQP 2020**

KEY idea
In situ = 'In' - Internal environment
Ex situ = 'Ex' – external environment

Ans. Differences between *in situ* and *ex situ* approaches of conservation of biodiversity are

In situ conservation	*Ex situ* conservation
This method involves protection of endangered species in their natural habitat.	It involves placing of threatened animals and plants in special care units for their protection.
It helps in recovering populations in the surroundings where they have developed their distinct features.	It helps in recovering populations or preventing their extinction under stimulated conditions that closely resemble their natural habitats.
e.g. national parks, biosphere reserves, wildlife sanctuaries, etc.	e.g. botanical garden, zoological parks, etc.

21. List six advantages of '*ex situ*' approach to conservation of biodiversity. **Delhi 2019**

Ans. *Ex situ* conservation strategies help

(i) To conserve those animals that have become extinct in wild, but can be maintained in zoological parks.

(ii) To preserve gametes of threatened species in viable condition through cryopreservation.

(iii) To propagate threatened plants *via* tissue culture.

(iv) To grow plants with recalcitrant seeds in orchards where all possible varieties are maintained.

(v) To conserve seeds of commercially important plants in seed banks.

(vi) To save endangered or threatened plants that need urgent measure to save it from extinction in botanical gardens.

22. Explain the '*ex situ* conservation' of biodiversity. How is the *in situ* conservation different from it? **2018C**

Ans. For *ex situ* conservation, refer to answer no. 6 (ii) and for difference answer no. 20.

23. *In situ* conservation can help endangered / threatened species. Justify the statement. **Delhi 2017**

Ans. *In situ* conservation involves the protection of species in their natural habitats. It helps in the conservation of threatened/endangered species *via* following means

(i) **Biodiversity hotspots** are regions with high levels of species richness and high degree of endemism (i.e. species confined to that region are not found anywhere else). Hotspots cover less than 2% of the earth's land area. (1)

(ii) **Protected areas** are ecologically unique and biodiversity rich regions. These are legally protected as biosphere reserves, national parks and sanctuaries. (1)

(iii) **Sacred groves** are forest areas set aside, all the trees and wildlife within it are venerated and given total protection. These are religious and cultural places, which are protected. (1)

24. Why should biodiversity be conserved? Explain giving three reasons. **Outside Delhi 2016C**

Ans. Biodiversity should be conserved for the following reasons

(i) The broadly utilitarian argument says that biodiversity plays a major role in many ecosystem services that nature provides. (1)

(ii) The narrow utilitarian argument says that humans derive countless direct economic benefits from nature and products of medicinal importance. (1)

(iii) The ethical argument for conserving biodiversity relates to what we owe to millions of plant, animal and microbe species with whom we share this planet. (1)

25. Many plant and animal species are on the verge of their extinction because of loss of forest land by indiscriminate use by the humans. As a biology student what method would you suggest along with its advantages that can protect such threatened species from getting extinct. **Delhi 2015**

Ans. As a biology student, I would suggest *ex situ* conservation approach for such animals.

It involves placing the threatened animals and plants in special care units for their protection. It includes off-site collections; botanical gardens, zoological parks, etc. and gene banks, seed banks, tissue culture, etc. (1½)

Advantages of *ex situ* conservation are

(i) Off-site collection can be used to restock depleted population, reintroduce species in the wild and restore degraded habitats.

(ii) It is useful in maintaining a large number of genotypes in small area, rapid multiplication of endangered species, through tissue culture, etc. (1½)

26. Compare narrowly utilitarian and broadly utilitarian approaches to conserve biodiversity, with the help of suitable examples. **Foreign 2015**

Ans. Comparison between narrowly utilitarian and broadly utilitarian approaches are

Narrowly utilitarian approach	Broadly utilitarian approach
It includes most of the resources required for our day-to-day life.	It includes most of the ecosystem services provided to us by nature.
e.g. food, oil, clothes, wood and drugs.	e.g. release of O_2 and fixation of CO_2.

27. There are many animals that have become extinct in the wild, but continue to be maintained in zoological parks.

(i) What type of biodiversity conservation is observed in this case?

(ii) Explain any other two ways which help this type of conservation. **Delhi 2014**

Ans. (i) Zoological parks are an example of *ex situ* conservation, in which threatened animals are kept in special conditions, away from natural habitat, in order to protect them. (1½)

(ii) The other ways of maintaining the endangered animals or species by *ex situ* conservation are botanical gardens and cryopreservation.

In **botanical garderns**, plants are grown in special conditions. Threatened and critically endangered plant species are grown here.

In cryopreservation, gametes and seeds of threatened species are preserved in viable condition at the temperature of around –196° C. (1½)

28. The sacred groves of Aravalli Hills and Ooty botanical garden both aim at biodiversity conservation. How do they differ in their approaches? Explain. **All India 2013C**

Ans. Sacred groves are undisturbed forest patches, surrounded by highly degraded landscapes where not even a single human activity is allowed, e.g. sacred groves of Aravalli hill is protecting many endemic species. In botanical gardens, the plants are raised outside their natural habitat under the supervision of skilled persons.

29. What are the two types of desirable approaches to conserve biodiversity? Explain with examples bringing out the difference between the two types. **Delhi 2012, All India 2012**

Ans. Conservation of biodiversity means the preservation of existing variable forms of life in their natural habitat, while deriving sustainable benefits from nature. It is done *in situ* (on-site) and *ex situ* (off-site). *In situ* preservation and conservation always aim to protect organisms in their natural habitats (e.g. sacred groves, biosphere reserves). *Ex situ* conservation helps to protect threatened plants and animals. In this method, these organisms are placed outside the natural habitat and are promoted to reproduce.

5 Marks Questions

30. (i) Why should we conserve biodiversity? How can we do it?

(ii) Explain the importance of biodiversity hotspots and sacred groves. **Delhi 2016**

Ans. (i) For reasons, refer to answer no. 24 and for methods, refer to answer no. 27. **(3)**

(ii) **Importance of biodiversity hotspots and sacred groves** Biodiversity hotspots are the regions of accelerated habitat loss. These can reduce the ongoing mass extinctions by almost 30%. Sacred groves are important in biodiversity conservation, as these are naturally protected by the native population without much efforts. In Meghalaya, the sacred groves are the last refuges for large number of rare and threatened plants. **(2)**

31. (i) Explain the narrow utilitarian, broadly utilitarian and ethical arguments in favour of conservation of biodiversity.

(ii) How is designation of certain areas as hotspots a step towards biodiversity conservation? Name any two hotspots in India. **Delhi 2014C**

Ans. (i) Refer to answer no. 24. **(3)**

(ii) Hotspots are regions exhibiting high degree of endemism and great species richness, therefore designating these areas as 'biodiversity hotspots' allows their maximum protection and reduce the ongoing extinction by about 30%.

Such hotspot regions in India are Western Ghats and Himalayas. **(2)**

Concept Enhancer Our country's *in situ* conservation efforts are reflected in its 14 biosphere reserves, 90 national parks, more than 450 wildlife sancturies and many sacred groves.

Case Based/Source Based/Passage Based Questions (Based on Complete Chapter)

1. Read the following passage and answer the questions that follow

It incredible that India's land area is only 2.4 per cent of the world's total land area whereas its share of the global species diversity is an impressive 8.1 per cent. However, in these estimates of species, prokaryotes do not figure anywhere.

Biologists are always keen on collecting data with respect to species diversity observed in different regions of the world. The data collected based on the survey conducted for species richness of groups of mammals in three different regions of the world is shown in the bar graph given below **CBSE 2024 (Set-I)**

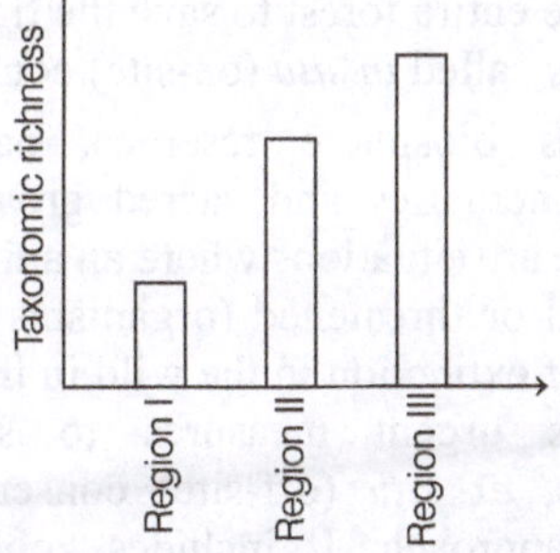

(i) Why is the species richness maximum in region III in the bar graph?

Or

(i) Why is the species richness minimum in region I in the bar graph?

(ii) Plants and animals do not have uniform diversity in the world but show rather uneven distribution. Mention what this kind of diversity is referred to as.

(iii) Why is it that prokaryotes do not have an estimated number of their species diversity as seen in plants and animals ? Explain.

Ans. (i) Species richness is maximum in region III of the bar graph as it contains the maximum count of different species present in a region or ecological environment, i.e. taxonomical richness. **(1)**

Or

(i) Species richness is minimum in region I of the bar graph as it contains the least count of different species present in a region or ecological environment, i.e. taxonomical richness. **(1)**

(ii) This kind of diversity is referred to as species diversity. **(1)**

(iii) Prokaryotes do not have an estimated number of their species diversity as seen in plants and animals as

- It is difficult to study prokaryotic species diversity using conventional taxonomic methods.
- They are microscopic and thus, their estimation is difficult.
- Most prokaryotic organisms are impossible to culture *in vitro* and hence cannot be studied properly. **(2)**

2. Read the following and answer the questions given below.

When we conserve and protect the whole ecosystem, its biodiversity at all levels is protected, we save the entire forest to save the tiger. This approach is called *in situ* (on-site) conservation.

It includes biosphere reserves, national parks, wildlife sanctuaries and sacred groves. However, when these are situations where an animal or plant is endangered or threatened (organisms facing a very high risk of extinction in the wild in the near future) and needs urgent measures to save it from extinctions, *ex situ* (off-site) conservation is the desirable approach. It includes zoological parks, botanical gardens, gene banks, etc.

(i) The numbers of national parks, biosphere reserves and wildlife sanctuaries in India, respectively are

(a) 90, 14, 448 (b) 158, 62, 10
(c) 58, 412, 10 (d) 96, 412, 10

(ii) In your opinion, which is the most effective way to conserve genetic diversity of the plant of an area?

(a) By tissue culture method
(b) By creating biosphere reserve
(c) By creating botanical garden
(d) By developing seed bank

(iii) Sacred groves in India are related with

(a) aesthetic pleasure
(b) the place where threatened species are protected
(c) the place where only artificial plant breeding is allowed
(d) forest patches around the places of worship

(iv) Cryopreservation of gametes of threatened species in viable and fertile condition can be referred to as

(a) *in situ* conservation of biodiversity
(b) advanced *ex situ* conservation of biodiversity
(c) *in situ* conservation by sacred groves
(d) *in situ* cryopreservation of biodiversity

(v) Refer to the given figure representing different zones of a biosphere reserve.

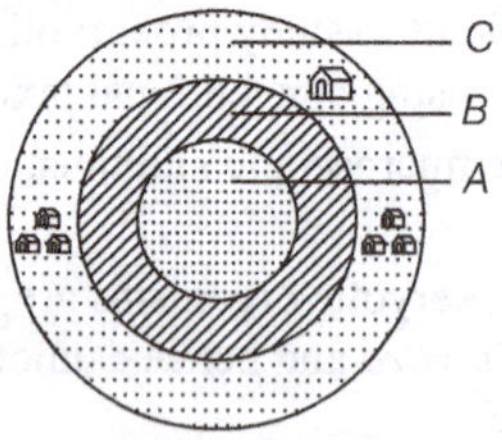

Choose the correct answer as per the statements given below.

I. Limited human activity is allowed such as for research and education.
II. An active cooperation occurs between reserve management and local people for activities like cropping, settlements, etc.
III. No human activity is allowed.

Codes

	I	II	III
(a)	A	B	C
(b)	B	C	A
(c)	C	A	B
(d)	C	B	A

Ans. (i)-(a), (ii)-(b), (iii)-(d), (iv)-(b), (v)-(b)

3. Read the following and answer the questions given below.

On earth day, a group of ecological activists took out a rally to aware people about biodiversity loss and its conservation. These activists told the public about various causes of biodiversity loss and how it could impact all our lives too. They also pronounced the various practices of biodiversity conservation.

(i) Enlist the consequences of biodiversity loss in a region.
(ii) What do you understand by 'The Evil Quartet'?
(iii) Mention the cause of extinction of passenger pigeon and Stellar's sea cow.
(iv) How does *in situ* conservation differ from *ex situ* conservation?

Ans. (i) Decline in plant productivity, increased variability in ecosystem processes, drought, etc. **(1)**

(ii) The Evil Quartet are four major causes of biodiversity losses which largely include human activities. These are habitat loss and fragmentation, overexploitation, alien species invasion and co-extinction. **(1)**

(iii) Overexploitation of natural resources by humans led to the extinction of passenger pigeon and Stellar's sea cow. **(1)**

(iv) *In situ* conservation involves on-site conservation in which organisms are conserved in their natural habitats only. In *ex situ* or off-site conservation, organisms are conserved outside their natural habitat, at special places like zoological or botanical parks. **(1)**

CHAPTER TEST

01 Mark Questions

Multiple Choice Questions

1 The species area relationship is a straight line described by the equation

(a) $\log S = \dfrac{\log C}{\log A}$ (b) $Z \log A = \dfrac{\log C}{\log S}$

(c) $\log S = \log C + Z \log A$ (d) $\log S = \log C - Z \log A$

2 Species-area relationship is represented on a log scale as

(a) curved (b) rectangular hyperbola
(c) linear (d) inverted

3 According to rivet popper hypothesis, the rivets on the wings represent

(a) abundant species (b) key stone species
(c) rare species (d) endangered species

4 One of endangered species of Indian medicinal plant is that of

(a) *Podophyllum* (b) *Ocimum*
(c) Garlic (d) *Nepenthes*

5 Which one of the following pairs of organisms are exotic species introduced in India?

(a) *Ficus religiosa* and *Lantana camara*
(b) Water hyacinth and *Lantana lamara*
(c) Water hyacinth and *Prosopis cineraria*
(d) Nile perch and *Ficus religiosa*

6 With reference to IUCN/Red List, which of the following statements are true?

I. IUCN stands for International Union of Conservation of Nature.
II. It has its headquarters in USA.
III. It maintains Red Data Book.
IV. Red Data Book was initiated in the year 1963.

(a) I and II (b) I and III
(c) I and IV (d) I, III and IV

Assertion-Reason Type Questions

Direction (Q. Nos. 7-10) *In the questions given below two statements an **Assertion** and a **Reason** are given. Give the appropriate response as*

(a) If both Assertion and Reason are true and Reason is the correct explanation of Assertion
(b) If both Assertion and Reason are true, but Reason is not the correct explanation of Assertion
(c) If Assertion is true, but Reason is false
(d) If Assertion is false, but Reason is true

7 **Assertion** *In situ* conservation means conservation of organism in their natural habitat, in which they naturally occur.

Reason Zoo is an *in situ* conserved area.

8 **Assertion** According to ecologists communities with more species tend to be more stable.

Reason They balance the nature by feeding upon each other.

9 **Assertion** Garden is an example of *ex situ* conservation.

Reason Garden is an artificial habitat resembling to the natural habitat of organisms.

10 **Assertion** Species with low genetic variability are usually at a great risk of extinction.

Reason Low genetic variability increases vulnerability to diseases, environmental changes and predators.

2/3 Marks Questions

11 What characteristics make a community stable?

12 Explain the levels of biodiversity at genetic specific and ecological levels with the help of one example each.

13 What is coextinction? Explain with a suitable example.

14 When and where was the world summit on sustainable development held? How many countries made commitment to it? What were its objectives?

15 What are sacred groves? Where are they found in India? Explain their importance in conservation.

16 Write a note on cultural and religious importance of biodiversity.

05 Marks Questions

17 Explain the status of Indian biodiversity. Give a brief account of loss of biodiversity.

18 How is biodiversity important for ecosystem functioning?

19 How can you as an individual, prevent the loss of biodiversity?

Answers

1. (c)	2. (b)	3. (b)	4. (a)	5. (b)
6. (d)	7. (c)	8. (b)	9. (a)	10. (a)

CBSE Unsolved

SAMPLE PAPER 01

Time : 3 hrs
Marks : 70

Biology

General Instructions

1. All questions are compulsory.
2. The question paper has five sections and 33 questions. All questions are compulsory.
3. **Section-A** has 16 questions of 1 mark each; **Section-B** has 5 questions of 2 marks each; **Section-C** has 7 questions of 3 marks each; **Section-D** has 2 case-based questions of 4 marks each; and **Section-E** has 3 questions of 5 marks each.
4. There is no overall choice. However, internal choices have been provided in some questions. A student has to attempt only one of the alternatives in such questions.
5. Wherever necessary, neat and properly labelled diagrams should be drawn.

Section-A

1. Cross-pollination through insect agent is called
(a) anthropophily (b) malacophily
(c) entomophily (d) ornithophily

2. Root cap enclosed in an undifferentiated sheath is called
(a) epicotyl (b) coleorhiza
(c) coleoptile (d) scutellum

3. Given below is a schematic representation of a *lac* operon in the absence of an inducer.

Identify *A* and *B* in it.

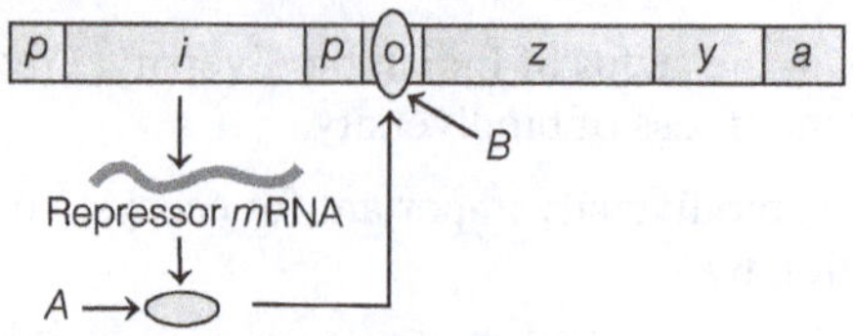

(a) *A* – Repressor; *B* – Operator
(b) *A* – *lac* mRNA; *B* – Repressor
(c) *A* – Operator; *B* – Repressor
(d) *A* – Operator; *B* – *lac* mRNA

4. Colour of human's skin is not just either black or white. There are different shades of human's skin.

Determination of skin colour is an example of
(a) codominance
(b) polygenic inheritance
(c) incomplete dominance
(d) pleiotropy

5. The carrying capacity of environment for a given population can be represented by the following equation.

(a) $dN = rN - \frac{N}{K}$ (b) $\frac{dN}{dt} = rN - \frac{N}{K}$
(c) $\frac{dN}{dt} = rN - \frac{1}{K}$ (d) $\frac{dN}{dt} = rN\left(1 - \frac{N}{K}\right)$

6. In analogy
(a) organs are functionally similar
(b) organs are functionally dissimilar
(c) organs are anatomically similar
(d) Both (b) and (c)

7. Which of the following *Bt* crops is being grown in India by the farmers?
(a) Maize (b) Cotton
(c) Brinjal (d) Soybean

8. From the given graph of population growth select the correct option having correct value of '*r*' and bar graph.

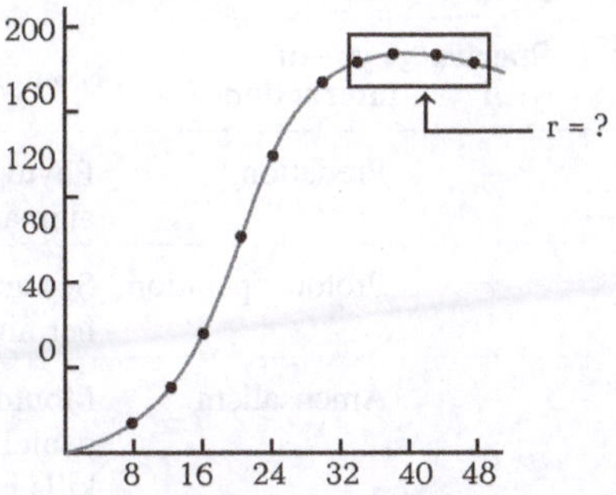

(a) $r = -$ve →  (b) $r = -$ve → 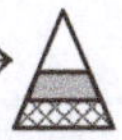

(c) $r = -$ve →  (d) $r = 0$ → 

9. Technique used to detect mutated genes is called
(a) gel electrophoresis
(b) polymerase chain reaction
(c) gene therapy
(d) autoradiography

10. Identify the incorrect pair w.r.t the ART and its feature.

	ART	Feature
(a)	ICSI	Injection of one sperm into egg cytoplasm.
(b)	GIFT	Fertilisation *in vitro*
(c)	AI	In case of no sperm in reproductive tract.
(d)	ZIFT	Embryo enters the uterus after 24 hours

11. What type of evolution supports strong evidence from embryology?
(a) Marsupials of Australia
(b) Darwin's finches
(c) Presence of gill clefts in all vertebrate embryos
(d) Both (a) and (c)

12. *Cry* II Ab and *Cry* I Ab produce toxins that control.

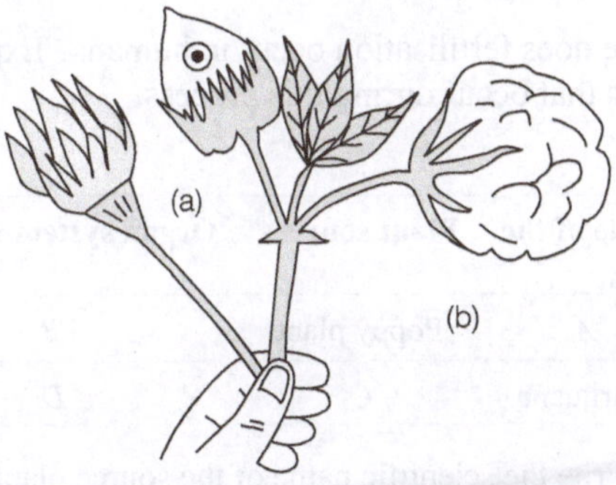

(a) Corn borer and cotton bollworm respectively.
(b) Cotton bollworms and corn bore, respectively
(c) Tobacco budworms and nematodes, respectively
(d) Nematodes and corn borer, respectively.

Direction (Q. Nos. 13-16) *In the questions given below two statements an* ***Assertion*** *and a* ***Reason*** *are given. Give the appropriate response as*
(a) If both A and R are true and R is the correct explanation of A
(b) If both A and R are true, but R is not the correct explanation of A
(c) If A is true, but R is false
(d) If A is false, but R is true

13. **Assertion** (A) The great Indian bustard is a critically endangered bird found in India.
Reason (R) It is vulnerable to extinction in the future.

14. **Assertion** (A) Antibody mediated immune response is provided by B-cells.
Reason (R) B-cells work chiefly by secreting substance called antibodies into the body fluids.

15. **Assertion** (A) Baculoviruses are broad spectrum insecticides.
Reason (R) These viruses are excellent choices for biocontrol in an ecologically sensitive area for integrated pest management.

16. **Assertion** (A) Alcohol consumption during pregnancy is harmful.
Reason (R) Alcohol causes physical and mental defects in the offspring called Foetal Alcohol Syndrome (FAS).

Section-B

17. Where does fertilisation occur in humans? Explain the events that occur during this process.

18.

Name of the drug	Plant sources	Organ system affected
A	Poppy plant	*B*
Marijuana	*C*	*D*

(a) Write the scientific name of the source plant of the drugs-marijuana and hashish and mention their effect on human body.

(b) Name the blank spaces *A*, *B*, *C* and *D* in the table given above.

19. The graph given below indicates the administration of first (*A*) and second dose (*B*) of a vaccine. The corresponding response of the body indicated by *X* and *Y*. Interpret the graph and briefly explain which type of the immunisation is shown in the graph.

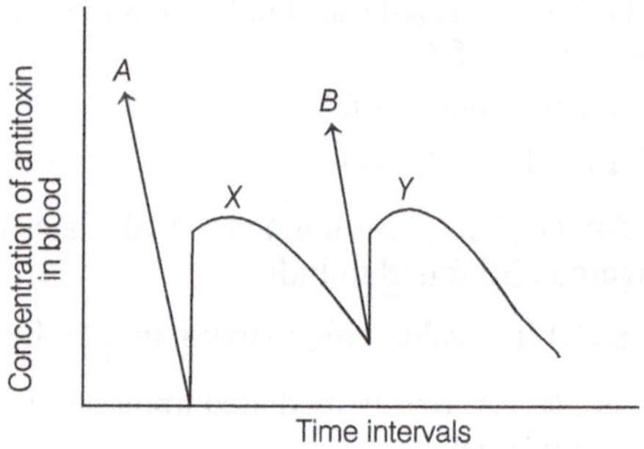

20. Study the diagram given below and answer the questions that follows

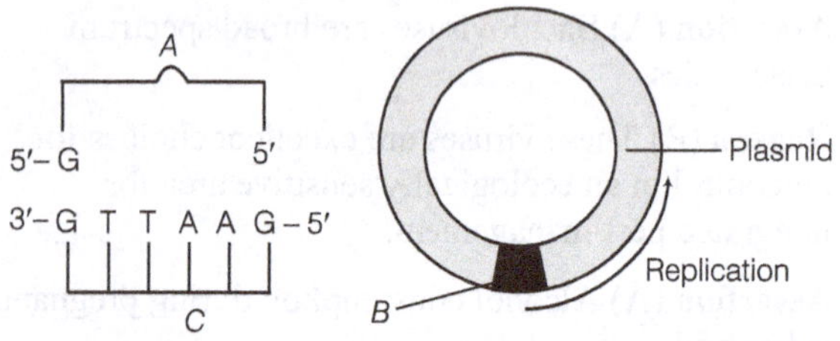

(i) Identify *A* and *B* illustrations in the above diagram.

(ii) Write the term given to *A* and *C* and why?

21. On his visit to a national park, Harshendra was very angry as the forest authorities did not allow him to enter a specified area.

On returning back, he discussed the matter with his friend, who explained him the reason.

(i) Which category of conservation strategy does national park belong to?

(ii) Name India's first national park. At present, how many national parks are there in India?

Or

The table given below depicts species *A*, *B* and the type of interaction with example. Study the information and answer the questions that follows.

Species *A*	Species *B*	Type of interaction	Examples
+	−	Predation	Phytophagous animal and plants.
+	+	Protocooperation	Sea anemone and hermit crab.
+	−	Amensalism	Mould secreting penicillin that kills bacteria while mould remain unaffected

What is predation? Explain with the help of suitable examples. Why is it required in a community with rich biodiversity?

Section-C

22. The figures given below show the pollination in plants *A* and *B*. Observe the given below figures and answer the questions.

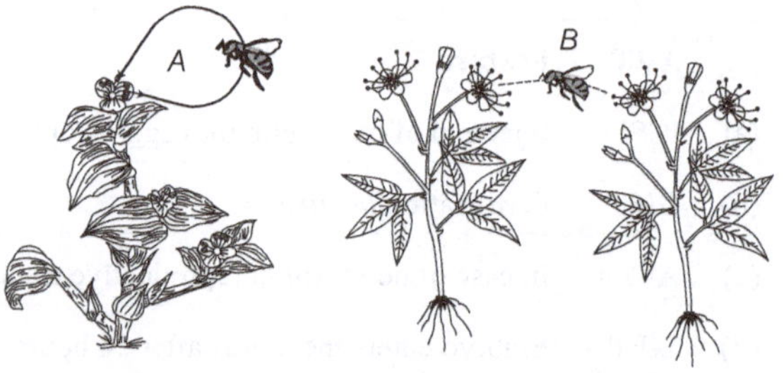

(i) Write four advantages of *B* over *A*.

(ii) Why does *A* not lead to seed formation in self-incompatible species?

23. Give an example of an autosomal recessive disease in humans. Explain its pattern of inheritance with the help of a cross.

24. A heavily bleeding and bruised road accident victim was brought to a nursing home. The doctor immediately gave him an injection to protect him against a deadly disease.

(i) List any two situations, when a medical doctor would recommend injection of preformed antibodies into the body of a patient. Name this kind of immunisation and mention its advantages.

(ii) Name the kind of immunity attained when instead of antibodies, weakened antigens are introduced into the body.

25. A schematic representation of Polymerase Chain Reaction (PCR) upto the extension stage is given below.

Give answers of the following questions.

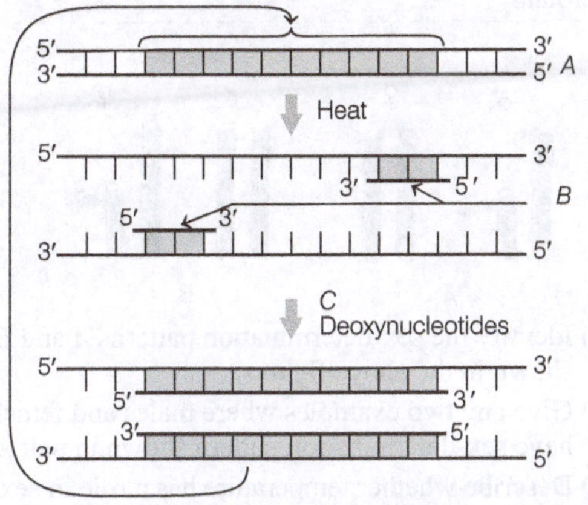

(i) Name the process *A* and identify *B*.

(ii) Identify *C* and mention its importance in PCR.

26. Write symptoms of haemophilia and colour blindness in humans. Explain how the inheritance pattern of the two diseases differs from each other.

27. The oral pills are generally taken daily for a period of 21 days starting within the first five days of menstrual cycle. A women has certain queries as listed below, before starting the contraceptive pills.

(i) (a) What do contraceptive pills contain and how do they act as contraceptives?

(b) What schedule should be followed for taking these pills?

(ii) Is the use of contraceptives justified? Give reason.

Or

Regarding family planning, married couples are advised to adopt birth control techniques.

(i) Name the temporary method, which is safe, effective and has long lasting effect for about 5 years.

(ii) Name a method adopted by males as barrier to avoid fertilisation.

(iii) Name the hormone used during subcutaneous implants for contraception.

28. Cheese is a particularly degraded content rate of milk, prepared by the action of microorganisms. How are different types of cheese characterised? Explain giving three examples.

Section-D

29. In the year 1963, the two enzymes responsible for restricting the growth of bacteriophage in *Escherichia coli* were isolated. One of these added methyl groups to DNA, while the other cut DNA. The later was called restriction endonuclease. These restriction enzyme are the part of bacterial immune system. Answer the following question on the basis of figure given below.

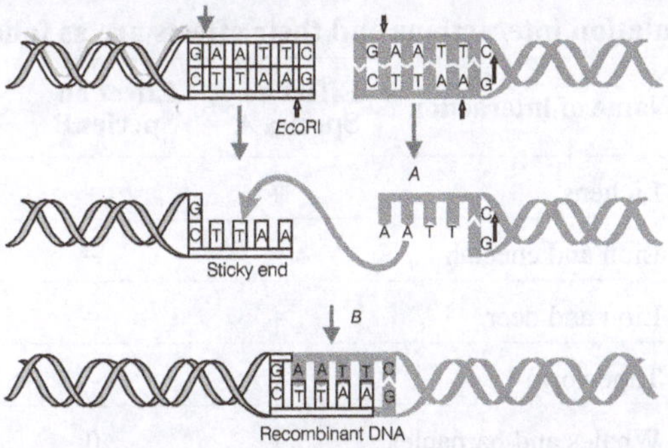

(i) *Eco*RI is a restriction endonuclease. How is it named so? Explain.

Or (i) Write the sequence of DNA bases that the enzyme recognise. Mention the point at which the enzyme makes a cut in the DNA segment.

(ii) *Eco*RI works on a specific sequence and produces DNA fragments with special ends, indicated by '*A*' in the above figure.

(a) Identify the *A* and write its significance.

(b) Identify enzyme *A* and explain its role in the above process.

(iii) Write any four ways used to introduce a desired DNA segment into a bacterial cell in recombinant DNA technology experiments.

30. Observe the global biodiversity distribution of the major plant taxa in the given diagram and answer the questions accordingly.

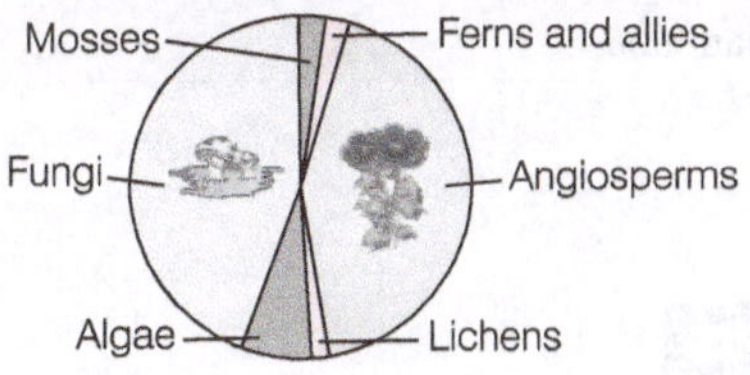

(i) Which group of plants are the most endangered?
(ii) Why are mosses/ferns so few? Give reason.
(iii) How do fungi that are heterotrophs sustain themselves as a large population?

Or

In nature, living organisms such as animals, plants and microbes, cannot live in isolation and therefore, interact in various ways to form a biological community. **Interspecific interactions** occur between the populations of two different species living together within a community. Intraspecific interactions occurs between members of the same species. These interactions could be beneficial (+), detrimental (–) or neutral (0) as shown in table below

Population interactions and their effects are as follows

Name of Interaction	Effect on Species A	Effect on Species B
Lichens	+	+
Lion and cheetah	–	–
Lion and deer	+	–
Tapeworm	+	–
Whales and barnacles	+	0
Penicillium	–	0

With the help of given example. Write the name of each interaction and explain briefly.

Section-E

31. Given below are organs of female reproductive system. Identify and write their location and function.

Organs	Location	Function
Ovaries		
Uterus		
Mammary glands		
Clitoris		
Fallopian tube		

Or

Given below are organs of male reproductive system. Identify and write their location and function.

Organs	Location	Function
Testes		
Penis		
Cowper's gland		
Vas deferens		
Scrotum		

32.

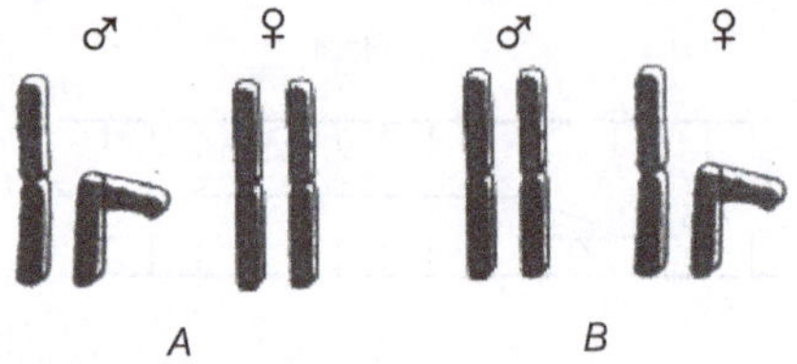

(i) Identify the sex-determination patterns *A* and *B* shown in the above figures.
(ii) Give any two examples where males and females have sex-determination pattern shown in pair *A*.
(iii) Describe whether temperature has a role in sex-determination.

Or

A pregnant women undergoes prenatal testing and the results reveal an extra copy of chromosome 21 in the foetus.

(i) Which condition is most likely to be present in the foetus and what are the features associated with this conditions?
(ii) Define aneuploidy? How is it different from polyploidy?
(iii) Describe the individuals having the following chromosomal abnormalities.
(a) XXX
(b) XO

33. Explain pleiotropy with reference to phenylketonuria.

Or Inheritance pattern of flower colour in garden pea plant and snapdragon differs. Why is this difference observed? Explain showing the crosses upto F_2-generation.

Answers

1. (c) 2. (b) 3. (a) 4. (b) 5. (d) 6. (a) 7. (b) 8. (d) 9. (d) 10. (b)
11. (c) 12. (b) 13. (b) 14. (a) 15. (c) 16. (a)

CBSE Unsolved

SAMPLE PAPER 02

Time : 3 hrs
Marks : 70

Biology

General Instructions

1. All questions are compulsory.
2. The question paper has five sections and 33 questions. All questions are compulsory.
3. **Section-A** has 16 questions of 1 mark each; **Section-B** has 5 questions of 2 marks each; **Section-C** has 7 questions of 3 marks each; **Section-D** has 2 case-based questions of 4 marks each; and **Section-E** has 3 questions of 5 marks each.
4. There is no overall choice. However, internal choices have been provided in some questions. A student has to attempt only one of the alternatives in such questions.
5. Wherever necessary, neat and properly labelled diagrams should be drawn.

Section-A

1. A nucleoside differs from a nucleotide. It lacks the
(a) base (b) sugar
(c) phosphate group (d) hydroxyl group

2. Antibodies are the glycoproteins which
(a) provide localised protection in external secretions against bacteria and viruses
(b) are involved in allergy and hypersensitivity
(c) help in complement activation
(d) All of the above

3. Table given below shows interaction between two organisms 1 and 2.

Population interactions

Organism 1	Organism 2	Names of interaction
+	+	Mutualism
–	–	*A*
+	–	Predation
+	–	*B*
+	0	Commensalism
–	0	*C*

'+' sign for beneficial interaction.

'–' sign for harmful (detrimental) interaction.

'0' sign for neutral interaction.

Find out what could be *A*, *B* and *C*.
(a) *A*–Amensalism, *B*–Parasitism, *C*–Competition
(b) *A*–Competition, *B*–Parasitism, *C*–Amensalism
(c) *A*–Competition, *B*–Amensalism, *C*–Parasitism
(d) *A*–Amensalism, *B*–Competition, *C*–Parasitism

4. Typhoid fever is confirmed using
(a) ELISA (b) Bone marrow transplantation
(c) Widal test (d) MRI

5. Person having genotype $I^A\ I^B$ would show the blood group as AB. This is because of
(a) pleiotropy (b) codominance
(c) segregation (d) incomplete dominance

6. C-peptide of human insulin is
(a) a part of mature insulin molecule
(b) responsible for formation of disulphide bridges
(c) removed during maturation of pro-insulin to insulin
(d) responsible for its biological activity

7. Coitus interruptus is the withdrawl method of natural contraception involving
(a) withdrawl of penis from vagina before ejaculation
(b) withdrawl of penis from vagina after ejaculation
(c) sex during ovulation
(d) no sex during ovulation

8. Find out *A*, *B* and *C* in the diagram given below.

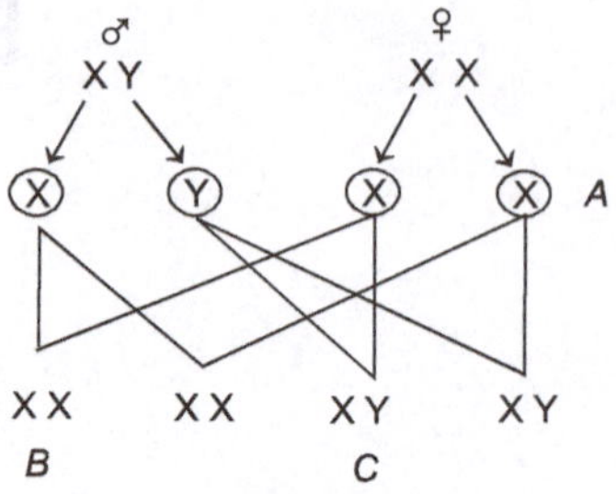

(a) *A*–Male gamete, *B*–Female, *C*–Gametes
(b) *A*–Male, *B*–Female, *C*–Sperm
(c) *A*–Female, *B*–Male, *C*–Gametes
(d) *A*–Gametes, *B*–Female, *C*–Male

9. Opioids are the drugs, which bind to specific opioid receptors present in our
(a) central nervous system
(b) gastrointestinal tract
(c) Both (a) and (b)
(d) urinogenital system

10. Identify the correct match for the given apparatus.

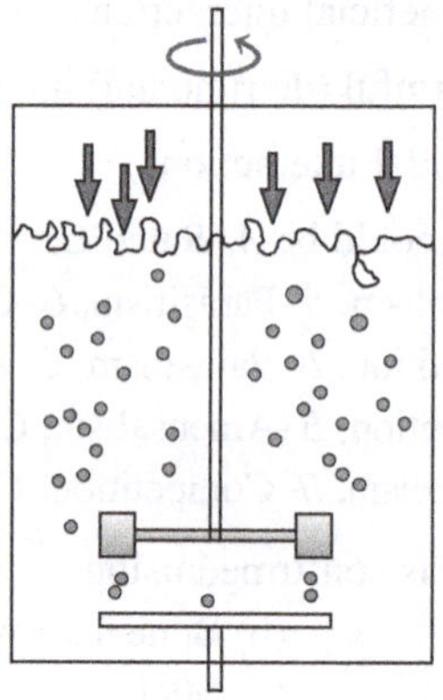

Apparatus	Functions
(a) Gene gun	Vectorless direct gene transfer
(b) Column chromatograph	Separation of chlorophyll pigments
(c) Sparged tank bioreactor	Carry out fermentation process
(d) Respirometer	Finding out rate of respiration

11. The BOD test measures the rate of uptake of oxygen by microbes in water bodies. The greater BOD of sample water, indicates that
(a) it is highly polluted
(b) it is not polluted
(c) it is moderately polluted
(d) pollution level cannot be determined

12. Study the diagram given below of translation and choose the correct option for labels *A, B, C, D* and *E*.

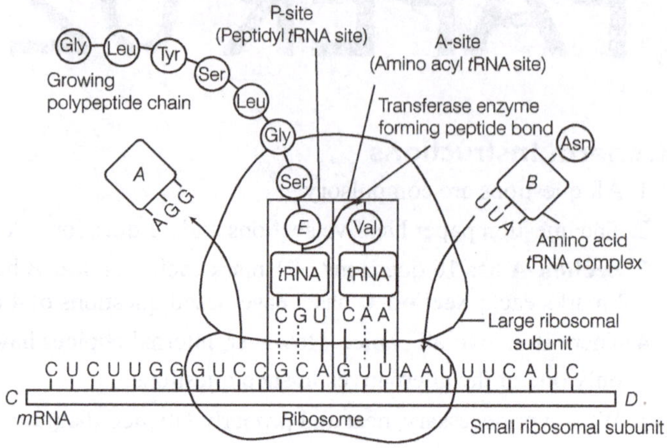

	A	*B*	*C*	*D*	*E*
(a)	Charged/ Aminoacylate d *t*RNA	Uncharged *t*RNA	5′ end	3′ end	Glycine
(b)	Uncharged *t*RNA	Charged/Amino -acylated *t*RNA	5′ end	3′ end	Alanine
(c)	Uncharged *t*RNA	Charged/Amino -acylated *t*RNA	3′ end	5′ end	Glycine
(d)	Uncharged *t*RNA	Charged/Amino -acylated *t*RNA	5′ end	3′ end	Lysine

Direction (Q. Nos. 13-16) *In the questions given below two statements an **Assertion** and a **Reason** are given. Give the appropriate response as*
(a) If both A and R are true and R is the correct explanation of A
(b) If both A and R are true, but R is not the correct explanation of A
(c) If A is true, but R is false
(d) If A is false, but R is true

13. **Assertion** (A) IUCN prepares and maintains a Red Data Book since 1964.

Reason (R) It is a catalogue which provides awareness about the degree of threat to the biodiversity.

14. **Assertion** (A) In flowering plants, zygote is formed inside the ovule.

Reason (R) The ovule develops into seed after fertilisation.

15. **Assertion** (A) In F_2-generation, the traits seen in the progeny were identical to their parents.

Reason (R) The progeny of the F_2-generation show no blending of traits.

16. **Assertion** (A) DNA acts as a genetic material in all organisms.

Reason (R) It is a double-stranded biomolecule in most organisms.

Section-B

17. Why both the strands of DNA are not copied during transcription? Explain.

18. Study the *m*RNA segment given below, which is complete and to be translated into a polypeptide chain.

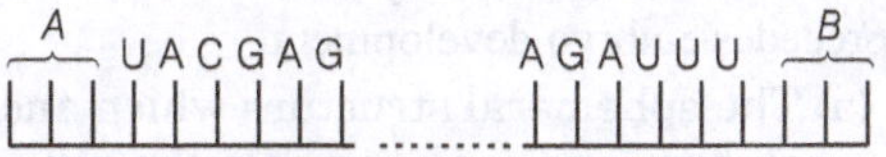

(i) Write the codons *A* and *B*.

(ii) How is peptide bond formed between two amino acids in the ribosome?

19. The diagram given below is that of a typical biogas plant.

Explain the sequence of events occurring in it. Identify *A*, *B* and *C*.

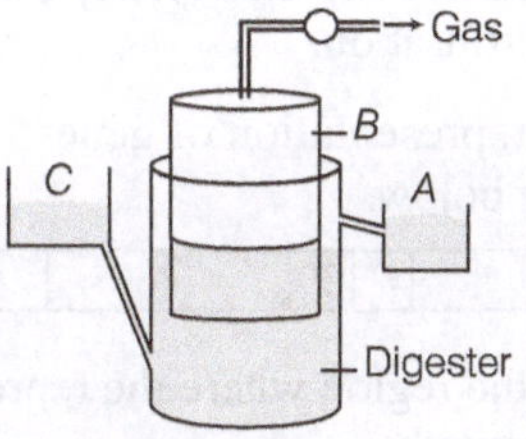

20. Study the given figure.

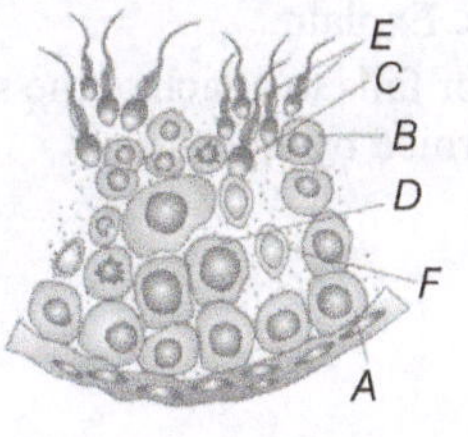

(i) Pick out and name the cells that undergo spermiogenesis.

(ii) Name *A* and *B* cells. What is the difference between them with reference to the number of chromosomes?

21. The DNA molecule that can carry a foreign DNA segment and replicate inside the host cell is called a vector. These vectors have the ability to replicate within bacterial cells independent of the control of chromosomal DNA.

Diagrammatically represent the experimental steps in cloning and expressing a human gene (say the gene for growth hormone) into a bacterium like *E. coli*.

Or

The following illustrates the linking of DNA fragments.

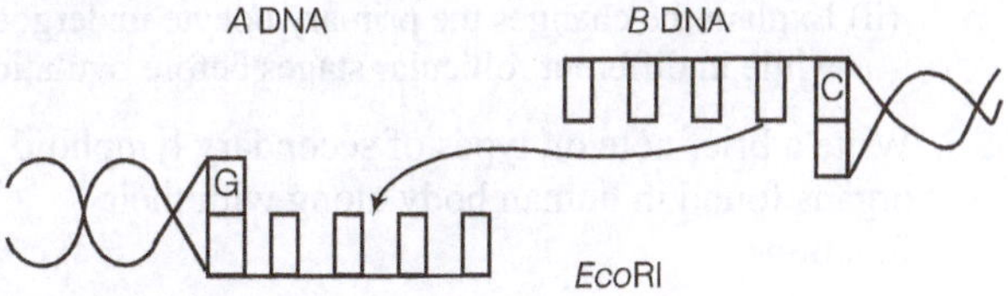

(i) Write the name of *A* and *B*.

(ii) Complete the palindrome which is recognised by *Eco*RI.

Section-C

22. Read the sequence of the nucleotides in the given segment of *m*RNA and the respective amino acid sequence in the polypeptide chain.

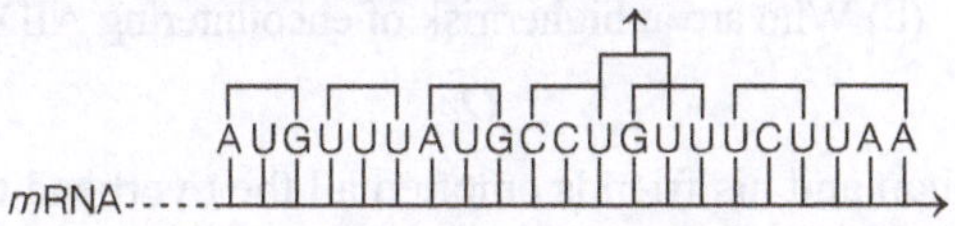

(i) Provide the triplet of bases (codon) for

(a) valine

(b) proline

(ii) Write the nucleotide sequence of the DNA strand from which this *m*RNA was transcribed.

23. Explain Verhulst-Pearl logistic growth of a population.

24. While teaching in class, teacher told the students that Mendel used the contrasting traits of pea plant to propose three basic laws of inheritance. She also said that these laws are not always universally applicable.

(i) When did Mendel performed hybridisation experiments and with how many traits of pea plants?

(ii) What phenotypic and genotypic ratio were obtained by Mendel in monohybrid cross? Give example of any two exceptions to Mendel's law of dominance.

25. Given below is the TS of human ovary.

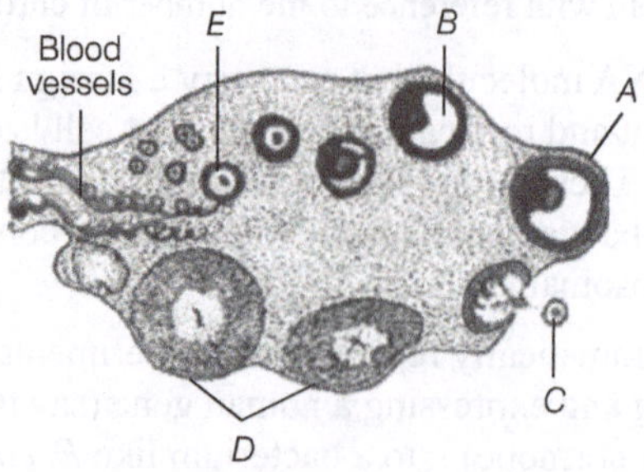

(i) Identify the following in the diagram.
Corpus luteum, secondary oocyte, antrum, primary follicle and primary oocyte.

(ii) Explain the changes the primary oocyte undergoes while in different follicular stages before ovulation.

26. Write a brief note on types of secondary lymphoid organs found in human body along with their functions.

27. Ankit attended a blood donation camp to donate blood and came to know that he was HIV positive. He lost interest in studies knowing that. He remained absent from school for a long time. The biology teacher visited his house and talked to him. Ankit started coming to school again and showed interest in studies.

(i) A person detected to be HIV positive should be isolated by the society. Do you agree? Why/why not?

(ii) (a) Write the processes through which AIDS does not spread.

(b) Who are at higher risk of encountering AIDS?

Or

Rohan and his friends emptied all the overhead tanks, which were not in use for last few months. Some people did not like this. Rohan and his friends explained and convinced them about the hygienic benefits of their act.

(i) What was the objective behind their act?

(ii) Explain in brief the stages of life cycle of a malarial parasite in human body.

(iii) Which pathogen is responsible for malaria?

28. Why are people quite apprehensive to use GM crops? Give three arguments in support of GM crops to convince the people in favour of such crop.

Section-D

29. Study the given diagram of a mature embryo below and answer the questions that follow

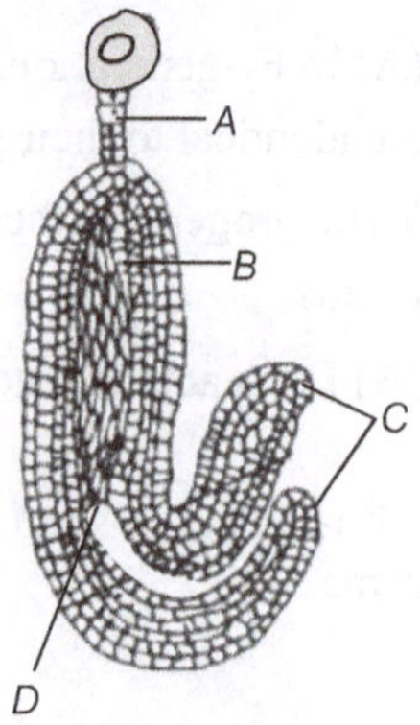

(i) Which of the following, an endosperm or an embryo, develops first in an angiospermic seed? Give reason for the precedence

Or

(i) State the role of endosperm in mature albuminous seed. Also comment why endosperm development precedes embryo development.

(ii) (a) The ephemeral structure which anchors the embryo and pushes it into the nutritional zone of the embryo sac is called

(i) A *(ii)* B *(iii)* C *(iv)* D

(b) Identify *A* in the figure showing a stage of embryo development in a dicot plant and mention its functions.

(iii) What is triple fusion? Where and how does it take place? Give the name of nuclei involved in triple fusion and also explains briefly the phenomenon of double fertilisation.

30. Observe the representation of genes involved in the *lac* operon given below.

(i) Identify the region where the repressor protein will attach normally.

(ii) Under certain conditions repressor is unable to attach at this site. Explain.

(iii) If repressor fails to attach to the site what products will be formed by *z*, *y* and *a*?

Or

(iii) Study the diagram given below. Name the linkage *X*, *Y*, *Z* and the respective molecule formed by them.

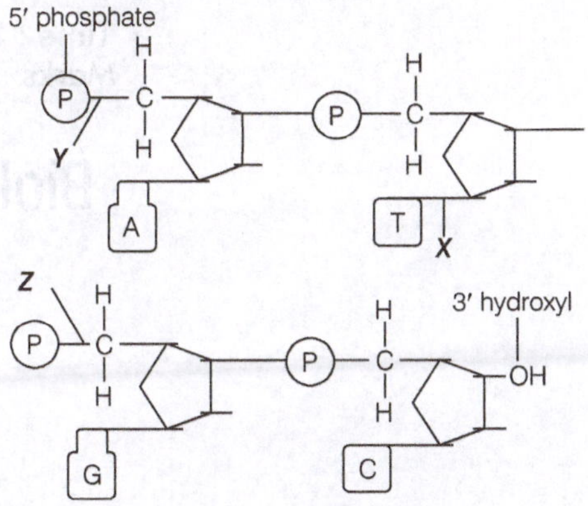

A polynucleotide chain

Section-E

31. Placed below are the details of pBR322 which has genes resistance for ampicilin and tetracycline and have different enzymes for different restriction sites.

	Restriction sites	**Enzymes**
1.	amp^R	*Pvu* I
2.	*rop*	*Sal* I
3.	tet^R	*Bam* HI
4.	amp^R	*Pst* I
5.	*ori*	*Sal* I

From the above given table select the incorrectly mentioned restriction site with their enzymes and justify your answer giving reason. Also state reason for other choices.

Or

The table shows some restriction enzymes, their sources and the target DNA sequence with cleavage site. Analyse and suggest the name of organism along with their ends produced.

Enzymes	**Organism**	**Target DNA sequence** (cleavage site marked by arrow)	**Ends produced**
Eco RI		5′—G↓ AATTC….. 3′ 3′ CTTAA↑ G…5′	
Hind II		5′...GTPy↓ Pu AC... 3′ 3′...CAPu↑Py TG... 5′	Blunt ends
Hae III	*Haemophilus aegyptius*	5′...GG↓ CC...3′ 3′ ...CC↑ GG...5′	
Hpa I		5′...GTT↓ AAC...3′ 3′...CAA↑ TTG... 5′	Blunt ends
Sma I	*Serratia marcescens*	5′...CCC↓ GGG...3′ 3′...GGG↑ CCC...5′	

32. Spermatogenesis is the formation of spermatozoa (sperms) in testes, which originate from the Primordial Germ Cells (PGCs). The process of spermatogenesis starts at puberty.

(i) Mention different stages in the process of spermatogenesis with its brief description.

(ii) State the ploidy of spermatogonial cell.

(iii) Which kind of cell division occurs in spermatogonia and what structure is formed?

(iv) State the differences between spermatogenesis and spermiogenesis.

Or

The process of spermatogenesis is completely under control of hormones. Keeping in mind the process, answer the following questions.

(i) State the role of Leydig and Sertoli cells.

(ii) Which hormone controls secretion of LH and FSH?

(iii) What is feedback mechanism? Explain with the help of diagram.

33. 'Analysis of age pyramids for human population can provide important inputs for long-term planning strategies'. Explain.

Or

Draw a pyramid of numbers of a situation, where a large population of insects feeds upon a very big tree. Explain why the pyramid of energy is always upright?

Answers

1. (c) **2.** (d) **3.** (b) **4.** (c) **5.** (b) **6.** (c) **7.** (a) **8.** (d) **9.** (c) **10.** (c)
11. (a) **12.** (b) **13.** (a) **14.** (b) **15.** (a) **16.** (d)

CBSE Unsolved

SAMPLE PAPER 03

Time : 3 hrs
Marks : 70

Biology

General Instructions

1. All questions are compulsory.
2. The question paper has five sections and 33 questions. All questions are compulsory.
3. **Section-A** has 16 questions of 1 mark each; **Section-B** has 5 questions of 2 marks each; **Section-C** has 7 questions of 3 marks each; **Section-D** has 2 case-based questions of 4 marks each; and **Section-E** has 3 questions of 5 marks each.
4. There is no overall choice. However, internal choices have been provided in some questions. A student has to attempt only one of the alternatives in such questions.
5. Wherever necessary, neat and properly labelled diagrams should be drawn.

Section-A

1. Promoter and terminator flanks the
   (a) house-keeping gene
   (b) structural gene
   (c) recon
   (d) transcription unit

2. Antibodies present in colostrum which protects the newborn from certain disease is of
   (a) IgG type (b) IgA type
   (c) IgD type (d) IgE type

3. ZZ/ZW type of sex-determination is seen in
   (a) platypus (b) snails
   (c) cockroach (d) peacock

4. Given below are some pairs of bacteria w.r.t. their products. Identify how many pairs are incorrect?

A.	Citric acid	1.	*Clostridium butylicum*
B.	Cyclosporin-A	2.	*Aspergillus niger*
C.	Statin	3.	*Monascus purpureus*
D.	Gobar gas	4.	*Trichoderma polysporum*

   (a) 1 (b) 2 (c) 4 (d) 3

5. The organisation which published the Red List of species is
   (a) ICFRE (b) IUCN (c) UNEP (d) WWF

6. Identify the incorrect label in the given figure of double fertilisation in angiospermic plant.

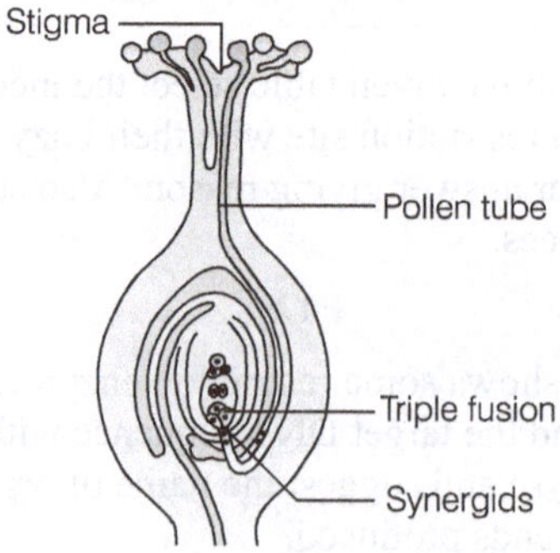

   (a) Stigma (b) Synergids
   (c) Triple fusion (d) Pollen tube

7. In DNA 20% bases are adenine. What percentage of bases are pyrimidines?
   (a) 30% (b) 60% (c) 50% (d) 20%

8. The given figure is the diagrammatic representation of the vector pBR322. Which one of the given options correctly identifies its certain component(s)?

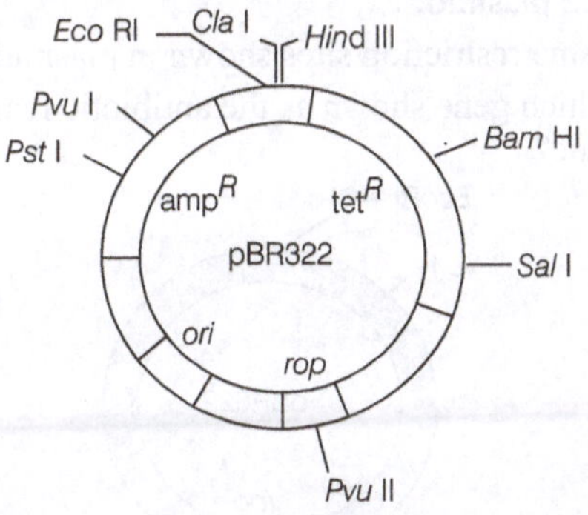

(a) *ori*–original restriction enzymes
(b) *rop*–reduced osmotic pressure
(c) *Hind* III, *Eco* RI–selectable markers
(d) amp^R, tet^R–antibiotic resistance genes

9. Identify what is indicated in the given diagram?

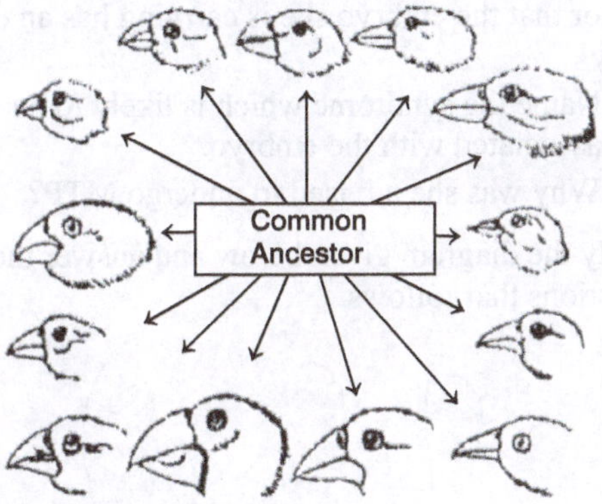

(a) Recombination
(b) Adaptive radiation
(c) Ecological succession
(d) Different species of penguins by mutation

10. Which vector can clone only a small fragment of DNA?
(a) Bacterial artificial chromosome
(b) Yeast artificial chromosome
(c) Plasmid
(d) Cosmid

11. Which of the following is used as 'clot buster' for removing clots from blood vessels of patient, who have undergone myocardial infarction?
(a) Ethanol (b) Statins
(c) Cyclosporin-A (d) Streptokinase

12. DNA-dependent DNA polymerase catalyses polymerisation in which direction?
(a) $5' \rightarrow 3'$ polarity strand
(b) $3' \rightarrow 5'$ polarity strand
(c) Both (a) and (b)
(d) None of the above

Direction (Q. Nos. 13-16) *In the questions given below two statements an* ***Assertion*** *and a* ***Reason*** *are given. Give the appropriate response as*
(a) If both A and R are true and R is the correct explanation of A
(b) If both A and R are true, but R is not the correct explanation of A
(c) If A is true, but R is false
(d) If A is false, but R is true

13. **Assertion** (A) Cannabinoids are known for their effects on cardiovascular system of the body.

Reason (R) Cannabinoids is a class of diverse chemical compounds that activate cannabinoid receptors present principally in brain.

14. **Assertion** (A) Barrier methods prevent conception.

Reason (R) These prevent the physical meeting of sperm and ovum.

15. **Assertion** (A) Zoological parks serves the purpose to protect the threatened species and provide special care.

Reason (R) Zoological parks are the examples of *in situ* conservation.

16. **Assertion** (A) The Sertoli cells are present in seminiferous tubules.

Reason (R) Sertoli cells provide nutrition to the germ cells and spermatozoa.

Section-B

17. Why is it that the father never passes on the gene for haemophilia to his sons? Explain.

18. Refer to the diagram given below and answer the questions that follow

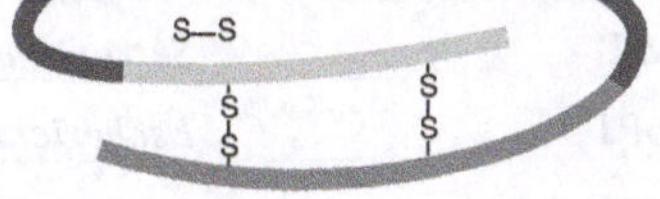

(i) The diagram shown above is insulin or proinsulin, justify.
(ii) How is mature insulin synthesised?

19. The diagram given below shows the schematic representation of spermatogenesis. Interpret the representation by naming the cells that represent *A*, *B*, *C* and *D* and also explain spermatogenesis.

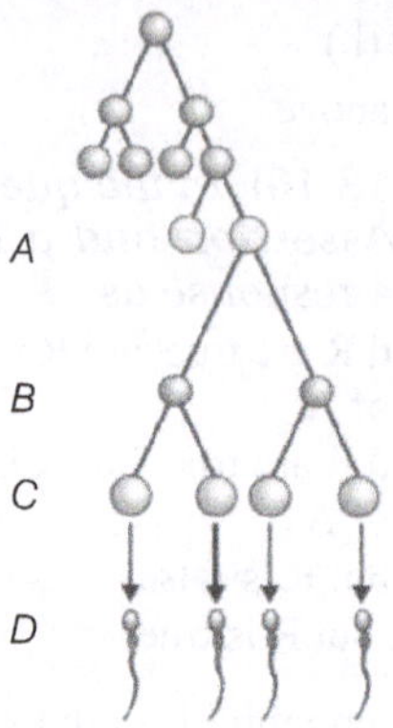

20. The diagram shows the structure of an antibody.

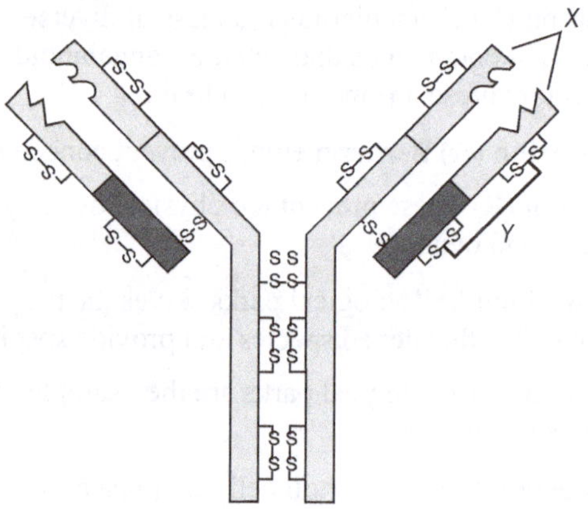

(i) Describe the role of *X*.
(ii) Identify the label *Y* and name the bonds present in the given diagram.

21. The PCR is a method widely used to rapidly make millions to billions of copies of a specific DNA sample, it allow scientists to take a very small sample of DNA and amplify it to a larger amount to study in detail. Draw and explain three simple steps of PCR technique.

Or Use the information provided in the table given below to answer the following questions.

	Restriction enzymes	Sources
A.	*Sma* I	*Serratia marcescens*
B.	*Eco*RI	*Escherichia coli* RY13
C.	*Bam*HI	....
D.	*Hind* II	*H. influenzae* Rd.

(i) Name the correct source for *C*.
(ii) What is the restriction site for *Eco*RI.

Section-C

22. The figure given below shows the schematic sketch of pBR322 plasmid.
(i) Name restriction sites shown in plasmid.
(ii) Which gene shown as the antibiotic resistance gene?

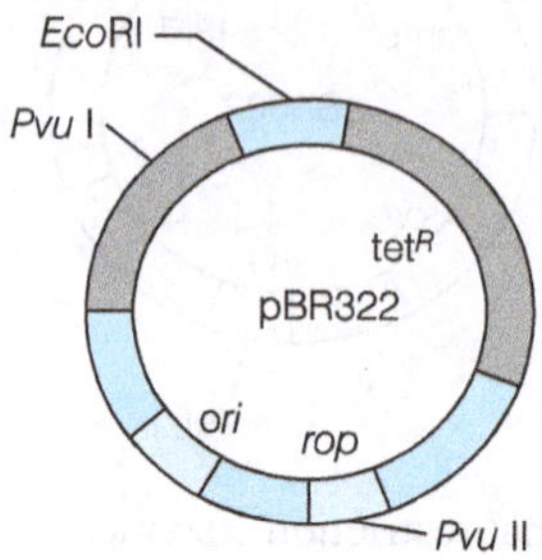

23. Explain gene therapy with reference to treatment of SCID.

24. A pregnant woman who had amniocentesis test was advised to undergo MTP. It was diagnosed by her doctor that the embryo she is carrying has an extra Barr body.
(i) Name the syndrome which is likely to be associated with the embryo.
(ii) Why was she advised to undergo MTP?

25. Study the diagram given below and answer the questions that follows.

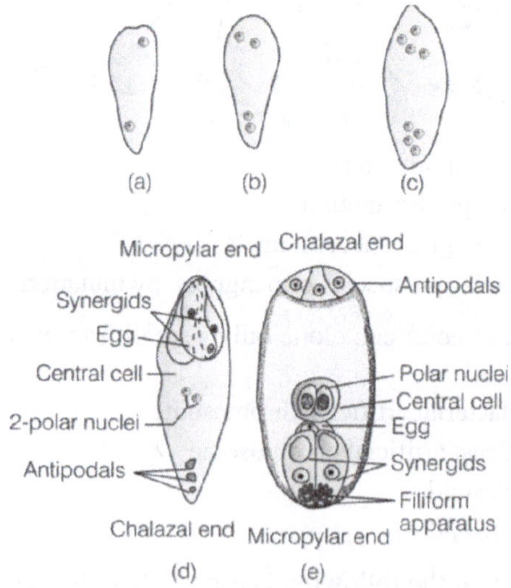

(i) How many cells are present in the mature embryo sac? State the function of each cell.
(ii) Name the collective term of the whole process happening in female part of the flower of angiosperm.

26. Give an example of a sex-linked recessive trait in humans. Explain its pattern of inheritance with the help of a cross.

27. Once Gita asked Sarita about her adrenaline and steroid medication. On this, Sarita told her that she is allergic to pollens and mites. Thus, she takes these medications. She also mentioned that she became allergic due to the protected environment provided to her in early life. Upon further conversation, Gita told her that she herself is suffering from an autoimmune disease.

(i) Name the antibody which is produced in response to allergens.
(ii) Mention few symptoms of allergic reactions.
(iii) How adrenaline and steroids would help Gita to relieve allergy?

Or

The outline structure of a drug is given below

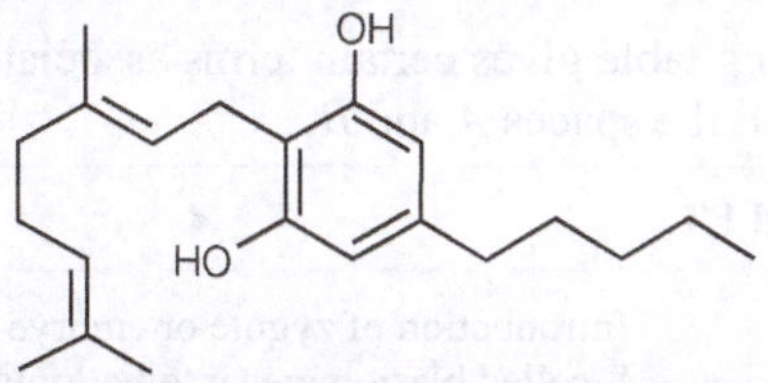

(i) Which group of drugs does this represent?
(ii) (a) What are the modes of consumption of these drugs?
(b) Name the organ of the body which is affected by consumption of these drugs.

28. Legumes fertilise the soil, but cereals do not. Comment on the statement with suitable examples.

Section-D

29. Refer to the diagram given below and answer the questions that follows.

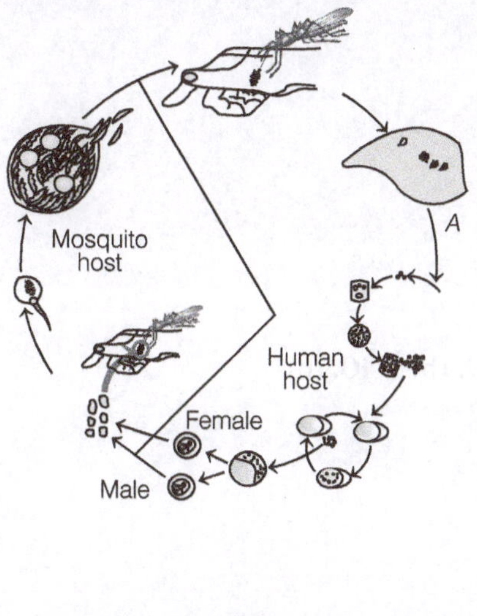

(i) The parasite reproduces in human host by which method?

Or

(i) What are sporozoites?
(ii) (a) The sexual stages of parasite are referred as.
(b) Which stage of the parasite life cycle invades the part labelled as *A* in the above diagram.
(iii) Where does the fertilisation and development of parasite takes place in mosquito's body?

30. Study the figure given below and answer the following questions.

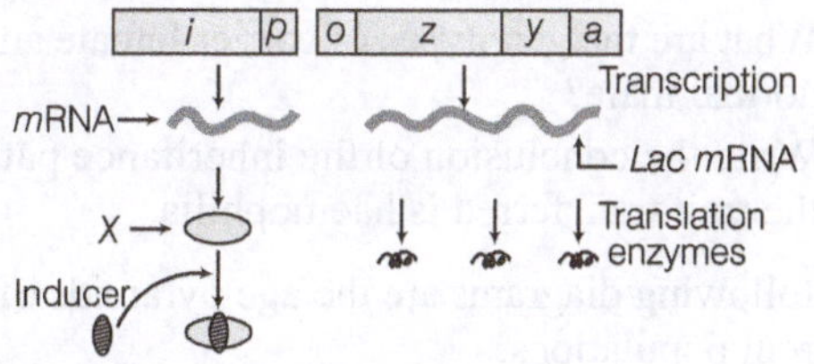

(i) Name the molecule '*X*' synthesised by *i* gene. How does this molecule get inactivated?
(ii) Which one of the structural genes codes for β-galactosidase?
(iii) When will the transcription of this gene stop?

Or

A cross between a normal couple resulted in a son who was haemophilic and a normal daughter. In course of time, when the daughter was married to a normal man, to their surprise, the grandson was also haemophilic.

Represent this cross in the form of a pedigree chart and give the genotypes of the daughter and her husband. Write the conclusion you draw of the inheritance pattern of this disease.

Section-E

31. Given below is a table showing the genotypes and the phenotypes of blood groups in the human population.

Genotypes	Phenotypes
W	*Y*
$I^B I^O$	*Z*
$I^A I^B$	O
X	O

(i) Identify the genotypes *W* and *X*, and the phenotypes *Y* and *Z*.
(ii) How is codominance different from incomplete dominance and dominance?

(iii) Name the pattern of inheritance exhibited by the phenotypes *Y* and *Z* in the table.

Or

With reference to the below schematic representation of pedigree analysis, answer the questions that follows

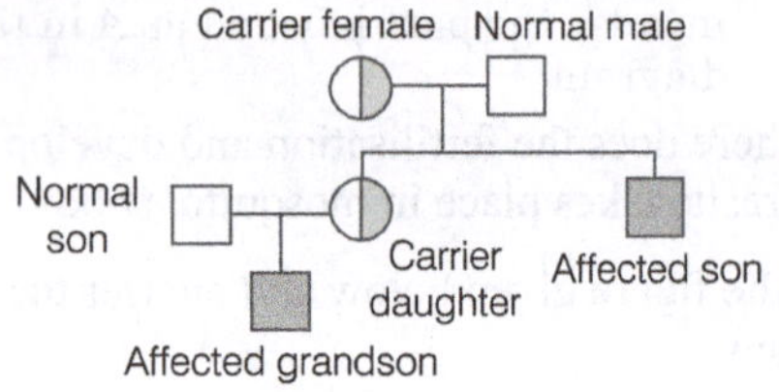

(i) What are the genotypes of carrier female and normal male?

(ii) Write the conclusion of the inheritance pattern if the trait transferred is haemophilia.

32. The following diagrams are the age pyramids of different populations.

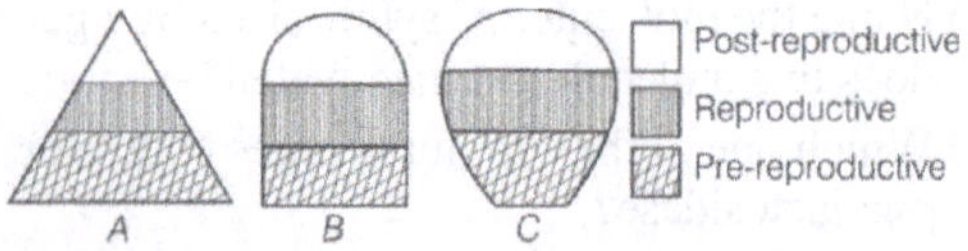

(i) What is depicted in all these three figures?

(ii) Which of the above mentioned structures shows expanding population and why?

(iii) Which shape is obtained for zero population growth rate?

Or

A large tract of old-growth forest is slated for clear-cutting to make way for a commercial developement. The forest is home to several endangered species.

(i) Why should we conserve biodiversity? How can we do it?

(ii) Explain the importance of biodiversity hotspots and sacred groves.

(iii) Define the following terms

(a) Endangered species

(b) IUCN

33. Double fertilisation is reported in plants of both, castor and groundnut. However, the mature seeds of groundnut are non-albuminous and castor are albuminous. Explain the post-fertilisation events that are responsible for it.

Or

Following table gives certain terms associated with ART. Fill the spaces *A* and *B*.

IVF and ET	*A*
B	Introduction of zygote or embryo with 8-celled blastomeres into Fallopian tube.

Identify *A* and *B*. Describe the significance of IVF technique along with the procedure of ICSI technique.

Answers

1. (b) **2.** (b) **3.** (d) **4.** (b) **5.** (b) **6.** (c) **7.** (c) **8.** (d) **9.** (b) **10.** (c)
11. (d) **12.** (a) **13.** (b) **14.** (a) **15.** (c) **16.** (b)